Julius Caesar's Battle for Gaul

New archaeological perspectives

edited by

Andrew P. Fitzpatrick
and Colin Haselgrove

OXBOW | books
Oxford & Philadelphia

First published in the United Kingdom in 2019. Reprinted in 2022 by
OXBOW BOOKS
The Old Music Hall, 106–108 Cowley Road, Oxford OX4 1JE

and in the United States by
OXBOW BOOKS
1950 Lawrence Road, Havertown, PA 19083

Paperback Edition: ISBN 978-1-78925-050-3
Digital Edition: ISBN 978-1-78925-051-0 (ePub)

A CIP record for this book is available from the British Library

Library of Congress Control Number: 2019946781

Typeset in India for Casemate Publishing Services. www.casematepublishingservices.com

For a complete list of Oxbow titles, please contact:

UNITED KINGDOM
Oxbow Books
Telephone (01865) 241249
Email: oxbow@oxbowbooks.com
www.oxbowbooks.com

UNITED STATES OF AMERICA
Oxbow Books
Telephone (610) 853-9131, Fax (610) 853-9146
Email: queries@casemateacademic.com
www.casemateacademic.com/oxbow

Oxbow Books is part of the Casemate Group

Cover credits:
The reconstructed Roman defences at the Muséoparc Alésia (photo A.P. Fitzpatrick).
Denarius issued by Julius Caesar in 48–47 BC showing a trophy with a Gaulish shield and Gaulish carnyx war trumpet, Crawford *Roman Republican Coinage* 452/2 (© Ashmolean Museum, University of Oxford, Accession no. HCR9986).

Contents

List of figures and tables

Figures

Tables

Ancient sources

The following ancient sources are referenced in the book. Where titles are cited in Greek or Latin, English translations are given below.

Aeneus Tacitus
Poliorketika (Defending the City)
Antonine Itinerary
Itinerarium Antonini Augusti (The Itinerary of the Emperor Antoninus)
Appian
Civil War
Caesar
de Bello Africo (The African War)
de Bello Civile (The Civil War)
de Bello Gallico (The Gallic War)
Cassius Dio
Roman History
Cicero
ad Atticum (Letters to Atticus)
Brutus
de Legibus (On the Laws)
Diodorus Siculus
Library of History
Florus
Epitome of Roman History
Horace
Odes
Julius Exsuperantius
History (of the Civil War)
Juvenal
Satires
Livy
Fragments (Fragments from The History of Rome)
Periochae (Summaries of The History of Rome)
Lucan
Pharsalia (On the Civil War)
Orosius
Historiarum Adversum Paganos (History Against the Pagans)
Philo of Byzantium
Mechanike Syntaxis (Compendium of Mechanics)
Pliny
Natural History
Plutarch
Life of Caesar
Life of Sertorius
Polybius
The Histories
Poseidonios
History
Ptolemy
Geography
Sallust
Histories
Fragments (Fragments from The Histories)
Strabo
Geography
Suetonius
Life of the Deified Caesars
Tacitus
Annals
Histories
Valerius Maximus
Memorable Deeds and Sayings
Vegetius
de Re militari (On Military Matters)

List of contributors

Eduard Ble
Departament de Prehistòria, Història Antiga i Arqueologia, University of Barcelona, Spain – eduard.ble@gmail.com

Manuel Fernández-Götz
School of History, Classics & Archaeology, University of Edinburgh, UK – M.Fernandez-Gotz@ed.ac.uk

Andrew P. Fitzpatrick
School of Archaeology & Ancient History, University of Leicester, UK – af215@le.ac.uk

Colin Haselgrove
School of Archaeology & Ancient History, University of Leicester, UK – cch7@le.ac.uk

Sabine Hornung
Vor- und Frühgeschichte und Vorderasiatische Archäologie, University of Saarland, Germany – sabine.hornung@uni-saarland.de

Philip de Jersey
Archaeology Officer, States of Guernsey – Philip.dejersey@gov.gg

Gilbert Kaenel
University of Geneva, Switzerland – gilbert.kaenel@unil.ch

Sophie Krausz
Ausonius-UMR 5607, University of Bordeaux Montaigne, France – Sophie.Krausz@u-bordeaux-montaigne.fr

Christopher Krebs
Department of Classics, University of Stanford, USA – cbkrebs@stanford.edu

Angel Morillo
Departamento de Prehistoria, Historia Antigua y Arqueología, University Complutense, Madrid, Spain – amorillo@ucm.es

Laurent Olivier
Musée d'Archéologie nationale, Paris, France – laurent.olivier@culture.gouv.fr

Carles Padrós
Catalan Institute of Classical Archaeology, Tarragona, Spain – cpadros@icac.cat

Lionel Pernet
Musée cantonal d'archéologie et d'histoire, Lausanne, Switzerland – lionel.pernet@vd.ch

Àngels Pujol
Association GIRA (Grup Independent de Recerca en Arqueologia), Barcelona, Spain – angelspcamps@hotmail.com

Ian Ralston
School of History, Classics & Archaeology, University of Edinburgh, UK – Ian.Ralston@ed.ac.uk

Michel Reddé
École Pratique des Hautes Études, Paris, France – michel.redde@ephe.sorbonne.fr

Nico Roymans
Faculty of Humanities, Free University (VU), Amsterdam, Netherlands – n.g.a.m.roymans@vu.nl

Xavier Rubio-Campillo
School of History, Classics & Archaeology, University of Edinburgh, UK – Xavier.Rubio@ed.ac.uk

Roger Sala
SOT Archaeological Prospection, Barcelona, Spain – roger_sala_bar@yahoo.es

Feliciana Sala-Sellés
Departamento de Prehistoria, Arqueología, Historia Antigua, Filología Griega y Filología Latina, University of Alicante, Spain – feliciana.sala@ua.es

Robert Tamba
Association GIRA (Grup Independent de Recerca en Arqueologia), Barcelona, Spain – roberttamba@riseup.net

Greg Woolf
Institute of Classical Studies, School of Advanced Study, University of London, UK – greg.woolf@sas.ac.uk

Introduction

Andrew P. Fitzpatrick and Colin Haselgrove

Julius Caesar's battle for Gaul is one of the most famous and dramatic episodes in European history. Caesar's own commentaries, *de bello Gallico* (*BG*), are a unique account of a war between Romans and Barbarians during the late Republic. Caesar was not the only Roman general of this time to ensure that an account of their campaigns was written, but his is the only one to survive intact. His account is, naturally, told from a Roman perspective and because it was written in the third person Caesar is the omnipresent narrator.

Traditionally both scholarly and popular studies of the battle have tended to mirror Caesar's approach by considering the war either in the context of Roman history or as a piece of military history. As ever, it is a history written by the victors.

But the battle was fought against many different peoples. Caesar famously began the first book of his commentaries with the statement that Gaul was divided into three parts, one of which was occupied by the Belgae, another by the Aquitani and a third by a people called in their own tongue Celtae, in the Latin Galli. The wars went on to involve the Germans and the Britons. Caesar provided the first written accounts of some of these peoples but in comparison with contemporary Rome, much more of their stories must be told through archaeological remains, and archaeology is the focus of this book. Recent considerations of many of the other topics within the wide canon of Caesarian studies can be found in recent volumes in English (*e.g.* Griffith 2009; Grillo and Krebs 2018). A new edition of the complete works of Caesar has also recently been published, accompanied by a series of web essays which provide archaeological, historical and literary context to these texts (Raaflaub 2017).

Although the identification of the places and natural features mentioned in the commentaries – be they settlements, battlefields or rivers – had occupied scholars for centuries, the systematic archaeological study of the battle for Gaul can be said to have begun in the mid-19th century AD. While the researches initiated by Napoléon III, successively President and Emperor of France between 1848–1870, were a statement of national and imperial intent, they also reflected a genuine interest in history and the rapidly emerging discipline of archaeology that extended far beyond Gaul (Laronde *et al.* 2011). Even so, the emperor was entranced by Julius Caesar. The best-known legacies of this fascination are his *Histoire de Jules César,* published in 1865, and what is today the National Archaeology Museum, which he opened in the Château de Saint-Germain-en-Laye in 1867 (Nicolet 2009).

The emperor surrounded himself with a circle of leading scholars, but he also used the considerable resources of the imperial treasury and the skills of his soldiers to undertake a systematic survey of the topography of Gaul, or more precisely the terrain in the area of places mentioned by Caesar. This work was carried out by the specially created *Commission de la Topographie des Gaules* (1858–1879) and comments in the *Histoire* and in the records of the commission indicate that a systematic attempt was made to locate all the sites mentioned in Caesar's wars, not just the battle for Gaul but also for the different campaigns in the Civil War. Several of the sites in France were ground-truthed by trenching, often on a considerable scale. The results included the identification of the site of the Battle of the Aisne in 57 BC and the Roman camp at Mauchamp, and the siege sites of Alesia and Uxellodunum dating to 52 and 51 BC respectively. The researches were not restricted to fieldwork and included what would now be called experimental archaeology and subjects as diverse as Roman artillery, a Roman galley, and part of the siege works defences at Alesia were replicated. It is fair to say that these researches laid a secure foundation for the study of the archaeology of the battle for Gaul.

Without the support afforded by the imperial treasury, subsequent progress was much slower and restricted to individual projects. In the later 20th century, however, attention began to be refocused on the archaeology of the war. A number of factors contributed to this: an upsurge in research on the Iron Age in France accompanied by an increasingly refined chronology which made it possible to identify features and finds of Caesarian date more accurately; a new study of Alesia was begun by a Franco-German team (Reddé and von Schnurbein 2001; 2008); and the establishment of the European Archaeological Centre at the Gaulish *oppidum* of Bibracte – supported by President François Mitterand – and the ensuing programmes of research. Independent of this trend, the massive increase in development-led archaeological fieldwork has led to the discovery of new sites while several new research projects are now revisiting the archaeology of the battle for Gaul and earlier Republican military campaigns in the west (Reddé 2018).

Some of those sites are in Britain and their recognition was the stimulus for a research project funded by the Leverhulme Trust at the University of Leicester to examine the archaeology of the British campaigns in their wider context. As part of the project a conference was organized in Oxford in 2017 with two aims. The first was to bring together researchers from different countries to present papers

Map showing location of key sites mentioned in the volume.

that through a mixture of geographically based or thematic approaches provided a balanced overview of recent archaeological and numismatic research across all the regions in which the war was fought. As much of the literature about this work has appeared in specialist archaeological publications and in a number of languages, the second aim was to make the overview readily available to scholars working in other disciplines, and in a single language. This book is the result.[1]

Three contributions set the scene: Krebs reiterates the fundamental role of Caesar's own account in shaping interpretations of the archaeological evidence for the war (Chapter 1) whilst Woolf sets the Gallic War in its Roman context (Chapter 2). Ralston then takes us to late Iron Age Gaul, where in recent years archaeology has fundamentally transformed our understanding of the complexity of Gaulish societies (Chapter 3). They were very different from Roman societies, but far more sophisticated than archaeologists could demonstrate only a quarter of a century ago.

Chapter 4 examines the now rapidly emerging archaeology of the Sertorian War in Spain (Morillo and Sala-Selés), which provides an important background to the Caesarian evidence from north-west Europe. Subsequent chapters focus on specific aspects of the Gallic War and are also largely geographical in scope (see map of key sites). Approaches range from the examination of individual sites and finds such as coin hoards in their context to national overviews. Further papers examine topics such as the social effects of fighting for Rome as auxiliaries and the ways in which archaeology has shaped concepts of ethnicity and identity.

It is not our intent to summarize the individual chapters here but rather to highlight some of the key themes that run through them. Some general points may also be made. Firstly, although the focus of this book is on the archaeology of the Gallic War, the authors integrate historical, archaeological and numismatic evidence. Secondly, the boundaries typically found in Anglophone work on research into Roman and prehistoric or protohistoric archaeology are mostly absent. While the influence of provincial Roman studies is also clear, the approaches presented here are distinct from most Roman military studies, particularly those focused on frontier studies of the Imperial period. In part this is because many of the authors are specialists in the Iron Age but also because in the mid-1st century BC the authority of Rome was still expanding and Caesar's army was very different from the Imperial one.

Romans at war

One of the most important developments in Roman military archaeology as a whole in recent years has been the increase in research undertaken in Iberia. This encompasses the whole of the Roman period but some of the most important work has been on the Republican period during which Rome fought many long and difficult wars in Iberia. For many years knowledge of Republican military sites was dominated by the research of Adolf Schulten in the earlier 20th century, who explored many sites – most notably the siege works encircling the *oppidum* of Numantia. Schulten used the excavation techniques of the day, typically establishing the outline of buildings by means of narrow trenches, and the results were interpreted primarily on the basis of the historical sources. This work undoubtedly provided many important results, but the small scale of the excavations restricted their value to subsequent archaeological research, as illustrated by Dobson's reanalyses of several of the sites examined by Schulten (*e.g.* 2008; 2013).

The research undertaken in recent decades has finally broken the shackles of what Morillo and Sala-Selés (Chapter 4) call the 'philological archaeology' approach practised by Schulten. A range of Republican military sites is now being recognized, from battlefields and siege works to fortresses and lookout posts. Although the detailed chronology of these sites is still emerging, one of the most important results in relation to the archaeology of the battle for Gaul is the identification of a number of sites that date to the Sertorian Wars, a Roman civil war that also involved many

Iberian communities. The war lasted from 80–72 BC and as less than a generation elapsed before the battle for Gaul began in 58 BC, the Roman bases associated with it provide an important baseline for what might be anticipated in Gaul.

There are a number of differences between sites of the Sertorian wars and those of the 2nd century BC explored by Schulten. The earlier camps did not always have defensive ditches, but they occur more frequently in ones of Sertorian date. The legionary base at Cáceres el Viejo has defensive ditches and is one the first camps with a rectangular plan and, unlike camps of Augustan and later date, the corners of the walls are right-angled rather than rounded. The oldest known Roman rampart made of earth and turf found is also dated to the Sertorian War, at Villajoyosa, Alicante. Although there is a trend to more rectangular camps, as Morillo and Sala-Selés observe, there is still considerable variety in the shape of camps and many campaign bases are essentially contour forts of irregular plan. As well as these military camps, destruction horizons are known at several settlements. As Morillo and Sala-Selés also note, it is likely that the horizon of sites currently attributed to the Sertorian Wars may well include some that may prove to date to the Spanish campaigns of the Great Roman Civil War of 49–45 BC. Although evidence for the attack of some settlements, such as Ilerda, has long been known (Engel and Paris 1901; Sievers 1997), the modern study of the settlements that were involved in this conflict is still in its infancy, as the case study on Puig Ciutat by Pujol *et al.* shows (Chapter 12).

The distinction between rectangular and irregularly shaped military camps is also evident in the Caesarian camps in Gaul, with the base at Mauchamp in northern France being rectangular but the forts and fortlets of the siege works at Alesia irregular. All these sites have earthen ramparts. Given the length and intensity of the campaigns in the battle for Gaul it is something of a surprise that even today, as Reddé observes (Chapter 6), so few certain Caesarian bases are known in Gaul (and several of these were identified during Napoléon III's researches).

In France as in Spain, fieldwork has contributed significantly to progress in recent years. In Spain extensive use has been made of non-invasive surveys, often involving metal detecting and, more recently, Lidar. In France aerial photography by Michel Boureux and Bernard Lambot among others has enhanced our understanding of the base at Mauchamp in the Aisne valley, but some of the most significant recent results have come from further work on the siege works at Alesia. A combination of air photography by René Goguey, painstaking archival research by Le Gall on the 19th-century excavation records and new excavations have allowed the reliability of the earlier work to be confirmed (Reddé and von Schnurbein 2001) and this provided a framework in which to reassess the older discoveries (Chapter 6).

A few new Roman bases have also been found but their identification is not always straightforward. The defensive ditch at Ebbsfleet, UK (Chapter 8), was first seen in a watching brief for a water pipeline and there was insufficient evidence to characterize the site until a large area was exposed in excavations in advance of a new road. Similarly, while some of the five camps now known at Valence, Drôme, are likely to be of Caesarian date, this has only become clearer as the size of the area excavated in advance of development has increased (Silvino *et al.* 2011; Conjard-Rethoré and Ferber 2013; Roumégous *et al.* 2016). In contrast, the camp at Hermeskeil (Chapter 11), part of which survives as an earthwork, has been known since the 19th century and one of several interpretations proposed for it was as a Roman camp. However, a number of small-scale excavations did not reveal anything distinctively military in character and the origins of the recent fieldwork was in a research project looking at late Iron Age settlement in the area (Hornung 2012).

The rectilinear base at Hermeskeil, which has an annexe, also had an earthen rampart but, surprisingly, the careful excavation of the south-west gate did not provide any evidence for a gate structure. The size of the defences indicates that Hermeskeil was not a marching camp and the discovery of rows of ovens there but no buildings, as at Valence and also at La Chaussée Tirancourt (Bayard and Fichtl 2016), indicates that the accommodation was in tents. With the exception of hobnails, only a few military objects have been found at Hermeskeil and this hints at why late Republican military sites can be hard to identify. The Roman army was developing from a citizen army to a standing army and allies were used extensively with the result that equipment was much less standardized than in the Imperial period.

Considerable progress has been made in the study of Roman militaria in recent years and the publication of a conference held in 2002 dedicated to the subject represents an important landmark (Poux 2008). Perhaps the most striking, not to say surprising, result of this work has been the recognition that the size and manufacturing techniques of hobnails provide a valuable means of not only indicating the presence of Roman soldiers at a site but also dating it. As a result, the size of the hobnails is one of the techniques used by Hornung to date Hermeskeil (Chapter 11) – and to date the camp east of the Rhine at Limberg (Meyer *et al.* 2013).

But, as Hornung shows, the scientific analysis of the other types of finds can make a major contribution. Provenance studies of the pottery and querns from Hermeskeil provide important information on the supply of the army and also on where its garrison, perhaps a combination of Roman legions and Gaulish cavalry, was previously stationed.

The study of defences, garrisons and military supply are well-established areas of study in the archaeology of the Imperial Roman army but some of the differences between the camps of the Republican and of the Imperial armies are striking. The battle for Gaul was fought for almost a decade yet to date not a single temporary marching camp of the types so well-known in northern Europe from the Augustan period onwards has been certainly identified. This includes parts of Gaul that have seen extensive aerial reconnaissance (*e.g.* Agache 1978 for Picardy) but also Italy. The civil war between Caesar and Pompey was preceded by other internal conflicts, yet to date the only base known is near Trieste in north-east Italy (Bernardini *et al.* 2015). During the Sertorian War some camps began regularly to have defensive ditches, but it is not clear that this extended to temporary camps.

The *hiberna*, the winter bases of Caesar's legions, are almost as elusive. Here the evidence from the *oppidum* at the Titelberg, Luxembourg, is thought-provoking. There, evidence for what is interpreted as a Roman trading post, replete with wall paintings and terrazzo and *opus spicatum* floors, dates to the period between the battle for Gaul and the Roman occupation under Augustus. Elsewhere in Gaul many late Iron Age *oppida* have yielded large quantities of Roman goods. These objects have usually been interpreted as evidence for trade with the Roman world but, as the buildings found at the Titelberg show, the objects could also indicate the presence of Romans, and perhaps suggest where the *hiberna* of Caesar's legions were.

But the battle for Gaul was not only fought on land. In 56 BC, the sea battle between the Venetii and Romans, probably in Quiberon Bay, north-west France, was the decisive battle of that year's campaigning. The invasion of Britain in 54 BC could not have been achieved without a major programme of ship building that was undertaken by the legions during the preceding winter, sometimes far from the coast. Although it has long been assumed that the Channel ports that were used had built harbour structures such as jetties and quays, this view is anachronistic and Fitzpatrick argues (Chapter 8) that these critical places for embarking and disembarking the army safely were essentially natural places, just beaches. One of the reasons behind the identification of Ebbsfleet as the place where the Roman fleet landed in Britain in 54 BC is its match with the topographic clues given, in passing, in Caesar's commentaries.

Gauls, Germans and Britons

The correlation of landscape with text in relation to events recounted by Caesar harks back to the methods of Napoléon III's *Commission de la Topographie des Gaules*. Many of these places were battlefields or towns that were besieged and although traditionally viewed as the sites of Roman victories, they involved many combatants, be they Gauls, Germans or Britons. Many *oppida* in Gaul can be equated, with varying degrees of certainty, with places mentioned by Caesar[2] and the sites of the sieges of Alesia and Uxellodunum have been identified though the archaeological evidence for the siege works and the battlefields.

Most *oppida* in Gaul already had fortifications, but in many cases, these ramparts had been built several decades earlier, had been conceived more with an eye to status than to practical considerations of defence, and were now in a state of some disrepair. The Gauls responded to Roman siege warfare by building carefully engineered defences designed to prevent siege engines or tunnels reaching the defences of the *oppida*. As Krauz shows (Chapter 9), these were massive engineering works and in regions such as Berry where several sites were fortified in this way, would have required a huge labour force.

There is also increasing evidence for attacks on settlements, whether through sieges or direct assaults, and for battlefields, most often in the form of assault or sieges on settlements. Spain provides evidence for assaults on settlements from both the Sertorian and Great Civil Wars (Chapters 4 and 12). The discovery of Roman lead sling bullets in the rampart of the hillfort at Thuin, Belgium, has led Roymans to identify it as the *oppidum* of the Aduatuci (Chapter 7). Identifying the sites of battles that did not take place near settlements is more difficult, as the continuing search for the site of the battle of Bibracte shows. While the most recent attempts to identify it are suggestive, they are not conclusive (Flutsch and Furger-Gunti 1987; Kaenel, Chapter 5). No such doubt attaches to the siege of Uxellodunum. The site was examined as part of the research of Napoléon III, but re-excavation and, as importantly, the full publication of the results has provided a graphic image of the assault. The fountain of Loulié was the only source of drinking water for the inhabitants of the *oppidum*, and part of the deadly barrage of projectiles that rained down on it has been found (Giraut 2013). As well as siege works, temporary battlefield obstacles were also built. The identification of Gergovia has also long been agreed, but it is only recently that work at the nearby *oppida* of Corent and Gondole and in the landscape between them has revealed the large scale of the temporary defences built by the Romans and the first details of the artillery attacks on some of the sites.

Outside Gondole several pits containing multiple burials of animals have been found, mainly of horses but also some of cattle and sheep. It is not clear if all of these burials were directly associated with the war (Deberge *et al.* 2014) but the famous grave of eight men and eight horses seems likely to represent the clearing of a battle site. The extent of the defences is a testimony to the number of combatants, particularly in 52 BC, when tens of thousands fought on each side. Identifying on whose side some soldiers were fighting is not straightforward, since Gauls and Germans fought alongside the Roman legions as either allies or auxiliaries, often using the same equipment as their opponents.

In the aftermath of battle, entire populations could sometimes be sold as slaves, as with the 53,000 people of the Aduatuci (Chapter 7), but the number of casualties could also run into many thousands and sometimes included non-combatants. The siege of Avaricum ended with the entire population being massacred by the Roman army and a similar fate had earlier befallen the Germanic tribes, the Tencteri and Usipetes. Using the topographical descriptions provided by Caesar, Roymans locates this battle at the confluence of the Waal and the Meuse, and associates with it a range of finds from the Meuse at Kessel and Lith. These include number of weapons, of both Iron Age and Roman types, and costume fittings of Germanic type. These finds have previously been interpreted as votive offerings. However, when set alongside the numerous human remains (some of them with weapon trauma) from the river that have been radiocarbon dated to the late Iron Age, and a small number of stable isotope analyses that indicate that the individuals were not local to area, Roymans reinterprets the objects as the belongings of the Tencteri and Usipetes.

This change in interpretation, from finds deposited as votive offerings over many years to the testimony of a single episode of genocide, also illustrates the practical difficulty in dating Iron Age objects precisely enough to allow them to be associated confidently with the battle for Gaul. This is seen most clearly in coinage. Iron Age gold and silver coins of the early to mid-1st century BC are very common both in hoards and as single finds; their uses undoubtedly included raising armies and paying soldiers. The large amounts of coins issued at this time are thus a good measure of the numbers of soldiers who fought in the war, and in both Celtic and Belgic Gaul, the minting of a wide range of gold and silver types, followed by the ending of gold coinage, has been more or less plausibly associated with the battle for Gaul for many years (*e.g.* Scheers 1972).

However, associating individual types of coins with individual historical events is far from easy, especially when, as with many late gold types, the coins are uninscribed and rarely if ever found in well-sealed and independently dated archaeological contexts (Haselgrove 1999). It is understandable that chronologies often gravitate towards historical events as a result (*e.g.* Roymans *et al.* 2012; Sills 2017), but there is a recurrent tension between this approach and an archaeological one that is based on associated finds, which often suggests an earlier dating (Chapter 13).

On occasion historically based chronologies can produce contradictory results. This is well illustrated by the massive number of coins from the Le Câtillon II hoard on Jersey, Channel Islands (Chapter 14). This is the largest hoard of Gaulish coins yet discovered. The great majority of the coins were issued in present-day Brittany and most of them are attributed to the Armorican people known as the Coriosolitae. The standard French chronology for these coins envisages their issue ceasing after the battle for Gaul and initially the hoard was interpreted as dating to the campaign in north-west France in 56 BC. However, the hoard was soon found to contain a small number of British coins. One of the chronologies commonly advanced for British coinage (Cottam *et al.* 2010; Sills 2017) sees the first large-scale minting of gold coins as not starting until 55 BC when Julius Caesar invaded Britain. As the coins in the Le Câtillon II hoard are not the earliest British types, that historically based chronology would place the deposition of the hoard up to 20 years later than the French historically based chronology. Both of these historically based chronologies could be wrong, but they cannot both be right (Chapter 13).

There is a temptation to associate exceptional finds such as the Le Câtillon II hoard, or ones that are clearly not of local origin with the Gallic War. The bronze Gaulish helmet found in a late Iron Age burial near Canterbury (Farley *et al.* 2012) is a good example of the latter. It is harder to identify the impact of the war on the pattern of settlement. When the Helvetii began their migration, Caesar reported that they burnt all of their settlements, from *oppida* to farms, and all their corn apart from what they could carry with them in order to remove all hope of returning home. But despite the painstaking excavation at several *oppida* in Switzerland, no unambiguous evidence for destruction horizons has been found. The same is true of those regions where a scorched-earth policy was adopted by one side or the other.

In regions where there was a considerable decrease in the population, whether due to death in battle, slavery, genocide or deliberate resettlement by Caesar, it might be anticipated that there would be archaeological evidence for a reduction in the number of settlements or some other form of discontinuity. The exponential increase in the quantity and quality of evidence for Iron Age rural settlements due to development-led projects across western Europe is beginning to provide a dataset that can be systematically examined for such changes (Chapter 7; Malrain *et al.* 2013). However, at present it is difficult to identify suitable evidence, which, while it may exist, is difficult to define because of the limitations of current dating methods. The difficulties in establishing fine-grained chronologies for when coins were issued are much more pronounced when dealing with pottery, which is still the most common dating material found on settlements. Large numbers of radiocarbon determinations are needed to undertake Bayesian modelling and while this can provide much more accurate date ranges, the modelled dates are statements of statistical probability and not conventional historical dates.

In Gaul, where long-term trends in Iron Age settlement type and location can now be clearly delineated (Malrain *et al.* 2013), one of the major changes in settlement pattern relating to the battle for Gaul seems not to have occurred until decades later, when many *oppida* were superseded by newly founded Roman towns that were typically located on valley floors rather than hilltops. Many areas of Gaul do show a pronounced decline in rural settlement numbers in the 1st century BC (La Tène D2), but it is clear that this does not constitute a single horizon; in some areas the Gallic War was very probably a contributory factor to the changes in settlement numbers, but this cannot yet be demonstrated with certainty and the war was not necessarily the most important cause (*e.g.* Haselgrove and Guichard 2013).

One change that had long-term effects was the use of auxiliaries by the Romans (Chapter 10). These included slingers and archers from the Mediterranean world, but all the cavalry seem to have come from either Gaul or Germany. Some of these men have been identified through the weapons placed in their graves which are often of Iron Age rather than Roman types. This would have caused the immediate displacement of large numbers of young men, and many continued to serve Caesar in the Civil War. In one sense this re-established the long-standing tradition of mercenary service in the Mediterranean world (Baray 2015), but it also provided an important way of maintaining peace after the war by removing men of fighting age from their homelands. One of the rewards for such service could be Roman citizenship, which was an important means of ensuring the peaceful administration of a new province. Beyond the provinces a network of client kings was established and there is clear evidence for this in Britain from coinage and the funerary record (Creighton 2000; Fitzpatrick 2007).

Future research directions

As the individual chapters all show there is a now considerable body of archaeological evidence for the battle for Gaul. Some is old, one of the legacies of the researches of Napoléon III, but there is much that is new, which will help hone the archaeological signature of the war and its aftermath, and this will doubtless stimulate the recognition of further evidence.

A prerequisite to enabling this is a more refined chronology. The finds from Alesia have long been used to provide a fixed point in the typologies of Iron Age objects (Chapter 15). Even when allied to Bayesian modelling, radiocarbon dating cannot yet offer equivalent precision but has the potential to establish whether a Caesarian dating should be considered. At present there are radiocarbon dates from only a few sites that can be confidently regarded as Caesarian: the Roman military ones at Ebbsfleet and Hermeskeil and the battlefield sites of Gondole and Kessel/Lith. There are also dates from some settlements that can be plausibly associated with the war, for example Bigberry and Thuin. In view of the evidence from Britain where some sites that can be confidently dated to the 1st century BC using object typologies have returned radiocarbon dates that are significantly earlier (Garrow *et al.* 2008; Fitzpatrick *et al.* 2017), the dating of material from sites that was deposited in a single year would help improve the understanding of the reasons behind the discrepancies. In contrast, agreeing the detailed chronology of the coinage that illuminates much of the war is perhaps more of a theoretical than a methodological issue.

Although Roman bases have now been identified in Germany and Britain, as yet there is no certain evidence from western and north-western France. In the same way that some evidence in Spain that is currently attributed to the Sertorian Wars may eventually be shown to derive from the Great Civil War, some of the evidence currently attributed to the battle for Gaul may also prove to be of different date. In central and southern France this includes the revolt of the Allobroges in 62 BC, and in northern France some Roman military sites date to early in the Principate and it is not certain to which historical episode they are to be associated. This is well illustrated by the evidence from the *oppidum* of La Chaussée-Tirancourt, Somme, which was used by Roman forces in both the battle for Gaul and in the early Principate (Fichtl 1995; Bayard and Fichtl 2016).

Identifying Roman bases of late Republican date is also not entirely straightforward. Their shapes may be different from what has often been anticipated and Roman militaria may comprise only a small component of the finds assemblage. Identifying the impact of the battle for Gaul on Iron Age settlements is harder still. The appearance of new types of defences, the identification of evidence for assaults on defended sites and/or their abandonment, and changes in the wider settlement pattern, are, superficially at least, relatively straightforward to interpret. Characterizing and identifying evidence for the provisioning and arming of the large numbers of men that were involved in the war is much harder.

However, archaeology is well equipped to take on such challenges and the quality and quantity of evidence is ever increasing. This book focuses on the material remains and only touches lightly on other important wider themes, such as identity and ethnicity, imperialism and nationalism. The battle for Gaul was a defining event in the history of many of the Iron Age societies of north-west Europe, and its archaeology, in all its aspects, merits renewed research. We hope that this book will encourage such research.

Acknowledgements

Our foremost thanks are to the contributors for sharing their research and for preparing their lectures and chapters in English. The conference was organized by the Department of Continuing Education, University of Oxford and our thanks are due to Dr Alison MacDonald and her colleagues for making the event so enjoyable. Pamela Lowther helped with the copy editing and preparing the final illustrations, while at Oxbow Books, Julie Gardiner and Jessica Scott have overseen the publication. The *In the Footsteps of Caesar* project at the University of Leicester is funded by a generous grant from the Leverhulme Trust.

Notes

1 The papers in this volume are largely as presented at the conference. Christopher Krebs' opening lecture in Oxford formed part of a wider project which he has since published (Krebs 2018) and he has instead kindly written a short new contribution. The volume also includes two chapters on topics not presented at the conference, one by Pujol *et al.* reporting on a potential Civil War fortified site in Catalonia, the other by Haselgrove on coinage and the Gallic War.

2 A few *oppida* named by Caesar have not been satisfactorily identified on the ground, despite the name being perpetuated in a major Roman town. Places where mid-1st-century BC occupation has yet to be conclusively demonstrated include Lutetia (Paris) and Samarobriva (Amiens). Possibly the name applied to the general locality or originated in a nearby late Iron Age focus, such as Nanterre or La Chaussée-Tirancourt.

Bibliography

Agache, R. (1978) *La Somme pré-romaine et romaine.* Amiens, Mémoire de la Société Archéologique de Picardie 24.

Baray, L. (2014) *Les mercenaires celtes et la culture de La Tene. Critères archéologiques et positions sociologiques.* Dijon, Éditions universitaires de Dijon.

Bayard, D. and Fichtl, S. (2016) Le 'Camp César' de la Chaussée-Tirancourt (Somme). *Oppidum* gaulois ou camp romain? In G. Blancquaert and F. Malrain (eds), Évolution *des sociétés gauloises du Second* âge *du Fer, entre mutations internes et influences externes (Actes du 38e colloque international de l'AFEAF, Amiens 2014)*, 343–362. Amiens, Revue Archéologique de Picardie Numéro spécial 30.

Bernadini, F., Vinci, G., Horvat, J., Min, A., de, Forte, E., Furlani, S., Lenaz, D., Pipan, M., Zhao, W., Sgambati, A., Potleca, M., Micheli, R., Fragiacomo, A. and Tuniz, C. (2015) Early Roman military fortifications and the origin of Trieste, Italy. *Proceedings of the National Academy of Sciences* 112, E1520–9. doi: 10.1073/pnas.1419175112.

Conjard Réthoré, P. and Ferber, E. (2013) Les camps romains du plateau de Lautagne à Valence (26) – état de la question. *Revue Archéologique Narbonnaise* 46, 201–220.

Cottam, E., de Jersey, P., Rudd, C., and Sills, J. (2010) *Ancient British Coins.* Aylsham, Chris Rudd.

Creighton, J. (2000) *Coins and Power in Late Iron Age Britain.* Cambridge, Cambridge University Press.

Deberge, Y., Baucheron, F., Cabezuelo, U., Caillat, P., Gatto, E., Landry, C., Leguet, D., Pasty, J.-F., Pertlweiser, T., Vermeulen, C. and Vernet, G. (2014) Témoignages de la Guerre des Gaules dans le bassin clermontois, nouveaux apports. *Revue archéologique du Centre de la France* 53, 1–47.

Dobson, M. (2008) *The Army of the Roman Republic. The Second Century BC, Polybius and the Camps at Numantia, Spain.* Oxford, Oxbow Books.

Dobson, M. (2013) No holiday camp: The Roman Republican army camp as a fine-tuned instrument of war. In J. De Rose Evans (ed.), *A Companion to the Archaeology of the Roman Republic*, 214–234. Oxford, Wiley-Blackwell.

Engel, A. and Paris, P. (1906) Une forteresse ibérique à Osuna (fouille de 1903). *Nouvelles archives des missions scientifiques et littéraires* XIII (4), 357–490.

Farley, J., Parfitt, K., Richardson, A., Antoine, D., Pope, R. and Sparey-Green, C. (2014) A late Iron Age helmet burial from Bridge, near Canterbury, Kent. *Proceedings of the Prehistoric Society* 80, 379–388.

Fichtl, S. (1995) Les fouilles de la porte intérieure du site fortifié de La Chaussée-Tirancourt (Somme). *Revue Archéologique de Picardie* 1/2 1995, 135–148.

Fitzpatrick, A.P. (2007) The fire, the feast and the funeral. Late Iron Age burial rites in southern England. In V. Kruta and G. Leman-Delerive (eds), *Feux des morts, foyers des vivants. Les rites et symboles du feu dans les tombes de l'Âge du Fer et de l'*époque *romaine*, 123–142. Villeneuve d'Ascq, Revue de Nord Hors Série, Collection Art et Archéologie 11.

Fitzpatrick, A.P., Hamilton, D. and Haselgrove, C. (2017) Radiocarbon dating and Bayesian modelling of the late Iron Age cremation burial cemetery at Westhampnett, West Sussex, GB. *Archäologisches Korrespondenzblatt* 47, 359–381.

Flutsch, L. and Furger-Gunti, A. (1987) Recherches archéologiques sur le site présumé de la bataille de Bibracte: campagne d'exploration d'une équipe suisse à Montfort', Département de Saône-et-Loire, France. *Zeitschrift für Schweizerische Archäologie und Kunstgeschichte* 44, 241–251.

Garrow, D., Gosden. C., Hill, J.D. and Bronk Ramsey, C. (2009) Dating Celtic art: a major radiocarbon dating programme of Iron Age and early Roman metalwork in Britain. *Archaeological Journal* 166, 79–123.

Girault, J.-P. (2013) *La Fontaine de Loulié au Puy d'Issolud. Le dossier archéologique du siège d'Uxellodunum.* Glux-en-Glenne, Collection Bibracte 23.

Griffith, M. (ed.) (2009) *A Companion to Julius Caesar.* Oxford, Wiley-Blackwell.

Grillo, L. and Krebs, C.B. (eds) (2018) *The Cambridge Companion to the Writings of Julius Caesar.* Cambridge, Cambridge University Press.

Haselgrove, C. (1999) The development of coinage in Belgic Gaul. *Numismatic Chronicle* 159, 111–168.

Haselgrove, C. and Guichard, V. (2013) Les Gaulois sont-ils dans la plaine? Reflections on settlement patterns in Gaul in the 1st century BC. In S. Krausz, A. Colin, K. Gruel, I. Ralston, T. Dechezleprêtre (eds), *L'âge du Fer en Europe. Mélanges offerts à Olivier Buchsenschutz*, 301–311. Bordeaux, Maison Ausonius.

Hornung, S. (2012) Ein spätrepublikanisches Militärlager bei Hermeskeil (Lkr. Trier-Saarburg). Vorbericht über die Forschungen 2010–2011. *Archäologisches Korrespondenzblatt* 43, 205–224.

Krebs, C. (2018) The World's Measure: Caesar's geographies of Gallia and Britannia in their contexts and as evidence of his world map. *American Journal of Philology* 139, 1 (no. 553), 93–122.

Laronde, A., Toubert, P. and Leclant, J. (eds) (2011) *Histoire et archéologie méditerranéennes sous Napoléon III (Actes du 21e colloque de la Villa Kérylos à Beaulieu-sur-Mer, les 8 and 9 octobre 2010).* Paris, Cahiers de la Villa 'Kérylos' 22.

Malrain, F., Blancquaert, G. and Lorho, T. (2013) *L'habitat rural du second âge du Fer. Rythmes de création et d'abandon au nord de la Loire.* Paris, Inrap/CNRS, Recherches archéologiques 7.

Metzler, J., Gaeng, C. and Méniel, P. (2016) *L'espace public du Titelberg.* Luxembourg, Dossiers d'archéologie du musée national d'histoire et d'art XVII.

Meyer, J., Schade-Lindig, S. and Schallmayer, E. (2013) De bello Gallico in Hessen – archäologische Spuren Caesars rechts des Rheins. *Denkmalpflege und Kulturgeschichte Hessen* 2013 (4), 2–9.

Nicolet, C. (2009) Caesar and the two Napoleons. In M. Griffith (ed.), *A Companion to Julius Caesar*, 410–417. Oxford, Wiley-Blackwell.

Poux, M. (ed.) (2008) *Sur les traces de César. Militaria tardo-républicains en contexte gaulois.* Glux-en-Glenne, Collection Bibracte 14.

Raaflaub, K.A. (2017) *The Landmark Julius Caesar: The Complete Works.* New York, Pantheon Books.

Reddé, M. (ed.) (2018) *L'armées romaines en Gaule à l'époque républicaine. Nouveaux témoignages archéologiques*. Glux-en-Glenne, Collection Bibracte 28.
Reddé, M. and Schnurbein, S. von (eds) (2001) *Alésia: fouilles et recherches Franco-Allemands sur les travaux militaires romains autour du Mont-Auxois (1991–1997)*. Paris, Mémoires de l'Académie des Inscriptions et Belles-Lettres 22.
Reddé, M. and Schnurbein, S. von (eds) (2008) *Alésia et la bataille du Teutoburg. Un parallèle critique des sources*. Paris, Francia Beiheft 66.
Roumégous, A., Zaaraoui, Y., Kielb, M. and Buffat, L. (2016) Des amphores par légions... Les contextes tardo-républicains des camps militaires romains de Lautagne (Valence, Drôme). In L. Rivet and S. Saulnier (eds), *Société française d'étude de la céramique antique en Gaule, Congrès d'Autun, 5–8 mai 2016*, 443–460. Marseilles, SFECAG.
Roymans, N., Creemers, G. and Scheers, S. (2012) *Late Iron Age Gold Hoards from the Low Countries and the Caesarian Conquest of Gaul*. Amsterdam, Amsterdam Archaeological Studies 18.
Scheers, S. (1972) Coinage and currency of the Belgic tribes during the Gallic War. *British Numismatic Journal* 41, 1–6.
Sievers, S. (1997) Alésia und Osuna. Bemerkungen zur Normierung der spätrepublikanischen Bewaffnung und Ausrüstung. In M. Feugère (ed.), *L'équipment militaire et l'armement de la république (IVe–Ier s. av. J.-C.), Roman Military Equipment Conference (ROMEC) X, Montpellier, septembre 1996*, 271–276. London, Journal of Roman Military Equipment Studies 8.
Sills, J. (2017) *Divided Kingdoms. The Iron Age Gold Coinage of Southern England*. Aylsham, Chris Rudd.
Silvino, T., Maza, G., Faure, P., Tran, N. and Argant T. (2011) Les origines de la colonie romaine de Valence (Drôme). *Gallia* 68.2, 109–154.

Chapter 1

Scylla, Caesar and Charybdis: (Mis)readings of the *Gallic War*

Christopher B. Krebs

'Vercingetorix' stands, some 20 feet tall, on top of Mont Auxois near Alise-Sainte-Reine; decked out with a cuirass and a necklace of pearls, and with his hands resting on the pommeled hilt of his hefty sword, he gazes, mournfully perhaps, into the distance. Commissioned by Napoléon III, sculpted by Aimé Millet, and erected in 1865 (Figure 1.1), he commemorates, as the second of two inscriptions specifies, Vercingetorix, Caesar's main antagonist in the great Gallic uprising of 52 BCE, who lost his final battle defending the *oppidum* of Alesia on this very hilltop.[1] It seems only proper, then, that the Roman leader is present too, inscribed, that is, into the statue's base; for the upper inscription reads: 'La Gaule unie, formant une seule nation, animée d'un même esprit, peut défier l'univers.' It is an adapted excerpt from a speech that Caesar, in his *Gallic War*, reports of Vercingetorix, who promises 'to effect one plan for all of Gaul; and not even the whole world can withstand its unanimity' (*unum consilium totius Galliae effecturum, cuius consensui ne orbis quidem terrarum possit obsistere*; *BG* 7.29).

To the keen eye, 'Vercingetorix' quickly disintegrates: archaeologists will be quick to point out that his anachronistic accoutrements date from a range of periods other than Vercingetorix's own, what with his armament from the Bronze Age, and his pantaloons Merovingian; and anyone familiar with Napoléon III will notice the *uncanny* resemblance (Le Gall 1970, 207–208). 'Vercingetorix', it appears, is doubly representative, albeit in starkly uneven measure: he tells today's observer a great deal about a modern ruler's infatuation with Caesar and his battle for Gaul, a great deal, too, about 'the' Gaul in the artistic imagination of the Second Empire;[2] and exceedingly little about his actual referent, Vercingetorix himself. As such, he may well be said to emblematize the mythical transmogrification the Gallic leader has undergone over the last century and a half.[3]

As the upper inscription neatly intimates, any interest in the Iron Age Gallic man underneath the 19th-century French monument ultimately leads to Caesar's

Figure 1.1 Nineteenth-century statue of Arvernian chieftain Vercingetorix by Aimé Millet, at Mont Auxois, Alise-Sainte-Reine, Côte-d'Or (courtesy Muséoparc Alésia, photo T. Clarté, Balloïde Photo).

Gallic War, as, first, it is the only extant contemporary account by an eyewitness (for the most part); second, it is highly uncertain to what – if any – extent later retellings of the campaigns (such as Plutarch's or Cassius Dio's) contain anything additional or contradictory to Caesar's account that is not owed to error, inference, condensation or rhetorical elaboration; and, lastly, even the coins that bear Vercingetorix's name by themselves tell us next to nothing other than that he seems to have been more important than any other of the five Arvernian leaders Caesar mentions, for whom we lack numismatic evidence.[4] 'Vercingetorix', in his statued embodiment as well as any other manifestation, owes his existence to Caesar; the ironies multiply.

What is true of the Gallic leader holds true also – if to a lesser degree – of the battle for Gaul in general; and this is another way in which 'Vercingetorix' may serve us as an emblem. For all the clarification and correction that archaeology – the only truly independent (or is it?) alternative source – has brought to our understanding of the Gallic campaigns, it bears recalling what Christian Goudineau stated in the middle of his review of archaeological findings concerning these campaigns some twenty years ago: 'à supposer que César n'eût pas écrit ses *Commentaires* et que nul auteur antique ne s'en fut inspiré, la recherche archéologique aurait été incapable d'imaginer qu'il s'était déroulé, entre 58 et 50 av. J.-C, une série d'expéditions militaires sur le territoire gaulois.'[5] Let us just think, once more, of the almost two-dozen coins bearing Vercingetorix's name and how difficult it would be to understand their full significance without Caesar's narrative. In consequence, for the purposes of this volume (and beyond), a contextual understanding and watchful reading of the *Gallic War* are imperative.

Caesar's 'Notes on events in the Gallic War', *commentarii rerum gestarum belli Gallici*, as its original title in all likelihood ran, have traditionally been read – and more often than not from the lectern – with an historical or linguistic interest: time and again, students of history and Latin (were) marched through their pages.[6] Caesar's style seems to encourage both: tendentiously characterized by none other than his political and intellectual rival Cicero as 'naked ... straight and charming, with all embellishment of speech stripped off just like a dress' (*nudi ... recti et venusti, omni ornatu orationis tamquam veste detracta*, *Brutus* 262), these 'Notes', as highlighted by the deprecatory title, suggest easy access to what happened in Gaul and (the learning of) the Latin language.

But both views require qualification. Cicero, again (*Brutus* 261), addressing Caesar's Latin more particularly, comments on how the latter 'correct[ed] faulty and corrupt usage with his pure and uncorrupted usage (*pura et incorrupta consuetudine*), aided by theory (*rationem adhibens*)'; and we now understand much better just how Caesar created his lapidary schoolbook-friendly regular idiom out of the irregular Latin of the time, with a discerning eye on the qualities of the language of the Roman state.[7] And just as Caesar shaped his own idiom, so he shaped his narrative, choosing the places, protagonists and occurrences to include as well as the (usually) small amount of detail to provide of them. There are several reasons for the often vague, sometimes misleading presentations of motivations, movements and military engagements. But his contemporaries already felt a certain malaise when reading an account for which one and the same man answered as both protagonist and author; and just so we have come to appreciate rather more fully how the author's political stake colours his (re) presentation of events and participants in the *Gallic War*. Caesar writes about 'Caesar', 'Vercingetorix', and 'the battle for Gaul', as it were: Michel Rambaud (1966), who half a century ago looked deeply into Caesar's *art de la déformation historique*, overshot, it seemed to most of his critics, when he suggested that the seemingly straightforward war narrative was in fact the product of *all*-pervasive rhetorical manipulation for political purchase; but it is in no small part Rambaud's legacy that any responsible reading of the *Gallic War* today must proceed at equidistance from both a naïve positivism and a radical scepticism.[8]

Just as political concerns warped the *Gallic War*, so did literary ones. Mostly forgotten today, to his (near) contemporaries Caesar was known not only as an efficient politician and quick-footed general but also as an eminent man of letters, whose list of accomplishments – in oratory and linguistics, in engineering and geography – was long. When the imperial encyclopaedist Pliny the Elder, a man of formidable learning, pondered Caesar with hindsight, he lamented his battle for Gaul, which 'I for one should not set down to his glory'; but he praised the man of

Figure 1.2 Gold stater of Vercingetorix from the hoard discovered at Pionsat, Puy-de-Dôme in 1852. Diameter 19mm. Delestrée and Tache (2007) type DT 3601 (© Musée Danicourt, Péronne / Bibracte, photo Antoine Maillier).

letters, whose 'intellectual excellence [was] capable of comprehending everything under the skies'.[9] As such Caesar knew that (ancient) histories were treated much the same way we today treat historical fiction: that around a core (often small) of sober historical facts, colourful details, pulled from the rhetorical and literary traditions and the author's poetic imagination, had to be woven into the text.[10] As has become increasingly apparent, the *Commentarii*, despite their dismissive and disarming title[11] and their first impression of simplicity, owe plenty to these traditions. This – more recent – third way of reading, often styled 'historiographical', differs from the more traditional historical one in that the former looks for evidence of rhetorical embellishment and borrowings from other Greek and Roman authors (historians amongst them) where the latter (more or less) simply assumes facts. It makes them both more interesting as literary text and more problematic as historical source: is 'Vercingetorix' characterized as a 'young man' (*adulescens*, *BG* 7.4.1), because he was in his 20s when he rose against Caesar; or because other famous enemies of Rome (such as Hannibal) had previously been characterized as young men in Greek and

Roman histories (Polybius 3.15.6 ἅτε νέος ... ὤν, 'for he [Hannibal] was young')? The youthful depictions of 'Vercingetorix' on contemporary coins (Figure 1.2) do not, unfortunately, offer any independent corroboration, as they, in turn, adhere to their own conventions (Nieto-Pelletier 2012, 243–245).

Once again, to dismiss all of the detail in the *commentarii* as 'commonplace' would be just as foolish as to accept it all as fact; indeed, it may on occasion be both: when Gergovia, Vercingetorix's most likely place of birth, is described as 'located atop a high mountain' (*posita in altissimo monte*), the topographical image is both realistic – the *Plateau de Gergovie* (formerly *Plateau de Merdogne*) rises about 1,000 feet above the terrain – and conventional, as for example passages in the poet Horace or the historian Tacitus show.[12] What appears clearly, however, is how careful a reading is required.

Where available, material finds (or other sources of information) can shed additional light on both the battle for Gaul and Caesar's (re)presentation thereof in his *Gallic War*; but it must be reiterated that there are no absolutes, since (much of) our understanding of the archaeological record of the Iron Age is fundamentally shaped by the *Gallic War*.[13] To this day, a certain kind of extant Gallic fortification is called *murus Gallicus*, 'Gallic wall', a designation used by Caesar in a highly Roman description of what he perceived to be the typical Gallic bulwark.[14] One may perhaps wonder what archaeologists would have made of the excavated fortifications without Caesar's description, just as one may wonder whether readers of the *Gallic War* passage would not still be struggling with some of the detail of the description and its general authenticity, if no *muri Gallici* had ever been found.[15]

Notes

1 'Napoléon III, empereur des Français, à la mémoire de Vercingétorix.' The history of the statue is discussed in Le Gall 1970; he quotes, among others, Henry Martin's poetic impression: 'L'attitude est grave, recueillie, méditative, l'aspect général est imposant et mélancolique.'

2 Le Gall (1970, 219) happily speaks of 'Vercingetorix' as 'un témoin de son temps'. On Napoléon III's fascination with Caesar, see Nicolet 2009, 414–417 and Olivier this volume; on the reception of his *Histoire de Jules César*, whose first volume appeared in the same year, 1865: Richardson 2016.

3 For an 'Historiographie d'un mythe', see Harmand 1989.

4 Discussion of contemporary accounts: Zecchini 1978 (though with implausible conclusions, see Pelling 1982); for a balanced summary and further literature, see Drummond 2013, 439 n. 63. For surveys of the tradition of the conquest of Gaul from Cicero to Orosius, see Sihler 1887 and Gelzer 1955. Vercingetorix's coins: Colbert de Beaulieu and Lefèvre 1963 (esp. 11 n. 1). On the hermeneutical difficulty: Nieto-Pelletier 2012, 235–236.

5 Goudineau 1991, 644 (while the review itself is now quite dated, its conclusion is not); along similar (but less emphatic) lines: Reddé 2008, 284 (but cf. note 13). For more recent overviews of the implications of archaeological finds for our understanding of the *Gallic War*, see Bénard 1996 (esp. 51, 56, 59–63), Reddé 2008 and this volume.

6 The title is reconstructed in Kelsey 1905. On the meaning(s) of '*commentarius*', see Riggsby 2006, 133–150. In point of fact, the Latin is ambiguous, and *commentarii rerum gestarum* might also be translated as 'notes for a (future) history'; I explore some possible implications in Krebs 2017.

Pascucci (1973, 502) elegantly summed up the ambivalent popularity of the *Bellum Gallicum* as a school text as 'la (s)fortuna di Cesare'.

7 I have attempted an updated overview of Caesar's style in Krebs 2018.

8 Rambaud (1966, 364) conceded that Caesar narrated real events, 'mais du côté qui convient à ses intérêts, et les formes de son récit suscitent chez le lecteur une impression fausse.' On 'Caesar constructing Caesar', see Batstone 2018.

9 Pliny, *Natural History* 7.91–92: *animi vigore praestantissimum arbitror genitum Caesarem dictatorem, nec virtutem constantiamque nunc commemoro nec sublimitatem omnium capacem quae caelo continentur, sed proprium vigorem celeritatemque quodam igne volucrem. ... nam praeter civiles victorias undeciens centena et nonaginta duo milia hominum occisa proeliis ab eo non equidem in gloria posuerim...* On Caesar as an intellectual, see Fantham 2009 and Schiesaro 2010. I am currently preparing a fuller treatment (Krebs forthcoming a).

10 Woodman 1983 develops this analogy nicely.

11 But see note 6 above.

12 *BG* 7.36.1. Horace, *Odes* 4.14.11–12 *arces / Alpibus impositas*, and Tacitus, *Annals* 4.46.5 *castella rupibus indita.*

13 Reddé 2008, 280 emphasizes how 'l'archéologie est en effet devenue, aujourd'hui, une science autonome, qui a ses protocoles et ses règles, fondées sur l'observation, l'analyse des contextes et la comparaison avec d'autres données issues de méthodes comparables. Mais elle ne peut éviter, en définitive, le dialogue avec les textes historiques, quand ceux-ci existent.'

14 *BG* 7.23.1: *muri autem omnes Gallici hac fere forma sunt*. Dozens of such walls have been excavated (Buchsenschutz and Ralston 2014 give an overview); but other types of rampart have been found in Gaul as well. Caesar's subsequent description is informed by Greco-Roman architectural theory, as, soon after, formulated by Vitruvius (as I discuss in my commentary on *BG* 7, Krebs forthcoming b).

15 I should like to thank Andrew Fitzpatrick and Colin Haselgrove for their kind invitation to speak at the conference (thus also enabling me to learn a lot in a short time) as well as for their comments on an earlier version of this contribution.

Bibliography

Batstone, W. (2018) Caesar constructing Caesar. In L. Grillo and C.B. Krebs (eds), *The Cambridge Companion to the Writings of Julius Caesar*, 43–57. Cambridge, Cambridge University Press.

Bénard, J. (1996) Alésia: du mythe à l'archéologie. In M. Reddé (ed.), *L'armée Romaine en Gaule*, 40–65. Paris, Editions Errance.

Buchsenschutz, O. and Ralston, I. (2014) Nouvelles remarques sur les *muri gallici*. In J. Bullinger, P. Crotti and C. Huguenin (eds), *De l'âge du Fer à l'usage du verre. Mélanges offerts à Gilbert Kaenel dit 'Auguste'*, 171–178. Lausanne, Cahiers d'archéologie romande 151.

Colbert de Beaulieu, J.-B. and Lefèvre, G. (1963) Les monnaies de Vercingétorix. *Gallia* 21, 11–75.

Delestrée, L.-P. and Tache, M. 2007. *Nouvel Atlas des Monnaies Gauloises, III: La Celtique, du Jura et des Alpes à la façade Atlantique.* Saint-Germain-en-Laye, Editions Commios.

Drummond, A. (2013) C. Asinius Pollio. In T. Cornell (ed.), *The Fragments of the Roman Historians*, Vol. 1, 430–446. Oxford, Oxford University Press.

Fantham, E. (2009) Caesar as an intellectual. In M. Griffin (ed.), *A Companion to Julius Caesar*, 141–156. Oxford, Wiley-Blackwell.

Gelzer, M. (1955) Vercingetorix. *Paulys Realencyclopädie der classischen Altertumswissenschaft* Band VIII A.1, 981–1008. Stuttgart, Alfred Druckenmüller Verlag.

Goudineau, C. (1991) La Guerre des Gaules et l'archéologie. *Comptes rendus des séances de l'Académie des Inscriptions et Belles-Lettres* 135, 641–653.

Harmand, J. (1989) Historiographie d'un mythe. L'invention de Vercingétorix de 1865 à nos jours. *Storia della storiagrafia* 15, 3–16.
Kelsey, F.W. (1905) The title of Caesar's work on the Gallic and Civil War. *Transactions of the American Philological Association* 36, 211–238.
Krebs, C.B. (2017) Caesar the historian. In K. Raaflaub (ed.), *The Landmark Julius Caesar*, 210–214. New York, Pantheon Books.
Krebs, C.B. (2018) A style of choice. In L. Grillo and C.B. Krebs (eds), *The Cambridge Companion to the Writings of Julius Caesar*, 110–130. Cambridge, Cambridge University Press.
Krebs, C.B. (forthcoming a) *The Mind of the Commander*. New York, W.W. Norton.
Krebs, C.B. (forthcoming b) *Caesar. Bellum Gallicum Book VII*. Cambridge, Cambridge University Press.
Le Gall, J. (1970) Cent ans après. Un témoin méconnu de l'histoire du Second Empire, la statue de Vercingétorix sur le Mont Auxois. *Mémoires de l'Académie des Sciences, Arts et Belles-Lettres de Dijon* 117, 199–219.
Nicolet, C. (2009) Caesar and the two Napoleons. In M. Griffin (ed.), *A Companion to Julius Caesar*, 410–417. Oxford, Wiley-Blackwell.
Nieto-Pelletier, S. (2012) Le portrait monétaire gaulois: les monnayages du Centre de la Gaule (IIIe–Ier siècles a. C.). *Cahiers des études anciennes* 49, 235–258.
Pascucci G. (1973) Interpretazione linguistica e stilistica del Cesare autentico. *Aufstieg und Niedergang der Römischen Welt* I.3, 488–522. Berlin, De Gruyter.
Pelling, C.B.R. (1982) Review of G. Zecchini, *Cassio Dione e la guerra gallica di Cesare*. *Classical Review* 32, 146–148.
Rambaud, M. (1966) *L'art de la déformation historique dans les commentaires de César* (2nd edn). Paris, Les Belles Lettres.
Reddé, M. (2008) Alésia: du texte de César aux vestiges archéologiques. In M. Reddé and S. von Schnurbein (eds), *Alésia et la bataille du Teutoburg. Un parallèle critique des sources*, 277–289. Paris, Deutsches Historisches Institut Beihefte der Francia 66.
Richardson, E. (2016) The Emperor's Caesar: Napoleon III, Karl Marx and the *History of Julius Caesar*. In T. Fögen and R. Warren (eds), *Graeco-Roman Antiquity and the Idea of Nationalism in the 19th Century: Case Studies*, 113–130. Berlin, De Gruyter.
Riggsby, A.M. (2006) *Caesar in Gaul and Rome. War in Words*. Austin, University of Texas Press.
Schiesaro, A. (2010) Cesare, la cultura di un dittatore. In G. Urso (ed.), *Cesare: precursore o visionario?*, 241–249. Pisa, I Convegni della Fondazione Niccolò Cabussio 9.
Sihler, E.G. (1887) The tradition of Caesar's *Gallic Wars* from Cicero to Orosius. *Transactions of the American Philological Association* 18, 19–29.
Woodman, A.J. (1983) Reading the ancient historians. *Omnibus* 5, 24–27.
Zecchini, G. (1978) *Cassio Dione e la guerra gallica di Cesare*. Milan, Università Cattolica del Sacro Cuore.

Chapter 2

The Gallic Wars in Roman history

Greg Woolf

Colonial wars

Caesar's campaigns north of the Alps during the 50s BC strongly resemble the colonial wars of recent centuries. Just as in modern colonial wars, their timing reflected priorities at the centre more than events at the periphery. As in modern colonial wars, they impacted on peripheral populations far more than on those of the metropolis. There were differences. Roman expansion in Caesar's day was no longer carried out in competition with expansive campaigns led by other powers, as had been the case before the destruction of Carthage in 146 BC and would be the case during the 19th century 'Scramble for Africa'. There was also less of a technology gap between Roman led armies and those they opposed than would be the case in most colonial wars of later periods. Yet the fundamental condition of colonial warfare applied to all these scenarios: conflict was asymmetrical.

Asymmetry applied at an economic level, at a military level, and in terms of information. Late prehistoric societies in Europe were not primitive – whatever sense we give to that term – and there is a broad consensus that during the last few centuries BC there was sustained demographic and economic growth across much of the continent (see Ralston this volume). That growth was manifested in increased agricultural and metallurgical production, in the construction of larger and more complex settlements, in increased levels of exchange within and beyond temperate Europe that went well beyond a trade in luxuries or prestige goods, and in periodic large-scale population movements. But European economies could not yet match Mediterranean ones. This mattered most in the capacity of Rome to field large well-equipped armies composed of soldiers who – if not yet formally professionalized – served for years at a time and underwent considerable training. Rome also had the financial resources to induce others to serve alongside them. The military resources of tribes and tribal states north of the Alps varied enormously in scale but even the most powerful groups seem to have disposed only of seasonal levies, whose training and equipment were inferior to those of Rome. The final asymmetry was information. Caesar and his senior commanders had a significant information advantage over their opponents. The scale of his ambitions must have come as a complete surprise to most populations north of the Alps. In that respect there is a very close analogy with the experience of the Aztec and the Inka, or numerous sub-Saharan African polities of later periods. Romans certainly gathered a great deal of information in the course of their campaigns – Caesar's account often dramatizes episodes in which he sought information from locals, or was brought it by allies – but at all times their knowledge of the enemy and its territory was much superior to whatever north European populations can have known about Rome. That information advantage allowed Caesar and his deputies to plan and coordinate their efforts better.

And as in most colonial wars, the outcome mattered more to the conquered populations than to the conquerors. Rome in this period was fighting wars in almost all directions, and some were more successful than others. Caesar himself benefited enormously from the success of his campaigns in Gaul: he was personally enriched, his prestige was enhanced and the soldiers he had fought with there helped ensure victory in the Civil Wars that followed. But Roman interests would not have been significantly harmed if his campaigns had ended in disaster, as did those of his ally Crassus in Syria. Even if the eventual northern frontier of the empire had rested on the Loire or the Elbe rather than the Rhine the long-term history of the empire might not have been so different. Put bluntly the Gallic Wars mattered more to Gauls than to Romans.

Caesar in his own words

The chronology of the wars in Gaul are well known and have recently been clarified in detail (Raaflaub and Ramsay 2017). Caesar was consul in 59 BC and on stepping down received a proconsular command giving him authority over Gaul on both sides of the Alps and an army of four legions. Apart from the five-year term this arrangement was on the face of it quite regular. In reality, elections and the allocation of provinces had, since 60 BC, been controlled by a faction led by Caesar, Crassus and Pompey. One of its aims was to give Caesar a command with a prospect of lucrative campaigning. Early in 58 BC he advanced west of the Alps and began a series of summer campaigns that lasted until 50 BC. Caesar's duties as governor included an annual tour of the assize centres. He also attempted to keep in close touch with events in Rome. Most years his army campaigned north of the Alps during the summer months, then settled into winter quarters while he returned to Transalpina and Cisalpina in September or October. In some years his troops fought in several parts of Gaul at the same time, and they were generally dispersed during the winter for logistical reasons as well as to ensure the occupation.

Caesar's campaigns are known almost entirely from his own account, *de bello Gallico* (On the Gallic War, henceforth *BG*). What other versions we have are heavily indebted to his own version. Apart from some letters of Cicero there is no other contemporary source of information. There is a briefer version in the *Roman History* of Cassius Dio, written about two and a half centuries later, and the Gallic campaigns feature in the lives of Caesar written by Plutarch and Suetonius in the late 1st and early 2nd centuries AD. Other accounts have been lost, significantly Livy's version which will have been written within a generation of Caesar's death. Just enough alternative testimony survives to demonstrate what we might have expected, that Caesar's version was selective and self-interested.

The care with which Caesar shaped his narrative to suit his immediate ends has long been appreciated (Stevens 1952; Rambaud 1966; Welch and Powell 1998). Take for instance the first book of *BG* which begins with a plot engineered by one of the chiefs of the Helvetii of the Swiss Plateau, plotting with disaffected chieftains among the Sequani and the Aedui to take control of the whole of Gaul. The conspiracy collapses almost immediately, but the Helvetii decide to launch a mass migration to what is now south-west France which would have involved them crossing the Roman province of Transalpina which extended up the middle Rhône valley. Caesar first enters the narrative in chapter 7 when he hears this news while still in Rome and at once set out for Gaul. Within two weeks he meets the Helvetii at Geneva and refuses them passage, allegedly because he remembered their participation in humiliating a Roman army during the Cimbric Wars, half a century earlier. The first half of the book relates Caesar's successful efforts to block the Helvetian migration, in the process becoming embroiled in rivalries among some of the major tribes of central France, among them the Aedui, the Sequani, the Bituriges and the Arverni. The Helvetii eventually suffer a devastating defeat (chapter 29) and their survivors flee to the territory of the Germans beyond the Rhine. The second half of the book begins with a general assembly of the Gauls. It emerges that all are terrified by the recent invasion of Gaul led by Ariovistus, a German king. Caesar undertakes to mediate but Ariovistus responds arrogantly. After he rejects repeated diplomatic overtures and continues to plunder the territory of some Gallic tribes, Caesar has no choice but to engage him. Ariovistus' army is destroyed just before the end of the campaigning season, his army disperses and the Germans turn on each other.

The narrative of *BG* book 1 is presented with a great deal of drama. There are some compelling set pieces such as the scene where the Sequani are too terrified of Ariovistus even to speak to Caesar, and their case has to be made by an Aeduan ally instead. Caesar's trademark speediness (*celeritas*) is repeatedly emphasized, as is his decisiveness. As in most Greek and Latin historical writing, moments of great significance are underlined by invented speeches. This is even truer of Dio's version which tells the story of Caesar's first year in Gaul in twenty chapters, eight of them comprising Caesar's speech to his troops on the eve of the battle with Ariovistus. There is more subtle persuasion at play too (Riggsby 2006). Caesar's book famously begins with 'All Gaul is divided into three parts', its broad ethnic divisions marked out by rivers. It is fairly clear that Gallia is a Roman concept, one that was progressively extended from parts of Italy north of the Apennines to include the Republican Province and eventually the whole area bounded by the Atlantic, the Channel and the Rhine (Williams 2001). None of its inhabitants were aware of 'Gaul' as an entity, yet Caesar tells us the Helvetii wanted to create an empire of all Gaul, and has Ariovistus draw a parallel between the Roman and German invasions of Gaul. Roman ethnography, the narrative of the Helvetian migration and Ariovistus' speech are suspiciously in agreement about the unity of Gaul and the possibility of its domination by one power. The great rivers too recur: Caesar prevents the Helvetii from crossing the Rhône and drives the Germans back over the Rhine. He will eventually cross the Rhine himself. The book has a dramatic unity and high level of closure. It concludes with these sentences:

> Caesar, having concluded two major wars in a single season, led his army into winter quarters among the Sequani, a little earlier than the time of year demanded. He put Labienus in charge of the winter-quarters, and he himself set out for Nearer Gaul to hold the assizes.

Caesar's version is naturally self-serving. The unspoken claim for glory through conquest is presented alongside explicit justifications for each campaign in terms of revenge for the losses in the Cimbric War, and the duty to protect Rome's allies. There are omissions too. Caesar in his account several times emphasizes that the crisis has been brewing since the consulship of Marcus Messala and Marcus Piso (61 BC). Yet Caesar's initial disposition of legions had three based at Aquileia and only one in Transalpina, suggesting he was gearing up for campaigns in the northern Balkans, perhaps against the Dacians. He also says nothing of the negative reactions at Rome to his defeat of Ariovistus, who was in fact a Roman ally. Roman reactions to his campaigns, which are always recorded at book-ends, are always positive as if daring the reader to dissent from the Roman popular appreciation of Caesarian achievement.

There are some other gestures to domestic political concerns. In the run up to the showdown with Ariovistus, Caesar encounters resistance from his own troops (*BG* 1.39). They have reached Besançon, the capital of the Sequani, far to the north of any point a Roman army has ever reached before, and they began to hear stories of the size and ferocity of the Germans. Stereotypes of this kind were part and parcel of ancient imaginings of northern barbarians (Krebs 2006; 2011), but an interesting Caesarian twist is that the panic spreads from the top down, from the tribunes and prefects and those who had followed Caesar out of friendship although inexperienced in war. It is staunched by Caesar's rhetoric and the experience of the centurions. This is an early appearance of what would become a *Leitmotiv* of *BG*, the heroism and dependability of ordinary centurions and the unreliability of some of their aristocratic commanders. This marks *BG* out as *popularis* history, a historical viewpoint that coheres with Caesar's consistent use of popular support in opposition to the politics of Sulla, Pompey and Cicero that in different ways tried to minimize the influence of the people in Roman politics.

For yet more discerning Roman readers Caesar's account of events at Besançon has other resonances. It recalls another mutiny famous in Caesar's day, the rebellion of Alexander the Great's army at the Hyphasis river in 326 BC, a mutiny that marked the end of Alexander's eastward advance. Alexander obsessed Romans of this day, especially Pompey, Caesar and Augustus. Suetonius' *Life of the Deified Caesar* (chapter 7) includes a story of the young Caesar coming across a statue of Alexander at Gades (modern Cadiz, another 'end of the world') and being upset that he had achieved so little at an age when Alexander had done so much. Caesar's success where Alexander had failed, at rallying his army at the edge of the known world, would not have been lost on some readers. Some of those readers would have been familiar with earlier works on which Caesar drew, and would have enjoyed observing how he handled familiar subjects like the exoticism of the Druids, episodes of individual heroism, or the nature of the ends of the earth (Romm 1992; Riggsby 2006; Woolf 2011).

The point of emphasizing the rhetorical skill with which *BG* was composed is not to convict Caesar of bias – we all write from one perspective or another, and all texts have aims and persuasive projects integral to them – nor to make *BG* seem less reliable – it is difficult to catch Caesar in an actual falsehood – but to situate his text in broader discourses of empire. There are subjects on which we must expect it to be vague: the habits and characteristics of particular peoples are poorly differentiated. It will have greater sympathy and concern for the wellbeing and reputation of Romans than of locals. *BG* exemplifies an imperial gaze, one in which the Gauls are objects to be observed, in which events in Gaul between 58 and 52 BC are given meaning in a larger narrative of Roman imperial expansion, the deaths in battle justified by Rome's manifest destiny. It offers a very partial view of the history of these years and of Caesar's activities during them. Affairs in Gaul occupy the bulk of the text and Caesar's annual absences are mentioned as briefly as possible. Caesar the general dominates our vision, excluding Caesar the politician, as if he were a full-time warrior only occasionally distracted by his other duties and concerns. In reality, the war in Gaul was for Caesar just an end to a different means, and the conquest of Gaul was a stepping stone to pre-eminence in Rome.

The Gauls between imperial expansion and civil war

Romans evolved their own story arc in each generation as they sought – sometimes with the help of Greek intellectuals – to make sense of the rolling out of empire. Recent studies have disentangled successive Roman understandings of empire and imperialism (Brunt 1978; 1990; Ferrary 1988; Steel 2001; Richardson 2008). Historians used to write as if the motivations of Roman leaders (if they could be established) would provide a sufficient explanation of Roman expansion. More recently attention has focused on the ideologies and structures that made Republican wars of expansion possible and perhaps for a time necessary (Hopkins 1978; North 1981; Rosenstein 2004). Roman imperialism had its roots in the 5th century BC and continued until the 2nd century AD (Raaflaub 1996). There were long-term continuities (Harris 1979; 2016) even if the pace of expansion was not uniform (Rich 1993).

Caesar was born in 100 BC and died in 44 BC. He lived through the first part of the most rapid phase of Roman territorial expansion, which began in the mid-60s BC with Pompey's extraordinary commands in the East and ended with the halt to Augustan expansion in the first decades AD. During Caesar's lifetime he also experienced the Civil War between Sulla and Marius after which he briefly had to flee Rome, the failed *coup d'état* of Catiline in 63 BC in which he was nearly implicated, and the Civil Wars he himself fought first with Pompey, and then with his successors. That last batch of wars interrupted his proconsulate in Gaul in 49 BC and continued off and on until his assassination. The origins of these civil conflicts are complex but in general reflect the inability of the political institutions of a city-state to deal with the security problems and economic transformations brought by control of the Mediterranean basin (Nicolet 1977; Woolf 2012).

The background of rapid expansion and periodic political collapse had several implications for warfare in Gaul. First, it was impossible for any Roman leader not to become involved in both civil politics and expansion. Caesar's war in Gaul always had a domestic political dimension. From the perspective of Rome his eagerness to get a province with an army, his willingness to take risks and escalate conflicts, his ruthless extraction of slaves and booty, and the close relationship he built in reality (and in *BG*) with common soldiers were all about preparing for civil conflict. Once again we see the typical subordination of colonial wars and the interests of peripheral populations to metropolitan priorities. Naturally Caesar's rivals were doing the same, or trying to, in other colonial arenas. Whatever the immediate priorities in those distant locales – in Egypt and Syria and Spain and so on – Roman commanders always had an eye on events in Rome.

Second, this scenario meant that the empire into which Gaul was being drawn was a chaotic and unstable one. This is a point of difference with the empires of Spain and Portugal in the early modern Americas and even with the African empires of European powers before 1914. Gaul and the Gauls were drawn into these conflicts in a range of ways. Most obviously Gallic communities – first in Cisalpina and Transalpina, and then in the rapidly enlarging circle of Roman allies – were compelled year on year to provide troops to support Roman armies. Many communities also had to provide provisions, for their own warriors and also for the Roman legions, which at their peak strength numbered around 50,000 and needed to be provisioned not only while on campaign but also while overwintering (Erdkamp 1998).

From the Roman perspective none of this was new. From the late 4th century BC peoples defeated by Rome were compelled to provide allied contingents for future wars (Gabba 1976). During the Republic an economy of violence developed, in which more and more of the human resources of first Italy and then of the Mediterranean basin as a whole were drawn into Rome's wars. Parallel to this was the mobilization of bullion to the political economy of the Roman state (Crawford 1985). Within temperate Europe, which had encountered Roman armies only recently and was not organized in terms of city-states with citizen armies, all this was new. Martial traditions, chiefly warbands and the like were recruited to a new cause.

Those campaigns were not limited to assisting Caesar against their traditional enemies and neighbours. When Caesar led his armies out of Gaul to engage those of Pompey, many Gauls came with him providing cavalry support for his legions. The impact on local societies and local elites was dramatic (Drinkwater 1978). One effect was a shift in power relations and in wealth, within Gallic communities. Another was to bring some Gallic élites into a much closer engagement with Mediterranean politics and culture (Woolf 1998). The same thing was, of course, happening all around the Mediterranean world (Woolf 2005; Yarrow 2006; Crawford 2008). The mobilization of European manpower to serve Roman expansion would continue long after Caesar's day with transformative effects (Roymans 2004; Haynes 2013).

Collateral damage

BG does not offer a comprehensive accounting of the war. There are several reasons for this. One is that it was apparently written episodically, one year at time. Caesar could not know at the start how many books, or years, there would be. The original term of his command would have ended at the end of 54 BC. The agreement to extend it was only made in the winter of 56 BC. One political context for the invasion of Britain in 55 BC was that Caesar had claimed such great successes for his first three years of campaigning that he badly needed new worlds to conquer. Once Caesar marched out of Gaul for the last time not much energy was devoted to reworking the individual books into a coherent narrative. As annual bulletins on his success they had, after all, served their purpose already. Besides, Caesar had other concerns from the moment he crossed the Rubicon at the beginning of 49 BC, leaving his province to march on Rome, until his death in 44 BC. Writing up the eighth and final book of *BG* was delegated to Aulus Hirtius.

For Caesar the wars in Gaul were a huge success. He had entered his province in 58 BC deeply in debt. A letter of Cicero (*ad Atticum* 4.16) written in the summer of 54 BC shows Caesar's plans for extravagant building on the Campus Martius were already underway. The impact of Caesarian campaigns on the precious metal coinages of Gaul is well known (Haselgrove 1984). Eight years campaigning in Gaul had also more than doubled the number of legionaries loyal to him, and added perhaps an equivalent member of Gallic auxiliaries. The number of Roman aristocrats who had benefited from his patronage – many had served with him as legionary commanders or more junior officers and been enriched as a result – was significant. Not all remained loyal, but many did. His credentials as a *popularis* champion and a victorious general were unrivalled. He had overtaken Pompey, and their former ally Crassus had been killed in a less successful act of colonial brigandage. Success in Gaul contributed in many ways to Caesar's success in the Civil Wars of the early 40s.

What about the Gauls? There clearly were some winners, at the level of tribes and at the level of individuals. But the stresses and strains of his campaigns were also significant. Many former allies joined Vercingetorix against Caesar in 52 BC. The loss of life and property as well as liberty was considerable. Plutarch, who presented the Gallic War as the turning point in Caesar's life offered the following reckoning (*Life of Caesar* 15):

> although he waged war in Gaul for less than ten years, he took by storm more than eight hundred cities, subdued three hundred nations, and fought pitched battles at different times with three million men, of whom he slew one million in hand to hand fighting and took as many more prisoners.

For Plutarch these casualty figures establish Caesar's military superiority to all other Roman generals, Sulla and Pompey included. Plutarch expresses no moral qualms about the human cost. Nor does Suetonius summarizing Caesar's achievements in Gaul in a single chapter (25) of his *Life of Deified Julius.*

> He achieved the following in the nine years in which he was in command. All of Gaul, which is bounded by the Pyrenees, the Alps and the Cevennes and by the Rhine and Rhone rivers, a circuit of around 3200 miles he turned into a province, all but a few allies whose loyalty had earned their independence. He imposed an annual tribute on it of 400 million sesterces. The Germans, who live beyond the Rhine, he was the first Roman to attack and he did so by building a bridge across and inflicting major casualties on them. He also attacked the Britons, a people previously unknown to us, and when he had defeated them he took money and hostages. During all these victories he encountered only three reverses: in Britain his fleet was almost destroyed, by the force of storm, in Gaul one of his legions broke and fled at Gergovia, and on the borders of Germany his legates Titurius and Aurunculeius were slaughtered in an ambush.

All of Gaul, victories at the edge of the world, booty and glory, collateral damage. Like all colonial wars, Caesar's campaigns north of the Alps were reduced to an historical note in a grander imperial story.

Bibliography

Brunt, P.A. (1978) Laus Imperii. In P. Garnsey and C.R. Whittaker (eds), *Imperialism in the Ancient World*, 159–191. Cambridge, Cambridge University Press. (Reprinted from Brunt, P.A. *Roman Imperial Themes*, Oxford, Oxford University Press, 288–323).

Brunt, P.A. (1990) Roman Imperial Illusions. *Roman Imperial Themes*, 433–480. Oxford, Clarendon Press.

Crawford, M.H. (1985) *Coinage and Money under the Roman Republic. Italy and the Mediterranean Economy.* London, Methuen.

Crawford, M.H. (2008) States waiting in the wings. Population distribution and the end of the Roman Republic. In L. de Ligt and S. Northwood (eds), *People, Land and Politics. Demographic developments and the transformation of Roman Italy 300 BC–AD 14*, 631–643. Leiden, Brill.

Drinkwater, J.F. (1978) The rise and fall of the Gallic Julii. *Latomus* 37, 817–850.

Erdkamp, P. (1998) *Hunger and the Sword. Warfare and food supply in Roman republican wars (264–30 B.C.)* Amsterdam, J.C. Gieben.

Ferrary, J.-L. (1988) *Philhellénisme et impérialisme: aspects idéologiques de la conquête romaine du monde hellénistique, de la Seconde Guerre de Macédoine à la Guerre contre Mithridate.* Rome, École Française de Rome.

Gabba, E. (1976) *Republican Rome, the Army and the Allies.* Oxford, Blackwell Publishers.

Harris, W.V. (1979) *War and Imperialism in Republican Rome, 327–70 B.C.* Oxford, Clarendon Press.

Harris, W.V. (2016) *Roman Power. A thousand years of empire.* Cambridge, Cambridge University Press.

Haselgrove, C.C. (1984) Warfare and its aftermath as reflected in the precious metal coinage of Belgic Gaul. *Oxford Journal of Archaeology* 3(1), 81–105.

Haynes, I. (2013) *Blood of the Provinces. The Roman Auxilia and the making of provincial society from Augustus to Diocletian.* Oxford, Oxford University Press.

Hopkins, K. (1978) *Conquerors and Slaves. Sociological Studies in Roman History I.* Cambridge, Cambridge University Press.

Krebs, C.B. (2006) 'Imaginary Geography' in Caesar's *Bellum Gallicum. American Journal of Philology* 127(1), 111–136.

Krebs, C.B. (2011) Borealism. Caesar, Seneca, Tacitus and the Roman Discourse about the Germanic North. In E. Gruen (ed.), *Cultural Identity in the Ancient Mediterranean*, 202–221. Los Angeles, Getty Research Institute.

Nicolet, C. (ed.) (1977) *Rome et la conquête du monde méditerranéen, 264–27 avant J.C.* Paris, Presses Universitaires de France.

North, J. (1981) The development of Roman imperialism. *Journal of Roman Studies* 71, 1–9.

Raaflaub, K. (1996) Born to be Wolves? Origins of Roman imperialism. In R.W. Wallace and E.M. Harris (eds), *Transitions to Empire. Essays in Greco-Roman History 360–146 B.C. in Honor of E. Badian*, 273–314. Norman and London, University of Oklahoma Press.

Raaflaub, K. and Ramsey, J.T. (2017) Reconstructing the Chronology of Caesar's Gallic Wars. *Histos* 11, 1–74.

Rambaud, M. (1966) *L'art de la déformation historique dans les 'Commentaires' de César.* Paris, Les Belles Lettres.

Rich, J. (1993) Fear, greed and glory: the causes of Roman war-making in the middle Republic. In J. Rich and G. Shipley (eds), *War and Society in the Roman World*, 36–68. London, Routledge.

Richardson, J.S. (2008) *The Language of Empire. Rome and the idea of empire from the third century BC to the second century AD.* Cambridge, Cambridge University Press.

Riggsby, A. (2006) *War in Words. Caesar in Gaul and Rome.* Austin, University of Texas Press.

Romm, J.S. (1992) *The Edges of the Earth in Ancient Thought. Geography, exploration, and fiction.* Princeton, Princeton University Press.

Rosenstein, N.S. (2004) *Rome at War. Farms, families and death in the middle Republic.* Chapel Hill, University of North Carolina Press.

Roymans, N. (2004) *Ethnic Identity and Imperial Power. The Batavians in the Roman Empire.* Amsterdam, Amsterdam Archaeological Studies 10.

Steel, C. (2001) *Cicero, Rhetoric and Empire.* Oxford, Oxford University Press.

Stevens, C.E. (1952) The 'Bellum Gallicum' as a work of propaganda. *Latomus* 11(1), 3–18.

Welch, K. and Powell, A. (eds) (1998) *Julius Caesar as Artful Reporter. The war commentaries as political instruments.* London and Swansea, Duckworth.

Williams, J.H.C. (2001) *Beyond the Rubicon. Romans and Gauls in Northern Italy.* Oxford, Oxford University Press.

Woolf, G. (1998) *Becoming Roman. The origins of provincial civilization in Gaul.* Cambridge, Cambridge University Press.

Woolf, G. (2005) Provincial perspectives. In K. Galinsky (ed.), *Cambridge Companion to the Age of Augustus*, 106–129. New York, Cambridge University Press.

Woolf, G. (2011) *Tales of the Barbarians. Ethnography and empire in the Roman west*. Malden (MA) and Oxford, Blackwell Publishers.
Woolf, G. (2012) *Rome. An Empire's Story*. New York, Oxford University Press.
Yarrow, L.M. (2006) *Historiography at the End of the Republic. Provincial perspectives on Roman rule*. Oxford and New York, Oxford University Press.

Chapter 3

The Gauls on the eve of the Roman conquest

Ian Ralston

Introduction

The Iron Age societies of temperate Gaul in the decades preceding the Gallic War were evolving, rapidly but unevenly, towards increasing complexity in economic, social and political terms. Well aware of the expansion of the military and political power of Republican Rome to their south, notably as a consequence of the late 2nd-century Roman conquest of the original *provincia*, Gallia Transalpina, in southern France, they also had strong trade and ancillary links towards the Mediterranean basin; this is at its most visible archaeologically through the importation of wine in quantity. Southern contacts were counterbalanced by other social and economic relations more widely across the temperate continent, including cross-Channel connections with southern Britain. Gallic economies displayed rapidly-developing secondary sectors, in which craft production of numerous relatively standardized products, sometimes on a scale not previously seen in the temperate European Iron Age, underpinned their increasing importance. In the primary sector, agriculture too bore witness to a range of developments; it displays evidence for a variety of strategies in terms of livestock and plant production, often intimately linked to the diversity of Gaul's landscapes, some of which were organized at a new and larger scale (Haselgrove 2006; Brun and Ruby 2008, 112–149; Fernandez-Götz 2014; Buchsenschutz 2015, 295–371; Blancquaert and Malrain 2016).

Understanding of the transformations then under way is currently enhanced by the results of numerous large-scale archaeological projects. These include investigations of major, dominantly settlement, sites including those at Corent (Poux 2012a) and nearby in the Puy-de-Dôme, as well as the long-term (since its relaunch as President Mitterand's final *Grand Projet* in 1984) research endeavour at Mont Beuvray in Burgundy (Bradley *et al.* 2016, 261–327). These investigations, and numerous others, have been complemented by major rescue projects related to the insertion of large-scale infrastructure: such undertakings are notably of significance both for investigating extensive lowland areas, in particular within the Paris Basin, and of sectors undergoing redevelopment within modern towns and cities. In places such as Nanterre within Paris, and Orléans, there is thus a growing later prehistoric 'urban archaeology' of successful places for settlement viewed in the long-term to complement the evidence recovered from long-abandoned rural locales (Buchsenschutz *et al.* 2009; Reddé and van Andringa 2015).

As has always been the case, study of the later Iron Age of Gaul remains in some aspects strongly 'text-aided' because of the survival of a range of Latin and Greek texts, the most famous and extensively used being Julius Caesar's *de Bello gallico* (*e.g.* Raaflaub 2017), the only extensive account by a Roman general of a war he fought. These – all composed externally to the Gallic societies which they described – too have been subject to renewed study and reinterpretation (*e.g.* Riggsby 2006), thereby nuancing in new ways the manner in which the evidence they contain can be deployed in relation to the archaeological record.

In light of the pace of changes in both scholarship and the evidential base on which it is erected, any brief overview must be highly selective and is likely to offer a rather blurry snapshot, restricted too in its viewpoint. This should be borne in mind in considering what follows.

Nested political and social geographies

The delineation of regional and other geographical variations within Gaul, versions of which are already conspicuously present in Caesar's text, is a significant underpinning of many overviews. The internal geographies of Gallia (Figure 3.1) at this time – in so far as they can be reconstructed – were complex and arranged at a variety of scales. The main regional sub-divisions, excluding the Mediterranean coastlands and the lower Rhone valley, already under Roman control by the later 2nd century BC, consisted of Gallia Belgica, north and east of the River Seine, Aquitania south of the Garonne in the south-west (a special case not considered in detail here), and Gallia Comata, occupying the intermediate area extending from Brittany to the north-west fringes of the Alps. Within these, the major territorial entities were termed in Latin, *civitates*. Over 60 in number, varying in scale (individually up to *c.* 20,000 km^2 in extent but with many distinctly smaller; and often with imprecise boundaries), these are named for the dominant tribes or peoples they contained, such as the Helvetii of much of the plateau of Switzerland or the Osismi within western Brittany (Fichtl 2012; 2013a).

By the latter part of the Iron Age, in the 1st century BC, the meaning of *civitas* seems to have embraced territories as well as socio-political groups. It was the elites which dominated such groups, whether kings, aristocrats or elected magistrates, with whom Julius Caesar in due course negotiated. *Civitates* enveloped a number of smaller units – we are particularly well-informed in the case of the four sub-divisions within the Helvetii because of Caesar's account (*BG* 1.5; 1.12). These latter were termed

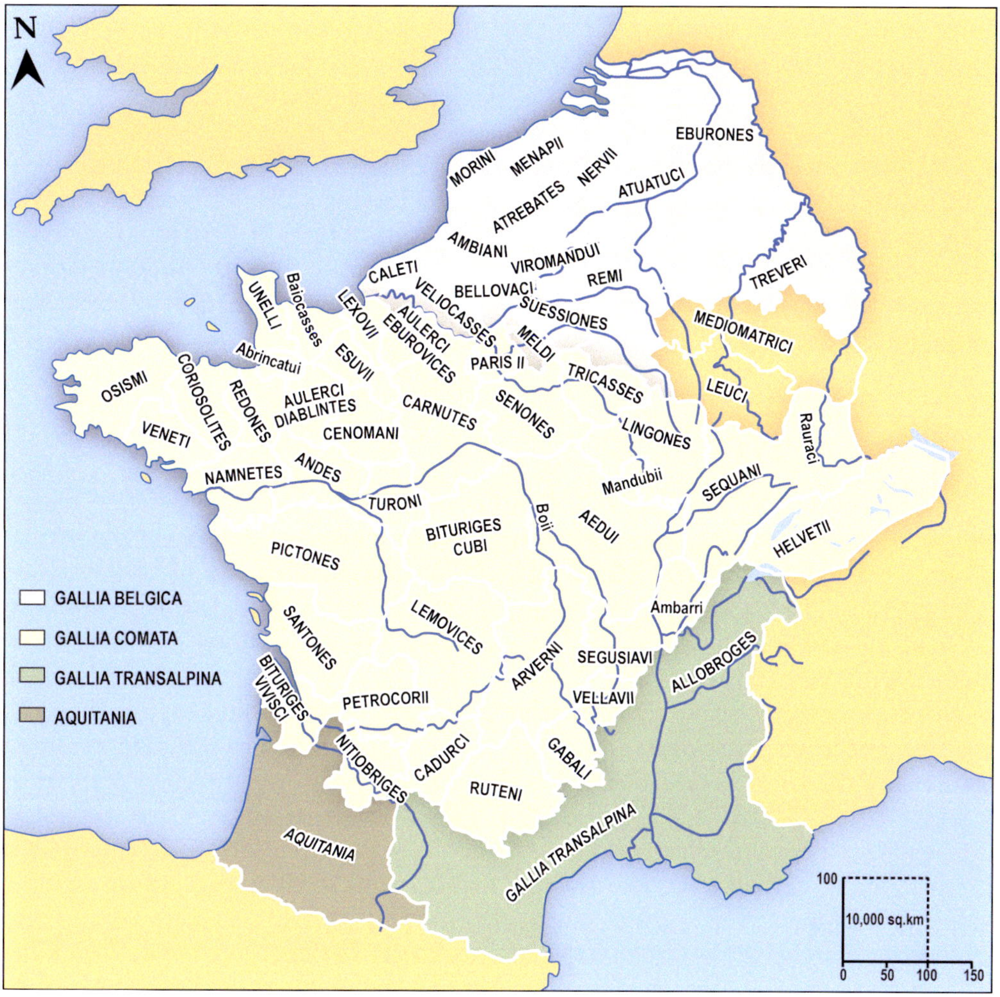

Figure 3.1 Gaul: civitates and major regional subdivisions in the decades prior to the Gallic War. The attribution of the Leuci and Mediomatrici to Gallia Belgica or Comata is unclear (after Fichtl 2013a).

pagi and were, at least in some cases, the units in which armies were mustered; the term too has a territorial connotation (a distant descendant is French *pays*). As with important families and other smaller social units, *civitates* could be linked through alliances and socio-political obligations such as clientship: in the case of the Aedui of east-central France, their 'confederation' in the 1st century BC included the Segusiavi and Ambarri on the northern fringes of the Roman *provincia* but also extended northwards across the Paris Basin through the territories of the Senones and Parisi to that of the Bellovaci in the department of Oise (Ralston 1992, fig. 59). It is important to stress, however, that any sense of a single nation or of Gaul itself as a meaningful entity in political terms was very under-developed, although Caesar tells us that during the Gallic War, members of the local elites came together temporarily on four occasions over successive years at one or other of the major Gallic settlements (termed *oppida*) in a body called the Council of All Gaul (*concilium totius Galliae*; Fichtl 2012, 122, map). Equally, the religious elites, the *druides*, shared a particular sacred place (*BG* 6.13), a *locus consecratus* set in the *civitas* of the Carnutes, centered on the Orléanais.

If most of these represent significant units and useful building-blocks towards the understanding of the spatial dimension of 2nd and 1st century BC Gaul, it is important not to read too much into their precise boundaries during the pre-Conquest period. It is likely that these were undergoing recurrent modifications, so that frontier zones would have waxed and waned. The mapped boundaries often now used are derived from the extents of early Christian bishoprics many centuries later, believed, at at least two removes, to be indicative of the extents of the pre-conquest *civitates*.

Changing fashions, increasing imports and the building of chronologies

During the middle (C) and late (D) La Tène periods, from approximately the middle of the 3rd century BC to the generation just after Caesar's conquest of Gaul between 58 and 51 BC, many aspects of the material culture record were developing rapidly, allowing at least some archaeological contexts and the phases they represent to be defined with the precision of approximately one generation (Barral and Fichtl 2012). In this regard, technological innovations – the reintroduction and rapid take-up of the slow and more particularly the fast potter's wheel is a case in point (represented on sites by the changing proportions of hand-made and wheel-finished pottery, to material wholly thrown on the fast potter's wheel) – are important (Le Dreff *et al.* 2017). Quickening changes (Guillaumet 1996) in the design and production (including the use of brass rather than bronze, and the manufacture of simpler types in multiple moulds) of 'fashion' items such as safety-pin brooches (*fibulae*) also considerably help in bringing some precision to dates for particular archaeological contexts. The same is true of imported coinage and the local numismatic products that were to varying extents indebted stylistically and/or metrically to them. Other imported material culture, and the local imitations thereof, help define such chronologies, as well as – for example, latterly in the adoption of flat ceramic plates – showing the uptake of new culinary habits.

Compendious recent work for the Auvergne – especially examining finds from specific contexts such as pit groups in lowland settlements within the Limagne basin and on upland *oppida* near Clermont-Ferrand – can stand as an example: here seven stages (*étapes* in French terminology) are distinguished between *c.* 250 BC and *c.* 30/20 BC, this latter marking the transition to the increasingly Romanized inventory present from the Augustan period. From the final phase of middle la Tène (C2/D1a: étape 7) beginning *c.* 160 BC, the successive stages identified each lasts notionally around 30 years (Figure 3.2; Mennessier-Jouannet and Deberge 2017). While similar schemes across the country vary in detail (Mennessier-Jouannet and Deberge 2017, fig. 491), consistent features include the accelerating pace of development over the

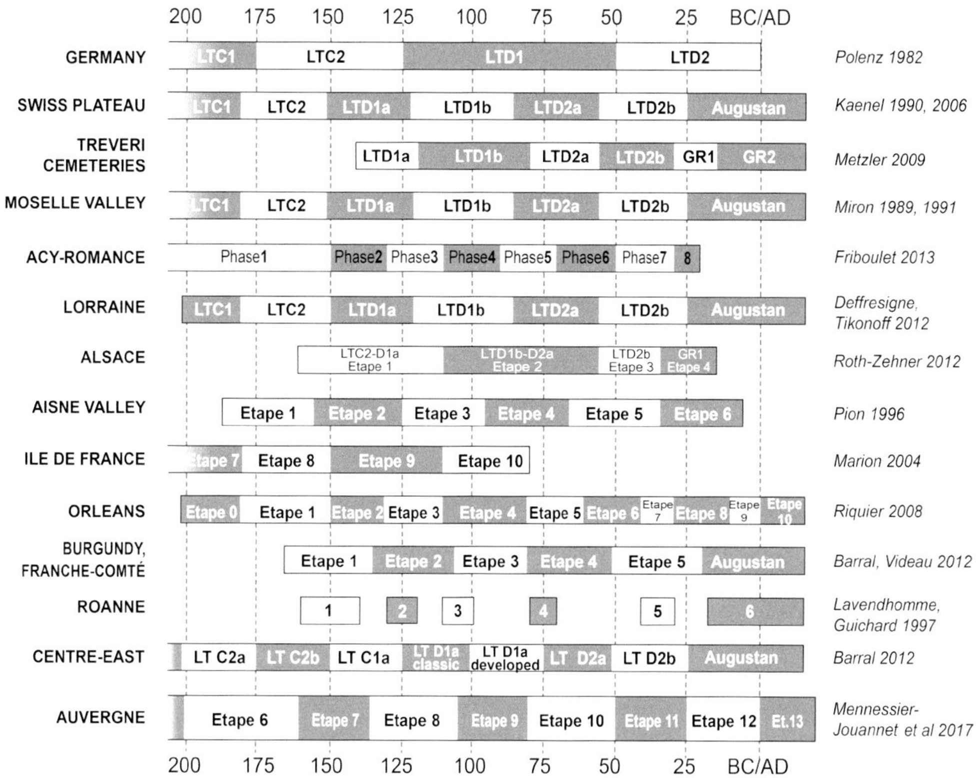

Figure 3.2 Chronological phases identified for selected sites and areas of non-Mediterranean France and adjacent areas from c. 200 BC to the time of Augustus (simplified from Messessier-Jouannet and Deberge 2017).

125 years or so before the Gallic War; and the fact that the end of that War coincided with a less complete change in material culture (La Tène D2a–b) than was to occur a generation later, in Augustus's time. This emphasizes that military conquest was not generally marked by straightforwardly dramatic impacts, readily perceptible in the archaeological record. Overall, however, rapid modifications to key series of object types allow rhythms of development to be approached at a broadly generational scale.

While the seriation of qualitative and quantitative changes in material culture is of key importance, other methods such as dendrochronology can assist by furnishing dating evidence that, on occasion, fits tantalizingly closely with the historical record. Rescue excavations on the Colline de Sainte Croix, within the city of Metz (Moselle), offer a classic case. Here, timberwork from the successive builds of an elaborate version of a timber-laced defensive wall in *murus gallicus* style (considered further below) provided felling dates firstly between 114 and 110 BC and then in 55 BC (Faye *et al.* 1990; Brkojewitsch *et al.* 2015). While caution is appropriate, the goodness of fit with the dates of Caesar's campaigns and, before that, of the marauding incursions of the Germanic Cimbri and Teutones, is noteworthy. The archaeological examination of the locations of historically documented events, more particularly those taking place during the Gallic War, such as the siege of Alesia (Alise-Sainte-Reine in Burgundy) in 52 BC, have long provided a further direct means of calibrating the historical and archaeological records (see Reddé this volume).

Major themes

This consideration will focus on the parts of Gaul set back from the Mediterranean coastlands, in essence those taken over by Rome in the 1st rather than the 2nd century BC. Over the decades preceding the Gallic War a number of key changes are identifiable in the archaeological record of this zone, but it is reasonable to propose that their impacts were variable across space and in time. Gallic societies, complex but not uniform, undoubtedly had their conservative elements as well as their innovators. Analysis of the very different numbers of imported wine amphorae in particular areas, for example, supports historical statements to the effect that some groups, such as the Nervii in Gallia Belgica, resisted the import of southern alcohol. In some other *oppida* and indeed lesser settlements, contrastingly, amphorae are copiously represented and bear witness to the huge volumes of (especially Italian) wine arriving at this time (Tchernia 1986, 77–94; Olmer *et al.* 2013). Matthieu Poux (2012a, 134) has estimated that 20,000 litres of Italian wine a year were arriving at the Arvernian *oppidum* of Corent in the early part of the 1st century BC.

The developing settlement record

As the named locations of some of the key events in the Gallic War, the major settlements (Caesar's *oppida*) of the 1st century BC have long attracted archaeological attention (Culture 2000; Fichtl 2005; Rieckhoff, 2014). Often extensive (their internal areas measured in tens and occasionally hundreds of hectares), and enclosed by large-scale ramparts, the best-preserved remain conspicuous monuments in the French countryside. Such sites were at the apogee of the later La Tène settlement record in the 1st century BC, when – as research particularly since the 1970s confirms – they complemented and/or replaced a huge diversity of smaller settlements marked primarily by the wide variety of 'negative features' – including pits, ditches, postholes, wells, sleeper-beam or palisade trenches, and semi-sunken workshops – mostly characteristic of the deployment of styles of earthfast timber architecture. Identified in their hundreds in the arable lowland 'zones of likely destruction', many of these represent farmsteads (again of many varieties and of different socio-economic statuses). Such areas, however, have also produced evidence for larger, open or lightly-enclosed, agglomerations (of scale order *c.* 10 ha and occasionally larger) which generally preceded the *oppida* chronologically whilst, albeit on a more modest scale, revealing many of the traits heralding increasing economic and social complexity that developed further on the *oppida* themselves (Buchsenschutz and Ralston 2012, 358–359). Such industrial villages, now identified across temperate France from Acy-Romance (Ardennes) to the Garonne valley, form the western component of a distribution of comparable sites which extends to central Europe (Barral and Nouvel 2012, fig. 14; Fichtl 2013b, fig. 1) and, like the shared items of copper alloy jewellery and other material culture they produce, emphasizes their linkages across this sub-continental area.

These sites mark the first steps in the resurgence of complex larger-scale settlements across this area since the demise of the late Hallstatt series, as illustrated in Burgundy by Mont Lassois, Vix, Côte d'Or, during the 5th century BC. Their development thus extends the beginnings of the making of larger settlement units, with considerable evidence for craft industries, back to the 3rd century BC, but more particularly to the 2nd century BC in Gaul. The internal organization of some sites appears more 'bottom-up' in their slightly haphazard arrangements than the greater degree of 'top-down' planning characteristic of at least some of the *oppida* which generally succeeded them in time, if often not directly in terms of location. While the drivers behind their coalescence can be debated, what such sites manifestly do is to substantially detach the increasing elaboration of Gallic settlements from complete dependence on Mediterranean models and influences.

Coinage and a market economy

Other key developments over the span considered here include the increasing penetration of a monetary economy, by the end of our period possessing (at least in some areas) a locally-produced trimetallic coinage, including low-value units, often with very restricted distributions, such as would have facilitated small-scale market exchanges. Equally the weights of some coin series, notably those produced within east-central France, were aligned on Mediterranean standards, such as those of the Roman *denarius* or the coinage of the important entrepot at Marseilles (Massalia), indicating that ready interchangeability with southern money-based economies was desired (Nieto-Pelletier 2013). One major change in our understanding of Gallic numismatics over recent years has been the recognition that, while normally conforming to Gresham's Law – whereby declining metal purity and falling coin weights intimate that 'bad money drives out good' – exceptions can occur. This perspective was one of the underpinnings of the idea that low value, cast copper alloy 'potin' coinages – as opposed to those struck in a die (Gruel *et al.* 2017) – were a very late development. In fact, their discovery – and that of the moulds to make them – on some of the open agglomerations mentioned above, such as Levroux-les-Arènes in Berry, indicates that *fiat* coinage of this kind was already in use in the 2nd century BC on that suite of sites, and thus at a much earlier chronological horizon than had been thought.

The very earliest Gallic coins, modelled on the later 4th century BC Macedonian staters of Philip and his son Alexander the Great, and always of high value and considerable rarity, likely served to store wealth or to make exceptional payments such as dowries, but from the 2nd century BC, the multiplication of these low-value coin series, often with distributions restricted geographically, intimates the deeper penetration of the market into areas of temperate Gaul – but not the Armorican west, for example. Not all such coinages were used in this way, however; some series are predominantly recovered from sanctuary sites, thus forming part of the burgeoning evidence for particular ritual practices at special locations, a characteristic of later Iron Age Gaul to be considered further below. Equally the need to pay for troops during the Gallic War for instance, provoked some very substantial emissions of coins, coinciding with declining metal standards and weights. On Jersey, the massive metal-detected Le Câtillon II hoard, substantially of base silver coins of the Armorican Coriosolitae, and one of several hoards of continental coinage from the island, belongs in this disturbed period of the Gallic War and its aftermath (see de Jersey this volume).

Transport and movement

Another key development during this broad period is the declining friction of distance indicated, inevitably very incompletely in the archaeological record, by evidence for various advances in transport. Key components of this include increasing evidence for bigger riding ponies, of fourteen hands or thereby, in place of the smaller beasts which previously, in pairs, had pulled chariots and carts. The military concomitant of this is the deployment of cavalry, well-attested in Caesar's text. Evidence for wheeled vehicles becomes more common, although their association principally with elite milieux declines (Buchsenschutz 2009). Accompanying infrastructure consists of at least some roads (*e.g.* Bruant and Touquet 2016) – 14 m wide in the case of the main transversal route within Mont Beuvray (Figure 3.5 below) – and increasing evidence for timber bridges across significant rivers to complement textual references, such as Caesar's description of the Loire crossing at Cenabum (Orléans) in 52 BC (*BG* 7.11). Less direct evidence perhaps survives for riverine and maritime connexions, but the development of harbour installations would include those on the Rhône at Genava, present-day Geneva, in the territory of the Allobroges at the Swiss border.

Albeit partial, this archaeological information helps give substance to the scale of, and resources reported to have been required for, the westward migration of the Helvetii in 58 BC (*BG* 1.3), the event which provided the immediate trigger for Caesar's intervention beyond the then *provincia* in southern Gaul (Kaenel this volume). Indeed the fluid nature of much of the campaigning across Gaul in which Caesar's armies were to be involved over the following years is itself proxy evidence for the prior existence of relatively well-developed transport networks and the consequent ease of movement of substantial forces within Gaul. It is thus not altogether surprising, for example, that the coins and pottery used by the auxiliaries garrisoning the *oppidum* of La Chaussée-Tirancourt in the Somme valley after the Gallic War strongly suggest that they originated from southern France (Bayard and Fichtl 2016).

The primary sector

Underpinning the complexity betokened by the three elements just introduced – settlements, coinage, transport – was a developed and successful agricultural sector, now known through the large-scale excavation of many farms and rural settlements, including the results of very significant associated environmental and zoo-archaeological work to determine their economies. Agricultural activities were of course not absent from the open agglomerations, as at Acy-Romance, where one sector of the site seems to have been used primarily by farmers and another by stockmen (Buchsenschutz 2004a, fig. 46; Ministère de la Culture n.d.), or indeed at *oppida* (*e.g.* Villeneuve-St-Germain, Aisne, where juxtaposed compounds each containing a substantial house, four-poster granary and cellar suggest the presence of numbers of well-off farmers inhabiting at least that part of the site: Paris 2017, fig. 3). That said, the most prolific building block for rural settlement in many areas within Gallia is undoubtedly the ditch-enclosed farmstead, generally broadly rectilinear in form and containing a few, often dispersed, buildings, along with four-post granaries, and sometimes storage pits and similar structures (*e.g.* Malrain *et al.* 2002; 2013; Bertrand *et al.* 2009). Wholly unenclosed sites are also known, but are markedly rarer. If some of these enclosed farmsteads are relatively humble installations, others are distinctly grander, as shown by the major buildings within them, and indications such as the recovery of wine amphorae and other southern imports from them. Amongst the latter, Batilly-en-Gâtinais in Loiret (Figure 3.3) exceeds 20 ha in overall enclosed area, is focused on a major internal building within a 2 ha enclosure, and has produced material culture intimating its elite status: it is one of a series of big enclosures known from aerial imagery and set about a kilometre apart in this sector of the southern Paris Basin, with their plans already heralding *villa* arrangements. Batilly was in use between La Tène D1a and D2a, and thus over approximately three generations culminating in the middle of the 1st century BC (Fichtl 2013c; 2016).

Overall, such farms show an admixture of short-lived examples and others which were in use for longer, as well as fairly infrequently, long-term use (exceeding the timeframe that is the primary focus here) including, in rare cases, development from ditched-and-palisaded farm through small enclosed site to lowland *oppidum*-in-the-making, as at Paule (Côtes d'Armor) in Brittany (Menez 2012; 2016). The enduring nature and success of this site, adjacent to an inland crossroads, is surely underpinned by the increasing wealth, power and status of its controlling family through time. In the case of sites investigated at Bazoches-lès-Bray (Seine-et-Marne) a rather different pattern is suggested – a sizeable quadrilateral enclosure dating to La Tène C2 at Près le Tureau aux Chèvres, with buildings both within and outwith its enclosure, was succeeded in La Tène D1b by a smaller and much more rectilinear farmstead less than half a kilometre away. The broader pattern for east-central France, of which this last example forms part is, however, one of a generally increasing number of occupied farms through La Tène C and D, superimposed on which are local sequences of the creation and (sometimes rapid) abandonment of individual units (Nouvel *et al.* 2009). Geographical and other factors, probably including property ownership (Lambot 2016), plainly influenced these patterns, not least in terms of the relative significance of river valley or elevated plateau locations.

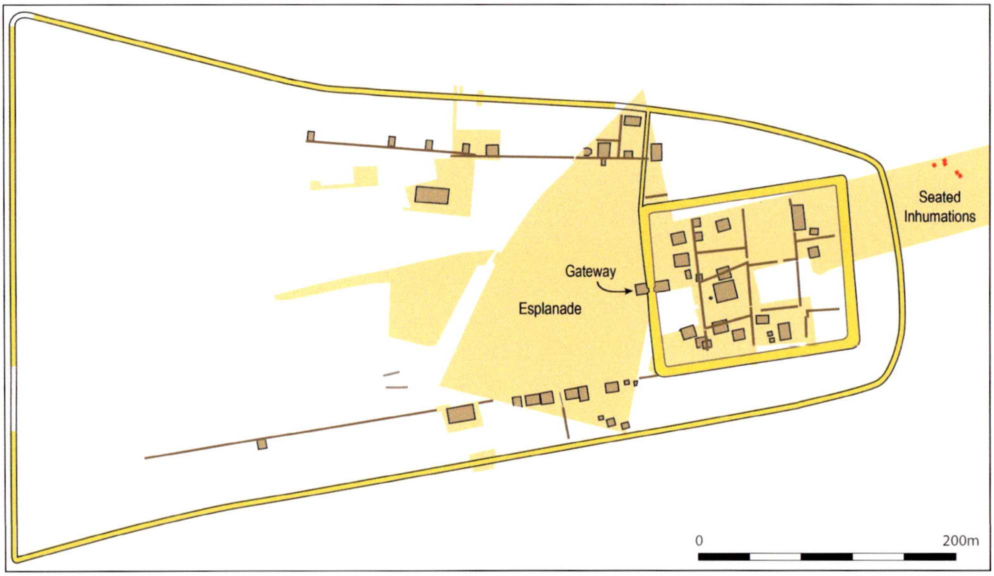

Figure 3.3 Plan of a late La Tène aristocratic farm at Batilly-en-Gâtinais, Loiret (adapted from Fichtl 2013c and a plan courtesy Stephan Fichtl).

Changes in agricultural production are also well documented. Cereal crops, in the earlier Iron Age often consisting of an admixture of species, were increasingly grown as pure stands. Recent overviews highlight the variability in cereal production, of stock-raising regimes and of storage technologies in use, for example across northern France between Brittany, Normandy and the west generally, and the zone to the east, and between middle and late La Tène (Zech-Matterne *et al.* 2013, fig. 1). Naked barley seems to have been the dominant crop in the eastern sector in middle La Tène, but increased in significance further west in the succeeding period; hulled wheats such as emmer and spelt were more common than free-threshing varieties, only represented in the east and only in late La Tène. Oats were more prevalent in the west, where the presence of both winter- and spring-sown cereals seems to indicate an increasing intensity of production, with individual fields being left fallow less often (Zech-Matterne and Brun 2016; Toulemonde *et al.* 2017). Superimposed on this, additional features can be seen: for example, non-local weeds begin to appear, suggesting that crops and seed-corn were being moved greater distances than previously as supply-chains lengthened. These adaptations should be seen alongside other major transformations during this time, notably the very rapid replacement of saddle- by rotary-querns primarily in the earlier part of middle La Tène, with consequent substantial gains in labour efficiency in flour production (Jaccottey *et al.* 2013, fig. 6).

In northern France, cattle are the dominant livestock represented (with pigs in second place in the north-east). Selective culling of young animals for meat is apparent, and is the dominant practice on some sites, whereas at other farms cattle were plainly

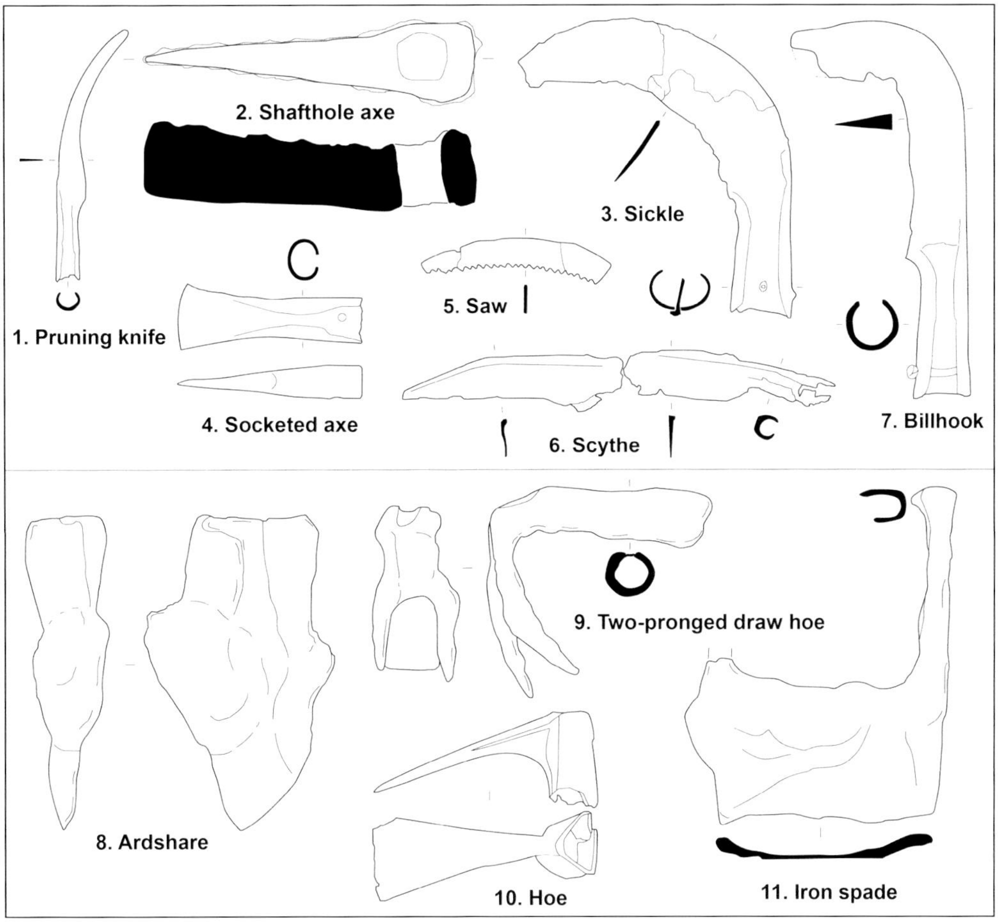

Figure 3.4 Selected agricultural iron tools of the later Iron Age, not to scale (source: Nillesse 2009).

retained for longer, whether for use as draught animals or as milk-producers. Some reliance on fodder for overwintering is indicated, and amongst a widening range of specialist iron tools for farming use (Figure 3.4), the appearance of scythes is thus noteworthy (Nillesse 2009; Nillesse and Buchsenschutz 2009; Toulemonde *et al.* 2017, figs 10–13). The increasing penetration of the agricultural sector by iron implements is a strong proxy for the rising availability of supplies of iron. Hypotheses suggesting the importation of bigger livestock from the south, especially of cattle and horses, need to be balanced as evidence for improvements through selective breeding begin to appear in the case of cattle at latest in La Tène D; in general evidence for bigger stock remains localized and proportionately relatively slight (Duval *et al.* 2013; Nuviala 2016). Horses are represented in both the north-western and north-eastern zones within Gaul and for both middle and late La Tène periods represent about 6% of the total livestock; their presence may accord with the cultivation of oats in some, but not all, areas where they are found. The slaughter, consumption and manipulation of animal carcasses in quantity which is attested on numerous sanctuary sites again underline the productivity of agricultural systems at this time.

Diverse structures were available for the storage of agricultural products: pits and cellars, as well as raised, often four-post, granaries, and (much more rarely) souterrains. This range is perhaps also an indication of increasing sophistication (and perhaps specialization) at this time in the storage of food products and seed crops. Other indications of such currents include consideration of the proxies for textile production. Whorls for spinning are ubiquitous on settlement sites, but the clay weights indicative of weaving are much less widely distributed, indicating the concentration of the latter activity at specific places. Superimposed on evidence for an increasingly-sophisticated and diversified agricultural sector, there are, however, other indications of internal differences within individual sites in terms of the availability of food-stuffs. At Acy-Romance, for instance, the discard pattern of animal bone debris across the site suggests that the inhabitants of some areas within it were consuming much more prime meat than their neighbours (Méniel 2001, 42–43). At the open industrial village of Levroux-les-Arènes (Indre), the pig bones (Duval *et al.* 2016, 584) dominantly derived from the front end of the carcass, with the implication that the prime hams were being consumed elsewhere. This was also the case with beef and mutton – the best cuts are less commonly represented on site.

Alongside at least some imported livestock, other food commodities were also arriving from the south – including both olives and cultivated grapes, as well as a selection of herbs. With olive oil a culinary tradition of frying develops, complementing earlier staples such as stews and gruels. These new consumables add to the indications of successful, diversified agricultural economies in which some commodities were exchanged over considerable differences. The continuing collection of wild fruits and berries is also attested and on a few sites hunted red deer are present as a sufficient proportion of the meat bones to suggest that these were pursued on horseback for sport. Overall, the evidence suggests a diversifying and successful primary sector well able to support what seems to have been – on the basis of the evidence for settlements – a rising human population.

The settlement record: *oppida*

If archaeologists consciously or unconsciously try to interpret the record of settlements in terms of the principal descriptors used by the Classical authors (such as the three terms dominantly used by Caesar of *aedificia* – isolated buildings or farmsteads; *vici* – villages or hamlets; and *oppida* – major settlements or towns), it is of course the case that attributes believed to have been characteristic of one of these series can, sometimes surprisingly, be identified elsewhere. Increasingly, archaeologists are aware that aspects of the archaeological record as it is recovered do not map straightforwardly on to this tripartite division. An example is represented in the case of *muri gallici*, the elaborate stone-faced and timber-laced wall type often identified by the presence of the iron spikes augered into their timber frames and thus recovered archaeologically within them, which were described by Caesar at his siege of Avaricum, the main *oppidum* of the Bituriges Cubi, now Bourges (Cher) in 52 BC (*BG* 7.23). Walls of this type (and variants with longitudinal timbers set in their wall-faces) have been widely recognized in the earlier 1st century BC on *oppida* across Gallia (Buchsenschutz and Ralston 2014). Elaborate and showy (see Krausz this volume), their occurrence at the external limits of major urban places such as Mont Beuvray is readily explicable, but less so is their appearance on much smaller sites akin to farmsteads in size. At Luant in Indre (Berry), a small enclosure of about one hectare is not only enclosed by a fortification of this type, but also possessed a miniaturized version of the inturned entrances characteristic of *oppida*. Here the traits of the enclosing walls of the major *oppida* have been appropriated to convey the status and power of what must have been an elite farm set within a rural estate. These major farms prefigure the grander villas established in rural Gaul from the 1st century AD.

Large-scale excavations have contributed to the identification of an increasing range of features within the *oppida*, whilst generally confirming their relatively short-lived character (the main occupations of many fit substantially within the 1st century BC), although successful sites retained at least some of their status into the Gallo-Roman period, and in some cases indeed beyond. The numbers of known examples thus continue to be enhanced not only by exploratory works within long-established French cities but also by new discoveries in the countryside. Moulay (Mayenne), an *oppidum* of the Aulerci Diablintes, falls into the latter category through the identification of a 135-ha promontory fort in rescue work by INRAP, where previously a much smaller enclosure of some 12 ha at its apex was all that was known (Le Goff 2016). Paule (mentioned above) too, latterly expanding towards 30 ha, intimates rapid growth late in the Iron Age; and this seems to be the case elsewhere, as at the *oppidum* of Hérisson in Allier. The only part of Gaul where *oppida* are noticeably lacking is the coastal flatlands of the far north, where the settlement pattern is dominated by small 'villages' and farmsteads (cf. Roymans this volume).

As a result of long-term excavations in the 19th century, and again since 1984, Mont Beuvray, Bibracte of the Aedui, remains one of the best-known of these sites. Unusually, however, over the course of its use, it shrank from an original enclosed extent of some 200 ha to 135 ha (Figure 3.5), defined by a monumental enclosing wall set further up the contours of the substantial hill, 810 m high, on which it was set; the superimposition of the inner, over the outer, enclosure wall makes it clear that this is not a case of a widely-spaced bivallate enclosure; indeed *oppida*, even when massive, are predominantly univallate. As was the case with the inner wall at Beuvray, numbers of these elaborate timber-laced walls, imposing architectural variants of a long-lived temperate European tradition, were enveloped by the middle of the 1st century BC in massive and well-engineered dump banks, fronted by a sizeable ditch, as at Châteaumeillant (Cher), Mediolanum of the Bituriges (see Krausz this

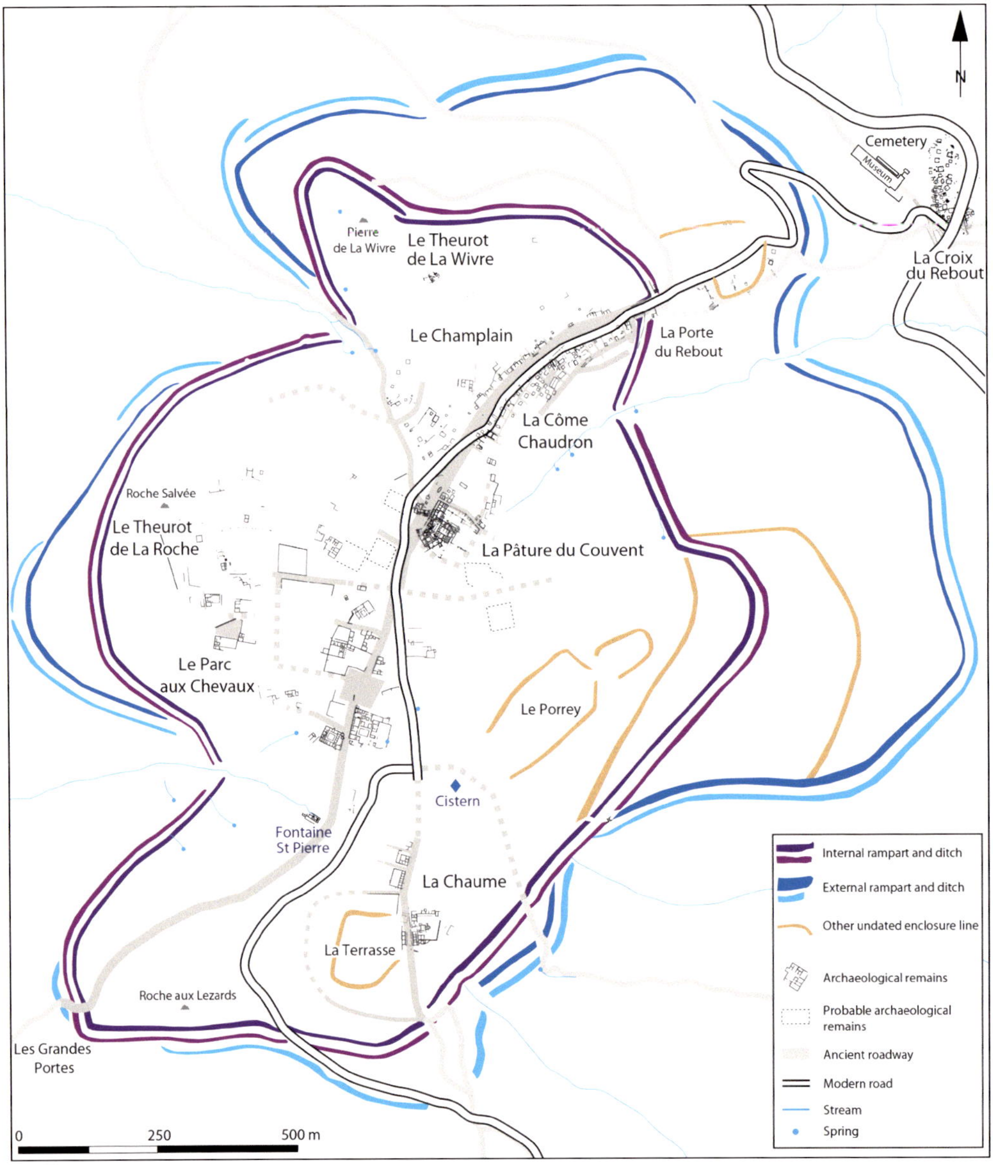

Figure 3.5 Plan of Mont Beuvray, Nièvre/Saône-et-Loire. The inner enclosure extends to 135 ha (courtesy Centre archéologique Européen, simplified).

volume). These imply refurbishment arguably in the face of a new threat, most likely Roman war machinery.

There are other unusual features of Mont Beuvray, notably that it is set on a hill which had formerly undergone substantial mining for iron ore – such that in modern jargon the *oppidum* was erected in part on a 'brownfield' site. Furthermore the settlement within the *oppidum* is matched from its developed stage by another contemporary, seemingly unenclosed, agglomeration of approximately the same extent set on a nearby hill (Moore *et al.* 2013). Even allowing for these places representing low-density forms of urbanism, the co-existence of these sites suggests a very substantial population at that time in this now very rural upland area.

Key characteristics of Mont Beuvray in the earlier 1st century BC include the frequently-modified monumental wall (again in *murus gallicus* style) fronted by a rock-cut ditch which surrounded it (in the case of the 135 ha enclosure this is over 5 km long), and the sub-division of its interior into different sectors in which a variety of activities prevailed. Inside the major, north-east inturned gateway of the Porte du Rebout, itself nearly 20 m wide and lacking any substantial gate-tower or similar structure, a major roadway progressed upslope, subdividing the internal space. Distributed along the road immediately inside the gate were areas for craftworking, with enamel-workers decorating a standardized range of copper-alloy jewellery and fitments on the left; and smiths, generally ironworkers, on the right. In at least one case near the Porte du Rebout a workshop was occupied successively by blacksmiths and then coppersmiths. Extensive excavations at the first substantial level area upslope from the gate (La Pâture du Couvent) have revealed a major stone-built tank of imported granite set longitudinally into the roadway, equipped with its own water supply arrangements. Flanking the road here were insula-like rows of houses set at right angles to the principal route. An indication of the wealth of their owners is that they were constructed over substantial cellars, initially sometimes wood-lined and latterly stone-built, accessed by wide stairways which suggests they were for the storage of commodities in quantity. Beyond these to the south is an area which served as a *forum*, again with stone buildings and the footings for columns, from the mid-1st century BC. By the following generation, its surroundings were to include further imposing Romanized stone buildings.

Further upslope, at Le Parc aux Chevaux, was an area with substantial houses, frequently remodelled on the same site, as is best demonstrated in the case of Parc aux Chevaux 1, which had five successive builds between *c.* 90 BC and 15 AD (Paunier and Luginbühl 2004). If latterly this was a substantial residence in atrium style, with tiled roof and many Romanizing traits such as *opus spicatum* floors, the initial phases, admittedly much less well preserved, seem to have been distinctly less imposing. Continuity in the use of the location, and the characteristics of this building by its Phase 3, suggest however that aggrandizement of the owners' status and wealth was already well underway by the mid-1st century BC. These buildings seem good candidates for the town houses of the elite, who at other times resided on their estates in the countryside, as well as of those benefiting from the upsurge in trade and manufacturing.

Alongside internal variations in the domestic and craft uses of space within Mont Beuvray, there are other areas given over to ritual use as sanctuaries, such as at the small summit enclosure of La Terrasse or the enclosure enveloping the source of one of the many streams which rise within the *oppidum* at La Fontaine St Pierre, which was embellished with increasingly complex architecture through time. There are strong indications that the uppermost parts of the hill around La Chaume were given over to cult and ritual and to public meetings and markets; indeed such activities long endured on the hill after settlement rapidly declined in the 1st century AD. As is the case with some other *oppida*, there were also less-intensively used sectors within the 135 ha enclosure, such as Le Verger near Les Grandes Portes.

Mont Beuvray, in its conspicuous upland (and now very rural) location in the Morvan, and early deserted by its elite inhabitants for the new Roman city of Augustodunum (Autun, Saône-et-Loire; Labaune and Kasprzyk 2015) in the lowlands some 20 km away, is one template for an *oppidum*. Others varied considerably from this model not only in scale (some are approximately a tenth of its size, a few are bigger) but in their landscape setting. Examples extend from low hills, to riparian settings on major navigable rivers, to the coastal edge. Some may have had their functions dispersed at a number of different locations, as is suggested for Corent–Gergovie–Gondole in the Auvergne (Poux 2014, fig. 14.4). In the longer term, some were rapidly found not to be successful nodes within developing urban and administrative networks, whereas others fared much better. A developing urban archaeology of protohistoric places provides a range of examples of the latter from Toulouse and Rodez to Orléans and Paris (Buchsenschutz *et al.* 2009). Variations in their size, chronological development (normally not from before the later 2nd century BC) and apparent complexity as particular urban places are thus readily apparent; indeed some such sites may have developed far less infrastructure, even on occasion remaining essentially walled places of refuge – the Puy d'Issolud, in Lot, scene of a battle late in the Gallic War (*BG* 8.40; Girault 2013; Reddé this volume), may be a case in point.

Sanctuaries, ritual and the funerary record

Mont Beuvray is far from the only *oppidum* where evidence of ritual and religion seems well-attested in the surviving record. Indeed in some cases and some areas – notably within Gallia Belgica – a good case can be mounted for the primary use of some upland sites which subsequently developed into *oppida* being related to their intermittent use as important sanctuaries (Fernández-Götz 2014; Metzler *et al.* 2016). Within Iron Age archaeology, the study of religion and ritual is undoubtedly the sub-field most transformed by new data and interpretations in recent decades (Poux 2012b).

The general tendency during the period considered here is for evidence for ritual and religion to be increasingly clearly – and separately in spatial terms – identifiable in the archaeological record. In the earlier decades, as within the settlement of Acy-Romance, such evidence tends to be closely juxtaposed with that for other activities (Lambot and Méniel 2000). Thereafter, the trend is for it either to be focused on specific areas within individual sites, as in the ditch-defined sector within the Titelberg *oppidum* in Luxembourg in the territory of the Treveri (Metzler *et al.* 2016), or for it to be established within separate, demarcated places in the countryside. These rural sanctuary sites have been identified particularly in Gallia Belgica where they seem in several cases to occur in frontier areas between *civitates*; the marking of their locations with special deposits and with special structures within enclosed spaces probably contributed to the definition and organization of territories then under way. Some sanctuaries thus have longer 'biographies' during the later Iron Age, with beginnings before the period under consideration. Sanctuaries and evidence of ritual practices (involving not only the processing of animal and sometimes human remains, but also material culture; Bataille 2008), however, also occur elsewhere across Gaul as at Mirebeau in east-central France (Barral *et al.* 2016) and west to Brittany, including special deposits of various kinds on Ouessant (Ushant) and at Tronoen in Finistère (Arcelin and Brunaux 2003). Many of these locations remained significant into Gallo-Roman times, as at Mandeure (Doubs), and often it was the monumental Roman-period structures which first intimated the importance of the place to the archaeologist, as at Ribemont-sur-Ancre (Somme) or Tintignac (Corrèze).

New discoveries, as made from 2006 onwards in rescue excavations at an altitude of nearly 600 m at Mormont in Vaud, Switzerland, have the potential to radically change and enlarge this record. Here a series of over 250 substantial pits seems to have been a short-lived sanctuary of the Helvetii for perhaps two generations around 100 BC: the pits, individually up to 5 m deep, contained special deposits including a wide range of everyday material culture and coins, along with some sherds of imported amphorae (Brunetti *et al.* 2014). There was also evidence including human skulls suggesting sacrifices (perhaps prisoners of war), human skeletons and those of animals, including some big (and probably imported) horses. There are indications that this exceptional site was located at an important node in the routeways through the surrounding mountains.

Of those sanctuaries directly associated with settlements, the relevant sector within the Titelberg is literally amongst the most clearly-delineated, by a major ditch which sub-divided the internal area of the *oppidum* (Metzler *et al.* 2016). The *oppidum* of Corent (Puy-de-Dôme) has also produced a remarkable rectilinear sanctuary enclosure (Figure 3.6). Within it, rigorous field archaeology has revealed in fine detail extraordinary practices including the use of swords to cut the necks of amphorae to allow the wine therein to run as libations into prepared basins set in the ground. A collection of iron weaponry recovered from the ditch perhaps initially formed a trophy set up on the margin of the sanctuary (Poux 2012a, 142–167; Poux and Demierre 2016).

Among the practices attested across this set of sites is the deposition of material culture, including, as has been noted, prestigious items such as weaponry. Often such

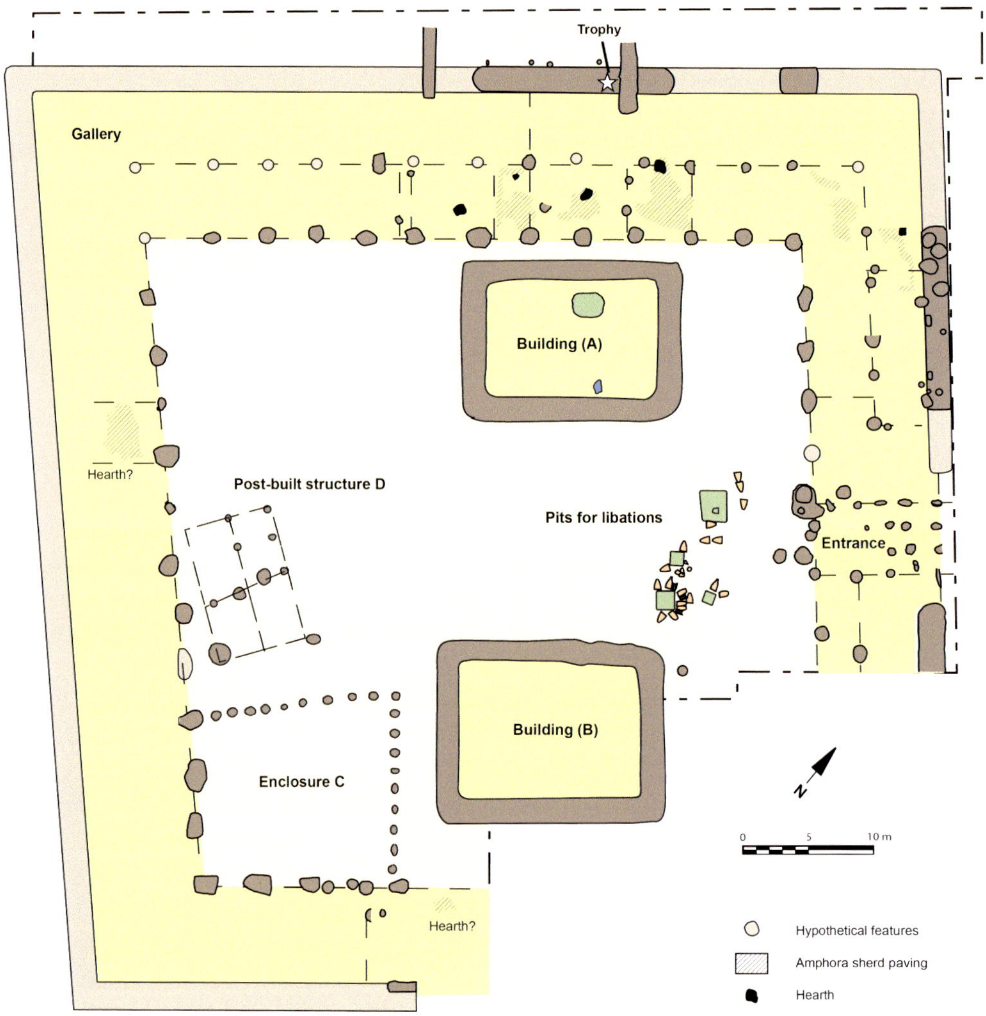

Figure 3.6 Corent, Puy-de-Dôme. Sanctuary within the oppidum. *Phase 2: earlier 1st century BC (adapted from Poux 2012a; 2016, courtesy Matthieu Poux).*

items have been bent or twisted or otherwise rendered unfit for further use, and this has been done recurrently in a way that implies a series of formal, ritualized gestures. Animal skeletons too may display indications of standardized patterns of killing, as in the poleaxed cattle skulls from Gournay-sur-Aronde (Oise). The differing nature of animal bone deposits intimate different activities ranging from on the one hand the sacrifice of individual animals (their deposited skeletons recovered from a pit or ditch remaining largely intact) to the large-scale consumption of young creatures, such as lambs or suckling pigs, where grouped but jumbled remains of a single species in a deposit may indicate a major feast – in essence a single event. Human remains also occur and can show a range of treatments, as at Ribemont-sur-Ancre, where three

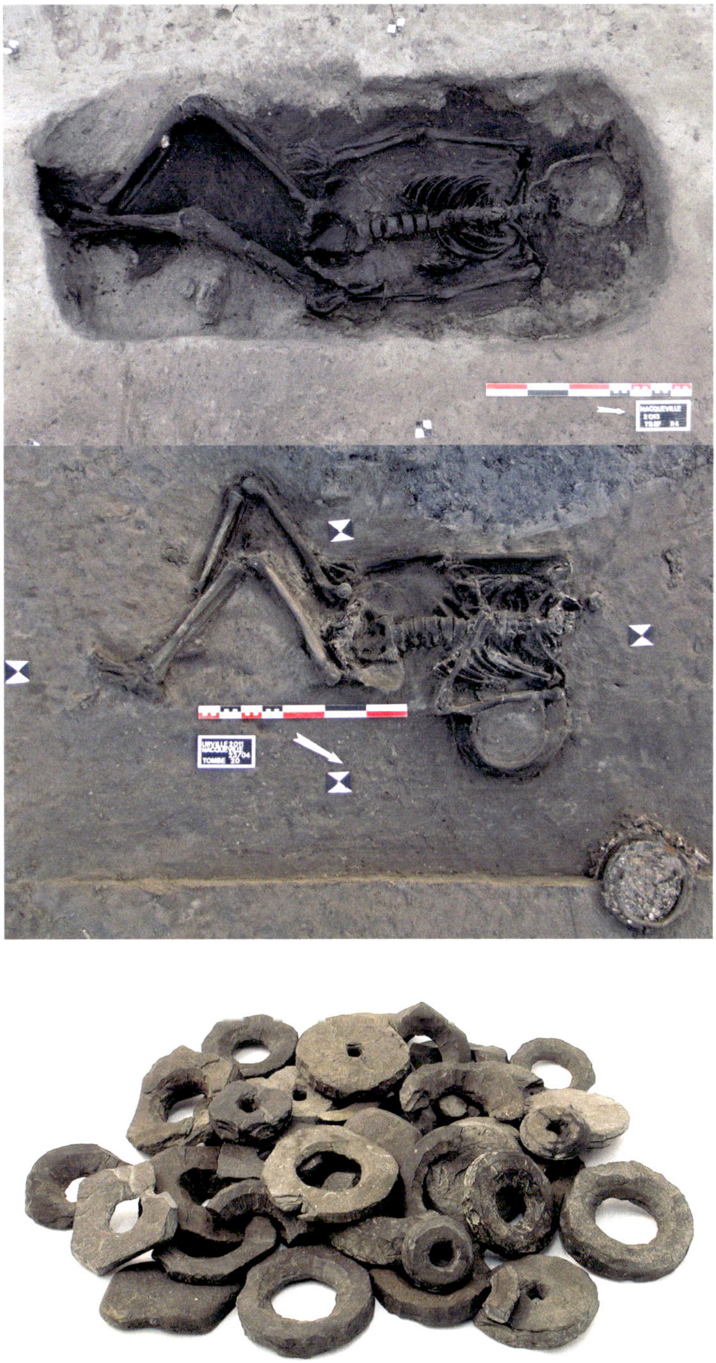

Figure 3.7 Urville-Nacqueville, Manche. Two inhumation burials from Les Dunes cemetery and collection of Kimmeridge shale bracelet rough-outs (photos Anthony Lefort, J.-Y. Yvon).

distinct procedures over time can be seen in the human remains: first, structures built of long bones set above individual pits and perhaps interpretable as altars; second, a large deposit of mixed partial human remains of males, but with no skulls, set outside the principal enclosure and perhaps representing a charnel house (these may be the remains of a defeated army which may – from the associated material culture – have come from Lower Normandy); and finally, a series of remains from another nearby enclosure, treated entirely differently and with skeletal elements pecked by large birds, which has been interpreted as a *heroon* (Brunaux 2004).

In sum, as archaeological evidence accumulates, the indications from sanctuaries and cult sites of a variety of kinds – including deposits in water – point to a hugely elaborate suite of ritual practices, sometimes showing considerable time-depth within the Iron Age, which are widely recognized as pervasive if not omnipresent on sites examined by archaeologists. This perspective completely contradicts earlier views in which religious practices at this time were considered essentially atectonic, substantially confined to natural settings, and more generally difficult to identify archaeologically.

Mont Beuvray is also one of the relatively few *oppida* with a known cemetery, in this case principally of relatively modestly accompanied cremations under little square ditched barrows distributed along the access route around La Croix de Rebout and upslope to the main north-east gateway (Figure 3.5 above). Although not as rare as once thought, the evidence for burials during the last two centuries BC forms a lesser component of the later Iron Age record in Gaul than it does for earlier periods. One key change is the increasing deployment of cremation, as at Beuvray and in the La Tène D (and later) cemetery of Lamadeleine on the upper skirts of the Titelberg hill, where inhumations are very rare (Metzler-Zens *et al.* 1999). In some areas, notably north-eastern France, small cemeteries – often including accompanied inhumations in middle La Tène, but predominantly cremations thereafter – are better known near farms and open agglomerations. They can be associated here with small, generally rectilinear, enclosures, as well as barrows and small post-built structures (Lambot 2002; Stead *et al.* 2006). In general, the status of individuals is now marked more by the presence of equipment associated with preparing food, eating and drinking, especially amphorae of imported wine, rather than the vehicles and high-status metalwork characteristic of earlier centuries.

Like other evidence considered here, there are marked regional differences. Late and rare instances of long-established elite rites – such as burial with a two-wheeled cart, or on occasion, components of a vehicle – occur, as at Nanterre in the Paris Basin (Olivier and Schönfelder 2002) and at Boé in Aquitaine (Schönfelder 2002). In some cases, wealthy graves are located at some distance from the *oppida* in contrast (as at the Titelberg) to less richly-accompanied ones in their immediate vicinity. Clemency, albeit still less than 10 km from the Titelberg, is a case in point. Here, in an oak chamber beneath a barrow, a male, cremated in a bearskin, was accompanied *c.* 80 BC by grave goods intimating feasting which included an imported copper alloy basin, a Campanian oil lamp, a grill, ten wine amphorae and four piglets. Pillaged in antiquity, other items including weaponry may have been removed. A rein-ring harks back to the cart-burial tradition, but in the main this is a very different presentation of an elite burial than characterized those of earlier La Tène times (Metzler 2002). The location of this grave across the valley from the Titelberg surely indicates a prominent male interred on his family landholding.

A series of similar individual but very rural elite inhumations, attributable to late La Tène as at Fléré-la-Rivière (Indre) and continuing into the early Gallo-Roman period occur in the *civitas* of the Bituriges Cubi (Ferdière and Villard 1993). They intimate that, if major political decisions were made in the *oppida*, the wealth and power of those who made them were often founded on rural resources. Such elites, as was also the case in more recent times in temperate Europe, were thus often peripatetic, dividing their time between public engagement – latterly extending to auxiliary service with Rome (see Pernet this volume) – and more private, domestic spheres remote from the central places. At other scales, too, the funerary record, very partial though it is, can indicate movement: a remarkable recent discovery at the north end of the Cotentin peninsula of Normandy is a cemetery containing some inhumations buried in a very Durotrigan fashion near the coastal settlement of

Figure 3.8 Four-sided, two-aisled structure found juxtaposed with settlement evidence and a small rectilinear enclosure, Ville Pollo, Trégueux, Côtes d'Armor (source: Allen et al. *2012, courtesy Tim Allen).*

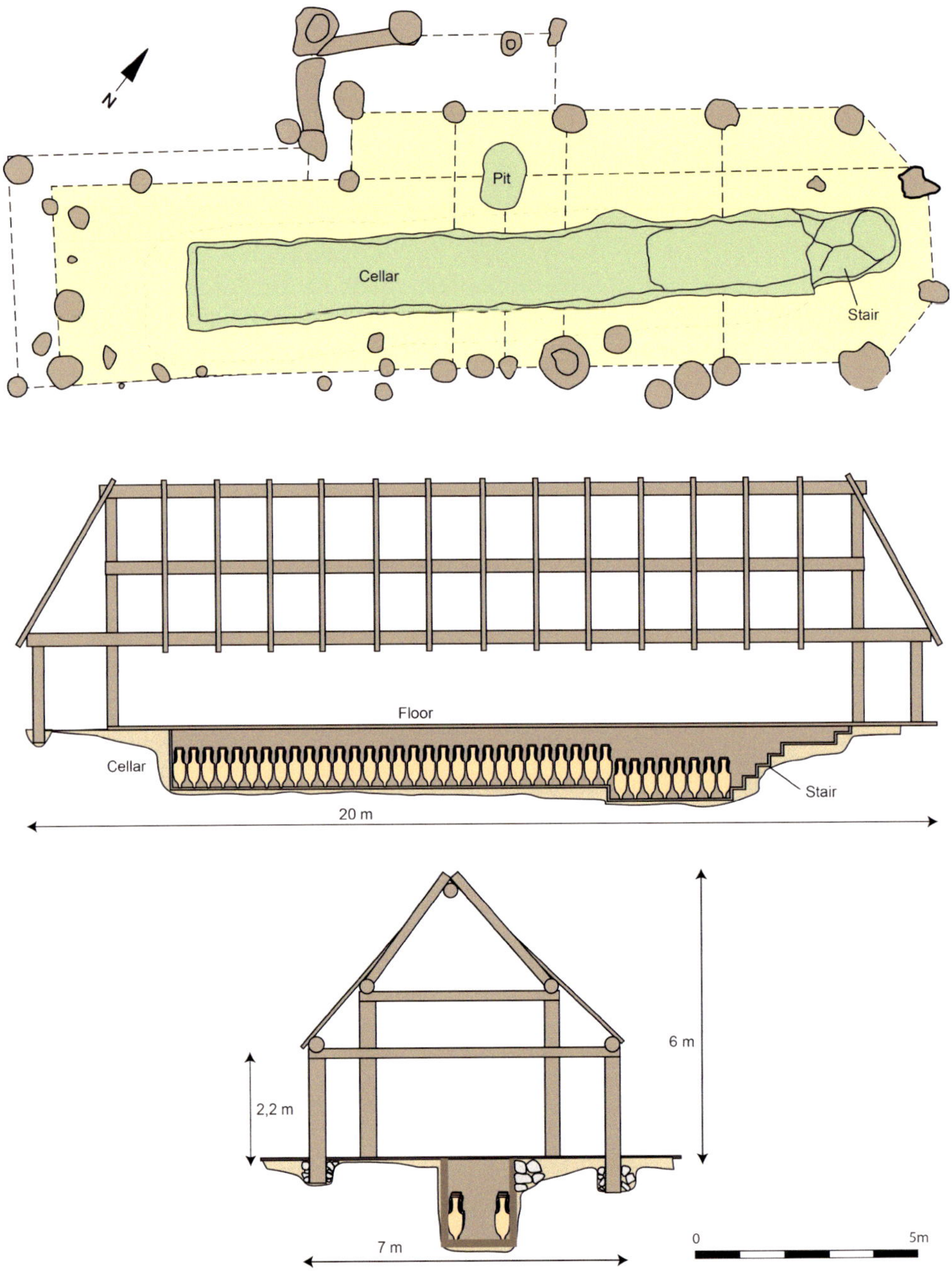

Figure 3.9 Corent, Puy-de-Dôme. Warehouse with a long narrow cellar for the storage of wine amphorae, of a type with parallels in Rome and Narbonne (after Poux 2012a, courtesy Matthieu Poux).

Urville-Nacqueville, which also yielded the footings of roundhouses and roughouts of Kimmeridge shale bracelets (Figure 3.7; Lefort *et al.* 2015). Arrivals from the Dorset area are strongly indicated here.

Conclusions

Archaeological knowledge of middle and late La Tène Gaul is increasing rapidly, on the one hand furnishing data on the layout of settlement sites and their environments at a scale previously unachievable and on the other through fieldwork and analyses providing radically new sorts of information. This last point may be illustrated simply by reference to the recent identification of new building types: substantial quadrangular two-aisled buildings as found at Trégueux (Côtes d'Armor) in Brittany (Menez and Allen 2016; Figure 3.8) and on Mont Beuvray; and a remarkable warehouse (or tavern?) with a cellar used for the storage of wine amphorae (Figure 3.9) within the *oppidum* of Corent (Poux 2012a, 117–134) may stand as examples. Alongside versions of *fora* at Beuvray and at Corent, there are also signs of an architecture related to public assemblies, as again at Corent or indeed the arrangement postulated as a support for voting in the early 1st century BC phase at the Titelberg (Metzler *et al.* 2016, fig. 60; overview at 420–436). And the late Christian Peyre (2000, figs 13–15) hypothesized that the remarkable timber arcades subdividing the slightly later (La Tène D2) lowland *oppidum* at Villeneuve-Saint-Germain may have fulfilled a similar function. Whilst some such features may encourage renewed comparisons with Italy and the urbanized Mediterranean world to the south more generally, it remains important to assess this temperate European evidence on its own terms.

The period under review is marked by plentiful indications of increasing production in both primary and secondary sectors, of rapidly developing major settlements, of religious and ritual complexity apparent in the archaeological record, and of population growth. But, as several episodes in Caesar's account make plain, all this was not achieved without on occasion – more likely recurrent – social and political pressures and discord. This was the second tranche of Transalpine Gaul the expanding Roman state had to deal with; if it was a semi-periphery in world system terms, it plainly contained numerous actors with considerable familiarity with the world to the south.

The distributions of *oppida* across some Gallic *civitates* and the accompanying evidence for lesser settlements and, in some instances, sanctuaries, strongly indicate the presence of state-level societies, not necessarily everywhere, nor all equally robust – or indeed fragile. The evidence of the organization of territories such as that of the Bituriges Cubi (Krausz 2016) certainly contributes to the perception that one reason Caesar was able to make relatively rapid military headway in temperate Gaul was that, setting aside all consideration of the effectiveness of Roman equipment and military organization, he was dealing with societies which were structured and operated in ways that in effect contributed in due course to their relatively straightforward assimilation within the late Republic and then early Empire (Buchsenschutz 2004b). Of course on occasion this process was delayed or met with resistance and setbacks, in some instances decades after Caesar's campaigns, but Caesar's military adventure into temperate Europe was undoubtedly to be hugely significant for the protagonists on both sides.

Acknowledgements

I am much indebted to colleagues for supplying graphic materials redeployed here: Mr Tim Allen (Oxford Archaeology) – Trégueux; Professor Stephan Fichtl (Strasbourg) – Batilly; Dr Vincent Guichard, Director of the Centre archéologique Européen, Mont Beuvray; Dr Anthony Lefort (INRAP, Normandie) – Urville-Nacqueville; and Professor Matthieu Poux (Lyons) – Corent. The graphics were expertly modified by Ms Leeanne Whitelaw. I am grateful to Colin Haselgrove and Andrew Fitzpatrick for the invitation to present the lecture at the Oxford conference from which this paper grew. All remaining errors are of course the author's responsibility.

Bibliography

Allen, T., Biddulph, E., Dodd, M., Donnelly, M., Gourlin, B. and Poole, C. (2012) Rocade d'agglomération briochine (Trégueux – Côtes d'Armor-Bretagne): enclos défensif, bâtiment public et habitat nucléé de la Tène 2, et leurs développements à la période gallo-romaine et à l'époque médiévale. Unpublished client report for the Conseil Général des Côtes d'Armor. Oxford, Oxford Archaeology.

Arcelin, P. and Brunaux, J.-L. (eds) (2003) *Cultes et sanctuaires en France à l'âge du Fer. Gallia* 60. Paris, CNRS.

Barral, P., Joly, M., Nouvel, P. and Thivet, M. (2016) Influences et modèles dans l'organisation et l'architecture de quelques sanctuaires laténiens et gallo-romains du centre-est de la Gaule. In G. Blancquaert and F. Malrain (eds), *Évolution des sociétés gauloises du second âge du Fer, entre mutations internes et influences externes (Actes du 38e colloque international de l'AFEAF, Amiens 2014)*, 447–452. Senlis, Revue Archéologique de Picardie numéro spécial 30.

Barral, P. and Fichtl, S. (eds) (2012) *Regards sur la chronologie de la fin de l'âge du Fer (IIIe–Ier siècle avant notre ère) en Gaule non méditerranéenne.* Glux-en-Glenne, Collection Bibracte 22.

Barral, P. and Nouvel, P. (2012) Le dynamique de l'urbanisation à la fin de l'âge du Fer dans le centre-est de la France. In S. Sievers and M. Schönfelder (eds), *Die Frage der Protourbanisation in der Eisenzeit. La question de la proto-urbanisation à l'âge du Fer (Akten des 34. internationalen Kolloquiums der AFEAF, Aschaffenburg 2010)*, 139–164. Bonn, Römisch-Germanische Kommission Kolloquien zur Vor- und Frühgeschichte 16.

Bataille, G. (2008) *Les Celtes: des mobiliers aux cultes.* Dijon, Editions universitaires de Dijon.

Bayard, D. and Fichtl, S. (2016) Le Camp César de la Chaussée-Tirancourt (Somme) – *oppidum* gaulois ou camp romain? In G. Blancquaert and F. Malrain (eds), *Évolution des sociétés gauloises du second âge du Fer, entre mutations internes et influences externes (Actes du 38e colloque international de l'AFEAF, Amiens 2014)*, 343–362. Senlis, Revue Archéologique de Picardie numéro spécial 30.

Bertrand, I., Duval, A., Gomez de Soto, J. and Maguer, P. (eds) (2009) *Habitats et paysages ruraux en Gaule et regards sur d'autres régions du monde celtique (Actes du 31e colloque international de l'AFEAF, Chauvigny 2007), Vol. 2.* Chauvigny, Association des Publications Chauvinoises Mémoire 35.

Blancquaert, G. and Malrain, F. (eds) (2016) *Évolution des sociétés gauloises du second âge du Fer, entre mutations internes et influences externes (Actes du 38e colloque international de l'AFEAF, Amiens 2014).* Senlis, Revue Archéologique de Picardie numéro spécial 30.

Bradley, R., Haselgrove, C., Vander Linden, M. and Webley, L. (2016) *The Later Prehistory of North-West Europe: The evidence of development-led fieldwork.* Oxford, Oxford University Press.

Brkojewitsch, G., Dreier, C. and Marquié, S. (2015) Metz/Divodurum, cité des Médiomatriques: apport de deux fouilles récentes. In M. Reddé and W. van Andringa (eds), *La naissance des capitales de cités en Gaule chevelue. Gallia* 72.1, 177–193. Paris, CNRS.

Bruant, J. and Touquet, R. (2016) Origines protohistoriques des voies de grands parcours antiques en territoire Carnute, Sénon et Parisii. Éléments fournis par l'archéologie préventive et l'archéogéographie. In G. Blancquaert and F. Malrain (eds), *Évolution des sociétés gauloises du second âge du Fer, entre mutations internes et influences externes (Actes du 38e colloque international de l'AFEAF, Amiens 2014)*, 19–33. Senlis, Revue Archéologique de Picardie numéro spécial 30.

Brun, P. and Ruby, P. (2008) *L'âge du Fer en France. Premières villes, premiers États celtiques.* Paris, La Découverte.

Brunaux, J.-L. (2004) *Guerre et religion en Gaule. Essai d'anthropologie celtique.* Paris, Errance.

Brunetti, C., Kaenel, G. and Méniel, P. (eds) (2014) *Les Helvètes au Mormont: une énigme dans le monde celtique. Archéothéma* hors-série 7.

Buchsenschutz, O. (2004a) *Les Celtes de l'Age du Fer dans la moitié nord de la France.* Paris, Maison des Roches.

Buchsenschutz. O. (2004b) Les Celtes et la formation de l'Empire romain. *Annales Histoire Sciences sociales* 59, 337–361.

Buchsenschuz, O. (2009) Chars, charettes et transport dans l'agriculture celtique. In I. Bertrand, A. Duval, J. Gomez de Soto and P. Maguer (eds), *Habitats et paysages ruraux en Gaule et regards sur d'autres régions du monde celtique (Actes du 31e colloque international de l'AFEAF, Chauvigny 2007), Vol. 2*, 85–92. Chauvigny, Association des Publications Chauvinoises Mémoire 35.

Buchsenschutz, O. (ed.) (2015) *L'Europe celtique à l'âge du fer.* Paris, Presses universitaires de France/ Nouvelle Clio.

Buchsenschtuz, O. and Ralston, I. (2012) Urbanisation et aristocratie celtiques. In S. Sievers and M. Schönfelder (eds), *Die Frage der Protourbanisation in der Eisenzeit. La question de la proto-urbanisation à l'âge du Fer (Akten des 34. internationalen Kolloquiums der AFEAF, Aschaffenburg 2010)*, 347–364. Bonn, Römisch-Germanische Kommission Kolloquien zur Vor- und Frühgeschichte 16.

Buchsenschutz, O. and Ralston, I. (2014) Nouvelles remarques sur les muri gallici. In J. Bullinger, P. Crotti and C. Huguenin (eds), *De l'âge du Fer à l'usage du verre. Mélanges offerts à Gilbert Kaenel dit 'Auguste', à l'occasion de son 65e anniversaire*, 171–178. Lausanne, Cahiers d'archéologie romande 151.

Buchsenschutz, O., Chardenoux, M.-B., Krausz, S. and Vaginay, M. (eds) (2009) *L'âge du Fer dans le boucle de la Loire: Les Gaulois sont dans la ville (Actes du 32e colloque de l'AFEAF, Bourges 2008).* Tours, Revue Archéologique du Centre de la France Supplément 35.

Culture 2000 (n.d.) Oppida: premières villes an nord des Alpes. http://www.oppida.org/ (accessed 1 July 2018).

Duval, C., Frémondeau, D., Lepetz, S. and Horard-Herbin, M.-P. (2016) L'élevage du porc: un savoir-faire gaulois? Apport croisé des études isotopique et ostéométrique des os de cochon. In G. Blancquaert and F. Malrain (eds), *Évolution des sociétés gauloises du second âge du Fer, entre mutations internes et influences externes (Actes du 38e colloque international de l'AFEAF, Amiens 2014)*, 583–596. Senlis, Revue Archéologique de Picardie numéro spécial 30.

Duval, C., Horard-Herbin, M.-P. and Lepetz, S. (2013) Morphological changes in domestic cattle in Gaul, from the second century BC to the fifth century AD: diversity of herds in the Seine valley (France) and northern Gaul. *Journal of Archaeological Science* 40, 3977–3990.

Faye, O., Georges, M. and Thion, P. (1990) Des fortifications de La Tène à Metz (Moselle). *Trierer Zeitschrift* 53, 55–126.

Ferdière, A. and Villard, A. (1993) *La tombe augustéenne de Fléré-la-Rivière (Indre) et les sépultures aristocratiques de la cité des Bituriges.* Saint-Marcel, Musée d'Argentomagus Mémoire 2.

Fernández-Götz, M. (2014) *Identity and Power. The transformation of Iron Age Societies in Northeast Gaul.* Amsterdam, Amsterdam Archaeological Studies 21.

Fichtl, S. (2005) *La ville celtique: les* oppida *de 150 av. J.-C. à 15 apr. J.-C.* (2nd edn). Paris, Errance.

Fichtl, S. (2012) *Les peuples gaulois IIIe–Ier siècle av. J-C.* Paris, Errance.

Fichtl, S. (2013a) Rome en Gaule: organisation territoriale de la Gaule de l'époque de l'indépendance au début de la période romaine. In S. Hansen and M. Meyer (eds), *Parallele Raumkonzepte (Topoi: Berlin Studies of the Ancient World)*, 291–304. Berlin, de Gruyter.

Fichtl, S. (2013b) Les agglomérations gauloises de la fin de l'âge du Fer en Europe celtique (IIIe–Ier siècle av. J.-C.). In D. Garcia (ed.), *L'habitat en Europe celtique et en Méditerranée préclassique – domaines urbains.* Paris, Errance.

Fichtl, S. (2013c) À propos des résidences aristocratiques de la fin de l'âge du Fer: l'exemple de quelques sites du Loiret. In S. Krausz, A. Colin, K. Gruel, I. Ralston and T. Dechezleprêtre (eds), *L'âge du Fer en Europe. Mélanges offerts à Olivier Buchsenschutz*, 329–343. Bordeaux, Ausonius Mémoires 32.

Fichtl, S. (2016) À l'origine des grandes *villae:* la résidence aristocratique de Batilly-en-Gâtinais. In G. Blancquaert and F. Malrain (eds), *Évolution des sociétés gauloises du second âge du Fer, entre mutations internes et influences externes (Actes du 38e colloque international de l'AFEAF, Amiens 2014)*, 393–401. Senlis, Revue Archéologique de Picardie numéro spécial 30.

Girault, J.-P. (2013) *La Fontaine de Loulié au Puy d'Issolud. Le dossier archéologique du siège d'Uxellodunum.* Glux-en-Glenne, Collection Bibracte 23.

Gruel, K., Nieto-Pelletier, S., Demierre, M. and Hiriart, E. (2017) Évaluation des indices de métallurgie monétaire au second âge du Fer. In S. Marion, S. Deffressigne, J. Kaurin and G. Bataille (eds), *Production et proto-industrialisation aux âges du Fer; perspectives sociales et environnementales (Actes du 39e colloque international de l'AFEAF, Nancy 2015)*, 497–518. Bordeaux, Ausonius Mémoires 47.

Guillaumet, J.-P. (1996) *L'artisanat chez les Gaulois.* Paris, Errance.

Haselgrove, C. (ed.) (2006) *Celtes et Gaulois. L'archéologie face à l'histoire: Les mutations de la fin de l'âge du fer.* Glux-en-Glenne, Collection Bibracte 12/4.

Jaccottey, L., Alonso, N., Defressigne, S., Hamon, C. *et al.* (2013) Le passage des meules va-et-vient aux meules rotatives en France. In S. Krausz, A. Colin, K. Gruel, I. Ralston and T. Dechezleprêtre (eds), *L'âge du Fer en Europe. Mélanges offerts à Olivier Buchsenschutz*, 405–419. Bordeaux, Ausonius Mémoires 32.

Krausz, S. (2016) *Des premières communautés paysannes à la naissance de l'État dans le Centre de la France.* Bordeaux, Ausonius Éditions, Scripta Antiqua 86.

Labaune, Y. and Kasprzyk, M. (2015) Autun/Augustodunum, cité des Éduens. In M. Reddé and W. van Andringa (eds), *La naissance des capitales de cités en Gaule chevelue. Gallia* 72.1, 195–216. Paris, CNRS.

Lambot, B. (2002) Noblesse, aristocratie et signes extérieurs de richesse à la Tène finale en Champagne. In V. Guichard and F. Perrin (eds), *L'aristocratie celte à la fin de l'âge du fer*, 87–108. Glux-en-Glenne, Collection Bibracte 5.

Lambot, B. (2016) Le territoire et la propriété au deuxième âge du fer en Champagne. In G. Blancquaert and F. Malrain (eds), *Évolution des sociétés gauloises du second âge du Fer, entre mutations internes et influences externes (Actes du 38e colloque international de l'AFEAF, Amiens 2014)*, 241–252. Senlis, Revue Archéologique de Picardie numéro spécial 30.

Lambot, B. and Méniel, P. (2000) Le centre communautaire et cultuel du village gaulois d'Acy-Romance dans son contexte régionale. In S. Verger (ed.), *Rites et espaces en pays celte et Méditerranéen. Étude comparée à partir du village d'Acy-Romance (Ardennes, France)*, 7–139. Rome, Collection de l'Ecole française de Rome 276.

Le Dreff, T., Roth-Zehner, M. and Séguier, J.-M. (2017) Les ateliers de potier au second âge du fer: premier bilan et perspectives de recherche. In S. Marion, S. Deffressigne, J. Kaurin and G. Bataille (eds), *Production et proto-industrialisation aux âges du Fer; perspectives sociales et environnementales (Actes du 39e colloque international de l'AFEAF, Nancy 2015)*, 155–178. Bordeaux, Ausonius Mémoires 47.

Lefort, A., Baron, A., Blondel, F., Méniel, M, and Rottier, S. with Nieto-Pelletier, S. and Querré, G. (2015) Artisanat, commerce et nécropole. Un port de La Tène D1 à Urville-Nacqueville. In F. Olmer and R. Roure (eds), *Les gaulois au fil de l'eau (Actes du 37e colloque international de l'AFEAF, Montpellier 2013)*, 441–74. Montpellier, Ausonius.

Le Goff, E. (2016) L'oppidum de Moulay, capitale gauloise des Aulerques Diablintes. In S. Fichtl, E. Le Goff, A. Mathiaut-Legros and Y. Menez (eds), *Les premières villes de l'ouest. Agglomérations gauloises de Bretagne et Pays de la Loire*, 123–138. Jublains, Deco 72.

Malrain, F., Blancquaert, G. and Lorho, T. (eds) (2013) *L'habitat rural du second âge du Fer. Rythmes de création et d'abandon au nord de la Loire.* Paris, INRAP/CNRS, Recherches archéologiques 7.

Malrain, F., Matterne, V. and Méniel, P. 2002 *Les paysans gaulois.* Paris, Errance.

Menez, Y. (2012) Die Entstehung städtischer Siedlungen bei besfestigten Adelssitzen der jüngeren Eisenzeit in Gallien. Das Beispiel von Paule (Côtes d'Armor). In S. Sievers and M. Schönfelder (eds), *Die Frage der Protourbanisation in der Eisenzeit. La question de la proto-urbanisation à l'âge du Fer (Akten des 34. internationalen Kolloquiums der AFEAF, Aschaffenburg 2010)*, 289–301. Bonn, Römisch-Germanische Kommission Kolloquien zur Vor- und Frühgeschichte 16.

Menez, Y. (2016) De la résidence rurale à l'agglomération. In S. Fichtl, E. Le Goff, A. Mathiaut-Legros and Y. Menez (eds), *Les premières villes de l'ouest. Agglomérations gauloises de Bretagne et Pays de la Loire*, 139–146. Jublains, Deco 72.

Menez, Y. and Allen, T. (2016) Résidence aristocratique et bourgade de la ville Pollo à Trégueux (Côtes d'Armor). In S. Fichtl, E. Le Goff, A. Mathiaut-Legros and Y. Menez (eds), *Les premières villes de l'ouest. Agglomérations gauloises de Bretagne et Pays de la Loire*, 160–167. Jublains, Deco 72.

Méniel, P. (2001) *Les Gaulois et les animaux: élevage, repas et sacrifice.* Paris, Errance.

Mennessier-Jouannet, C. and Deberge, Y. (eds) (2017) *Chronologie du mobilier archéologique du second âge du Fer en Auvergne, Vol. 1: Monographies des ensembles de référence.* Tours, Revue Archéologique du Centre de la France Supplément 65.

Metzler, J. (2002) Réflexions sur les sépultures aristocratiques en pays trévire. In V. Guichard and F. Perrin (eds), *L'aristocratie celte à la fin de l'âge du fer*, 175–186. Glux-en-Glenne, Collection Bibracte 5.

Metzler, J., Gaeng, C. and Méniel, P. (2016) *L'espace public du Titelberg, Vols 1–2.* Luxembourg, Centre National de Recherche Archéologique, Dossiers d'Archéologie XVII.

Metzler-Zens, N., Metzler-Zens, J. and Méniel, P. (1999) *Lamadelaine. Une nécropole de l'oppidum du Titelberg.* Luxembourg, Musée Nationale d'Histoire et d'Art Dossiers d'Archéologie VI.

Ministère de la Culture (n.d.) *2200 years ago – Acy-Romance – Les Gaulois des Ardennes.* http://archeologie.culture.fr/gaulois-ardennes/en (accessed 1 July 2018).

Moore, T., Braun, A., Creighton, J., Cripps, L., Haupt, P., Klenner, I., Nouvel, P., Ponroy, C. and Schönfelder, M. (2013) *Oppida*, agglomerations and suburbia: the Bibracte environs and new perspectives on late Iron Age urbanism in central-eastern France. *European Journal of Archaeology* 16, 491–517.

Nieto-Pelletier, S. (ed.) (2013) Monnaies gauloises: origine, fabrication, usages. *Dossiers d'Archéologie* 360.

Nillesse, O. (2009) Activités. Métiers, vie quotidienne dans les établissements ruraux de l'Ouest de la France à travers l'instrumentum. In I. Bertrand, A. Duval, J. Gomez de Soto and P. Maguer (eds), *Habitats et paysages ruraux en Gaule et regards sur d'autres régions du monde celtique (Actes du 31e colloque international de l'AFEAF, Chauvigny 2007), Vol. 2*, 45–83. Chauvigny, Association des Publications Chauvinoises Mémoire 35.

Nillesse, O. and Buchsenschutz, O. (2009) Les faux et la datation de l'outillage agricole des dépôts de l'âge du Fer. In M. Honegger, D. Ramseyer, G. Kaenel, B. Arnold and M.-A. Kaeser (eds), *Le site de La Tène: bilan des connaissances – état de la question*, 157–165. Neuchâtel, Archéologie neuchâteloise 43.

Nouvel, P., Barral, P., Deffressigne, S., Riquier, V., Séguier, J.-M., Tikonoff, N. and Zehner, M. (2009) Rythmes de création, fonctionnement et abandon des établissements ruraux de la fin de l'âge du Fer. In I. Bertrand, A. Duval, J. Gomez de Soto and P. Maguer (eds), *Habitats et paysages ruraux en Gaule et regards sur d'autres régions du monde celtique (Actes du 31e colloque international de l'AFEAF, Chauvigny 2007), Vol. 2*, 109–151. Chauvigny, Association des Publications Chauvinoises Mémoire 35.

Nuviala, P. (2016) La production des «grands bœufs» dans l'est de la Gaule: entre évolutions gauloises et influences romaines. In G. Blancquaert and F. Malrain (eds), *Évolution des sociétés gauloises du second âge du Fer, entre mutations internes et influences externes (Actes du 38e colloque international de l'AFEAF, Amiens 2014)* , 597–609. Senlis, Revue Archéologique de Picardie numéro spécial 30.

Olivier, L. and Schönfelder, M. (2002) Nanterre (Hauts-de-Seine): un char de parade de la Tène moyenne. In V. Guichard and F. Perrin (eds), *L'aristocratie celte à la fin de l'âge du fer*, 113–118. Glux-en-Glenne, Collection Bibracte 5.

Olmer, F., Girard, B., Verrier, G. and Bohbot, H. (2013) Voies, acteurs et modalités du grand commerce en Europe occidentale. In A. Colin and F. Verdin (eds), *L'âge du Fer en Aquitaine et sur ses marges. Mobilité des hommes, diffusion des idées, circulation des biens dans l'espace européen à l'âge du Fer (Actes du 35e colloque international de l'AFEAF, Bordeaux 2011)*, 665–691. Bordeaux, Aquitania Supplément 30.

Paris, P.-E. (2017) Economy and society of the Remi and Suessiones in Gallia Belgica during the last two centuries BC through the prism of archaeozoology. *Environmental Archaeology* 22, 298–317.

Paunier, D. and Luginbühl, T. (2004) *Bibracte – le site de la maison 1 du Parc aux Chevaux (PC1) des origines de l'oppidum au règne de Tibère*. Glux-en-Glenne, Collection Bibracte 8.

Peyre, C. (2000) Documents sur l'organisation publique de l'espace dans la cité gauloise: le site de Villeneuve-Saint-Germain et la bilingue de Verceil. In S. Verger (ed.), *Rites et espaces en pays celtes et Méditerranéen. Étude comparée à partir du village d'Acy-Romance (Ardennes, France)*, 155–206. Rome, Collection de l'École française de Rome 276.

Poux, M. (ed.) (2012a) *Corent: voyage au coeur d'une ville gauloise* (2nd edn). Paris, Errance.

Poux, M. (2012b) Religion, sanctuaires et pratiques cultuelles en Gaule: quarante ans d'innovations. In L. Olivier (ed.) *Le Musée d'Archéologie Nationale et les Gaulois du XIXe au XXIe siècle*,151–169. Saint-Germain-en-Laye, Musée d'Archéologie Nationale.

Poux, M. (2014) Enlarging *oppida*: multipolar town patterns in late Iron Age Gaul. In M. Fernández-Götz, H. Wendling and K. Winger (eds), *Paths to Complexity. Centralisation and Urbanisation in Iron Age Europe*, 156–166. Oxford, Oxbow Books.

Poux, M. and Demierre, M. (2016) *Le sanctuaire de Corent (Puy-de-Dôme, Auvergne). Vestiges et rituels.* Paris, Gallia Supplément 62.

Raaflaub, K. (ed.) (2017) *The Landmark Julius Caesar*. New York, Pantheon Books.

Ralston, I. (1992) *Les enceintes fortifiées du Limousin. Les habitats protohistoriques de la France non-méditerranéenne*. Paris, Documents d'archéologie française 36.

Reddé, M. and van Andringa, W. (eds) (2015) *La naissance des capitales de cités en Gaule chevelue. Gallia* 72.1. Paris, CNRS.

Rieckhoff, S. (2014) Space, architecture and identity in Gaul in the 2nd/1st centuries BC. In M. Fernández-Götz, H. Wendling and K. Winger (eds), *Paths to Complexity. Centralisation and Urbanisation in Iron Age Europe*, 101–110. Oxford, Oxbow Books.

Riggsby, A. (2006) *Caesar in Gaul and Rome. War in Words.* Austin, University of Texas Press.

Schönfelder, M. (2002) *Das spätkeltische Wagengrab von Boé (Lot-et-Garonne): Studien zu Wagen und Wagengräbern der jüngeren Latènezeit*. Mainz/Bonn, Römisch-Germanisches Zentralmuseum Mainz Monografien 54.

Stead, I., Flouest, J.-L. and Rigby, V. (2006) *Iron Age and Roman Burials in Champagne*. Oxford, Oxbow Books.

Tchernia, A. (1986) *Le vin de l'Italie romaine. Essai d'histoire économique d'après les amphores.* Rome, Bibliothèque des Écoles françaises d'Athènes et de Rome 261.

Toulemonde, F., Zech-Matterne, V., Wiethold, J., Brun, C., Malrain, F., Riquier, V., and Durand, F. (2017) Reconstitution des pratiques agricoles du Ier millénaire en France orientale, d'après le croisement des données carpologiques et archéologiques. In S. Marion, S. Deffressigne, J. Kaurin and G. Bataille (eds), *Production et proto-industrialisation aux âges du Fer; perspectives sociales et environnementales (Actes du 39e colloque international de l'AFEAF, Nancy 2015)*, 29–50. Bordeaux, Ausonius Mémoires 47.

Zech-Matterne, V., Auxiette, G. and Malrain, F. (2013) Essai d'approche des systèmes agricoles laténiens. Données carpologiques, archéozoologiques et archéologiques. In S. Krausz, A. Colin, K. Gruel, I. Ralston and T. Dechezleprêtre (eds), *L'âge du Fer en Europe. Mélanges offerts à Olivier Buchsenschutz*, 397–404. Bordeaux, Ausonius Mémoires 32.

Zech-Matterne, V. and Brun, C. (2016) Vers une agriculture extensive? Étude diachronique des productions végétales et des flores adventices associées, au cours de la période laténienne, en France septentrionale. In G. Blancquaert and F. Malrain (eds), *Évolution des sociétés gauloises du second âge du Fer, entre mutations internes et influences externes (Actes du 38e colloque international de l'AFEAF, Amiens 2014)*, 623–638. Senlis, Revue Archéologique de Picardie numéro spécial 30.

Chapter 4

The Sertorian Wars in the conquest of Hispania: From data to archaeological assessment

Ángel Morillo and Feliciana Sala-Sellés

Hispania was a frontier region of the Roman state for two centuries, from 218 to 19 BC, when the northern territories were finally conquered (Figure 4.1).[1] The first contact with the Roman army took place in the Second Punic War (218–201 BC). During this conflict Iberia was the main source of manpower and silver for the Carthaginian army. Gnaeus Cornelius Scipio landed at the Greek colony of Emporion with two legions and established a camp there. Occupation of the Punic bases in the east and south of Spain such as Carthago Nova (Cartagena), Castulo and Gades (Cádiz) was necessary to defeat his enemies. In 206 BC, the last Carthaginian forces left Hispania. After the war, Rome divided Spain into two provinces – Hispania Citerior, on the east coast, and Hispania Ulterior, in the south. Both provinces, but particularly Ulterior Baetica, were rich in silver and other precious metals. During the Second Punic War, the local tribes switched between supporting the Carthaginians and the Romans, but when the war finished they all turned against the Romans in simultaneous and independent rebellions.

The second phase of the Roman conquest of Hispania began in 195 BC when Marcus Porcius Cato (the Elder) was given command of both provinces. This period saw the end of the revolts and the conquest of new territory on the borders of the new provinces. There were two main opponents: the Lusitani, on the west coast and the central and western plains (Portugal and Spanish Estremadure), and the Celtiberians,[2] living between the Ebro valley and the central plains of Castille. During the Lusitanian Wars, the tribes rebelled on two occasions (in 155 and 146 BC). Viriathus became leader of the Lusitanians in 146 BC until his murder in 139 BC and the conflict finished three years later.

The Celtiberian Wars (153–133 BC) were the single most important conflict in the conquest of Spain. Rome had to send a large number of legions to control the tribes and finally it needed a brilliant general, Publius Cornelius Scipio Aemilianus, who had defeated Carthage, to end the wars. The tribal resistance was broken by the Roman siege

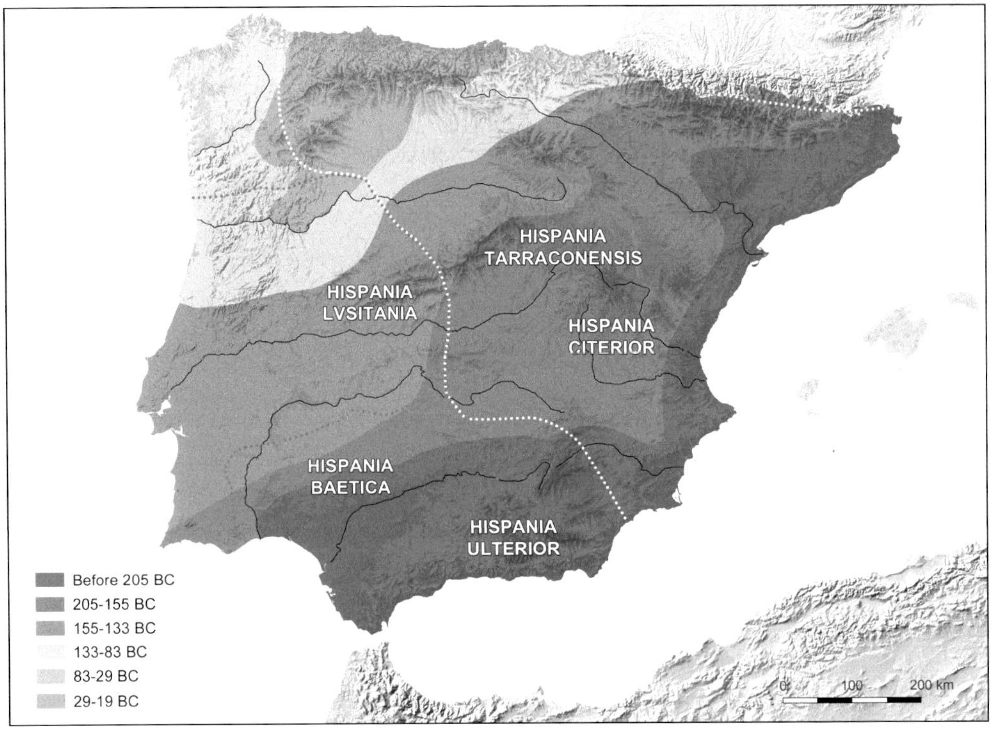

Figure 4.1 Stages in the Roman conquest of Hispania.

and destruction of Numantia, the centre of Celtiberian resistance, in 133 BC, after which only the northern and north-western parts of Hispania were not occupied by Rome.

A new episode in the relationship between the Roman army and Hispania began as a consequence of social and political conflict in Rome when the first Civil War between Lucius Cornelius Sulla and Gaius Marius broke out in Italy (88–87 BC and 82 BC). The Roman provinces of Hispania suffered directly from the civil conflict in Rome. The Sertorian Wars (82–72 BC) were a phase of intense military activity in the Iberian Peninsula, and have always been well known thanks to classical sources, mainly Plutarch (*Sertorius*) and Sallust (*Histories* 1.77).

In 82 BC Sulla defeated Marius and in 81 BC he became dictator and embarked on systematic repression of the *populares*, among whom was Quintus Sertorius, the designated governor of Hispania Citerior. Sertorius had great military and political talent. Although Roman officials in Hispania did not recognize his authority, he took control of Hispania with his army. Sertorius decided to confront Sulla's dictatorship and from 82 to 72 BC he waged a Civil War against the Republic. He was forced to flee to North Africa in 81 BC but a year later, the Lusitanians rose against Rome and asked Sertorius to return to lead them, which he did. Rome's legal governor in Lusitania was defeated by Sertorius at the battle of the Baetis (Guadalquivir river, 80 BC) and Sertorius quickly obtained the indigenous support of the Citerior province, especially of the Celtiberians. Sertorius' work was reflected in his establishment of the capital at Osca (Huesca), where he based the administrative and military organization, a Senate with Roman exiles, and founded a school where the sons of Roman citizens and local chieftains were educated together. He organized an army in the Roman manner with an indigenous element and he took advantage of the discontent of the provincials towards the abuses of the Romans. In some regards Sertorius was an early example for Julius Caesar, who would threaten Rome from his own base in the provinces.

Sulla sent an army commanded by Quintus Metellus Pius to quash the revolt, but it was defeated by Sertorius' forces. By 77 BC, Sertorius, a brilliant commander, controlled most of both provinces of Hispania, except for part of Baetica and the maritime bases of Tarraco and Carthago Nova. Sertorius was in league with the Cilician pirates and was in communication with Mithridates VI of Pontus. In 76 BC, a new Roman army under Pompey the Great marched from Italy over the Pyrenees to join forces with Metellus, but Sertorius outwitted them in a series of campaigns (76–73 BC). However, Pompey gradually began to overcome the Sertorian troops and when Marcus Perpenna helped murder Sertorius and assumed command of the army, the rebellion was finally crushed (72 BC).

The archaeological evidence: military camps

The Sertorian Wars are well documented thanks to the classical sources, but only recently have we begun to identify archaeological evidence of this conflict. In the last few years, different approaches to the conflict have been adopted. Some studies take only a historical perspective (García Morá 1991; Salinas 2006; Schulten 2013), whereas others incorporate archaeological evidence (Beltrán Lloris 2002; Pérez Gutiérrez 2011; Salinas Romo 2014).

One of the main strands of evidence is provided by Roman camps. The prolonged conquest of Hispania, which lasted two centuries (218–19 BC), and the significance of episodes such as the Celtiberian and Sertorian Wars, have traditionally drawn researchers to the Republican camps and forts. Spain has the best collection of surviving Roman Republican military sites, as Schulten's research in the early 20th century revealed – sites such as Numantia, Renieblas, Cáceres el Viejo and Aguilar de Anguita. All were built entirely or partly in stone. However, Schulten's work has not been continued and his extensive monographs on the Numantia camps (Schulten 1927; 1929) have been largely ignored by Spanish researchers.

Schulten's methodology is a good example of 'philological archaeology'. This means forcing the archaeological data to fit the narrative of the written sources, sometimes going even further, to the extent of modifying the texts so that they 'fit' with the discoveries, the best example of which is the study of the circumvallation of Numantia. The problem is the excessively imaginative interpretations of many structures and the absence of stratigraphy and the method has had negative consequences for research (Morillo 2003, 45, 54; Morillo *et al.* 2017, 179–182).

The last two decades have seen a complete renewal of methodological approaches and qualitative advances in the knowledge of the military bases. The archaeological data available make it possible to define defensive architecture templates that

Figure 4.2 Aerial view of the Roman Republican camp at Cáceres el Viejo, Cáceres (source: Abásolo et al. 2008).

were used in Republican military sites. These could be simple earth and timber constructions, turf ramparts with an earth core or defences using stone for the foundations, parapets or the complete walls (Morillo 2014; Morillo and Adroher 2014a).

Our knowledge of Sertorian military sites has increased considerably. Only two decades ago, confirmed Sertorian camps were limited to little more than the well-known site of Caceres el Viejo, some 3 km north-east of Cáceres. The first mention

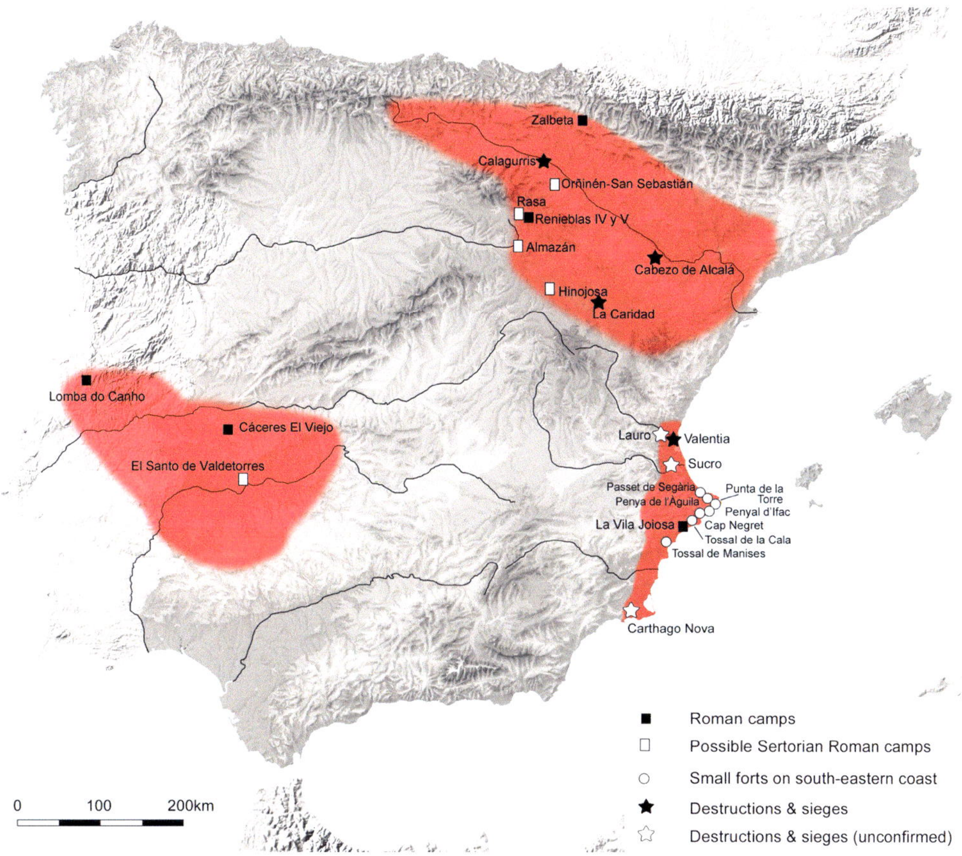

Figure 4.3 Military sites of the Sertorian Wars (mapped onto on-line IGN cartography, www.ign.es/web/ign/portal/recursos_educativos).

of this site as a Roman military installation was in the 18th century. By the following century, the fortress had already been associated with the campaigns of Caecilius Metellus and identified as the legionary base Castra Caecilia mentioned by Pliny the Elder (*Natural History* 4.117) and in the Antonine Itinerary (433.4). In the early 20th century, Schulten excavated at the site and published preliminary reports (Schulten 1918; 1928; Paulsen 1928; 1930; 1932), but no final monograph. In the later 20th century, the coins and pottery were studied by Beltrán Lloris (1973–1974) before Ulbert (1984) re-examined Schulten's excavations and conclusions. The latest archaeological work has validated some of Schulten's results (Abásolo *et al.* 2008, 122).

The base has a rectangular shape, with right-angled corners, and encloses an area of *c.* 24 ha (Figure 4.2). The defences consist of two rock-cut ditches with irregular U- and V-shaped cross-sections; behind them, the 3.5–4 m wide rampart still stands to a height of *c.* 1 m and was constructed of slate using the *emplecton* technique. In this, large worked, but unmortared, stones were used to build vertical wall faces (1.4 m high externally, 0.9 m high internally), very like a rough ashlar facing, while smaller stone

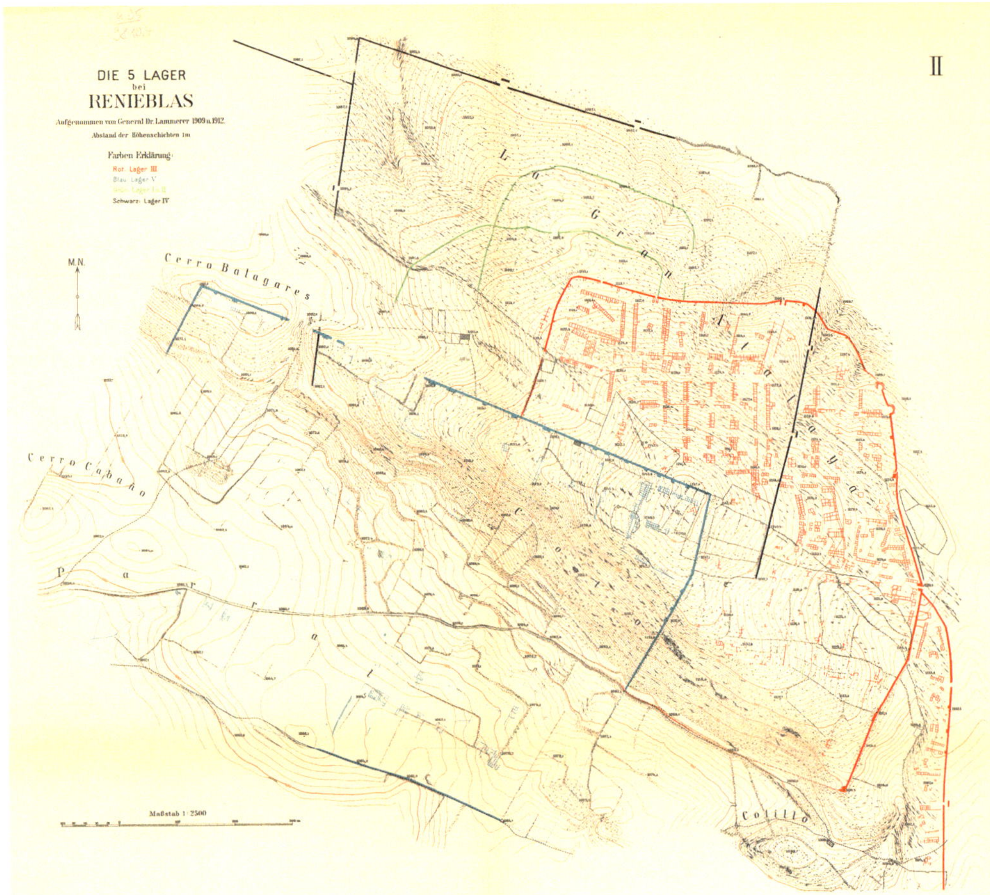

Figure 4.4 Renieblas, Soria: plan of Camps I–V (Schulten 1929, pl. II). Key: green – Camps I and II; red – Camp III; black – Camp IV; blue – Camp V.

rubble was used for the wall core (Ulbert 1984; Morillo 2003; Abásolo *et al.* 2008, 122). Transverse walls locked together the external faces of the wall. These walls appear to have been unbonded; the absence of mortar would have prevented the wall from being more than 1.5 m high.

The solid construction of the defences as well as the internal buildings make a long-term occupation of Cáceres el Viejo highly plausible. Based on the size of imperial legionary fortresses, the area is large enough to accommodate one legion. Finds of Iberian clothing elements and weaponry could indicate the presence of local auxiliaries. The base undoubtedly belongs to the first quarter of the 1st century BC, but a more exact construction date is still uncertain. However, analysis of the bronze coinage allows us to date its destruction to between 80 and 72 BC. At least the southern part was destroyed extensively by a fire, and some would see this as evidence of military destruction.

The recent reinterpretation of some other military sites allows us to include them in this Sertorian period (Figure 4.3). Among those currently under review are the last two camps at Renieblas (Renieblas IV and V). They are rectangular in plan, with right angled corners, and their size and method of construction are very different from those of the earlier Numantine Wars.

About 8 km east of Numantia, near Renieblas, is the hill 'La Gran Atalaya'. Our knowledge of the camps on it is still based mainly on the excavations of Schulten between 1909 and 1912 (Schulten 1929), although recently the complex has been the subject of renewed archaeological and topographic research (Luik 2000; Luik and Valdhör 2012). Schulten said nothing about his excavation methods, but it is clear that following the practices of the time, he dug narrow trenches along the walls. Only what were considered outer walls or easily recognizable inner walls of buildings were uncovered. The interiors of the buildings and the areas between buildings were not investigated, and, compared to modern standards, the stratigraphy and the context of the finds were barely documented.

The first three camps at Renieblas are polygonal in shape (Figures 4.4–4.5). Camp III (*c.* 45.3 ha) is still the best surviving example of a military camp of the Roman Republic. It had a 3 m wide stone rampart with stone faces. A walkway along the top was possibly reached by a series of ramps and there is evidence for a total of 27 towers, usually 30 m apart. On the south-east side there was a large annexe. The defences of the annexe described a wide arc to the south (making the total length a remarkable 850 m). The two known gateways each had a *titulum*. Camps IV and V both had rectangular ground-plans with sharply angled corners.

The defences of Camp IV were *c.* 3 m wide and made use of the *emplecton* technique. Its plan can be reconstructed almost completely: *c.* 795 m (south side) × *c.* 740 m (west side) × 855 m (north side) × 670 m (east side), giving an area of 58.9 ha. All eight gateways were provided with a *titulum*. No obvious remains of internal buildings were found by Schulten (1929).

Camp V is one of the largest Roman camps known, occupying an area of 61.2 ha. Its northern defences, consisting of two facing walls (width 4–4.4 m) in the *emplecton* technique, were completely uncovered (length 925 m). Sixteen towers were added for protection; their width varied considerably but their depth was uniformly 2.8 m; these towers always projected inwards from the rampart rather than outwards. There are at least two entrance passages along the northern side (gateways 1–2) and there may have been a third. Schulten's investigations revealed internal structures, which may be interpreted as the men's quarters and other buildings such as granaries (Schulten 1929; Luik 2002).

The chronology of camps was deduced by Schulten on historical grounds, with the small finds from the excavations playing only a secondary role. Camp I was associated with the campaign of M. Porcius Cato against Numantia in 195 BC. Some finds dating from the early 2nd century BC support this theory. No clear statements were made by Schulten concerning the date of Camp II, but Camp III was identified as the winter garrison of Q. Fulvius Nobilior in 153/152 BC, and indeed most of the small finds currently known date from the middle decades of the 2nd century BC (Luik 2002).

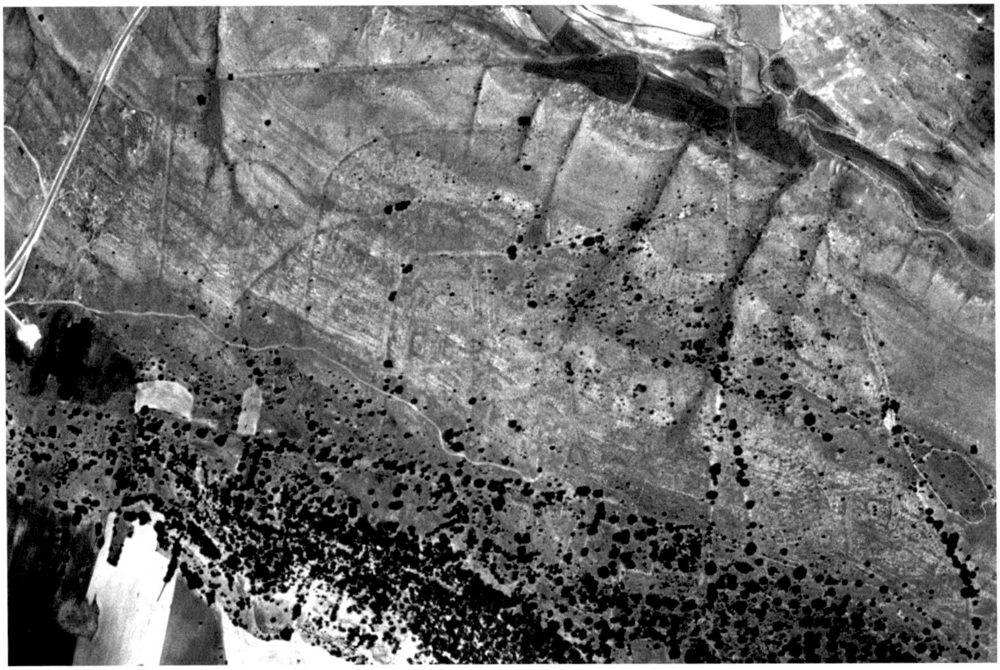

Figure 4.5 The Roman camps at Renieblas from the air (photo F. Didierjean, Instituto Ausonius, Burdeos).

Schulten connected Camp IV closely with Camp V mainly because they shared the same 'ideal' rectangular shape. According to Schulten, Camp V was constructed during the Sertorian Wars in 75/74 BC to house troops loyal to Pompey (Schulten 1929, 146–155). In recent decades, however, it has repeatedly been suggested that Camps IV and V should be back-dated to the 2nd century BC (Hildebrandt 1979; Romero Carnicero 1990; Sanmartí and Principal 1997). There is, however, no well-founded basis for this opinion and so much indisputably early 1st-century BC material has been found that no other dating is really possible (Luik 2000; 2002; Gómez-Pantoja and Morales 2002; Morillo and Morales 2015).

From their planning and construction techniques, other military sites like Rasa and Almazán could also be of Sertorian date. Schulten included the camp of Rasa in the Numantia siegeworks of 133 BC (Schulten 1927). His research there brought to light a 300 m long and 2.85 m wide length of rampart that ran across a level, but significant scarp; the rampart had two gates with a *titulum* on the east side, indicating that the camp lay to the west of the rampart. Schulten assumed that the camp was 200 m wide and therefore had an area of 6 ha. The excavations in the interior uncovered neither walls nor any finds, and it differs from the other camps and forts of the Scipionic circumvallation in its regular ground-plan, different rampart construction, and absence of archaeological finds, internal buildings and also traces of the circumvallation. Consequently, the camp at Rasa must be excluded from the Scipionic siege works. It could date a little later than the Numantine Wars (Dobson and Morales 2008; Morillo and Morales 2015).

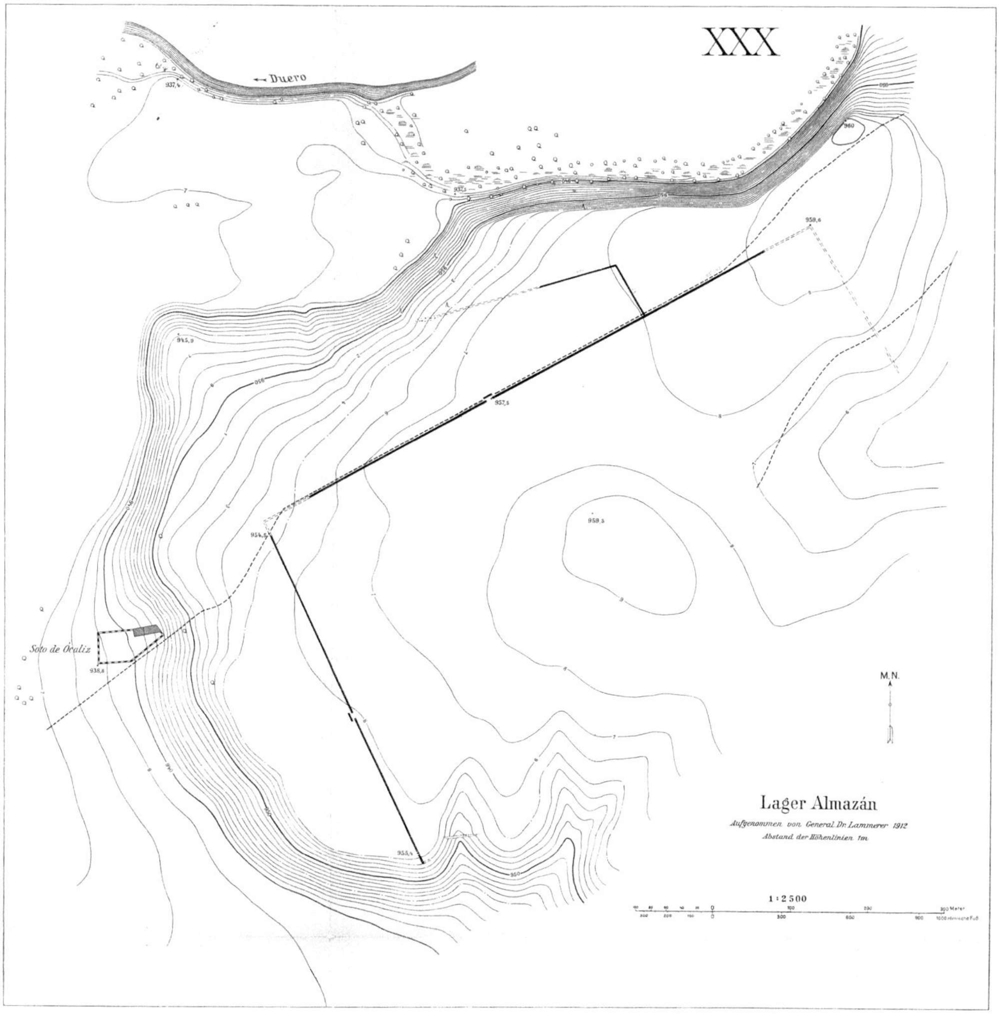

Figure 4.6 Plan of the Roman camp at Almazán, Soria (Schulten 1929, pl. XXX).

The camp of Almazán (Soria) lies 30 km south of Numantia (Figure 4.6). The site was built on a terrace overlooking the south bank of the river, on an ancient meander. Schulten was the first to point out that there could be a Roman military base here (Schulten 1912, 96–99). In 1927, new fieldwork demonstrated the presence of structures (Schulten 1927, 198–200) and in 1968 a rescue excavation established its real date (Gamer and Ortego 1969). More recently, a targeted intervention was undertaken to investigate the state of preservation. What we know about this camp is that there was a stone wall with external facings infilled with a core of large pebbles. The wall is now badly preserved, but in 1912 it stood almost 1 m high. Apparently, the camp has a rectangular plan with right-angled corners, and covers 38 ha. The remains of a ditch and a gate are located on the western side, with another gate on the northern side. Both entrances were protected by a *titulum*. To the north, a wall 252 m long that

Figure 4.7 The Roman Republican camp at Vila Joiosa, Alicante: the ditch during excavation (photo A. Espinosa).

describes an almost right-angled turn, runs from the defences down to the river and may have been an outer defence. The southern and the eastern sides of the camp have almost completely disappeared (Morillo 2003, 49–50).

According to Schulten, the camp may be linked to the campaign of Nobilior when he passed through this area in 153 BC on his way to Numantia. Scholars who have researched Nobilior's campaigns using the historical sources, suggest the existence of a summer camp in the area between Ocilis and Numantia on the route from the valley of the river Jalón towards the upper plateau. The dating evidence from the 1968 excavation could fit with this episode (Morillo 2003, 49–50), but a later date cannot be ruled out.

The settlement of El Santo de Valdetorres (Badajoz) has some similarities. It is possibly rectangular in plan, although only a section of a straight wall about 200 m long and 4.7 m wide is known. It is stone-built, apparently with two facing walls, an internal pebble core, and transverse inner walls. The ceramics seem to confirm a Sertorian dating (Heras 2009), but there are still many doubts about the identification of this settlement as a military site (*e.g.* the complete absence of militaria).

In recent decades, the first earth and timber camps of this period have been identified. The best example is Vila Joiosa, Alicante (Espinosa *et al.* 2014). This site, whose plan has yet to be determined, has a V-profiled ditch (*fossa fastigata*) 4.25 m wide and 3 m high (Figure 4.7). The presence of earth and turves in the fill of the ditch confirms that the rampart had a turf core, the oldest of its kind known in Hispania (Morillo and Adroher 2014b). It is dated to around the Sertorian Wars.

Another earth and timber fort has been identified on the hill called Alto de Santa Cruz at Zalbeta (Navarra), close to modern Pamplona, the ancient Pompaelo. This name is thought to be composed of the latin *nomen* Pompeius and the native suffix *iri/ili*, which in Basque means city. Archaeology has so far provided no evidence for this supposed origin of Pompaelo, so the hypothesis is based on a comment in Sallust about the Sertorian Wars (*Histories* 2.93): 'Pompeius settled down in the land of the Basconum in the winter of 75–74, near to the routes of food supply coming from Gallia'. The fort is polygonal in shape tending to rectangular, with an area of just over 2.5 ha (Armendáriz 2006), clearly delimited by an earthwork around the whole perimeter. At the weakest points, on the south-east and south-west, the rampart was reinforced by two ditches. Two lead sling bullets (*glandes*) from the site bearing the inscription *Q.(uintus) Ser-tor(ius) proco(n)s(ul) Pietas* can be dated between 76 and 74 BC.

Some researchers suggest that there was another Sertorian camp in Ormiñen-San Sebastián (Fitero y Cintruénigo, Navarra). No structural remains have been found and the site is inferred from finds of several sling bullets inscribed *Q. Serto(rius) Pietas*, together with militaria and coins (Medrano Marqués and Ramírez 2009). These researchers equate this settlement with the Castra Aelia of the classical sources (Livy *Fragments* 91.3), which was a winter camp of Sertorius in 77/76 BC. However, this identification has generated much controversy. Recently an alternative location for Castra Aelia has been proposed at La Cabañeta (El Burgo de Ebro, Zaragoza). This site is rectangular in plan, has ditches on three sides, and was later the site of a Roman town (Ferreruela and Mínguez 2006).

In Portugal, Lomba do Canho (Arganil) possibly belongs to the Sertorian period. This fort occupies a promontory partially surrounded by the river Alva. The site was quarried for stone before the presence of archaeological remains was recognized and this, combined with dense vegetation in some areas, makes it very difficult to understand what its shape and defences were like. Archaeological excavations revealed poorly constructed buildings and a large number of Roman weapons, mainly iron catapult bolts (*pila catapultaria*). A large square building, about 25 m long, interpreted as a *praetorium*, was excavated along with a smaller building (perhaps a bath-house), large warehouses and small barracks (Nunes *et al.* 1988; Fabião 2006). The camp seems to have been built in the second quarter of the 1st century BC and the large number of artefacts strongly suggest a hasty abandonment of the camp in the mid-1st century BC. The settlement could be related to the exploitation of local gold resources. Lastly, the Sertorian dating of another military site at Hinojosa in Guadalajara (Cerdeño and Gamo 2016) has not been verified archaeologically.

The Sertorian period is the first where we can verify archaeologically the use of camps with a rectangular plan by the Roman army, a fact which is of great importance in understanding the development of Roman castrametation (the making or laying out a military camp). Writing in the 2nd century BC, Polybius described camps as quadrangular in shape and based on the unit of measurement the *actus quadratus* (*Histories* 6.28.10; 6.42.6). Dobson has pointed out the problems of Schulten's reconstruction of the camps at Numantia and tries to combine Polybius' information with the archaeological evidence from Renieblas and the forts of the circumvallation, identifying them as early cohort-based camps (Dobson 2013, 224). The archaeological evidence does not confirm the use of rectangular plans at this date so perhaps Polybius' type of camp was only an ideal that only became real over time (Morillo 2008, 79). It has been suggested that the reforms of Gaius Marius at the beginning of the 1st century BC and the integration of troops of Italic allies (*socii*) as citizens within the structure of the Roman army (Lenoir 1986; Miller and De Voto 1994) could have motivated the regularization and enlargement of the layout of camps, which then began to be built in a rectangular form (Morillo 2014, 41–42).

This new rectangular model with right angles coexisted for more than a century with camps and forts of polygonal shape, as we know from Alesia (Reddé and von Schnurbein 2001; Reddé this volume) and some Augustan camps and forts in Germany. It seems that regular plans were adopted for more permanent camps while siege and marching camps kept to the old polygonal models which were more adaptable to topography. Size could be also important. This evolution does not appear to have been a linear process but was instead flexible (Morillo 2016, 29).

Sieges and destructions

In addition to these camps, there is also evidence of destruction and sieges. One of the best examples of destruction has been identified in the present-day city of Valencia, Roman Valentia (Ribera 2006). The historical sources mention two events: the foundation of the town by D. Iunius Brutus in 138 BC (Livy *Periochae* 55) and its destruction in 75 BC during the Sertorian Wars (Sallust *Histories* 2.54, 2.98). This was followed by a period of abandonment and a new foundation during the Augustan period.

The archaeological evidence of the destruction by Pompey's army in 75 BC is impressive. The buildings of the Republican period – *horreum* (warehouse), baths, sanctuary – were completely destroyed by fire and as well as the burnt buildings, the mutilated skeletons of some 13 males were found scattered over an open area that may have been the Republican *forum*. The bodies display signs of torture and violent death, such as tied or severed hands, ropes around their necks, and one man had been impaled on a spear. These are surely traces of an exemplary punishment to the Sertorian troops. Several weapons typical of this period and a coin of 77 BC were also found, together with pottery of the earlier 1st century BC (Ribera 2006, 80).

The destruction of Valentia is easy to understand because it had supported the Sertorian troops in a strategic position on the eastern coast of the Tarraconensis, close to Dianium (modern Denia, Valencia), the main maritime base of the insurgents.

La Caridad de Caminreal (Teruel), in the lower Ebro valley also seems have been destroyed, in this case following a siege. Located on the left bank of the river Jiloca, the settlement developed in the 2nd century BC and was destroyed in 74 BC, although the precise circumstances of the assault are not known. A great diversity of weapons (offensive and defensive, indigenous and Roman) have been discovered, including a very well-preserved Roman torsion catapult or *scorpio* (Figure 4.8) and numerous spearheads, sling bullets and the heads of *pila catapultaria* (Vicente *et al.* 1997; Ezquerra Lebrón 2006).

Other towns in the Ebro valley also show signs of siege during the period of the Sertorian Wars. Calagurris (Calahorra, La Rioja) was an allied city that remained faithful to Sertorius until the end of the war. It was besieged and destroyed by Pompey in 72 BC, in one of the best-known episodes of the *bellum Sertorianum*.[3] Some years ago, a group of 200 sling bullets with inscriptions related to the Pompeian troops came to light (Velaza *et al.* 2003; Díaz Ariño 2008).

Figure 4.8 Roman torsion catapult (scorpio) *found at La Caridad de Caminreal, Teruel (source: Vicente et al. 1997).*

The destruction of El Cabezo de Alcalá (Azaila, Zaragoza) may also be associated with the Sertorian Wars. The discovery of a siege ramp, 26 m wide, 75 m long and 5 m high, built with the debris of the houses of the *oppidum* mixed with lime mortar has been linked to the assault of the Pompeian troops (Beltrán Lloris 1976, 181; Sáez Abad 2009, 1086). Inside the citadel, two catapults and large concentrations of catapult projectiles were found near the gates. Classic sources mention other besieged cities (*e.g.* Contrebia Carbica, Osca, Tiermes, Pallantia, Uxama, Clunia). Perhaps for this reason, archaeologists have usually connected the evidence of destruction at several settlements with the Sertorian Wars, particularly those in the Ebro valley, but also in the central plateau. In many cases, however, the archaeological data does not allow a direct relationship to be established.

The small forts of the south-eastern coast: a new model of Republican military site

During the last decade, a number of sites that do not follow previously known Roman military architectural forms of the 1st century BC have been recognized. They are fortified settlements of irregular shape, that are hardly more than a hectare in size and are perfectly adapted to their topography. However, their chronological and cultural attribution is not easy. The construction methods are clearly Roman, but regional differences are apparent, each linked to local cultural traditions. The finds indicate the presence of the late Republican Roman army (Morillo and Adroher 2014a, 236; Morillo 2016, 29–41).

These sites should be considered as small Roman forts or fortlets, but in the current Spanish literature they are called *castella*, which leads to considerable confusion (Morillo 2016, 12–13). These forts were part of a strategy of occupation and economic and territorial control, and each had different objectives according to their position. They can be interpreted as a new pattern of occupation at a time of crisis such as the civil conflicts of the 1st century BC.

The small forts on the coast of Alicante, ancient Contestania, provide one of the best-known examples of this phenomenon (Sala *et al.* 2014a; 2014b). These sites, no bigger than half a hectare, are located on coastal hills that lack agricultural resources but which are well suited as anchorages or shelters for ships. Such sea side locations are unusual in the traditional pattern of Iberian settlement. Mountain ranges and valleys that run down to the sea create a coastline of alternating steep cliffs and small coves. Overland movement was complicated, but the coast was advantageous for navigation and this region lies opposite the island of Ibiza, which is a great reference point in navigation. All of these sites were able to maintain visual contact and their hilltop locations ensured total control of the coast, which was especially important when looking out for vessels sailing round Cap de la Nau (Figure 4.9).

Excavations at Tossal de la Cala in the mid-20th century exposed some simple square rooms adapted to the topography. The lower ones were attached to a wall 1 m thick; the entrance to the fortification is described as a corridor gate open to the

Figure 4.9 The coast of Alicante south of Cap de la Nau viewed from Punta de la Torre. The next promontory is Penyal d'Ifac; in the distance is the small fort of Tossal de la Cala.

west. Recent excavations confirm the use of a typical Italic building technique and also revealed Roman militaria, late Republican coins and Iberian and Roman ceramic vessels together with Roman and Punic amphorae (Sala *et al.* 2014b, 80–82).

At Cap Negret, an excavation in 1987 revealed part of the wall built only 3 m above sea level, which may be the reason why it was reinforced with a V-shaped ditch (Sala *et al.* 2014b, 82). A plan of Penyal d'Ifac made by J. Belda in 1964 shows an irregular semicircle on the highest part of the outcrop, defining a fortified area described as 'shelter Roman citadel'. Finds confirm that the building of the fort was linked to military occupation at the beginning of the 1st century BC. Further north, less is known about the settlement of Punta de la Torre, as all the existing information is from surface investigation. Only a few scattered walls and no defensive buildings remain, but the finds confirm that it is a similar type of construction (Sala *et al.* 2014b, 83).

North of Cap de la Nau, the sites of Penya de l'Àguila and Passet de Segària are not located on hills next to the sea, but on high ground near the coast, and helped to maintain control over the whole gulf of Valencia. On the western side of the Montgó mountain range, about 484 m above sea level, rocky outcrops form a long narrow plateau known as Penya de l'Àguila (Sala *et al.* 2014b, 83–88). Three walls ranging in width from 2.4–4 m were built across the plateau; the distance between the first and the third walls is about 1200 m (Figure 4.10). In the 1960s, Schubart published a plan of the area, concluding that the fortifications had to be a response to an important crisis related to the Second Punic War or to the location of the Sertorian naval base at Dianium (Schubart 1963, 83–85).

Figure 4.10 Aerial photograph of Penya de l'Àguila, Alicante.

Just a few kilometres north of Penya de l'Àguila on the Segària mountain range, Passet is a strong fortification of 260 × 70 m defended by discontinuous drystone terraces made from large unworked stones (sometimes called pseudo-cyclopean) that run across the steep slope (Figure 4.11). The northern, western and southern sides are defended in this manner but on this last there is also a regularly built ashlar wall 2.5 m high that runs for at least for 82 m (Sala *et al.* 2014b, 86–88).

The finds assemblages from all these forts are quite similar (Figure 4.12), with weapons, militaria, soldiers' personal belongings, tools, lead objects, coins and ceramics, all dating to the first quarter of the 1st century BC (Bayo 2014; Domenech 2014; Sala *et al.* 2014a; 2014b). This shows how the Contestania region related to Sertorian strategic interests, housing a network of military garrisons along the north coast of Alicante, intended on the one hand to control maritime traffic, and on the other to obtain supplies for the army. Since the port of Cartagena further south down the Mediterranean coast belonged to Sulla and Pompey, Sertorius chose the port at Dianium as his naval base around the year 77 BC. It must have been then that he created the network of these small coastal sites. Controlling the traffic of senatorial vessels near Cap de la Nau was key to Sertorius, because Ebusus and Carthago Nova were already out of his reach (Sala *et al.* 2014b, 88–89).

We should note that Livy mentions the Contestani as Sertorian allies. Part of this alliance was undoubtedly the provisioning of troops, which would explain the many amphorae and Iberian storage vessels found in the coastal forts. Iberian Contestani could also have served Sertorius as auxiliaries and have been stationed at the small coastal sites. However, there is a high percentage of Roman ceramics. We know that the troops drank wine from Campania and Apulia and ate salted fish from Cádiz. If the

Figure 4.11 The small fort of Passet de Segària, Alicante. Insets: the different construction techniques of the defences.

official trade channels were controlled by the senatorial troops, these products might have been supplied by Cilician pirates. Some historical sources associate pirates with Sertorius and his naval base at Dianium. The tactics of piracy are well suited to the rocky north coast of Alicante: small boats could hide in the coves that lay at the foot of the forts, then sail out to surprise senatorial vessels on their way to Carthago Nova (Sala *et al.* 2014a, 198–199; 2014b, 89). In this vein, a recent study of the Roman Republican fort of Tossal de Manises, suggests that it was constructed by Pompeian forces, with a wall strengthened with solid towers of square stones built using the *opus quadratum* technique to dissuade Cilician vessels from raiding towards Cartagena (Olcina *et al.* 2014).

Evidence without context: an archaeological problem

We have numerous pieces of artefactual evidence of the conflict, often without context: lead sling bullets with marks of Q. Sertorius or Gn. Pompeius, Roman and Iberian silver *denarii* issued in this period, and late Republican militaria. There is no doubt that some of these finds are direct evidence of conflicts, sieges and troop movements of either side. However, they need to be analysed on a case-by-case basis. The weapons and military dress of this period could fit perfectly well in either the Sertorian Wars or the later struggle between Caesar and Pompey and the same may be said about coin hoards and coins of the period (Arévalo and Marcos 1998, 27; Blázquez Cerrato 2002, 171–181; Rodríguez Casanova 2008). In contrast, the lead sling bullets with inscriptions of Pompey or Sertorius undoubtedly relate directly to the conflict and are very common in the regions affected by the Sertorian War (Díaz Ariño 2008).

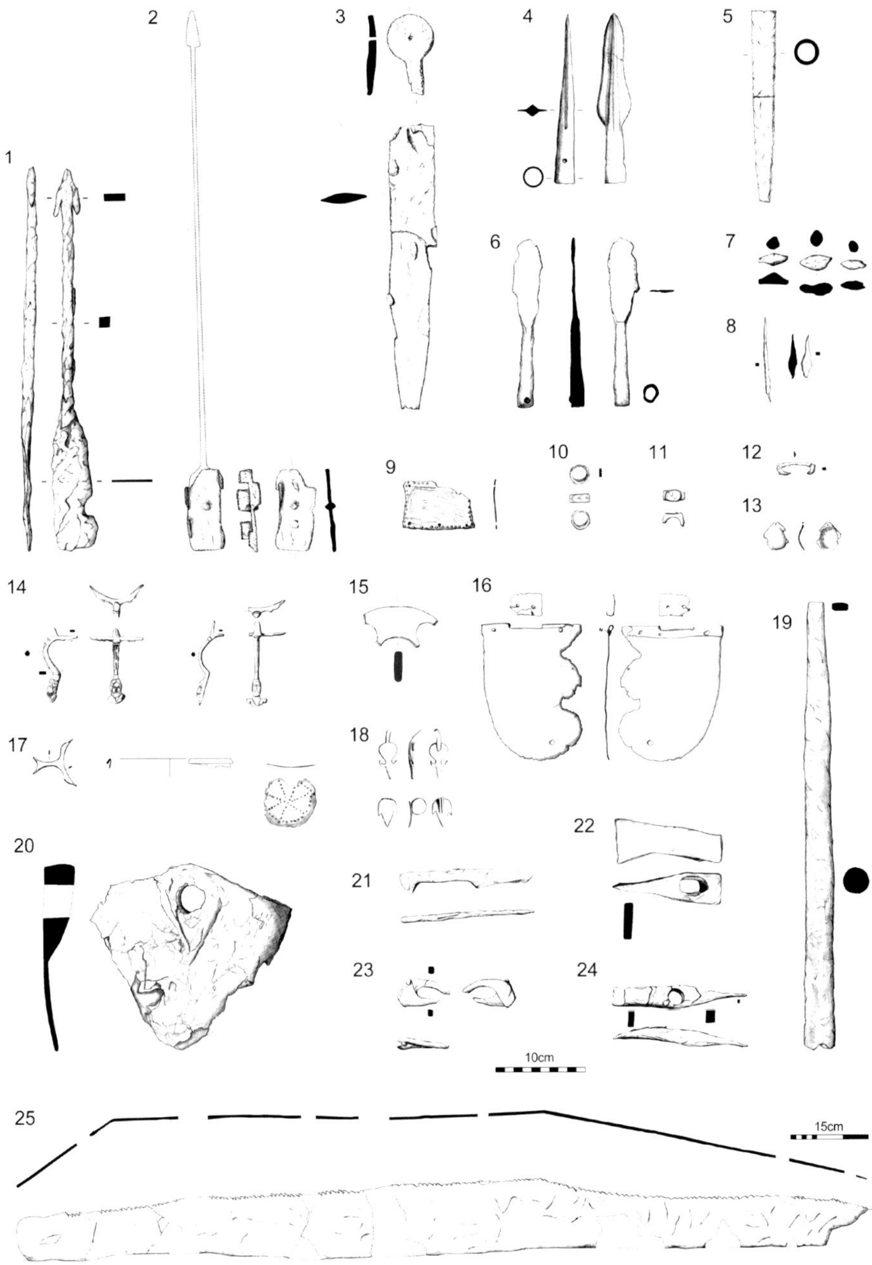

Figure 4.12 Militaria and other finds from the small coastal forts in Alicante: (1–2) pila; *(3)* gladius; *(4–6) spearheads; (7) lead sling bullets; (8) spears; (9) cavalry harness fitting or belt plaque; (10–11) bone and iron rings; (12) strike-a-light; (13) seal box (*bulla*); (14–15, 18) bronze jug handles and situla fragment; (16) cheekpiece from Montefortino type helmet; (17) fragments of strainer (*trulla*); (19–25) various tools (drawings S. Bayo). Nos 1, 4, 6, 8–9, 11–12, 16–17, 19–24 Penya de l'Àguila; No 7 Passet de Segària; Nos 2–3, 5, 10, 13–15, 18, 25 Tossal de la Cala.*

Many of them can be very accurately dated thanks to these inscriptions. We can also reconstruct the distribution patterns of the bullets on the ground, allowing us to compare the information from the classical sources with the actual landscapes in which the clashes took place.

One of the most important collections of Sertorian sling bullets (some 2000 *glandes plumbeae*) was found on the hill of the castle of Azuaga (Badajoz). Some bear the inscription *Q(uintus) Me(tellus)*, who is identified with the governor of Ulterior who fought against Sertorius in south-west Hispania between 79–76 BC (Domergue 1970; Díaz Ariño 2008). There is also evidence of lead working nearby and this may have been to supply the troops on campaign.

Final considerations: 'deconstructing' Sertorius

The availability of an increasing amount of archaeological evidence relating to the 1st century BC – camps and forts, destructions and sieges of Roman towns and Iberian *oppida*, new small forts to control the coast and sea, sling bullets with the names of the opponents, late Republican militaria, Roman and Iberian *denarii* – allows us to link some of these archaeological remains directly with the Sertorian conflict.

This new dataset permits a reconstruction of the struggle between Sertorius and Pompeius. Nevertheless, the absence of a clearly defined material cultural sequence for the 1st century BC in most cases prevents us from determining whether all the archaeological evidence does really belong to the Sertorian period or if some is later. Only better knowledge of the chrono-stratigraphy of the individual military sites will allow us to correctly distinguish the Sertorian phase from later periods.

The recent discoveries described above have transformed the Sertorian War from a mere period in which specific military events were known to have taken place in specific regions of Hispania, into a complex archaeological phenomenon or set of phenomena spaced over several decades, which are generalized across the entire Iberian Peninsula. It is a good example of the new 'philological archaeology'. In modern Spanish and Portuguese archaeological literature, it is common to find references to abandoned *oppida*, destroyed towns, dismantled walls, camps and forts that date to the 1st century BC and for them to be associated directly to the Sertorian Wars. Any group of coins (even 4 or 5 bronzes) is immediately classified as a hoard and related to a violent episode of military confrontation. A region where there are no settlements during the 1st century BC is deemed an area punished for its affiliation to Pompey or Sertorius. While lead sling bullets with inscriptions of Pompey or Sertorius do confirm the presence of troops of this period, they could still represent anything from a casual loss to a full-scale siege. Often, archaeological evidence directly connected with this historic episode simply does not exist.

Apart from the presence of an army, there may be other explanations for this archaeological evidence, for example troop movements or a consequence of cities taking the side of one party or the other. To be able to identify real testimony of this conflict, we need to reassess the 'Sertorian phenomenon'. New, well-dated archaeological information from military sites or *oppida* could help us advance understanding of this topic, as could holistic analysis of the archaeological objects – weapons, military clothing, coins, pottery. Starting from the correct definition of the military or civilian sites from the Sertorian period will allow us to define the material context of other conflict episodes in 1st-century BC Hispania.

Finally, a still virtually unknown aspect of the 1st century BC is the confrontation between Caesar and Pompey in 49–45 BC, some decades after the Sertorian conflict ended (Pujol *et al.* this volume). Although the clash had great repercussions for Hispania, archaeological evidence for this episode is as yet very scarce (Beltrán Fortes 2008) and we know very little about its camps and forts. The site of Alto dos Cacos in the Low Tajo, in the environs of Santarem, may belong to the period (Pimenta *et al.* 2014; Guerra *et al.* 2014), as may Cabeça de Vaiamonte, Monforte (Rita Pereira 2014) and Castelo das Juntas, Moura (Mataloto 2014) in southern Portugal. Several small forts in south-east and south-west Hispania also share the same chronology (Brotons and Murcia 2008; Morillo and Adroher 2014b with bibliography). The archaeological evidence from civil settlements has undoubtedly been underestimated: Contrebia Belaisca (Botorrita, Zaragoza) suffered a second siege and destruction in Caesar's time. However, the coinage in circulation differs little from that of the Sertorian period, since coins minted between 72 and 49 BC are very scarce in Hispania. Roman black glazed pottery of the middle decades of 1st century BC that might help date sites more closely is also uncommon.

Our hypothesis is that some of the archaeological evidence currently assigned to the Sertorian period may instead relate to the confrontation between Caesar and Pompey. It is necessary to review the ceramic dating within its stratigraphic framework and to interpret each deposit according to its own archaeological context to establish the chronology. In short, we need to re-calibrate the 'Sertorian phenomenon'.

Notes

1 This research was undertaken as part of the I+D Project HAR2011-24095 *Military Camps and Territories in Hispania*, led by Professor Ángel Morillo and endorsed by the Ministry of Science and Innovation on 1 January 2012, and the I+D Project HAR2016-76917-P: *Traces of the Roman Civil Wars in the South-East of Hispania. Conflict and cultural transformations*, led by Professor Feliciana Sala, funded by the Ministry of Economy and Competitiveness from 1 January 2017.

2 Made up of the Arevaci, Belli, Titti and Lusones.

3 See: Livy *Fragments* 91, *Periochae* 93; Strabo *Geography* 3.4.10; Appian *Civil War* 1.12, 112; Sallust *Histories* 3, *Fragments* 86–87; Valerius Maximus 7.6.3; Juvenal *Satires* 15.93–96; Florus *Epitome of Roman History* 2.10.9; Orosius *Historiarum Adversum Paganos* 5.23.14; Julius Exsuperantius 8.

Bibliography

Abásolo, J.M., González Fernández, M.L. and Mora Serrano, B. (2008) Recientes investigaciones en el campamento de Cáceres el Viejo. In P.J. Sanabria (ed.), *Arqueología Urbana en Cáceres. Investigaciones e intervenciones recientes en la ciudad de Cáceres y su entorno*, 115–143. Cáceres, Memorias Museo de Cáceres 7.

Arévalo, A. and Marcos, M.M. (1998) *El depósito monetal de Torelló d'en Cintes (Mahón, Menorca)*. Barcelona-Madrid, Colección A. Vives Escudero 9.

Armendáriz Martija, J. (2006) Zalbeta camp. In A. Morillo and J. Aurrecoechea (eds), *The Roman Army in Hispania: An archaeological guide*, 287–289. León, Universidad de León.

Bayo Fuentes, S. (2014) Identificación del uso del espacio y su momento histórico a partir de los contextos materiales. In F. Sala and J. Moratalla (eds), *Las guerras civiles romanas en Hispania. Una revisión histórica desde la Contestania*, 99–114. Alicante, Universidad de Alicante-Museo Arquelógico Provincial de Alicante.

Beltrán Fortes, J. (2008) La arqueología cesariana de la provincia Hispania Ulterior. In M.P. García-Bellido, A. Mostalac and A. Jiménez (eds), *Del Imperium de Pompeyo a la Auctoritas de Augusto. Homenaje a Michael Grant*, 67–83. Madrid, Consejo Superior de Investigaciones Cientificas, Anejos Archivo Español de Arqueología 47.

Beltrán Lloris, M. (1973–74) Problemas de la arqueología cacereña: el campamento romano de Cáceres en Viejo (Cáceres). Estudio numismático. *Numisma* 23/24, 255–310.

Beltrán Lloris, M. (1976) *Arqueología e Historia de las ciudades antiguas del Cabezo de Alcalá de Azaila (Teruel)*. Zaragoza, Institución Fernando el Católico, Monografías Arqueológicas 19.

Beltrán Lloris, M. (2002) La etapa de Sertorio en el Valle del Ebro. Bases arqueológicas. *Pallas* 60, 49–52.

Blázquez Cerrato, C. (2002) *Circulación monetaria en el área occidental de la península ibérica. La moneda en torno al 'Camino de la Plata'*. Archéologie et Histoire Romaine 6. Montagnac, Éditions Monique Mergoil.

Brotons, F. and Murcia, A. (2008) Los *castella* republicanos romanos de la cuenca alta de los ríos Argos y Quípar (Caravaca, Murcia). Aproximación arqueológica e histórica. In M.P. García-Bellido, A. Mostalac and A. Jiménez (eds), *Del Imperium de Pompeyo a la Auctoritas de Augusto. Homenaje a Michael Grant*, 49–66. Madrid, Consejo Superior de Investigaciones Cientificas, Anejos Archivo Español de Arqueología 47.

Cerdeño, M.L. and Gamo, E. (2016) Estudio preliminar del campamento romano de La Cabeza del Cid (Hinojosa, Guadalajara, España). *Gerion* 27.1, 169–184.

Díaz Ariño, B. (2008) *Epigrafía latina republicana de Hispania (ELRH)*. Barcelona, Universitat Autònoma de Barcelona.

Dobson, M. (2013) No holiday camp: The Roman Republican army camp as a fine-tuned instrument of war. In J. De Rose Evans (ed.), *A Companion to the Archaeology of the Roman Republic*, 214–234. Oxford, Wiley-Blackwell.

Dobson, M. and Morales Hernández, F. (2008) Monedas inéditas de los campamentos romanos republicanos del cerco de Escipión y de la Gran Atalaya de Renieblas, y algunas consideraciones cronológicas sobre el campamento V de Renieblas. *Archivo Español de Arqueología* 81, 71–92.

Domenech, C. (2014) El conflicto sertoriano en el Sureste peninsular a través de los registros numismáticos. In F. Sala and J. Moratalla (eds), *Las guerras civiles romanas en Hispania. Una revisión histórica desde la Contestania*, 91–98. Alicante, Universidad de Alicante-Museo Arquelógico Provincial de Alicante.

Domergue, C. (1970) Un témoignage sur l'industrie minière et métallurgique du plomb dans la région d'Azuaga (Badajoz) pendant la guerre de Sertorius. *XI Congreso Nacional de Arqueología (Merida 1968)*, 608–626. Zaragoza, Universidad de Zaragoza.

Espinosa Ruiz, A., Ruiz Alcalde, D., Marcos González, A., Peña Domínguez, P. and Martínez Sánchez, A.M. (2014) El campamento militar de las guerras sertorianas en Villajoyosa. In F. Sala and J. Moratalla (eds), *Las guerras civiles romanas en Hispania. Una revisión histórica desde la Contestania*, 115–126. Alicante, Universidad de Alicante-Museo Arquelógico Provincial de Alicante.

Ezquerra Lebrón, B. (2006) La ciudad romana de 'La Caridad' (Caminreal, Teruel). In *Celtíberos. Tras la estela de Numancia*, 205–212. Soria, Junta de Castilla y León.

Fabião, C. (2006) The Roman army in Portugal. In A. Morillo and J. Aurrecoechea (eds), *The Roman Army in Hispania: An archaeological guide*, 107–126. León, Universidad de León.

Ferreruela, A. and Mínguez Morales, J.A. (2006) Secundum oppidum quod Castra Aelia vocatur. In A. Morillo (ed.), *Arqueología militar romana en Hispania. Producción y abastecimiento en el ámbito militar*, 671–682. León, Universidad de León.

Gamer, G. and Ortego Frías, T. (1969) Neue Beobachtungen am römischen Lager bei Almazán (Prov. Soria). *Madrider Mitteilungen* 10, 172–184.

García Morá, F. (1991) *Un episodio de la Hispania republicana: la guerra de Sertorio*, Granada, Universidad de Granada.

Gómez-Pantoja, J. and Morales, F. (2002) Sertorio en Numancia: una nota sobre los campamentos de la Gran Atalaya. In A. Morillo (ed.), *Arqueología Militar Romana en Hispania*, 303–310. Madrid, Consejo Superior de Investigaciones Científicas & Polifemo, Anejos de Gladius 5.

Gómez-Pantoja, J. and Morales, F. (2008) Los etolios en Numancia. *Salduie* 8, 37–58.

Guerra, A., Pimenta, J. and Sequeira, J. (2014) Conjunto de Glandes plumbeae do sítio arqueológico do Alto dos Cacos-Almeirim. *Cira Arqueológica* 3, 293–321.

Heras Mora, F.J. (2009) El Santo de Valdetorres (Badajoz, España). Un nuevo enclave militar romano en la línea del Guadiana. In A. Morillo, N. Hanel, E. Martín Hernández (eds), *Limes XX. Actas del XX Congreso Internacional de Estudios sobre la Frontera Romana*, 315–327. Madrid, Consejo Superior de Investigaciones Cientificas & Polifemo, Anejos de Gladius 13.

Hildebrandt, H.J. (1979) Die Römerlager von Numantia. Datierung anhand der Münzfunde. *Madrider Mitteilungen* 20, 238–271.

Lenoir, M. (1986) Le camp romain et l'urbanisme hellénistique et romain. In *La fortification dans l'histoire du monde grec. Colloque international*, 329–336. Paris, CNRS.

Luik, M. (2000) Die römischen Lager bei Renieblas, Prov. Soria (Spanien). Ergebnisse der Vermessungskampagnen 1997–2000. In P. Freeman, J. Bennett, Z.T. Fiema and B. Hoffmann (eds), *Limes XVIII. Proceedings of the XVIIIth International Congress of Roman Frontier Studies*, 771–778. Oxford, Archaeopress, British Archaeological Reports International Series 1084.

Luik, M. (2002) *Die Funde aus den römischen Lagern um Numantia im Römisch-Germanischen Zentralmuseum.* Mainz, Römisch-Germanisches Zentralmuseum Mainz, Katalog vor- und frühgeschichtlicher Altertümer 31.

Luik, M. and Valdhör, M. (2012) Forschungen in Renieblas 2009 und 2010. *Madrider Mitteilungen* 53, 289–309.

Mataloto, R. (2014) A propósito de um conjunto de glandes plumbeae: o Castelo das Juntas (Moura) no contexto do episódio Sertoriano das Guerras Civis na margem esquerda do Guadiana. *Cira Arqueológica* 3, 343–384.

Medrano Marqués, M. and Ramírez Vallejo, S. (2009) Nuevos testimonios arqueológicos romano-republicanos procedentes del campamento de Sertorio en el curso bajo del río Alhama (Cintruénigo-Fitero, Navarra). In J. Andreu (ed.), *Los vascones de las fuentes antiguas: en torno a una etnia de la antigüedad peninsular*, 371–402. Barcelona, Universitat de Barcelona.

Miller, M.C.J. and De Voto, J.G. (1994) (eds) *Polybius and Pseudo-Hyginus: The fortification of the Roman camp*. Chicago, Ares.

Morillo, A. (2003) Conquista y defensa del territorio en la Hispania republicana: los establecimientos militares temporales. In A. Morillo, F. Cadiou and D. Hourcade (eds), *Defensa y territorio en Hispania de los Escipiones a Augusto (espacios urbanos, rurales, municipales y provinciales)*, 41–80. León/Madrid. Universidad de León/Casa de Velázquez.

Morillo, A. (2008) Criterios arqueológicos de identificación de campamentos romanos en Hispania. *Salduie* 8, 73–93.

Morillo, A. (2016) Campamentos y fortificaciones tardorrepublicanas en Hispania. Una nueva línea de investigación en arqueología militar romana. In J. Pera and J. Vidal (eds), *Fortificaciones y control del territorio en la Hispania republicana*, 1–51. Zaragoza, Libros Portico.

Morillo, A. and Adroher, A. (2014a) El patrón arqueológico de carácter material: un criterio imprescindible de identificación de recintos militares romano-republicanos. *Cira Arqueológica* 3, 25–43.

Morillo, A. and Adroher, A. (2014b) Modelos de arquitectura defensiva e implantación territorial de los campamentos republicanos en Hispania. In R. Mataloto, V. Mayoral and C. Roque (eds), *La gestación de los paisajes rurales entre la Protohistoria y el periodo romano. Formas de asentamiento y procesos de implantación*, 227–252. Mérida, Consejo Superior de Investigaciones Cientificas, Anejos Archivo Español de Arqueología 70.

Morillo, A. and Morales Hernández, F. (2015) Campamentos romanos de la Guerra de Numancia: la circunvalación escipiónica. In M. Bendala (ed.), *Los Escipiones en Hispania*, 275–297. Alcalá de Henares, Museo Regional Comunidad de Madrid.

Morillo, A., Morales Hernández, F. and Durán Cabello, R. (2017) Schulten y los campamentos romano republicanos en Hispania: una mirada desde el siglo XXI. In E. Baquedano and M. Arlegui (eds), *Schulten y el descubrimiento de Numantia*, 174–200. Alcalá de Henares, Comunidad de Madrid.

Nunes, J.C., Fabião, C. and Guerra, A. (1988) *O Acampamento Militar Romano da Lomba do Canho (Arganil)*. Arganil, Ayuntamiento de Arganil.

Olcina, M., Guilabert A. and Tendero E. (2014) Fortificaciones tardorrepublicanas de *Lucentum* (Hispania citerior). In F. Sala and J. Moratalla (eds), *Las guerras civiles romanas en Hispania. Una revisión histórica desde la Contestania*, 127–138. Alicante, Universidad de Alicante-Museo Arquelógico Provincial de Alicante.

Paulsen, R. (1928) Die Fundegegenstände aus dem Lager Cáceres. *Archäologischer Anzeiger (Jahrbuch Deutschen Archäologischen Instituts)*, 14–30.

Paulsen, R. (1930) Die Fundegegenstände aus dem Lager Cáceres. *Archäologischer Anzeiger (Jahrbuch Deutschen Archäologischen Instituts)*, 58–67.

Paulsen, R. (1932) Die Fundegegenstände aus dem Lager Cáceres. *Archäologischer Anzeiger (Jahrbuch Deutschen Archäologischen Instituts)*, 348–387.

Pérez Gutiérrez, M.L. (2011) El bellum Sertorianum y los lusitanos. *Anas* 24, 97–114.

Pimenta, J., Mendes, H. and Henriques, E. (2014) O Acampamento militar romano do Alto dos Cacos-Almeirim. *Cira Arqueológica* 3, 256–291.

Reddé, M. and von Schnurbein, S. (2001) *Alésia. Fouilles et recherches franco-allemandes sur les travaux militaires romains autour du Mont-Auxois (1991-1997)*. Paris, Mémoires de l'Académie des Inscriptions et Belles-Lettres 22.

Ribera, A. (2006) The Roman foundation of Valencia and the town in the 2nd–1st c. B.C. In L. Abad, S. Keay and S. Ramallo (eds), *Early Roman Towns in Hispania Tarraconensis*, 75–89. Portsmouth (RI), Journal of Roman Archaeology Supplement 62.

Rita Pereira, T. (2014) Entre Sertório e César: as marcas do exército no sítio arqueológico de Cabeça de Vaiamonte (Monforte/Portugal). *Cira Arqueológica* 3, 322–342.

Rodríguez Casanova, I. (2009) Tesoros sertorianos: nuevas perspectivas desde datos antiguos. In A. Arévalo (ed.), *Actas XIII Congreso Nacional de Numismática. Moneda y Arqueología*, I, 337–352. Madrid/Cádiz, Universidad de Cádiz/Museo Casa de la Moneda.

Romero Carnicero, M.V. (1990) Lucernas republicanas de Numancia y sus campamentos. *Boletín del Seminario de Estudios de Arte y Arqueología* 56, 257–296.

Sáez Abad, R. (2009) Evidencias arqueológicas de la poliorcética en la Península Ibérica. In A. Morillo, N. Hanel, E. Martín Hernández (eds), *Limes XX. Actas del XX Congreso Internacional de Estudios sobre la Frontera Romana*, 1079–1088. Madrid, Consejo Superior de Investigaciones Cientificas & Polifemo, Anejos de Gladius 13.

Sala, F., Abad, L., Bayo, S. and Domenech, C. (2014a) Las huellas de las guerras sertorianas en el sureste de Hispania. In F. Cadiou and M. Navarro (eds), *La guerre et ses traces dans la péninsule Ibérique. Conflicts et sociétés en Hispanie à l'époque de la conquête romaine (IIIe-Ier siècle av. J. C.)*, 181–202. Bordeaux, Ausonius.

Sala, F., Moratalla, J. and Abad, L. (2014b) Los fortines de la costa septentrional alicantina: una red de vigilancia de la navegación. In F. Sala and J. Moratalla (eds), *Las guerras civiles romanas en Hispania. Una revisión histórica desde la Contestania*, 79–89. Alicante, Universidad de Alicante-Museo Arquelógico Provincial de Alicante.

Salinas, M. (2006) Geografía real y ficticia de la epopeya sertoriana. In G. Cruz, P. Le Roux and P. Moret (eds), *La invención de una geografía de la Península Ibérica I. La época republicana*, 153–174. Málaga/Madrid, Diputación de Málaga/Casa de Velázquez.

Salinas Romo, M. (2014) Apuntes en torno a las guerras sertorianas: evolución e impacto sobre el poblamiento y la ordenación territorial del valle del Ebro. *Espacio, Tiempo y Forma, Serie II. Historia Antigua* 27, 15–53.

Sanmartí, E. and Principal, J. (1997) Las cerámicas de importación, itálicas e ibéricas, procedentes de los campamentos numantinos. *Revista d'Arqueologia de Ponent* 7, 35–75.

Schubart, H. (1963) Untersuchungen an den Iberischen Befestigungen des Montgó bei Denia (Prov. Alicante). *Madrider Mitteilungen* 4, 51–85.

Schulten, A. (1912) Ausgrabungen in Numantia VI. *Archäologischer Anzeiger* 27, 81–99.

Schulten, A. (1918) Ein römischer Lager aus der sertorianischen Kriege. *Jahrbuch des Deutschen Archäologischen Instituts*, 75–106.

Schulten, A. (1927) *Numantia. Die Ergebnisse der Ausgrabungen 1905-1912, III. Die Lager des Scipio.* Munich, F. Bruckmann.

Schulten, A. (1928) Campamentos romanos en España. *Investigación y Progreso* 5, 34–36.

Schulten, A. (1929) *Numantia. Die Ergebnisse der Ausgrabungen 1905-1912, IV. Die Lager bei Renieblas.* Munich, F. Bruckmann.

Schulten, A. (2013) *Sertorio* (1st published 1926). Seville, Renacimiento.

Ulbert, G. (1984) *Cáceres el Viejo. Ein spätrepublikanisches Legionslager in Spanisch-Extremadura.* Mainz, Madrider Beiträge 9.

Velaza Frías, J., Cinca Martínez, J.L. and Ramírez Sádaba, J.L. (2003) Un depósito de proyectiles de catapulta hallado en Calahorra (La Rioja). *Archivo Español de Arqueología* 76, 263–271.

Vicente, J., Punter, M.P. and Ezquerra, B. (1997) La catapulta tardo-republicana y otro equipamiento militar de 'La Caridad' (Caminreal, Teruel). *Journal of Roman Military Equipment Studies* 8, 167–199.

Chapter 5

58 BC: The Helvetii, from the Swiss Plateau to Bibracte… and back

Gilbert Kaenel

The title of this contribution – 58 BC – indicates that we will focus on the first 3 months of the Gallic War and emphasise the role played by the Helvetii in the confrontation between Rome and the Celts. We shall proceed in two stages, from history to archaeology: first we will summarize the historical sources, and then we will try to find archaeological evidence that may be related to the events described in the texts.

History

A brief summary of the historical sources and the history of research

There are three major historical dates that relate to the Helvetii:

- 107 BC: at a battle near Agen in south-west France, the Tigurini, a Helvetian tribe according to Caesar and most scholars, inflicted a humiliating defeat on the Roman legions, who were forced to pass under the yoke. Between 111 and 101 BC, the Tigurini followed the Germanic peoples who invaded the Roman provinces of southern France and northern Italy during the last two decades of the 2nd century BC, the period of the Cimbrian Wars.
- 58 BC: the migration of the Helvetii provided a *casus belli* for Caesar, marking the beginning of the Gallic War. The migrants (a coalition of Helvetii and associated tribes) intended to settle in south-west France, the far west of Gaul, but Caesar stopped them definitively at a battle near Bibracte (Mont Beuvray) in Burgundy. The Helvetii returned by order of the Roman general to their 'home' on the Swiss Plateau.

- 52 BC: the battle and defeat of the Gallic coalition at Alesia, also in Burgundy, led to the end of the Gallic War. According to Caesar, 8,000 Helvetian warriors were sent to join the revolt of Vercingetorix in Gaul.

These events have had a major influence on the history of research. The Helvetii were very famous in the 19th century, not only in patriotic processions but in the history of Switzerland and the Swiss 'nation'. All young children learnt in school about the lake dwellings, the life of the *Lacustres* in the Neolithic and Bronze Age, as well as the story of the Helvetii and their chieftain Divico. Even after their defeat by the Romans, the return of the Helvetians to their 'home' in the summer of 58 BC when ordered by Caesar brought 'civilisation' to the Swiss Plateau... Divico acceded to the status of a mythical hero, as famous as legendary national heroes such as Wilhelm Tell and Arnold von Winkelried (*Les Helvètes* 1991; Kaeser 2014; Kaenel 2016, 9–10). And the name chosen following the constitution of 1848 in Switzerland was, and still is today, the *Confoederatio Helvetica* (Swiss Confederation).

Let us conclude by recalling that the earliest mention of the name Helvetii was by Poseidonios of Apameia about 100 BC – 'a people rich in gold but peaceful' (7.2.2). The Greek historian and geographer unfortunately does not say where they lived. A graffito on a pottery cup found in Mantua, northern Italy, mentions *ELUVEITIE*, written from right to left in Etruscan writing, a dative form that means, by extrapolation, 'this cup belongs to me, the Helvetian'. The vessel is dated to about 300 BC. We do not know where our Helvetian came from – southern Germany according to some ancient sources (Plutarch, Tacitus, Ptolemy) – or from another country (Kaenel 2016, 17–23; Aberson *et al.* 2017).

Events of the year 58 BC

We will not discuss here the details of the arguments about, or the veracity (or otherwise) of Caesar's text. Many books deal with this subject, from Walser (1988) who does not believe in the story of the Helvetii related by Caesar, stressing Caesar's own use of propaganda, to Goudineau (1990, 161–166) and Kaenel (2016, 36–37) who are more trusting of the Roman general's *Commentaries*. After his consulate in 59 BC, Caesar was made proconsul of the Roman provinces of Gallia Cisalpina and Illyricum (northern Italy and the Dalmatian coast). Following the death of the proconsul of Gallia Transalpina (south and south-west France, from the Mediterranean to Geneva), the Roman Senate also gave him charge of the province of Gallia Narbonensis. Let us note some 'facts', whilst accepting that the ancient sources do not provide any alternative scenarios.

The two or three years leading up to 58 BC witnessed the 'conspiracy' of Orgetorix, the instigator of the migration project, who was in contact and dealing with the Sequanian Casticos and the Aeduan Dumnorix. This situation was certainly well understood in Rome, echoing the first triumvirate of Caesar, Crassus and Pompey in 60 BC (Gerhard 1991). Orgetorix 'disappeared' (though the exact circumstances are

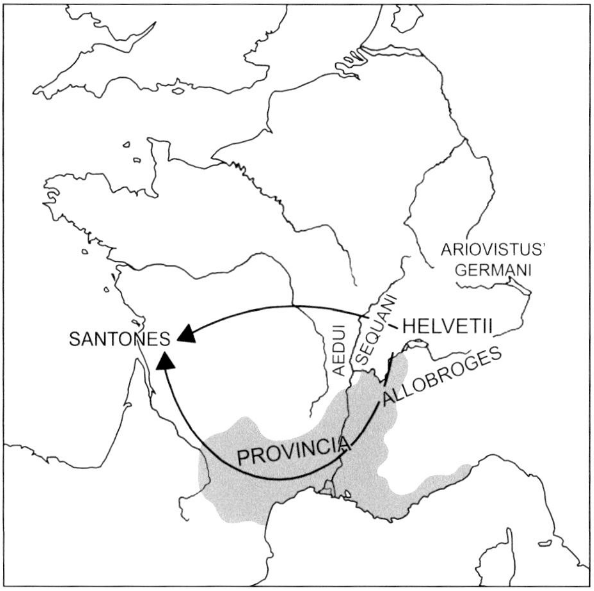

Figure 5.1 The two main routes for the migration of the Helvetii and associated tribes in 58 BC, from the Swiss Plateau to south-west France (after Goudineau 1990, 135).

unknown: was he killed or did he commit suicide?), because according to Caesar he attempted to seize power. Nevertheless, the Helvetii can be seen as one of the leading Gallic tribes at that time. The project for the whole population to migrate was known in Rome. Cicero (*ad Atticum* 1.19.2) wrote to Atticus in 60 BC that the Helvetians took up arms and intended to make raids into Gallia Narbonensis (Figure 5.1). Why? Caesar argues that the pressure exerted by the Germans moving into southern Germany and eastern France – like Ariovistus and the Suebi in 58 BC – contributed to the decision of the Helvetii to leave their homeland and settle in the territory of the Santones, contacts having been made with the tribes who would be affected. Other factors could have included economic, political or internal events but this is a matter of conjecture.

Geography and territory of the Helvetii

According to Caesar, 'the Helvetii are closed in on all sides by natural boundaries. On one side is the Rhine river, extremely wide and, which divides the Helvetian territories from the Germans. On another side is the Jura, a very high mountain range between the Sequani and the Helvetii. Separating them from the Province on the third side are Lake Lemannus and the Rhône river' (*BG* 1.2; Figure 5.2). He describes how the Helvetii thought that their territory was too small, as it was only 240 miles long and 180 wide. If we translate the distances given by Caesar into metric measurements, the length of 360 km is only slightly too big, whereas the width of 290 km is far too large! Around 80–90 km would be more correct for the width of the Swiss Plateau. This could be due to a mistake in copying the numbers (CLXXX instead of LXXX) or perhaps Caesar was referring to earlier times? It should be remembered that he did not enter the Helvetian area with his army.

In another famous passage, which has been central to Swiss archaeology since the birth of the subject in the 19th century, Caesar states the numbers of towns, villages and farms (*oppida, vici, aedificia*) in the territory of the Helvetii in 58 BC:

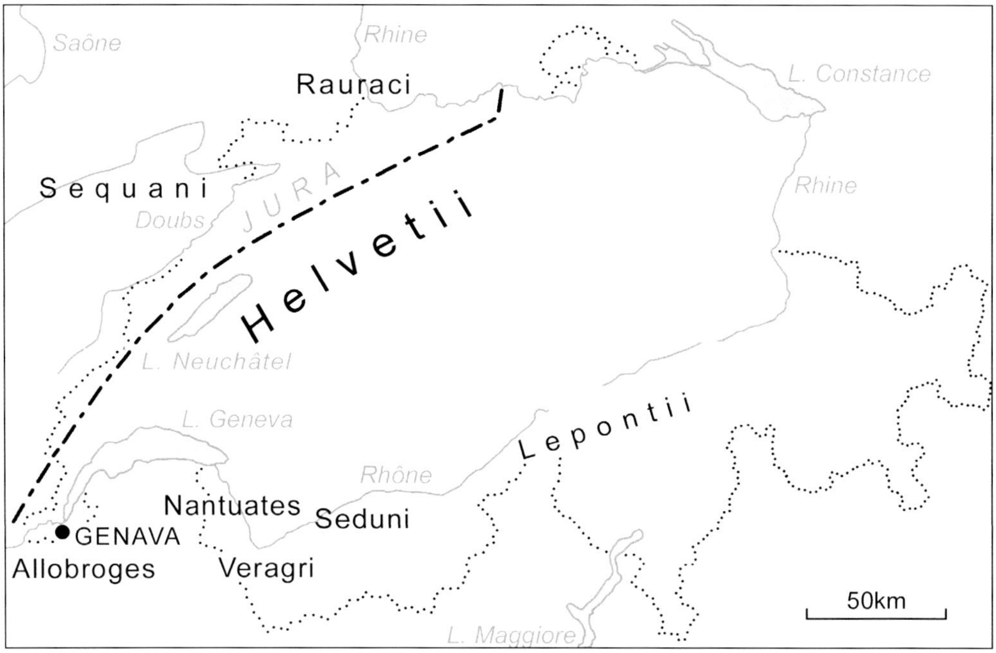

Figure 5.2 The limits given by Caesar for the territory of the Helvetii in 58 BC (after Stöckli 2016, Abb. 21).

> After Orgetorix's death, the Helvetii did not give up their attempts to realise their intention to migrate form their country. When they thought that they were ready to go, they set fire to all their towns, about twelve of them, as well as their roughly 400 villages, and all their other private buildings; furthermore they burned up all the grain beyond what they were going to carry with them – all this in order to eliminate any hope of returning home, so that they would be more fully committed to undergo all dangers, finally, they ordered every person to take with him three months' worth of already-ground-up rations from his home. They persuaded their neighbours, the Rauraci, the Tulingi, and the Latobrigi to adopt the same plan, burn down their towns and villages and emigrate with them. Also, they welcomed in their territory and adopted as their allies the Boii, who had settled across the Rhine but then crossed over into the territory of Noricum and attacked the town of Noreia (*BG*, 1.5).

In late March, the migrants gathered in the vicinity of Geneva with the intention of crossing into the territory of the Allobroges, the best route to south-west Gaul being through the Roman *provincia* (Figure 5.3). But the proconsul intervened by rushing to Genava (the northernmost town in the province, *extremum oppidum allobrogum*; *BG* 1.6), where he demolished the bridge over the Rhône. War began... Peace negotiations started, but failed.

In mid-April, Caesar refused to allow the Helvetii to pass through the *provincia*. In the meantime, he had raised troops and fortified the southern bank of the river Rhône with 'a wall 19 miles long and 16 feet high, along with a trench, all the way from Lake Lemannus [...] to the Jura' (*BG* 1.8). The Helvetii were forced to change their plans

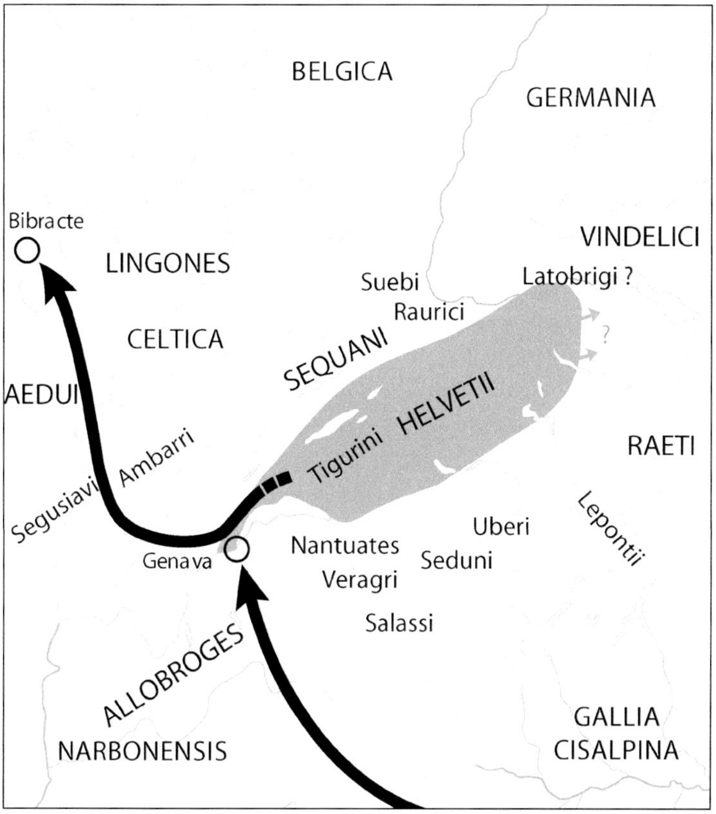

Figure 5.3 The Helvetii, their neighbours and the migration of Spring 58 BC: Caesar reached Geneva with his legions after a forced march, and pursued the coalition of Helvetii and other tribes through the Jura and the Saône plains, until the final battle that took place south of the oppidum *of Bibracte in Burgundy (after Kaenel 2016, 25).*

and march north-west. After crossing the Jura, they headed for the river Saône, the alternative route to south-west France (Figure 5.3). During the river crossing, which took some days, the Roman legions slaughtered those Tigurini who had not yet crossed the river. The migrants send Caesar an embassy 'headed by their chieftain Divico, who had been commander of the Helvetii, in the war against Cassius' (*BG* 1.13).[1] According to Caesar, Divico even threated Rome, making reference to the battle of Agen 107 BC,

> if Caesar received hostages them, to convince him that they would do what they have promised and if they would make amends to the to the Aedui for the harm done to them and to their allies, and if they would satisfy the Allobroges likewise, he [Caesar] would make peace with them. Divico answered that among the Helvetii it had been an established practice to receive hostages, not to give them; this is what they were used to doing. The Roman people could testify to this. That was the reply he gave before leaving (*BG* 1.14).

The negotiations failed once more.

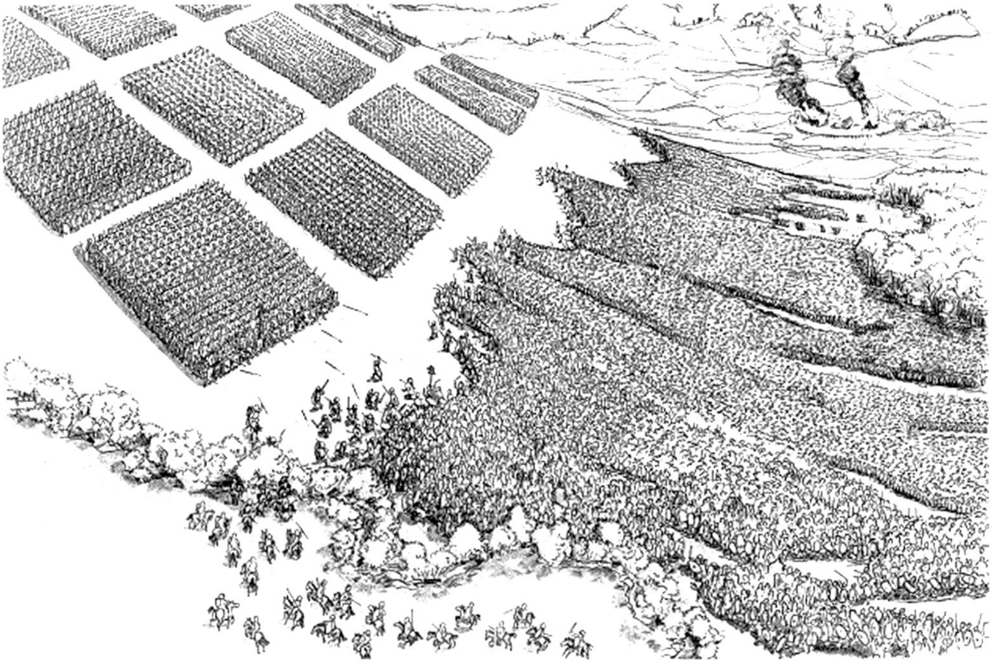

Figure 5.4 The battle near Bibracte begins: the Helvetii attack the Roman legions arranged on the flank of the hill (after Müller and Lüscher 2004, 154–155; drawing P. Schirm).

Early June... The battle near Bibracte, which took place 18 Roman miles (about 25 km) south of the main *oppidum* of the Aedui. The camp of the migrants was in the plain, that of Caesar and his legions was on a hill, where they were attacked by the Helvetii (Figure 5.4). The details of the different phases of the battle cannot be reconstructed from Caesar's description (Goudineau 1990, 278–280) but the result was a disaster for the migrants and Caesar was proud to revenge the shame of the defeat at Agen, nearly 50 years earlier, and so argue to the senate that it was a 'just war'. But the Romans also sustained heavy losses as Caesar spent three days burying the dead and treating the wounded before pursuing the survivors who were marching northwards. However, they were forced to surrender in the territory of Lingones and Caesar demanded hostages and their weapons. So ended the Helvetian War.

Let us quote another famous passage where Caesar gives numbers, which is often presented as a model of Gallic social organization and a way to approach the 'demography' of the Helvetii in the spring/summer of 58 BC:

> In the Helvetian camp, tablets were found containing documents in Greek script, and these were brought to Caesar. They were complete records with names, listing among the number of emigrants the men of military age and separately the children, old men, and women. As a total of all these categories, there were 263,000 Helvetii, 36,000 Tulingi, 14,000 Latobrigi, 23,000 Rauraci 23,000, and 32,000 Boii. Out of all these, close to 92,000 were capable of bearing

> arms. The whole migration comprised almost 368,000 persons. When a census was taken, as Caesar ordered, of those who returned home, their number was found to be 110,000 (*BG* 1.29).

Using these numbers (following Curdy and Buchsenschutz 1991), we can construct a theoretical 'demography' of the Helvetii using simple arithmetic, based on Caesar's total of 263,000. By suggesting 2,000 inhabitants for each *oppidum*, 200 for each *vicus* and 40 for each *aedificium*, we arrive at an estimate of 33 *vici* and 330 *aedificia* for each *oppidum*. If multiplied by 12 – in line with Caesar's statement that there were 'about 12 *oppida*' (*ad duodecim*) – this results in a total slightly smaller than Caesar's number for the population.

After their defeat, Caesar sent the Helvetii back to their former territory under a treaty (*foedus*), to prevent, so he claims, the settlement of Germans from across the Rhine on the Swiss Plateau which was close to the *provincia* (Frei-Stolba and Paunier 2014; Sanchez 2016).

52 BC

Although the Helvetii were no longer directly concerned with Caesar and the war, 8,000 warriors were sent in 52 BC to take part in the Gallic coalition under the command of Vercingetorix and, *de facto*, the treaty was broken. Only six years after the disaster at Bibracte, we can see that a new, young generation of warriors was able to make war. Perhaps they were drawn from the children who had escaped death and returned to the Swiss Plateau in the summer of 58?

Archaeology

The migration process

We must admit that it is difficult to find clear traces or direct evidence for the migration as recounted by Caesar. As early as the 19th century, some traces of charcoal found in Bern (Brenodor) were thought to be associated with the events of spring 58 BC, but this interpretation does not correspond with the archaeological evidence and its current dating (Fellmann 1999). The 1981 excavations at Mont Vully brought a surprise, in the form of a thick burnt layer beneath a destroyed rampart. It was suggested that this layer was related to the events of March 58 BC ('they set fire to all their towns'), but if that was plausible 35 years ago, it is no longer valid today: the chronology of the late La Tène period has been revised and the relative dating has been moved earlier (Kaenel *et al.* 2004). The burning of Mont Vully is now attributed to the end of the La Tène D1b phase, *c.* 80 BC, at least one generation before the events of 58 BC. With this chronological revision, the only trace of this famous episode of the Helvetii disappeared.

Genava (Geneva)

The harbour of the *oppidum* at Genava has been excavated, yielding dendrochronological dates of 123–105 BC. Caesar might even have seen the large oak statue, which is dated

Figure 5.5 The harbour at Genava (Geneva) at the end of the 2nd or beginning of the 1st century BC. Oak statue with trophy, which Caesar might have seen (after Curdy and Kaenel 2008, fig. 297; drawing A. Houot).

Figure 5.6 28 March 58 BC: at Genava, Caesar has destroyed the bridge over the Rhône, between the Allobroges in the Roman provincia and Helvetian territory north of Lake Geneva, where the migrants wait (after Curdy and Kaenel 2008, fig. 356; drawing A. Houot).

to about 80 BC (the last ring without bark is 101 BC), with trophy, weapons and human bones (Figure 5.5). But no trace of the bridge that Caesar destroyed has yet been found, nor can any other archaeological evidence be clearly linked to his presence or of the Helvetii on the other side of the Rhône (Figure 5.6).

Nor is there any sign of the long, high wall that Caesar states was built from Lake Geneva to the Jura, despite the investigations undertaken by Colonel Eugène-Céleste Stoffel in 1861 – a Swiss citizen, *officier d'ordonnance* of the Emperor, sent on mission there by Napoléon III – or the 1940s excavations by cantonal archaeologist Louis Blondel, and at the end of the 1980s by the Swiss National Museum in Zurich (Flutsch 1991).

The battle near Bibracte

In 1863, as part of Napoléon III's project, Stoffel proposed that the location of the battlefield was the Mont de Jaux at Montmort in southern Burgundy. The Emperor preferred a different location but in 1886 the Emperor's former *aide de camp* returned to Montmort, opening several cuttings and discovering a ditch that he interpreted as a Roman work. A hundred years later, researchers from the Swiss National Museum located this ditch running perpendicular to the hill slope for about 120 m, and excavated part of it: it was 5–6 m wide and 2 m deep (Figure 5.7). Two or three iron nails were found, but no weaponry. Radiocarbon dates from the fill of the ditch fall in the 2nd or 3rd century AD, but even if direct proof has not been established, what could the function of such a substantial defence be, if it is not military (Flutsch 1991)?

Oppida *after the return of the Helvetii*

If we can observe continuity of occupation from the 2nd to the 1st century BC and onwards through Roman times at Geneva in the territory of the Allobroges, we find similar archaeological continuity in Helvetian territory, especially at some of the *oppida* on the western part of the Swiss Plateau. An example is Bern, an open settlement that became the biggest and most important *oppidum* on the Swiss Plateau in the 1st century BC. There is no evidence here that strictly attests to either the departure or the return of many people, although there are no absolute dates from dendrochronology.

The *oppidum* of Yverdon-les-Bains occupies a very favourable location in the western part of the plateau, on the west coast of Lake Neuchâtel. It too shows continuity of occupation from the 3rd or 2nd century BC up to the present day. In 81/80 BC, a rampart was constructed over the remains of an earlier open settlement (based on dendrochronologically dated oak from the rampart structure). This defence was destroyed in 60/50 BC, dismantled and then covered by lake deposits of sand (Brunetti *et al.* 2007). The excavations showed that there was a clear hiatus in occupation after these events, though its length is unknown (10, 20 years?), before new structures were built over the ruins. At the same time, in the mid-1st century BC,

Figure 5.7 Excavations in 1986 at Mont de Jaux, Montmort, Saône-et-Loire, uncovered a substantial ditch of military appearance at what may be the site of the battle near Bibracte (photo G. Kaenel).

a rampart was erected on the hill of Sermuz, 2 km to the south (Figure 5.8 A). Unlike the rampart at Yverdon-les-Bains, this one was not a *Pfostenschlitzmauer* (rampart with frontal posts) but a *murus gallicus* (Figure 5.8 B).

In the eastern part of the Swiss Plateau, Windisch (Vindonissa) and Zurich were occupied at the end of the 2nd and beginning of the 1st century BC. So was the Altenburg, on the German side of the Rhine, although its counterpart on the opposite bank at Rheinau[2] was founded slightly later, with occupation lasting until the mid-1st century BC. None of these sites, however, have yielded evidence that can be dated definitively to 58 BC, even where structures and material of the second or third quarter of the 1st century BC are present. There is also some doubt, on the basis of coins and pottery, as to whether Altenburg-Rheinau actually belonged to the territory of the Helvetii (Stöckli 2016, 230).

Open settlements, farms, roads, bridges and graves

Most later Iron Age settlements on the Swiss Plateau were occupied during La Tène C2–D1, in the later 2nd and early 1st century BC. Sites belonging to the earlier 2nd or even late 3rd century BC, such as Bern and Yverdon-les-Bains, are much rarer, just as with the later *oppida* in the later 1st century BC. In this context, we should mention

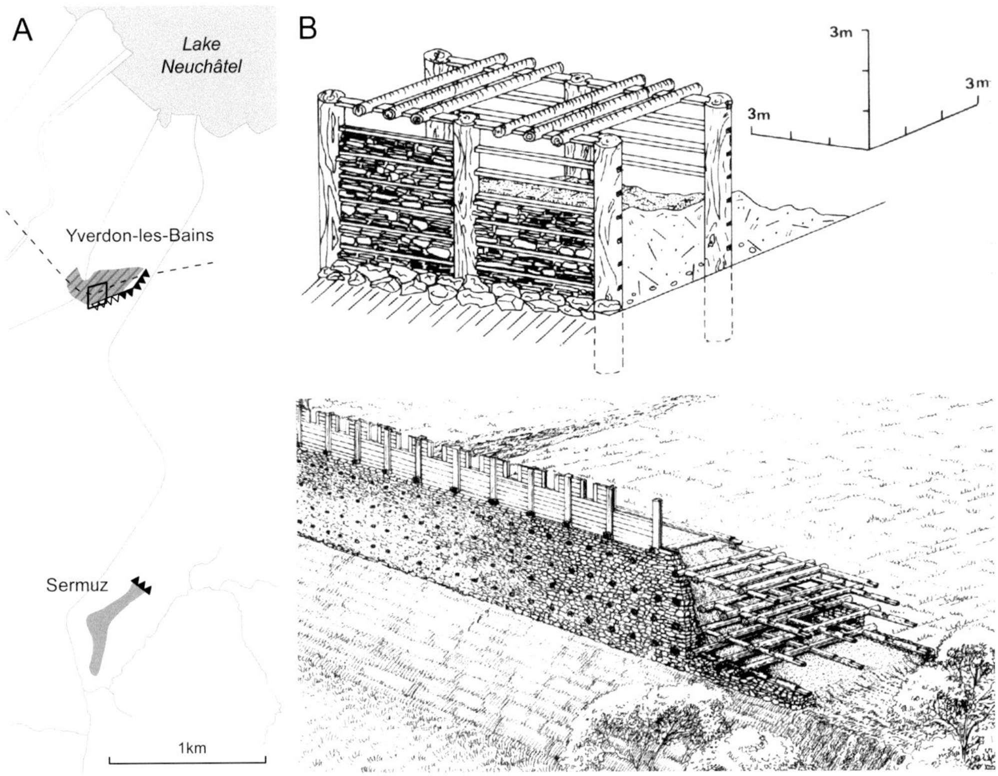

Figure 5.8 (A) The location of the oppida *of Yverdon-les-Bains and Sermuz, south-west of Lake Neuchâtel, Vaud (drawing Archeodunum, Gollion). (B)* Pfostenschlitzmauer *at Mont Vully, Fribourg, c. 100 BC, and* murus gallicus *at Sermuz, c. 50 BC (after Kaenel 2016, 84).*

a recently discovered settlement of the 2nd century BC at Vufflens-la-Ville, between Lake Geneva and Yverdon-les-Bains (Demierre *et al.* 2017).

Roads and bridges are known, for example at Payerne, between Yverdon-les-Bains and Avenches, which is dated to 70/69 BC by dendrochronology. This bridge stood during the Gallic War, and the Roman, medieval and modern roads, down to the motorway constructed in the 1990s all followed this route (Castella and Eschbach 2014). However, graves are very rare in the La Tène C2–D1 period and are almost unknown after 100 BC (Jud and Ulrich-Bochsler 2014), during the Gallic War and up to the mid-1st century AD (Sauteur 2017).

Archaeological methods and relative chronology cannot therefore bring us direct proof of Caesar's account. It is difficult to argue and date the evidence more precisely than to within a generation.

Roman military presence on the Swiss Plateau, 50–20 BC

After the destruction of the rampart at Yverdon-les-Bains and the temporary abandonment of the *oppidum*, the site of Sermuz was built 2 km to the south. Here a *murus gallicus* was erected to protect the 7 ha plateau. Surface finds cover the late Republican and early Augustan periods and include brooches of Alesia type, traditionally dated to La Tène D2b and attributed to the Roman military, and more than 100 identifiable coins (61 Iron Age and 44 Republican), 2 silver flans and even a coin die of Naevius Balbus (79 BC) used to produce Roman silver *denarii* after the Gallic War (Geiser 2017a). More than 50% of the pottery is Roman and the finds are interpreted as deriving from a military occupation, perhaps with auxiliaries from eastern Gaul. This phase, dated to between 50 and 20 BC – which Stöckli has labelled the 'Sermuz horizon' rather than La Tène D2b – corresponds to the first phase of the Roman period in the western part of the Swiss Plateau (Stöckli 2010; 2016; Martin-Kilcher 2011).

A hoard found at the Belpberg, south of Bern, comprises 101 coins in the same proportions as at Sermuz (61 Gaulish *quinarii* and 40 Republican *denarii*), and has been interpreted as the pay of the Roman military, again auxiliaries (Nick 2017). At Lausanne, the first buildings of the *vicus* of Lousonna are also dated to 50–20 BC and were constructed in La Tène tradition. They are not located on the hill around the cathedral, but about 3 km to the south-west on the shore of Lake Geneva. Although the Roman poet Lucan tells in his *Pharsalia* how the Caesar's army camped on the shore before marching to Italy and crossing the Rubicon in early 49 BC, no archaeological evidence for this has been found (Frei-Stolba 1999, 32–36).

In 45/44 BC, only a few years after the end of the war and just before his assassination in Rome, Caesar founded Colonia Iulia Equestris for cavalry veterans at Nyon, in territory seized from the Helvetii. The new *colonia* controlled the south-westerly access to Gallia Narbonensis. Excavations there have so far brought to light a few finds contemporary with the foundation, but no structures. The north-eastern border of the Helvetii was similarly controlled by Colonia Raurica (Augst), which was founded by Lucius Munatius Plancus in 44 BC.

There is, however, some evidence of military activity that is not attested in the written texts. At the Col des Etroits on the road across the Jura mountains from Besançon (Vesontio) in Franche-Comté to Yverdon-les-Bains and at a height of 1080 m, prospection in 2008 and subsequent trial excavations uncovered Roman hobnails, coins (an east Gaulish *quinarius* with the legend *TOC*, a Republican *denarius* with Roma on a chariot, and half a *dupondius* of Nîmes dating from 27 BC onward), as well as finds dating to the second half of the 1st century BC (Demierre *et al.* 2015). Roman military equipment has also been found in the Alps in the region of the Saint-Bernard pass which leads from Italy to the Valais, in the territory of the Veragri (hobnails and rare military finds from Liddes can be dated to the last two-thirds of the 1st century BC; Andenmatten and Pignolet 2017), and in eastern Switzerland, between the lakes of northern Italy and Lake Constance (nails, lead sling bullets and other finds are dated *c.* 40–20 BC; Martin-Kilcher 2011; 2015).

Aventicum

Finally, Avenches (Aventicum) was the future capital of the Flavian civitas Helvetiorum. The Roman *colonia* is situated in the plain, about 10 km from the La Tène D1 *oppidum*

Figure 5.9 View from the Bois de Châtel looking towards Avenches, Vaud, where a late La Tène settlement underlies Roman Aventicum, and the oppidum *of Mont Vully (photo G. Kaenel).*

of Mont Vully, on the top of a hill between Lake Morat and Lake Neuchâtel, to the north-east, with another *oppidum* nearer still, at Bois de Châtel, directly to the south (Figure 5.9). Mont Vully was no longer occupied at the time of the Gallic War. Surface surveys at Bois de Châtel have yielded coins mostly of the 1st century BC, especially *Büschelquinarii* and a silver *quinarius* with the legend *VATICO*. Vatico, like Orgetorix and Divico, was probably a leading member of the Helvetian elite (Kaenel and von Kaenel 1983; Geiser 2017b).

Our understanding of Avenches has changed fundamentally in the last 20 years. Originally, only a coin of *VATICO* and a die for gold staters of the late 2nd century BC, both stray finds, were known from the site. Since then a late La Tène settlement has come to light beneath Roman Aventicum. In 1998, two cremation burials dating to the second half of the 2nd century BC were excavated in the zone subsequently occupied by Roman temples, in the western part of the town, and in 2003, pottery, coins, as well as pellet mould fragments and a coin flan were found, all of which date to the second quarter of the 1st century BC, just before or at the time of the Gallic War. Rescue excavations have also brought to light extensive traces of late La Tène occupation in the area later occupied by the western part of the Roman town, which shows continuity in occupation from the second half of the 2nd century BC to the Augustan period and beyond. The late La Tène open settlement, which covers many hectares, shows a horizontal stratigraphy and west to east organization along the road from Yverdon-les-Bains, via Payerne with its bridge, to the future centre of

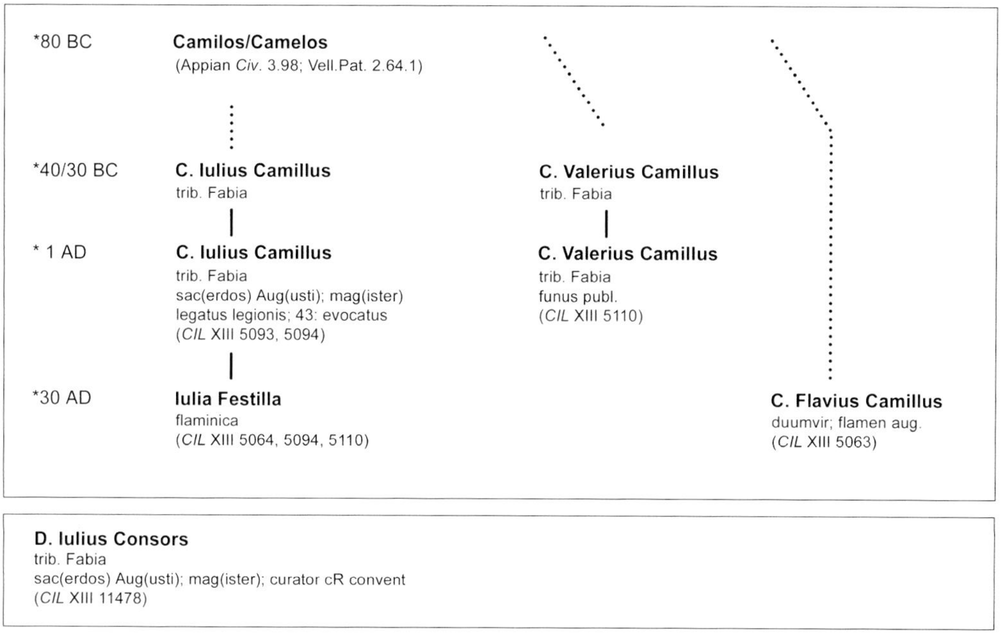

Figure 5.10 The names of prominent Helvetii known from texts and archaeology (coins): from Camilos at the time of the Gallic War to the famous Camilli, Roman citizens of Aventicum and western Switzerland (after Kaenel and Martin-Kilcher 2002, ill. 9).

Aventicum along the later *decumanus maximus* (Amoroso and Castella 2016). Finally, in 2015, excavations brought to light a dense and continuous stratigraphic sequence containing many finds that date from 50 BC to the Augustan period, with more than 50% of the material being Roman, including black- and early red-slipped wares, and amphorae of types known in the *provincia*, at Vienne and Geneva for instance, which were also imported to Bibracte in the post-war years, *c.* 50–20 BC (Schenk *et al.* 2016).

As an example of this continuous occupation, we can cite the discovery of two bodies buried in a seated position, with no accompanying finds. The individuals are radiocarbon dated to the 3rd or 2nd century BC, but eight or ten generations later, an Augustan round temple was built at the same place. The location of the two bodies, placed as they were in a position of majesty, under the entrance of the temple (Morel and Blanc 2008, 39–41), is clearly no coincidence and plausibly evokes the memory of revered Celtic ancestors. Were these people already Helvetii? (Kaenel 2016, 144–145; Aberson *et al.* 2017). It is difficult to say, even if we can suggest that the Tigurini (who, according to Caesar, were a *pagus* of the Helvetii in the 1st century BC), settled on the Swiss Plateau following their return from the Cimbrian Wars after 101 BC.

Conclusion

We know some Helvetii by name (Figure 5.10): Divico and Orgetorix are the most famous, but we can also mention Nammeius and Verucloetius, who negotiated in vain with Caesar in Geneva, and Ninno, Viros and Vatico, are named on coins. Additionally, Pliny refers to the perhaps mythical figure of Helico in older times. Of considerable interest is the case of Camilos/Camelos, mentioned by Appian: the Camilli, who became Roman citizens (with the full *tria nomina*), were one of the most influential Helvetic families in Aventicum and western Switzerland during the 1st century AD (Kaenel and Martin-Kilcher 2002).

In conclusion, let us imagine a hypothetical scenario: Camilos could have taken part in the migration of the Helvetii in 58 BC, and escaped death or slavery. Perhaps it was him who arrested Decimus Brutus, one of Caesar's assassins, in the Jura mountains, in the territory of the Sequani, not far from the Col des Etroits, where militaria from the decades after the Gallic War have been found (above). Nevertheless, we must admit that without Caesar and his *Commentaries*, archaeologists would never have been able to conceive a scenario like the migration of all the Helvetii along with many other tribes! But even if we have no objective, precisely dated archaeological traces of the Gallic War, we can introduce indirect arguments (as for example for Yverdon), combining history and archaeology, to help us construct hypotheses – and abandon some of them – in the hope that in future there will be more archaeological evidence and it will play a greater role in the debate about the battle for Gaul.

Notes

1 '*cujus legationis Divico princeps fuit qui bello Cassiano dux Helvetiorum fuerat*'.

2 The twin defended sites at Altenburg and Rheinau occupy opposing peninsulae defined by a double bend of the Rhine.

Bibliography

Aberson, M., Geiser, A. and Luginbühl, T. (2017) Les Helvètes en marche: confrontation de sources. *Revue historique vaudoise* 125, 175–197.

Amoroso, H. and Castella, D. (2016) Un habitat gaulois aux origines d'*Aventicum*. Les fouilles de *Sur Fourches* (2009/2015). *Bulletin de l'Association Pro Aventico* 56, 2014/2015, 7–72.

Andenmatten, R. and Pignolet, A. (2017) Recherches archéologiques autour du mur (dit) d'Hannibal à Liddes: des sites fortifiés de haute montagne dans la région du Grand-Saint-Bernard (Suisse/Valais, Italie/Val d'Aoste). *Bulletin de l'Association française pour l'étude de l'âge du Fer* 35, 41–44.

Brunetti, C., Curdy, P., Geiser, A. *et al.* (2007) *Yverdon-les-Bains et Sermuz à la fin de l'âge du Fer*. Lausanne, Musée cantonal d'archéologie et d'histoire, Cahiers d'archéologie romande 107.

Castella, D. and Eschbach, F. (2014) Le pont celtique des Avanturies à Payerne (Vaud, Suisse). In J. Bullinger, P. Crotti and C. Huguenin (eds), *De l'âge du Fer à l'usage du verre. Mélanges offerts à Gilbert Kaenel*, 207-216. Lausanne, Musée cantonal d'archéologie et d'histoire, Cahiers d'archéologie romande 151.

Curdy, P. and Buchsenschutz, O. (1991) L'habitat helvète sur le Plateau Suisse. *Archéologie Suisse* 14–1, 89–97.

Curdy, P. and Kaenel, G. (2008) Les Celtes de l'âge du Fer. In A. Gallay (ed.), *Des Alpes au Léman. Images de la préhistoire* (2nd edn), 260–325. Gollion, Infolio.

Demierre, M., Luginbühl, T. and Montandon, M. (2015) Militaria tardo-républicains au Col des Etroits (Jura vaudois, Suisse). Données et essai d'analyse. In G.A. Lehmann and R. Wiegels (eds),

Über die Alpen und über den Rhein. Beiträge zu den Anfängen und zum Verlauf der römischen Expansion nach Mitteleuropa, 283–297. Berlin, De Gruyter, Abhandlungen der Akademie der Wissenschaften zu Göttingen 37.

Demierre, M., Schopfer, A., Julita, B., and Steudler, A. (2017) L'agglomération laténienne de Vufflens-la-Ville. Organisation spatiale, quartiers et fonctions. *Archéologie vaudoise, Chroniques 2016*, 34–45. Lausanne, Archéologie cantonale.

Fellmann, R. (1999) Das Zink-Täfelchen vom Thormebodewald auf der Engehalbinsel bei Bern und seine keltische Inschrift. *Archäologie im Kanton Bern* 4B, 133–175. Bern, Archäologischer Dienst.

Flutsch, R. (1991) La localisation de la bataille de Bibracte: historique et bilan des recherches récentes. *Revue Suisse d'art et d'archéologie* 448, 38–48.

Frei-Stolba, R. (1999) Recherches sur les institutions de Nyon, Augst et Avenches. In M. Dondin-Payre and M.-Th. Raepsaet-Charlier (eds), *Cités, Municipes, Colonies. Les processus de municipalisation en Gaule et en Germanie sous le haut-Empire romain*, 29–95. Paris, Publications de la Sorbonne.

Frei-Stolba, R. and Paunier, D. (2014) Die römische Epoche. Integration in die Mittelmeerwelt. In G. Kreis (ed.), *Die Geschichte der Schweiz*, 38–70. Basel, Schwabe Verlag.

Geiser, A. (2017a) Yverdon-les-Bains (VD), *oppidum* de Sermuz 'Sur Châtillon'. In J. Genechesi and L. Pernet (eds), *Les Celtes et la monnaie. Des Grecs aux Surréalistes*, 122–124. Gollion, Infolio.

Geiser, A. (2017b) Des facies monétaires celtiques qui fondent l'histoire des Helvètes? In J. Genechesi and L. Pernet (eds), *Les Celtes et la monnaie. Des Grecs aux Surréalistes*, 94–95. Gollion, Infolio.

Gerhard, Y. (1991) Orgétorix l'Helvète et le *Bellum Gallicum* de César. *Les études classiques* 59, 267–274.

Goudineau, C. (1990) *César et la Gaule*. Paris, Errance.

Jud, P. and Ulrich-Bochsler, S. (2014) *Bern, Reichenbachstrasse. Neue Gräber aus dem latènezeitlichen Oppidum auf der Engehalbinsel*. Bern, Archäologischer Dienst des Kantons Bern.

Kaenel, G. (2016) *L'an -58. Les Helvètes. Archéologie et histoire d'un peuple celte* (2nd edn). Lausanne, Presses polytechniques et universitaires romandes, Le Savoir Suisse 82.

Kaenel, G. and Martin-Kilcher, S. (2002) Où et qui sont les aristocrates helvètes? In V. Guichard and F. Perrin (eds), *L'aristocratie celte à la fin de l'âge du Fer (IIe s. avant J.-C. -1er s. après J.-C.)*, 153–166. Glux-en-Glenne, Collection Bibracte 5.

Kaenel, G. and von Kaenel. H.-M. (1983) Le Bois de Châtel près d'Avenches à la lumière de trouvailles récentes: oppidum celtique? et castrum du Bas-Empire. *Archéologie suisse* 6–3, 110–119.

Kaenel G., Curdy, P. and Carrard, F. (2004) *L'oppidum du Mont Vully: un bilan des recherches: 1978–2003*. Fribourg, Archéologie fribourgeoise 20.

Kaeser, M.-A. (2014) Helvetier, Römer, Pfahlbauer. Die Archäologie und die mytischen Ahnen der Schweiz. In G. Kreis (ed.), *Die Geschichte der Schweiz*, 31–34. Basel, Schwabe Verlag.

Les Helvètes (1991) *Les Helvètes et leurs voisins en tant que figure d'identification: théories et effets*. Basel, Archéologie Suisse 14–1.

Martin-Kilcher, S. (2011) Römer und gentes Alpinae im Konflikt – archäologische und historische Zeugnisse des 1. Jahrhunderts v. Chr. In G. Moosbauer and R. Wiegels (eds), *Fines imperii – imperium sine fine?*, 27–62. Rahden, Marie Leidorf, Osnabrücker Forschungen zu Altertum und Antike-Rezeption 14.

Martin-Kilcher, S. (2015) Archäologische Spuren der römischen Okkupation zwischen Alpen und Hochrhein und die städtische Besiedlung der *civitas Helvetiorum* im 1. Jh. V. Chr. In G.A. Lehmann and R. Wiegels (eds), *Über die Alpen und über den Rhein. Beiträge zu den Anfängen und zum Verlauf der römischen Expansion nach Mitteleuropa*, 235–281. Berlin, De Gruyter, Abhandlungen der Akademie der Wissenschaften zu Göttingen 37.

Morel, J. and Blanc, P. (2008) Les sanctuaires d'Aventicum. Evolution, organisation, circulations. In D. Castella and M.-F. Meylan Krause (eds), *Topographie sacrée et rituels. Le cas d'Aventicum, capitale des Helvètes (Actes du colloque international d'Avenches 2-4 novembre 2006)*, 35–50. Basel, Archéologie suisse, Antiqua 43.

Müller, F. and Lüscher, G. (2004) *Die Kelten in der Schweiz*. Stuttgart, Theiss.

Nick, M. (2017) Le trésor de la fin de l'âge du Fer du Belpberg (BE). In J. Genechesi and L. Pernet (eds), *Les Celtes et la monnaie. Des Grecs aux Surréalistes*, 128–129. Gollion, Infolio.

Sanchez, P. (2016) Les Helvètes ont exigé qu'aucun de leurs ressortissants ne devienne romain. *Passé simple* 14, 17–19.

Sauteur, E. (ed.) (2017) *À la Montagne. Une nécropole du Ier siècle après J.-C. à Avenches*. Lausanne, Musée cantonal d'archéologie et d'histoire, Aventicum 21/Cahiers d'archéologie romande 167.

Schenk, A., Amoroso, H. and Blanc, P. (2016) Route du Faubourg, Avenches. *Bulletin de l'Association Pro Aventico* 56, 2014/2015, 190–230.

Stöckli, W.-E. (2010) Der Auszug der Helvetier von 58 v. Chr.: Die Aussage der Münzen und Fibeln. In C. Ebnöther and R. Schatzmann (eds), *Oleum non perdidit, Festschrift für Stefanie Martin-Kilcher*, 105–117. Basel, Archéologie suisse, Antiqua 47.

Stöckli, W.-E. (2016) *Urgeschichte der Schweiz im Überblick (15 000 v. Chr.-Christi Geburt)*. Basel, Archéologie suisse, Antiqua 54.

Walser, G. (1988) *Bellum Helveticum. Studien zum Beginn der caesarischen Eroberung von Gallien*. Stuttgart, Franz Steiner, Historia Einzelschriften 118.

Chapter 6

Recent archaeological research on Roman military engineering works of the Gallic War

Michel Reddé

Caesar's account of the Gallic War teems with the names of places and peoples that are often hard to identify. This is particularly true of battlefields, which the proconsul generally describes succinctly. Sometimes just a few words suffice. On the siege of the hillfort of Vellaudunum, which we cannot locate for certain – it was possibly Nevers – the proconsul writes *oppugnare instituit idque biduo circumvallavit* ('He determined to assault the place and in two days invested it', *BG* 7.11). There is nothing more. But that was enough, because everyone understood what was going on when a Latin technical term like *circumvallavit* was used, indicating the building of fortifications to encircle a stronghold. In contrast, no fewer than twenty-one chapters are given over to the episode of Alesia, which is by far the lengthiest in the entire account. But then again it was the final victory that was to ensure Caesar of glory – the duel with the opponent the *imperator* had picked out for himself. This difference in treatment is obviously a bias for the modern historian who does not always have the necessary information to identify any particular one of the numerous sites of battle in this war of conquest.

Another difficulty is that the narrative is extremely succinct and the geographical descriptions are only cursory. This can be explained both by Caesar's personal style of writing, his *brevitas* (concision) and by the fact that ancient military accounts were to be read without any maps or sketches. To weigh them down with detailed descriptions was not only contrary to good literary taste but also contrary to common sense. It was enough to set out the gist of the matter for it to be understood by the reader. Needless to say, these were all accounts composed after the event by the victor.

These preliminary indications explain why it is so difficult for archaeologists to identify the battle sites of the Gallic War. In the 19th century, Napoléon III spent substantial sums on this, launching French archaeology's first great programmes

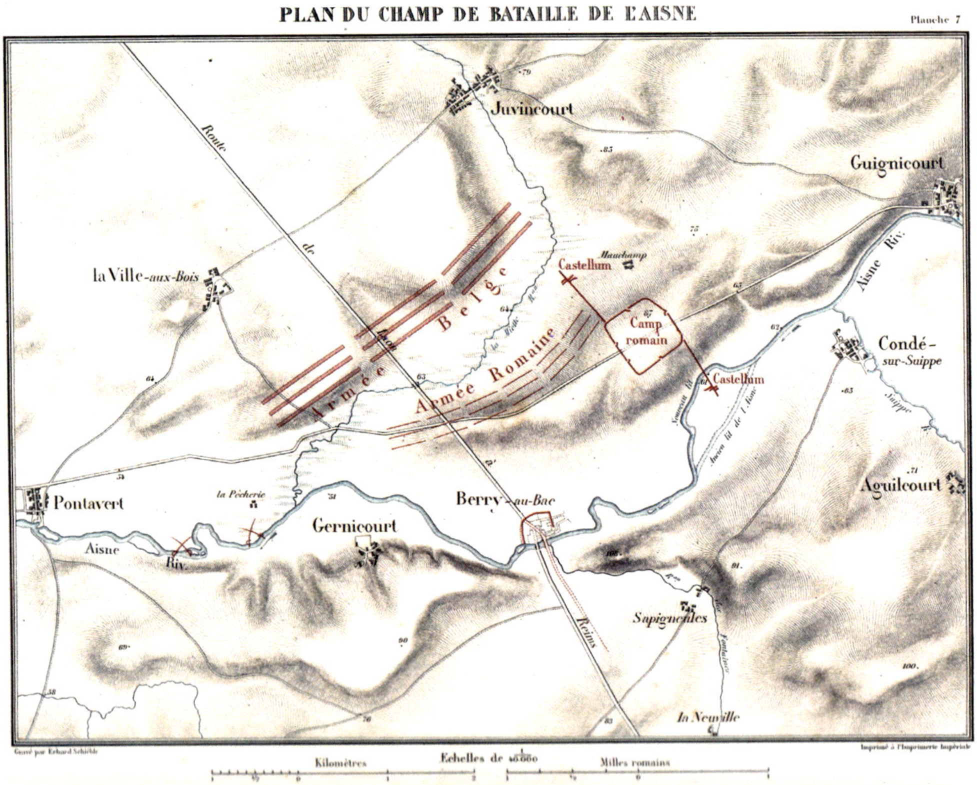

Figure 6.1 Plan of Mauchamp, Aisne, from Napoléon III's Histoire de Jules César, *pl. 7.*

of works, with undeniable successes and incontrovertible failures (Napoléon III 1865–1866). Today we still take that pioneering research as our starting point, to confirm, clarify and possibly challenge it. Here I shall review recent research on the subject, emphasizing first that the following examples, which number just four in all, are all that we can present with certainty today, apart from the recent discovery of Hermeskeil, in Germany. For example, so major an episode as the siege of Bourges has still not yielded an archaeological context categorically related to Caesar's account. The sites of the battles against the Helvetii in 58 BC or the Germans of Ariovistus that same year remain to be proved.[1]

The battle of the Aisne and the camp of Mauchamp

This episode relates to the campaign of the year 57 BC. Caesar was attempting to subdue the Belgae who, except for his allies the Remi, were leagued against him. The event took place in the Aisne valley, not far from the *oppidum* of Bibrax, which was under siege from the coalition of the Belgae. Caesar's arrival lifted the siege; there followed a pitched battle in the valley against the Gallic forces (Figure 6.1):

> At first Caesar determined, because of the vast numbers of the enemy and their excellent reputation for valour, to avoid an engagement. By cavalry combats, however, he sought daily to prove what the valour of the enemy could do and what our men could dare. Then, perceiving that our men were not inferior, he chose a ground before the camp naturally suitable and appropriate for forming line of battle; for the hill where the camp had been pitched, standing up but a little from the plain, offered to the front as broad a space as a line deployed could occupy; on either flank it fell away, while in front by a gentle slope it came down gradually to the level of the plain. On either flank of that hill he dug at right angles a protecting trench of about four hundred paces, and at the ends of the trenches he constructed forts and there posted his artillery, so that, when he had formed line, the enemy might not be able, because of their great superiority of numbers, to surround the Romans fighting on the flanks (*BG* 2.8).

Caesar's position is clear, then: a hill on the northern bank of the Aisne. On the strength of these indications, Napoléon III and Stoffel, his *aide de camp*, had long trenches dug out from the road that crosses the site along the crest. The excavations eventually brought to light a series of ditches forming an almost square complex measuring 658 × 655 m (about 42 ha), with rounded corners, the north-east side being at an angle. Five gateways, two of which were to the west, provided access. These gateways were defended by internal *claviculae*, that is, semi-circular ditches barring the way and forcing any assailant to present his unshielded, right-hand side. Two large ditches some 750 m long ran one from the north-west corner of the camp to a small stream, the Miette, that it virtually joined up with; and the other from the south-east corner towards the river Aisne, so that Mauchamp hill was completely barred off and any outflanking manoeuvre rendered impossible. Some smaller ditches, the layout of which is unclear, cut off crosswise the tip of the northern arm; no equivalent ditches have been found to the south, perhaps having been eroded by a change in the course of the Aisne, but they are dotted on Napoléon's map. The archaeologists who have worked on the case generally debate three points: the consistency between the published map and Caesar's description; the material character of the remains discovered; and the chronology of the site.

On the first point, it has to be observed that the plan drawn up by Napoléon does bear similarities to the details in *de Bello Gallico*. Peyre (1979) proved convincingly that each of the topographical indications given by Caesar matches a feature on the ground; but even if some interpretation or other of the Latin text is challenged, the account and the excavations are strikingly consistent on the main point: the presence of long ditches on either side of the hill (Figure 6.2). True, the Roman redoubts have not been found, but these *castella*, which were necessarily made of wood, would only have left postholes, and around 1860 it was barely known how to recognize such features. Aerial photographs taken by Bernard Lambot have revealed a *clavicula*, and recent excavations at Alesia attest that these were already in use in Caesar's time (Reddé 1995). It therefore seems a sound hypothesis today to attribute the camp at Mauchamp to the battle against the Belgae in the year 57 BC, particularly because the identification of the *oppidum* of Bibrax with the site of Vieux-Laon, 12 km from

Figure 6.2 Air photograph of Mauchamp (courtesy Bernard Lambot).

Mauchamp, has recently been confirmed by the exceptional discovery of a Balearic coin attributed to Caesar's slinger auxiliaries (Lambot and Casagrande 1997). It was not the usual type of coinage in circulation in northern Gaul.

The siege of Gergovia

In 52 BC, the seventh year of the war, Caesar had to face the emergence of a vast coalition led by a young noble of the Arverni, Vercingetorix. After a brilliant start to his campaign, in which he systematically avoided confronting the legions directly, Vercingetorix had to fall back before the end of the summer on Gergovia, the *oppidum* of the Arverni, which was threatened by the Roman army. The proconsul's description of the stronghold is cursory and has fuelled much controversy.

> Having reconnoitred the position of the city, which was set upon a very lofty height, with difficult approaches on every side, he despaired of taking it by storm, and he determined not to attempt a blockade until he had secured his corn-supply. Vercingetorix, for his part, had pitched camp near the town, and posted the contingent of each state separately at short intervals around himself. Every eminence on the ridge from which a bird's-eye view was possible had been seized, and the appearance was formidable ... Opposite the town there was a hill at the very foot of the mountain, an exceedingly strong position, precipitous on every side. If our troops secured this they thought they could cut off the enemy at once from a great part of their water-supply and from freedom of foraging. The post was held, however, by the enemy

> with a garrison, albeit not a very strong one. None the less, Caesar marched out of camp in the silence of night, dislodged the garrison before it could be reinforced from the town, and made himself master of the position. He posted two legions there, and ran a double ditch, twelve feet broad in each case, from the greater to the lesser camp, so that even single soldiers could pass to and fro safe from a sudden onset of the enemy (*BG* 7.35).

Napoléon III and Stoffel proposed to identify the site of Gergovia with the volcanic plateau of Merdogne (70 ha), south of Clermont-Ferrand, and their excavations revealed a large camp of 35 ha to the east of the *oppidum* and a small camp of about 5.5 ha to the south of it, on the hill of La Roche Blanche. Traces of a linear fortification were recognized joining the two. This evidence has, though, long been contested, like all the work of the Second Empire. It must be said that, while the plateau of Merdogne was enclosed, it does not seem to have been inhabited at the end of the Iron Age. The confusion has recently been intensified by the discovery of very dense protohistoric settlement at two nearby *oppida* (Figure 6.3): Gondole, immediately east of Merdogne plateau, and Corent, a few kilometres south of Gondole. While Gondole had a rampart, although not yet necessarily dated with any certainty, Corent did not, at least as far as we know for now, but the two sites were inhabited at the time of the Gallic War, even if Corent lost some of its importance after the conquest (Poux 2011; Poux *et al.* 2015, 505–530). Might not one of these settlements have been the Arvernian capital, rather than the plateau of Merdogne? Very recent excavations, though, have shown beyond doubt that the rampart of Merdogne, dating to the late Hallstatt period, had been substantially remodelled, with a dry-stone rampart erected towards the middle of the 1st century BC, at the time of the Gallic War (Pertlwieser *et al.* 2010). So what is to be concluded from this? A programme of recent research conducted over more than 20 years around Gondole in particular, but also research into the remains identified by Napoléon III as Caesarian military engineering works, has been synthesized recently and I will summarize it here (Deberge *et al.* 2014; 2018) (Figure 6.4).

- The existence of the 'large camp', almost square in shape, has been confirmed by a series of trial excavations on its western and eastern sides, and its north-western and south-eastern corners. Its perimeter takes the form of a V-shaped ditch with a very regular profile that is often extremely eroded. In the south-east corner, the scant material found comprises a few pottery vessels and an iron fibula associated with a skeleton. The iron rim of a shield was recovered from the northern ditch. It seems that all of the finds can be attributed to the middle of the 1st century BC, given the known typologies.
- The existence of the small camp has also been confirmed by a series of excavations that traced its north-eastern side over some 250 m. The ditch was 3.5 m wide and 1.8 m deep. Unfortunately the small scale of the excavations meant it was impossible to look for a rampart. Various Dressel 1 amphora bodies, two iron catapult bolts, and three granite projectile balls attest to the use of the site by the Roman military (Guichard and Deberge 2006).

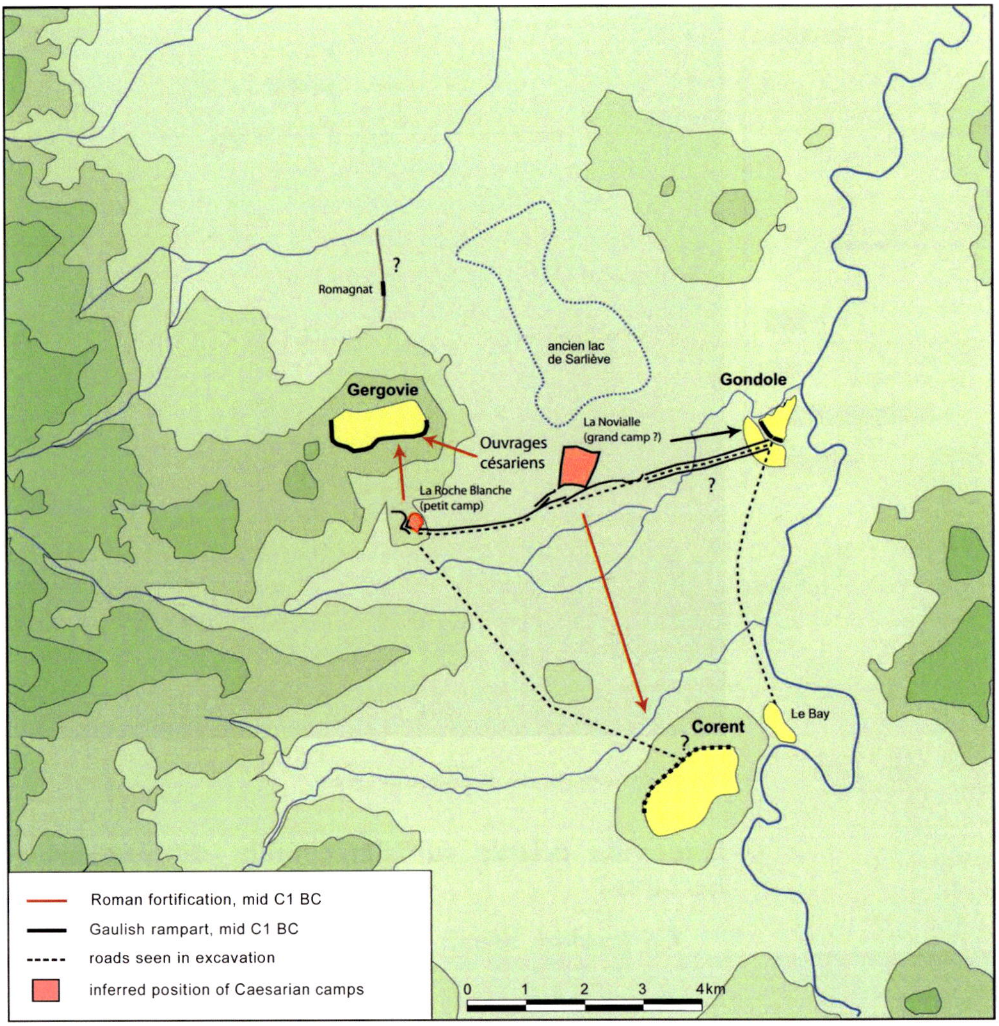

Figure 6.3 Map of Celtic oppida *and Roman siegeworks in the Limagne, Puy-de-Dôme (after Poux 2011, 243, courtesy Mathieu Poux).*

- The trace of the intermediate fortification has also been verified and established in four places. The single ditch, which is often truncated by erosion, had an asymmetric fill, suggesting a rampart on its southern side. It is not known how this engineering work connected up with the two camps.
- Various other ditch-type engineering works, unknown to the Second Empire excavations, have recently been unearthed in the lowlands and at the foot of the *oppidum*. These include a ditch associated with a wooden palisade to the north of the large camp in the ancient lake of Sarliève, which was cultivated land at the time, before the paludization (development of marshy conditions) of the lake, which

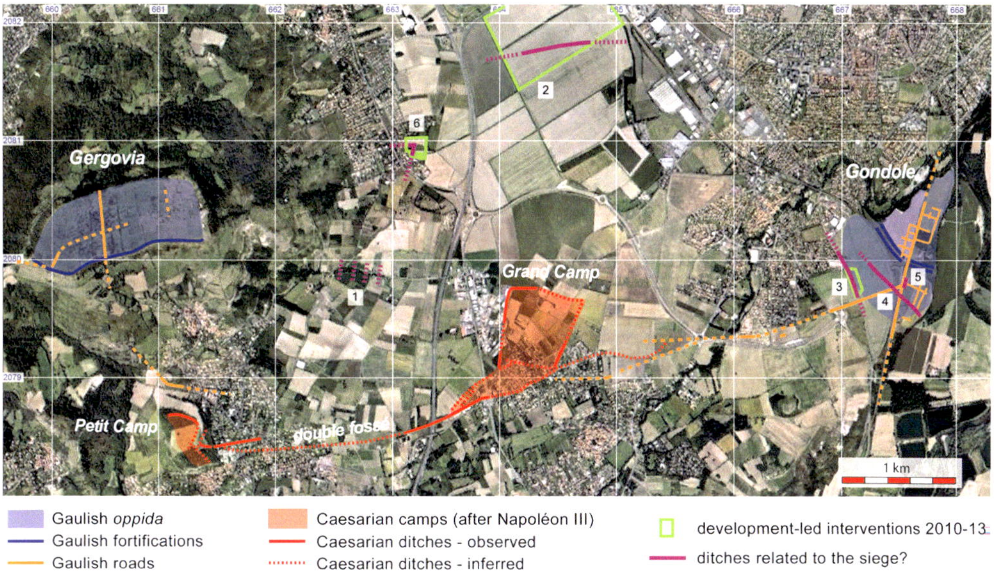

Figure 6.4 The Roman siegeworks between Gergovia (top left, in blue) and Gondole (on the right, in blue), Puy-de-Dôme (courtesy Y. Deberge).

occurred shortly afterwards, in the early Roman period (Trément *et al.* 2007). This type of arrangement is very much like that discovered in the Roman siegeworks of Alesia at the foot of Mont Réa. Another identical ditch segment over 200 m long has been discovered opposite the *oppidum* of Gondole. It is irregular in form, even if it is predominantly V-shaped with relatively steep sides and a flat bottom. A final trace of linear engineering work has been identified opposite the exit from the oppidum where it bars access routes to the fortification.

Finally, the entire site contains a series of finds of militaria that are entirely consistent in their typology with those from Alesia (Figure 6.5). A *scorpio* (catapult) tip lodged in the south-western rampart of Merdogne is especially noteworthy.

Can it be concluded from this set of old and new evidence that a positive identification has been made? It will be observed first that the archaeological works of the Second Empire have indeed been confirmed. The location of the small camp at La Roche Blanche is an excellent argument for locating the Gauls' stronghold at Merdogne rather than Gondole. As for Corent, which was not fortified, it obviously does not count any more than other fanciful sites suggested in recent years. Was Gondole itself even fortified? The question is apparently still under debate, but it is clear that Merdogne offered a far more daunting defensive position, above all because, as said, its rampart had been rebuilt. The position of the large camp on the low-lying land at the centre of the arrangement, between the two high points, and its protection by ditches lined with fences to the north and east are good arguments for seeing this as effective protection against an attack from the rear. This threat, which

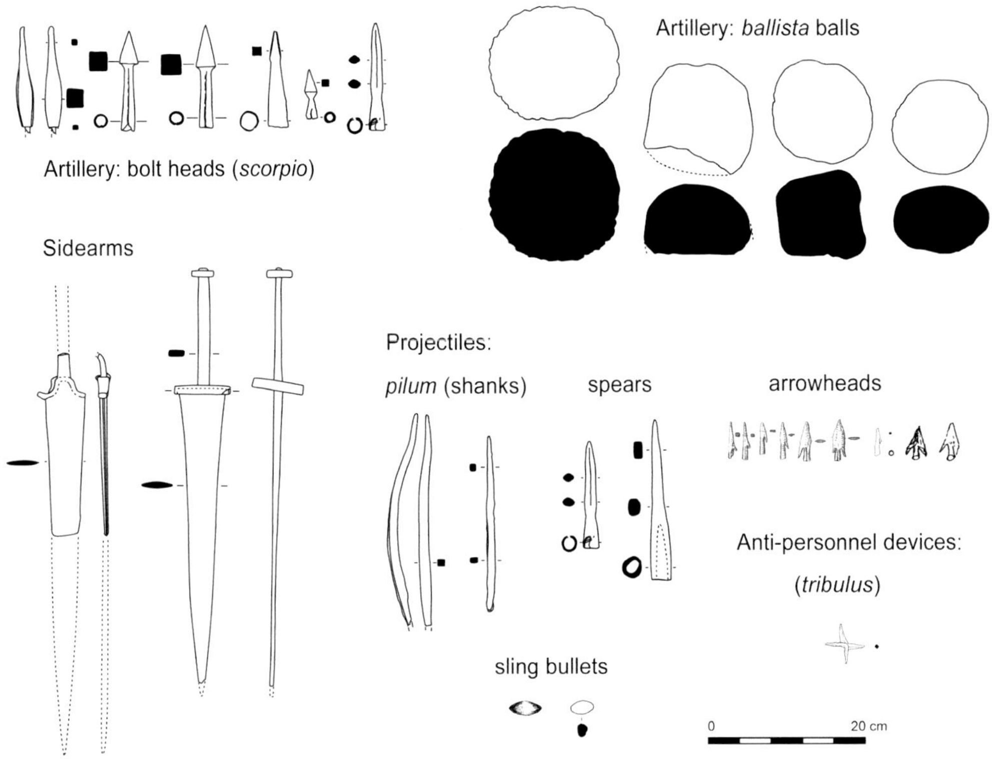

Figure 6.5 Types of weapons discovered around Gergovia (courtesy Y. Deberge).

Caesar's text accounts for since the Aedui had then gone over to Vercingetorix's side and were attacking Caesar in his back was real enough (*BG* 7.38–40). As the position of the Gauls was too strong, the Roman troops were forced to lift the siege after several fruitless assaults and to move back north.

Although not completely elucidated, much headway has been made with the Gergovia dossier in recent years. The physical identity of the capital of the Arverni and the settlement does, however, remain a problem that has not been definitively solved. It could not have been Merdogne, which may just have been a stronghold brought back into service at the time of the Gallic War, in anticipation of threats to come. M. Poux has argued for a 'multi-polar' Gergovia (Corent + Gondole + Merdogne) around a fertile plain, which is a brilliant and attractive hypothesis, because the locations are so close. But it is a novel and unproven hypothesis to date (Poux 2011).

The siege and battle of Alesia

Few ancient battlefields are as well documented as Alesia both through Caesar's writings (*BG* 7.68–69) and archaeological excavations. The events occurred at the end of the summer of 52 BC, after those of Gergovia. The account closes Caesar's book and is its climax, earning the *imperator* an unprecedented 20 days of official thanksgiving in Rome as if the conquest were already complete. That at any rate was what the conqueror wanted people to believe, concerned about good propaganda at a time when his political adversaries in Rome were becoming a threat. In point of fact, the fighting was to go on for another two years.

The circumstances are common knowledge: having been thwarted at Gergovia, the Roman army moved north and rebuilt its strength around Langres during the summer, before setting off back for southern France. It was a considerable military force of 10 to 12 legions or 40,000 to 60,000 men, allowing for losses in previous engagements. The army of the Gallic coalition, including the Aedui, blocked his path somewhere in the Saône valley. There ensued a first battle between Caesar's German cavalry and Vercingetorix's cavalry. At the end of this indecisive fight, Vercingetorix took refuge in the *oppidum* of the Mandubii at Alesia. For once, Caesar gave a relatively detailed description (Figures 6.6, 6.7)

> 69: The actual stronghold of Alesia was set atop of a hill, in a very lofty situation, apparently impregnable save by blockade. The bases of the hill were washed on two separate sides by rivers. Before the town a plain extended for a length of about three miles; on all the other sides there were hills surrounding the town at a short distance, and equal to it in height. Under the wall, on the side which looked eastward, the forces of the Gauls had entirely occupied all this intervening space, and had made in front a ditch and a rough wall six feet high. The perimeter of the siege-works which the Romans were beginning had a length of eleven miles. Camps had been pitched at convenient spots, and three-and-twenty forts had been constructed on the line. In these pickets would be posted by day to prevent any sudden sortie; by night the same stations were held by sentries and strong garrisons...

> 72: [Caesar] dug all round [the Gallic stronghold] two trenches, fifteen feet broad and of equal depth; and the inner one, where the ground was level with the plain or sank below it, he filled with water diverted from the river. Behind the trenches he constructed a ramp and palisade twelve feet high; to this he added a breastwork and battlements, with large fraises [stakes] projecting at the junction of screens and ramp, to check the upward advance of the enemy; and all round the works he set turrets at intervals of eighty feet... 73: Caesar... thought proper to make a further addition to these works, in order that the lines might be defensible by a smaller number of troops. Accordingly, trunks or very stout branches of trees were cut, and the tops thereof barked and sharpened, and continuous trenches five feet deep were dug. Into these the stumps were sunk and fastened at the bottom so that they could not be torn up, while the bough-ends were left projecting. They were in rows of five fastened and entangled together, and anyone who pushed into them must impale himself on the sharpest of stakes. These they called 'markers'. In front of these, in diagonal rows arranged like a figure of five [V], pits three feet deep were dug, sloping inwards slightly to the bottom. In these, tapering stakes as thick as a man's thigh, sharpened at the top and fire-hardened, were sunk so as to project no more than four fingers' breadth from the ground; at the same time, to make all strong and firm, the earth was trodden down hard for one foot from the bottom, and the remainder of the pit was covered over with twigs and brushwood to conceal the trap. Eight

Figure 6.6 Plan of Alesia, Côte-d'Or, from Napoléon III's *Histoire de Jules César*, pl. 23.

Figure 6.7 Air photograph of Alesia, from the west (courtesy R. Goguey).

> rows of this kind were dug, three feet apart. From its resemblance to the flower the device was called a 'lily'. In front of all these, logs a foot long, with iron hooks firmly attached, were buried altogether in the ground and scattered at brief intervals all over the field, and these they called 'spurs'. 74: When all these arrangements had been completed Caesar constructed parallel entrenchments of the same kind facing the other way, against the enemy outside, following the most favourable ground that the locality afforded, with a circuit of fourteen miles. This he did to secure the garrisons of the entrenchments from being surrounded by a host, however large it might chance to be.

Then comes the account of the siege, which breaks down into several episodes and probably lasted several weeks, while a sizeable army of Gauls marched to support Vercingetorix. In a final battle that probably involved the entire theatre of operations and during which the Romans, caught in crossfire, risked annihilation, Caesar's army, which was well protected by its defences, won out. The following day Vercingetorix was handed over by his troops and the Gauls surrendered.

Despite this account, the site of the siege would probably not have been easy to identify if an old historical tradition had not associated it with Alise-Sainte-Reine, near Montbard, in Burgundy. It should be added that the discovery in 1839 of a large stone inscription in the Gaulish language mentioning the place-name *ALISIIA* (*Corpus Inscriptionum Latinarum* XIII, 2880) supported this traditional location. Extensive excavations were therefore undertaken from 1861 to 1865 under the Second Empire and were resumed more recently by a Franco-German team from 1991–1997 (Reddé and von Schnurbein 2001). So what, then, is the current archaeological state of play?

First it should be recalled that the Second Empire excavation work proceeded by cutting narrow sections across uneven ground that was strewn with ancient vineyard trenches on the slopes and palaeochannels in the floodplain. Despite inevitable mistakes among these various types of natural and man-made structures and despite hesitations and changes of heart, Napoléon III's men managed to identify most of the Roman military installations: a number of camps and the two main linear defensive systems set up by the Roman army, and known as the 'contravallation' for the inner line besieging the *oppidum* and the 'circumvallation' for the outward-facing defensive line designed to hold off the relief army. At the same time, a substantial quantity of finds was unearthed, of which only the coins and weapons were kept in the 19th century. Commendable records (Figure 6.8) were kept at the time, especially plan views and cross-sections (Le Gall 1989; Olivier and Reddé 2015). Even so, the classical method of the day was unable to identify small features that were difficult to interpret, especially postholes and traps. It should be added that the terrain has been unevenly eroded since the events of the year 52 BC and the structures have not all been conserved identically everywhere. The ancient soil horizons, in particular, have only been preserved in rare locations, meaning that the shallow traps described by Caesar are not always observable in the field. Lastly, Napoléon III himself often imposed his own views and choices, considerably simplifying the complexity of the excavation data in the publication of the finds.

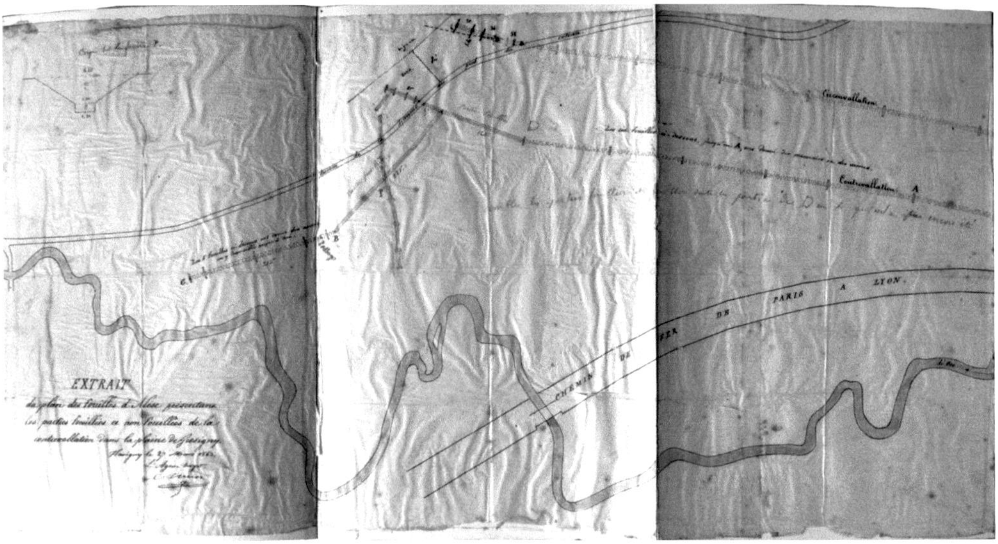

Figure 6.8 Excavations at the foot of Mont Réa. The plan records the location of the trenches and the ditch profile, with annotations indicating where finds were made (drawing by P. Millot, March 1863; from the Alesia archive).

The recent Franco-German project has identified anew Caesar's siegeworks and checked the claims of the Second Empire investigators. Napoléon III had identified several camps, located on the hills and in the low-lying areas of the site. Three have been confirmed by the recent excavations: Camps A, B and C. The last two, located facing one another to the north and south of the Roman installations, were also the largest (approximately 7 ha). Their shape followed the contours, which, contrary to what is often believed, was common in Caesarian and Augustan military engineering works. Their siting on hilltops accounts for the form of construction with dry-stone walls of locally extracted material. They are incontrovertibly Roman camps, because of the presence at their gateways of characteristic obstacles – the *titulum* and *clavicula*[2] – and military material found in their ditches. Camp C has, moreover, been identified as that of Labienus, Caesar's first lieutenant, because two pieces of slingshot marked with his name were found there (Figure 6.9, 1). Camp A, which was much smaller (2.3 ha), was protected by a sloping earth rampart topped by wooden posts. It has yielded quite rich finds (fibulae, coins, weapons, a ladle, pottery), and in particular a piece of leather tenting. The camps in the floodplain identified by Napoléon III's excavators cannot be systematically confirmed because of modern development that has destroyed the western part of the site. In other instances, especially at the foot of Mont Réa (Camp D) and in the floodplain of Les Laumes (Camp I), it is clear that Napoléon III's men came to mistaken conclusions. From this review, it can be concluded that a number of Caesar's troop emplacements remain to be discovered, especially on Mont Réa to the north and Pennevelle to the east.

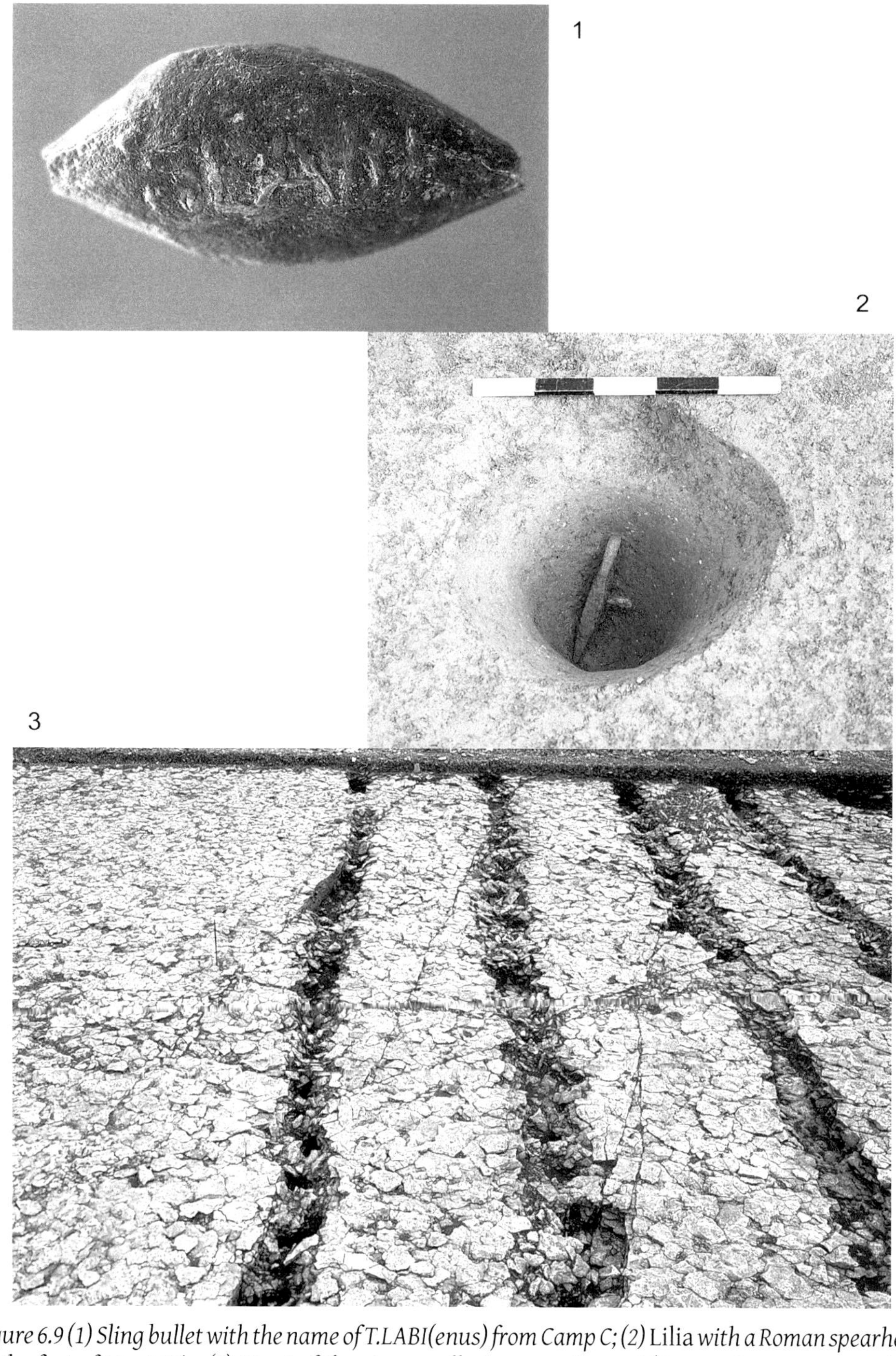

Figure 6.9 (1) Sling bullet with the name of T.LABI(enus) from Camp C; (2) Lilia *with a Roman spearhead at the foot of Mont Réa; (3)* Cippi *of the circumvallation near Camp C (Franco-German excavations, photos R. Collot and P. Barral).*

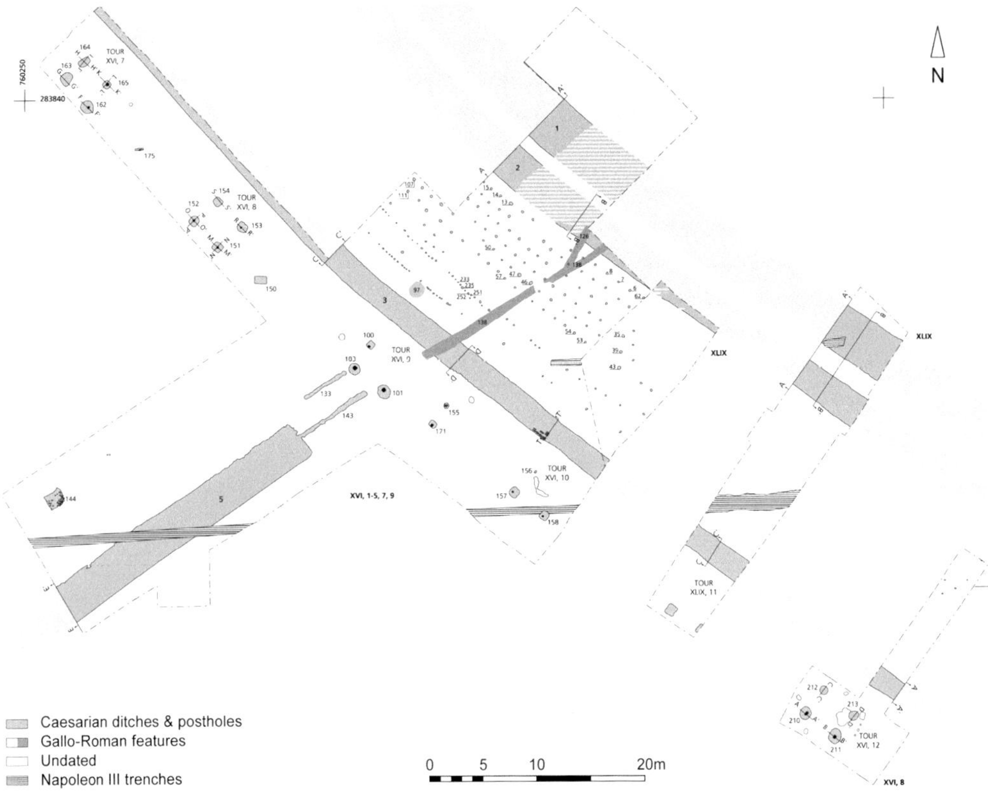

Figure 6.10 German excavations (RGK) in the Plaine des Laumes (after Reddé and von Schnurbein 2001, pl. hors texte 11).

The forts (*castella*) were not excavated in the recent campaigns. A previously unknown fort was identified at l'Épineuse crossroads, at the eastern end of the town of Les Laumes. It was located between the two defensive lines and covered a square of about 100 m × 100 m, blocking off the dangerous narrow corridor in which the Roman legionaries were massed. Other devices of this type are surely waiting to be discovered.

The contravallation has been recognized in various places where Napoléon III had identified it (Figures 6.10, 6.11); the circumvallation, however, is more problematic. It was the less complete of the two lines of defence, having been built subsequently as protection from an attack from the rear. Some of the ditches were probably not fully dug, and the system of traps was probably less developed; above all the line cannot be traced with certainty on the slopes of Mont Réa because of the erosion that has affected the Caesarian works on what is sometimes quite a steep slope. This is certainly one of the sectors where future research would be beneficial.

The recent excavations have above all shown the extreme variability of the defensive system from one line and one sector to another (Figure 6.12). The topography and the nature of materials available locally dictated the actual form the Caesarian siegeworks took. They were in keeping with a general plan that examination reveals

Figure 6.11 Reconstruction of the contravallation in the Plaine des Laumes (drawing J.-P. and C. Adam).

was not specific to Alesia but was based on familiar practice for the Romans. Numerous applications of it are found over time, in particular at the siege of Numantia against the Celtiberians in 134–133 BC.

On the limestone plateaux, the construction method used for the defensive lines was identical to that of the camps: slabs known in French as *lozes* dug locally from the ground were built into a dry-stone wall, some 5.4 m wide; in the floodplain, where clay and turf prevailed, unfired bricks or sods were assembled on the spot, much like breeze blocks, in a manner well-known in the Roman army. The rampart was as thick as that of the defensive lines on the plateau, and, judging from Caesar's writings, stood about 3.5 m high, without the breastwork.

The wall was flanked by wooden towers, which were clearly observed in the recent excavations, spaced at variable distances apart depending on how much of a threat there was in each sector. The wall was generally protected by two or even three ditches in part of the very exposed floodplain of Les Laumes. The types of obstacle fit Caesar's description: metal spikes (*stimuli*), pits (*lilia*) (Figure 6.9, 2), and branches (*cippi*) planted in several rows parallel to the ditches, have all been identified (Figure 6.9, 3). However, the layout of these systems of traps is subject to marked variations according to the extent of the threat locally.

Can this divergence with Caesar's writings be explained? A detailed description of all the traps put in place by Caesar around Alesia would have taken up a great deal of space in the book with a wealth of unnecessary detail; it would have pointlessly blurred the account for readers who, it should be remembered, had neither maps, nor

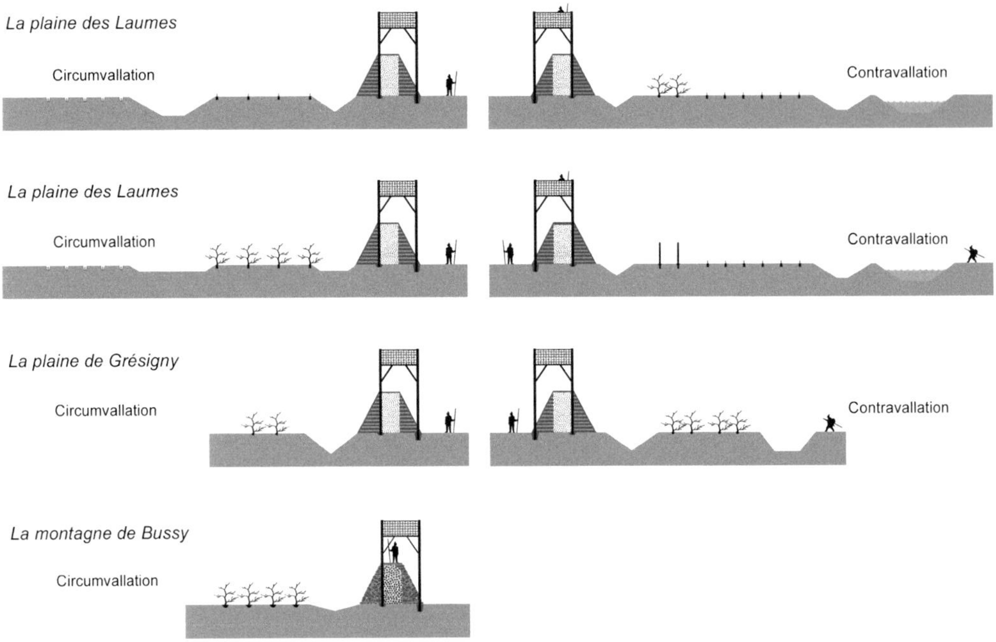

Figure 6.12 Types of Roman defences at Alesia (after Reddé and von Schnurbein 2001, figs 296–297).

plans, nor obviously photos! An understanding of events required a description that was not detailed like an archaeology book, but that was generic, so to speak, and in keeping with the historiographical tradition of the time. All told, each of the devices Caesar describes are indeed found in the field at Alesia, and that is the essential point. Their practical implementation was a matter of detail of little interest to readers who would not readily have understood it for want of convenient topographical markers.

Studies of the material unearthed both in the 19th century and in the recent excavations have allowed useful comparison with chronologically similar collections. They confirm the material is essentially homogeneous, barring a few obvious exceptions. This provides a valuable reference context for the middle of the 1st century BC. The Franco-German studies of 1991–1997 have provided a renewed scientific basis for the study of the Caesarian siegeworks at Alesia, that have now been exhaustively published, which was not the case for the Second Empire excavations (Reddé and von Schnurbein 2001). Obviously, this does not mean that all questions have been answered: on the contrary, the new research has highlighted the limits of our knowledge, especially when it comes to the site's topography.

Uxellodunum

The siege of Uxellodunum, the final stronghold of the Gauls, in 50 BC, is narrated by Hirtius, Caesar's lieutenant and his literary continuator since he was the one who wrote

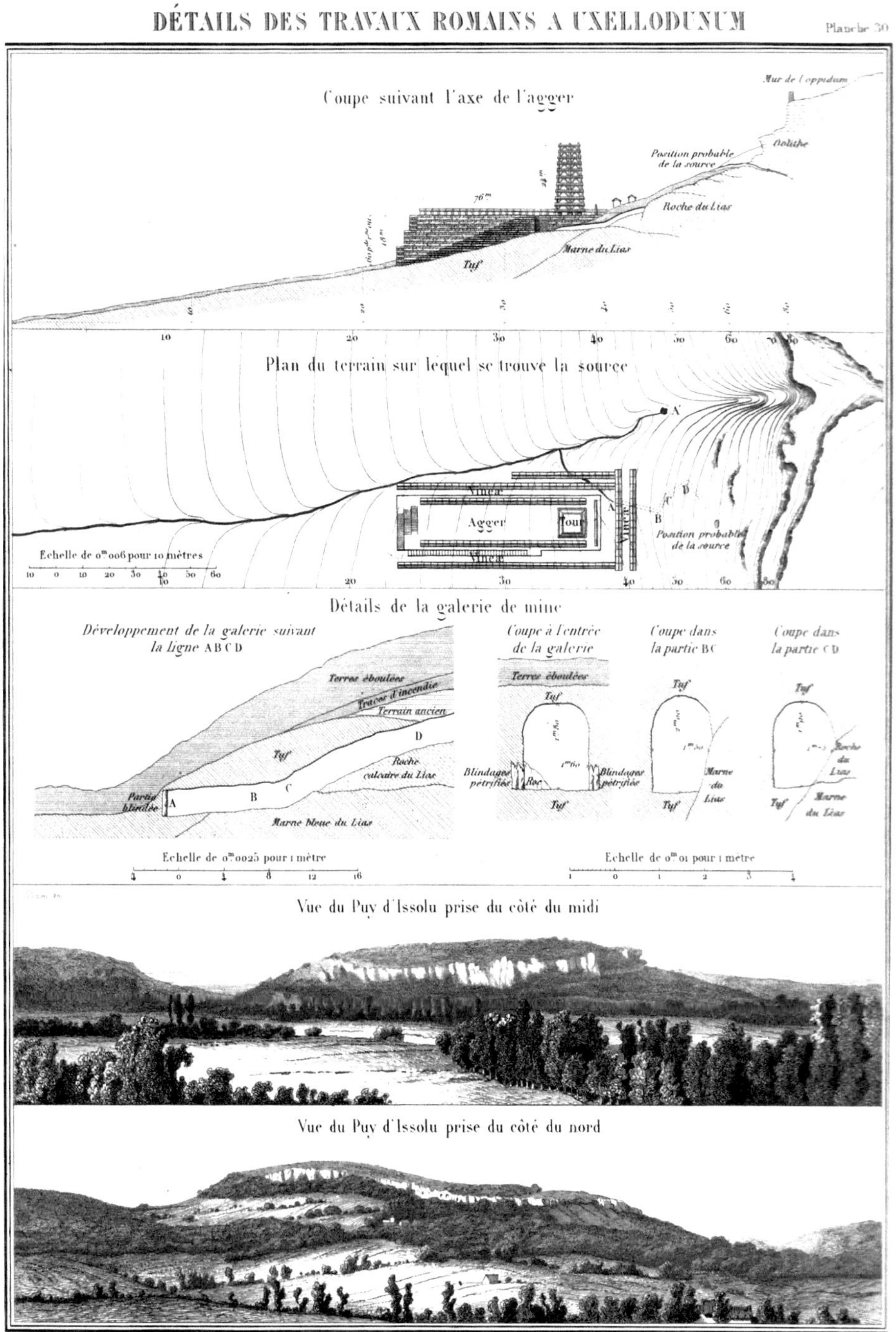

Figure 6.13 The Roman siegeworks at Uxellodunum, Lot, from Napoléon III's Histoire de Jules César, *pl. 30.*

the final book of the *Commentaries*. It will be recalled that after Alesia, the proconsul had to quell uprisings throughout the country. One of the noteworthy final episodes was among the Cadurci (in the Cahors region): Caesar's legates, C. Caninius and C. Fabius, came to grips with the Gallic chieftains Drappes and Lucterios, who had taken refuge in the naturally well-defended *oppidum* of Uxellodunum. C. Caninius began by setting up three camps on the high land around the site and constructing siegeworks. This is the classic scheme already seen at Alesia. Then Caesar himself came to direct operations that focused on a spring below the Gallic stronghold which was the water supply for the besieged. Caesar decided to cut off access to it (Figure 6.13).

> He began, just opposite the place, to push up mantlets against the hill and to build a ramp with great effort and continual fighting; for the townsfolk ran down from the higher ground and engaged without risk at long range, wounding many men as they doggedly worked upwards. However, our troops were not to be deterred from thrusting the mantlets forward and from defeating the local difficulties by sheer labour of engineering. At the same time they were pushing forward covered mines from the mantlets to the head of the spring; and this kind of work involved no risk, and could be done without suspicion on the part of the enemy. The ramp was built up to a height of sixty feet, and upon it was set a turret of ten stories, not, indeed, to reach the level of the walls, for no siege-works could effect that, but to overtop the level of the spring. When the artillery from the turret began to discharge missiles upon the line of approach to the spring, and the townsfolk could not get water without danger, not only cattle and beasts of burden, but even the great host of the enemy, were like to die of thirst. Terror-struck by this trouble, the townsfolk filled tubs with grease, pitch, and shingles, and rolled them burning on to the works, at the same time engaging with the utmost ferocity in order that the danger of the fight might prevent the Romans from extinguishing the fire. A mighty flame suddenly shot forth in the midst of the works; for everything that was discharged over the escarpment was held up by the mantlets and the ramp, and set fire to the particular object which checked its course. On the other hand, our soldiers, though handicapped by the dangerous character of the fighting and by the disadvantage of position, none the less endured every difficulty in the most gallant spirit. For the action went on at a considerable height and in sight of our army, and great shouting arose on both sides. So each man, in as conspicuous a fashion as he could – the better to make his valour known and approved – faced alike the missiles of the enemy and the flames.
>
> Seeing not a few of his men wounded, Caesar ordered cohorts to climb the height from every side of the town and under pretence of attacking the walls to raise a shout all round. This action terrified the townsfolk, and in their uncertainty as to what was going on in the other quarters they recalled their men-at-arms from the attempt on the works and set them along the walls. So our men, when the fighting ceased, speedily extinguished or cut away the parts of the works which had caught fire. Although the townsfolk continued to resist stoutly, and stuck to their resolve, even when they had lost a great part of their number through thirst, at last by means of the mines the feeders of the spring were cut off and diverted. This caused the perpetual spring suddenly to dry up... And so necessity forced them to surrender (*BG* 8.41–42).

The archaeological identification of Uxellodunum was based essentially on the account of this crucial episode. The narration of this stratagem fuelled the military literature of the time. Napoléon III's excavators haphazardly investigated other sites before finally

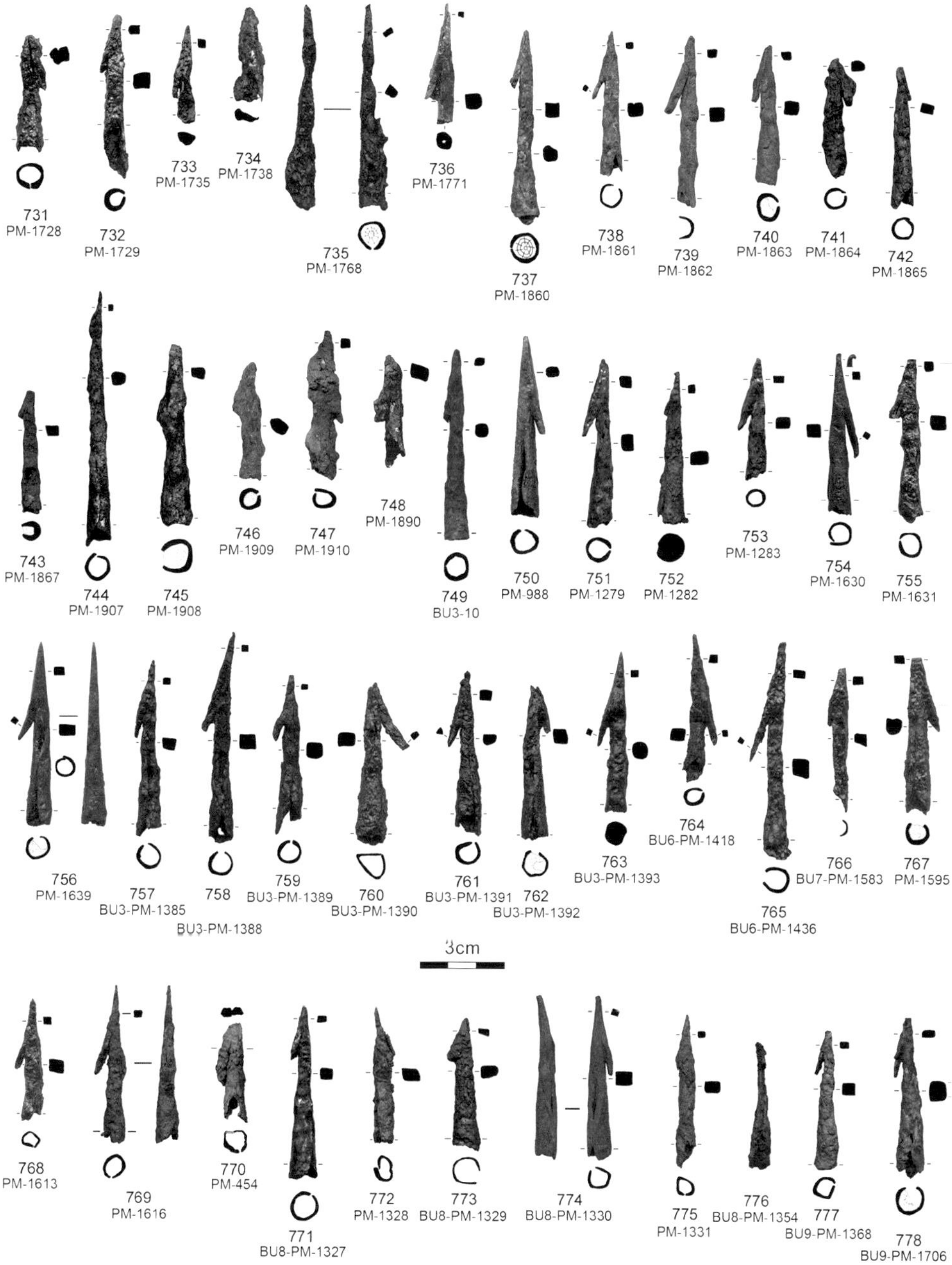

Figure 6.14 Arrowheads discovered at Uxellodunum (after Girault 2013).

turning to Le Puy d'Issolud. Neither the camps nor the siegeworks are known to date. The Second Empire excavations concentrated around the Fontaine de Loulié, where the initial digging by J.-B. Cessac in 1865 had revealed a spring, galleries leading to its head, catapult bolts at the foot of the *oppidum* and layers of burning. After being continued and then resumed in the 1990s by J.-P. Girault the research has recently been published (Girault 2013).

The main outcome of these recent campaigns is to accord credence to this 19th-century localization by revealing a whole complex of saps, the plan of which is not always clear, associated with a considerable amount of Roman militaria similar to what has been found at Alesia, primarily arrowheads and catapult bolt heads. We can add helmet parts, spearheads, *pila*, tools, hobnails, shield rims, coins and ceramics that fit perfectly with the archaeological context of the mid-1st century BC (Figure 6.14).

Sapping techniques had been practised for centuries by the time of the events. They are expounded by Aeneas Tacticus in the middle of the 4th century BC in his *Art of Siege* (*Poliorketika* 37.1–2) and then by Philo of Byzantium in his *Compendium of Mechanics* (*Mechanike Syntaxis* 5, C 7; Garlan 1974, 307). They applied essentially to attacking ramparts. Specialized sappers (*cunicularii*) featured besides under the command of the *praefectus fabrum*, the prefect of workmen, if the testimony of Vegetius is to be believed (*de Re Militari* 2.10). The finest archaeological example known is provided by the mine dug by the Sassanids under the rampart of Dura-Europos, which Simon James has recently shown to have been the theatre of an underground combat with chemical weapons, after a counter-mine dug by the besieged burst into the gallery (James 2011). These techniques borrowed from miners were not exclusive to Mediterraneans: the Gauls besieged at Avaricum, Caesar tells us (*BG* 7.22), toppled the Roman earthworks by mining beneath them. The concentration of missiles over a small surface area of a few hundred square metres is exceptional. It is all the more remarkable as a number of projectiles are lodged in the ground.

Conclusion

The archaeological record of Caesar's time in Gaul is both very scant and very rich. It is scant indeed considering that all those years of conflict have yielded just four sites of battles or sieges that have been truly identified and explored, although so much fighting went on! But it must also be considered, conversely, that without them archaeology would have no material traces of that war, made famous by the account of the great Latin writer who waged it and won it.

Had the proconsul's account not been written and preserved, would we be able to identify and understand the sites of the war? First of all, it is far from certain that we would even have looked for them; and we would not necessarily know how to interpret some of the remains that have been brought to light. It is the overlapping of both literary and archaeological sources that has enabled us, at Alesia, to look for what was not known and to interpret it, to relate some of the evidence uncovered in the field with the text, and in return to understand the literary mechanisms by which the account was drafted and matters were simplified.

Obviously, we must allow for the circumstances in which the ancient historians wrote, their motives, their sources, and the discrepancy between their conception of history and our own. In the cases of Alesia and Gergovia, told by the main protagonist, Caesar himself, we cannot ignore the political circumstances of the time: the Roman general was grappling with substantial military difficulties, at a time when a struggle for power was raging in Rome and the account of the Gallic War, told to the Senate and the Roman people, was by no means an academic exercise seeking to be scientifically objective, but a work designed to further Caesar's political career and justify his actions. The *imperator*, as careful studies have shown, made a habit of twisting the truth for his own benefit, although naturally without completely misrepresenting it, so as to hide his failures, ensure his political propaganda, and hone his image for posterity (Rambaud 1953). It should not be forgotten, either, that the idea of 'objectivity' in history is a recent one, and a world away from the practice of the ancients, save a few notable exceptions such as Thucydides and Polybius. Cicero himself explains that history is a 'rhetorical' art, meant to move the reader and depict events as 'drama' (*de Legibus* I.2). It is this interplay between the various sciences used in investigating the ancient world that today provides us with fresh and fertile insights into classical sources.

Notes

1 For discussion of these sites see the chapters by Hornung, Krausz and Kaenel in this volume.
2 The *titulum* was a straight-line obstacle (ditch and fence or embankment) in front of a gateway to block it off.

Bibliography

Deberge, Y., Baucheron, F., Cabezuelo, U., Caillat, P., Gatto, E., Landry, C., Leguet, D., Pasty, J.-F., Pertlweiser, T., Vermeulen, C. and Vernet, G. (2014) Témoignages de la Guerre des Gaules dans le bassin clermontois, nouveaux apports. *Revue archéologique du Centre de la France* 53, 2014. Available at http://journals.openedition.org/racf/2071 (accessed 15 June 2017).

Deberge, Y., Foucras, S., Pasty, J.-F., Hulin, G., Jud, P., Leguet, D., Millet, M. and Simon, F.-X. (2018) Présence militaires romaines dans le bassin clermontois. In M. Reddé (ed.), *L'armée romaine en gaule à l'époque républicaine. Nouveaux témoignages archéologiques.* 73–112. Glux-en-Glenne, Collection Bibracte 28.

Garlan, Y. (1974) *Recherches de poliorcétique grecque.* Paris, Bibliothèque des Écoles Françaises d'Athènes et de Rome 223.

Girault, J.-P. (2013) *La fontaine de Loulié au Puy d'Issolud. Le dossier archéologique du siège d'Uxellodunum.* Glux-en-Glenne, Collection Bibracte 23.

Guichard, V. and Deberge, Y. (2006) La Roche-Blanche / Gergovie / Gergovia. In M. Reddé, R. Brulet, R. Fellmann, J.K. Haalebos and S. von Schnurbein (eds), *L'architecture de la Gaule romaine. Les fortifications militaires,* 371–373. Paris/Bordeaux, Documents d'Archéologie Française 100/ Ausonius éditions.

James, S. (2011) Stratagems, Combat, and 'Chemical Warfare' in the Siege Mines of Dura-Europos. *American Journal of Archaeology* 115–1, 69–101.

Lambot, B. and Casagrande, P. (1997) Une monnaie d'Ebusus sur l'oppidum de « Vieux-Laôn » à Saint-Thomas (Aisne). Nouvelles données archéologiques sur Bibrax et le camp de Mauchamp (*César B.G. II*). *Bulletin de la Société Archéologique Champenoise* 90–2, 15–29.

Le Gall, J. (1989) *Fouilles d'Alise-Sainte-Reine 1861–1865.* Paris, Mémoires de l'Académie des Inscriptions et Belles Lettres 9.

Napoléon III (1865–1866) *Histoire de Jules César.* Paris, Champion.

Olivier, L. and Reddé, M. (2015) L'Album des fouilles d'Alise redécouvert dans les archives de la Commission de la Topographie des Gaules. *Antiquités nationales* 45, 69–79.

Pertlwieser, T., Deberge, Y. and Ott, I. (2010) Das südliche Befestigungswerk des Oppidums von Gergovia (Puy-de-Dôme). In S. Fichtl (ed.), *Murus Celticus: architecture et fonctions des remparts de l'âge du Fer,* 281–296. Glux-en-Glenne, Collection Bibracte 19.

Peyre, C. (1979) Le champ de bataille de l'Aisne (*César, B.G. II, 8–9*). *Revue des Études Latines* 56, 175–217.

Poux, M. (ed.) (2011) *Corent: Voyage au cœur d'une ville gauloise.* Paris, Errance.

Poux, M., Demierre, M., Garcia, M. and Laurenson, R. (2015) *Le sanctuaire de Corent (Puy-de-Dôme, Auvergne): vestiges et rituels.* Paris, Gallia supplément 62.

Rambaud, M. (1953) *L'art de la déformation historique dans les Commentaires de César.* Paris, Les belles Lettres.

Reddé, M. (1995) Titulum et clavicula. A propos des fouilles récentes d'Alésia. *Revue Archéologique de l'Est* 46, 349–356.

Reddé, M. and von Schnurbein, S. (eds) (2001), *Alésia. Fouilles et recherches franco-allemandes sur les travaux militaires romains autour du Mont-Auxois (1991–1997).* Paris, Mémoires de l'Académie des Inscriptions et Belles-Lettres 22.

Trément, F., Rialland, Y., Prat, B., Milcent, P.-Y., Mennessier-Jouannet, C., Marinval, P., Macaire, J. J., Lopez Saez, J.-A., Loison, G., Liabeuf, R., Fournier, G., Fourmont, A., Dousteyssier, B., Cabanis, J M., Bréhéret, G. and Argant, J. (2007) Un ancien lac au pied de l'oppidum de Gergovie (Puy-de-Dôme): interactions sociétés-milieux dans le bassin de Sarliève à l'Holocène. *Gallia* 64, 289–351.

Chapter 7

Caesar's conquest and the archaeology of mass violence in the Germanic frontier zone

Nico Roymans

Roman imperialist expansion and the study of mass violence

Historical evidence convincingly shows us that the formation and expansion of the Roman empire, like that of other empires in antiquity, was very much the result of an aggressive military expansion. A standard feature of the wars of conquest was the combination of overwhelming military superiority and the use of brutal violence against populations that resisted Roman domination. The theme of mass violence and imperial expansion has until now generated little serious archaeological research. Scholarship has been dominated by the Romanization debate and the myth of the *Pax Romana*. However, this situation has started to change in the last two decades under the influence of post-colonial theory and the corresponding critical view of imperialism and militarism. There is also the impact of the general increase of military conflict and aggression in our modern society where the theme of violence dominates public debate. However, most important is the availability of new and better archaeological evidence that enables us to develop a more accurate picture of the Roman conquests and their direct social impact on the subjected societies.

My paper focuses on the situation in the Germanic frontier zone in the extreme north of Gaul during the period of the Caesarian conquest, thereby discussing the topic of Roman imperialist expansion and the use of mass violence. I hope to demonstrate that archaeology has the potential to make a serious contribution to the study of the scale, spatial dimension and local social impact of historically documented cases of mass violence in the conquest period. I will do this by addressing the new domain of conflict archaeology that has stimulated the historical-archaeological research of battlefields, military infrastructure and massacre sites. Recently the first steps have been taken towards a more systematic approach to the archaeology of mass violence and genocide (Roymans and Fernández-Götz 2015; Quesada-Sanz 2015; see also Guilaine and Sémelin 2016). It is my aim to contribute to the further development of this field.

Since the development of the processual paradigm in the 1970s, there has been a kind of taboo in Anglophone archaeology on the study of Caesar's military campaigns in Gaul. It was seen as a return to a traditional historical archaeology that was just interested in famous men, major military events, and aimed at tracing battles in the archaeological record (Lloyd 1986, 41). However, by focusing on the themes of mass violence, genocide and imperialism, this research has something to offer that history, classics and military history cannot provide. Because of its anthropological and sociological orientation, and its link with both the natural sciences and modern historical research on ancient warfare (Hanson 2007), conflict archaeology has a wider scope than the traditional domain of military history, and asks different questions that also include the social, cultural and ritual aspects of warfare.

Caesar's conquest of the Germanic frontier zone

Caesar's *Commentaries* on his conquest of Gaul (*BG*) are a unique document for the study of the violent aspects of Roman imperial expansion, as they represent a detailed eye-witness account by the leading general himself. Especially in the Germanic frontier zone, the conquest had dramatic negative effects. The numbers of enemy casualties he reports are often extremely high and his descriptions of mass violence are often pitiless and explicit, making his actions appear excessively cruel and unethical by modern standards (Bellemore 2012). Consequently, these instances have been interpreted in modern literature as massacres, atrocities, or even genocide, and they raise the question of the value associations of mass violence in the Roman imperial discourse.

However, the interpretation of Caesar's war narrative is not without its problems. How reliable are his commentaries, and to what extent can his 'war in words' be qualified as propagandistic rhetoric? There are different opinions on the local social impact of Caesar's conquest. Some scholars accept his descriptions of mass violence as an historical reality, while others strongly put into perspective its scale and societal impact, regarding Caesar's claims as exaggerations (Henige 1998) or even as a type of deliberate historical deformation.[1] Only archaeology has the potential to evaluate the impact of Caesar's conquests with an independent dataset.

Caesar describes three methods of mass violence against groups in the Germanic frontier zone that resisted Roman domination:

a. mass-enslavement and deportation of an entire group;
b. massacring a complete community, including its non-combatant population, after a battle;
c. annihilating a dispersed community by employing a scorched earth policy.

The archaeological record of the different types of mass violence is clearly quite different, as are the methodologies we need for gathering and interpreting the evidence. Below I will discuss examples of the above strategies and show in what ways archaeology can be used to get a more accurate picture of them.

The mass enslavement of the Aduatuci (57 BC)

A major source of income for Caesar during his Gallic Wars was the large-scale taking of prisoners among enemy groups and selling them as slaves. In Book 2 of his narrative he describes the dramatic case of the conquest of the *oppidum* of the Germanic Aduatuci in modern Belgium, after which its entire population of 53,000 individuals were sold as slaves and deported to Italy. After this disastrous event, the Aduatuci no longer played a role of political significance, and soon completely disappeared from the tribal map.

One of the more spectacular discoveries of the last few years is the plausible identification of a late Iron Age fortification at Thuin (Belgium) as the *oppidum* of the Aduatuci (Roymans and Scheers 2012). This fortification (Figure 7.1) occupies a plateau of more than 13 ha and can be reached on the eastern side via a narrow finger of land 60 m wide. Several strands of evidence suggest that this was the *oppidum* conquered by Caesar, as argued in our 2012 publication: a radiocarbon date for charcoal from the rampart giving a date between 90 BC and AD 60; the location of this late Iron Age fortification in the territory of the Aduatuci; the absence of finds from the early Roman period which means that the fortification did not survive into Roman times; the match with the topography described by Caesar; the discovery of several gold hoards that can be dated to the early 50s BC and which seem to reflect a single event; and finally, and very importantly, concentrations of Roman lead sling bullets indicating a siege by the Roman army. The sling bullets appeared in two separate concentrations: on the wall near the main entrance of the fortification and on the other side of the river Biesmelle. Their concentration at the main rampart suggests that they were in fact used by the attacking side. With the identification of the *oppidum* of the Aduatuci at Thuin we have probably located one of the major 'crime sites' from the period of the Roman conquest.

The massacre of the Tencteri and Usipetes (55 BC)

In Book 4 of *BG*, Caesar describes the dramatic fate of the Tencteri and Usipetes, two tribes from the interior of Germania who had yielded in the preceding years to the pressure of Suebian tribes and who had consequently given up their homeland. In the winter of 56/55 BC they crossed the Rhine and lived on the stores of the Menapii. When Caesar was informed of this he directly advanced with his complete army against the two tribes (Figure 7.2). The Germans gathered all their able-bodied men, women and children with all their possessions in a central encampment, while Caesar concentrated his troops in a camp 12 km away. A strategic advance by the Roman army provoked the Usipetes and Tencteri into a cavalry fight, which gave Caesar the excuse he needed to attack them.

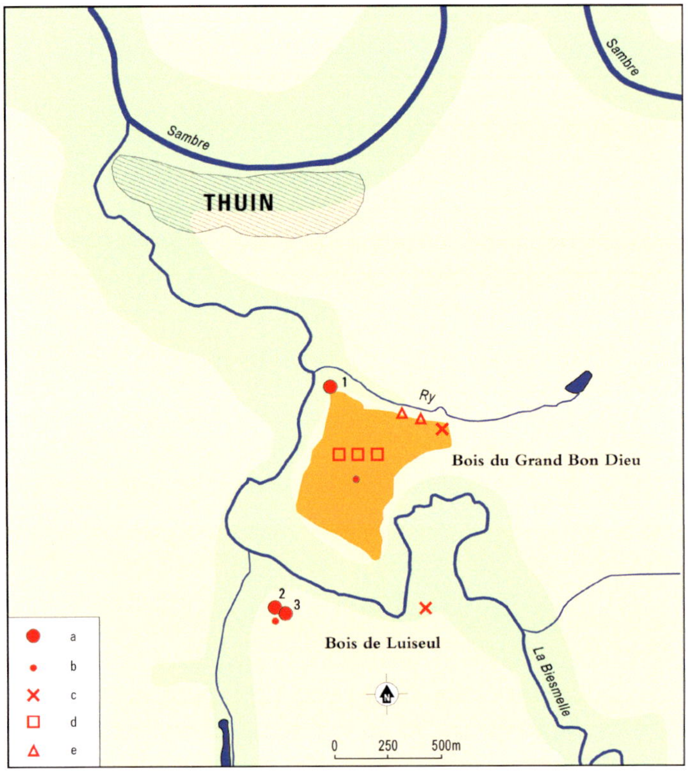

Figure 7.1 Thuin, Belgium: topography of the late Iron Age fortification (shaded orange) and the location of gold hoards (1–3) and clusters of Roman lead sling bullets (x). Key: a – gold hoards, b – isolated gold coin, c – sling bullets, d – metal tools, e – bronze ornaments.

The conquest of the enemy camp can hardly be called a battle; in the absence of their leaders the Germans completely panicked and fled *en masse*. Caesar subsequently ordered his troops to cut down as many as possible, including women and children. At the confluence of the Rhine and the Meuse the fleeing Germans could not go any further. Here they were slaughtered in great numbers or drowned in the nearby river. The total number would have come to 430,000, which is highly implausible if not absurd. Caesar proudly reports that his army did not lose a single man and that only a few were wounded.

Caesar's narrative is vague about the exact topography of his operations against the Tencteri and Usipetes. The main geographical point of reference is his statement that the final massacre took place at the confluence of the rivers Rhine and Meuse where the fleeing Germans were trapped.[2] This situates Caesar's action in the region between the Waal – the main branch of the Lower Rhine – and the Meuse (Figure 7.2). Several Roman authors mention the Meuse/Waal junction. However, the complex dynamics of river systems in a Holocene delta make it impossible to simply read the confluence

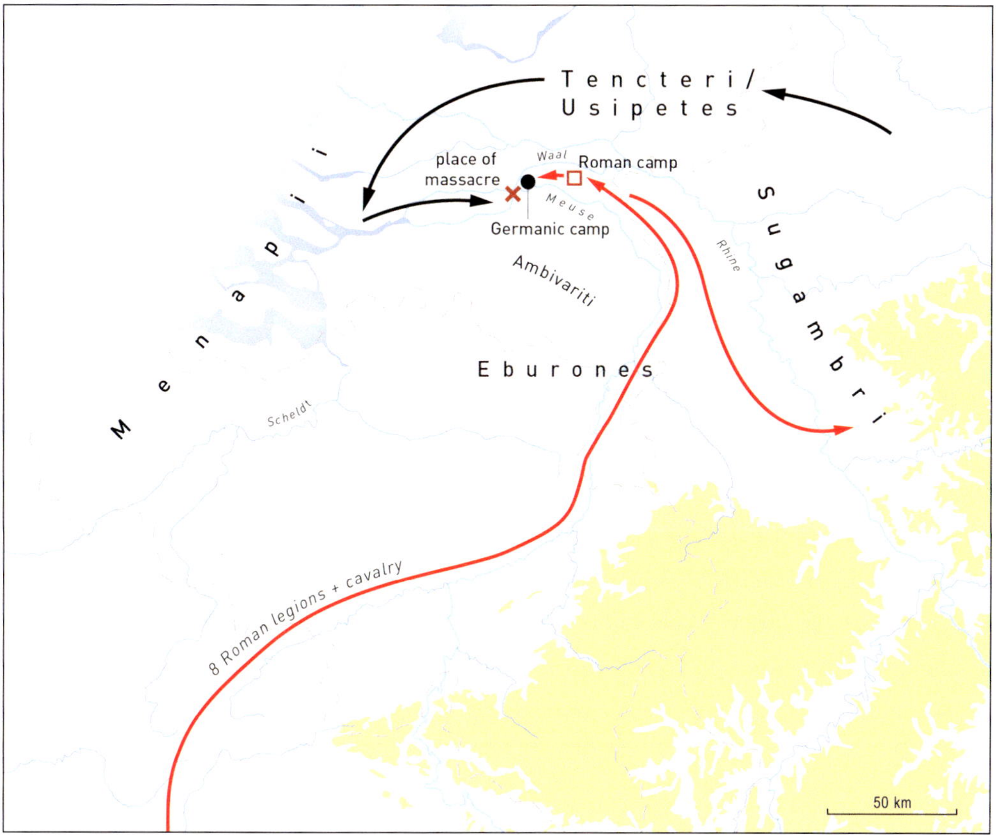

Figure 7.2 Geographical reconstruction of Caesar's Germanic campaign of 55 BC.

from modern topographical maps. We should proceed here from a palaeogeographical reconstruction based on physical-geographical surveys (Figure 7.3). This demonstrates that in the early 1st century AD the main Meuse/Waal confluence was situated near Rossum some 80 km from the Dutch coast. There are geological, historical and archaeological arguments to support this location (Roymans 2018).

Starting from this location, the camp of the Tencteri and Usipetes should be placed directly to the east. Caesar reports that the fleeing population was pursued by the Roman army after the fall of the Germanic camp. We are dealing here with the usual brief pursuit of the defeated enemy on the day of the battle, which means that the Germanic camp should be sought within a short distance of only a few kilometres east of the river junction at Rossum. We should accordingly expect Caesar's camp some 12 km further east.

The historical and palaeogeographical evidence permits the following scenario of Caesar's attack, as presented in Figure 7.3. The Germanic camp was situated at a strategic location with natural defences on all sides, except for its open east flank. Caesar reports that he marched against the enemy camp with his army in three columns and with the cavalry bringing up the rear. On reaching the camp, fierce fighting broke out amidst carts and baggage wagons. The camp must have covered an area of several square kilometres, since it also included the non-combatant population and several thousand wagons, draught animals and other livestock.

Does archaeology have anything to contribute to the above historical-geographical reconstruction? Is there any archaeological evidence in the micro-region of the Meuse/Waal confluence that can be linked to the battle of 55 BC? It is our hypothesis that archaeological remains of the Germanic encampment and of the slaughter of the fleeing Germans have been identified at Kessel/Lith, only a few kilometres east of the ancient river confluence (Figure 7.4; Roymans 2018). A large late Iron Age find complex has been identified at this location, part of which may relate to the battle of 55 BC. This find complex was collected by amateur archaeologists over the past four decades during large-scale dredging operations in a former bed of the Meuse. The fact that we are dealing with dredged finds seriously hampers their interpretation; furthermore, it is important to realize that only a tiny fraction of the finds has been recovered – most of the material (more than 95%) was lost undocumented.

The material dredged at Kessel/Lith covers a long period from the Bronze Age into the late medieval period, but with a clear peak in the late Iron Age and Roman period. The find spectrum from the late Iron Age begins in the 3rd century BC and can be characterized as settlement material: animal bones, pottery sherds, spindle whorls, loom weights, fragments of rotary querns, etc. However, the material from the late Iron Age differs in two respects from that of contemporary settlements in the Dutch river area: the presence firstly of large quantities of human skeletal remains, and secondly, of weaponry and other metalwork. Both find categories will be discussed briefly below.

The conflict-related nature of part of the find complex dredged at Kessel/Lith is above all reflected in the massive presence of human skeletal remains. A total of some 722 skeleton parts, belonging to at least 70 individuals, has been preserved (Ter Schegget 1999; Pintar 2016). A sample of 42 bones has been radiocarbon dated. The chronological pattern that emerges is twofold (Figure 7.5): a diffuse spread over a long period from the early Bronze Age to the pre-modern period, and a clear clustering in the late Iron Age or the period between 200 and 50 BC (Figure 7.6).[3] The great variation in skeleton parts and the absence of traces of gnawing by dogs indicate the direct deposition of complete bodies in open water. What also stands out is the mixed composition of the bones in terms of age and sex: adult males predominate, but the population also includes women, children and the elderly. Moreover, traces of injuries – mostly of peri-mortem nature – were found on six of the 21 radiocarbon-dated late Iron Age bones (Figure 7.7). A dramatic case is the skull of an adult aged between 40 and 60 (No. 1) with part of the frontal bone cut off, probably inflicted by a sword blow. A skull of an adult male aged between 30 and 40 shows a perforation in the skull caused by a spear (No. 4). A skull of an adult female of between 40 and 60 years (No. 2) has a circular hole above the left eye from a *pilum*, arrow or *gladius* point. The perforation in the skull of an adult male between 40 and 60 years of age was probably caused by an axe (No. 3), and the injury on an adult tibia was probably inflicted by a spear (No. 5).

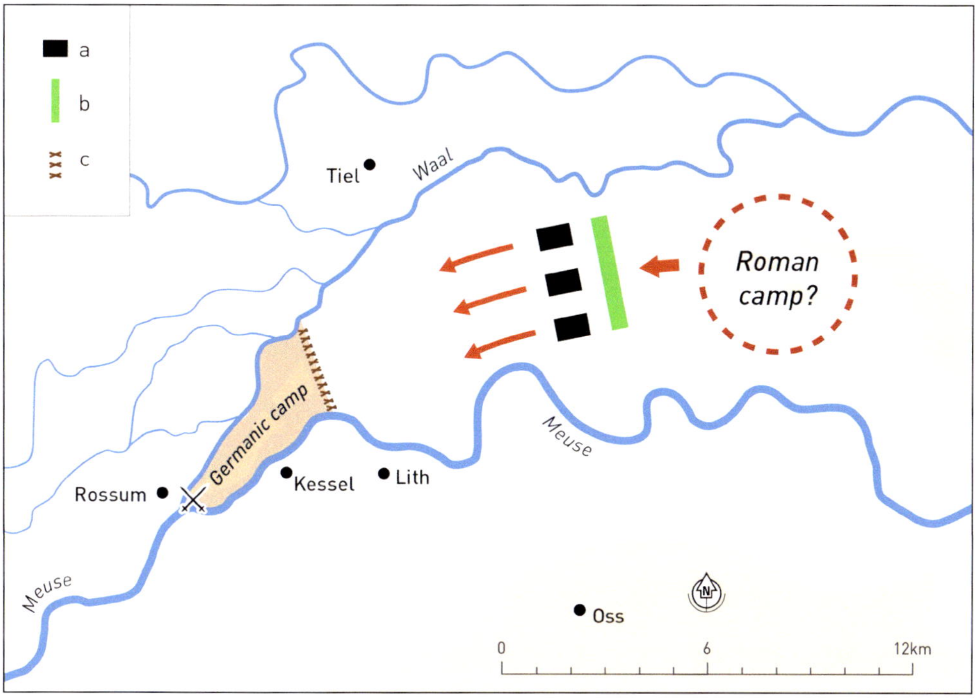

Figure 7.3 Hypothetical scenario of the Roman attack on the Germanic camp, based on Caesar's war account and palaeogeographic reconstruction. Key: a – Roman infantry, b – Roman cavalry, c – open east side of Germanic camp.

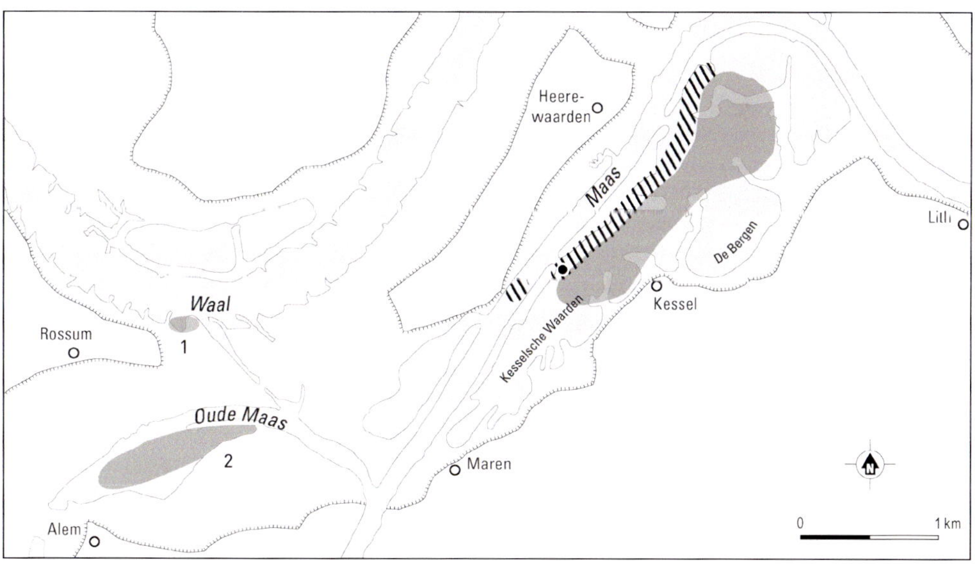

Figure 7.4 The modern topography of the Kessel/Lith area, Netherlands, showing the actual courses of the Meuse and Waal rivers and the main find concentrations (hatched) in fossil Meuse channel in the late Iron Age/early Roman period. 1 – location of probable early Roman military settlement, 2 – Roman vicus.

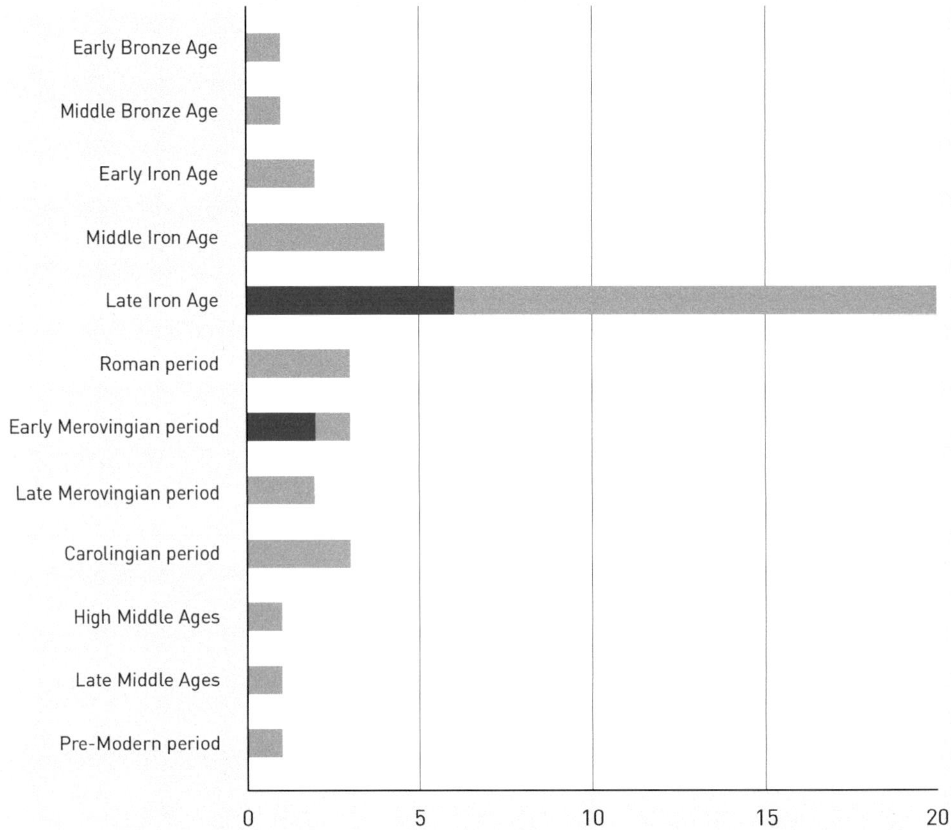

Figure 7.5 Chronological ordering of 42 radiocarbon-dated human bones dredged from the Meuse at Kessel/Lith. Dark shading: bones with weapon injuries.

The dental remains of a selection of four late Iron Age individuals were investigated by means of isotope analyses in order to determine whether or not these people were of local origin. The values for strontium indicate that none of the individuals were native to the Holocene Dutch river landscape, but immigrants from other landscape types.[4]

Among the late La Tène metal finds collected from the ancient river bed at Kessel/Lith are 23 iron swords or sword scabbards (Figure 7.8), some spearheads, an iron helmet and 22 bronze belt hooks. A characteristic group of long swords have bronze discs slid around the hilt tang. They can be dated to La Tène D2 and their extreme similarity suggests that they were products of the same workshop. The same date applies to 18 bronze band-shaped belt hooks of the types Kessel A and B (Roymans 2004). They are of Germanic origin and were probably elements of female attire. They, too, are identical in many respects and may well be products of the same workshop. Finally, the Meuse bed at Kessel/Lith has also produced pieces of Roman military equipment (Figure 7.9). Some of them belong to the imperial period, but a

Human bones Kessel-Lith			
MK 362	femur	GrN-29219	2150 ± 30 BP
MK 370	femur	GrN-29220	2120 ± 30 BP
MK 373	femur	GrN-29222	2080 ± 30 BP
MK 376	femur	GrN-29223	2125 ± 30 BP
MK 416	femur	GrN-29229	2100 ± 30 BP
MK 359	femur	GrN-20587	2100 ± 20 BP
MK 617	maxilla	GrA-64833	2110 ± 30 BP
MK 618	maxilla	GrA-64834	2095 ± 30 BP
MK 95	skull	GrA-64835	2090 ± 30 BP
MK 2	mandibula	GrA-64837	2140 ± 30 BP
MK 1004	tibia with injury	GrA-65832	2090 ± 30 BP
LH-1	skull	GrA-65833	2120 ± 30 BP
LH-5	skull with injury	GrA-65840	2135 ± 30 BP
Caesarian camp Hermeskeil			
Hermeskeil	wooden twigs	Erl-16189	2078 ± 30 BP
Hermeskeil	wooden twigs	Erl-16187	2107 ± 30 BP

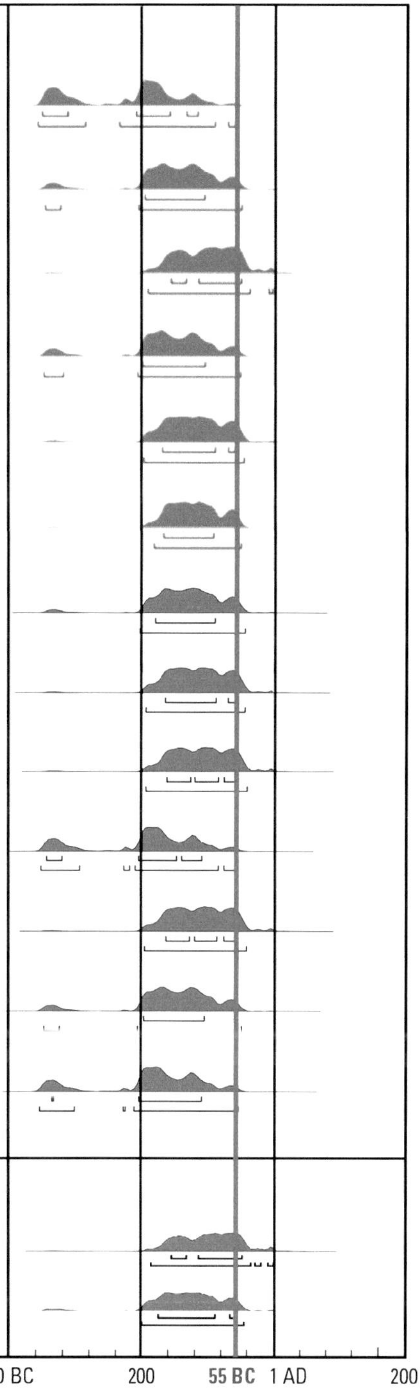

Figure 7.6 Radiocarbon-dated human bones from Kessel/Lith with error ranges of no more than 30 years, and radiocarbon dates from the Caesarian camp at Hermeskeil near Trier.

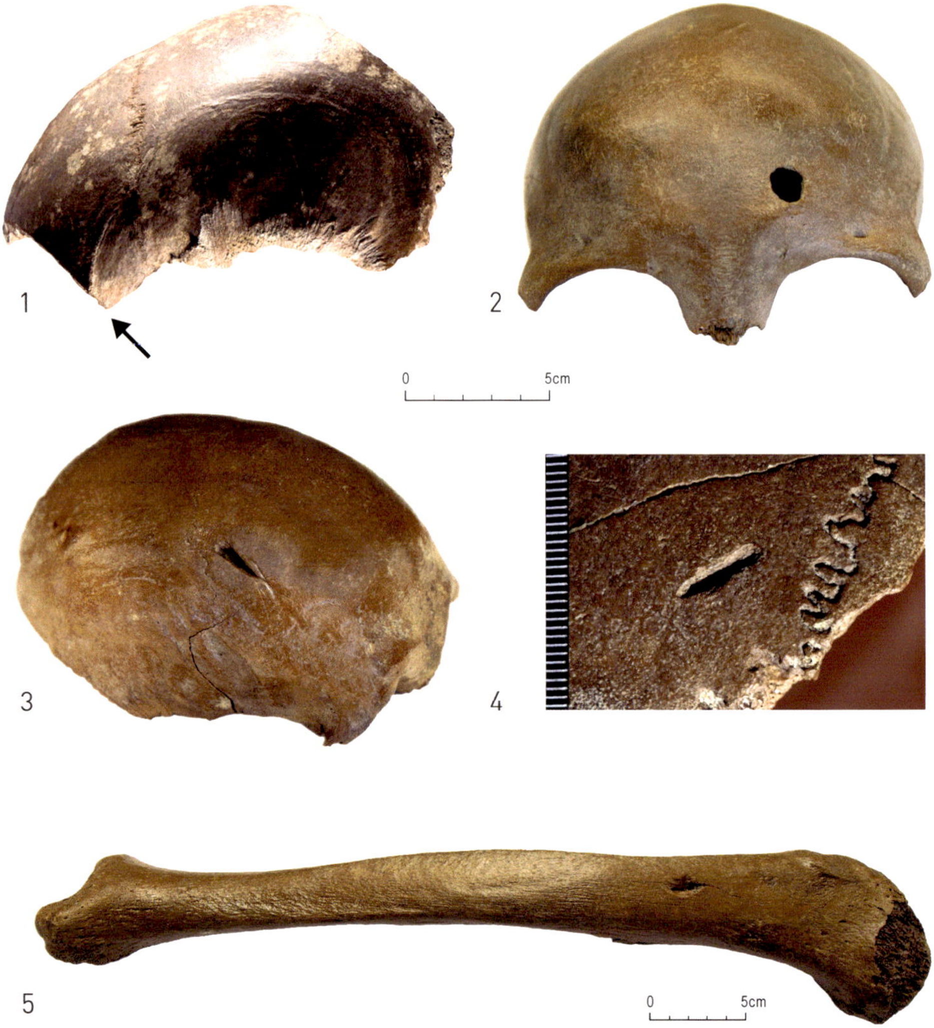

Figure 7.7 Radiocarbon-dated human bones with traces of trauma from the Meuse at Kessel/Lith.

fragment of a *gladius*, an iron umbo with a conical boss and some spearheads could be placed in the late Republican period. The latter date is certainly plausible for a horn-shaped helmet fitting and an iron helmet ornamented with 'eyebrows' and horn motifs at the front. We are dealing with a helmet of the Port type with a riveted neck guard, a type worn by Gallic auxiliary soldiers in the Roman army in the mid-1st century BC (see Pernet this volume).

As already mentioned, in the absence of high-quality contextual information and with limited chronological resolution, it is difficult to interpret the find complex in the ancient Meuse bed at Kessel-Lith. However, a significant portion of the late Iron Age find complex is battle-related and may well reflect a single event. Although hard

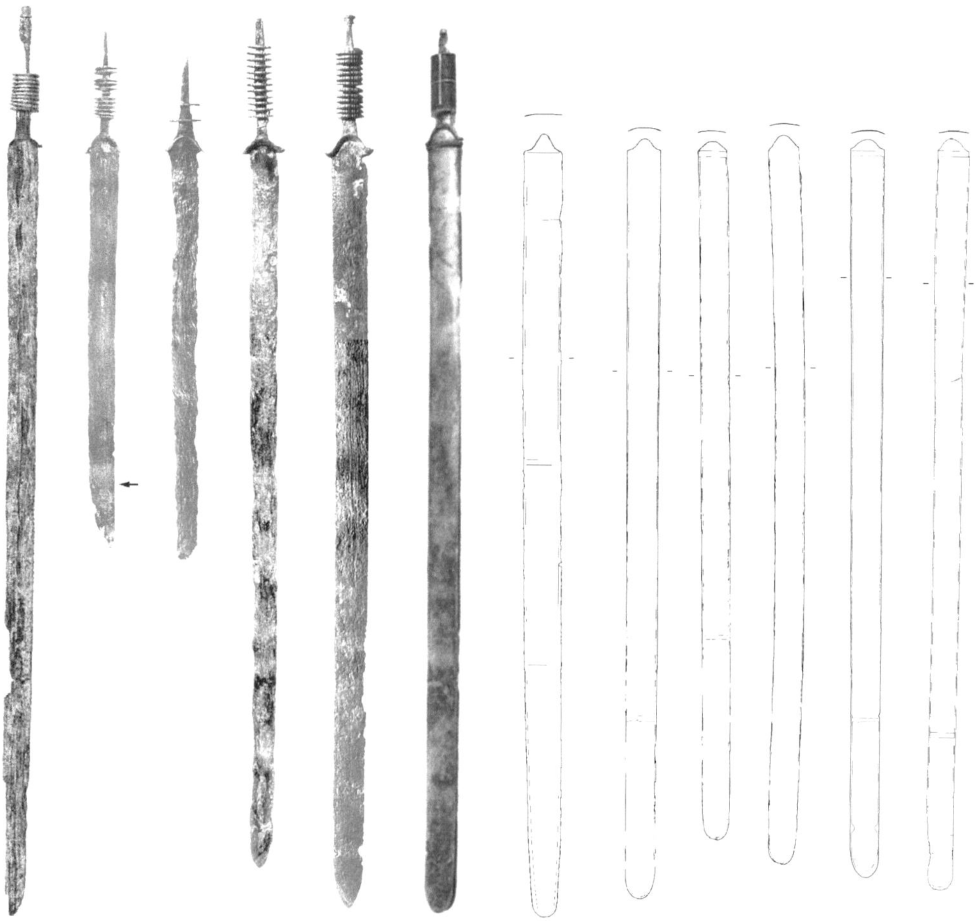

Figure 7.8 La Tène D2 swords and associated bronze scabbard plates found in an ancient bed of the Meuse at Kessel-Lith.

proof cannot be given, the characteristics of the human bone assemblage and part of the metal objects are suggestive of a massacre scenario as described by Caesar. The finds were collected at precisely the place where we can locate Caesar's annihilation of the Germans, and the historical date of the massacre falls within the chronological range of the archaeological material presented above. The victims include women and children, as is evident from the bones and ornaments (belt hooks), and the isotope analyses point to a non-local origin of the dead. This specific anthropological profile of the human remains accords surprisingly well with details in Caesar's account, and the geographical spread of the human bones in the Meuse bed across a zone of about 3 km argues for a link to a major battle rather than a cult place interpretation, as I suggested earlier (Roymans 2004, 133–148).

Although hard proof cannot be given, the *combination* of historical, palaeogeographical and archaeological evidence makes the location of Caesar's battle of 55 BC near Kessel

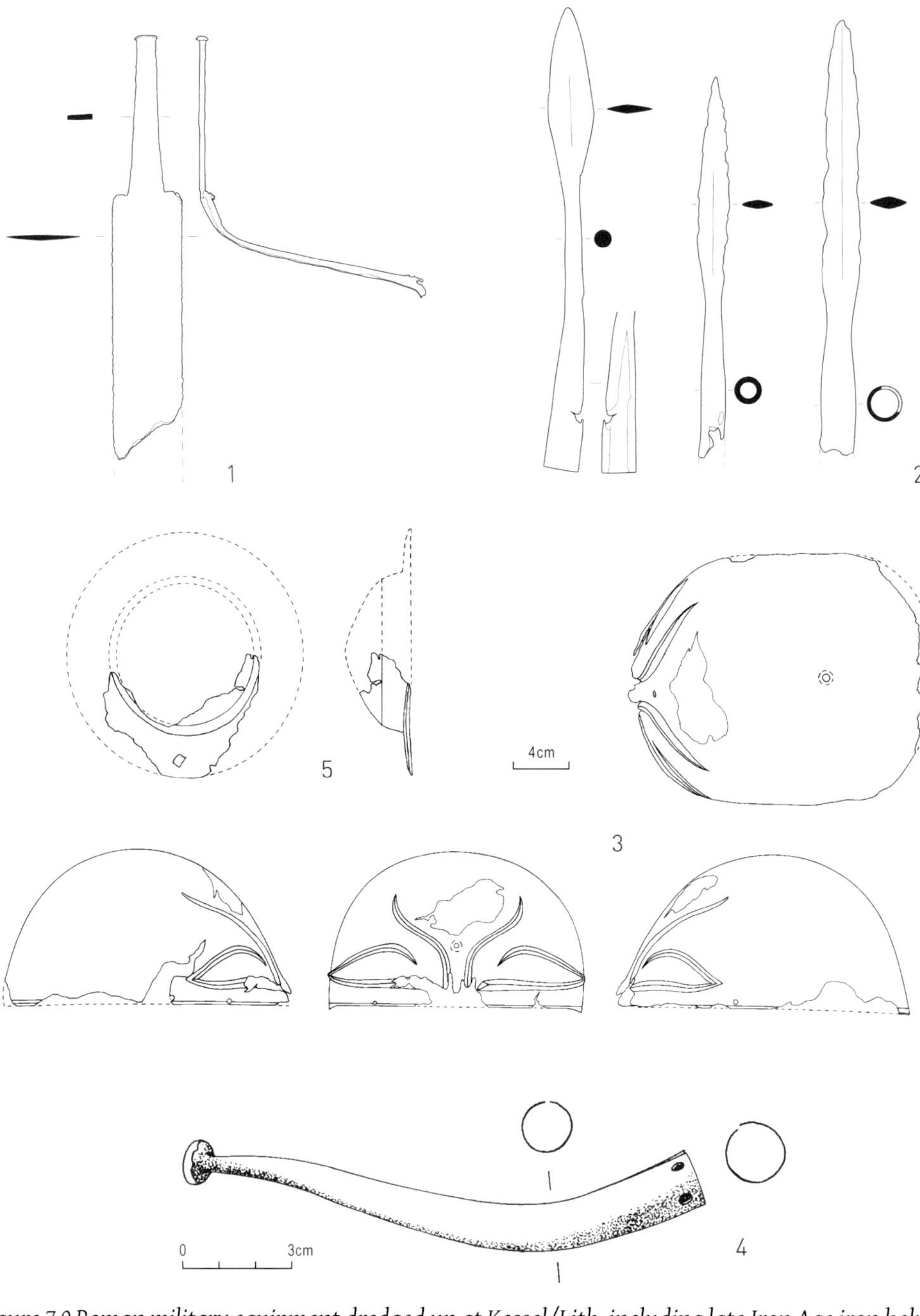

Figure 7.9 Roman military equipment dredged up at Kessel/Lith, including late Iron Age iron helmet of Port type.

a highly plausible interpretation. If we accept this interpretation, then we have located one of the largest massacre sites described in Caesar's war account.

Scorched earth policy and the creation of a landscape of terror

Most tribes in the Germanic frontier zone were confronted with another variant of mass violence: scorched earth policy. This policy was practised against resistant groups who avoided open battle and turned to guerrilla warfare, like the Menapii, the Morini, the Sugambri and above all the Eburones in the years after their revolt of 54 BC. The Roman strategy came down to the large-scale (involving several legions) burning to the ground of settlements, taking prisoners, carrying off cattle and destroying the harvest in the fields. Because of the massive troop deployments and the systematic planning, the scorched earth campaigns will have had a disastrous effect on the subsistence basis of the indigenous populations and may even have threatened their survival as a political community. The systematic ravaging of the countryside will also have put its stamp on the physical appearance of the inhabited areas, which were transformed into landscapes of trauma and terror.

The study of demographic discontinuities

The described forms of mass violence, when taken seriously, can all be interpreted as genocidal practices that must have had a dramatic impact on local societies in the extreme north of Gaul.[5] However, we do not know to what extent Caesar's descriptions are biased by propagandistic rhetoric, self-glorification, exaggeration and delusion, which makes it difficult to assess the real scale and societal impact of the violence. Indeed, his narrative contains several reports of an almost total annihilation of a group (Nervii, Eburones, Aduatuci),[6] but later passages show that such claims should be put into perspective. On the other hand, one reason for not playing down the impact of his activities too much is the almost complete reshuffle of the Caesarian tribal map of the Germanic frontier zone in the post-conquest period, in combination with reports about the influx of new Germanic groups from the east bank of the Rhine (Figure 7.10). For the Batavians, Tacitus (*Histories* 4.12) even explicitly mentions that they settled in a *vacua cultoribus* in the Rhine delta.

The key question is to what extent archaeology is able to test the historical model of Roman mass violence and destruction just discussed. Until recently, scepticism prevailed among archaeologists.[7] It is a fact that the intensive settlement investigations of the past few decades have hardly produced any evidence for Caesar's disastrous activities. But what does that say? Burnt houses, killed people, stolen cattle and destroyed harvests leave little or no physical trace, certainly not when we realize that the surviving archaeology usually lies some 40 cm below the level of the late Iron Age ground surface. Yet, I believe that the archaeological settlement evidence does offer possibilities for testing the historical model.

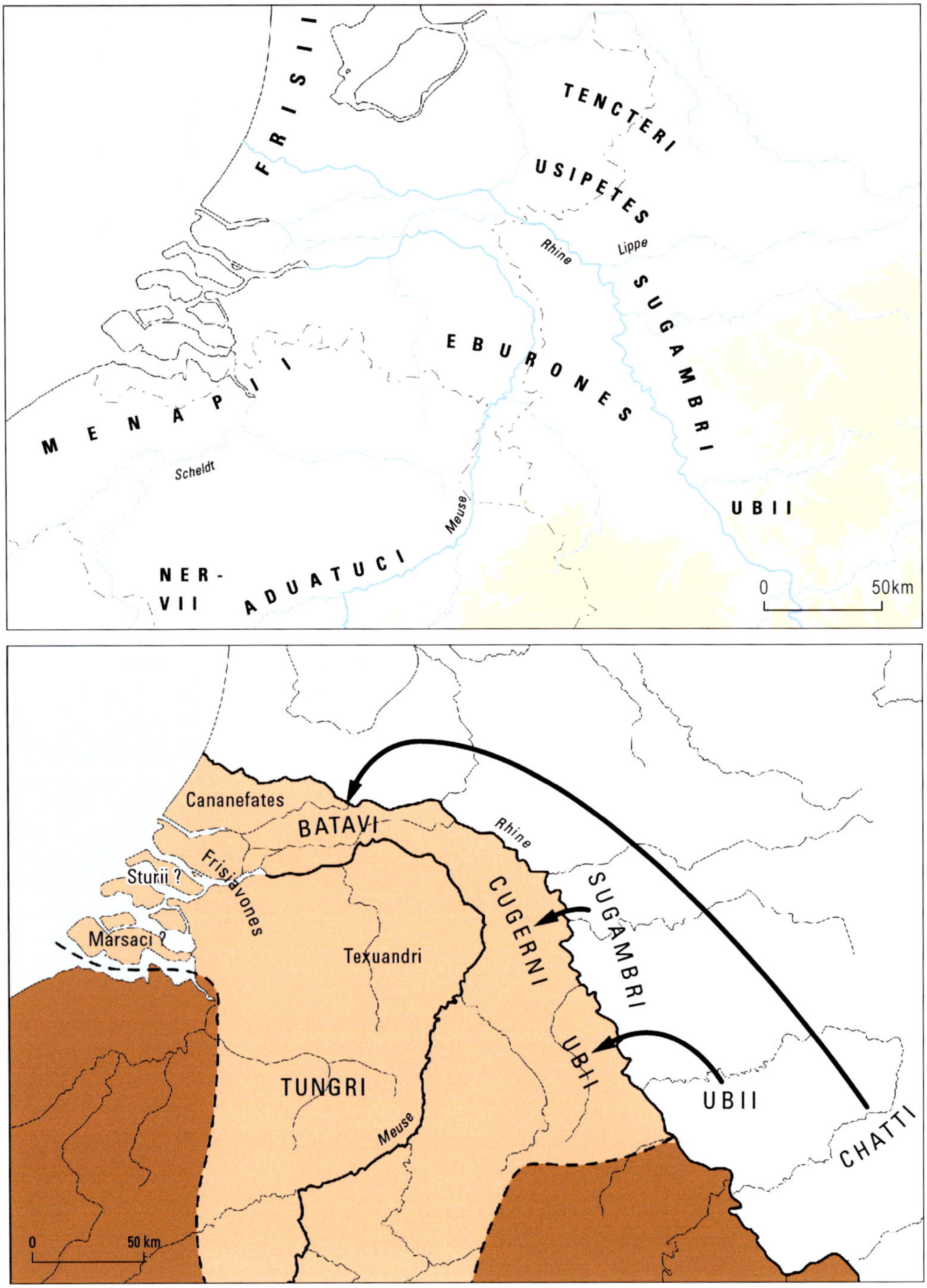

Figure 7.10 Tribal map of the Germanic frontier zone in the Caesarian period (above) and the Augustan/Tiberian period (below).

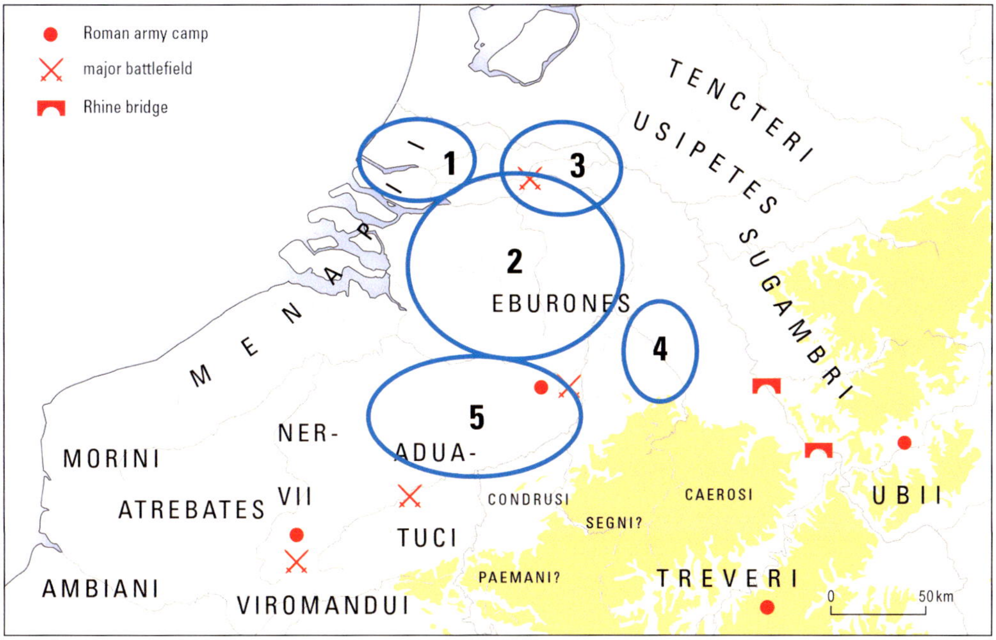

Figure 7.11 Test regions with high-quality settlement evidence: (1) South-Holland, (2) Meuse-Demer-Scheldt region, (3) Dutch eastern river area, (4) Cologne hinterland, (5) Tongres area.

The most practical method would be the investigation of 1st-century BC regional settlement trajectories, with a special attention paid to discontinuities in habitation, assuming that Caesar's activities – if taken at face value – will have caused a substantial depopulation in many regions. We are confronted, however, with the problem of the limited chronological resolution of late Iron Age material culture, which rarely allows a more specific date than '1st century BC'. On the other hand, the precision of dating has increased considerably in recent decades thanks to the growth of the number of excavations, the improved typo-chronology of building structures and material culture and systematic metal detection. Habitation discontinuity can also be established by studying 1st-century AD Roman settlements. The basic questions are: to what extent are these settlements simply continuations of late Iron Age sites? What is the relative proportion of newly founded settlements? And is there any evidence for regional variation in recolonization trends?

I will briefly discuss here the available evidence of five test regions where many data have been gathered in the past decades (Figure 7.11).[8] This research is still ongoing, but the main trends can already be given.

The first region covers the province of South Holland in the Dutch coastal area. The settlement research of the past decades has been synthesized by Jasper de Bruin (2017). Proceeding from a sample of some 50 mostly partially excavated sites, he concludes that almost every rural settlement starts in the Claudian period, which points to a large-scale colonization of the land. The construction of the longhouses and the hand-made pottery types suggest that the new settlers came from coastal areas north of the Rhine. All this implies a more or less total depopulation of the region, which can be dated, judging from the pottery evidence, to the late Iron Age, and more specifically to the early 1st century BC (Van Heeringen 1989, 233, 243).

The second region is the sandy Meuse/Demer/Scheldt (MDS) region of the southern Netherlands and northern Belgium. Thanks to intensive archaeological research in past decades we now have a much better understanding of late Iron Age and early Roman habitation. About 50 settlements of this date have been fully or partially excavated. What is striking is that most of the Roman settlements appear to be new foundations of the Augustan period (Hiddink and Roymans 2015, 84), pointing to a substantial influx of settlers from another area.[9] Furthermore, some Roman cemeteries have been excavated which start in the late Iron Age, but continuity is not in the least certain. Significant is the absence of metal finds (fibulae, belt hooks) that are characteristic for the advanced stage of La Tène D2, which may point to a break in the use of the cemeteries. Anyway, in this region, too, a scenario of a substantial population decrease in the 1st century BC seems plausible.

The third region is the Dutch eastern river area, in the Roman period the homeland of the Batavi. Here too, 50 rural settlements from the late Iron Age/early Roman transition have been fully or partially excavated (Heeren 2009). Most striking is that many of these Roman settlements were already inhabited in the final stage of La Tène D2, a generation earlier than in the MDS region. They seem to be new foundations of the period between *c.* 50 and 20 BC; bronze rainbow staters (Roymans 2004) and La Tène D2 spoonbow fibulae (Heeren and Van der Feijst 2017, 49 ff.) occur frequently at these sites. Conversely, only three settlements display continuity from La Tène D1 into the Roman period.[10] For this region Heeren (2009, 258) proposes a model of a partial regression in habitation around the mid-1st century BC, which shortly afterwards was compensated by an influx of an immigrant population. The immigrants came from the east bank of the Rhine, as is suggested by the coin evidence and the 'Germanization' of the handmade pottery tradition (Van den Broeke 2012, 142 ff.).

Our fourth region corresponds to the lignite mining area in the hinterland of Cologne, where we again see a completely different picture (Joachim 2007; Gaitzsch 2011). Some 69 Roman rural settlements have been excavated here which often develop into small villa sites in the later 1st and 2nd centuries AD. Almost all Roman sites appear to be new foundations *ex nihilo* from the Tiberian but above all the Claudian period. A small number of late Iron Age settlements have been investigated, all of which had been abandoned in the 1st century BC (Hornung 2016, 282–290). In this region, too, we are confronted with an almost total settlement discontinuity and a dramatic demographic decline in the 1st century BC, a picture that is further strengthened by pollen-analytical research (Kalis and Meurers-Balke 2007).

The fifth region is the fertile Hesbaye region in central Belgium, where Fanny Martin (2017, 395) has studied some 34 sites dating to La Tène C–D. The great majority

Table 7.1. Degree of settlement discontinuity in five test regions with high-quality settlement evidence. The numbering of the regions corresponds to that in Figure 7.11.

Region	Degree of settlement discontinuity	Date BC	Period of settlement intensification
1 South Holland	total	1st century	Claudian
2 Meuse/Demer/Scheldt area	substantial	1st century	Augustan
3 Dutch eastern river area	partial	mid-1st century	50–30 BC
4 Cologne hinterland	total	1st century	Claudian
5 Tongres region	substantial	1st century	Augustan

seem to have been abandoned towards the end of La Tène D, suggesting a dramatic decline in population. Roman settlements appear to be new foundations *ex nihilo* from the Augustan period onward.

Overviewing the evidence from the five investigated regions (Table 7.1), we can say that our knowledge of habitation trajectories during the late Iron Age/early Roman transition period has substantially increased in the last few decades. Quantitative analysis of the data is still ongoing, but the evidence clearly indicates that the 1st century BC was indeed a period of substantial settlement abandonment and depopulation in all five regions. Nowhere do we observe a simple habitation continuity from La Tène D1 into the Roman period. Furthermore, interesting regional patterns become apparent in the repopulation of the investigated regions. In the Batavian river area, the foundation of new settlements starts in the period 50–20 BC in La Tène D2, in the MDS region and probably also the Hesbaye area a generation later in the Augustan period, and in South Holland and the Cologne hinterland (where the depopulation was most dramatic) another generation later in the Claudian period.

But the key question remains to what extent our evidence for a substantial demographic regression in our study areas in the 1st century BC can be explained as an effect of Caesar's genocidal practices. My opinion is that a link with Caesar's activities is indeed plausible, although hard proof cannot be given. The problem remains that the date of the 1st century BC settlement abandonment cannot be specified exactly. The depopulation may have been a more gradual process with multiple causes.[11] In this context it is interesting to observe that the 1st century BC is in many parts of continental Europe a period of significant change in the settlement record. In France the La Tène D2 rupture in the settlement record (Figure 7.12) has been explained recently as the result of a move of rural populations from their farms to nearby fortified *oppida* in the context of a 'Celtic urbanization process' (Haselgrove and Guichard 2013; Malrain *et al.* 2013; Malrain and Lorho 2016). However, this alternative explanation for the 1st-century BC depopulation of the countryside has little relevance for the northern frontier zone of Gaul, where urbanized *oppida* are absent. Although the causes for the serious settlement abandonment and demographic regression in this zone may have been more complex (including factors like disease, ecological

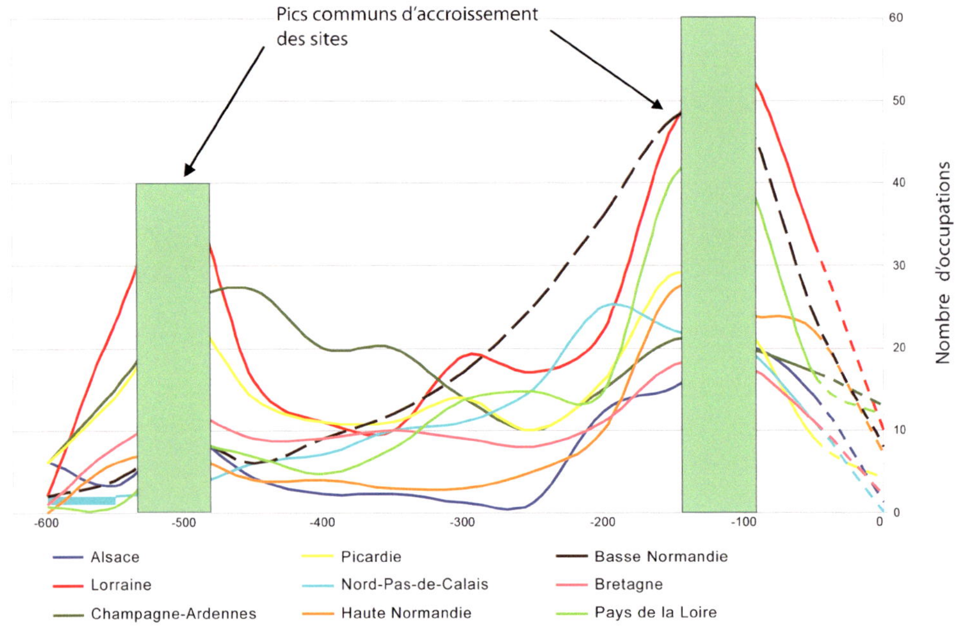

Figure 7.12 Reconstructed demographic fluctuations in various French regions during the later Iron Age (source: Malrain and Lorho 2016).

crisis and migration), the Roman conquest seems to have been a major explanatory factor here.

Conclusion and discussion

With the increase of the quantity and quality of evidence, archaeology is becoming better equipped for a regional contextualization of Caesar's activities, in this way generating new questions and discussions. It is still too early to come up with hard conclusions and test the historical model. However, we can say that there is increasing archaeological evidence that may confirm that Caesar's conquest indeed had dramatic consequences in the northern Germanic frontier zone. Here Roman imperialism seems to have revealed itself in its most dramatic form. Several interrelated explanations can be given for the high degree of violence in this frontier area: the absence of central places or heavily defended *oppida* that could be used by Caesar as military targets; the employment by Germanic groups of a strategy of decentralized, guerrilla-type warfare, and of course Caesar's motivation to revenge the successful ambushing of a Roman army by the Eburonean leader Ambiorix.

But there remains the intriguing question whether the extreme violent behaviour in this zone was also influenced by anti-Germanic ethnic stereotyping and racism by the Romans, including Caesar himself. We can point to his extremely negative framing of Germanic ethnicity in his *Commentaries* (*BG* 4.1–3; 6.21–28). Germani are presented as the barbarians par excellence, a warlike, semi-nomadic race that formed a threat to the Roman provinces and even to Italy.[12] His geography of Germania can – in contrast to that of Gallia and Britannia – be characterized as a 'geography of exclusion'. In *BG* 6.9, we read that the Germanic Ubii feared becoming the victims of 'a general hatred of the Germans' (*communi odio Germanorum*). This hatred no doubt reflected the general opinion of the Roman soldiers and may well have contributed to the moral justification for the genocidal activities of the Roman army in the Germanic frontier zone.

Notes

1 Cf. the interview of Professor Hugo Thoen (Ghent University) in the Belgian newspaper *De Morgen*, 7 April 2006.

2 For a more extensive and fully referenced study of the massacre of 55 BC and its location in the Dutch river delta, see Roymans 2018.

3 It is striking that these radiocarbon dates belong to exactly the same horizon as those obtained recently for the Caesarian camp at Hermeskeil near Trier, dated archaeologically to the late 50s BC; see Hornung this volume. Information kindly provided by Professor Sabine Hornung.

4 Analyses carried out by Lisette Kookter, Faculty of Earth and Life Sciences, Vrije Universiteit Amsterdam. The results will be published elsewhere.

5 We adhere to an historic definition of genocide as the practice of mass killing of a national, ethnic or religious group in combination with the intent (be it successful or not) to annihilate that group (cf. Bloxham and Moses 2010). The concept, first coined by the Polish lawyer Raphael Lemkin in 1943, has been employed for cross-cultural comparative studies from antiquity onwards. See Van Wees 2010; Kiernan 2007, 46, 71; Quesada-Sanz 2015. Kiernan (2014) has shown us that conceptions of genocide-like 'general massacre' and 'extermination' long pre-date the modern coining of the term.

6 *BG* 2.28 (Nervii), 2.33 (Aduatuci), 6.34–35, 6.43, 8.24–25 (Eburones).

7 See, for example, the recent study by Sabine Hornung (2016, 275–318) of the archaeological evidence from the Eburonean area.

8 For some regions recent syntheses were available. For the MDS area and the Dutch eastern river area I have intensively used site reports of development-led excavations. The full results will be published elsewhere.

9 It has been debated whether this influx can be linked to the introduction at this time of a new, much sturdier type of longhouse (the Alphen-Ekeren house). The high degree of stability of farmhouses from the Augustan period onward, compared to the more diffuse spread of farmsteads from the late Iron Age, is also noteworthy.

10 Significantly, use of the regional cult place at Empel shows a clear peak in the second half of La Tène D2, pointing to a substantial rural population at this period.

11 In the Cologne hinterland, the demographic downturn may already have started in the pre-Caesarian period; if so, other historical contexts may have played a role (Hornung 2016). Van Heeringen (1989, 233) relates the break in habitation in the early 1st century BC in South Holland to the flooding of large parts of the peatlands.

12 Caesar *BG* 1.33. Cf. Riggsby 2006, 60–61 on Caesar's qualification of Germani as outcasts and 'terrorists'.

Bibliography

Bellemore, J. (2012) The Roman concept of massacre. Julius Caesar in Gaul. In P.G. Dwyer and L. Ryan (eds), *Theatres of Violence. Massacre, Mass Killing and Atrocity Throughout History*, 38–49. Oxford and New York, Berghahn Books.

Bloxham, D. and Moses A.D. (eds) (2010) *The Oxford Handbook of Genocide Studies.* Oxford, Oxford University Press.

De Bruin, J. (2017) *Rurale gemeenschappen in de Civitas Cananefatium 50-300 na Christus.* Ph.D. thesis, University of Leiden.

Gaitzsch, W. (2011) Roman villa landscapes of the lignite mining areas in the hinterland of Cologne. In N. Roymans and T. Derks (eds), *Villa Landscapes in the Roman North: Economy, Culture and Lifestyles*, 285–300. Amsterdam, Amsterdam Archaeological Studies 17.

Guilaine, J. and Sémelin, J. (eds) (2016) *Violences de guerre, violences de masse. Une approche Archéologique.* Paris, La Découverte.

Hanson, V.D. (2007) The modern historiography of ancient warfare. In P. Sabin, H. van Wees and M. Whitby (eds), *The Cambridge History of Greek and Roman Warfare, Vol. 1: Greece, the Hellenistic World and the Rise of Rome*, 3–21. Cambridge, Cambridge University Press.

Haselgrove, C. and Guichard, V. (2013) Les Gaulois sont-ils dans la plaine? Reflections on settlement patterns in Gaul in the 1st century BC. In S. Krausz, A. Colin, K. Gruel, A. Ralston and T. Dechezleprêtre (eds), *L'Âge du Fer en Europe. Mélanges offerts à Olivier Buchsenschutz*, 317–327. Bordeaux, Ausonius Éditions Mémoires 32.

Heeren, S. (2009) *De romanisering van rurale gemeenschappen in de* civitas Batavorum*: de casus Tiel-Passewaaij.* Ph.D. thesis, Vrije Universiteit Amsterdam. Amersfoort, Rijksdienst Archeologie Cultuurlandschap en Monumenten.

Heeren, S. and Van der Feijst, L. (2017) *Prehistorische, Romeinse en Middeleeuwse fibulae uit de Lage Landen. Beschrijving, analyse en interpretatie van een archeologische vondstcategorie.* Amersfoort, Eigen Beheer.

Henige, D. (1998) He came, he saw, we counted: the historiography and demography of Caesar's Gallic numbers. *Annales de démographie historique 1998-1*, 215–242.

Hornung, S. (2016) *Siedlung und Bevölkerung in Ostgallien zwischen Gallischem Krieg und der Festigung der römischen Herrschaft.* Mainz, Römisch-Germanische Forschungen 73.

Hiddink, H. and Roymans, N. (2015) Exploring the rural landscape of a peripheral region. In N. Roymans, T. Derks and H. Hiddink (eds), *The Roman Villa of Hoogeloon and the Archaeology of the Periphery*, 45–86. Amsterdam, Amsterdam Archaeological Studies 22.

Joachim, H.-E. (2007) Die späte Eisenzeit am Niederrhein. In M. Hegewisch (ed.), *Krieg und Frieden. Kelten Römer Germanen*, 48–58. Darmstadt, Primus Verlag.

Lloyd, J. (1986) Why should historians take archaeology seriously? In J. Bintliff and C. Gaffney (eds), *Archaeology at the Interface: Studies in archaeology's relationships with history, geography, biology and physical science*, 40–51. Oxford, British Archaeological Reports International Series 300.

Kalis, A.J. and Meurers-Balke, J. (2007) Landnutzung im Niederrheingebiet zwischen Krieg und Frieden. In M. Hegewisch (ed.), *Krieg und Frieden. Kelten Römer Germanen*, 144–153. Darmstadt, Primus Verlag.

Kiernan, B. (2007) Classical genocide and early modern memory. In B. Kiernan (ed.), *Blood and Soil: A world history of genocide and extermination from Sparta to Darfur*, 42–71. New Haven (CT), Yale University Press.

Kiernan, B. (2014) Is 'genocide' an anachronistic concept for the study of early modern mass killing? *History* 99, 530–548.

Malrain, F. and Lorho, T. (2016) Base de données sur les établissements ruraux du Second âge du Fer. Quelques résultats sur le monde rural laténien. In M. Reddé (ed.), *Méthodes d'analyse des différents paysages ruraux dans le nord-est de la Gaule Romaine*, 47–61. Available at https://hal.archives-ouvertes.fr/hal-01253470 (accessed 9 October 2017).

Malrain, F., Blancquaert, G. and Lorho, T. (2013) *L'habitat rural du second âge du Fer. Rythmes de création et d'abandon au nord de la Loire*. Paris, Inrap/CNRS Recherches archéologiques 7.
Martin, F. (2017) *Atuatuques, Condruses, Éburons... Culture matérielle et occupation du sol dans le territoire de la future* civitas Tungrorum, *de la fin de l'âge du Fer au début de l'époque gallo-romaine*. Ph.D. thesis, Université Libre de Bruxelles.
Pintar, A. (2016) *Rivers Keep Many Secrets. Bronze and Iron Age depositions of human remains in river and settlement contexts*. MA thesis, Vrije Universiteit Amsterdam.
Quesada-Sanz, F. (2015) Genocide and mass-murder in Second Iron Age Europe. Methodological issues and case studies in the Iberian Peninsula. In C. Carmichael and R.C. Maguire (eds), *The Routledge History of Genocide*, 9–22. London, Routledge.
Riggsby, A. (2006) *Caesar in Gaul and Rome. War in Words*. Austin, University of Texas Press.
Roymans, N. (2004) *Ethnic Identity and Imperial Power. The Batavians in the Early Roman Empire*. Amsterdam, Amsterdam Archaeological Studies 10.
Roymans, N. (2018) A Roman massacre in the far north. Caesar's annihilation of the Tencteri and Usipetes in the Dutch river area. In M. Fernández-Götz and N. Roymans (eds), *Conflict Archaeology. Materialities of Collective Violence in Late Prehistoric and Early Historic Europe*, 167–181. London, Routledge.
Roymans, N. and Fernández-Götz, M. (2015) Caesar in Gaul. New perspectives on the archaeology of mass violence. In T. Brindle, M. Allen, E. Durham and A. Smith (eds), *TRAC 2014. Proceedings of the Twenty Fourth Theoretical Roman Archaeology Conference*, 70–80. Oxford, Oxbow Books.
Roymans, N. and Scheers, S. (2012) Eight gold hoards from the Low Countries. A synthesis. In N. Roymans, G. Creemers and S. Scheers (eds), *Late Iron Age Gold Hoards from the Low Countries and the Caesarian Conquest of Northern Gaul*, 1–46. Amsterdam, Amsterdam Archaeological Studies 18.
Ter Schegget, M. (1999) Late Iron Age human skeletal remains from the river Meuse at Kessel. A river cult place? In F. Theuws and N. Roymans (eds), *Land and Ancestors. Cultural Dynamics in the Urnfield Period and the Middle Ages in the Southern Netherlands*, 199–240. Amsterdam, Amsterdam Archaeological Studies 4.
Van den Broeke, P. (2012) *Het handgevormde aardewerk uit de IJzertijd en de Romeinse tijd van Oss-Ussen. Studies naar typochronologie, technologie en herkomst*. Ph.D. thesis, University of Leiden. Leiden, Sidestone Press Dissertations.
Van Heeringen, R.M. (1989) The Iron Age in the Western Netherlands V: Synthesis. *Berichten van de Rijksdienst voor het Oudheidkundig Bodemonderzoek* 39, 157–267.
Van Wees, H. (2010) Genocide in the ancient world. In D. Bloxham and A.D. Moses (eds), *The Oxford Handbook of Genocide Studies*, 239–258. Oxford, Oxford University Press.

Chapter 8

Caesar's landing sites in Britain and Gaul in 55 and 54 BC: Critical places, natural places

Andrew P. Fitzpatrick

In the late Republic the nature of Roman imperialism and warfare were such that success was defined by defeating the enemy in battle; victory did not require the permanent occupation of a territory. Accordingly, Caesar's invasions of Britain were not intended to lead to a permanent garrison. The intention was always that once victory had been achieved the army would return to Gaul at the end of the campaigning season. Thus, the landing places in Britain and Gaul were the single most important places in both Roman invasions of Britain because of the need to protect the fleet while it was in Britain and to secure an unopposed landing on its return to Gaul.

The location of these critical places has been considered almost entirely on the basis of the historical sources. While these sources provide the essential framework and much important information, they rarely give sufficient detail to allow individual landing sites to be identified. In some instances, notably the identification of the 'Itian port' from which the fleet set sail from Gaul in 54 BC, the evidence is contradictory. Now, archaeological discoveries combined with an assessment of the types of ships in the Roman fleets allow the landing sites – the places of both embarkation and disembarkation – to be assessed from a different perspective. An important aspect of this approach is understanding the modifications of the landscape caused by coastal change and land reclamation because, unlike much of the archaeology of the battle for Gaul, which focuses on battlefields and camps, the archaeology of the landing sites used in 55 and 54 BC is also an archaeology of natural places.

The historical sources and the crossings

As the accounts of Greek and Roman writers provide the framework for understanding where Caesar's fleets sailed from and landed, it is necessary to begin by reviewing them briefly. Caesar's own dramatic accounts of the outward crossing and landings in *de Bello Gallico* are the prime source, but Cassius Dio and Strabo also provide relevant comments.

Caesar described how, in 55 BC, he decided to invade Britain from the territory of the Morini, who inhabited the coastal parts of the modern department of Pas-de-Calais, because the shortest crossing to Britain was from there. He tried to gather information from the traders about the places in Britain that would be suitable for a large number of ships to land. When those attempts were unsuccessful, he dispatched Gaius Volusenus with a single galley to reconnoitre the coast and report back.

Shortly afterwards Caesar sailed overnight for Britain with a fleet of about 80 ships that carried two legions. The fleet left without the cavalry because some ships could not reach the place where the others had gathered. Accordingly, the cavalry was instructed to ride to join those ships at a port further down the coast (the *ulteriorem portum*, *i.e.* to the north) and to sail to Britain independently. The passage of the main fleet was uneventful, but Caesar described how, as they neared the shore the following morning, he could see armed Britons on all the heights. He then described how at the first place they attempted to land the sea was surrounded by steep ground from which projectiles could be thrown down onto the shore. Deciding that this was an unsuitable place to land, Caesar sailed on for about seven Roman miles. The legionaries hesitated before disembarking but, after fierce fighting, the landing was successful. A site was selected for the camp, the warships beached, and the transports anchored.

When the cavalry did eventually set sail and were within sight of the camp, a storm prevented them from landing and also damaged the rest of the fleet. Although twelve of the ships were irreparable, the remainder, albeit damaged, were able to make an uneventful return apart from two transports that were unable to make the same port as the rest and landed a little lower (*infra*) down the coast.

In 54 BC the force was much larger: five legions and 2,000 cavalry, and the fleet amounted to over 800 vessels. Caesar states that the 'most convenient' crossing was to be used, a distance of about 30 Roman miles, and that the fleet was to land at the place that he had learnt the year before was the 'best place for disembarkment'. The fleet sailed from the Itian port (*portus Itius*) and Titus Labienus was left with the remaining three legions and 2,000 cavalry to guard the ports, implying that more than one port was used for the return crossing. Again, the fleet sailed overnight, with the intention of using the ebb tide to take it north and the south-westerly wind to help it sail westwards across the Channel. Around midnight the wind dropped, and the fleet could not maintain its course. At first light Caesar saw Britain far behind him on the port (left) side. By dint of hard rowing the fleet made landfall around midday. Again, the Britons had gathered to oppose the landing but, taken aback by the size of the fleet, they retreated. The site of the camp was chosen and at first light the next day Caesar marched out with most of the army leaving the fleet riding at anchor. The next night almost all of the fleet was damaged in a storm.

As well as setting about the repair of the fleet, Caesar sent instruction that new ships should be built on the Continent. In the end, some 40 ships could not be repaired, so at the end of the campaign, the army returned from Britain in two divisions intending that the ships used in the first passage would return accompanied by the newly-built vessels. When very few of these ships returned, the remaining troops boarded the available ships. After an uneventful crossing the ships were beached in Gaul.

Cassius Dio also gave a short account of the crossings in his *Roman History* (39.51, 1–2), which is more dispassionate than Caesar's. For example, Dio wrote that Caesar coveted Britain and if the particular reason that he gave for invading had not been forthcoming, he would have found another one. Dio also said that the place at which Caesar first tried to land in 55 BC was not well chosen, adding that the fleet had sailed along a projection (προέχουσαν) – either a headland or a promontory – then back down the other side before landing. Dio wrote in the early 3rd century AD and while his principal source was Caesar's account, which he generally summarized accurately, he drew on at least one other contemporary source that is now lost. This is thought to be the history of Asinius Pollio, perhaps via Livy (McDougall 1991; cf. Morgan 2000).

Strabo's *Geography*, written in the early 1st century AD, states that Caesar sailed to Britain from *Ition* in the territory of the Morini; he arrived the next day about the fourth hour, and the passage was 320 stadia (4.5.2). The language used to describe *Ition* suggests that it was a headland or promontory. While Strabo did not say to which year he was referring, the time of arrival is consistent with Caesar's account of 55 BC. However, the distance – 320 stadia – equates to 40 Roman miles (as Strabo usually counted 8 stadia to a Roman mile), whereas Caesar gave the distance as 30 miles. This could be due to a transcription error, but it sounds a cautionary note about the reliability of the historical sources, a point illustrated amply by the final one – Ptolemy's *Geography*.

Also writing in Greek, but in the 2nd century AD, Ptolemy (*Geography* 2.9.1) described *Ition* as a headland or cape located between the river Phrudis, identified as the Somme, and Gesoriacum (Boulogne). The coordinates were given in degrees and minutes: *Ition* (22° 15': 52° 30') and Gesoriacum (22° 30': 52° 30') are located at the same latitude, with *Ition* further to the west. Beyond Gesoriacum the coastline runs east, with the rivers Tabula (Scheldt) and Mosa (Meuse), and Lugdunum Batavorum (Brittenberg) being named. As a result, Cap Alprech, immediately south of Boulogne, has been identified as the Itian port mentioned by Caesar but many commentators believe it to be Cap Griz-Nez, which stands north of Boulogne, and that the port was at Wissant where today a long and wide sandy beach stands in the lee of the cape.

Cap Gris-Nez forms the continental side of the Straits of Dover, the narrowest part of the English Channel, and also marks a pronounced change in the direction of the French coast. South of the cape, the coast runs approximately north–south, and to the north of it, roughly south-west to north-east. For a sailor it is a striking landmark and on a clear day it is easily visible from England. While Cap Gris-Nez is widely recognized as the most obvious location for Ptolemy's *Ition*, this requires accepting that there is an error in the schedule of places. Although Ptolemy underestimated the size of the equator, and hence the earth, this is a systematic error that can be compensated for. In contrast, the accuracy of the information he was working from was variable and this is thought to be the cause of several of the errors in his schedules. Much of the extensive debate about portus Itius, the older chapters of which were rehearsed by Rice Holmes (1907, 552–595), has revolved around whether Ptolemy or a later scribe made an error, perhaps transposing the names of *Ition* and Gesoriacum and repeating the same latitude. The question cannot be resolved on the available evidence and with the inconsistencies in Strabo's comments, it serves as a reminder of the limitations of the historical sources.

The Roman fleets

The battle for Gaul is usually thought of as a land war, but the sea also played an important role. Caesar fought several naval campaigns and by the start of the battle for Gaul in 58 BC he already had considerable naval experience in waters that ranged from the Black Sea to the Atlantic (Schulz 2000). This experience is reflected in the careful preparations made for the fleets used in the campaigns of 56–54 BC.

The core of the fleet used to invade Britain in 55 BC was the one assembled the previous year for the campaign against the Veneti and their allies in north-west France. That campaign culminated in the famous sea battle that probably took place in Quiberon bay, Morbihan. As no wrecks of late Republican Roman warships or of Gaulish vessels are known (McGrail 2001, 215–218) we are reliant, for the present, on the historical sources (Figure 8.1). Caesar states that in the winter of 57–56 BC he had warships built on the Loire in preparation for this campaign (*BG* 3.9). In addition, there were Gaulish ships from the Pictones and Santones and other pacified regions, presumably also on the Atlantic coast between the Loire and the Garonne (*BG* 3.11). Dio also stated that the ships used in the sea battle with the Veneti were brought from the Mediterranean and 'had been built rather light in the interest of speed, after the manner of our naval construction' (*Roman History* 39, 40, 3–4).

The fleet of 55 BC may have contained other Gaulish ships. Caesar stated that he commanded that ships be brought from the districts that neighboured the Morini, that is to say along the north coast of Gaul, to add to his fleet of 56 BC. If these ships were local Gaulish vessels, they would have needed to be adapted to serve as transports, but they could also have included ships built by the legions in the winters of 57–56 and 55–54 BC. In the winter of 56–55 BC the legions were stationed in the territories of the tribes in north-west Gaul who had joined the rebellion in 56 BC, with the Aulerci and Lexovii being named. The Lexovii inhabited modern Calvados which faces the Channel and the eastern boundary of their territory may have been the Seine. Although in 55 BC Caesar sailed for Britain late in the campaign season, it is clear that the invasion was planned long before, and preparations may have included building ships during the preceding winter.

Figure 8.1 Model of a Roman galley of the 1st century BC or AD, based on a graffiti on the podium of a temple at Alba Fucens, Abruzzo, Italy (photo V. Iserhard and R. Müller, Museum für Antike Schiffahrt des RGZM, Mainz).

In 55 BC the two legions crossed the Channel in about 80 vessels. A further 18 ships that were unable to reach the port of concentration because of adverse winds were allocated to the cavalry (*BG* 4.21–2). Caesar's description of his fleet is inconsistent. The 80 or so ships were described initially as transports (*BG* 4.22), but warships (*naves longes*), transports (*onerarias*) and scout ships (*speculatoria*) are all mentioned subsequently, and it is also stated that the troops had been transported in warships (*BG* 4.29).

The fleet of 54 BC was almost ten times bigger, some 800 ships. It comprised the surviving vessels of the 55 BC fleet (perhaps around 80), about 600 specially designed transport ships and 28 warships that the army had built over the winter, and private vessels which individuals (presumably officers) had built for their own convenience (*BG* 5.2; 5.8). What types of ships these private vessels were is not known, but at the Battle of Actium in 31 BC personal ships were warships.

The building of the new transports was a major logistical exercise and the design of ships was adapted for the local waters. Tidal range varies according to the terrain, the depth of the sea and other factors. In the Mediterranean, it is rarely greater than 0.3 m, whereas in Britain the average tidal range is 6 m (McGrail 1998, 259; Votruba 2017, 18–19). As a result, ships built in the Roman tradition were not well suited to northern waters where vessels were grounded regularly by the falling tide. In 56 BC Caesar commented that the keels of the Venetic ships were considerably flatter than Roman ones and were able to weather shoals and ebb tides more easily (*BG* 3.13). In 55 BC he also observed that the size of the Roman ships made it difficult for them to be run aground in shallow waters (*BG* 4. 24).

The new transports had lower hulls for easier beaching and were also broader to facilitate the transport of cargo and draught animals. The new vessels were equipped with oars and sails, which may imply that the transports of 55 only had sails. If Dio's comments about changing the design of the ships refer correctly to 57–56 BC, and not 55–54 BC, design adaptation may have been a continual process. These adapted transports may have been the prototype of the Gallic style vessels used in the Civil War (*de Bello Civili* 3.29) in 48 BC, and perhaps also of the Roman *ponto* ship depicted and named on a later mosaic (McGrail 2001, 217–218).

Some of the transports were built far inland. In the winter of 55–54 BC all eight legions wintered in Belgic Gaul and, in passing, Caesar mentioned that in 54 BC, 60 ships built in the territory of the Meldi had difficulty in joining the rest of the fleet. The Meldi inhabited the region of Meaux (Seine-et-Marne), so this means that the ships were built on the river Marne, *c.* 40 km north-east of Paris, some 200 km from the sea. The ships' tackle was brought from Spain, most probably from Gades (modern Cadiz) on the Atlantic coast.

Although the soldiers could help build the fleet and row the transports, sailors were also needed. For the campaign of 56 BC Caesar ordered rowers to be drafted from the *provincia* (Transalpine Gaul in southern France) and for seamen and steersmen to be got together (*BG* 3.9). The rowers were probably for the galleys built on the Loire, whose fighting complement would have been, as was usual, legionaries, but the seamen and steersmen could also have been responsible for transports. Seamen and steersmen were mentioned again in 54 BC when Caesar records that the transports were rowed (*BG* 5.10).

The scale of the ship building undertaken in preparation for these naval campaigns and the extensive supply network needed to procure equipment and crews is often overlooked. They were building programs that required careful planning and entailed considerable expense.

Iron Age landing sites

These Roman fleets had to use the existing Iron Age landing sites and assumptions about the nature of these places have played an important role in many previous discussions.

In the early 20th century the British scholars Haverfield and Rice Holmes had a long-running debate over the location of the Itian port (*e.g.* Haverfield 1913). They did not reach agreement, but they did concur that the port/s of embarkation in Gaul were harbours protected from the open sea. For Rice Holmes this was 'a port properly called', that is to say one in a bay or an estuary as opposed to one on an open beach or where the sea was sheltered from the wind by land or by submerged sandbanks (1907, 438, 569–570). In *Ancient Britain and the Invasions of Julius Caesar* Rice Holmes envisaged Boulogne in 55 BC – before the arrival of the Roman army – as follows:

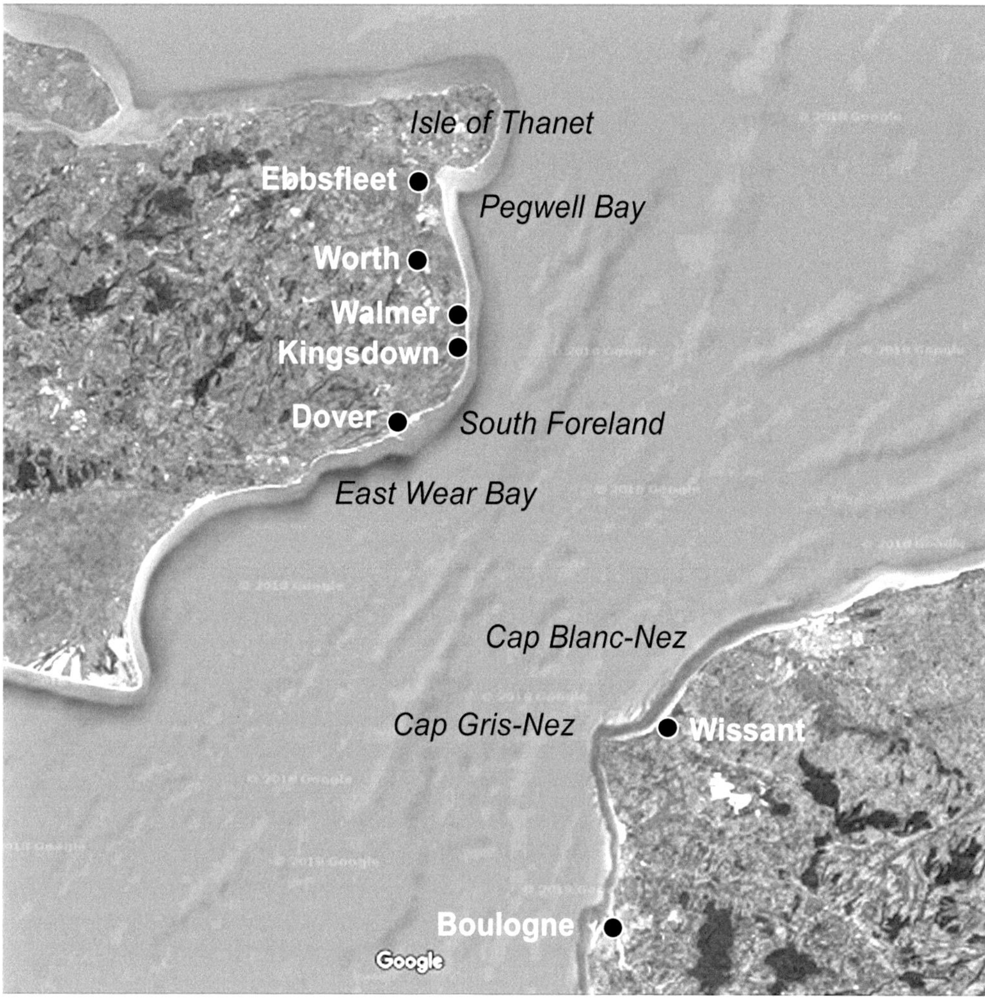

Figure 8.2 The location of coastal places in Kent and Pas-de-Calais mentioned in the text (author, on © Google Earth background image).

> The estuary, longer, wider and deeper than it is now, was protected from every gale by the bold, bluff of land which on the west throws out the promontory of Alprech, and which then projected northward considerably beyond its present limit. Vessels of light draught could enter the harbour at low tide. Shipyards lined its banks. Roads connected it with the interior; and timber in abundance could be floated down the river from the forest of Boulogne (Rice Holmes 1907, 306–307).

As Rice Holmes believed that a similar harbour existed at Dover (Figure 8.2), it was the obvious place for Caesar to attempt to land, even if doing so was not without difficulties because of the narrow and steep sided valley of the river Dour which the army would had to have fought its way up.

In the intervening century a considerable body of evidence has been amassed for Roman harbours, but almost none for Iron Age ones of the type envisaged by Rice Holmes and Haverfield. Instead, a consensus has developed amongst coastal and marine archaeologists that most prehistoric landing sites were in bays or areas of sheltered water with a gently shelving beach. Instead of mooring boats at a jetty or quay or altering the shoreline to accommodate ships, it is widely agreed that the shallow-draughted vessels were simply beached by taking the ground on a falling tide (*e.g.* McGrail 1983; 1990, 46–47; 1997, 219–220; 1998, 267–274; Ilves 2013, 320).

Two contemporary late Iron Age sites on opposite sides of the Channel are examples of this type of landing place. The site at Urville-Nacqueville (Manche) on the Cotentin peninsula was used in the late 2nd to earlier 1st centuries BC. According to calculations based on distance, prevailing winds, visibility and the presence of hazards, the Cotentin lies on one of the safest and most reliable Channel crossings, between the estuary of the Rance in Brittany, and Christchurch and Poole harbours in Dorset (McGrail 1983, Route 5; 1997, 219; 1998, 272–273, fig. 13.7, tab. 13.4). At the east end of the 2.5 km long sandy beach that faces the Channel are the rocky outcrops of the Rocher de Nacqueville headland. A manufacturing and trading site was established next to these outcrops (Lefort *et al.* 2015). As no rivers discharge into the sea along the length of the beach, there cannot have been any significant inlets here, so it is likely that boats used the small sandy bay east of, and in the lee of, the Rocher de Nacqueville. The manufacturing site may have been protected by dune formations that had developed against the rocks. Given its exposed position, the site is likely to have been used seasonally and as McGrail noted, it has no obvious access to the hinterland (1983, 324).

One of the sites with which Urville-Nacqueville was linked was Hengistbury Head, Dorset. This site has even more wide-ranging evidence for production, and for exchange with its hinterland and with Gaul (Cunliffe 1987; Cunliffe and De Jersey 1997). Hengistbury is located within the sheltered waters of Christchurch harbour into which the rivers Avon and Stour flow. The Iron Age port lies in a small bay close to the harbour entrance, protected from the prevailing south-westerly winds by the headland of Hengistbury Head. As at Urville-Nacqueville, manufacturing took place right next to the shore but there is some evidence for a harbour structure in the form of a gravel hard or layer that was found in a small inlet next to this bay. The hard is suggested to have been built to provide a standing for beached ships (Cunliffe 1987, 120–122; 1990, 29–31), perhaps to prevent them from settling into the muddy shore. It has also been suggested that Hengistbury Head was only used seasonally (Fitzpatrick 2001).

At both ports the ships seem likely to have been tide-beached. While Christchurch harbour could accommodate a large number of ships, the small bay at the Rocher de Nacqueville could not. This is not to say that harbour structures are unknown. In Britain, Poole harbour, Dorset, a few kilometres west of Hengistbury Head, provides an even larger natural harbour. Here, two separate timber jetty structures dated to the 4th to 2nd centuries BC have been found, one running from Ower peninsula on the mainland towards Green Island (one of several large islands in the harbour), the other from Green Island towards the Ower peninsula (Mankey *et al.* 2002; Wilkes 2013, fig. 8). Whether these are the remains of a single causeway, two jetties or even mole-like structures built to control access to the harbour by restricting the width of access, is, however, uncertain.

Elsewhere, structures more confidently interpreted as jetties or other harbour features are known, for example at Geneva (Kaenel this volume). Although Lake Geneva is astride the river Rhône – a major communications artery throughout prehistory – the harbour at Geneva could only accommodate a small number of vessels (Bonnet *et al.* 1989, 4–6, figs 2–3). Even Lattes, which was one of the largest ports in the Mediterranean and stood on the edge of a lagoon into which the river Lez debouched, could not have accommodated a hundred large ships. Harbour structures in the form of stone quays are first documented at Lattes in the 2nd century BC, probably in response to the increased size of Roman ships that had begun to sail regularly along the western Mediterranean coast (Garcia 2008).

It is also now clear that Roman ports with harbour structures in the Mediterranean were usually associated with cities. Contrary to the assumption of Haverfield and Rice Holmes, few ports were built at river mouths, partly because of the difficulties of navigation in many estuaries and coastal rivers, and partly because of the difficulty of keeping harbours navigable because of silting. It was only after the invention of hydraulic concrete in the 2nd century BC that it became easier to create larger coastal harbours by building breakwaters and other substantial structures (Blackman 1982; Oleson 2013). The Latin *portus* is a generic term for a landing site and does not imply the presence of built structures.

In short, there is no evidence to suggest that in western Europe in the late Iron Age there were landing sites with harbour structures that could accommodate a fleet of 100 large vessels, let alone 800. Instead, sheltered waters – typically beaches or bays – were used. The Roman fleets would have to have used these same sites and the evidence provided by Caesar and Dio is consistent with this. What will have distinguished the Roman embarkation and landing sites in Gaul and Britain is the need for the fleets to be defended.

The landing sites

The individual landing sites used by the fleets in 55 and 54 BC are not described in any detail but incidental comments about how the fleet was moored provide important information about the type of locations that were chosen.

In both years Caesar describes landing in Britain on open shores or beaches. In 55 BC the beach was described as even and open and the warships were hauled out above the tide (*in aridum subdexeret*), while the transports rode at anchor. This is presumably because the wine-glass shaped hulls and pronounced keels of the galleys could, if moored close to the shore in deep water, become unstable on the rising and falling tides (as Caesar described in 56 BC). The beach used in 54 BC was described as sandy or soft and open, and the best place for disembarkation. Presumably the water there was shallower because of a gently sloping beach profile, and the whole fleet rode at anchor. When the remainder of the fleet returned to Gaul that year, it was beached. As the fleet was able to both embark and disembark at the intended ports in 54 BC, this indicates that beaches were the preferred type of landing site.

All four of the main crossings were undertaken at night, presumably to allow embarkation and disembarkation to be undertaken in daylight and in a single day. This would allow the soldiers, horses and draught animals to board the ships from shallow water and wait for the tide to rise before setting sail. The precise time of sailing was determined by the tides.

Using the Blackfriars 1 shipwreck as a paradigm, Grainge (2002, 60–61) assessed the size of the landing fronts in Britain in 55 and 54 BC. The Blackfriars 1 ship was built in the mid-2nd century AD in the Romano-Celtic tradition (McGrail 1998; 2001, 196–197; Nayling and McGrail 2004, 208–209, 228) and sank, probably after a collision, in the Thames at London not long after. She had a beam of 6.12 m. If the Caesarian transports of 55 BC were of similar beam, and all of them came inshore at 20 m intervals, in order to provide sufficient space between their oars and also room for the soldiers to disembark between them, a landing front over 1.5 km wide would have been necessary. As the fleet of 54 BC was tenfold larger – over 800 vessels – it required a very much larger landing front. Because of this it seems unlikely that the whole fleet was able to land at the same time, and indeed in 55 BC, Caesar reported that the galleys provided support for the legionaries as they came ashore by firing artillery and launching projectiles. But even if the exact details are lacking, it is clear that, as the armies were disembarked rapidly in both 55 and 54 BC, wide landing fronts were needed.

Grainge also considered how different methods of anchoring and mooring up could be used to reduce the space needed for the fleet once the army had disembarked (Grainge 2002, 61). However, in 54 BC the fleet was struck by a storm on the first night and the ships were thrown up onto the shore when their cables and anchors could not hold. This suggests that the ships were moored to the shore, secured by stern lines, probably both port and starboard, that were fixed to wooden stakes on the shore, and by anchors cast from the bow (cf. Vortuba 2017, 16–17). This seems likely to have been because there had not been enough time on the first day to move them to deeper water to ride at anchor. It is also possible that the ships were moored several deep, one attached to another with only the vessels at the shore being secured to it (cf. Whitehead 1993, fig. 18.1). In 55 BC the much smaller number of transports were riding at anchor in deeper water when the storm struck, the galleys having been hauled out.

This evidence makes it is clear that the preferred landing sites were gently shelving beaches. It was relatively easy to embark and disembark large numbers of men and animals in a single day on such beaches and to moor the galleys to the shore and leave the transports at anchor. If such gently shelving beaches were unavailable, a beach where the galleys could be hauled up out of the sea – a task that required considerable labour – would be chosen. The first priority would have been the safe disembarkation of the soldiers, the second, the safety of the fleet.

The identification of the landing sites

Gaul

As we have seen, the Itian port and the port from which the fleet sailed in 55 BC (if different) remain to be identified. Strabo's account has been interpreted as showing that Caesar sailed from the Itian port in both 55 and 54 BC. Strabo stated that Caesar used *Ition* as a naval station when he sailed for Britain and the time of arrival he gave is consistent with the time that Caesar gave for 55 BC. However, Caesar himself made a distinction between the shortest and the most convenient crossings, stating that he had been advised that the most convenient was from the Itian port (*BG* 5.2). This can be read as meaning that it was not used in 55 BC.

Boulogne has often been identified as portus Itius on the basis of Ptolemy's *Geography* and the fact that in the Imperial period it became the main base of the *classis Britannica*. It was the site preferred by the *Commission de la topgraphie de la Gaule* and Napoléon III, and it was also favoured by Haverfield, and sometimes by Rice Holmes. One of the main reasons for the long running debate between Haverfield and Rice Holmes was Rice Holmes' indecision as to whether the Itian port was Boulogne or Wissant. The main reason for this equivocation was that while the Liane estuary at Boulogne was more sheltered than the open beach at Wissant, Rice Holmes doubted that the large fleet of 54 BC could have left the estuary on a single tide.

Even though there has been considerable archaeological work in Boulogne, as yet neither it nor Wissant have yielded any evidence to suggest that they were used regularly as landing sites in the late Iron Age (Seillier 2007; Blamangin *et al.* 2015, 14–15; Reddé 2015, 30). The port from which the cavalry sailed in 55 BC (the further port) is contingent upon identification of the port of concentration. If that port is held to be Boulogne, Ambleteuse is usually suggested; if Wissant, then Sangatte is usually proposed. The site at which the two transports landed in 55 (BG 4.37) cannot be identified beyond the fact that it was within a few hours ride of the camp, which is presumed to have been close to the shore.

Britain

Nearly all the contenders for the continental port/s are located within the territory of the Morini. In contrast, the locations of the British landing sites have ranged from Sussex on the Channel coast to Norfolk on the North Sea coast, with most writers preferring Sussex or Kent.

This wide geographical range is primarily due to the limited evidence and, perhaps surprisingly, a debate about the tide. Caesar did not give the date of the landing in 55 BC but reported that the storm that damaged the fleet occurred at a full moon four days later. By calculating the dates of the lunar cycle, that night can be fixed as 15/16th September 55 BC in the modern civil calendar. This would fix the date of the landing (depending on whether or not the night was counted as part of the preceding day) as the 12th or 13th. For many years it was considered that the fleet made landfall at Dover and that the tides there were consistent with Caesar having arrived mid-morning and waiting until the afternoon to sail north with the flood tide.

This calculation was based on the time of low water but in 1851 George Airy recognized that low water does not coincide with the change in the tidal stream. Instead it is over three hours before the tidal stream begins to run. This means that when Caesar sailed on, the tide would have been flowing south and the fleet would have been carried towards Sussex. However, scholars such as Rice Holmes remained adamant that the 'projection' that Dio said Caesar sailed around was the South Foreland, which is north of Dover. Rice Holmes attempted to resolve this contradiction by arguing that the favourable wind that Caesar mentioned was strong enough to counter the force of the tidal current.

In 1936 Collingwood suggested that this apparent contradiction may have been caused by a scribal error: 'I suspect that something has gone wrong with the numeral *quartem* in [*BG*] iv.28; if the interval was more like a week, the stream would be running north-eastwards when he weighed' (Collingwood and Myres 1936, 37, n. 1). In this emendation the number iiii is replaced by viii giving a landing date of September 8th, 55 BC, a date on which the tidal currents do match the times that Caesar gave (Olson *et al.* 2008), thus supporting the view that he landed in Kent.

In this interpretation it has been almost universally assumed that the intended landing site was Dover because the shortest Channel crossing is between there and Cap Gris-Nez. It was only when it was discovered that it was unsafe to land at Dover that the fleet sailed on for about seven miles to between Walmer and Deal.

There has been less certainty about the landing site of 54 BC. It has often been suggested that the same site was used, but Caesar's statement that fleet intended to land at the place that they had learnt the previous year was the best place of disembarkment implies a different port. A location further north, near Worth or Sandwich has often been proposed (*e.g.* Rice Holmes 1907, 335, 674; Hawkes 1977, 157–159).

Rice Holme's identifications have largely gone unchallenged and are regularly repeated (*e.g.* Hawkes 1977, 155; Raaflaub 2017, 123) but the identifications of Dover as the intended landing site and between Walmer and Deal as the actual one, are not without difficulties. As noted, Dover would not have been a very good landing site for a large army as the mouth of the river Dour is less than 1 km wide and its steep-sided valley is overlooked by higher ground. As with Boulogne, there is presently no evidence that Dover was a port in the late Iron Age (Parfitt 2004a, 266; 2004b, 101–102) but there is strong evidence that there was one *c.* 10 km to the west at East Wear Bay, Folkstone (Parfitt 2013, 36–37).

The comment that British warriors stood on the heights is generic rather than specific and could describe anywhere from East Wear Bay to Kingsdown where the cliff line falls rapidly (Figure 8.3) or even to the 10 m high brickearth terrace behind

Figure 8.3 View looking south towards the northern end of the cliffs of Dover at Kingsdown. The shingle beach, which is the southern end of the Sandwich Bay spit, extends from the end of the cliffs. The descent of the groyne illustrates the steepness of the beach face at this point (photo A.P. Fitzpatrick).

the beach at Kingsdown. Nor is it clear that the intended landing site that was described was necessarily the same location as the heights on which the Britons stood. The description of the steep slopes at the landing site and the fact that it was possible to throw projectiles down onto the shore could also refer to a steeply shelving shore.

Today, the coast between Walmer and Deal is such a steeply shelving shingle beach. Rice Holmes argued that the difference between this shore and the soft open shore and the fighting in the shallows along it described by Caesar was due to coastal change (*e.g.* Rice Holmes 1907, 523–525, 653–654). However, this is most unlikely. The shingle beach was created by longshore drift which has been continuous since the land bridge with the Continent was broken after the last Ice Age. To the north of Deal the shingle beach becomes a spit and this had reached as far as Worth by the 2nd century AD (Parfitt 2000).

Occasionally, reservations have also been expressed about the practicality of landing on the beach between Walmer and Deal (*e.g.* Wacher 1979, 2; Waite 2011, 51–52) and these are deepened by a consideration of the practicalities of hauling the galleys ashore, which Caesar reports doing. Athenian triremes of the Classical period (*c.* 5th–4th centuries BC) were rarely hauled up slopes greater than 1:10 because of the need to support the length of the keel (Coates 2012, 139). It would have been almost impossible to haul ashore the Roman galleys – which were larger and heavier (Morrison with Coates 1996) – between Walmer and Deal if the beach profile in the 1st century BC was at all similar to the modern one, whose angle of slope varies between 1:10 and 1:20, without having to excavate slipways to reduce the slope and increase the length of support for the hull (Figures 8.4–8.5).

To summarize, the belief that in 55 BC the Roman fleet tried to land at Dover is predicated on the belief that there was an Iron Age harbour there. If this presumption is set aside, Caesar's account is also consistent with an intended landing site at the northern end of the cliff line and an eventual landing further north on an even and open shore with shallows. Whatever the precise location of this site, the principle roles of the camp that was built close by were to defend the army and protect the fleet. The landing site of 54 BC was not necessarily the same as in the previous year, and this camp was certainly close to the shore and its principle role was to protect the fleet. It seems probable that the two camps would have occupied similar topographic positions.

Figure 8.4 View to the north from the same position on Walmer beach (photo A.P. Fitzpatrick).

Figure 8.5 View to the west from the foot of the beach face at Walmer at low tide. The man, who is c. 2 m tall, is standing at the top of the beach face (photo A.P. Fitzpatrick).

New evidence: the Ebbsfleet enclosure

The recent identification of a 1st-century BC defensive enclosure at Ebbsfleet on the Isle of Thanet, as the base built to protect the fleet in 54 BC (Fitzpatrick 2015; 2018a; 2018b) provides a new perspective on the landing sites in Gaul and Britain. Its topographic setting is consistent with the preferred type of Roman landing place but there has been significant landscape change during the intervening two millennia.

Identified in excavations in advance of road building (Andrews *et al.* 2015), the Ebbsfleet enclosure is sited on a low peninsula next to Pegwell Bay, the largest bay on

Figure 8.6 Aerial view of the Ebbsfleet enclosure looking east towards Pegwell Bay and the chalk cliffs at Ramsgate. In the foreground, part of the western side of the defences under excavation. The two fields beyond the road are on the Ebbsfleet peninsula. The area between these fields and the coast is reclaimed land (drone photo Dean Barkley).

the coast of east Kent (Figure 8.6). The full circuit of the enclosure is not yet established; only the western, landward side has been traced with certainty (Figure 8.7). Due to a combination of natural silting and land reclamation, the sea now lies *c.* 1 km to the east, but in the 1st century BC it would only have been a few hundred metres away. It is difficult to establish the precise sea level at this time, although it has been rising steadily since the end of the last Ice Age due to long-term climatic and geological factors, the position of the coastline is determined by local factors including coastal change. This is well illustrated by the fact that in the 1st century BC, the west side of the Ebbsfleet peninsula was flanked by the former Wantsum Channel (Figure 8.8). This area of wetland once contained a channel that ran between the east/Channel coast of Kent and the Thames estuary on the north coast. The Wantsum Channel separated the Isle of Thanet from mainland Kent until the Middle Ages and was navigable to sea-going vessels until a combination of natural silting and land reclamation made it impassable.

The Ebbsfleet enclosure is dated to the 1st century BC by coins, pottery and radiocarbon determinations. The ditch is typically *c.* 5 m wide and 2 m deep, its walls slope at 45 degrees and the base is flat. There is no certain evidence for a rampart having eroded into the ditch, so the ditch may have been backfilled deliberately. The enclosure is interpreted as a Roman base because on the one hand it would be a very unusual defensive enclosure in the local late Iron Age context, and on the other the best parallels for the ditch in terms of its size, shape and the large area it enclosed are the

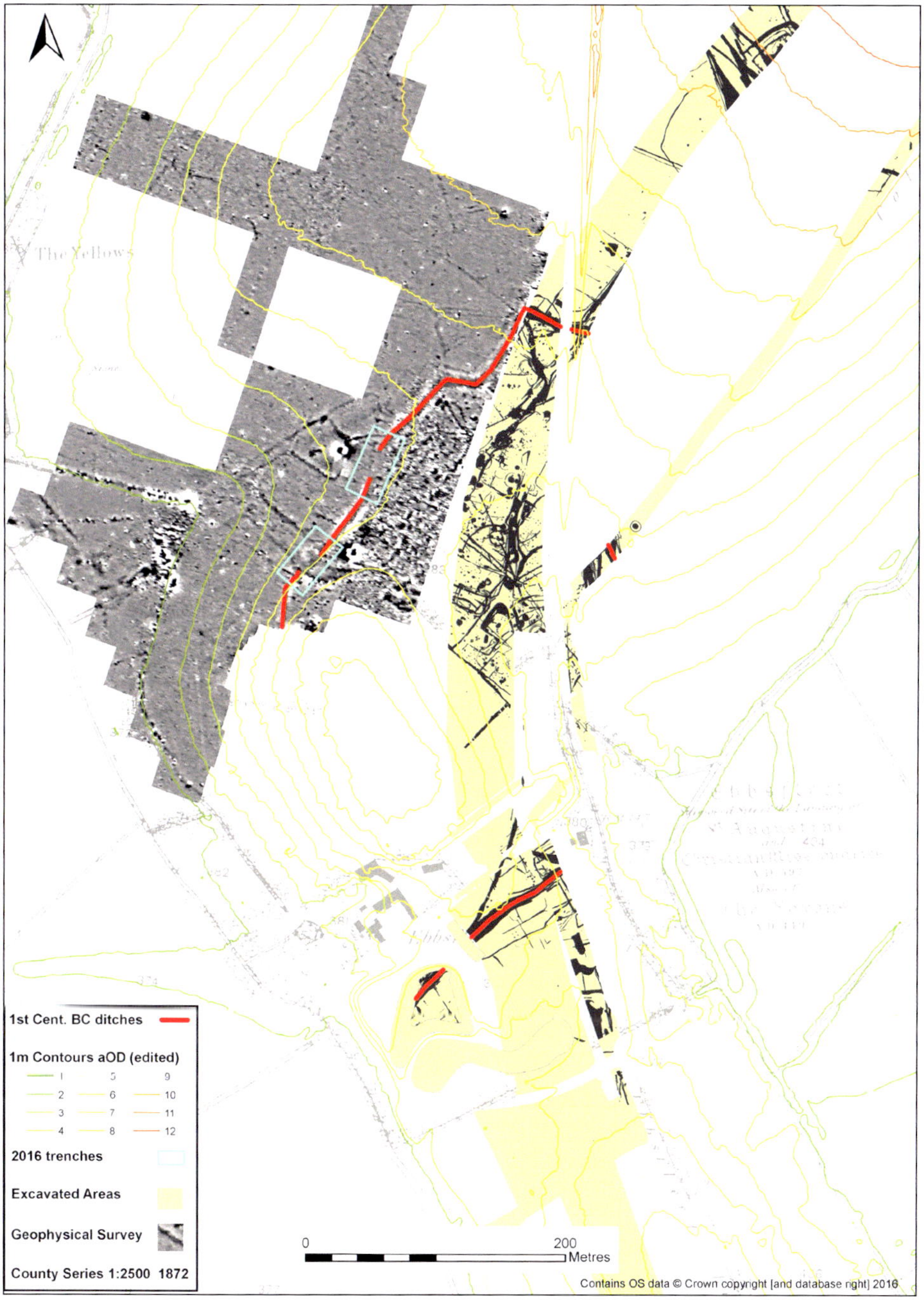

Figure 8.7 Plan of the Ebbsfleet enclosure showing the results of the geophysical survey and the routes of the new road and a pipeline to the east of it. Ebbsfleet Hill is covered by a wood and was not surveyed. The defensive ditch is marked in red and the sites of the recent excavations outlined in light blue. The contours are taken from the Ordnance Survey map of 1872 because of changes to the topography caused by recent landscaping for a golf course to the east of the road, visible in Figure 8.6.

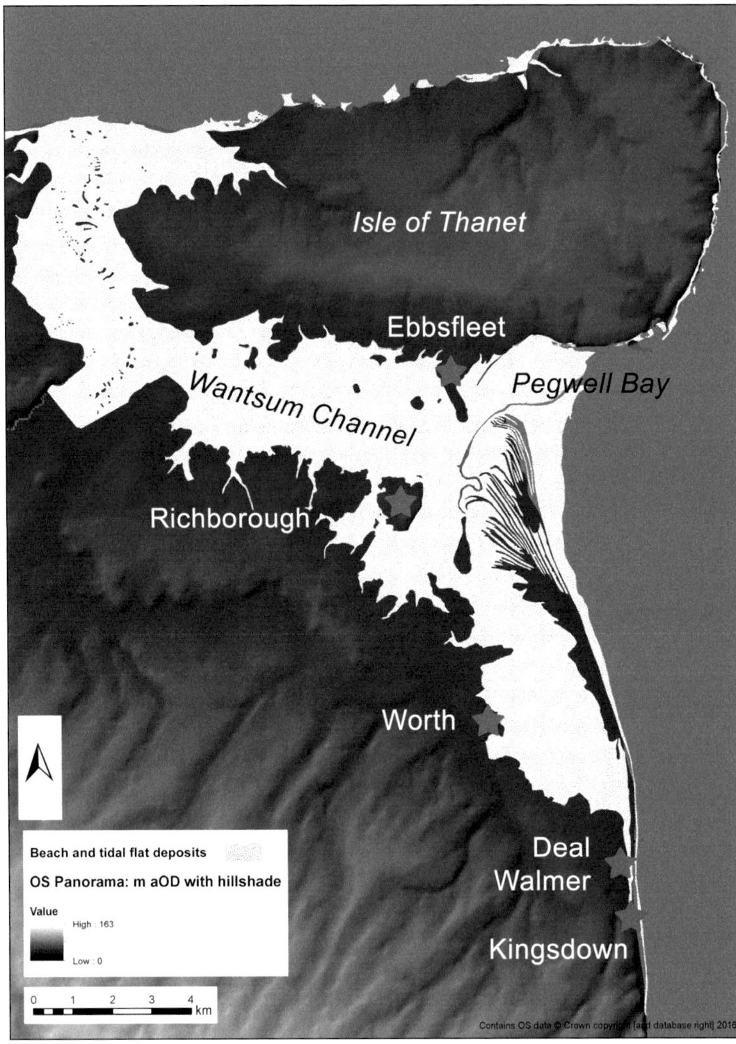

Figure 8.8 Lidar model of the topography of north-east Kent, showing the location of selected places mentioned in the text (Lidar render by Matt Beamish, University of Leicester Archaeological Services).

outer ditch of the circumvallation at Alesia (Reddé and von Schnurbein 2001; Reddé this volume), together with its coastal location. The similarity of the ditch to those at Alesia suggests that this particular type of defence was used to defend large areas rather than camps, which had v-shaped ditches. In this case it was the fleet, which had been hauled out of the sea, that was being defended. The one entrance identified so far at Ebbsfleet has similarities to the east entrance of the fortress at Hermeskeil (Hornung 2016; this volume). In each of the ten sections excavated across the ditch at Ebbsfleet, a smaller, later, ditch was found cut into the outer side of the infilled ditch. Conservation of the iron objects is ongoing, but a *pilum* tip of Republican type has been identified.

Figure 8.9 View of Pegwell Bay from Cliffs End, looking south. The flat, muddy, beach is backed by salt marsh and a narrow width of sand. Deal pier is on the far left of the horizon (photo A.P. Fitzpatrick).

The coastal location of the Ebbsfleet enclosure is one of the most important factors in interpreting it as a Roman base. The wide, open and gently shelving shore of Pegwell Bay would have made it well-suited for disembarking an army that may be conservatively estimated to comprise 20,000 men and at least 2,000 horses as well as numerous draught animals in a single day; this, however it was effected, must have required a landing front of several kilometres (above; Figure 8.9). The bay is also consistent with Caesar's comment that in 54 BC the fleet went to the place that they had learned the previous year to be 'the best place of disembarkation' and which he described as having a soft or sandy open shore. The chalk cliffs to the north of Pegwell Bay (Figure 8.10) are also consistent with Caesar's comment that when the fleet failed to hold its course in 54 BC and was carried too far to the north and east, Britain was visible far away to the left. Only high ground such as these cliffs would have been visible from far out at sea.

At first light on the day after they landed, Caesar took most of the army inland, where they defeated the Britons and captured a hillfort that was almost certainly Bigberry near Canterbury *c.* 23 km away (Thompson 1983). Almost immediately afterwards news arrived that the fleet had been badly damaged in a storm. Caesar led the army back to the coast, where he decided to beach the ships and protect them by building a single line of defence connecting the ships with the camp. The army worked for ten days and nights to haul the ships ashore and build the defence. When the base was 'strongly fortified', Caesar left the original garrison and all the skilled

Figure 8.10 Looking north towards the cliffs at Cliffs End and Ramsgate with Pegwell Bay mudflats in the foreground (photo A.P. Fitzpatrick).

workmen in the legions to repair the ships and led the rest of the army back inland to restart the advance.

The archaeological evidence and the topographic clues given by Caesar are all consistent with the Ebbsfleet enclosure being part of the Roman defences built to protect a fleet in 54 BC. It follows from this conclusion that the smaller, 1st century AD ditch cut into the outer part of the original ditch might be associated with the Claudian invasion of AD 43. The profile recorded on the north side of the enclosure is similar to the inner ditch of the Claudian defences at Richborough, less than 4 km to the south (Bushe-Fox 1932, 10, pl. i, sections 33 and 35; 1949, 15, pl. iv, b). A few pieces of Claudio-Neronian military equipment have also been found at the enclosure, including belt fittings and fragments of scabbard binding (Scott 2015, 55–57). This suggests that the Claudian army may have re-cut the circuit of the Caesarian defences, which though largely infilled will still have been visible as a surface depression.

Conclusions

The ports used in 55 and 54 BC were some of the most important places in the battle for Gaul. They were critical for ensuring the safe return of the fleets because Julius Caesar always intended that the army would return to Gaul at the end of each campaigning season.

The building of the fleets, their fitting out and the recruitment of their crews was a considerable, and expensive, logistical challenge that required careful planning. Even so, the fleets had to set sail from and land on open shores. The evidence from the late Iron Age sites at Urville-Nacqueville and Hengistbury Head on either side of the Channel is consistent with the view that prehistoric landing sites were used seasonally and rarely had harbour structures. The descriptions of how the ships were moored in Britain in 55 and 54 BC, of how they were damaged in storms and how the design of the new ships for the fleet of 54 BC was adapted, are all consistent with the preferred landing places being long, gently shelving beaches. In 54 BC, and probably also in 55, a camp was built close to the shore to protect the Roman fleet and on both occasions the camps provided the base to repair the damaged vessels. There is no evidence to support the long-held view that there were large sheltered harbours with built structures such as jetties and piers that could accommodate large fleets. It is this belief that has underpinned the long-held view that in 55 BC Caesar originally intended to sail from Boulogne and land at Dover.

The scale of landscape change around the Ebbsfleet peninsula since the 1st century BC emphasizes the importance of reconstructing the contemporary topography in attempting to locate the landing sites. Those changes have been caused by a combination of natural coastal change and land reclamation, processes which have altered both sides of the Channel in the last 2,000 years. In France there have been extensive changes in the low-lying landscapes of the north-east coast and amongst the extensive dune formations that protect it (*e.g.* Grenier 1944). In Britain the Lydden valley south of Ebbsfleet is largely a reclaimed landscape and the landing site of 55 BC is likely to be located within it. As the landing sites in Gaul were already secured by the presence of the Roman army, they are unlikely to have had major defences of the type needed in Britain in 54 BC, but it is very probable that their topography was similar to those of the landing sites in Britain.

Acknowledgements

I am grateful to Dr Roland Bockius of the Museum für Antike Schiffahrt des RGZM, Mainz, for his assistance regarding the ships of the 2nd and 1st centuries BC. The research for this paper was undertaken at the University of Leicester as part of the *In the Footsteps of Caesar* project, directed by Professor Colin Haselgrove and funded by the Leverhulme Trust.

Bibliography

Andrews, P., Booth, P., Fitzpatrick, A.P. and Welsh, K. (2015) *Digging at the Gateway. Archaeological Landscapes of South Thanet, Vol. 1: The Sites; Vol. 2: The Finds, Environmental and Dating Reports.* Oxford and Salisbury, Oxford Wessex Archaeology Monograph 18.

Blackman, D.J. (1982) Ancient harbours in the Mediterranean. Part 2. *International Journal of Nautical Archaeology and Underwater Exploration* 11, 185–211.

Blamangin, O., Demon, A. and Révillion, S. (eds) (2015) *Actualité de la recherche archéologique à Boulogne-sur-Mer*. Villeneuve d'Ascq, Revue du Nord Hors série, Collection Art et Archéologie 22.

Bonnet, C., Zoller, G., Broillet, P., Haldimann, M.-A., Baud, C.-A., Kramar, C., Simon, C., Olive, C. and Billaud, Y. (1989) Les premières ports de Genève. *Archéologie Suisse* 12, 12–24.

Bushe-Fox, J.P. (1932) *Third Report on the Excavations of the Roman Fort at Richborough, Kent*. London, Reports of the Research Committee of the Society of the Antiquaries of London 10.

Bushe-Fox, J.P. (1949) *Fourth Report on the Excavations of the Roman Fort at Richborough, Kent*. London, Reports of the Research Committee of the Society of Antiquaries of London 16.

Coates, J. (2012) On slipping and launching triremes from the Piraeus shipsheds and beaches. In B. Rankov (ed.), *Trireme* Olympias. *The Final Report: Sea trials 1992–4. Conference Papers 1998*, 134–141. Oxford, Oxbow Books.

Collingwood, R.G. and Myres, J.N.L. (1936) *Roman Britain and the English Settlements*. Oxford, Clarendon Press.

Cunliffe, B. (1987) *Hengistbury Head, Dorset, Vol. 1: The Prehistoric and Roman Settlement 3500 BC–AD 500*. Oxford, Oxford University Committee for Archaeology Monograph 13.

Cunliffe, B. (1990) Hengistbury Head: A late prehistoric haven. In S. McGrail (ed.), *Maritime Celts, Frisians and Saxons*, 27–31. York, Council for British Archaeology Research Report 71.

Cunliffe, B. and de Jersey, P. (1997) *Armorica and Britain: Cross-Channel Relationships in the Late First Millennium BC*. Oxford, Oxford University Committee for Archaeology Monograph 45/Studies in Celtic Coinage 3.

Fitzpatrick, A.P. (2001) Cross-Channel exchange, Hengistbury Head and the end of hillforts. In J.R. Collis (ed.), *Society and Settlement in Iron Age Europe (Actes du XVIIIe colloque de l'AFEAF, Winchester 1994)*, 82–97. Sheffield, Sheffield Archaeological Monograph 11.

Fitzpatrick, A.P. (2015) The Ebbsfleet defensive enclosure. In P. Andrews, P. Booth, A.P. Fitzpatrick and K. Welsh, *Digging at the Gateway. Archaeological Landscapes of South Thanet, Vol. 1: The Sites; Vol. 2: The Finds, Environmental and Dating Reports*, 194–215. Oxford and Salisbury, Oxford Wessex Archaeology Monograph 18.

Fitzpatrick, A.P. (2018a) Ebbsfleet, 54 BC. *Current Archaeology* 337, 26–32.

Fitzpatrick, A.P. (2018b) L'enceinte d'Ebbsfleet sur l'île de Thanet (Kent). Un camp césarien en Angleterre. In M. Reddé (ed.), *L'armée romaine en Gaule à l'époque républicaine. Nouveaux témoignages archéologiques*, 273–284. Glux-en-Glenne, Collection Bibracte 28.

Garcia, D. (2008) Le port de *Lattara* (Lattes, Hérault): premiers acquis sur les phases préromaines et romaines. *Gallia* 65, 131–149.

Grainge, G. (2002) *The Roman Channel Crossing of A.D. 43: The Constraints on Claudius's Naval Strategy*. Oxford, British Archaeological Reports British Series 332.

Grenier, A. (1944) Deux ports romains du Pas-de-Calais, Portus Itius et Portus Aepatiacus. *Comptes rendus des séances de l'Académie des Inscriptions et Belles-Lettres* 88, 372–386.

Haverfield, F.J. (1913) Portus Itius. *Classical Review* 27, no. 8, 258–260.

Hawkes, C.F.C. (1977) Britain and Julius Caesar. *Proceedings of the British Academy* 63, 125–192.

Hornung, S. (2016) *Siedlung und Bevölkerung in Ostgallien zwischen Gallischem Krieg und der Festigung der römischen Herrschaft: eine Studie auf Basis landschaftsarchäologischer Forschungen im Umfeld des Oppidums 'Hunnenring' von Otzenhausen (Lkr. St Wendel)*. Mainz, Römisch-Germanische Forschungen 73.

Ilves, K. (2013) Widening perspectives in the archaeological study of maritime landing sites: a model suggestion. In M.-A. Daire, C. Dupont, A. Baudry, C. Billard, J.-M. Large, L. Lespez, E. Normand and C. Scarre (eds), *Anciens peuplements littoraux et relations Homme/Milieu sur les côtes de l'Europe Atlantique / Ancient Maritime Communities and the Relationship between People and Environment along the European Atlantic Coasts*, 319–328. Oxford, British Archaeological Reports International Series 2570.

Lefort, A., Baron, A., Blondel, F., Méniel, M, and Rottier, S. with Nieto-Pelletier, S. and Querré, G. (2015) Artisanat, commerce et nécropole. Un port de La Tène D1 à Urville-Nacqueville. In

F. Olmer and R. Roure (eds), *Les gaulois au fil de l'eau (Actes du 37e colloque international de l'AFEAF, Montpellier 2013)*, 441–474. Montpellier, Ausonius.

Markey, M., Wilkes, E. and Darvill, T. (2002) Poole Harbour: An Iron Age port. *Current Archaeology* 181, 7–11.

McDougall, I. (1991) Dio and his sources for Caesar's campaigns in Gaul. *Latomus* 50, 616–638.

McGrail, S. (1983) Cross-Channel seamanship and navigation in the late first millennium BC. *Oxford Journal of Archaeology* 2, 299–337.

McGrail, S. (1990) Boats and boatmanship in the late prehistoric southern North Sea and Channel region. In McGrail, S. (ed.), *Maritime Celts, Frisians and Saxons*, 32–48. York, Council for British Archaeology Research Report 71.

McGrail, S. (1997) *Studies in Maritime Archaeology*. Oxford, British Archaeological Reports British Series 256.

McGrail, S. (1998) *Ancient Boats in North-West Europe. The Archaeology of Water Transport to AD 1500* (2nd edn). London, Longman.

McGrail, S. (2001) *Boats of the World from the Stone Age to Medieval Times*. Oxford, Oxford University Press.

Morgan, L. (2000) The autopsy of C. Asinius Pollio. *Journal of Roman Studies* 90, 51–69.

Morrison, J.S. with Coates, J.F. (1996), *Greek and Roman Oared Warships*. Oxford, Oxbow Books.

Nayling, N. and McGrail, S. (2004) *The Barland's Farm Romano-Celtic Boat*. York, Council for British Archaeology Research Report 138.

Oleson, J.P. (2014) The evolution of harbour engineering in the ancient Mediterranean world. In S. Ladstätter, F. Pirson and T. Schmidts (eds), *Häfen und Hafenstädte im östlichen Mittelmeerraum von der Antike bis in byzantinische Zeit. Neue Entdeckungen und aktuelle Forschungsansätze; Istanbul. 30.05.-01.06.2011/Harbors and harbor cities in the Eastern Mediterranean from Antiquity to the Byzantine period. Recent discoveries and current approaches*, 509–522. Istanbul, BYAS 19/Sonderschriften des Österreichischen Archäologischen Institutes 52.

Olson, D.W., Doescher, R.L. and the Texas State Honors Students (2008) Caesar's invasions of Britain. *Sky & Telescope* August 2008, 18–23.

Parfitt, K. (2000) A Roman settlement site at Dickson's Corner. *Archaologia Cantiana* 120, 107–148.

Parfitt, K. (2004a) Discovery and excavation. In P. Clark (ed.), *The Dover Bronze Age Boat*, 9–22. London, English Heritage.

Parfitt, K. (2004b) A search for the prehistoric harbours of Kent. In P. Clark (ed.), *The Dover Boat in Context: Society and Water Transport in Prehistoric Europe*, 99–105. Oxford, Oxbow Books.

Parfitt, K. (2013) Folkestone before Folkestone: Prehistoric Times. In I. Coulson (ed.), *Folkestone to 1500: A Town Unearthed*, 9–30. Canterbury, Canterbury Archaeological Trust.

Raaflaub, K.A. (ed.) (2017) *The Landmark Julius Caesar: The Complete Works*. New York, Pantheon Books.

Raaflaub, K. T. and Ramsey, J. T. (2017) Reconstructing the chronology of Caesar's Gallic Wars. *Histos* 11, 1–74.

Reddé M. (2015) Boulogne-sur-Mer dans le dispositif militaire de l'Empire romain. In O. Blamangin, A. Demon and S. Révillion (eds), *Actualité de la recherche archéologique à Boulogne-sur-Mer*, 29–39. Villeneuve d'Ascq, Revue du Nord Hors série, Collection Art et Archéologie 22.

Reddé, M. and Schnurbein, S. von (2001) *Alésia. Fouilles et recherches Franco-Allemandes sur les travaux militaires romains autour du Mont-Auxois (1991–1997)*. Paris, Mémoires de l'Académie des Inscriptions et Belles-Lettres 22.

Rice Holmes, T. (1907) *Ancient Britain and the Invasions of Julius Caesar*. Oxford, Clarendon Press.

Ridgeway, W. (1891) Caesar's invasions of Britain. *Journal of Philology* 19, 138–146.

Schulz, R. (2000) Caesar und das Meer. *Historische Zeitschrift* 271, 281–309.

Scott, I. (2015) Iron Age, Roman and post-Roman metalwork. In P. Andrews, P. Booth, A.P. Fitzpatrick and K. Welsh, *Digging at the Gateway. Archaeological Landscapes of South Thanet, Vol. 1: The Sites;*

Vol. 2: The Finds, Environmental and Dating Reports, 43–110. Oxford and Salisbury, Oxford Wessex Archaeology Monograph 18.

Seillier, C. (2007) De Gesoriacum à Bononia: bilan de trente ans de recherches archéologiques à Boulogne-sur-Mer. In R. Hanoune (ed.), *Les villes romaines du Nord de la Gaule: Vingt ans de recherches nouvelles (Actes du 25e colloque international de HALMA-IPEL UMR CNRS 8164)*, 133–146. Villeneuve d'Ascq, Revue du Nord Hors Série, Collection Art et Archéologie 10.

Thompson, F.H. (1983) Excavations at Bigberry, near Canterbury 1978–80. *Antiquaries Journal* 63, 237–278.

Votruba, G.F. (2017) Did vessels beach in the ancient Mediterranean? An assessment of the textual and visual evidence. *The Mariner's Mirror* 103, 7–29.

Wacher, J.S. (1979) *The Coming of Rome*. London, Routledge Kegan Paul.

Waite, J. (2011) *To Rule Britannia. The Claudian Invasion of Britain AD 43*. Stroud, History Press.

Whitehead, I. (1993) Mooring. In T. Shaw (ed.), *The Trireme Project. Operational Experience 1989–90: Lessons Learnt*, 95–98. Oxford, Oxbow Monograph 31.

Wilkes, E. (2013) Iron Age ports, harbours and structures in the northern Channel coast. In M.-A. Daire, C. Dupont, A. Baudry, C. Billard, J.-M. Large, L. Lespez, E. Normand and C. Scarre (eds), *Anciens peuplements littoraux et relations Homme/Milieu sur les côtes de l'Europe Atlantique / Ancient Maritime Communities and the Relationship between People and Environment along the European Atlantic Coasts*, 275–282. Oxford, British Archaeological Reports International Series 2570.

Chapter 9

Gauls under siege: Defending against Rome

Sophie Krausz

Introduction

Ever since the 19th century, many French and British scholars have pondered over Julius Caesar's strategies in the Gallic War, endeavouring to reconstruct the famous sieges that enabled him to defeat the Gauls between 58 and 51 BC. Looking through the books of the time by Camille Jullian (1920), Colonel Eugène Stoffel (1887) or Rice Holmes (1903), it is noticeable that the authors sided mostly with the Romans, openly admiring the art of war as practised by Julius Caesar. Some of those scholars, like the emperor Napoléon III (1865), a great admirer of Vercingetorix, attempted to understand how the Gauls defended themselves against the Romans. But they could not get very far with this approach since the Gauls almost always lost their battles against the Romans and were massacred after the great sieges as at Avaricum and Alesia in 52 BC. In the end, scholars came to believe that the Gauls were just too poorly organized to hope to get the upper hand over the Romans; they could not match their opponents' military skills. Admittedly, in defence of our 19th-century predecessors, very little evidence can be found in Caesar's *Commentaries* about Gallic military strategies and tactics. Caesar speaks primarily about himself, his style of command, and his military successes. His description of how the Gauls defended themselves against the Roman army are far less detailed and we have to read between the lines or even guess at what might have happened.

Alongside the literary sources, the archaeology of fortifications can play a fundamental role in reconstructing the forms of defence implemented by the Gauls before and during the Gallic War. The study of ramparts has the advantage of being scientifically objective because, unlike textual analysis, it does not adopt a Roman perspective. On the contrary, it can be used to provide some degree of understanding of the point of view and the intentions of the Gauls. Archaeological study can also determine whether or not the ramparts were specifically designed for warfare, and what social, cultural and political function they might have had. This archaeological approach does not exclude recourse to what Caesar wrote and the testimony of the proconsul of Transalpine Gaul remains highly valuable. His text may take on new meaning and ultimately is of enhanced worth when set against the archaeological sources. In this contribution, I will show that the design of Gallic ramparts extends beyond the context of architecture alone. Constructing effective fortifications presupposes mastery of specific technology, combining knowledge of architecture and military engineering specifically adapted to defensive works. In the ancient world, the standard reference was Greek siegecraft, which developed from the 6th century BC onwards and reached a peak under the Macedonian kings. It took highly skilled engineers to design the defensive systems of Philip II of Macedon and his son Alexander the Great and to come up with new war machinery capable of launching projectiles. The earliest treatises on the art of siege warfare that have come down to us date from the 4th and 3rd centuries BC; that of Aeneas Tacticus (the Tactician) around 355 BC, and then Philo of Byzantium in the 3rd century BC. In the 1st century BC, the treatise on war machines by Vitruvius was the first of its kind in Latin. The generals of the Roman Republic like Caesar had most certainly read the Greek and Latin theorists. In a world where the art of warfare had been cultivated and developed for centuries, it may well be asked what the designers of the Gallic ramparts knew about the subject.

The Bituriges up against Caesar in 52 BC

The territory of the Bituriges is well known today from the many archaeological excavations conducted there in the last 40 years especially in the agglomerations and *oppida* of the Gauls (Augier and Krausz 2012). This territory formed one of the largest *civitates* of central Gaul and its ancient boundaries coincide with those of the modern province of Berry (Figure 9.1). Caesar indicates that Avaricum (Bourges) was the capital of the Bituriges (*BG* 7.13) and mentions the name of this people for the first time in Book 7, which relates the events of the dreadful year 52 BC. Book 7 begins with the massacre of Cenabum, now the city of Orléans (Loiret), and ends with Vercingetorix's capture at Alesia (Reddé this volume). Between these two events, Caesar confronted the peoples of central Gaul on several occasions (Figure 9.2). In the winter of 53–52 BC, the Roman legions were quartered in north-eastern Gaul in the lands of the Lingones and Senones. The proconsul had returned to Rome for the winter, believing the region was peaceful enough. This was precisely the moment the Gauls chose to rise against the Romans and it was the Carnutes who were first to revolt: two men organized the massacre of several Roman traders based at Cenabum (*BG* 7.11). Among the victims was Caius Fufius Cita, a Roman knight whom Caesar had made quartermaster. The murders signalled the Gauls' intent to interfere with the Roman army's supplies, and the moment was particularly propitious as Caesar was away from Gaul. News of the Carnutes' action reached the Arverni in a matter of hours (*BG* 7.3). It is at this point in his account that Caesar introduces Vercingetorix, a young leader of the Arverni,

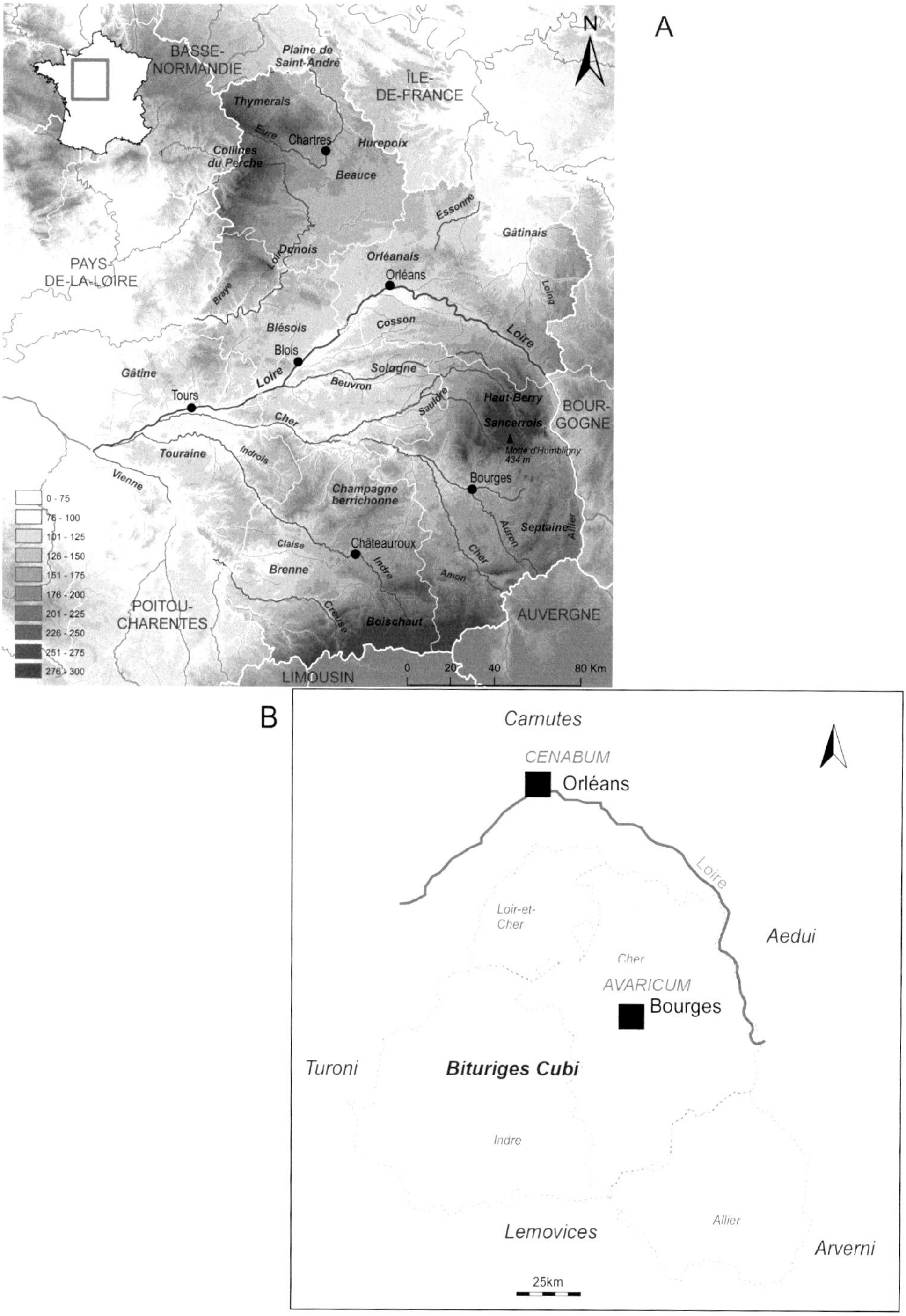

Figure 9.1 (A) Map of the Centre-Val de Loire region, France. (B) Map of the territory of the Bituriges and modern Berry (S. Krausz).

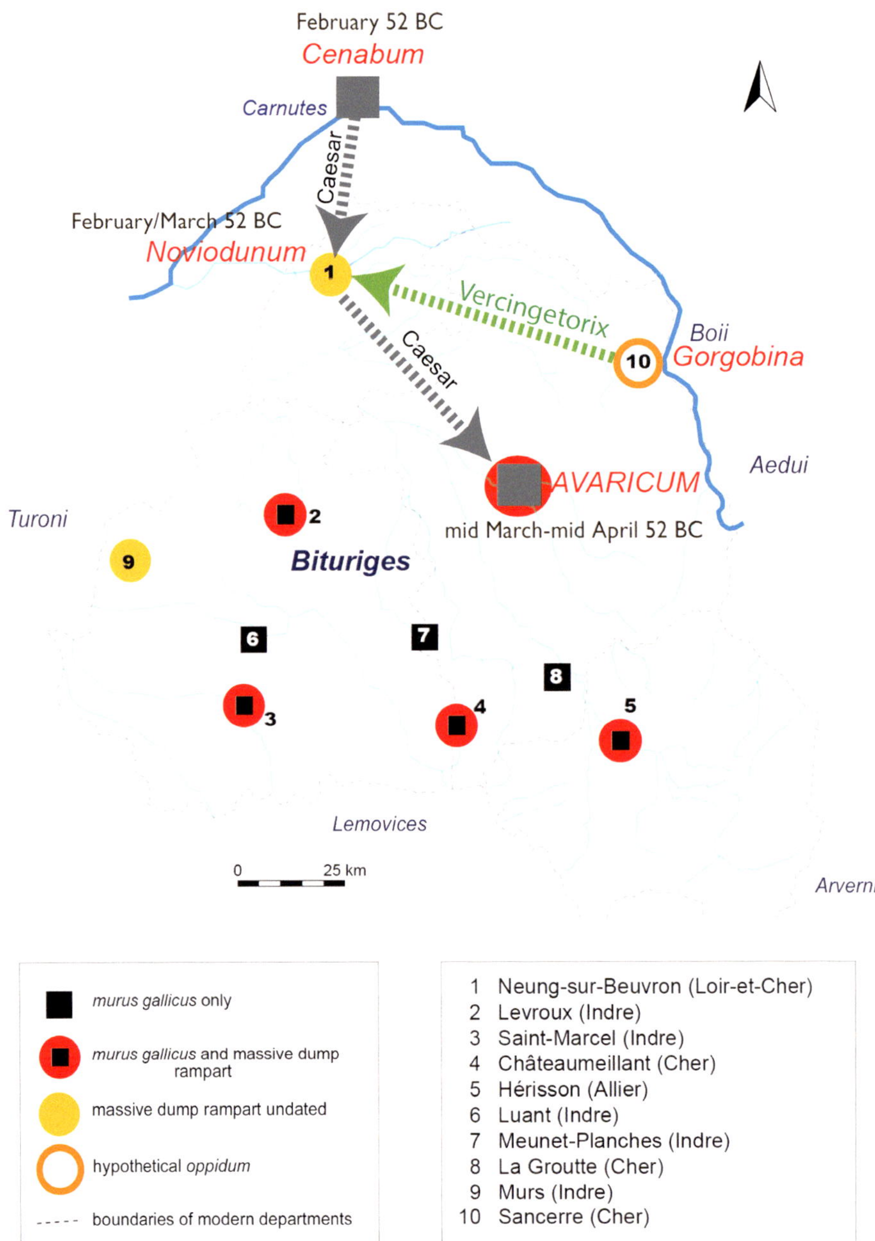

Figure 9.2 The main movements of Caesar and Vercingetorix between February and April 52 BC (S. Krausz).

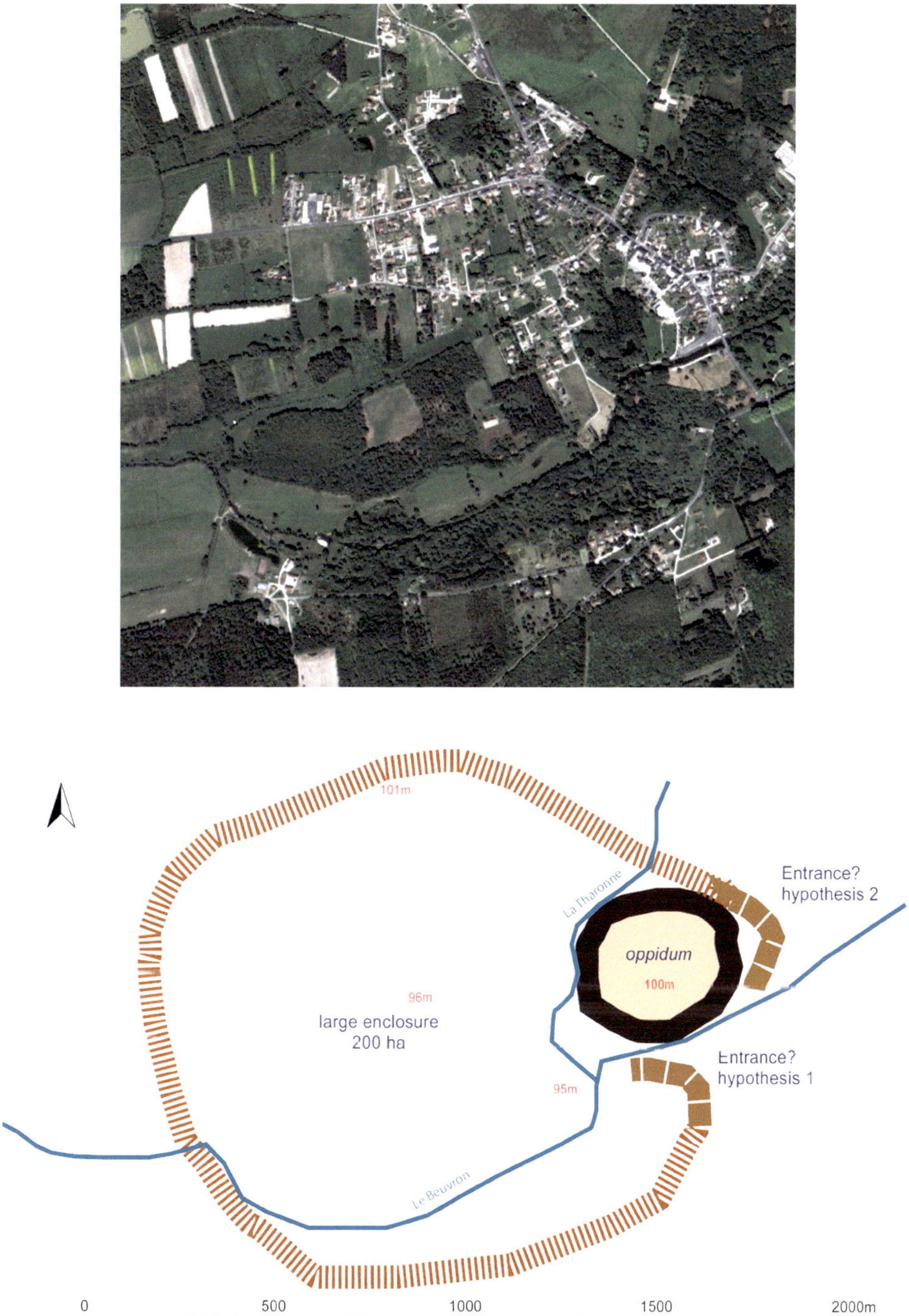

Figure 9.3 Neung-sur-Beuvron, Loir-et-Cher: plan of the oppidum *(Noviodunum biturigum) and potential territory or* pagus *(S. Krausz, on © Google Earth background image).*

who calls on the peoples of Gaul to rise against Rome: the Arverni, Carnutes, peoples of the Seine, of the middle and lower Loire and also the tribes of western Gaul joined Vercingetorix, who was proclaimed king. The Aedui, who were allies of Rome and known to the other Gauls as 'Brothers of the Republic', hesitated to join the coalition. Caesar's trust in the Aedui wavered and he undertook violent reprisals against the Gauls: first he took Cenabum to avenge the death of the Roman citizens there, then he destroyed the capital of the Bituriges and massacred the population of Avaricum. This episode was the beginning of a game of cat and mouse between Caesar and Vercingetorix that was to end at Alesia in September 52 BC.

The *oppidum* of Noviodunum

After the massacre of Cenabum, Caesar headed for Avaricum and arrived at the *oppidum* of Noviodunum which he decided to attack immediately (*BG* 7.12). The inhabitants had no wish to fight, though, and begged Caesar to spare them. Being pressed for time, Caesar accepted their surrender in exchange for arms, hostages and horses. But just when the inhabitants of Noviodunum had started to accede to Caesar's demands, they saw Vercingetorix's cavalry coming up from Gorgobina.[1] With fresh hope at the sight of the leader of the coalition of the Gauls arriving with reinforcements, the inhabitants of Noviodunum changed their minds about surrendering. They closed the gates of the *oppidum* and began to fight, supported by Vercingetorix's cavalry. The battle raged, but Caesar won the day with the support of his 400 German cavalrymen.

Recent archaeological research has identified a small *oppidum* of about 10 hectares at Neung-sur-Beuvron, within a larger enclosure of 200 ha, which probably marked the boundary of its territory or *pagus* (Figure 9.3) (Krausz 2015). There is an enormous rampart 10 m high at Neung-sur-Beuvron with a large flat-bottomed ditch in front of it. It was probably behind this rampart that the Bituriges of Noviodunum protected themselves against Caesar's army. The rampart has never been excavated but its shape and height indicate it was a massive dump rampart of the kind found at other *oppida* in the territory of the Bituriges.

Gorgobina, city of the Boii

The impressive promontory of Sancerre towers 168 m above the Loire, a little more than 2 km from the river's left bank (Figure 9.4). 'La montagne de Sancerre', as this prominent hill is called locally, would have made a splendid *oppidum*. But no Iron Age remains have so far been found, nor any trace of a rampart. Numerous historical and philological indications make it very likely that Gorgobina, the *oppidum* of the Boii, was indeed in the Sancerre area (Krausz 2015, 20). The Boii were Celts who originated in Bohemia, and Caesar tells us they were part of the migration of the Helvetii and fought at Bibracte in 58 BC (*BG* 1.28; Kaenel this volume). After the Helvetii had been defeated, Caesar placed the Boii under the protection of the Aedui, who gave them land within their *civitas*, probably Gorgobina.

A Roman agglomeration was excavated in the 1960s at Saint-Satur, a village next to Sancerre. A series of excavation campaigns have revealed a settlement area beside the Loire at the locality of Saint-Thibault. Moreover, a few years ago archaeologists discovered traces of two Gallo-Roman bridges in the bed of the river, indicating that a major highway crossed the Loire there (Dumont 2011). Re-examination of the 1960s excavation reports has revealed the presence of late Iron Age fibulae and coins among the objects attributed to the Gallo-Roman period. Poorly dated at the time of the excavations, they confirm the existence of a Gaulish settlement beside the Loire. The remains suggest that an agglomeration on the left bank of the river had a port, which might have been controlled by the Boii, probably for the benefit of the Aedui. This discovery suggests it might have been wrong to look for an *oppidum* on the mountain of Sancerre because Gorgobina, the town of the Boii, could well have been a port associated with a lowland *oppidum* at Saint-Satur on the left bank of the Loire.

The siege of Avaricum

After taking the *oppidum* of Noviodunum, Caesar raced directly for Avaricum. He was anxious to subjugate the Bituriges who were a serious threat for Rome at this point in the war. Vercingetorix asked the Bituriges to burn their towns and villages as part of a 'scorched earth' policy to prevent the Roman army from securing supplies. The Bituriges accepted the sacrifice and burnt down more than 20 of their towns with the neighbouring *civitates* doing the same (*BG* 7.15). But the inhabitants of Avaricum implored Vercingetorix to spare their capital. The leader of the Gauls agreed not to burn Avaricum but the subsequent story shows that he left the Bituriges to deal with Caesar by themselves and made no move to help them during the siege. The siege tied Caesar and his six legions down for 25 days between mid-March and mid-April of the year 52 BC in particularly harsh conditions as it was cold and rained non-stop. Caesar reported that he would have preferred to build a circumvallation around Avaricum and impose a blockade, but it was impossible to do so because the *oppidum* was surrounded by marshland on all sides. Caesar saw only a narrow passage to gain access to the promontory (Figure 9.5). The narrow passageway to the south-east of the *oppidum* probably led to the main gate of Avaricum and Caesar set up his main camp opposite it. This location, now Place Séraucourt in Bourges, is where ditches were discovered in the 19th century that may have been part of the Roman camp (Krausz and Ralston 2009). As he could not build a circumvallation, Caesar decided to build an assault ramp (*agger*) up which two towers could be rolled enabling him to reach the Gallic rampart and enter the city over the top of the fortifications. Caesar gives precise measurements of his assault ramp: 330 feet long and 80 feet high, that is about 100 m long and 24 m high. It was an enormous earthwork that cost the Roman legionaries 25 days of very hard toil not just in the cold and pouring rain but under a constant hail of missiles from the Gauls. But Caesar reports that his men were not discouraged because they thought only of avenging the murders of the Roman traders at Cenabum. The assault ramp should be thought of not as a major monument built to

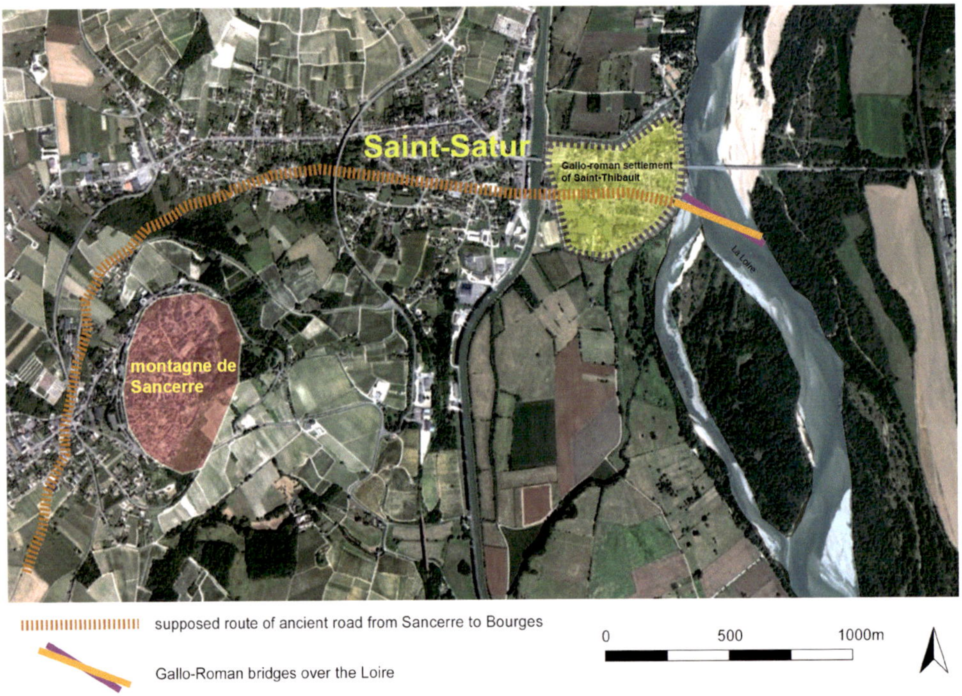

Figure 9.4 Gorgobina: location of the Montagne de Sancerre and the agglomeration of Saint-Satur, Cher (S. Krausz, on © Google Earth background image. Ancient road from Sancerre to Bourges after Chénon 1922, 46; Gallo-Roman bridges after Dumont 2011).

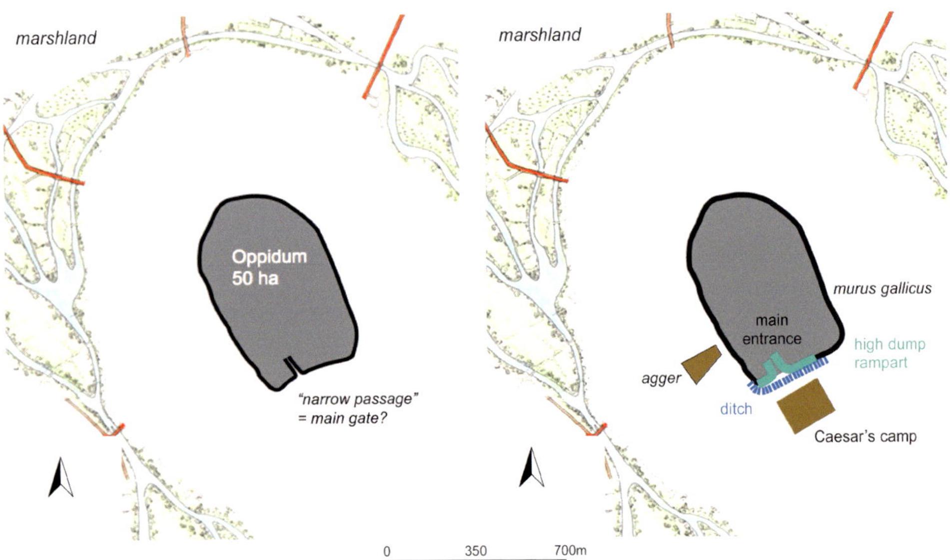

Figure 9.5 Bourges-Avaricum, Cher: sketch plans of the oppidum *and the Gaulish fortifications and supposed location of Caesar's siege installations (S. Krausz).*

last, as 19th-century scholars described it, but rather as an enormous earthwork made up of a heap of sundry material – earth, stones and probably a wooden framework to make it rigid. The assault ramp can be compared with two other ancient examples that still survive, built as banked up 'runways' around a wooden frame: the assault ramp at Masada in Israel built against the Zealots by the Roman general Silva in AD 73 and that of Dura-Europos in Syria built by the Persians in the 3rd century AD (Krausz 2019).

During the 25 days of the siege, the Gauls of Avaricum tried to destroy the Roman siegeworks as they were being erected: they set fire to the assault towers and the sheds that protected the Roman troops on the embankment. At the same time they dug galleries beneath the ramp to make it collapse and they set fire to the wooden frame. Caesar relates in Book 7.14 that the *agger* was smoking. The Gauls forced the Romans to rebuild the ramp several times; they fought hard to try and stave off the fatal outcome of the siege. Of Caesar's two assault towers, only one eventually reached the rampart. The other was most certainly burned by the Gauls or collapsed because of sapping, but Caesar does not dwell on the matter. One of the upper storeys of the tower must have contained a battering ram to open a breach in the wall. And at the top of the tower, there was probably a boarding bridge that the troops could drop down over the rampart in order to cross into the *oppidum*. Once the legionaries finally managed to enter Avaricum over the top of the ramparts, Caesar had the entire population of the capital slain. No one was spared, not old men, nor women, nor children. Only 800 out of 40,000 are said to have escaped the slaughter.

Despite the many archaeological excavations at Bourges in the last 30 years, no material evidence of the siege has yet been found. This is probably because Roman and then medieval urbanization have removed virtually all traces of the late Iron Age, given that the city of Bourges was extensively redeveloped from the Augustan period onwards. However, it is possible to form some idea of the morphology of the ramparts of Avaricum by comparing the text with archaeological data for the other ramparts of the Bituriges.

The Gallic rampart of Bourges is known from Caesar's famous description of it at precisely the time of the siege of Avaricum (*BG* 7.23). The Roman general gives details of how Gallic ramparts were built: he calls the rampart a *murus gallicus* and archaeologists have adopted this term to refer to this type of fortification (Figure 9.6), a rampart constructed with wooden beams, held together by large iron nails. It was clad externally with stones among which the ends of the beams were visible, either in rows or staggered in a diamond pattern. The *murus gallicus* was not a very tall rampart, generally measuring 4–6 m high, but could be topped by a wooden parapet or palisade. More often than not there was no ditch in front. Excavations of several examples of the *murus gallicus* in Berry reveal that they were constructed between 100 and 80 BC. These dates indicate that the *muri gallici* were not constructed out of fear of Roman sieges, because the Romans were not a perceived threat at the beginning of the 1st century BC. But, if Caesar is to be believed, it was behind their *murus gallicus* that the Gauls of Avaricum sought to hold out against the Roman army. The Roman general specifies that during the siege, the Gauls raised the height of the *murus*

Figure 9.6 The reconstructed murus gallicus at Bibracte, Mont-Beuvray, Nièvre/Saône-et-Loire (photo Antoine Maillier).

gallicus using wooden towers connected by planking to match the growing height of Caesar's own assault towers (*BG* 7.22). This detail shows that the Gauls were able to rearrange and develop their rampart to make it more effective, even in the thick of the action when under siege.

Although the archaeologists at Bourges have not yet been fortunate enough to see the *murus gallicus* attacked by Caesar, a stout defensive feature was discovered in an excavation in 1987 on the site of Bourges town hall, at the top of rue Moyenne (Krausz 2014). This was an enormous V-shaped ditch, measuring 25 m wide and 10 m deep (Figure 9.7). The amount of material extracted from the ditch indicates it formed part of a massive dump rampart. The archaeological finds confirm that it was backfilled in Augustan times, having been dug in the middle of the 1st century BC and had in all likelihood been in place at the time of the siege in 52 BC.

Close to the narrow passage mentioned by Caesar, the ditch reveals the existence of a gate fortified by a type of rampart that was far taller than a *murus gallicus*. While the *murus gallicus* must have formed an unbroken ring around the *oppidum* of Avaricum, the massive dump rampart formed a barricade protecting the main entrance, consolidating a major weak spot in the narrow passage described by Caesar. Since the 19th century, scholars have presumed that Caesar's assault ramp was built in this narrow passageway between the gate of Avaricum and Caesar's camp

A

B

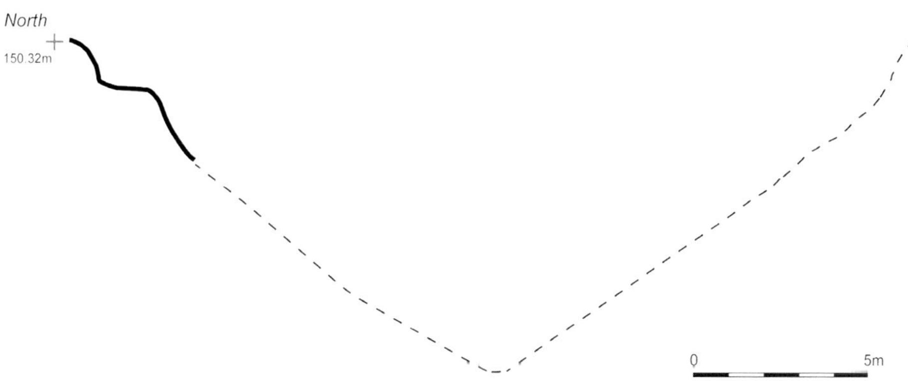

Figure 9.7 Bourges, ditch at the top of rue Moyenne, 1987 excavations by J. Troadec. (A) The upper ditch fills, seen in cross-section during the excavation. (B) Reconstructed ditch profile. Solid line, profile surveyed in 1987; dashed line, projected basal and southern sides (photo J. Troadec, Service archéologique de Bourges Plus; reconstruction S. Krausz).

(Napoléon III 1865; Duruy 1881). But Ian Ralston and I have shown that the ramp could not have been set up at this spot, something that the 19th-century scholars could not have known before the discovery of the big ditch in 1987 (Krausz and Ralston 2009). Caesar did not build his ramp opposite the gate but against one of the curtain walls of the *murus gallicus*. We can be sure of this because he clearly states that the legionaries entered Avaricum over the top of the rampart and not through a gateway (*BG* 7.27).

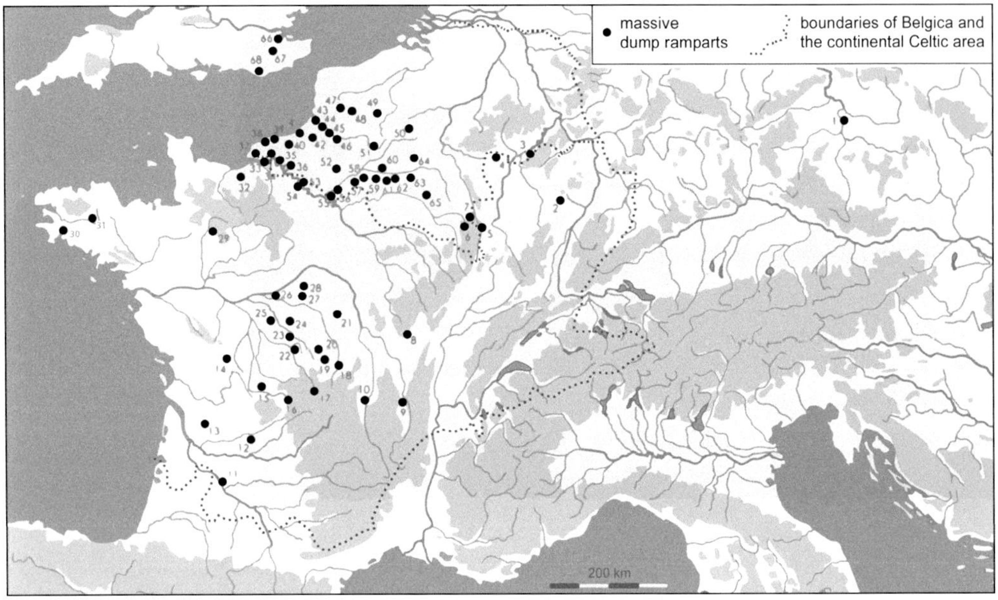

Figure 9.8 Map of massive dump ramparts in France (after Fichtl 2010, fig. 14, with additions).

Although there is no trace of the assault ramp at Avaricum, it might well have been built opposite one of the long sides of the *oppidum*: on the western side, for example, the present-day rue d'Auron has a 20 m rise between its low point in the valley and the top of the promontory. If we add 4 m to this for the average height of a *murus gallicus*, we have 24 m in all. This could explain the height of the assault ramp; the 24 m figure claimed by Caesar does not seem to be an exaggeration.

The massive dump rampart: the ultimate Celtic model

The massive dump rampart was the final model the Gauls invented. This was an embankment of earth or stones with many variants, the archetype being the Fécamp type rampart with a broad flat-bottomed ditch in front of it, defined by Mortimer Wheeler (Wheeler and Richardson 1957; Fichtl 2010). Earth and stone fortifications were common in Britain; they were low but often multivallate, as at Maiden Castle and a string of sites across Normandy inventoried by Wheeler. Ian Ralston (1992, 114) has shown that massive dump ramparts are found throughout Celtic Europe with two main concentrations: one in north-eastern France around the Seine valley and the other in central France (Figure 9.8). The tallest earthworks, some exceeding 10 m, are found in Berry and Limousin in central France (Buchsenschutz *et al.* 2010). Unlike the *murus gallicus* whose defensive function is not always very clear, the massive dump rampart is very much a rampart for war, an emergency fortification. In the territory of the Bituriges, dates for these fortifications centre on the 1st century BC, which means we can associate them with the Gallic War (Krausz 2014).

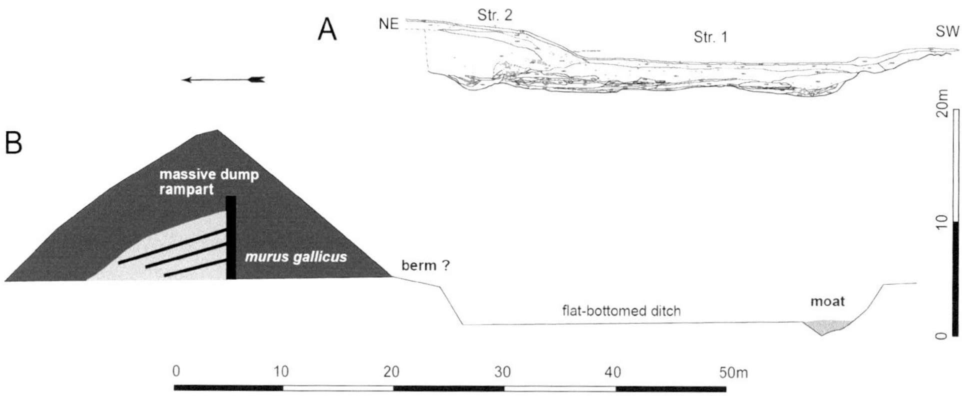

Figure 9.9 Rampart and ditch at Châteaumeillant, Cher. (A) Stratigraphic section of the large flat-bottomed ditch. (B) Reconstruction of the flat-bottomed ditch and ramparts (S. Krausz).

Châteaumeillant's massive dump rampart

Châteaumeillant was another of the principal *oppida* of the Bituriges, at the southern extremity of their territory on the edge of the Massif Central (Figure 9.2). This *oppidum* has the highest preserved rampart in central France, still standing 12 m high in places. It sits on a low promontory that rises to 10 m at most at its southern tip. The Latin name Mediolanum, meaning 'in the middle of the plain' or 'the middle plain', may be related to its situation between two near-parallel rivers. The natural promontory covers an area of 60 ha, but the fortification encloses just 24 ha at the southern end of the plateau. The site was excavated in the 19th century, and again from the 1950s until 1984 (Krausz 2009). For my part, I resumed excavations on the Gaulish fortifications and settlement in 2001 and research is ongoing. I present here only the pattern of fortifications and the early results from new excavations in 2018 of the massive dump rampart.

Massive dump ramparts are distinctive in that they combine two inseparable elements: a huge bank and a very large ditch. The bank is usually made up of the material dug out from the ditch; the rampart is therefore the positive counterpart of the excavated ditch. At Châteaumeillant, excavation of the ditch in 2002 revealed that it was 3 m deep, 45 m wide and that it had a flat bottom. The rampart now rises to a height of 10–12 m, but as it has been eroded by agriculture,[2] it could have been 14 or 15 m high originally (Figure 9.9). A parapet along the top would have added an extra 2 m, so the rampart might have stood 16–17 m high. Unlike stone ramparts, which have vertical or slightly tapered walls, earth ramparts slope distinctly at the front. The angle stabilizes the rampart's outer slope limiting slippage and making it easier to maintain. It also keeps siege machines at a distance, the Roman army's rolling towers being unsuitable for approaching embankments of this kind. Moreover, as it was made of earth, the rampart could not be set on fire or undermined to bring it down. So the classical Roman tactics of sapping,[3] firing and using assault towers were ineffective against this type of rampart. As for the ditch, analysis of its fill shows that it was marshy. Being supplied by one of the two rivers that flowed on either side of the *oppidum*, the ditch could have been wet or muddy for all or part of the year. This marsh would have made it impossible for an approaching army to gauge the depth of the ditch. In addition, a water-filled moat 10 m wide and 4 m deep to the front of the ditch provided an extra obstacle; it too was probably supplied by one of the rivers. This very large defensive ditch would have been a particularly effective impediment not just against siege machinery but also against infantry and cavalry. Even if the attackers managed to cross it, we then have to imagine a wall of earth nearly 16 m high looming over them, or in fact 19 m from the bottom of the ditch.

All the examples of *murus gallicus* ramparts of the main *oppida* in the territory of the Bituriges, as at Châteaumeillant, are covered by massive dump ramparts. This seems to be a systematic and deliberate architectural development to counter Roman siegecraft during the Gallic War. Could the *murus gallicus* have continued to play a part within the massive dump rampart? Its presence would have provided considerable military advantages (Figure 9.10):

- First, there was already a solid core in place, meaning less material had to be moved to form the dump rampart.

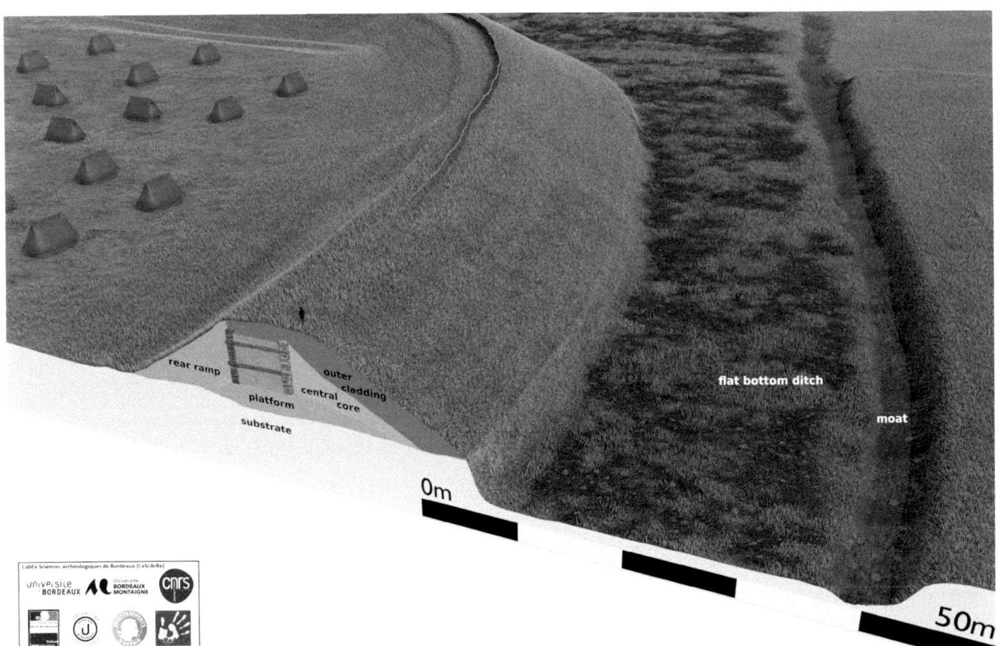

Figure 9.10 3D reconstruction of the fortifications at the oppidum of Châteaumeillant (Florent Comte, UMR5607 Ausonius).

- Next, the massive bank repaired and camouflaged the old ramparts built 50 to 70 years earlier, the beams of which had rotted and the facing slipped away.
- Lastly, from a military perspective, it could be considered that the massive embankment both completed and extended the *murus gallicus.*

The masonry core formed by the *murus gallicus* would have played a key role inside the embankment by solidifying it, which was particularly important for an earth rampart. While the earth embankment could not be set alight, it could be mined,[4] either at its base or part way up. The masonry core would have formed an effective anti-mining device. Too few massive dump ramparts have been excavated for their exact composition to be understood, whether at the core or on the inner and outer slopes. In most cases, it is not known how the slopes of the bank were constructed, but it is likely they were not just piles of earth. Some examples, such as the rampart at Bibracte and other ramparts in Berry, suggest that the outer slopes of the embankments were covered with cobbles or stones, forming an anti-mining device much like a tortoise shell (Krausz 2018).

The initial results from the summer 2018 excavation of the Châteaumeillant rampart reveal a complex, three-part architecture (Figure 9.11):

- A central core (st.705): a bank of orangey-red clay was built above the *murus gallicus*. This clay derives from the upper layers excavated from the ditch. The bank forms a highly compact and homogenous core; the clay is pure and not mixed with other material.
- The outer cladding (st.706): a series of grey clay layers were placed against the outer part of the central core. Some have varying contents of mica schist that are either crushed or form small pebbles. These clays come from the deeper layers of the Châteaumeillant subsoil. They form a highly compact and dense shell, which I interpret as a sort of external armour-plating forming the defensive part of the rampart. It is hard to penetrate these highly compact layers with digging tools. They are made up of a mixture of various sediments and several sorts of crushed

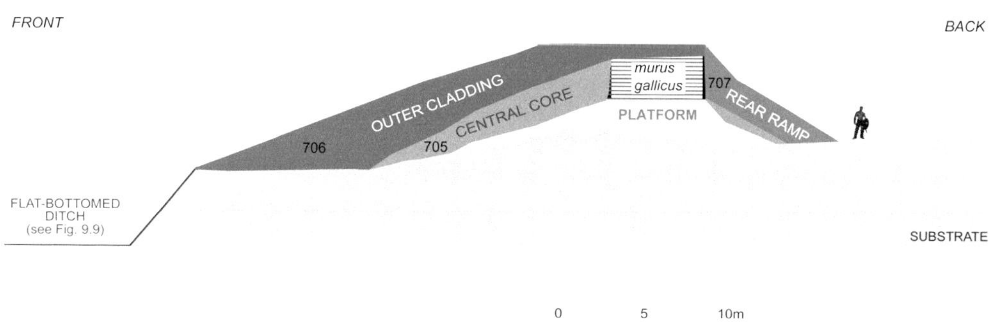

Figure 9.11 The massive dump rampart at Châteaumeillant: Hypothetical reconstruction of the different layers of construction (S. Krausz).

and ground rock; so this is by no means just a heap of earth, but a mixture of carefully selected geological resources customized to provide a material with specific properties.

- The rear ramp (st.707): as at the front, this is an embankment resting against the central core, on the inner side of the *oppidum*. The embankment is made up exclusively of a mass of broken down mica schist and amphibolites that is not mixed with clay, *i.e.* this blue-green layer is made up solely of ground rock. It is compact but seems less dense than the armoured cladding on the outer side. This embankment forms an access ramp to the rear of the rampart, which would have been used for moving around and climbing quickly to the top.

The observations of 2018 show that the massive dump rampart of Châteaumeillant was a complex structure and far more than just a mound of earth. On the contrary, it was a technological construction made up of several components with specific functions, and the outer face in particular seems to have formed a highly elaborate armour plating, the defensive shell of the rampart. The section dug in 2018 seems to show that the monument is perfectly and fully preserved in its initial form. No disturbance or reworking of the fortification has been observed.

The role of the rampart in the Gauls' defensive strategy

To understand the role of their ramparts, the archaeological approach has to be supplemented by analysing the defensive strategy the Gauls implemented. This means returning to Caesar's text, which gives many clues about how the Roman army attacked *oppida* and occasionally mentions how the Gauls defended themselves. Although sparse, Caesar's observations on the Gauls' means of defence can be used to some extent to evaluate the role of the Gallic rampart. During the Gallic War, Caesar employed classic methods familiar to all the generals of the Roman Republic. The legionaries knew how to implement three main tactics by the rules-of-the-art: combat in open country, direct assault and laying siege. The last two were suitable for capturing cities:

- **Storm** (*oppugnatio repentina*) was a quick and sudden method implemented *ex itinere*, that is, immediately after the troops arrived. The legionaries scaled the walls with ladders, archers and slingers drove off the defenders from the top of the ramparts, and the gates were set alight or smashed in.
- **Siege** (*oppugnatio longinqua*) was a protracted affair, implemented when it was not possible to take a city by storm.
- It went along with **investment** (*obsidio*), which consisted of blockading a city with one or more circumvallations to contain the besieged and prevent their resupply or support from outside. Siege warfare was 'mechanized' – battering rams and machinery were made ready, sometimes with a ramp (*agger*) to reach the defences and roll forward the assault towers.

Laying siege was undoubtedly the preferred method of Roman generals because it limited loss of life by keeping men out of hand-to-hand fighting. In some instances, the mere threat of such preparations, with the machinery being demonstrated and ostentatiously paraded, dispensed with any direct confrontation. This happened, for example, with the Senones at Vellaudunum (52 BC, just before Cenabum was taken; *BG* 7.11): Caesar set about building a circumvallation, but after two days' work the Senones surrendered so as to avoid the assault. We saw a similar situation at Noviodunum where the Bituriges were unwilling to fight the Romans. During the Gallic War, fewer cities were stormed than were besieged. There was the storming of Cenabum (Orléans), which Caesar ordered at night by setting fire to the gates. At Gergovia, he abandoned the siege because the topography was unsuitable and he was forced to attempt an assault that failed. Finally, at Alesia, he set up the greatest blockade of his career, a spectacular installation not unlike that at Numantia in Iberia, captured by Scipio Aemilianus in 133 BC (see also Morillo and Sala-Sellés this volume). Roman generals were assisted by military specialists, engineers and architects who advised them on the use of machinery and the calculations for setting out their siegeworks. For example, in the 2nd century BC, Scipio Aemilianus was accompanied by the Greek historian Polybius, a leading specialist in siegecraft, who was at his side at Carthage in 146 BC and Numantia in 133 BC. Caesar might have been accompanied at times during the Gallic War by the famous architect Vitruvius, or by other engineers whose names have not come down to us. Like the Roman army, the Gauls too might have had specialists in military, strategic and technical matters on their general staff. They may well have been members of the elite, able to read Greek and familiar with the theoretical questions in the treatises on siege warfare. It is known that some – including Vercingetorix and Ambiorix king of the Eburones – had had practical experience in the Roman army. Like young Roman noblemen, young Gallic aristocrats were invited to learn the art of warfare in the Roman army alongside famous generals. After such service, they would have had a very precise idea of the defensive strategies that would need to be implemented in the event of an attack on the *oppida* and would not have been taken aback or at a loss when up against the Roman army that they knew well.

In theory, defensive strategy could be passive or active. To be effective a rampart had to be adapted to the chosen form of defence:

- In adopting a passive defence, the besieged stayed back behind the rampart and relied on its solidity. The fortification was designed to resist attack through a combination of the height and width of the rampart, its ditches, towers, defensive gates, firing platforms, and so on. The fortifications did not have posterns as the designers did not anticipate any counter-offensives or sallies.
- In active (to very active) defence, the principle was to attack before being attacked, that is, to seek out the fight so as to control it. The most widely used tactic was the sally, forcing the aggressors to fight outside the city, so keeping them at a distance.

At Avaricum, the Gauls opted for active defence; they sallied out by day and by night and constantly harassed the Romans wherever they were, in order to keep Caesar's army away from the rampart. A final question concerns the connection between the strategy of active defence implemented by the Gauls and the capabilities of their ramparts. In other words, were the Gauls' ramparts specifically designed for active defence? Or was that defensive strategy used in the Gallic War to offset the shortcomings of certain ramparts? Or the shortcomings of certain topographical positions? Or both?

Conclusion

Throughout the Iron Age, the diversity of Gaulish ramparts as perceived through archaeology indicates how dynamic fortification design was. At the end of the Iron Age, the complex technology of the massive dump rampart reveals the capacity of the Gauls to adapt, and attests to their knowledge of classical siegecraft. The complex morphology of their ramparts shows that the Gallic designers mastered not only the principles of architecture but also of mathematics, geometry and even hydraulics. The ditch at Châteaumeillant, that includes a moat supplied by rivers, must have required expert calculations for it to fill up at certain times of the year, or to remain wet at all times. This knowledge of hydraulics was also a feature of Caesar's army, as indicated by the diverting of the springs at Uxellodunum in 51 BC (*BG* 8.40) and the flooding of the ditches during the siege of Alesia (*BG* 7.72). Caesar probably applied the recommendations of the handbooks on siege warfare he had read, those of Aeneas Tacticus and Philo of Byzantium, the latter advising – back in the 3rd century BC in his *Poliorketika* – to 'divert the waters that flow into the stronghold'.

If Roman generals were instructed in the theory and practice of Greek siegecraft, it is likely that some Gauls or Celts were too. Their practical knowledge could have been handed down by Celtic mercenaries from Greek and Carthaginian armies; but it may be that young Gallic aristocrats like Vercingetorix, who were later to hold political and military office in their *civitas*, had also garnered such practical and theoretical knowledge at first hand. If we accept that there were specialists in military strategy among the Gauls and more generally among the Celts, as there were in the Greek and Roman armies, it is conceivable that there were engineering corps in the armies of some Gaulish *civitates*. An archaeological clue is provided by the massive dump ramparts of the *oppida* of the Bituriges. The similarities of their design indicate that the ramparts might have been the work of a military section of the *civitas*, capable of coordinating huge engineering works and forming a common front against Caesar by means of a very well-organized strategy of defence.

Notes

1 Gorgobina or Gortona was an *oppidum* of the Boii, who were resettled in Aeduan territory after the defeat of Bibracte in 58 BC (*BG* 7.9). Vercingetorix besieged them early in 52 because the Boii, allies of the Aedui, were called on by Caesar to resupply his army. Was the leader of the Gauls trying to prevent this or to rally the Celtic populations to his coalition?

2 The rampart banks were covered with vines until the First World War. Châteaumeillant produces various AOC wines including a grey wine speciality.
3 Sapping was a classic Roman technique, consisting of loosening the base of a stone rampart so that it would collapse.
4 Like sapping, mining was a standard Roman technique by which one or more galleries (mines) were dug beneath a rampart through which to enter the city.

Acknowledgements

The author would like to thank Christopher Sutcliffe for translating this paper into English.

Bibliography

Augier, L. and Krausz, S. (2012). Du complexe princier à l'oppidum: les modèles du Berry. In S. Sievers and M. Schönfelder (eds), *Die Frage der Protourbanisation in der Eisenzeit. La question de la proto-urbanisation à l'âge du Fer (Akten des 34 internationalen Kolloquiums der AFEAF, Aschaffenburg 2010)*, 167–192. Bonn, Römisch-Germanische Kommission Kolloquien zur Vor- und Frühgeschichte 16.

Buchsenschutz, O., Krausz, S. and Ralston, I. (2010) Architecture et chronologie des remparts celtiques du Berry et du Limousin. In S. Fichtl (ed.), *Murus Celticus. Architecture et fonctions des remparts de l'âge du Fer.*, 297–313. Glux-en-Glenne, Collection Bibracte 19.

Chénon, E. (1922) *Les voies romaines du Berry*. Bar-le-Duc, Contant-Laguerre.

Dumont, A. (2011) Saint-Satur, Cher, ponts sur la Loire. In G. Barruol, J.-C. Fiches and P. Garmy (eds), *Les ponts routiers en Gaule romaine (Actes du colloque tenu au Pont du Gard, 8–11 octobre 2008)*, 213–216. Montpellier, Revue archéologique de Narbonnaise supplément 41.

Duruy, V. (1881) *Histoire des Romains depuis les temps les plus reculés jusqu'à l'invasion des Barbares*. Paris.

Fichtl, S. (2010) Réflexions sur les remparts de type Fécamp. In S. Fichtl (ed.), *Murus Celticus. Architecture et fonctions des remparts de l'âge du Fer*, 315–334. Glux-en-Glenne, Collection Bibracte 19.

Jullian, C. (1920) *Histoire de la Gaule. Tome 3: La conquête romaine et les premières invasions germaniques*. Paris, Hachette.

Krausz, S. (2009). L'oppidum de Châteaumeillant-Mediolanum (Cher). In O. Buchsenschutz, M.-B. Chardenoux, S. Krausz and M. Vaginay (eds), *L'âge du Fer dans le boucle de la Loire: Les Gaulois sont dans la ville (Actes du 32e colloque de l'AFEAF, Bourges 2008)*, 67–73. Tours, Revue Archéologique du Centre de la France Supplément 35.

Krausz, S. (2014) Stratégie et défense des *oppida* celtiques: les remparts de guerre des Bituriges Cubi. In O. Buchsenschutz, O. Dutour and C. Mordant (eds), *Archéologie de la violence et de la guerre dans les sociétés pré et protohistoriques (Congrès national du CTHS, Perpignan, mai 2011)*, 193–207. Paris, Éditions du CTHS.

Krausz, S. (2015) En 52 avant J.-C., les Bituriges Cubi face à César: l'énigme de *Noviodunum* et de *Gorgobina*. *Études Celtiques* 41, 7–30.

Krausz, S. (2018) L'art de la fortification celtique: architecture et ingénierie des systèmes défensifs. In A. Villard-Le Tiec, Y. Menez and P. Maguer (eds), *Architectures de l'âge du Fer en Europe occidentale et centrale (Actes du 40e colloque international de l'AFEAF, Rennes 2016)*, 239–255. Rennes, Presses universitaires de Rennes.

Krausz, S. (2019) Julius Caesar's assault ramp at the *oppidum* of Avaricum in 52 BC. In T. Romankiewicz, M. Fernández-Götz, G. Lock and O. Buchsenschutz (eds), *Enclosing Space, Opening New Ground: Iron Age Studies from Scotland to Mainland Europe*, 29–36. Oxford, Oxbow Books.

Krausz, S. and Ralston, I. (2009) Le siège d'Avaricum en 52 avant J.-C. ou comment les Gaulois se sont-ils défendus contre les Romains. In O. Buchsenschutz, M.-B. Chardenoux, S. Krausz and M. Vaginay (eds), *L'âge du Fer dans le boucle de la Loire: Les Gaulois sont dans la ville (Actes du 32e colloque de l'AFEAF, Bourges 2008)*, 145–155. Tours, Revue Archéologique du Centre de la France Supplément 35.

Napoléon III (1865) *Histoire de Jules César*. Paris, Champion.

Ralston, I. (1992) *Les enceintes fortifiées du Limousin: les habitats protohistoriques de la France non méditerranéenne*. Paris, Documents d'Archéologie Française 36.

Rice Holmes, T. (1903) *Caesar's Conquest of Gaul*. London, Macmillan.

Stoffel, E. (1887) *Histoire de Jules César: Guerre civile*, Vols 1–2. Paris, Imprimerie nationale.

Wheeler, R.E.M. and Richardson, K.M. (1957) *Hill-Forts of Northern France*. Oxford, Society of Antiquaries of London Research Report 19.

Chapter 10

Fighting for Caesar: The archaeology and history of Gallic auxiliaries in the 2nd–1st centuries BC

Lionel Pernet

Introduction

Written sources often refer to Gallic auxiliaries fighting for Rome. The aftermath of a battle that took place near Ruspina in 46 BC, during the Civil War, was described by the writer known as pseudo-Caesar as follows:

> Caesar ordered the retreat to be sounded and withdrew all his cavalry inside his own fortifications; and it was then, when the field had been cleared, that his attention was caught by the amazing bodies of the Gauls and Germans: some of whom had followed Labienus from Gaul in deference to his authority; others had been induced to join him by rewards and promises; and there were yet others who, having been made prisoners after Curio's defeat and their lives being spared, had been anxious to give proof of their unswerving gratitude by maintaining a correspondingly unswerving loyalty. These were the men whose bodies, amazing in their beauty and stature, were lying mutilated and prostrate here and there all over the battlefield (*de Bello Africo* 40, 5–6).

We need not, however, rely solely on the written sources: the archaeology of the Gallic auxiliaries who served in Roman armies in the 2nd and 1st centuries BC can also shed light on the military relations between Gauls and Romans. The research presented here originated in a study of the Giubiasco cemetery in the Ticino valley in Switzerland, during which it became apparent that some graves contained a surprising mixture of weapons from different traditions – Celtic, Roman and local (Pernet and Carlevaro 2006; Pernet 2008; Figure 10.1). These graves dated to the end of the Iron Age. In conjunction with historical information about the Roman conquest of this alpine valley, this led to the hypothesis that the burials might be those of auxiliaries, a status that held a particular meaning at the end of the Republican period, to which we will return. This was followed up by research that encompassed Cisalpine and Transalpine Gaul, from

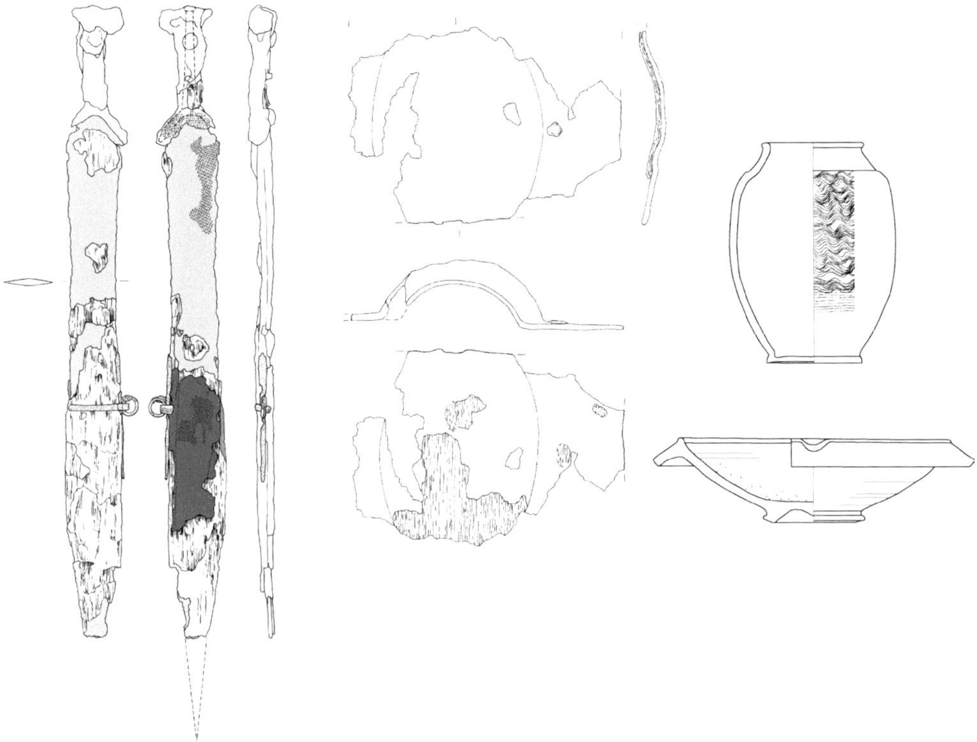

Figure 10.1 Giubiasco Grave 108, Tessin, Switzerland. The sword shows mixed influence: the hilt is in the Celtic tradition, the wood and bronze sheath is more of a Roman fashion. The umbo of the shield is Celtic, and the pots are local. Various scales. Surviving length of sword 69 cm; its original length can be estimated as around 80 cm (after Pernet and Carlevaro 2006).

northern Italy to the Rhine, the aim being to assess comparable grave groups with weapons and examine whether an archaeology of auxiliary service could be considered on a larger scale, even in the total absence of written sources for some regions. The study area was divided into five zones: northern Italy, the Alpine area, Transalpine Gaul (Narbonensis), Celtic Gaul and Belgic Gaul (Figure 10.2).

Goals and method

It is at the start of the 2nd century BC that the idea of Celtic mercenaries disappears from the written sources and is replaced by references to Gallic auxiliaries. Indeed, the Romans did not use the word 'mercenary' to describe the foreign soldiers who fought alongside them, even when they were paid and used *de facto* as mercenaries. The recruitment of mercenaries was in fact rare. Most foreign troops fighting on the Roman side were either allies or peoples who had fought and lost against Rome, and were forced to provide troops as part of a treaty (*foedus*) that stipulated the military and financial obligations of the subject people (Pernet 2010, 28). In the absence of texts or

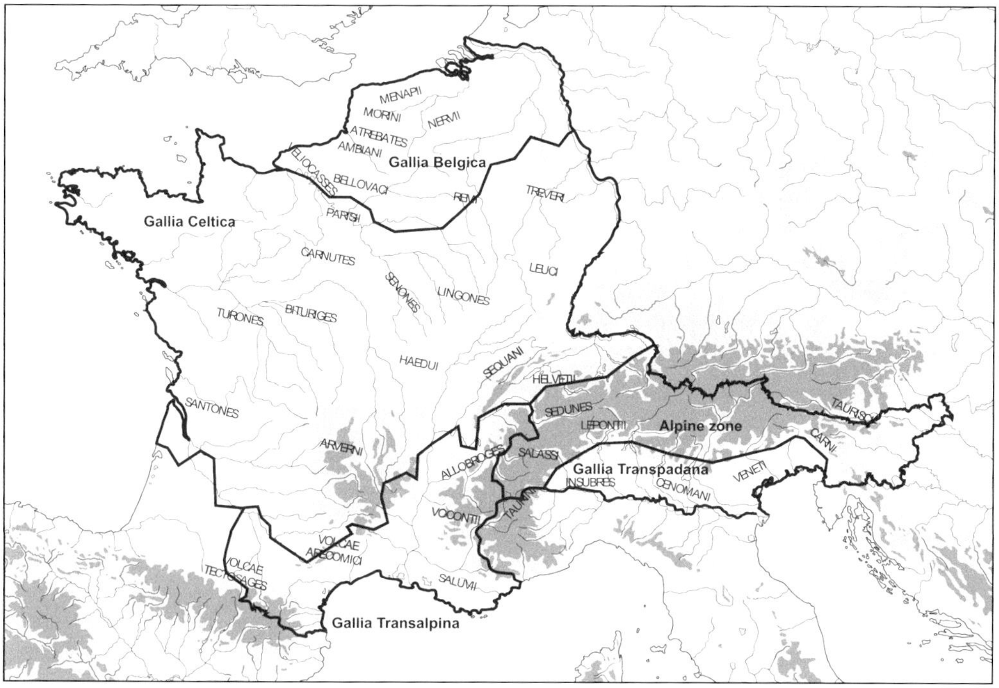

Figure 10.2 Map of the areas examined in the study of Gallic auxiliaries in the 2nd and 1st centuries BC, with the names of the peoples known from written sources and their location.

inscriptions, the exact role and status of men buried with weapons can only be based on the clues found in the closed archaeological context of their graves. Accordingly, burials were preferentially chosen for a corpus that comprises 145 sites with some 450 graves with weapons, including some previously overlooked and unpublished finds. Selection was made according to a protocol that took into account the presence of weapons, their exact location and dating, as well as an analysis of the goods placed with the deceased, in particular the weapons (Figure 10.3).

One might think that Roman auxiliaries can easily be identified from the presence of Roman weapons in their graves, but it became apparent very quickly in the course of studying the Giubiasco cemetery that weapons of the late Republican period were not as standardized as those of later, imperial, date. Indeed, these Republican weapons were sometimes inspired by non-Roman types following wars conducted by Rome in various regions, for example the Iberian Peninsula. To this complex situation must be added the almost complete absence of weapons in contemporary graves in Italy and Latium, which makes it difficult to identify weapons as certainly legionary. To avoid circular argument, weapons found in the study area that are considered Roman were excluded from the analysis.

Iconographic, written and archaeological sources from the Mediterranean world (Italy, Iberia, Greece, Egypt and Turkey) were analysed to determine the recurrent characteristics of Roman Republican weaponry. Attention was particularly focused on swords, spears,

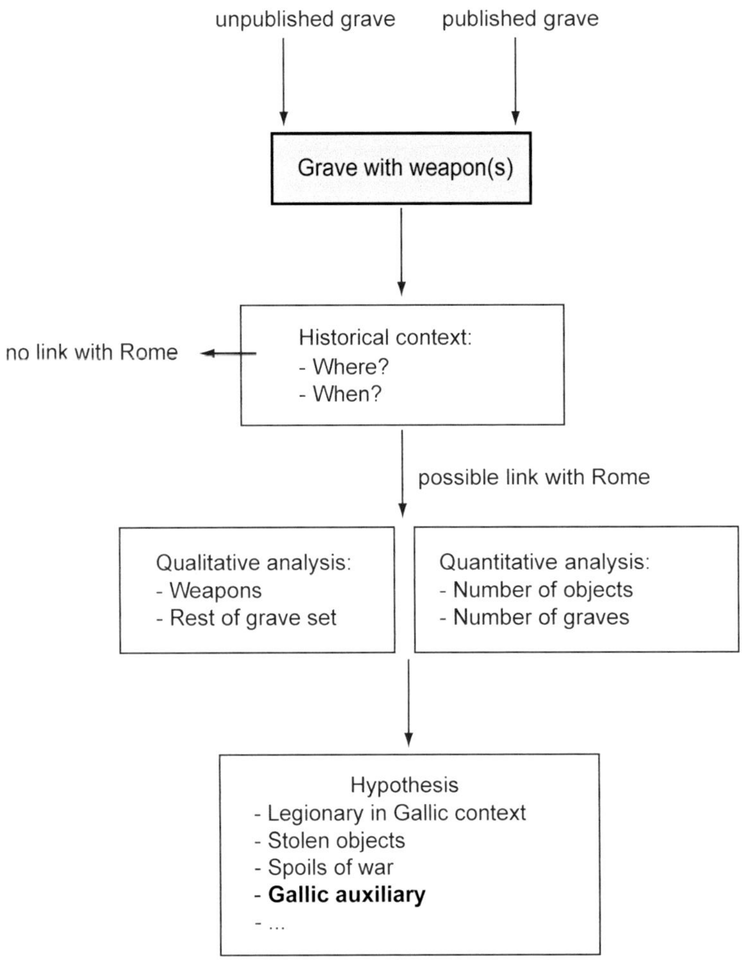

Figure 10.3 Selection method for the graves used in the study of auxiliaries in the 2nd and 1st centuries BC.

helmets and shields from Gaulish graves. A similar analysis was then undertaken of contemporary Celtic weapons. This also provided an opportunity to update the typology of late Iron Age weapons and thus distinguish weapon traditions rather than the origins of the weapons, while avoiding prejudging their makers' identity.

Swords of Roman tradition are distinguishable from Celtic ones by their waisted blades and their scabbards, which were made of organic materials such as leather or wood with edge bindings of bronze or iron. Swords of Celtic tradition are straight-edged and have metal scabbards. In the Celtic tradition, projectiles are represented mostly by leaf-shaped spearheads while the range of Roman weapons is wider, including various types of *pilum* that were fixed to the shaft by either rivets or tangs, and javelins. Artillery was also used. Some types of helmet, such as the so-called

Coolus-Mannheim type, that were previously thought to date to the Caesarian period (Waurick 1990), were shown by new finds in closed contexts to have already appeared in the 2nd century BC in the Celtic zone (Pernet 2010; 2016; 2017). In contrast, helmets of Roman tradition have a button on top for attaching a plume. These variations allowed us to distinguish weapons with Roman influence from weapons of Celtic tradition (Figures 10.4–10.5).

The distribution of the cemeteries examined is shown in Figure 10.6 and listed in the appendix. In all some 300 of the 450 graves analyzed were identified as potentially those of auxiliaries, according to the date of the burial, the status of the peoples or tribes concerned or the types of weapons present. Full details of the graves and the results of the regional analyses can be found in Pernet (2010).

Gallic auxiliaries before Roman conquest

In some cases, auxiliaries were recruited before their homeland was actually conquered. Some of the best examples are from the Alpine zone, especially among the Lepontii (Ticino, Switzerland) and the Carnii (Slovenia). In the absence of written sources, the challenge was to correlate the presence of Celtic and Roman weapons found in large cemeteries such as Giubiasco and Ornavasso (Piedmont, Italy) with possible auxiliary status. While the Roman weaponry from some graves seemed to provide sufficiently strong evidence to identify the deceased as auxiliaries, graves that only contained Celtic swords, spears or shields were more problematic. In the case of the Lepontii, these were graves dated between La Tène C2 and La Tène D1 (150–80 BC), and some of La Tène D2 (80–30 BC), which contained a panoply of Celtic weapons (Pernet and Carlevaro 2006).

Collaboration of the local elites with Rome seems likely to have begun following the completion of the conquest of Transpadane Gaul in the early 2nd century BC, even though these Alpine valleys were not part of the conquered territory. This does not necessarily mean that the men buried in these cemeteries served in the Roman army. In exchange for remaining autonomous, the Lepontii may have agreed to hold the Alpine passes and to monitor southward crossings. It was only later, in the 1st century BC, that some warriors, whose equipment included some Roman weaponry, served as auxiliaries. Similarly, the Carnii could have been charged very early on, after the establishment of the treaty with Rome (at the latest in 171 BC), with the supervision of the eastern Alpine border.

Auxiliaries enlisted during military conquest

The timing of the Roman conquest – which, depending on the particular region of Gaul, may have taken a long time – was an important factor in the process that led some Gallic aristocrats and their men to fight alongside the Romans. It must be remembered that, for Rome, conquest of territory was an opportunity to create circles of friends, allies

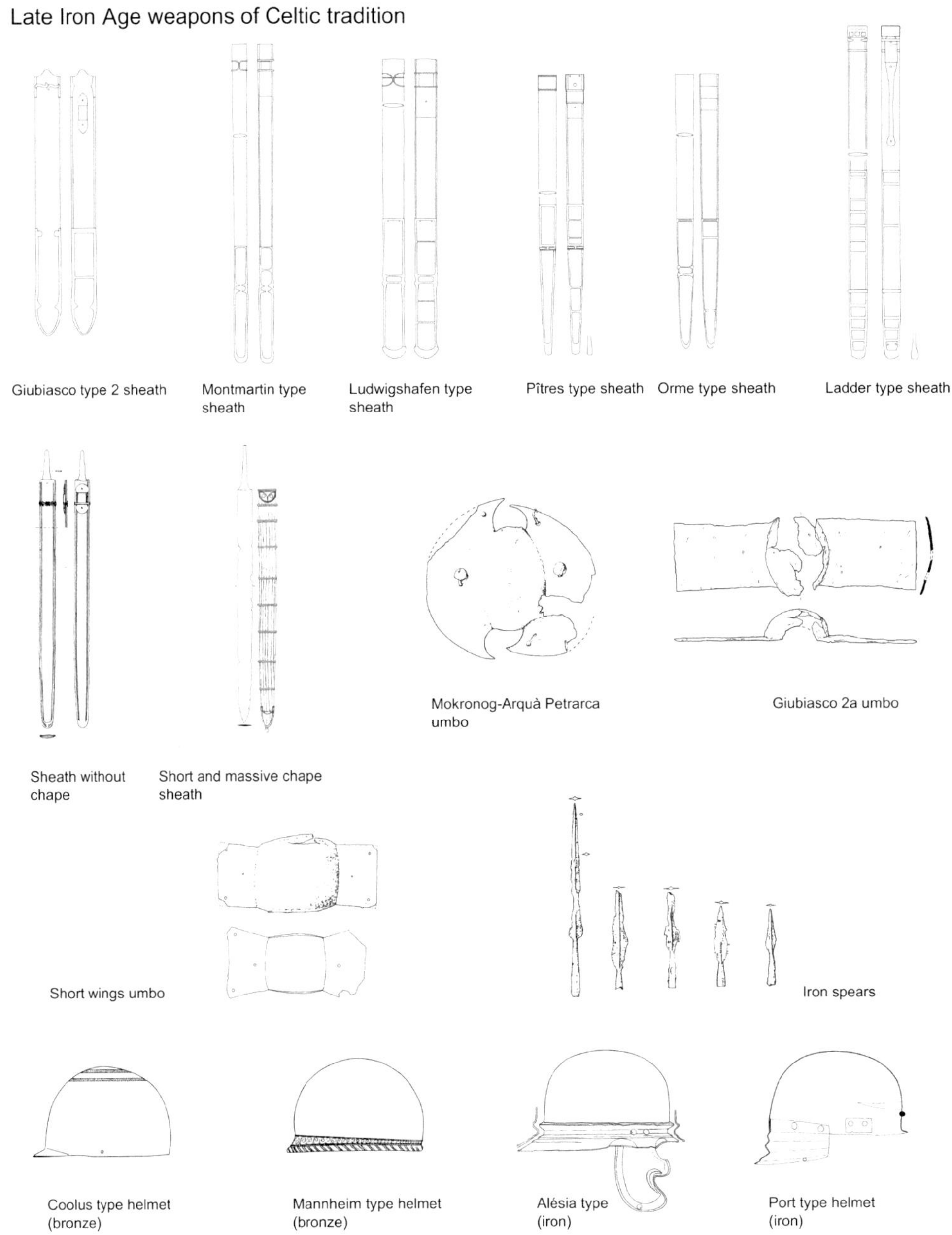

Figure 10.4 Late Iron Age weapons of the Celtic tradition.

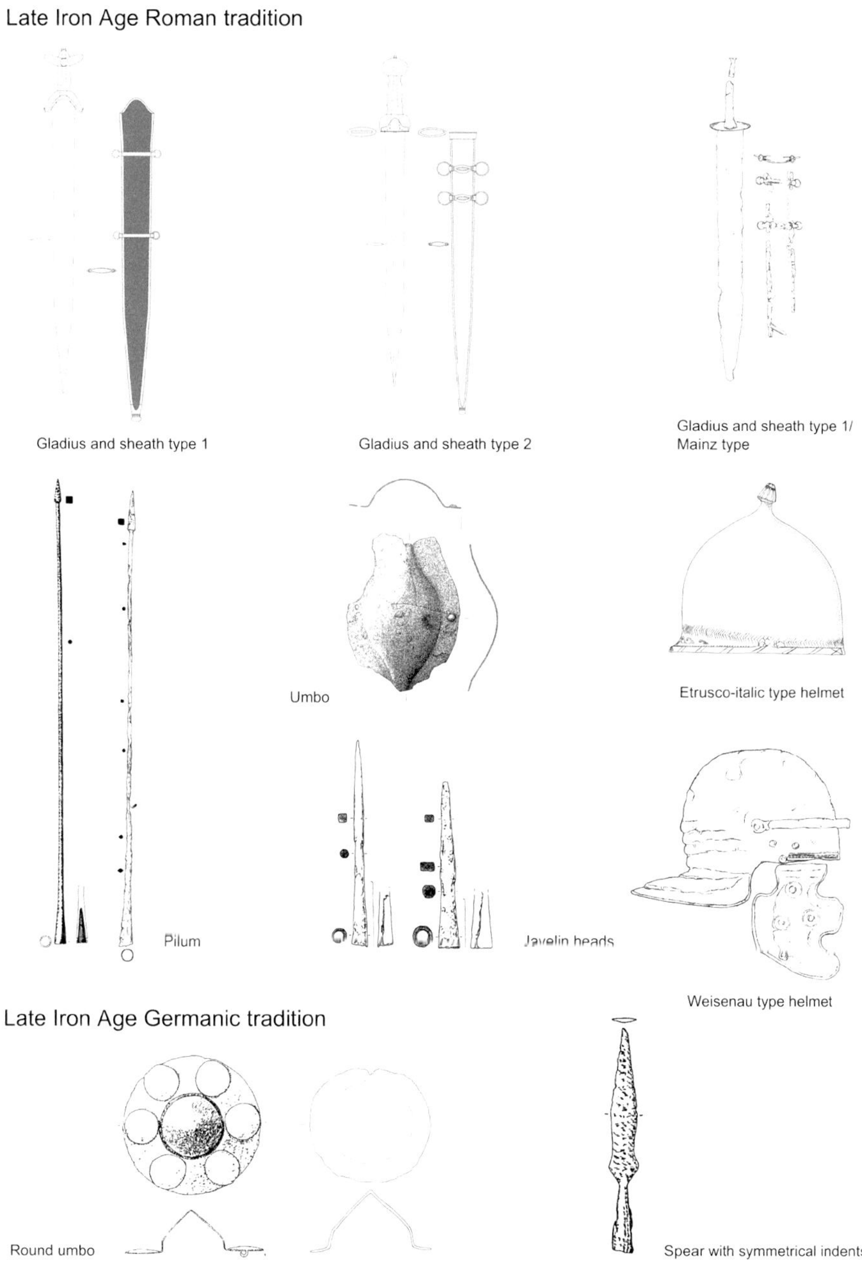

Figure 10.5 Late Iron Age weapons of the Roman and Germanic traditions.

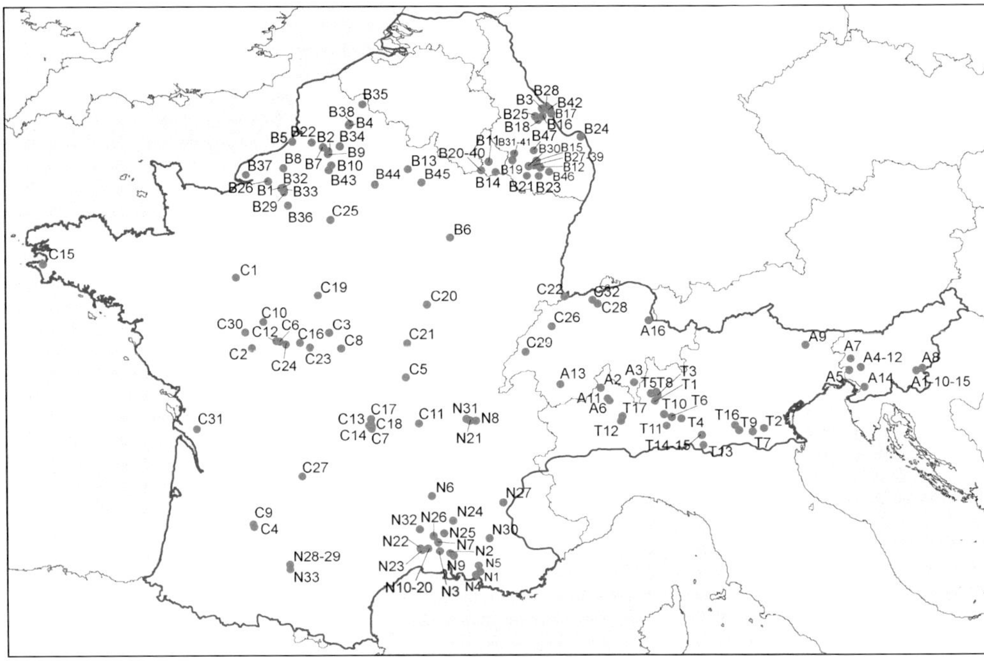

Figure 10.6 Location of the sites analysed (see Appendix for details).

or clients (Le Roux 2006), or, where such links existed already, to strengthen them, as with the Lepontii and Carnii. 'Those who then tried to betray [Rome] became *inimici* and would join the lot of *hostes* of the Roman people. They risked exemplary punishments and could not hope to find *fides* again in the eyes of the conqueror for a very long time' (Le Roux 2006, 23). Numerous Gallic tribes suffered such punishments, including the Boii, Atuatuci, Veneti, Eburones and Mandubii. Conditions varied for other conquered peoples, but they often included paying tribute and participating in Roman wars.

In this conquest phase, archaeological sources assume a greater significance. They naturally intersect with written sources that tell us 'in real time' about the participation of Gauls in Roman wars but they require further interpretation as the warrior may have died many years after these events. For the archaeological sources, two basic concepts encountered in the analysis of the funerary data were explored: continuity and rupture.

The five study regions were conquered at quite different times: Transpadane Gaul in the 190s BC, Transalpine Gaul in the 120s, Celtic and Belgic Gaul in the 50s, and the Alps not until the Augustan period. There are, however, many common points to highlight and, while paying attention to the particular contexts of individual sites, some broad guidelines can be proposed.

We may begin with funerary sites where clear continuity is observed between the period before and after the Roman conquest. The earliest of these are in Transalpine Gaul. In the (admittedly few) small cemeteries of the territory of the Volcae Arecomici, the custom of placing weapons in graves began well before the Roman conquest,

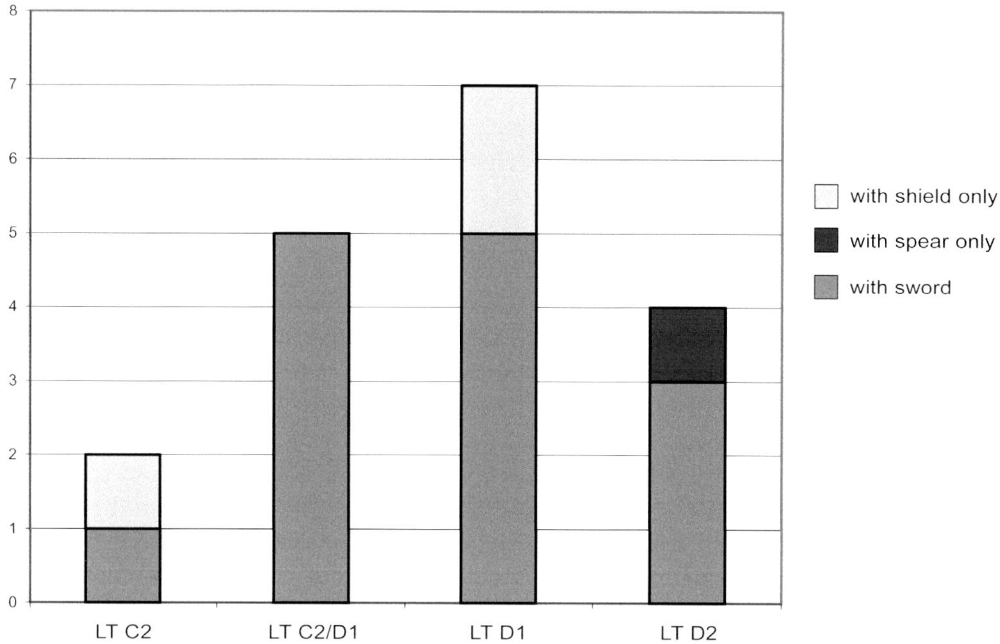

Figure 10.7 Chronological distribution of weapon graves between c. 200–30 BC in the Nîmes, Gard, region.

at the start of the 2nd century BC. The virtual absence of early La Tène C graves in Languedoc – except for the cemetery of Ensérune (Hérault), where there is a significant proportion of La Tène C1 weaponry (Schwaller *et al.* 2001) – makes it difficult to assess whether there was continuity in the placing of weapons in graves in this region from the early Iron Age to the 2nd century BC, the period of interest to us. However, the available evidence suggests that in the Nîmes region, for example, weapon deposition resumed in the early 2nd century BC. This raises the question of what triggered the marking of the aristocratic and warrior statuses of the deceased? At Nîmes and Beaucaire (Gard), weapons were placed with warriors who died before the Roman conquest in the 120s BC, and with those who were born at this time and afterwards (Figure 10.7). The practice spans the whole La Tène D period and both the number of tombs and the panoplies in which the sword figures prominently are consistent. In our opinion, the families who used these small cemeteries over a long period were those who retained their local power with the consent of both Rome and Marseille, as the latter city continued to levy a tribute on the Volcae. Throughout the conquest period and until after the revolt of the Volcae in 77–76 BC, there are no traces of a break in the archaeological evidence. In fact, the customs of the warriors who are identified as having served as auxiliaries may not have changed very much, because they remained within the Massiliote sphere of influence from before the conquest until the defeat of Marseille in 49 BC during the civil war.

In contrast, the conquest period saw a much more mixed picture among the Treveri in Belgic Gaul. Some large cemeteries such as Hoppstädten or Wederath

(Rheinland-Pfalz, Germany) were used continuously before and after the conquest, but many new cemeteries developed in or soon after the 50s BC (*e.g.* Lebach or Goeblingen-Nospelt in Luxembourg). Despite the obvious continuity of use apparent at Hoppstädten and Wederath, this does not extend to the graves containing parts of chariots or weapons. Following Ralf Gleser (2005), we interpret in social terms the difference between graves of La Tène D2a date at Hoppstädten in which chariot parts and other goods such as tuyères and briquetage containers symbolized the political and economic power of the deceased, and those of La Tène D2b in which chariot parts are absent. The transmission of power previously seen over several generations ceases, and although weapon graves still occur, the auxiliaries – even if they were of the same lineage as their predecessors – have lost, both symbolically and materially, the political and military prerogatives of their ancestors. In this cemetery, there are no graves of the warriors who lived during and just after the Gallic War, possibly as a result of harsh repercussions on the male population of this community (Gleser 2005, 265).

This is not the case at Goeblingen-Nospelt (Luxembourg), a cemetery that provides a snapshot of the generation who lived just after the conflict. In these exceptional graves, there are no noticeable changes in the ways that the elite presented themselves over these two or three generations, with their weaponry and spurs (Figure 10.8), and many objects that attest to regular contact with the Mediterranean world. They chose a funerary architecture (a wooden chamber below an earth mound), that links them to the great aristocratic burials of the 3rd to early 1st centuries BC, such as Tartigny (Oise) and Vieux-lès-Asfeld (Ardennes) in France, or closer to hand at Clémency (Luxembourg), or even to burials of Hallstatt D and La Tène A date (Metzler *et al.* 1991, 149; Metzler-Zens and Metzler 1998, esp. fig. 4). However, what is interesting at Goeblingen-Nospelt in terms of rupture is the choice of a new location, which apparently had not been used previously, for staging this grandiose burial (Metzler and Gaeng 2009). Was it a way of marking in the landscape a new lineage,[1] who had chosen the 'right side' in the Gallic Wars? These would be aristocrats who had pledged their allegiance to Caesar in the context of the disturbed relationship between the Treveri and the Romans during the Gallic Wars (*BG* 5.3; 5.58; 6.8; 8.44; see Hornung this volume).

We know that the Aedui of east central France collaborated with the Roman army, but this time there is little or no funerary evidence. Caesar's account nevertheless gives us a good idea of the extent of their help to him – including providing the bulk of his cavalry – as well as that of other Gallic peoples (*e.g. BG* 1.18; 2.5; 2.10; 5.54; 7.33; 7.50). Where there is burial evidence from Celtic Gaul, it varies between individual sites, but most fall into one of two groups, either small cemeteries or individual graves with large wooden chambers. Small cemeteries, such as Esvres-sur-Indre (Indre-et-Loire), Feurs (Loire) or Tavant (Indre-et-Loire), all in western central France, were used continuously both before and after the conquest, indicating that these social groups maintained their status after the war.

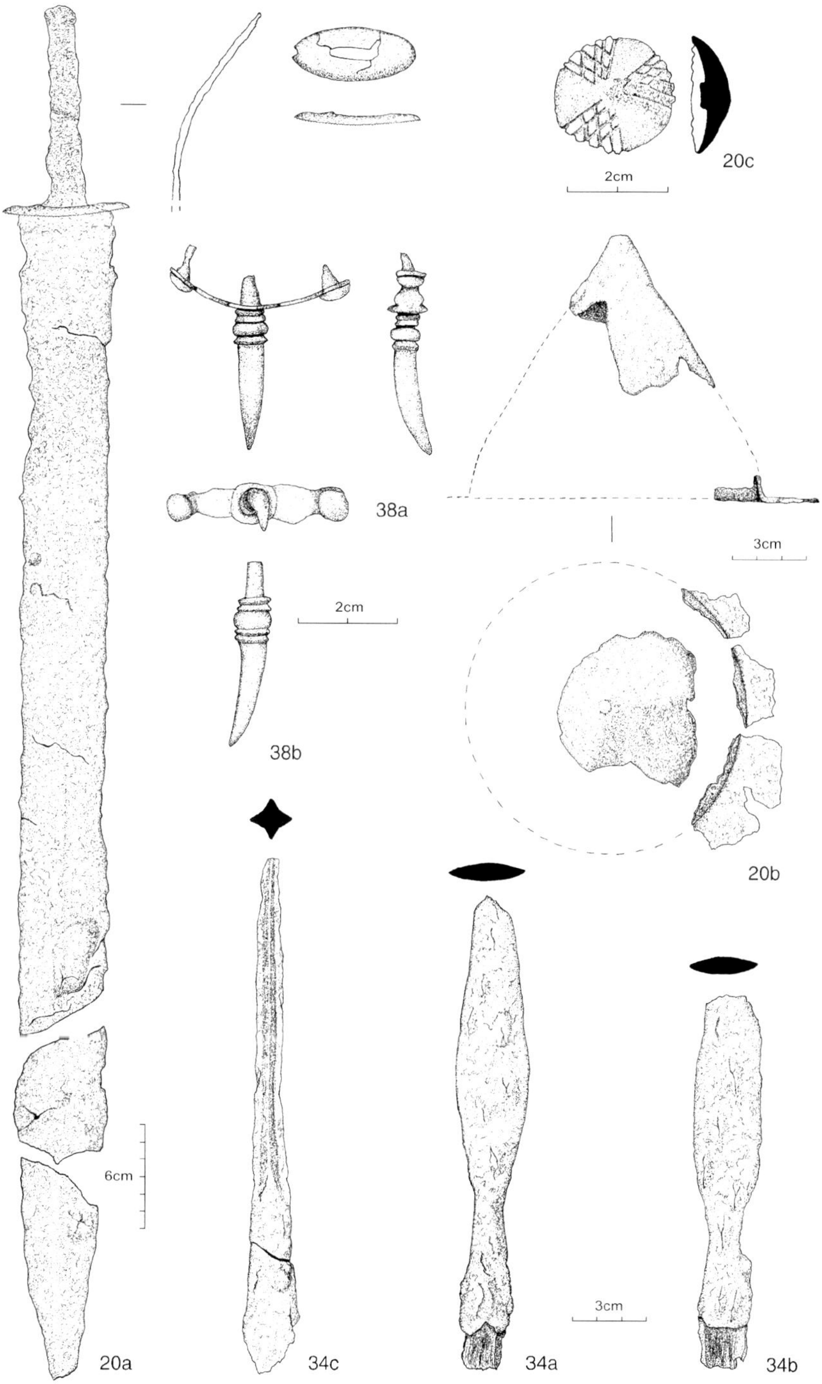

Figure 10.8 Weaponry and spurs from funerary chamber A at Goeblingen-Nospelt, Luxembourg. The sword (20a) is an iron gladius in the Roman tradition (after Metzler and Gaeng 2009, fig. 46).

The most striking phenomenon is the increase in the number of graves with large burial chambers, such as Fléré-la-Rivière (Indre), Antran (Vienne), Ménestreau-en-Villette (Loiret), Berry-Bouy (Cher) and Neuvy-Pailloux (Indre) (Figures 10.9–10.10). However, this tradition of large tombs began before La Tène D2b. Several examples show that this funerary architecture, which had been abandoned at the beginning of the 4th century BC, was reintroduced in La Tène D1. The reappearance of such graves cannot therefore simply be linked to the exceptional status acquired by these aristocrats after the conquest. Even so, it is difficult not to see a link between these richly-furnished burials in central France and those of Goeblingen-Nospelt, or similar graves at Saint-Nicolas (Pas-de-Calais), Boé (Lot-et-Garonne) and Verna (Isère). All mark a desire to highlight a power that was most probably acquired from the hands of the Roman conqueror, for good and loyal services rendered in the war. These tombs marked the construction of a new identity and power inherited from the Roman conqueror in both the landscape and the consciousness of their contemporaries.

After the conquest: coinage and auxiliary camps

The Gallic Wars allowed Caesar to establish close relations with the Gallic aristocrats who remained most faithful to him. This is illustrated by the arrangements he made in 49 BC during the civil war as he prepared to leave for Spain to fight against the Pompeian forces:

> Caesar had sent forward six legions into Spain, five thousand auxiliary infantry and three thousand cavalry which he had had with him during all his former wars, and an equal number from Gaul, which he had himself pacified, having specially called to arms all the men of conspicuous rank and bravery from every state; to these he had added men of the best class from among the *Aquitani* and the mountaineers who border on the province of Gaul. He had heard that Pompeius was marching at the head of his legions through Mauritania into Spain and would very soon arrive. At the same time he borrowed sums of money from the tribunes and centurions and distributed them among the soldiers. By this proceeding he gained two results: he established a pledge on the loyalty of the centurions and purchased by the bounty the goodwill of the troops (*de Bello Civili* 1.39).

This literally means that Caesar called up all the most noble and bravest men from Gaul who were faithful to him. These chiefs each had to recruit their own contingents. With this levy, we are at the heart of the Caesarian military system, which was based on Gallic leaders bringing their clients with them, sometimes forming an ethnically homogeneous group, sometimes combining warriors from different groups.

We know the name of some of these leaders, such as Epasnactos the Arvernian, who issued coins depicting a winged standard (*signum*) held by a soldier in Roman military kit on the reverse. Epasnactos could have commanded a cavalry unit, as did Atectorix, another Gallic leader (probably from Aquitania) after whom the *ala Atectorigiana* was named, and who issued coins at the end of the 1st century BC. Nor

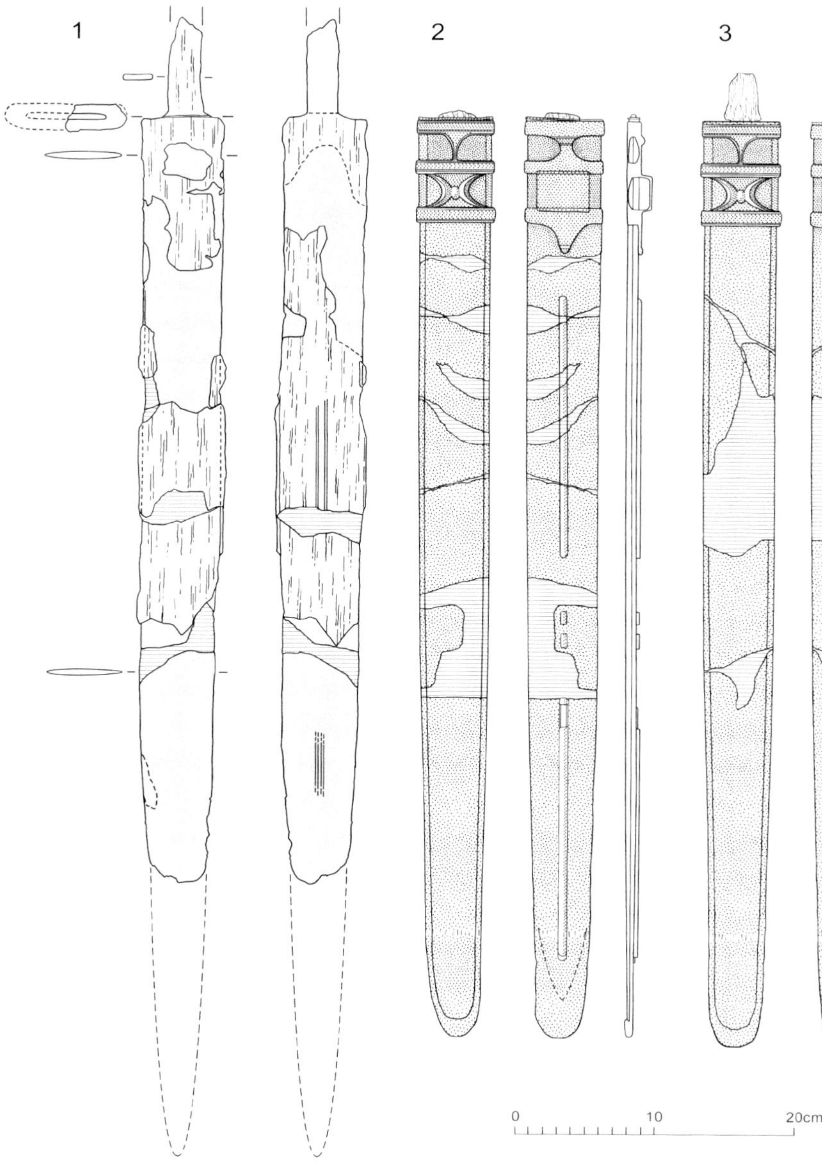

Figure 10.9 Swords in their scabbards from the chamber grave at Fléré-la-Rivière, Indre. (1) Roman tradition iron gladius with wooden sheath; (2–3) iron swords in bronze sheaths of Celtic tradition (after Pernet 2010, pl. 167).

						BC	AD				
Graves	**60-50**	**50-40**	**40-30**	**30-20**	**20-10**	**10-1**	**1-10**	**10-20**	**20-30**	**30-40**	**40-50**
Esvres F135 (C10)	■	■									
Ménestreau (C19)			■	■							
Berry-Bouy (C3)				■	■						
Fléré-la-Rivière (C12)					■	■					
Antran (C2)							■	■			
Chassenard (C5)										■	
Neuvy-Pailloux (C23)											■

Figure 10.10 Burial period of selected graves containing weapons from central France. The age of the warriors is unknown, but assuming an average age of 30–40 years at death, we can reflect on their status during and after the Gallic Wars (after Pernet 2010, fig. 115).

were the Transalpine Gauls left out at this time either, as the well-known case of Roucillos and Ecos reminds us. These two noblemen of the Allobroges accompanied Caesar to Greece with their own cavalry units but then embezzled the money for the horsemen's pay before defecting to Pompey:

> He had bestowed on them for these reasons offices of great dignity in their own homes, had arranged that they should be chosen on the tribal senate out of due course, had assigned to them lands in Gaul taken from the enemy and large prizes of money, and had raised them from poverty to wealth. These men, on account of their worth, were not only held in honour by Caesar, but were also regarded with affection in the army (*de Bello Civile* 3.59).

As we have seen, the Gallic military aristocracy who won the war with Caesar often issued their own coins (Martin and Pernet 2017). Part of these issues served to pay their troops, as can be seen at several sites. At the *oppidum* of La Chaussée-Tirancourt near Amiens (Somme, France), a geophysical survey in 2014 confirmed the military character of the site, which had already been suggested by the large number of surface finds of coins (Bayard and Fichtl 2016). The proportion of silver coins is very high. A large part of the assemblage comprises 'Mediterranean' silver issues, in this case Massiliote obols rather than Roman *denarii*, while the Gaulish coins are mostly from outside the region. Similar coin assemblages have been identified on other sites that were only occupied just before or during the Gallic War, such as Sermuz near Yverdon-les-Bains in Switzerland (Brunetti *et al.* 2007; see Kaenel this volume), Gondole (Puy-de-Dôme, France; Deberge *et al.* 2009) and Arras Actiparc (Pas-de-Calais, France; Jacques and Prilaux 2008). Sermuz (Figure 10.11), Gondole and La Chaussée-Tirancourt are all located on promontories defended by cross-ramparts of *murus gallicus* type (which were praised by Caesar in *BG* 7.23; see Krausz this volume). None of these fortified sites has the roughly rectangular plan of the Roman bases that became more common from the Augustan period, but all could have contained mixed garrisons of legionaries and auxiliaries, or perhaps just auxiliaries.

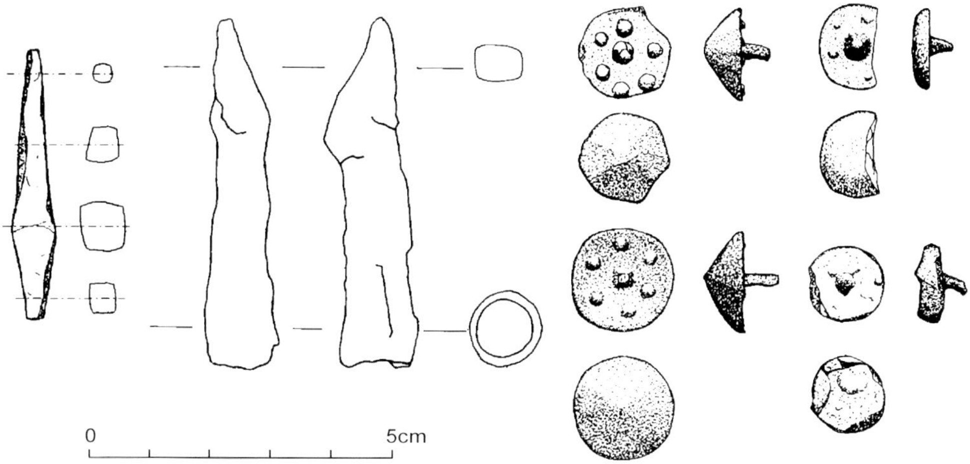

Figure 10.11 Roman Republican iron catapult bolts and hobnails from the oppidum *of Sermuz, Vaud, Switzerland (authorized prospections and drawings by Pierre-Alain Capt).*

Auxiliaries and 'Romanization'

At the time of their conquests there was a high degree of homogeneity across the study area in terms of 'civilization'. Whether northern Italy at the beginning of the 2nd century BC or Celtic Gaul in 58 BC, these zones had much in common and allow an overall assessment of the impact of auxiliary service on the process of Romanization in terms of the economic, political and military contacts these territories had with Rome.

All of the regions had experienced significant urbanization well before the Roman conquest: from the 5th century BC in southern France, from the 3rd century BC in northern Italy and from the 2nd century BC in Celtic Gaul. At the time of the Caesarian war, several peoples (*e.g.* the Aedui, the Helvetii or the Arverni) had an oligarchic mode of social and political organization. Roads were well developed, one of the reasons why Caesar was able to make such rapid progress across Gaul. Along the Rhone valley, Gaulish coinages were aligned on the Roman *denarius*, so military service as Roman auxiliaries was an additional component in a rapprochement that had started before the arrival of Roman troops on Gaulish soil. But the proximity of the Gallic auxiliaries to the Roman army and its organization, its supply system, its religions, its cuisine and its ability to produce coins, weapons and tools – including using new alloys such as brass (Istenic 2005, 200) – acted as a catalyst that accelerated this process (Poux 2008, 428–429).

In addition, the auxiliaries Caesar raised in Gaul to fight for him in the civil war against Pompey deprived Gaul of the youth that could have fuelled a revolt. As the anti-Roman parties were wiped out during the Gallic Wars, the auxiliaries effectively helped bring about 'complete' Romanization (through contact, exchanges, discipline, language etc.), while their absence did not impede – or even facilitated – the reorganization required by Rome. While the relationships of the Gallic elites with the Roman army, whether in conflict or cooperation, cannot on their own explain how Gaul entered the process of Romanization, they represent a significant aspect of it.

Nonetheless it is difficult to assess to what extent the auxiliaries assented. To what extent did they feel Roman? Without epigraphic evidence, it is a difficult question to answer because their exact status remains unknown. We have argued on the basis of weapons placed in their graves and their date, that some warriors may have been auxiliaries. Yet, until at least the Augustan period, their military equipment remained in the Celtic tradition and the material culture of the aristocracy was not radically different from that of the two or three preceding generations or their predecessors. Certainly, their mindsets did not change immediately. Gallic military organization was based on strong ties of patronage and the Romans exploited this relationship by simply adding an additional tier to the existing military hierarchy. Gallic aristocrats continued to command dedicated warriors while they swore loyalty to Caesar, who offered them gifts and benefits in exchange (money, land, citizenship...). It was only in the Augustan period, when weapons completely disappeared from graves, that mentalities changed (Le Roux 2006, 26).

Conclusion

The detailed study summarized here is based on a large corpus of late La Tène weapons that was brought together for the first time. Typological analysis allowed traditions of weapon manufacture (Gallic, Roman, Germanic) to be identified independently of the identity of the user. Although this distinction is important, it is also one of the limitations of the study. In order to determine the users' identities, the analysis needs to be supported by other criteria, such as funerary ritual, the nature of the deposits and the dating and context of the grave. For sanctuaries, battlefields and settlements, this question is much more difficult – do Roman weapons signify the presence of legionaries or of natives equipped with Roman weapons? – and often remains unanswered. This work, however, avoids the pitfall of confusing the tradition of a weapon and its origin, which has often led to erroneous arguments about Roman auxiliaries.

Archaeology is not an exact science, and no one expects it to deliver results from which indisputable laws can be drawn. It is nonetheless a scientific discipline insofar as one can test and validate the interpretations proposed. Verification is based on the statistical richness of the data (both qualitative and quantitative), which makes it possible to identify trends and especially regularities in the phenomena highlighted. Whilst none of the deceased fighters studied can unquestionably be identified as auxiliaries (this would require epigraphic evidence from their tombstones), we believe that the regularity with which we have identified fighters on the basis of their weapons in contexts that date to conquest periods or immediately after, justifies the tackling of this topic, which is fundamental for the understanding of the Romanization of Gaul.

To do so, it was necessary to consider the written sources on the same level as archaeological ones (Sauer 2004): where archaeology and ancient history meet. This is the only way, to quote Laurent Olivier, to really bring history into archaeology. For if history reconstructs 'what happened', archaeology tells us 'what happened to the existing (beings and things)' of the past. In this perspective, archaeology does not illustrate the past, it becomes 'a field of observation that enriches the history of diversity of all the individual trajectories developed by the subjects of the material universe' (Olivier 2008, 280). Behind the corpus of graves lie difficult choices, fighters broken and glorified by war, decimated communities and identity crises revealed by funerary deposits: human adventures, in all their richness. Where the written sources give us names, and anecdotes, archaeology brings us back their materiality.

Note

1 Other pointers to the existence of this new lineage are the clustering of smaller tombs around the five main burials at Goeblingen-Nospelt and the presence in the mound covering Grave 14 of repeated offerings of burnt bone and coins, which suggests an 'ancestor cult' (Metzler and Gaeng 2009, 504).

Bibliography

Bayard, D. and Fichtl, S. (2016) Le 'Camp de César' de la Chaussée-Tirancourt (Somme): *oppidum* ou camp romain? In G. Blancquaert and F. Malrain (eds), *Évolution des sociétés gauloises du second âge du Fer, entre mutations internes et influences externes (Actes du 38e colloque international de l'AFEAF, Amiens 2014)*, 343–361. Amiens, Revue archéologique de Picardie No. Spécial 30.

Brunetti, C., Curdy, P., Geiser, A. *et al.* (2007) *Yverdon-les-Bains et Sermuz à la fin de l'âge du Fer*. Lausanne, Musée cantonal d'archéologie et d'histoire, Cahiers d'archéologie romande 107.

Deberge, Y., Cabezuelo, U., Cabanis, M., Foucras, S., Garcia, M., Gruel, K., Loughton, M., Blondel, F. and Caillat, P. (2009) L'oppidum arverne de Gondole (Le Cendre, Puy-de-Dôme). Topographie de l'occupation protohistorique (La Tène D2) et fouille du quartier artisanal: un premier bilan. *Revue archéologique du Centre de la France* 48, 33–130.

Gleser, R. (2005) *Studien zu Sozialen Strukturen der historischen Kelten in Mitteleuropa aufgrund der Gräberanalyse. Die keltisch-römische Nekropole von Hoppstädten-Weiersbach im kontext latènezeitlicher Fundgruppen und römischer Okkupation*. Bonn, Saarbrücker Beiträge zur Altertumskunde 81

Istenic, J. (2005) Brooches of the Alesia group in Slovenia. *Arheoloski vestnik* 56, 187–212.

Jacques A. and Prilaux G. (2008) Arras – Les fouilles Actiparc (62). Le mobilier à caractère militaire découvert dans un vaste complexe césaro-tibérien. In M. Poux (ed.), *Sur les traces de César. Militaria tardo-républicains en contexte gaulois*, 47–62. Glux-en-Glenne, Collection Bibracte 14.

Le Roux, P. (2006) Rome et le monde celtique à la veille de la conquête césarienne. In D. Paunier (ed.), *Celtes et Gaulois. L'archéologie face à l'Histoire. La romanisation et la question de l'héritage celtique*, 12–28. Glux-en-Glenne, Collection Bibracte 12/5.

Martin, S. and Pernet, L. (2017) Le monnayage celtique de la guerre des Gaules à l'avènement d'Auguste (60–30 av. J.-C.). In J. Genechesi and L. Pernet (eds), *Les Celtes et la monnaie. Des Grecs aux Surrealistes*. Gollion, Infolio.

Meztler, J., Waringo R. and Metzler-Zens N. (1991) *Clémency et les tombes de l'aristocratie en Gaule Belgique*. Luxembourg, Musée National d'Histoire et d'Art Dossiers d'archéologie I.

Meztler, J. and C. Gaeng *et al.* (2009) *Goeblange-Nospelt. Une nécropole aristocratique trévire*. Luxembourg, Musée National d'Histoire et d'Art Dossiers d'archéologie XIII.

Metzler-Zens, N. and Metzler, J. (1998) Die spätkeltische Aristokratie in Gallien. Überlegungen zur Selbstdarstellung einer sozialen Gruppe. In A. Müller-Karpe, H. Braandt, H. Jöns, *et al.* (eds), *Studien zur Archäologie der Kelten, Römer und Germanen in Mittel- und Westeuropa Alfred Haffner gewidmet*, 417–427. Rahden, Marie Leidorf.

Olivier L. (2008) *Le sombre abîme du temps. Mémoire et archéologie.* Paris, Seuil.

Pernet, L. (2008) L'armement républicain des nécropoles de Giubiasco et d'Ornavasso. In M. Poux (ed.), *Sur les traces de César. Militaria tardo-républicains en contexte gaulois*, 275–293. Glux-en-Glenne, Collection Bibracte 14.

Pernet, L. (2010) *Armement et auxiliaires gaulois (IIe–Ier siècles avant notre ère).* Montagnac, Editions Monique Mergoil.

Pernet, L. (2016) L'ensemble de Sigoyer (Hautes-Alpes), un assemblage d'armement singulier de la fin de l'Âge du Fer: témoin de la mobilité de personnes ou de biens? *Bulletin d'études préhistoriques et archéologiques alpines* 2016, 185–196.

Pernet, L. (2017) La casque gaulois. In C. Nitu (ed.), Le Mormont, une décennie de recherches archéologiques. *Archéologie vaudoise chroniques 2016*, 57.

Pernet, L. and Carlevaro, E. *et al.* (2006) *La necropoli di Giubiasco. Vol. II, Les tombes de La Tène finale et d'époque romaine.* Zurich, Musée Suisse Collectio Archaeologica 4.

Poux M. (2008) L'empreinte du militaire tardo-républicain dans les faciès mobiliers de La Tène finale. Caractérisation, chronologie et diffusion de ses principaux marqueurs. In M. Poux (ed.), *Sur les traces de César. Militaria tardo-républicains en contexte gaulois*, 299–432. Glux-en-Glenne, Collection Bibracte 14.

Sauer, E.W. (ed.) (2004) *Archaeology and Ancient History: Breaking down the boundaries.* London, Routledge.

Schwaller, M., Marchand, G, Lejars, T., Orliac, D., Rapin, A. and Sanmarti, E. (2001) Echanges, influences, productions dans la nécropole du deuxième âge du Fer d'Ensérune (Hérault). *Documents d'archéologie méditerranéenne* 24, 173–184.

Waurick, G. (1990) *Helme in Caesars Heer.* Mainz, Römisch-Germanisches Zentralmuseum.

Appendix: Sites analysed in the study

A Alpine area		
A1	Bela Cerkev	large cemetery
A2	Domodossola	isolated grave
A3	Giubiasco	large cemetery
A4	Grad pri Reki (Reka)	battlefield
A5	Grad pri Šmihelu (Šmihel)	battlefield
A6	Gravellona Toce	large cemetery
A7	Idrija pri Bači	small cemetery
A8	Mihovo	large cemetery
A9	Monte Sorantri	settlement
A10	Novo Mesto	large cemetery
A11	Ornavasso	large cemetery
A12	Reka pri Cerknem	small cemetery
A13	Sion	small cemeteries
A14	Škocjanske Jame/ Grotte di San Canziano	sanctuary?
A15	Verdun pri Stopičah	large cemetery
A16	Wartau	sanctuary
B Belgic Gaul		
B1	Alizay	small cemetery
B2	Amiens	settlement/ military camp?
B3	Andernach	small cemetery
B4	Arras Actiparc	Roman fortlet
B5	Bois l'Abbé	sanctuary
B6	Le Châtelet de Gourzon	*oppidum*
B7	La Chaussée-Tirancourt	*oppidum*/military camp
B8	Cottévrard	small cemetery
B9	Dury	isolated grave
B10	Folleville	sanctuary
B11	Goeblingen-Nospelt	small cemetery
B12	Grügelborn	small cemetery
B13	Hannogne	isolated grave
B14	Hellange	isolated graves
B15	Hoppstädten-Weiersbach	large cemetery
B16	Kerben	small cemetery
B17	Koblenz-Neuendorf	small cemetery
B18	Kollig	small cemetery
B19	Konz-Filzen	small cemetery
B20	Lamadelaine	large cemetery
B21	Lebach Die Motte	large cemetery
B22	Liercourt-Erondelle	*oppidum*/military camp
B23	Mainzweiler	small cemetery

(*Continued*)

B24	Mainz-Weisenau	isolated graves
B25	Mayen	small cemetery
B26	Mesnil-sous-Jumièges	small cemetery
B27	Neunkirchen/Nahe	isolated grave
B28	Neuwied-Heimbach-Weis	small cemetery
B29	Notre-Dame-du-Vaudreuil	small cemetery
B30	Otzenhausen	*oppidum*
B31	Petrisberg	*oppidum*/military camp?
B32	Pîtres	large cemetery
B33	Poses	cemetery
B34	Ribemont-sur-Ancre	sanctuary
B35	Ronchin	small cemetery
B36	Rouvray, Forêt de	isolated grave
B37	Saint-Aubin-Routot	small cemetery
B38	Saint-Nicolas	small cemetery
B39	Sötern	small cemetery
B40	Titelberg	*oppidum*/military camp
B41	Trier-Olewig	isolated graves
B42	Urmitz	large cemetery
B43	Vendeuil-Caply	sanctuary
B44	Villeneuve-Saint-Germain	*oppidum*
B45	Ville-sur-Retourne	small cemetery
B46	Wahnwegen	large cemetery
B47	Wederath	large cemetery
C Celtic Gaul		
C1	Allonnes	sanctuary
C2	Antran	isolated grave
C3	Berry-Bouy «Fontillet»	isolated grave
C4	Boé	isolated grave
C5	Chassenard	isolated grave
C6	Châtillon-sur-Indre	isolated grave
C7	Corent	*oppidum*/sanctuary
C8	Dun-sur-Auron	isolated grave or deposit?
C9	L'Ermitage	*oppidum*
C10	Esvres-sur-Indre	small cemetery
C11	Feurs Rue Saint Antoine	small cemetery
C12	Fléré-la-Rivière	isolated grave
C13	Gergovie/Merdogne	*oppidum*/battlefield
C14	Gondole	*oppidum*
C15	Landudec	isolated grave
C16	Levroux	isolated graves
C17	Malintrat Chaniat	small cemetery
C18	Les Martres-de-Veyre	cemetery
C19	Ménestreau-en-Villette	isolated grave
C20	Mont-Auxois	*oppidum*/battlefield/military camp
C21	Mont-Beuvray	*oppidum*
C22	Münsterhügel	*oppidum*/military camp
C23	Neuvy-Pailloux	isolated grave
C24	Palluau	isolated grave
C25	Paris	grave?
C26	Port	sanctuary/bridges
C27	Le Puy d'Issolud	*oppidum*/battlefield
C28	Remetschwil	isolated grave

(*Continued*)

C29	Sermuz	*oppidum*/military camp?
C30	Tavant	small cemetery
C31	Tesson	isolated grave
C32	Vindonissa	military camp

N Transalpine Gaul (Narbonensis)		
N1	Le Baou-Roux	*oppidum*
N2	Les Baux-de-Provence	small cemetery
N3	Beaucaire	small cemetery
N4	La Cloche	*oppidum*
N5	Entremont	*oppidum*
N6	Jastres	*oppidum*
N7	Lafoux	isolated grave
N8	Mépieu	small cemetery
N9	Mouriès	small cemetery
N10	Nîmes Camplanier	isolated graves
N11	Nîmes Forum des Carmes	small cemetery
N12	Nîmes Forum Kinepolis	isolated graves
N13	Nîmes La Ranquette	isolated grave
N14	Nîmes Mail Romain	isolated graves
N15	Nîmes Mas de Vignoles	small cemetery
N16	Nîmes Mas des Abeilles	small cemetery
N17	Nîmes Octroi de Beaucaire	isolated graves
N18	Nîmes Pissevin	isolated graves
N19	Nîmes Rue de Seyne	isolated grave
N20	Nîmes Valdegour	isolated grave
N21	Optevoz	isolated grave
N22	Saint-Côme	isolated grave
N23	Saint-Dionisy	isolated grave
N24	Sainte-Cécile	isolated grave
N25	Saint-Laurent des Arbres	isolated grave
N26	Saint-Siffret	isolated grave
N27	Sigoyer	isolated grave
N28	Toulouse Estarac	settlement
N29	Toulouse Saint-Roch	settlement
N30	Vachères	uncertain
N31	Verna	isolated grave
N32	Vié-Cioutat	*oppidum*
N33	Vieille-Toulouse	*oppidum*

T Transpadane Gaul		
T1	Acquate	isolated graves
T2	Arquà Petrarca	small cemetery
T3	Barzio	isolated grave
T4	Coccaglio	isolated grave
T5	Esino	isolated graves
T6	Ghisalba	isolated grave
T7	Gomoria	isolated grave
T8	Introbio	small cemetery
T9	Isola Rizza	large cemetery
T10	Mariano al Brembo	isolated grave
T11	Misano di Gera d'Adda	isolated grave
T12	Oleggio	large cemetery
T13	Piadena	small cemetery
T14	Remedello Sopra	isolated graves
T15	Remedello Sotto	small cemetery
T16	Santa Maria di Zevio	large cemetery
T17	Somma-Lombardo	isolated grave

Chapter 11

The Hermeskeil fortress: New light on the Caesarian conquest of eastern Belgic Gaul and its aftermath

Sabine Hornung

In contrast to the detailed record of the Battle for Gaul given by Julius Caesar himself in *de Bello Gallico*, archaeological evidence connected to the events described is still sparse. Until 2010 not a single site from his campaigns in the territory of the Treveri – a tribe who lived west of the Rhine, in the Hunsrück and Eifel regions and as far as Luxembourg in the west (*BG* 3.11.1; 4.10.3; 5.3.4) – was known. Only recently has landscape archaeological research in the vicinity of Hermeskeil, a town 35 km south-east of Trier (Rheinland-Pfalz, Germany) brought to light the remains of a late Republican military camp (Hornung 2012a; 2012b; 2014; 2015; 2016a, 129–164; 2018). This site is situated strategically, in clear view of a late La Tène *oppidum*, the so-called 'Hunnenring' near Otzenhausen, on the Dollberg mountain just 5 km away (Figure 11.1). What is more, the Hermeskeil fortress controls access to two major axes of communication, one of which leads directly towards the Hunnenring to the south and the Trier basin to the north (Hornung 2014, 197; 2016a, 129). While the western part of the Hermeskeil camp lies in arable land, which was deforested in the 18th and then cultivated from the 19th century onwards, its eastern part is covered by dense woods. Consequently, the rampart is quite well preserved on its north-eastern and south-eastern sides, where it still reaches a height of up to 1 m. This remarkable state of preservation has also helped to protect the camp in recent years. Long considered a relic of medieval or modern woodland boundaries, it thus escaped the systematic plundering which has destroyed many archaeological sites in the region up to the present day.

The fortress: archaeological evidence

After eight years of intensive research, it is possible to reconstruct the fortress and its structure in some detail. It has an overall size of about 31 ha and consists of a main

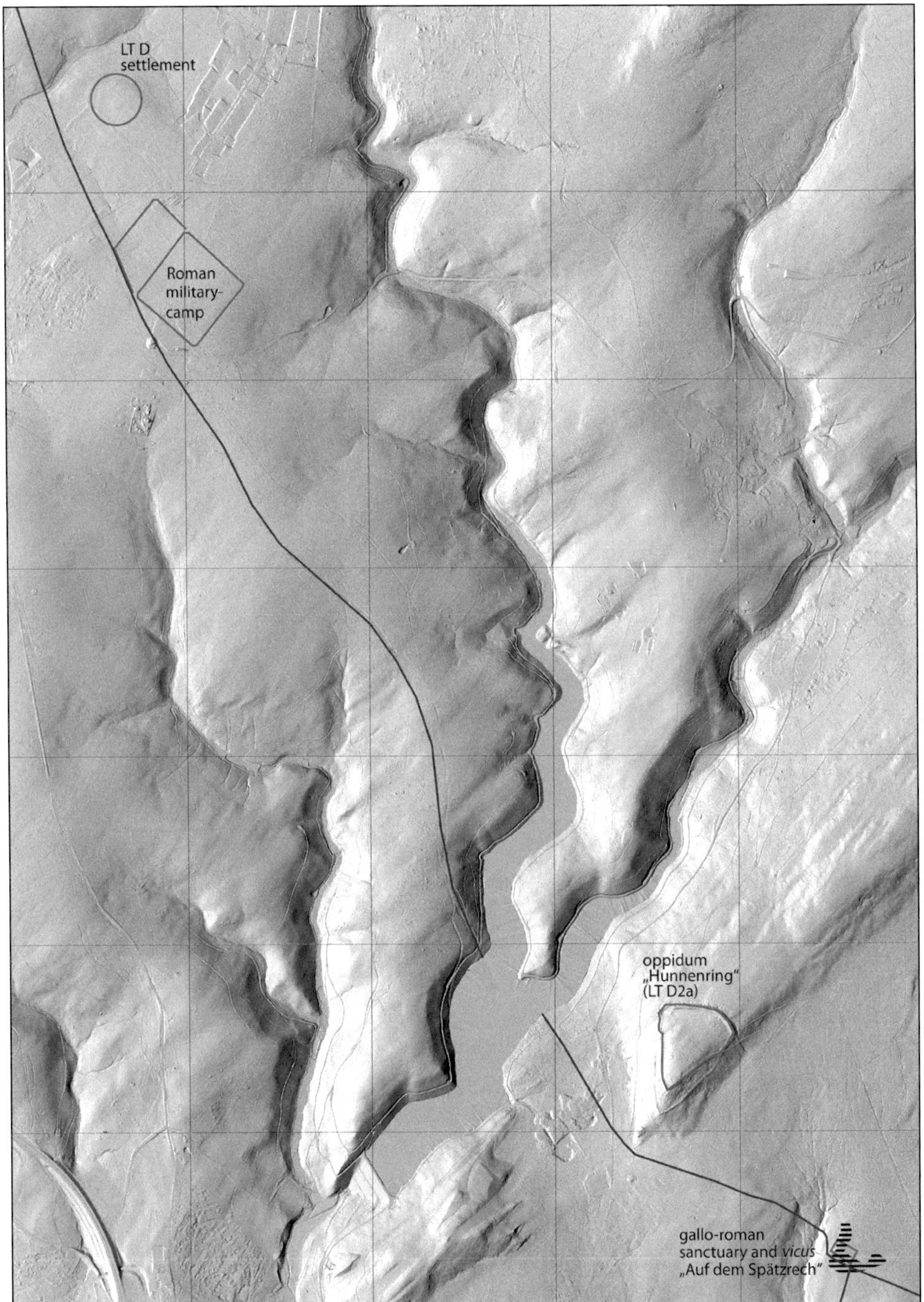

Figure 11.1 Map of the archaeological sites mentioned in the text and the reconstructed course of the Iron Age road connecting the Roman military camp at Hermeskeil and the Hunnenring oppidum *near Otzenhausen, Rheinland-Pfalz (image S. Hornung; LiDAR-Scan: LVermGeo Rheinland-Pfalz).*

camp and an adjacent annexe (Figure 11.2). The main camp is roughly square with rounded corners and covers around 19.5 ha (see Hornung 2015, 105–111 and 2016a, 129–142 for a more detailed description), the fortifications consisting of a rampart and a V-shaped ditch. The north-eastern third is partitioned off by another rampart and a more U-shaped ditch. There are indications that this internal fortification marks a subsequent reduction of the main camp's surface area, with its larger southern part still over 12 ha in size. To the north-west, an annexe of another 11.2 ha connects to the main camp. Its defences – again consisting of a rampart and ditch – enclosed a well, thus securing water supplies for the troops. The pottery discovered in this part of the camp includes mainly coarse, often handmade, wares belonging to vessels used for transporting foodstuffs, storage and cooking. There are indications that the annexe protected auxiliaries.[1] The south-western side lies at an angle, following the course of the ancient road leading towards the Hunnenring, which must therefore date to the late Iron Age or earlier. On the opposite side, a large late La Tène and Roman cemetery extends over several hundred metres. Some 42 graves have been excavated so far, but stray finds indicate a much larger area (Dehn 1951, 23; Fritsch 2010a, 64–67; 2010b; Hornung 2016a, 132).

Figure 11.2 Plan of the Caesarian military camp at Hermeskeil (S. Hornung).

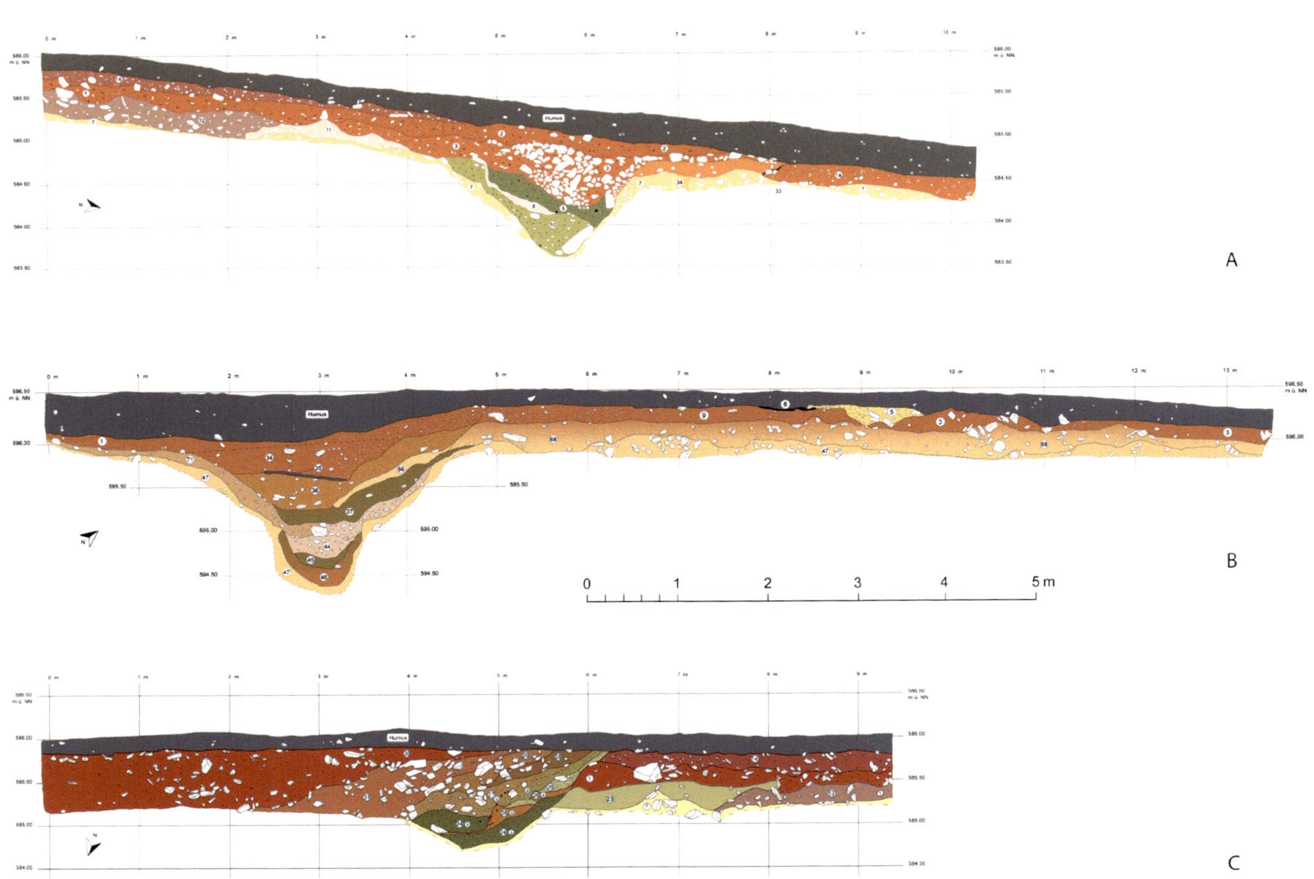

Figure 11.3 Sections through the defences at Hermeskeil. (A) The north-west side of the camp, 2010 excavation. (B) South-west gate, 2011 excavation: the ditch west of the entrance with traces of secondary cleaning. (C) The western end of the main camp's internal ditch and bank, 2010 excavation (images A. Braun).

The outer defences: rampart and ditch

The outer ditch is quite well preserved, even in those parts of the fortification which have been under the plough since the 19th century. Still, due to erosion its dimensions vary considerably, the ditch usually being between 2.5 and 3.5 m wide and 1.1 to 2.2 m deep (Fritsch 2011; Hornung 2016a, 134–140). All the trenches excavated between 2011 and 2017 have a similar stratigraphic fill sequence and the lowest layers at the bottom of the ditch have a distinctive greenish colouring (Figure 11.3, A–B). This colour is the result of organic material being mixed with the loamy soil. These layers were clearly deposited over a very short period, and probably mark the remains of turves, which once stabilized the bank and protected it from erosion. They would have been removed when the camp was abandoned, thus destabilizing the bank and preventing reuse of the encampment. On the other hand, the uppermost fill of the ditch usually consists of stones that were deposited when the area was turned over to arable during the 19th century. Only the ditches on the south-west side of the main camp showed traces of cleaning in the form of a secondary indentation or slot (Figure 11.3, B; Hornung 2012a, 210), but nevertheless this indicates that the fortress must have been in use over a longer period and cannot be considered a mere marching camp. The scale of the rampart and ditch at Hermeskeil closely resemble the defences of camp B at Alesia, and at Dorsten-Holsterhausen camps B and F, the temporary camp at Haltern (both Nordrhein-Westfalen) and the possible Caesarian camp I at Limburg an der Lahn (Hesse), all of which are associated with Roman campaigns in enemy territory (Reddé and von Schnurbein 2001, 234, 254–256, 264; Kühlborn 2006, 285; Ebel-Zepezauer *et al.* 2009, 16–21; Hornung forthcoming).[2]

The rampart at Hermeskeil would originally have been significantly higher than the 1 m that still survives in the woodland, and was surmounted by a wooden parapet, constructed mainly from branches. This very simple form of fortification was observed in all parts of the encampment except for the southern side of the annexe, which followed the ancient road. The latter must have cut deeply into the hill slope, leaving a scarp, so it was probably unnecessary to dig a ditch here. Since there was no upcast to use for a bank, the Roman army chose a different type of defence, in the form of a two-faced wooden wall, of which only two parallel gullies, both small and shallow, survive.

Gates

No traces of wooden structures belonging to towers or gates have so far been uncovered at Hermeskeil. The gates seem to have been simple gaps in the defences. This lack of timber architecture cannot be explained by the state of preservation or poor visibility of cut features, because when excavating the south-western gate in 2011 the original Roman surface was found partly intact (Figure 11.4) and there were no traces of postholes (Hornung 2012a, 210; 2016a, 134–136). Furthermore, several other features were clearly visible, such as the dark fills of the ditches. In the same

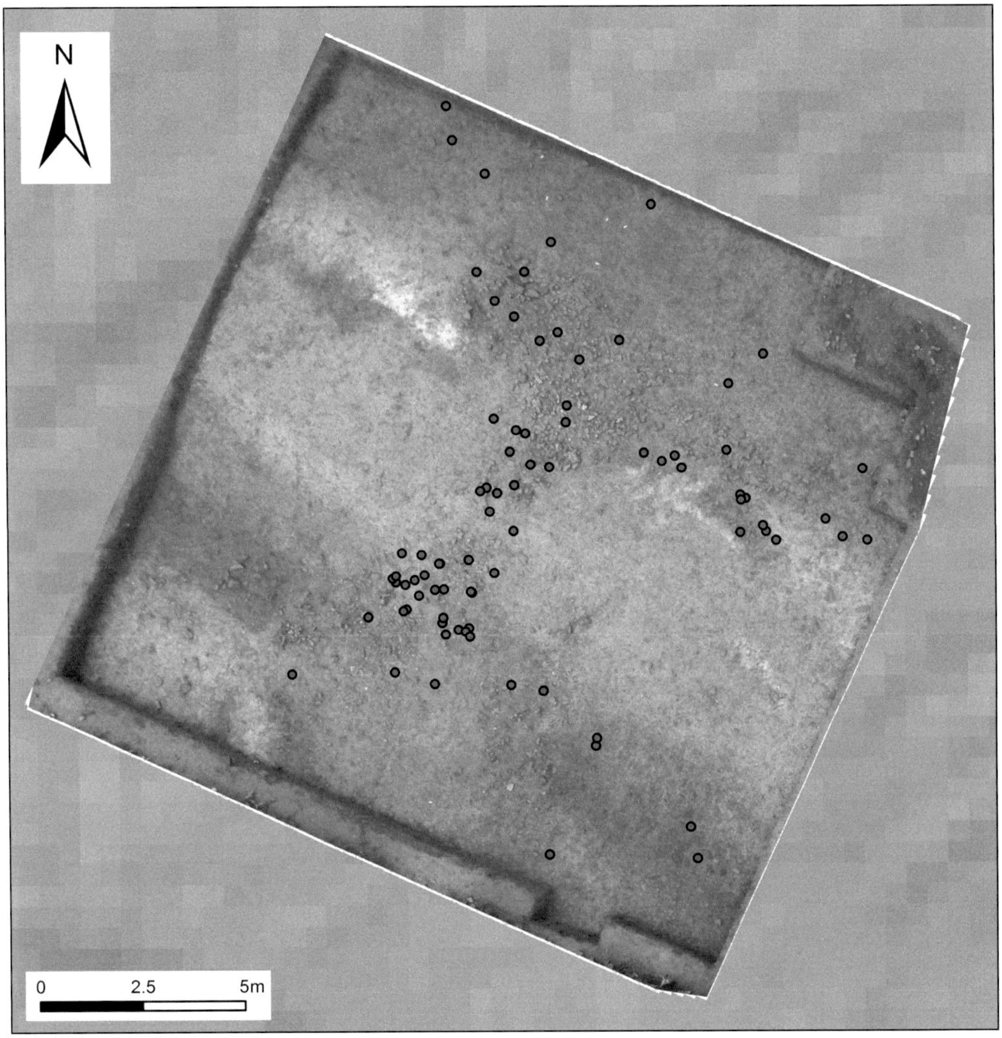

Figure 11.4 The south-west gate of the main camp. Dots: hobnails (image D. Rieth).

way, the berm was marked by a more yellowish color and the rampart behind it by a streak of greyish-ochre. A large reddish patch adjacent to the bank contained the remains of a wooden mat made of twigs that had been set on fire and this had burnt the surrounding soil. It is likely that the mats were part of a drainage system for the rampart to prevent rainwater from collecting behind it. Similar features are known, for example, from the Augustan site at Hedemünden in Germany, and from later sites such as Corbridge, Caermote and Llandovery in Britain, Valkenburg in the Netherlands and Altenstadt and Butzbach in Germany. The preservation of such mats is usually due either to waterlogging or to burning (Johnson 1987, 71–72; Grote 2008, 182; 2012, 61). In the case of Hermeskeil, this also indicates the intentional demolition of the fortress:

the Roman army set fire to all the wooden parts of the defences before leaving the camp, thus preventing its reuse by the enemy.

The gateway was only 3.3–3.5 m wide, its floor paved with slabs of local sandstone that showed clear traces of wear and partial repair, again indicating that the fortress was occupied for some time. The cleaning of the ditches and the relatively large quantity of finds point in the same direction. The very simple architectural form of the gates is paralleled in numerous Roman camps of the Augustan and possibly Caesarian periods, as for example at Dorsten-Holsterhausen, Wilkenburg, the temporary camp at Haltern and both the camps at Limburg an der Lahn (Kühlborn 2006, 285; Ebel-Zepezauer *et al.* 2009, 16–21; Haßmann *et al.* 2016, 23; Hornung forthcoming).

The north-western gate between the main camp and the annexe was built in a very similar way. Here too, the defences left a simple gap of about 7 m, about twice the width of the south-western gate. This was potentially the most important of the camp's entrances, being frequented each day by thousands of soldiers going in and out of the annexe to get water from the well. Therefore, it would have been particularly important to control access to the camp's interior. Two rectangular fire-pits, which partly blocked the entrance and still had thick layers of charcoal at the base, might have served this purpose. Again, the pits seem to have been backfilled by the army because large parts of storage vessels were found in their fills. If these vessels had been left lying on the surface for a long period, they would have been far more fragmented. It seems probable that the pits were levelled when the army left the camp in order to allow access for the carts needed to transport equipment. A small shallow ditch set at an angle to the outer defences was probably for drainage, because the gate occupied the slope of the hill and water would have run off the poorly draining loamy subsoil during heavy rain.

The inner ditch and bank

The internal ditch and bank differ slightly from the outer defences (Figure 11.3, C). The ditch has a more U-shaped profile and is up to 3.5 m wide (Hornung 2012a, 212; 2016a, 139). This implies a different function, best explained as a reduction in the size of the camp. In all the trenches excavated in the area under arable, the backfill of this inner ditch – whose stratigraphy closely resembled that of the outer ditch of the main camp – pointed towards the existence of a bank on its southern side. Again, this bank would have been reinforced with turves and dismantled when the Roman army left. Some vestiges of this shallow bank are still visible in the LIDAR scan of the wooded part of the fortress.

Internal organization

During geophysical prospection, a large number of anomalies were recorded in the interior of the camp that potentially related to Roman activity and thus warranted

Figure 11.5 Ovens in the interior of the Hermeskeil fortress. (A) Oven of type 1 with adjacent operating pit. There is no clear evidence for the former existence of a cupola. (B) Oven of type 1 with part of clay cupola still preserved to a height of c. 20 cm. The rest of the oven superstructure has collapsed into the pit. (C) Oven of type 2 with most of the stone-paved floor and two stones framing a former opening in the oven superstructure still intact (photos S. Hornung).

further investigation. Excavations in 2015 showed that a circular structure in the southern part of the main camp was a drainage ditch for a charcoal kiln of the 17th or early 18th century. Major charcoal production throughout the Hunsrück area followed the development of the local iron industry and marks one of the most extensive phases of land use in the region. In this case, it pre-dates the 18th-century clearance of this part of the fortress. However, several smaller magnetic anomalies proved to be Roman ovens, set at regular distances from one another (5–6 m) and roughly aligned in rows. The Roman pottery and hobnails from them confirm that they were part of the camp's original plan.

Two types of oven have been distinguished. The most common type (type 1) consists of a shallow round or slightly oval pit whose floor and sometimes walls are burnt red by the heat of the fire. An adjacent pit contains the ashes from these fires, often showing several distinct layers from different firings. Large stones were regularly pushed into these pits and these may well originally have framed them (Figure 11.5, A). It is unclear if we can presume the existence of domed superstructures on a regular basis. An oven of type 1 excavated in 2017 produced the first clear evidence for a clay cupola, which had collapsed into the pit (Figure 11.5, B). Unusually, this oven did not contain stones. Parallels for ovens of type 1 are known from many other Roman fortresses in Germany, such as the Augustan marching camps at Friedberg and Dorsten-Holsterhausen and the more permanent Claudian-Vespasianic camp at Groß-Gerau-Wallerstädten, to which we may add further examples from Augustan military complexes like Porta-Westfalica-Barkhausen, Hedemünden, Marktbreit and the possibly Caesarian camp II at Limburg an der Lahn (Pietsch *et al.* 1991, 300–302; Ebel-Zepezauer *et al.* 2009, 27–28; Tremmel 2011; Grote 2012, 80–81; Maurer 2013; Lindenthal 2014, 94–95; Hornung forthcoming).[3]

Only two type 2 ovens have been found so far. For these, a domed superstructure can be reconstructed with some certainty, because two stones, which once framed an opening, were discovered *in situ* in one of them (Figure 11.5, C). In this case, the circular floor of the pit was paved with sandstone slabs that were badly heat-damaged and the soil underneath was burnt red as well. The pit in front of the oven had a clearly defined rectangular shape and was filled with several layers of ash and large fragments of charred wood.

Similar anomalies in the magnetometry results seem to be roughly aligned in rows with a concentration in the area adjacent to the *intervallum* – the road running directly behind the rampart was obviously kept clear. Rows of ovens are also known in the interior of the camp and from their distribution we can virtually reconstruct the system of roads and details of the internal organization. What is more, type 1 ovens occur in all parts of the fortress, including the annexe, which must therefore have seen regular use too. The absence of timber or stone buildings indicates that the soldiers were accommodated in tents (Hornung 2015, 109). These would have been aligned in rows or blocks, divided by the internal roads.

Finds and dating

The Hermeskeil fortress has produced a large number of archaeological finds associated with its late Republican occupation. Some later objects are easily explained by the camp's proximity to other sites, for example the cemetery mentioned above which was used between the 2nd century BC and the 4th century AD, and a Roman villa (Dehn 1951, 23; Fritsch 2010b; Hornung 2016a, 132). These more recent finds all come from the topsoil, however, and may have been moved by ploughing or other forms of human activity in the area.

Pottery

The pottery from Hermeskeil – apart from imported amphorae – lacks any Roman types. As would be expected in a late Republican context, the Dressel 1 amphora is dominant. While most sherds belong to the Dressel 1B variety, there are also occasional finds of Dressel 1A, indicating a date no later than the mid-1st century BC (Hornung 2016a, 146).

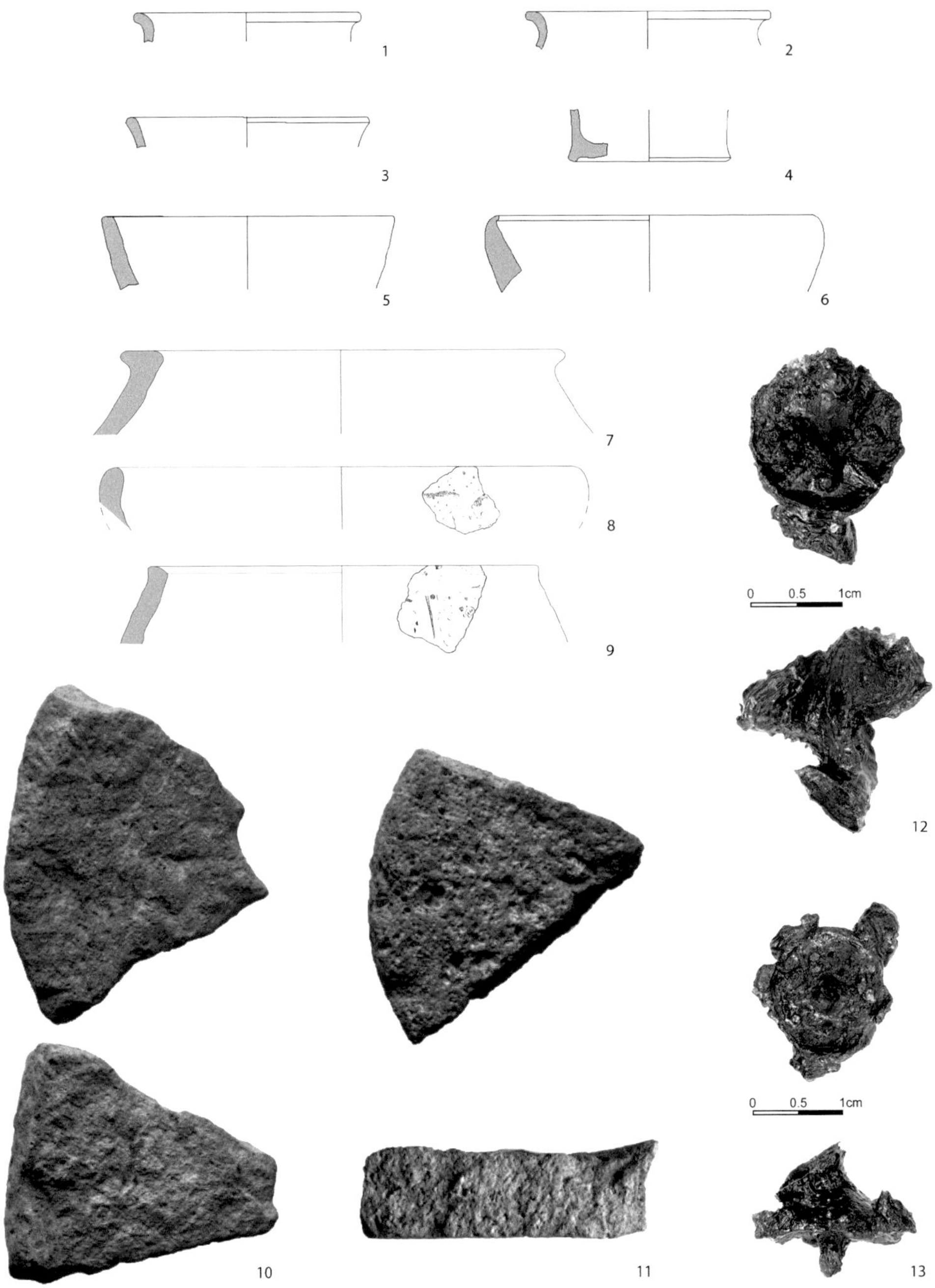

Figure 11.6 Selection of finds from Hermeskeil: (1–4) wheel-thrown pottery; (5–9) handmade pottery; (10) late La Tène type quern made of basaltic lava from Mayen; (11) legionary quern made of basaltic lava from the Massif Central; (12) caligae *hobnail of type D; (13)* caligae *hobnail of type C (images S. Hornung, A. Braun).*

All the other vessels and types are well known from non-Roman La Tène D2 contexts (Figure 11.6, 1–9); in particular, the wheel-thrown pottery closely resembles local wares of this date (Hornung 2016a, 143–146; 2018). That this pottery is mostly of local origin can be concluded from preliminary X-ray fluorescence analyses. The Hermeskeil sherds have been compared to samples from the Hunnenring *oppidum* and other Treveran centres, proving consistent with material from the neighbouring settlement (below).[4] On the other hand, most of the coarse handmade vessels seem to have been imported and have a very different chemical composition. Sometimes a non-local provenance is macroscopically visible too. For example, there are some sherds of graphite-tempered ware, which is otherwise completely absent in the Hunsrück. This type of pottery is frequently found in southern Germany, Bohemia and occasionally west of the Rhine.

Most of the pottery from Hermeskeil was recovered from the ditch fills, with a marked concentration at the very bottom and on the inner side. This indicates that the sherds originally came from the bank side and were probably deposited when it was dismantled by taking down the turves. The sherds may well have been used as a kind of paving to reinforce the walkway on the top of the rampart (Hornung 2015, 112).

Military equipment

Whereas very few, mostly fragmentary pieces of military equipment of little chronological significance have been found, there are a large number of hobnails. Most of these came to light during the excavation of the south-western gate (Hornung 2016a, 148–152), where they were stuck between the paving stones. The dominant type of hobnail compares well to type D from Alesia (Figure 11.6, 12), in which the heads bear a cross and four knobs. Type C is the second most frequent type, characterized by a circle of knobs (Figure 11.6, 13). Type D comprises about 75% of all finds, whereas type C accounts for only just over 10%. A similar predominance of type D occurs at Alesia camp B. In Alesia camps A and C, hobnails with a cross and four knobs are still the most frequent type but comprise only 40–50% of the hobnails (Brouquier-Reddé and Deyber 2001). That type D is in fact specific to late Republican sites becomes evident when the Hermeskeil finds are compared with ones of Augustan date. At Hedemünden, which is associated with the Augustan campaigns on the right bank of the Rhine, and the neighbouring small camp of Kring, type C predominates, whereas hobnails of type D are completely absent (Grote 2012, 253–261). The same predominance of type C can be observed for the camp on the Petrisberg near Trier, which was built during the Treveran revolt in 30/29 BC (Löhr 2003; Löhr and Trunk 2008).[5] According to these comparisons, the Hermeskeil fortress seems to be significantly earlier. This is supported by the size of the hobnails (14–26 mm), which compares well to the finds from sites like Gergovia, Uxellodunum and Vernon (Figure 11.7). Furthermore, only the hobnails from Alesia offer a close parallel at the upper end of the range (Poux 2008, 380; Martin-Kilcher 2011, 35). Thus, on the basis of the hobnails,

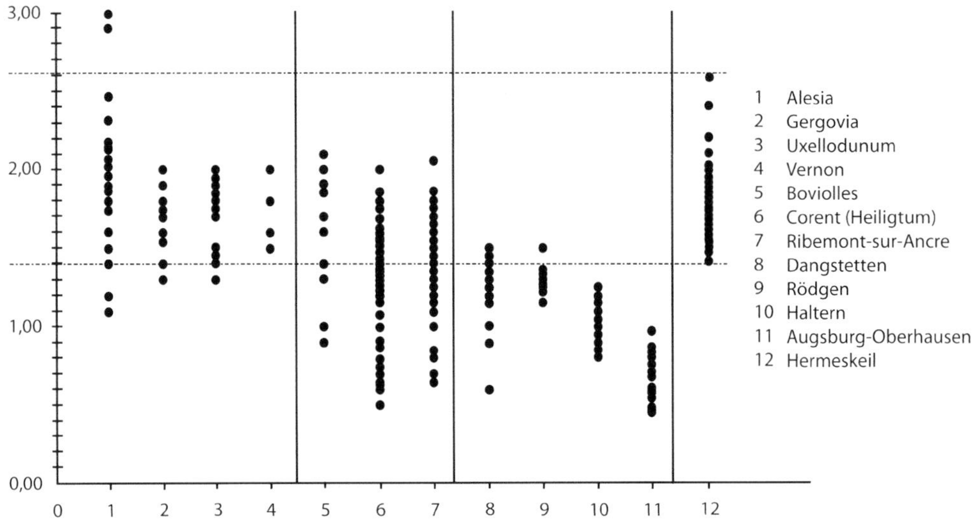

Figure 11.7 Comparison of the size of caligae *hobnails from different sites dating to the Caesarian and Augustan periods (after Hornung 2012a, fig. 8).*

a date for Hermeskeil in the mid-1st century BC – potentially Caesar's Gallic War – is quite probable.

Coins

The coin assemblage from Hermeskeil is quite small and bronzes in particular are often badly preserved. Most of the coins are Republican *asses*. In a Caesarian military context like Alesia, *asses* are mostly found whole, as at Hermeskeil (5 whole, 3 halved), whereas in the Augustan fortresses along the Rhine frontier they were usually halved (Martin 2011, 938–939). Only five Iron Age coins have been found so far at Hermeskeil. A Sequani type D2/1 potin is the youngest coin in the entire series and was minted from just before 50 BC at the earliest (Nick 2000, 38–42; 2015, 107). There are two eastern Gaulish *quinarii*,[6] which may indicate that the troops stationed at Hermeskeil had recently spent time in that region, potentially in the territory of the Sequani or Rauraci. This might be a primary chronological indicator, because Caesar's general Labienus, who conquered the Treveri in 51 BC, had his winter camp of 52/51 BC with the Sequani (*BG* 7.90.4). It is highly probable that he brought with him cavalry from that region when he started his campaign in the north the following summer.

Querns

In narrowing down our dating of the Hermeskeil fortress, the large number of quern fragments discovered during the 2010, 2011 and 2016 excavations become important.

Figure 11.8 Map of the Roman military campaigns in 52 BC and location of winter camps (blue squares) during the winter of 52/51 BC in relation to the provenance of querns discovered at Hermeskeil. Yellow shading: distribution areas of vaugnerite querns from the northern Morvan and La Salle rhyolite querns (image A. Kronz and S. Hornung).

These are of particular interest with regard to the provenance of the stone from which they are made. Caesar's army must originally have been provisioned with querns from quarries that were supplying the Romans before the start of the Gallic War. During the subsequent years of campaigning, broken querns were replaced with local products from the areas in which the troops were operating. The local supply of querns is reflected directly in the material from Hermeskeil (Hornung *et al.* 2015; in preparation).[7]

As would be expected for the final years of the conquest, only one of the small light querns regularly used by the Roman army, the so-called legionary quern, has so far been discovered (Figure 11.6, 11). It is made from the volcanic rock quarried at Cap d'Agde in the Roman province of *Gallia Transalpina,* which functioned as main base of operations during the battle for Gaul. Some of the legionaries who served in the war were recruited from the province (*BG* 1.7.2). Therefore, it comes as no surprise that the quarries at Cap d'Agde provided the army with the small querns used on campaign. The Hermeskeil quern from Cap d'Agde might thus be a survivor of the kit that a part of Caesar's army was equipped with at the start of the war, although we cannot rule out the possibility that it was acquired at a later stage of the campaigning – there were troop movements that make this possible and every year new recruits were added to legions.

The other querns from Hermeskeil are all of the slightly taller and heavier late La Tène type, which is less suitable for transport and would only have been chosen as replacements for broken legionary querns during the Roman campaigns. Several are made of basaltic lava from Mayen in the Eifel region (Figure 11.6, 10). Since the distribution of Mayen querns spreads as far west as north-eastern France and Belgium, with the river Rhine also being a major axis of distribution, these might have been acquired sometime during Caesar's campaigns in the area of Gallia Belgica from 55 BC onwards (Hornung 2018).

A late La Tène type quern made from vaugnerite from the northern Morvan gives a more important clue to the dating of Hermeskeil. Being made of an inferior raw material, at least compared to vesicular lava, these vaugnerite querns came from a quarry distributing querns on a regional scale. Their distribution covers an area *c.* 200–300 km across (Figure 11.8), extending from eastern Burgundy (Châlons-sur-Saône), via northern Burgundy (Alesia, Sens, Vertault) and southern Champagne (Troyes), to the southern Ile-de-France (Châteaubleau; Boyer *et al.* 2006; Boyer and Fronteau 2011). At Bibracte, capital of the Aedui, about 15% of the querns found at the *oppidum* consist of vaugnerite (Boyer *et al.* 2006). Thus, only Roman troop movements in east-central Gaul (either of legionaries and/or auxiliaries) before Hermeskeil went into disuse can account for the presence of the vaugnerite quern there. The same is true of a rhyolite quern from La Salle, another quarry producing on a regional scale. The distribution of late La Tène type querns made of La Salle rhyolite extends between the south-eastern territory of the Mediomatrici in the upper Saône valley and the north-western part of the territory of the Leuci, with a noticeable concentration in Lorraine, indicating that the Hermeskeil quern must have been acquired in that area.

Only the troop movements of 52 BC would account for all the quern provenances documented at Hermeskeil (Hornung *et al.* 2015; forthcoming; Hornung 2018). From 55 BC onward, the entire Roman army operated on several occasions within the distribution area of Mayen basaltic lava querns, whereas after the very first year of Caesar's battle for Gaul, they only re-entered the distribution area of querns from the Massif Central in 52 BC. And only in or after 52 BC would there have been any possibility of acquiring a vaugnerite quern from the northern Morvan and a rhyolite one from La Salle to the east (Figure 11.8). On the basis of the quern evidence, 52 BC is therefore the earliest possible date for the end of the Hermeskeil fortress (Hornung 2018; Hornung *et al.* forthcoming).

Historical sources

From the dating of the excavated finds, an association of the Hermeskeil fortress with Caesar's battle for Gaul seems highly likely. This is further supported by two radiocarbon dates on charred twigs, which were once part of the wooden parapet that surmounted the rampart (Hornung 2016a, 142–143),[8] although clearly these do not provide precise chronological evidence. In trying to narrow the camp's dating down to a single Roman campaign in Treveran territory, it is now necessary to reconsider Caesar's *de Bello Gallico*.

As a starting point, we should bear in mind that the fortress was in use for some weeks or even months. This rules out its interpretation as a marching camp. Use as a winter camp also seems highly unlikely; the Hunsrück region has very poor soils and it would have been hard to procure food for several thousand soldiers with no easy river access for transporting supplies (Metzler 1995, 598–600; Erdkamp 1998, 25, 152, 247). Therefore, the fortress must have been built during an active campaign, which is perhaps supported by its proximity to the Hunnenring *oppidum* (Hornung 2016a, 155). The Roman campaigns against the Treveri in 53 and 51 BC, both under the command of Caesar's general Titus Labienus, are thus the most likely options. Taking the quern provenances into consideration, a use in 51 BC can be considered likely. In 51 BC Labienus commanded two legions, whereas in 53 BC he had three. The southern part of the fortress is just over 12 ha in size, hardly enough space for three legions (Hornung 2016a, 155–156) but quite sufficient for two. In addition, the provenances of the Gaulish coins from Hermeskeil is best explained by the troops having recently spent time in eastern Gaul, which is exactly where several *hiberna* were located in the winter of 52/51 BC. Indeed, Labienus himself wintered in the territory of Sequani and must have brought Gaulish cavalry to join his campaigns in 51 BC. Hermeskeil can thus in all probability be considered the base from which he and his two legions conquered the Treveri in 51 BC. This obviously only applies to the second phase of the camp with its reduced size (Phase 2). Given its size of 19.5 ha, the original main camp is, however, large enough to have accommodated three legions, and so in its initial form (Phase 1), Hermeskeil might also have functioned as Labienus' main base in 53 BC when he was on the march with three legions.

An attempt at reconstructing a chapter of the battle for Gaul

This proposed association with historical events leaves archaeology with the question of whether it is possible to detect the impact of the Roman army's presence at Hermeskeil on the indigenous population. Our best chance is to look at nearby settlements in order to investigate questions of continuity and discontinuity. Unfortunately, it

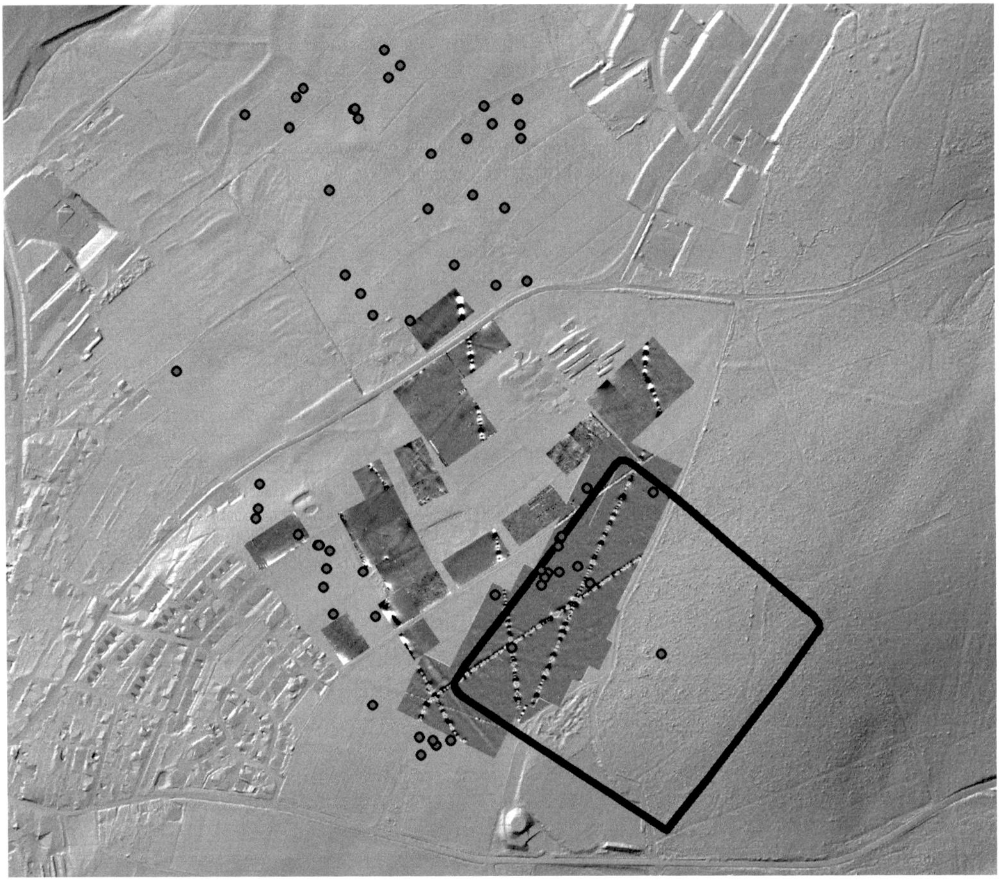

Figure 11.9 Distribution of sherds of imported amphorae found near the Hermeskeil fortress (after Hornung 2016a, fig. 109).

is a methodological challenge to identify unenclosed Iron Age settlements: in this region, they can only be located by systematical fieldwalking combined with geophysical survey.

In fact, some concentrations of imported amphora sherds were recorded during prospection (Figure 11.9), a rather large scatter south-west of the fortress being associated with the late Iron Age and Roman cemetery mentioned above (Hornung 2016a, 132). Some of the excavated late La Tène burials contained parts of amphorae as a *pars pro toto* and symbols of wealth, and wine also seems to have played an important role in the funerary practices (Fritsch 2010b). Another scatter of amphora sherds about 400 m north of the fortress correlates with a concentration of pits noted in magnetometry. These can be interpreted as the postholes of wooden buildings belonging to a late Iron Age village about 5 ha in size (Figure 11.10). A rectangular structure in the middle of this settlement is thought to be a small sanctuary. It is quite likely that its period of use goes back to the late Iron Age because a small lead wheel (*rouelle*) found during fieldwalking can be regarded as a typical votive deposit of the period. All the surface finds from the area of the settlement date to the middle decades of the 1st century BC, and there is no evidence whatsoever for a Roman settlement.

On the contrary, at the very end of the late La Tène period, settlement activity seems to have shifted to the opposite side of the valley. A Gallo-Roman vicus developed at the crossing of two major roads, the east–west connection between the Rhine and the Mosel valley along which the Roman houses were aligned, and the road that led south towards the Hunnenring and north towards the Trier basin (Figure 11.10). Magnetometry shows a marked concentration of pits in the western part of the vicus, possibly postholes of more wooden buildings. Most of the Iron Age coins and late La Tène pottery found in the vicus come from this area. On the other hand, the tiles typical of Roman style buildings are almost completely absent in this part of the settlement. It is likely, therefore, that this area marks the original core of the settlement, which must have been founded around the middle or during the second half of the 1st century BC. Later on, the focus shifted slightly towards the Roman road. These

Figure 11.10 The Hermeskeil fortress, the neighbouring late Iron Age settlement and the Roman vicus on the opposite side of the valley. Marked in white are the courses of several ancient roads (image P. Mertl).

developments leave us with an obvious discontinuity in local settlement structures, but no real basis to argue for a connection with the events of the Roman conquest. Therefore, we need to consider a broader picture.

The Hunnenring *oppidum* with its direct connection to the Hermeskeil fortress via an ancient road is another important site for reconstructing settlement developments. Pottery and a coin series ending with issues from the second quarter of the 1st century BC indicate that the *oppidum* was abandoned sometime around the transition from La Tène D2a to D2b, which is about the time of the Roman conquest. Despite large-scale excavations in the 1930s and since 1999 no traces of destruction have so far been uncovered (Wiegert 2002; Fritsch 2010a; Hornung 2016a, 27–69; 2016b). If occupation at the Hunnenring did continue into the second half of the 1st century BC, it must have been at a much-reduced level and only for a short period.

As at Hermeskeil, a shift took place around the mid-1st century BC. Only *c.* 1.3 km from the *oppidum*, the Saarland Antiquities Department have unearthed one of the largest Gallo-Roman temples in the entire Treveran territory (22.8 × 21 m) in 1984/85 (Burger 2016). According to the latest results from fieldwalking, geophysics and excavation, the temple was surrounded by a small *vicus* (Figure 11.11). The distribution of Roman tile suggests that this vicus was 8 ha in size (Hornung *et al.* 2012; Lang 2016). Occupation started during the first half of the 1st century AD, leaving an

Figure 11.11 The Roman sanctuary 'Auf dem Spätzrech' near Schwarzenbach, Saarland, and its adjacent vicus *with archaeologically documented features (after Lang 2016).*

obvious break between the abandonment of the Hunnenring and the foundation of the vicus some 50–100 years later (Hornung 2016a, 127–128). Remarkably enough this break is not visible in the finds from the temple itself, since the oldest pottery and coins from here date to the mid-1st century BC at the latest (Burger 2016, 156–160, 184–185). This might indicate that the temple was a direct successor to a supposed late Iron Age sanctuary at the heart of the nearby *oppidum* (Hornung 2014, 194–195; 2016a, 127–128). Such sanctuaries were not only ritual centres, but also had political and socio-economic functions, as markets and places of assembly (Fernández-Götz 2014; Metzler and Gaeng 2016). For some reason, the sanctuary was then moved to a place more suited from an infrastructural point of view. This development dates to La Tène D2, around the same time as a similar dislocation at Hermeskeil. This leaves us with the obvious question of whether these local settlement discontinuities were actually consequences of the Roman conquest, in particular when considering the presence of the nearby Roman fortress.

A history of economics or war?

When it comes to interpreting these observations on late Iron Age and Roman settlement in the vicinity of the Hermeskeil fortress, we must remember that archaeological data mainly reflect long-term changes rather than episodic crises. It is thus almost impossible to prove a direct connection between these noteworthy developments and Caesar's battle for Gaul. Indeed, we also need to consider alternative explanations for these changes in the settlement record. For example, they might instead reflect fundamental shifts in socio-economic structures around the mid-1st century BC.

This alternative view derives strong support from other Treveran *oppida* which were the main regional centres of production and trade (Hornung 2016a, 166–198). A marked increase in population and economic importance is observed at all of them during the first half of the 1st century BC. At the same time, a number of smaller fortifications were gradually abandoned, reflecting the ongoing process of centralization visible in the rise of the proto-urban settlements. After the Roman conquest, however, we see diverging developments for the Treveran *oppida* (Figure 11.12). Only the Titelberg in Luxemburg in the far west of the Treveran territory witnessed a marked increase in economic power which is clearly reflected in the archaeological finds from the *oppidum* (Metzler 1995). Apart from Kastel-Staadt, where the nature of developments is not yet fully understood (Nortmann 2002; Buchhorn 2016), all the other Treveran *oppida* declined after the Gallic War. There was a complete break in settlement at the Donnersberg (Zeeb-Lanz 2008; Wigg-Wolf 2009) and the Hunnenring; the Martberg (Nickel *et al.* 2008; Nickel 2013) and Wallendorf (Krausse 2006), both north of the Mosel, also experienced economic decline as well as a significant decrease in settlement activity. The latter is reflected, for example, in the coin finds from the Martberg: up to the mid-1st century BC their distribution covered the entire settlement, whereas after the war they are concentrated in the area of a late La Tène and Roman sanctuary in the

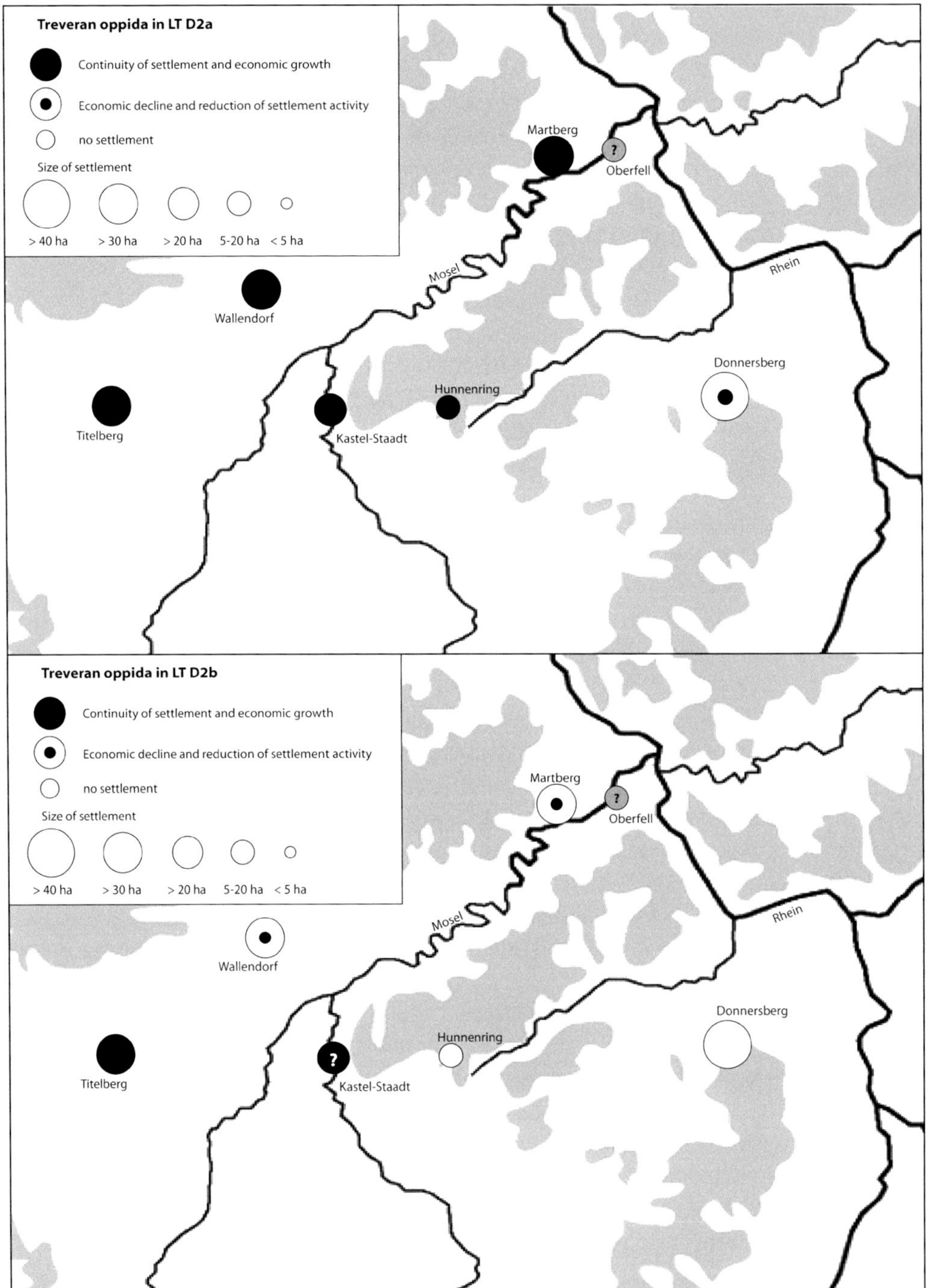

Figure 11.12 Economic development of Treveran oppida *in La Tène D2 (after Hornung 2016a, figs 157–158).*

heart of the *oppidum*. This might indicate some demonetarization of the local economy, with coins being deposited as votive offerings, in contrast to a much-reduced use of coinage in economic transactions (Wigg 2000).

The same structural changes are reflected in the distribution of imported wine amphorae. Before the Roman conquest, these finds display a regular distribution throughout Treveran territory. In contrast, from the second half of the 1st century BC amphorae are confined to its western part, in the vicinity of the Titelberg (Hornung 2016a, 262). Here a Roman trading station existed before the conquest (Metzler and Gaeng 2009, 519–528) and amphorae are regularly found as prestige goods in elite burials. This marked change in distribution seems to be due to the Titelberg being economically favoured by its close connection to one of the major axes of trade in eastern Gaul, along the Rhône-Saône and Mosel rivers. It is clear therefore that the impact of economic changes on settlement patterns should not be underestimated (Hornung 2016a, 429–520).

Conclusion

Against this broader backdrop, it is difficult to explain settlement developments at the Hunnenring or Hermeskeil solely by the events during Caesar's conquest of Gaul. Still, it might be possible to bridge the gap between the archaeological and historical record in a different way. In his account of events in 54 BC, Caesar tells us that the Treveri were divided into a pro-Roman party led by Cingetorix and an anti-Roman faction under Indutiomarus. The Romans killed the latter, but his relatives continued their resistance against Rome and were then defeated in 53 and 51 BC (*BG* 5.58; 6.5; 6.7; 8.24–25).

In view of the wider economic background summarized above, it seems unlikely that an anti-Roman faction lived in the western part of Treveran territory. The people there had close trade relations with Rome and even profited from the conquest. What is more, Roman troops were stationed at the Titelberg for several decades after the war, which also illustrates the political situation in an indirect way. On the other hand, it seems logical that the people who did not profit from participating in the growing economic networks of Gaul – mainly because their territory was on the very periphery of the empire – were bound to rise against the conquerors. Thus, although it is hard to prove short-term crises from the often-partial archaeological record, it is still possible to look at the broader picture. In this way, we can at least make a good case that the area around the Hunnenring *oppidum* and the Roman fortress at Hermeskeil might indeed have been where the Treveri were defeated in 53 and 51 BC.

Notes

1 An earlier example for the separate stationing of auxiliaries is found in camp III at Renieblas (Soria, Spain), which probably dates to the campaigns of Q. Fulvius Nobilior in 153/152 BC (Johnson 1987, 250; Luik 2005, 55–56, fig. 73; Morillo and Salla-Sellés this volume, Figures 4.4–4.5).

2 Alesia, camp B: ditch 2.4 m wide × 1.5 m deep; Dorsten-Holsterhausen, camp B: ditch 2.1 m wide × 1.5 m deep; camp F: 2 m wide × 1.4 m deep; Haltern: ditch 2.5 m wide × 1.5 m deep; Limburg I: max. 2.5 m wide × 1.5 m deep.

3 The same type of oven is known from the *vicus* next to the stone camp at Hofheim (Hesse) and from Carnuntum in Austria. See Stiglitz 1997, 19, figs 5–6.
4 M. Helfert pers. comm. A larger number of samples is currently under investigation.
5 The author thanks H. Löhr for the opportunity to inspect the hobnails found on the Petrisberg.
6 The author thanks D. Wigg-Wolf, who is currently working on the coins from Hermeskeil.
7 The author thanks A. Kronz and T. Gluhak for preliminary insights into their ongoing research on the Hermeskeil querns.
8 Erl-16189: 2078±30 BP; 1σ: 156–134 cal. BC (15.4%) and 115–48 cal. BC (52.9%), 2σ: 183–37 cal. BC (92.5%), 28–21 cal. BC (1.1%), 10 cal. BC–1 cal. AD (1.8%). Erl-16187: 2107±30 BP; 1σ: 175–91 cal. BC (63.5%) and 68–60 cal. BC (4.8%), 2σ: 200–46 cal. BC (95.4%).

Bibliography

Boyer, F. and Fronteau, G. (2011) Les géomatériaux meuliers: de l'identification des sources géologiques à la définition de catégories de gisements. In O. Buchsenschutz, L. Jaccottey, F. Jodry, and J.-L. Blanchard (eds), *Évolution typologique et technique des meules du Néolithique à l'an mille (Actes des IIIe Rencontres Archéologiques de l'Archéosite gaulois)*, 121–134. Bordeaux, Aquitania supplément 23.

Boyer, F., Buchsenschutz, O., Hamon, C., Jaccottey, L., Lagadec, J.-P., Milleville, A., Thomas, É. and Triboulot, B. (2006) Production et diffusion des meules du néolithique à l'antiquité: quelques exemples français. In A. Belmont and F. Mangartz (eds), *Mühlsteinbrüche. Erforschung, Schutz und Inwertsetzung eines Kulturerbes europäischer Industrie*, 5–13. Mainz, Römisch-Germanisches Zentralmuseum Tagungen Band 2.

Brouquier-Reddé, V. and Deyber, A. (2001) Fourniment, harnachement, quincaillerie, objets divers. In M. Reddé and S. von Schnurbein (eds), *Alésia, fouilles et recherches franco-allemandes sur les travaux militaires romains autour du Mont-Auxois (1991-1997)* , 294–333. Paris, Mémoires de l'Academie des Inscriptions et Belles-Lettres 22.

Buchhorn, A. (2016) Kastel-Staadt. Keltisches Oppidum und römischer vicus. Neue Ergebnisse zur Besiedlungsgeschichte. In M. Koch (ed.), *Archäologentage Otzenhausen 2. Beiträge des internationalen Symposiums zur Archäologie in der Großregion vom 19-22.02.2015*, 57–76. Otzenhausen, Europäische Akademie.

Burger, D. (2016) Der gallo-römische Umgangstempel „Auf dem Spätzrech" bei Schwarzenbach (Saarland). Auswertung der Grabung 1984/85. In S. Hornung, P. Brengel, M. König and D. Burger, with T. Lang, M. Smettan and A. Kronz (eds), *Mensch und Umwelt II - Vom Oppidum „Hunnenring" bei Otzenhausen zum römischen Tempelbezirk und vicus „Auf dem Spätzrech" bei Schwarzenbach, Gem. Nonnweiler, Lkr. St Wendel*, 137–292. Bonn, Universitätsforschungen zur Prähistorischen Archäologie 289.

Dehn, W. (1951) Vorgeschichtliche Denkmäler und Funde um Hermeskeil. *Trierer Zeitschrift* 20, 1–67.

Ebel-Zepezauer, W., Grünewald, C., Ilisch, P., Kühlborn, J.-S. and Tremmel, B. (2009) *Augusteische Marschlager und Siedlungen des 1. bis 9. Jahrhunderts in Dorsten-Holsterhausen. Die Ausgrabungen 1999-2002.* Mainz, Bodenaltertümer Westfalens 47.

Erdkamp, P. (1998) *Hunger and the Sword: Warfare and Food Supply in Roman Republican Wars (264–30 BC).* Amsterdam, J.C. Gieben, Dutch Monographs on Ancient History and Archaeology 20.

Fernández-Götz, M. (2014) *Identity and Power: The Transformation of Iron Age Societies in Northeast Gaul.* Amsterdam, Amsterdam Archaeological Studies 21.

Fritsch, T. (2010a) Zehn Jahre archäologische Forschungen am keltischen Ringwall Otzenhausen – die neuesten Ergebnisse im Überblick. In Terrex gGmbH (ed.), *Kelten und Römer im Sankt Wendeler Land. Die Ausgrabungen der Terrex gGmbH am „Hunnenring" und im vicus Wareswald*, 27–79. Sankt Wendel, Edition Schaumburg.

Fritsch, T. (2010b) Ein spätlatènezeitliches Waffengrab aus dem Gräberfeld „Ringgraben" bei Hermeskeil, Lkr. Trier-Saarburg. In S. Hornung (ed.), *Mensch und Umwelt I. Archäologische und naturwissenschaftliche Forschungen zum Wandel der Kulturlandschaft um den „Hunnenring" bei Otzenhausen, Gem. Nonnweiler, Lkr. St. Wendel*, 133–154. Bonn, Universitätsforschungen zur Prähistorischen Archäologie 192.

Fritsch, T. (2011) Archäologische Sondierungen in der Schanzanlage „Grafenwald" von Hermeskeil (Kr. Trier-Saarburg, Rheinland-Pfalz, BRD). *Bulletin de la Société Préhistorique Luxembourgeoise* 33, 55–74.

Grote, K. (2008) Hedemünden – Ein römisches Militärlager an der Werra-Weser-Linie im rechtsrheinischen Germanien. In M. Zelle (ed.), *Terra Incognita? Die nördlichen Mittelgebirge im Spannungsfeld römischer und germanischer Politik (Akten des Kolloquiums im Lippischen Landesmuseum Detmold vom 17. bis 19. Juni 2004)*, 177–186. Mainz, Philipp von Zabern.

Grote, K. (2012) *Römerlager Hedemünden. Der augusteische Stützpunkt, seine Außenanlagen, seine Funde und Befunde*. Dresden, Sandstein Kommunikation, Veröffentlichungen der Archäologischen Sammlungen des Landesmuseums Hannover 53.

Haßmann, H., Ortisi, S. and Wulf, F.-E. (2016) Luftbild mit Überraschung. Ein römisches Marschlager bei Hannover-Wilkenburg. *Varus-Kurier* 18, 21–23.

Hornung, S. (2012a) Ein spätrepublikanisches Militärlager bei Hermeskeil (Lkr. Trier-Saarburg). Vorbericht über die Forschungen 2010–2011. *Archäologisches Korrespondenzblatt* 42, 205–224.

Hornung, S. (2012b) Eine Episode des Gallischen Krieges auf deutschem Boden? Aktuelle Forschungen im spätrepublikanischen Militärlager von Hermeskeil, Lkr. Trier-Saarburg. *Funde und Ausgrabungen im Bezirk Trier* 44, 28–38.

Hornung, S. (2014) Caesar's conquest of Gaul – a factor of crisis or consolidation? The Otzenhausen oppidum and its environment. In M. Fernández-Götz, H. Wendling and K. Winger (eds), *Paths to Complexity: Centralisation and Urbanisation in Iron Age Europe*, 193–204. Oxford, Oxbow Books.

Hornung, S. (2015) Das spätrepublikanische Militärlager bei Hermeskeil (Lkr. Trier-Saarburg) – Überlegungen zu den Auswirkungen der römischen Eroberung auf die spätlatènezeitliche Besiedlung im Treverergebiet. In G.A. Lehmann and R. Wiegels (eds), *Über die Alpen und über den Rhein – Anfänge und früher Verlauf der römischen Expansion nach Mitteleuropa*, 103–132. Berlin, de Gruyter, Abhandlungen der Akademie der Wissenschaften zu Göttingen N.F. 37.

Hornung, S. (2016a) *Siedlung und Bevölkerung in Ostgallien zwischen Gallischem Krieg und der Festigung der römischen Herrschaft – Eine Studie auf Basis landschaftsarchäologischer Forschungen im Umfeld des Oppidums „Hunnenring" von Otzenhausen (Lkr. St Wendel)*. Mainz, Römisch-Germanische Forschungen 73.

Hornung, S. (2016b) Aktuelle Forschungen zur Besiedlungsentwicklung des Oppidums „Hunnenring" von Otzenhausen (Lkr. St Wendel, Saarland). In S. Hornung, P. Brengel, M. König and D. Burger, with T. Lang, M. Smettan and A. Kronz (eds), *Mensch und Umwelt II – Vom Oppidum „Hunnenring" bei Otzenhausen zum römischen Tempelbezirk und vicus „Auf dem Spätzrech" bei Schwarzenbach, Gem. Nonnweiler, Lkr. St Wendel*, 13–102. Bonn, Universitätsforschungen zur Prähistorischen Archäologie 289.

Hornung, S. (2018) Tracing Julius Caesar – The late-Republican military camp at Hermeskeil and its historical context. In M. Fernández-Götz and N. Roymans (eds), *Conflict Archaeology: Materialities of Collective Violence in Late Prehistoric and Early Historic Europe*, 193–203. London, Routledge.

Hornung, S. (forthcoming) Die Militärlager von Limburg im Vergleich. In *Die Vorgeschichte des Greifenberges über Limburg a. d. Lahn – Spuren von der Jungsteinzeit bis zur römischen Republik*. Hessen Archäologie Sonderband 4. Stuttgart, Theiss.

Hornung, S., Gluhak T. and Kronz, A. (2015) Die Provenienz der Mühlsteinfragmente aus dem spätrepublikanischen Militärlager von Hermeskeil (Lkr. Trier-Saarburg) – Eine Brücke zur historischen Überlieferung? In T. Gluhak, S. Greiff, K. Kraus, and M. Prange (eds), *Archäometrie und Denkmalpflege 2015, Jahrestagung Mainz, 25.–28. März 2015*, 126–128. Bochum, Deutsches Bergbaumuseum, Metalla Sonderheft 7.

Hornung, S., Jung, A., Braun, A. and Lang, T. (2012) Aktuelle Forschungen zum gallo-römischen vicus „Auf dem Spätzrech" bei Schwarzenbach, Lkr. St Wendel. *Jahresbericht Denkmalpflege des Saarlandes* 2012, 17–22.

Hornung, S., Gluhak, T.M., Kronz, A., Breedveld, G. and Gätjen, J. (forthcoming) The querns from the Roman military camp at Hermeskeil (Rhineland-Palatinate) – bridging the gap to Caesar's *De Bello Gallico. Journal of Lithic Studies.*

Johnson, A. (1987) *Römische Kastelle des 1. und 2. Jahrhunderts n. Chr. in Britannien und in den germanischen Provinzen des Römerreiches.* Mainz, Kulturgeschichte der Antiken Welt 37.

Krausse, D. (2006) *Eisenzeitlicher Kulturwandel und Romanisierung im Mosel-Eifel-Raum. Die keltisch-römische Siedlung von Wallendorf und ihr archäologisches Umfeld.* Mainz, Römisch-Germanische Forschungen 63.

Kühlborn, J.-S. (2006) Haltern. In M. Reddé, R. Brulet, R. Fellmann, J.K. Haalebos, and S. von Schnurbein (eds), *L'architecture de la Gaule romaine. Les fortifications militaires*, 185–290. Paris, Éditions de la Maison des sciences de l'homme, Documents d'archéologie française 100.

Lang, A. (2016) Ergebnisse der aktuellen Forschungen im Bereich des gallo-römischen vicus „Auf dem Spätzrech" bei Schwarzenbach (Gem. Nonnweiler, Lkr. St Wendel). In S. Hornung, P. Brengel, M. König and D. Burger, with T. Lang, M. Smettan and A. Kronz (eds), *Mensch und Umwelt II - Vom Oppidum „Hunnenring" bei Otzenhausen zum römischen Tempelbezirk und vicus „Auf dem Spätzrech" bei Schwarzenbach, Gem. Nonnweiler, Lkr. St Wendel*, 293–318. Bonn, Universitätsforschungen zur Prähistorischen Archäologie 289.

Lindenthal, J. (2014) Neues römisches Marschlager in Friedberg entdeckt. *Hessen Archäologie* 2014 (2015), 92–95.

Löhr, H. (2003) Das frührömische Militärlager auf dem Petrisberg bei Trier. Landesgartenschau und Archäologie. *Funde und Ausgrabungen im Bezirk Trier* 35, 21–30.

Löhr, H. and Trunk, M. (2008) Ein neues Militärlager auf dem Petrisberg bei Trier. In M. García-Bellido, A. Mostalac and A. Jiménez (eds), *Del Imperium de Pompeyo a la Auctoritas de Augusto. Homenaje a Michael Grant*, 141–150. Madrid, Editorial CSIC.

Luik, M. (2005) *Der schwierige Weg zur Weltmacht. Roms Eroberung der Iberischen Halbinsel 218–19 v. Chr.* Mainz, Philipp von Zabern.

Maurer, T. (2013) Eine Großbäckerei der Römerzeit? Antike Ofenbatterie in Wallerstädten entdeckt. *Hessen Archäologie 2012*, 105–108.

Martin, S. (2011) Monnaies romaines, usagers gaulois et vice versa. L'exemple de la Gaule de l'Est. In M. Reddé, P. Barral, J.-P- Guillaumet, M. Joly, J.-Y. Marc, P. Nouvel, L. Nuninger and C. Petit (eds), *Aspects de la Romanisation dans l'Est de la Gaule*, 937–944. Glux-en-Glenne, Collection Bibracte 21.

Martin-Kilcher, S. (2011) Römer und gentes Alpinae im Konflikt – archäologische und historische Zeugnisse des 1. Jahrhunderts v. Chr. In G. Moosbauer and R. Wiegels (eds), *Fines imperii - imperium sine fine? Römische Okkupations- und Grenzpolitik im frühen Principat.*, 27–62. Rahden, Marie Leidorf, Osnabrücker Forschungen zu Altertum und Antike-Rezeption 14.

Metzler, J. (1995) *Das treverische Oppidum auf dem Titelberg.* Luxembourg, Musée National d'Histoire et d'Art Dossiers d'Archéologie III.

Metzler, J. and Gaeng, C. (2009) *Goeblange-Nospelt - une nécropole aristocratique trévire.* Luxembourg, Musée National d'Histoire et d'Art Dossiers d'Archéologie XIII.

Metzler, J. and Gaeng, C. (2016) *L'espace public du Titelberg.* Luxembourg, Musée National d'Histoire et d'Art Dossiers d'Archéologie XVII.

Nick, M. (2000) *Die keltischen Münzen vom Typ „Sequanerpotin". Eine Studie zur Typologie, Chronologie und geographischen Zuweisung eines ostgallischen Münztyps.* Rahden, Marie Leidorf, Freiburger Beiträge zur Archäologie und Geschichte des ersten Jahrtausends 2.

Nick, M. (2015) *Die keltischen Münzen der Schweiz: Katalog und Auswertung. Inventar der Fundmünzen der Schweiz 12.* Bern, Schweizerische Akademie der Geistes- und Sozialwissenschaften.

Nickel, C. (2013) *Martberg. Heiligtum und Oppidum der Treverer, III. Die Siedlung.* Koblenz, Gesellschaft für Archäologie an Mittelrhein und Mosel, Berichte zur Archäologie an Mittelrhein und Mosel 19.

Nickel, C., Thoma, M. and Wigg-Wolf, D. (2008) *Martberg. Heiligtum und Oppidum der Treverer, I. Der Kultbezirk.* Koblenz, Gesellschaft für Archäologie an Mittelrhein und Mosel, Berichte zur Archäologie an Mittelrhein und Mosel 14.

Nortmann, H. (2002) Murus Gallicus. Die Modellrekonstruktion einer keltischen Mauer zum Oppidum Kastel. *Funde und Ausgrabungen im Bezirk Trier* 34, 7–16.

Pietsch, M., Timpe, D. and Wamser, L. (1991) Das augusteische Truppenlager Marktbreit. Bisherige archäologische Befunde und historische Erwägungen. *Bericht der Römisch-Germanischen-Kommission* 72, 263–324.

Poux, M. (2008) L'empreinte du militaire césarien dans les faciès mobiliers de La Tène finale. Caractérisation, chronologie et diffusion de ses principaux marqueurs. In M. Poux (ed.), *Sur les traces de César. Militaria tardo-républicains en contexte gaulois*, 299–432. Glux-en-Glenne, Collection Bibracte 14.

Reddé, M. and von Schnurbein, S. (2001) *Alésia, fouilles et recherches franco-allemandes sur les travaux militaires romains autour du Mont-Auxois (1991-1997)*. Paris, Mémoires de l'Academie des Inscriptions et Belles-Lettres 22.

Stiglitz, H. (1997) *Das Auxiliarkastell Carnuntum, 1. Forschungen 1977-1988*. Vienna, Österreichisches Archäologisches Institut Sonderschriften 29.

Tremmel, B. (2011) Augusteische Marschlager in Porta Westfalica-Barkhausen „Auf der Lake". *Archäologie in Westfalen-Lippe* 2010 (2011), 79–81.

Wiegert, M. (2002) *Der „Hunnenring" von Otzenhausen, Lkr. St Wendel. Die Siedlungsfunde und Bebauungsstrukturen einer spätlatènezeitlichen Höhenbefestigung im Saarland*. Rahden, Marie Leidorf, Internationale Archäologie 65.

Wigg, D.G. (2000) Der Beitrag des Martberges zur eisenzeitlichen Numismatik. In A. Haffner and S. von Schnurbein (eds), *Kelten, Germanen, Römer im Mittelgebirgsraum zwischen Luxemburg und Thüringen (Akten des Internationalen Kolloquiums zum DFG-Schwerpunktprogramm „Romanisierung" in Trier vom 28. bis 30. September 1998)*, 485–496. Bonn, Kolloquien zur Vor- und Frühgeschichte 5.

Wigg-Wolf, D. (2009) The coin finds from the Donnersberg, Rheinland-Pfalz, Germany. In J. van Heesch and I. Heeren (eds), *Coinage in the Iron Age. Essays in Honour of Simone Scheers*, 399–419. London, Spink & Son.

Zeeb-Lanz, A. (2008) *Der Donnersberg. Eine bedeutende spätkeltische Stadtanlage. (Archäologische Denkmäler in der Pfalz 2)*. Speyer, GDKE Direktion Landesarchäologie, Außenstelle Speyer.

Chapter 12

Archaeology of the Roman Civil Wars: The destruction of Puig Ciutat (Catalonia, Spain) and Caesar's campaign in Ilerda (49 BC)

Àngels Pujol, Manuel Fernández-Götz[1], *Roger Sala, Carles Padrós, Eduard Ble, Robert Tamba and Xavier Rubio-Campillo*

The archaeology of Julius Caesar: from *de Bello Gallico* to *de Bello Civili*

Recent years have witnessed an important increase in archaeological research on conflict archaeology related to the late prehistoric and early historic periods (see Fernández-Götz and Roymans 2018). The archaeology of Julius Caesar's military campaigns against tribal groups in Gaul continues to provide evidence that complements and expands the discoveries made since the mid-19th century at iconic sites such as Alesia (Reddé 2018; this volume). Recent research in north-eastern Gaul is proving particularly fruitful, with the identification of new Roman military camps such as Hermeskeil near Otzenhausen (Hornung 2018; this volume), assaults on indigenous fortified sites such as Thuin in Belgium (Roymans *et al.* 2012, 20–24; Roymans and Fernández-Götz 2015), and the interpretation of Kessel/Lith in the Dutch River area as a massacre deposit and the crime scene of Caesar's genocidal policy against the Tencteri and Usipetes (Roymans 2018; this volume). In addition, the first direct evidence of Caesar's crossing of the Channel has now been uncovered (Fitzpatrick this volume).

In sharp contrast to this rich material evidence for the Caesarian conquest of new territory, material remains from the Civil Wars fought by Caesar against other Roman leaders – most notably Pompey the Great – are much scarcer (although see Maschek 2018). Here we present a case study from north-eastern Iberia: the late Republican site of Puig Ciutat, its destruction seemingly linked to Caesar's campaign of 49 BC in Ilerda (Lleida).

Puig Ciutat: the discovery and investigation of a late Republican site

The site of Puig Ciutat (Oristà, Barcelona) is located in inner Catalonia, near the city of Vic, between the basins of the rivers Ter and Llobregat (Figure 12.1). Therefore, it is positioned on one of the main natural communication routes that connect the

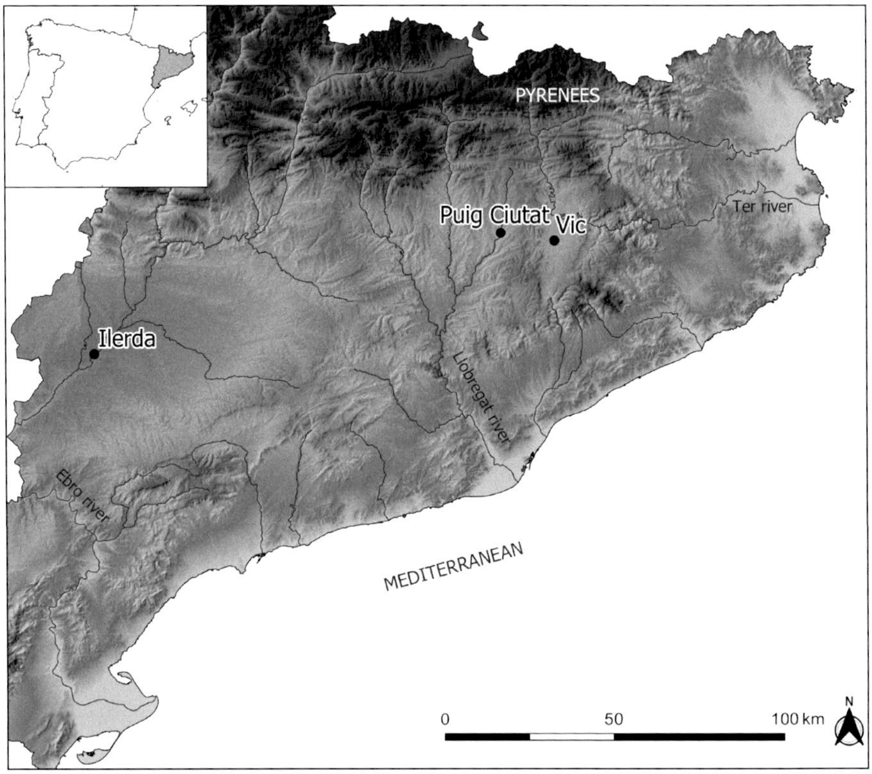

Figure 12.1 Location of Puig Ciutat and Ilerda in Catalonia (authors).

Pyrenees with the territory of Lleida and inland Spain. The site lies on a fluvial terrace that forms a plateau promontory covering approximately 5 ha. The eastern slope is less steep, which explains why it is here that the excavations have discovered an entrance and the main evidence of defensive walls. The hill is surrounded by a meander of the Gavarresa stream, just before the waters of the Olost flow into it (Figure 12.2). A twin hill where the medieval Tornamira castle is situated lies to the north-west of Puig Ciutat.

At the beginning of the 1980s, earthmoving for gravel extraction revealed a large quantity of archaeological finds and various structures. News of the discovery attracted the attention of clandestine excavators, who began systematically to loot the site. By the early 1990s, several local enthusiasts were in possession of numerous Iberian- and Roman-period finds from Puig Ciutat (Padrós *et al.* 2014, 101–102). In 2005 and 2007, a team from SOT Archaeological Prospection, under the direction of Roger Sala, carried out preliminary geophysical survey. This seminal study revealed a complex organization of the site, with a large central building (Building 1, below) and possible evidence that the settlement had been destroyed by fire.

Systematic study of Puig Ciutat began in 2010 (Padrós *et al.* 2014, 102–103; Pujol *et al.* 2014; 2016). Excavation is still ongoing, but we have a good preliminary idea of the internal organization of the site, its chronology and its eventful history (Figure 12.3).

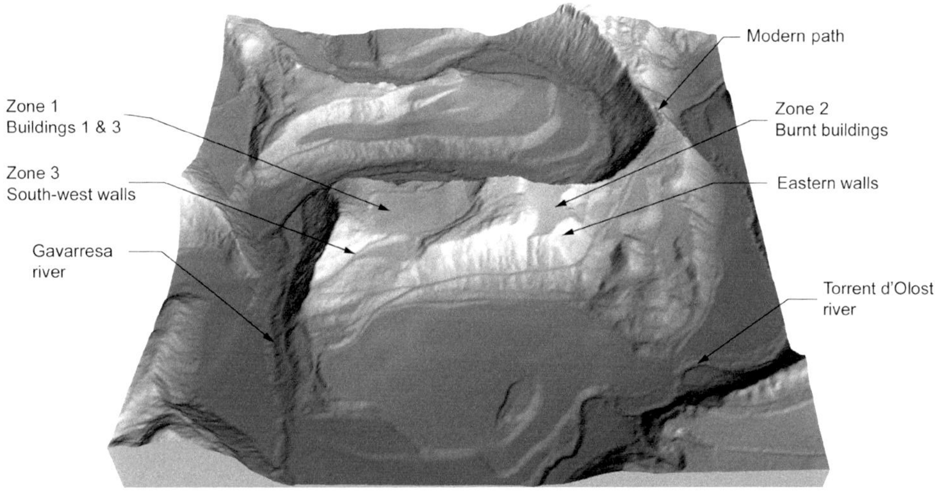

Figure 12.2 3D relief model of the setting of Puig Ciutat, showing the principal archaeological remains and natural features (authors).

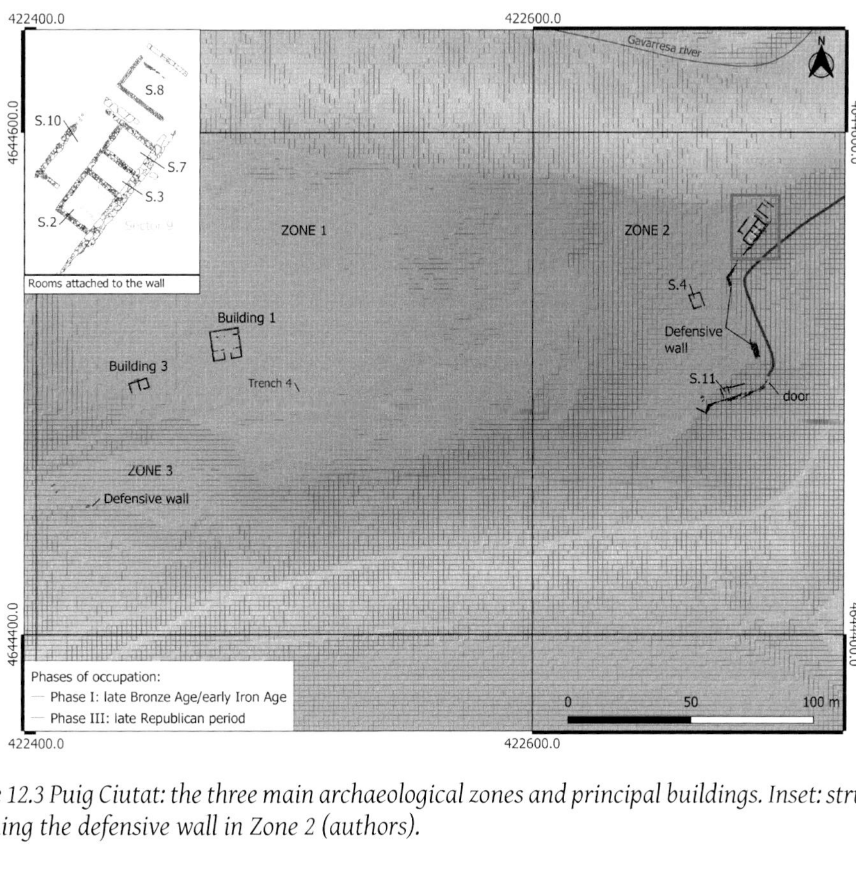

Figure 12.3 Puig Ciutat: the three main archaeological zones and principal buildings. Inset: structures adjoining the defensive wall in Zone 2 (authors).

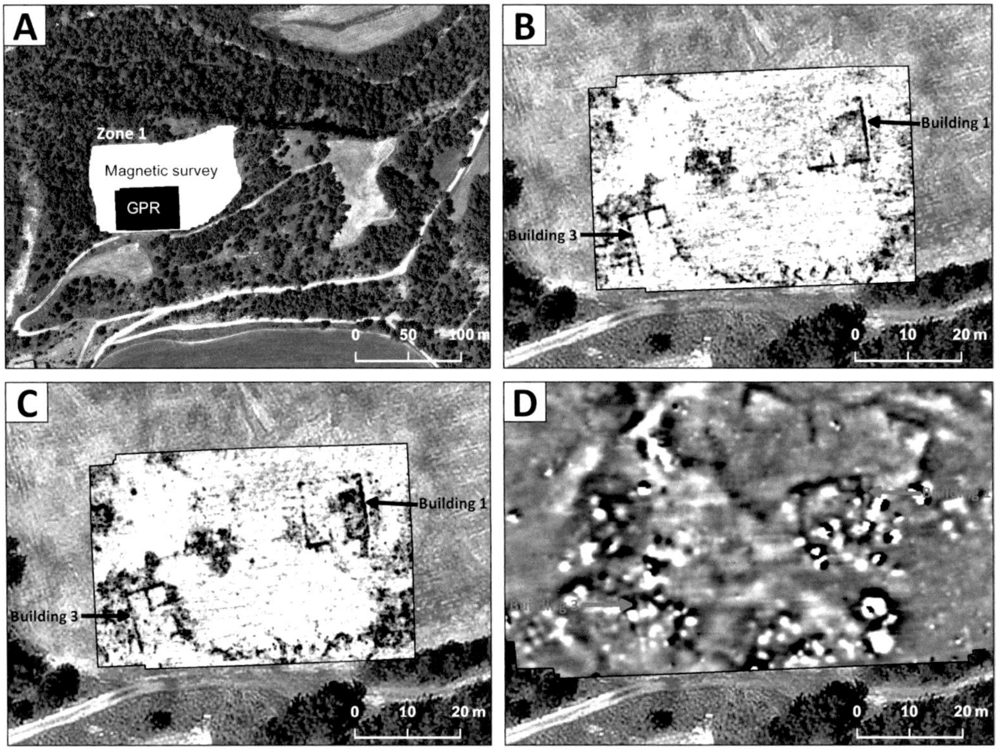

Figure 12.4 The geophysical surveys carried out in Zone 1 at Puig Ciutat (A) location; (B–C) GPR time slices; (D) magnetometry (authors).

Geophysical survey

Since the start of systematic archaeological investigation, various methods of geophysical survey have been used, including geomagnetic and ground penetrating radar. In general, the surveys show an apparently unplanned settlement layout, with empty spaces and, above all, the presence of fires across the entire investigated area. The results from the different zones explored are as follows:[2]

Zone 1 (Figure 12.4)

Practically all the anomalies detected in the geomagnetic survey can be interpreted as archaeological features, with those that present the greatest contrast probably indicating areas of burning. The survey results suggest a complex settlement layout, with no obvious orthogonal organization. Within this layout, strips of positive polarity have been interpreted as possible streets. In the middle of Zone 1, a series of linear anomalies arranged in almost cardinal alignments seem to reflect a single structure, designated Building 1.

In the south-eastern part of Zone 1, where agricultural activity had brought building material and pottery to the surface, geomagnetic survey revealed high-contrast anomalies suggestive of burning. The results from Zone 1 were complemented by the information obtained using ground penetrating radar, which provided more details of some of the groups of buildings. Building 3, detected in the south-west of the surveyed area, was one of the most clearly defined structures, corresponding to a rectangular anomaly approximately 11 × 8 m with an observable internal division.

Zone 2

The geomagnetic survey here mapped numerous anomalies representing archaeological structures, some of which contained evidence of burning. However, the ground penetrating radar revealed a division crossing the field from north to south, caused by two areas of highly reflective anomalies, which, according to tests from the soil samples, can be interpreted as bedrock. East of this division, groups of orthogonal anomalies are interpreted as parts of buildings. At the north-eastern end there are structures adjoining the defensive wall documented archaeologically in the 2010 campaign. Based on the geomagnetic data, the trial trench was extended southwards until the enclosing wall of the building was found.

In the middle of Zone 2, another group of orthogonal anomalies coincides with the burnt areas detected by the geomagnetic survey, suggesting the existence of a group of buildings that were burned down. Of particular interest is a linear space with no anomalies in the southern part of Zone 2, which is likely to be a street. If it is confirmed that the southern end of this feature links with the road that climbs from the east of the defensive wall, the area without anomalies could indicate an entrance to the fortified site.

The excavations

The excavations since 2010 have allowed us to define three clear phases of occupation at Puig Ciutat:

- Phase I, late Bronze Age/early Iron Age. Various pottery sherds of this date were found on the surface of the eastern slope of the hill. During the excavations in Zone 2, a large amount of late Bronze Age/early Iron Age pottery was found in Test Trench 15 in levels beneath Sector 9. Although the finds were very fragmented and came from archaeological infill, not structures, their quantity is significant and could indicate a more or less stable use of the site during the 9th and 8th centuries BC.
- Phase II, intermediate. Below the occupation level of Sector 2, another structure (Sector 9) corresponds to a phase prior to the Roman Republican period. This structure had been almost completely razed to the ground. It extends below the

late Republican wall, suggesting that, in its final phase, the size of the settlement was reduced at its eastern end. The material culture from Phase II is very sparse and fragmented and it has not been possible to specify a precise chronology for the remains; although the finds establish a *terminus post quem* in the Full Iberian period, no imported items have been found that would allow us to give a more accurate chronology.

- Phase III, late Republican period (1st century BC). This is the best-defined period of occupation at Puig Ciutat. A defensive wall, various buildings and a large number of archaeological finds have been documented. The wall, composed of large stone blocks, is 1.1 m wide. In general, it appears to have been built on the debris from the preceding phase, although in some places, as at the south-eastern end, it could have been built either on the wall of the preceding phase or on the rock itself. Various habitation spaces were identified in this final phase, of which the most outstanding are presented here:

Zone 1

Identified in the centre of Zone 1 through the geophysical surveys, Building 1 was a structure of *c.* 11 × 11 m (equivalent to 40 Italic feet). The remains had been badly damaged by farming, but the complexity and size of the building leads us to hypothesize a possible *praetorium* or *principia* from the late Republican period, similar to that identified at the Monteró 1 site (Camarasa, Lleida; Principal *et al.* 2015, 319–323). Interestingly, a burned beam was found at the building's entrance, which, together with carbonized remains in one of the rooms, suggests destruction of the building by fire, a phenomenon also observed in other structures from this phase across the site.

At the south-eastern end of Zone 1, where modern agriculture had brought a large amount of archaeological material to the surface, removal of the surface layer in Test Trench 4 (10.5 × 1.5 m) revealed two walls that marked the ends of various structures, along with burned areas, pottery and metalwork. The ceramics included Campanian C wares (corresponding to one or more types of the Lamboglia 7 form), coarse wares and amphorae of various origins (Circle of the Straits of Gibraltar, Africa, the Adriatic and Italy). Among the metal finds were various iron objects which could be scissors and the hilt of a bidiscoidal dagger (the predecessor of the Roman *pugio*).

Building 3, also detected by geophysical survey, was partially excavated in 2017. Located west of Building 1, it appears to comprise a courtyard or large room to the south, with two smaller rooms on the northern side. Only these smaller rooms have been excavated so far; they have provided evidence of burning in the form of numerous fragments of burnt beams. Among the finds are two *kalathoi* and an amphora, and other objects such as a pair of weights (*pondi*) and coins from various Iberian mints. Additionally, a sling bullet was discovered in the destruction layer.

Zone 2

Adjoining the large wall in Zone 2, Sector 2 is a room measuring 4.20 × 3.40 m. In the lower part of the collapse layer from this structure, a large number of ceramic vessels were found *in situ*. This group of ceramics included a *dolium*, late-Cales and Campanian C black-glazed wares, oxidized wares, white slip wares and reduced wares. Various spindle whorls and a weight were also found. The accumulation of pottery in the southern half of the room and its distribution suggest that the objects had been placed on a shelf or in a cupboard that fell, leaving the pottery strewn across the occupation level. Of particular interest is the quantity of metal objects recovered from the room, especially items of weaponry, such as two catapult bolt heads, several arrowheads, sling bullets and a *pilum* shank.

Sector 3 is another room, measuring 3.5 × 2 m and adjoining the wall, immediately north of Sector 2. Finds from the lower part of the collapse level here included a door key, iron nails and abundant faunal remains. Above the occupation level, in the south-eastern corner, was a group of four horizontal slabs. At the northern end of the west wall an entrance was found.

Figure 12.5 Zone 2, Sector 7 during excavation (authors).

Sector 7, a third room of 3.50 × 2.60 m adjoined the wall, next to Sector 3. In its collapse levels, a dolium and an amphora were found, the latter of Adriatic origin. These objects, however, do not appear to belong with the use of the room, but rather to have come from the demolition of an upper structure (Figure 12.5). The occupation level of Sector 7 yielded a series of pottery sherds (black-glazed, coarse ware, amphorae, etc.) and various pieces of metal. It should be emphasized that the occupation surface is compacted and consists of marl, making it easily identifiable.

Sector 10 lay west of sectors 2, 3 and 7. The northern and western walls of this building had been almost completely destroyed. There was a hearth next to the western wall. The building presents a destruction level very similar to that of the areas adjoining the wall, with an abundance of throwing weapons (sling bullets and catapult bolt heads). A rich pottery assemblage included a dolium, two amphorae of Dressel 1B type (products of the Straits of Gibraltar Circle and Tarraconensis), various pieces of Cales black-glazed wares, and locally produced wares. Seven Iberian-tradition coins from the mints of Iltirkesken, Ilturo, Kese and Bolskan were found in this structure, marking it out from the surrounding areas. Sectors 2, 3, 7 and 10 probably formed part of the same complex building, which has been designated Building 2. Sectors 3 and 7 seem to have been used for storage, whereas the hearth in Sector 10 could indicate a cooking area.

Separated from the previous sectors by a street, Sector 8 has a surface area of about 5.5 × 4.5 m, much larger than the previous rooms adjoining the wall. At the north-western end there appears to be a doorway. Excavation of this room yielded a large number of macro-faunal remains, especially cattle and horse bones, which showed signs of trauma.

Metal detector survey

Given the evidence of destruction documented within the interior, a survey using metal detectors and GPS devices was carried out in the area outside the settlement, with two main objectives of (1) identifying evidence of an assault from outside the walls, in order to confirm an anthropogenic cause for the destruction and an external origin for the attack; and (2) defining the routes taken by the possible attacking army.

The first surveys were carried out on the eastern and south-western slopes of the hill on which the settlement is located, since these were the only two possible access points. Some hobnails (*clavii caligae*) and a sling bullet were recovered on the eastern slope, whereas the results were negative on the south-western slope. A metal detector survey in 2017 confirmed the lack of evidence from the south-western area; thus, the idea of an attack from this side can be discarded.

The survey was extended northwards, following the trail of hobnails (*clavii caligae*) across the Collet d'en Roca pass. In this direction, overlooking both the pass and the settlement itself, is Pla Revell, an elevated plain initially proposed as a possible site of the camp of the attacking army on account of its geographical position. During the survey a sling bullet was found. Another plain known as Vila Granada lies south-west of Puig Ciutat on the other side of the Olost river; when surveyed, this area produced a Roman legionary hobnail.

The evidence recovered to date thus suggests an assault on Puig Ciutat by an external army, rather than a siege. Interestingly, the two projectiles documented from outside the site are very different from those recovered in the interior, which could indicate that they belonged to the defenders and attackers respectively.

Chronology and interpretation

The finds from Puig Ciutat include imports of late-Cales and Campanian C black-glazed wares, both clearly produced in the 1st century BC (90–20 BC). On the other hand, none of the sectors has yielded *in situ* finds of pre-*terra sigillata* or Arretine ware, the production of which peaked in the last quarter of the 1st century BC. This allows us to more accurately delimit Phase III to the period between 80 and 35–25 BC. Among the amphorae, those of Italic origin (Tyrrhenian and Adriatic) stand out, as well as Roman-tradition products from the Iberian Peninsula, such as those from the Circle of the Strait of Gibraltar and Tarraconensis. Of particular note in the two last groups is a piece of Rinconcillo ware (Algeciras) in the Circle of the Strait of Gibraltar with the stamp SCG. According to the latest studies, this dates to around 70 to 35–25 BC. Also relevant here is the presence of an Ovoid 4 amphora from the province of Cadiz, produced from around 70 BC, with a *floruit* between 50 and 25 BC. The Tarraconensian amphorae, which have 'Roman tradition' fabrics, have a date range of *c.* 65–40 BC (Figure 12.6).

As indicated above, an important outcome of the excavations has been the identification of traces of violent destruction across the different parts of the site. Since the 1980s, there has been a major methodological debate regarding archaeological indicators that could attest the violent destruction of settlements by human agency (Pesez and Piponnier 1988, 11–16; Hourcade 2008, 239–260; Noguera *et al.* 2013). Among the possible indicators, we can cite archaeological evidence of fire with various origins; large amounts of pottery preserved *in situ*; a concentration of weapons; and the presence of human and/or faunal remains in anatomical connection and/or with signs of violence.

These archaeological markers are fundamental elements for interpreting other destruction events that took place in the Iberian Peninsula at the end of the 1st millennium BC, such as at Valentia (Ribera and Calvo 1995, 19–40) and El Cerro de la Cruz (Quesada-Sanz *et al.* 2010, 75–95; Quesada-Sanz *et al.* 2014), and can also be applied to Puig Ciutat (Padrós *et al.* 2015, 287). The last site meets all the criteria except, to date, the presence of articulated human remains on the occupation levels. And it is interesting to note that in addition to the burned buildings and militaria (Figure 12.7) at Puig Ciutat, the excavations have also uncovered the articulated skeletal remains of

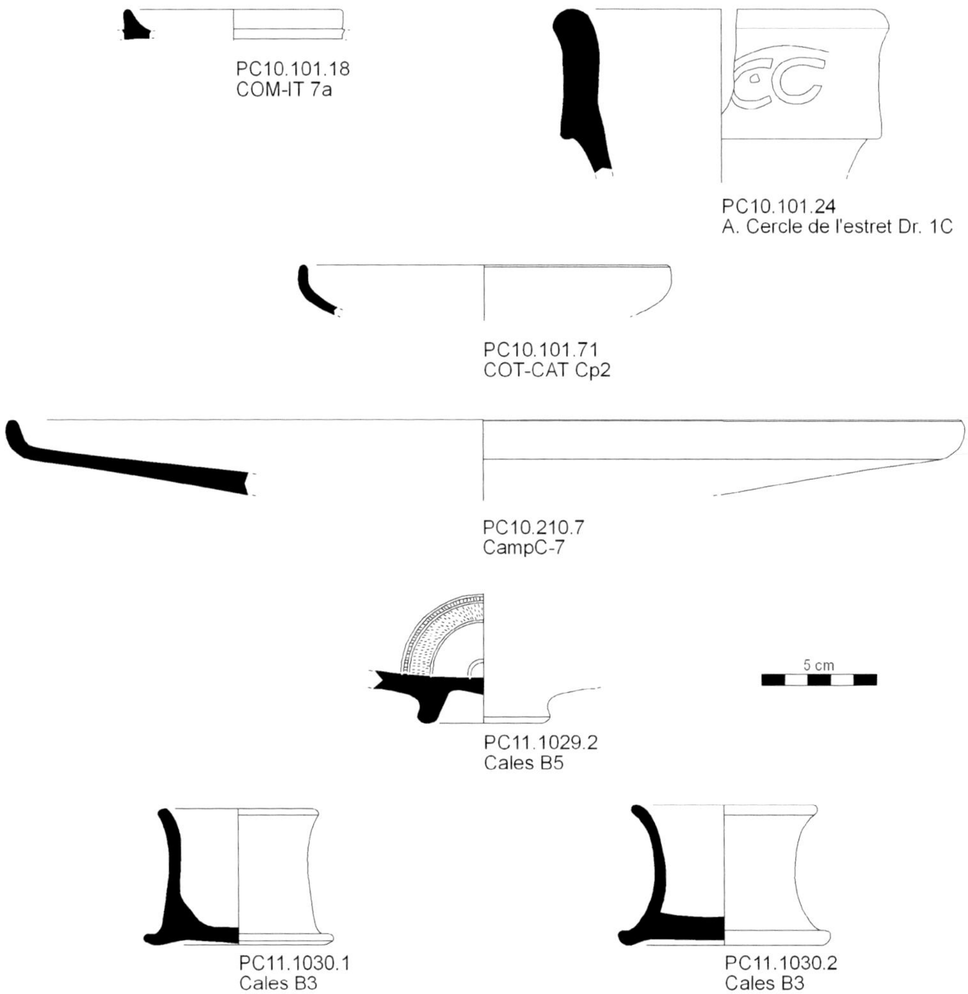

Figure 12.6 Ceramics characteristic of the late Republican occupation at Puig Ciutat (authors).

two dogs, one of them chained up at the time of its death (Padrós *et al.* 2015, 286–287), suggesting that they died during the attack on the site. In sum, the evidence seems to indicate an assault on and destruction of Puig Ciutat by an external army.

The historical context: the prelude to the battle of *Ilerda*

Based on the recovered evidence, in its final phase Puig Ciutat can be considered to be a late Republican Roman garrison, guard post or *praesidium*. It may have been a billet for a detachment of Roman soldiers occupying the site of a former indigenous settlement, which had been either abandoned or evacuated. The soldiers would have

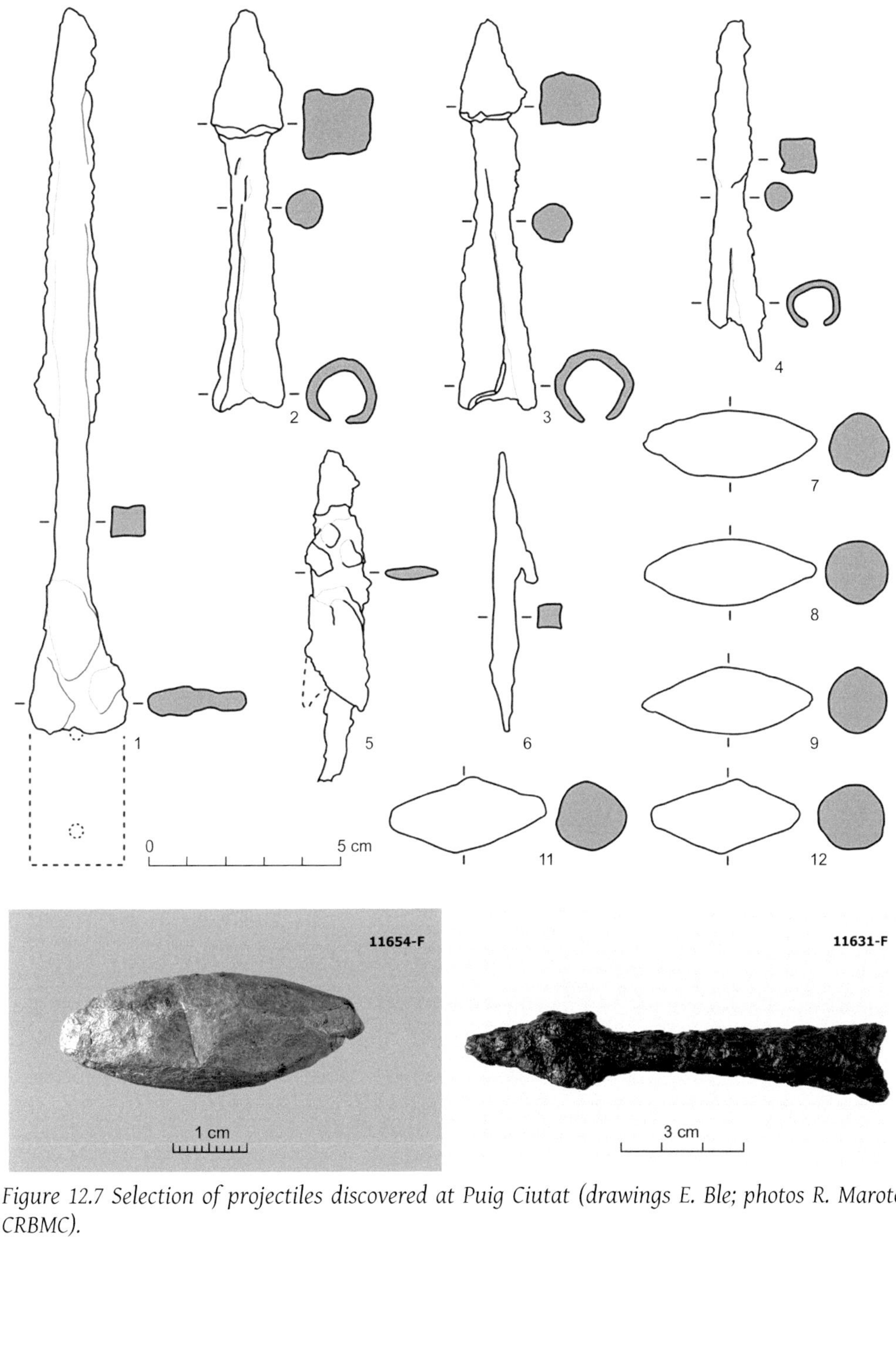

Figure 12.7 Selection of projectiles discovered at Puig Ciutat (drawings E. Ble; photos R. Maroto, CRBMC).

been charged with guarding the pass on the route between the Pyrenees, the Plain of Vic and the interior of the Iberian Peninsula.

The chronology offered by the finds suggests a context for the final moments of the site around the mid-1st century BC. This brings to mind an episode of the Civil War between Caesar and the supporters of Pompey (49–45 BC). We are specifically thinking of the preparations made during 49 BC in Hispania Citerior by Pompey's legate, Lucius Afranius, who would have installed a series of *praesidia* along the Pyrenean passes to impede or hinder the march of Caesar's supporters (Caesar *de Bello Civili* 1.37. 1–3; Cassius Dio 41.20.2). According to the written sources, while Caesar was preparing to march from Italy, he sent his legate Fabius in advance to Hispania, along with three legions he had left wintering in Narbo. Caesar's orders to Fabius were clear: quickly to take possession of the passes across the Pyrenees, at that time apparently occupied by detachments under Lucius Afranius. Fabius began a forced march towards Afranius' army (*de Bello Civili* 1.37.1–3), probably crossing the Pyrenees through La Cerdanya (Coll de la Pértiga; Pons 1986–89, 221). From that point, following the right bank of the river Segre, at least with the bulk of his troops, he would have arrived at the Plain of Lleida, in the vicinity of Ilerda, where Afranius and Petreius were waiting for him, entrenched there with a hastily formed army including troops from Hispania Citerior and Ulterior.

The characteristics of the settlement at Puig Ciutat – its location, chronology and the evidence for violent destruction (notably the Roman militaria indicating an exterior attack and the presence of burned buildings) – all suggest that the site was destroyed as part of the military operations that preceded the battle of Ilerda between the forces of Julius Caesar and the Spanish army of Pompey the Great in June 49 BC. In this sense, we can hypothesize that Puig Ciutat was occupied by followers of Pompey as part of the attempt to control the strategic route between the Pyrenees and the area of Ilerda. They were attacked by the approaching Caesarian army, which destroyed the site apparently without reoccupying it. Thanks to the archaeological programme, we are uncovering the remains of a short, rather marginal military event, but one that was directly linked to the wider theatre of operations of the Civil Wars in the dying days of the Roman Republic.

Acknowledgements

The research at Puig Ciutat since 2010 has been undertaken with the support of the Department of Culture of the Catalan Regional Government, SOT Archaeological Prospection, Oristà Town Council and the El Lluçanès Consortium of Municipalities. The project also had the scientific support of the Archaeological Museum of Catalonia and the DIDPATRI group, University of Barcelona. More recently, the investigations have been incorporated into a project entitled *El NE de la Citerior d'Escipió Emilià a Cèsar: la militarització del paisatge com a model de gestió territorial (2014–2017)*, which includes other sites such as El Camp de les Lloses (Barcelona) and Monteró 1 (Lleida). Since 2017, the fieldwork at Puig Ciutat has been carried out in collaboration with the University of Edinburgh, under the joint direction of Àngels Pujol, Roger Sala, Manuel Fernández-Götz and Xavier Rubio-Campillo. We would like to thank the Consorci del Lluçanès and the Leverhulme Trust for their support of the 2017 fieldwork at Puig Ciutat and in the production of this paper.

Notes

1 Corresponding author: Dr Manuel Fernández-Götz.
2 This paper employs the nomenclature used in previous publications on Puig Ciutat in Catalan and Spanish: 'zones' = main areas of the site and 'sectors' = building structures, mostly rooms.

Bibliography

Fernández-Götz, M. and Roymans, N. (eds) (2018) *Conflict Archaeology: Materialities of Collective Violence from Prehistory to Late Antiquity*. New York, Routledge.

Hornung, S. (2018) Tracing Julius Caesar. The Late Republican military camp at Hermeskeil and its historical context. In M. Fernández-Götz and N. Roymans (eds), *Conflict Archaeology: Materialities of Collective Violence from Prehistory to Late Antiquity*, 193–203. New York, Routledge.

Hourcade, D. (2008) Les 'évidences' archéologiques de siège et de prise de villes dans l'Hispanie républicaine: quelques faux indices. *Salduie* 8, 239–260.

Maschek, D. (2018) *Die römischen Bürgerkriege. Archäologie und Geschichte einer Krisenzeit.* Mainz, Philipp von Zabern.

Noguera, J., Asensio, D., Ble, E. and Jornet, R. (2013) The beginnings of the Roman conquest of Hispania. Archaeological evidence of the assault and destruction of the Iberian city of Castellet de Banyoles (Tivissa, Tarragona). *Journal of Roman Archaeology* 27, 60–81.

Padrós, C., Pujol, A. and Sala, R. (2014) El jaciment tardorepublicà de Puig Ciutat (Oristà, Osona): nous mètodes aplicats a l'arqueologia de recerca. *Tribuna d'Arqueologia 2012-2013*, 100–120.

Padrós, C., Pujol, A. and Sala, R. (2015) Puig Ciutat (Oristà, Barcelona): Un praesidium pompeià als peus dels Pirineus? *Revista d'Arqueologia de Ponent* 25, 277–290.

Pesez, J.M. and Piponnier, F. (1998) Traces matérielles de la guerre sur un site archéologique. In A. Bazzana (ed.), *Castrum, 3. Guerre, fortification et habitat dans le monde méditerranéen au Moyen Âge*, 11–16.

Pons, J. (1986–89) Aportacions al coneixement d'una comarca de l'alta conca del Segre en temps romans: L'Alt Urgell. *Empúries* 48–50, 218–225.

Principal, J., Camañes, P. and Padrós, C. (2015) Un edifici singular al castellum romanorepublicà de Monteró 1 (Camarasa, la Noguera), i l'urbanisme complex d'un post avançat del nord-est de la Citerior. *Revista d'Arqueologia de Ponent* 25, 309–325.

Pujol, A., Padrós, C. and Sala, R. (2014) El jaciment de Puig Ciutat (Oristà, Osona) i el seu entorn. Resultats de les campanyes de prospecció i excavació 2010–2012. *II Jornades d'Arqueologia de la Catalunya Central*, 129–136.

Pujol, A., Padrós, C. and Sala, R. (2016) Puig Ciutat (Oristà, Osona). Resultats de la campanya de 2013. *III Jornades d'Arqueologia de la Catalunya Central*, 158–161.

Quesada, F., Kavanagh, E. and Moralejo, J. (2010) El asentamiento de época ibérica en el Cerro de la Cruz. In I. Muñiz and F. Quesada (eds), Un drama en tres actos. Dos milenios de ocupación humana en el Cerro de la Cruz (Almedinilla, Córdoba). *Oikos* 2, 75–95.

Quesada-Sanz, F., Muñiz Jaén, I. and López Flores, I. (2014) La guerre et ses traces. Destruction et massacre dans le village ibérique du Cerro de la Cruz (Córdoba) et leur contexte historique au

IIe s. av. J.-C. In F. Cadiou and M. Navarro Caballero (eds), *La guerre et ses traces. Conflits et sociétés en Hispanie à l'époque de la conquête romaine (IIIe–Ier s. a.C.)*, 231–271. Bordeaux, Ausonius.

Reddé, M. (2018) The battlefield of *Alesia*. In M. Fernández-Götz and N. Roymans (eds), *Conflict Archaeology: Materialities of Collective Violence from Prehistory to Late Antiquity*, 183–191. New York, Routledge.

Ribera Lacomba, A. and Calvo, M. (1995) La primera evidencia arqueológica de la destrucción de *Valentia* por Pompeyo. *Journal of Roman Archaeology* 8, 19–40.

Roymans, N. (2018) A Roman massacre in the far north. Caesar's annihilation of the Tencteri and Usipetes in the Dutch River Area. In M. Fernández-Götz and N. Roymans (eds), *Conflict Archaeology: Materialities of Collective Violence from Prehistory to Late Antiquity*, 167–181. New York, Routledge.

Roymans, N., Creemers, G. and Scheers, S. (eds) (2012) *Late Iron Age Gold Hoards from the Low Countries and the Caesarian Conquest of Northern Gaul.* Amsterdam, Amsterdam Archaeological Studies 18.

Roymans, N. and Fernández-Götz, M. (2015) Caesar in Gaul: New perspectives on the archaeology of mass violence. In T. Brindle, M. Allen, E. Durham and A. Smith (eds), *TRAC 2014: Proceedings of the Twenty-Fourth Annual Theoretical Roman Archaeology Conference*, 70–80. Oxford, Oxbow Books.

Chapter 13

The Gallic War in the chronology of Iron Age coinage

Colin Haselgrove

> La plupart des dates proposés par divers numismates n'ont aucune base scientifique.
> (Blanchet 1905, 175)

By the time of Julius Caesar's conquest of Gaul and invasions of Britain, Iron Age precious and base metal coins were used across much of north-west Europe, and the Gallic War looms large in numismatic chronologies, on the presumption that both sides used coins to pay soldiers and finance the fighting. While regional differences in types and metals suggest that the roles and functions of Iron Age coins were not identical over this vast zone, as a medium sensitive to economic and political circumstances, we can reasonably expect their production and circulation to reflect an upheaval on the scale of the battle for Gaul. In the Hellenistic world, coinage was used to hire mercenaries, induce treachery or paid as indemnity or tribute. Under the late Republic, the volume of Roman coinage minted was largely determined by the level of military expenditure at the time (Crawford 1974, 694, table 8; Hopkins 1980, 110–111, fig. 3); long wars often led to the exhaustion of metal resources and, on more than one occasion, to debasement. Other expressions of conflict in the Mediterranean world included the dispersal of coins far beyond their home territories and the use of coin imagery and legends to express their issuers' allegiances or vaunt their triumphs.

A familiar example of this last is provided by *aurei* and *denarii* struck by Caesar himself in 48–47 BC on campaign and in 46–45 BC in Spain (RRC 452; RRC 468).[1] These coins – one of which adorns the cover of this book – depict Gallic weapon trophies and captives, and were probably struck from war booty. Major conflicts can also give rise to periods of intensified hoarding and non-recovery of buried valuables – well-documented instances range from the late Republic (Crawford 1985, 192–193) again, to the English Civil War (Besly 2015) – but so too can other kinds of crisis or instability. Moreover, without direct testimony or good contextual evidence, emergency hoards can be exceedingly difficult to distinguish from other forms of deposits, such as sacrificial offerings of wealth to seek divine protection or the dedication of booty after a successful campaign (Bland *et al.* forthcoming).

It was of course the large quantity of coins found in the 1860s at Alesia that established a direct archaeological link between coinage and the Gallic War (Colbert de Beaulieu 1955a; Scheers 1987). In their way, the 466 Gaulish coins found in the imperial explorations have had as profound an impact on Iron Age coin studies as the discovery of iron weapons had at the time on La Tène archaeology (Olivier this volume) – although unlike the weapons, the coins were not initially mired in controversy, but only became so later, as we shall see. That said, Alesia remains one of the few firm fixed points for Gaulish coin chronology. The 1991–97 investigations (Reddé this volume) added over 200 more coins, mostly through controlled metal detecting, raising the total to 679 identifiable Gaulish coins and 145 Roman to 54 BC, without much changing the overall picture (Fischer 2001; Popovitch 2001, 74–75). Today, few would disagree that these coins provide a good sample of military circulation at this point in the war, if skewed on the Gaulish side towards peoples actively involved in the siege or rescue attempt (on either side) – and with the *caveat* that some coins may be later losses and not subject to the absolute *terminus ante quem* of 52 BC provided by the siege.

The only other direct numismatic link with the Gallic War is through coin legends. A handful of individuals named on coins are clearly the same as Gaulish leaders mentioned in the *Commentaries*, notably Vercingetorix. Moreover, some of his staters were brass rather than gold (Nieto 2004), perhaps symptomatic of a shortage of precious metal at this stage of the war. Less easy to explain from a modern perspective, given Vercingetorix's career, is why his coins depict a Roman wine amphora – shared with another broadly contemporary Arvernian series inscribed Cas (DT 3570–3575), some of whose coins are also brass. However, in identifying legends with individuals named by Caesar, we are already entering subjective territory. In an article published in the wake of the Alesia discoveries, Saulcy (1867) claimed to have recognized as many as 28 names on Gaulish coins, but in his *Traité des monnaies Gauloises*, Blanchet (1905, 81–82) reduced the certain identifications to eight. Most scholars today would accept a figure of no more than ten (Colbert de Beaulieu 1962; Gruel 1989, 126–130; Colbert de Beaulieu and Fischer 1998).[2]

The need for such caution is illustrated by some central Gaulish bronze issues inscribed Sedvllvs (DT 3713). A ruler of the Lemovices called Sedulis was killed at Alesia (*BG* 7.88), but a link is nowadays ruled out for two reasons: first, the head on these coins seemingly copies a *denarius* not issued until 47 BC (RRC 454/1) and second, because the type is not represented at Alesia (Gruel 1989, 130). In ignoring the cardinal principle that absence of evidence is not the same as evidence of absence, this second argument is weak, although this has not prevented the absence of other coin types from Alesia being regularly deployed in debates about the dating of Gaulish coinage.

Other individuals named on Gaulish coins are either unknown to history or later than Caesar,[3] and Iron Age coins in Armorican and Belgic Gaul and Britain were in any case not inscribed until a late date. They cannot therefore simply be dated by cross-reference to the historical framework which provides the mainstay for deducing absolute dates for Classical coins in the last few centuries BC. Even where Gaulish coins imitate Hellenistic or Roman prototypes (Scheers 1969; 2004), this yields only a *terminus post quem*, often compromised by uncertainty over the dating of the prototype (as with many bronze coins of Marseille), the time lapse before copying, or even incorrect derivation. Writing when all potin coins were thought to be late, Scheers (1977, 171) accepted that an animal depicted on the Belgic torc-bearer type (S191) might copy the elephant *denarius* of Caesar (RRC 443/1), which Crawford (1974) dates 49–48 BC[4] – but we now know that these potin coins are around a century older (Haselgrove 1995); nor is the animal, whatever its identity, an elephant! Similarly, given how long Republican *denarii* remained in circulation, their association with Gaulish coins in hoards and other contexts far beyond their core circulation area may well be a poor guide to the actual date of deposition.

Deprived of an independent means of dating Iron Age coins, scholars have struggled over the years to develop an accurate and reliable chronological framework for the myriad regional series found in Gaul and Britain. In recent decades, as we will see, great strides have been made in dating Gaulish silver and base-metal issues from archaeological evidence, revealing deep flaws in older historically-based models. That said, although the overall nature of monetary developments through the mid-1st century BC is now relatively well understood, few series can be dated with the degree of precision that most numismatists would like, while for the uninscribed gold and billon issues that circulated in large numbers in the 2nd and 1st centuries BC in northern Gaul and Britain the problems of dating remain acute.

Iron Age gold coins rarely occur in archaeological contexts. Their dating still relies heavily on traditional numismatic methods: typology and stylistic considerations, die studies and overstriking, metrology and fineness, and hoard evidence. While the relative chronologies these produce are generally robust within series, they are less reliable for ordering related series, where imitation could go either way, or for dating regional coinages relative to one another, since these may adhere to different rules of weight or fineness for cultural reasons. Other standard numismatic rules-of-thumb cannot necessarily be relied on. For example, the degree of wear on coins in a hoard is often used to estimate their relative ages, but this presupposes that all issues were used in the same ways; moreover it is hard to distinguish between wear on the designs of coins arising from the use of worn dies and wear caused by circulation (Sills 2017, 724; Talbot 2017, 121–122; see below).

Partly as a result of these complexities, the slender historical framework remains the main source of absolute dating, which is inexorably pulled towards episodes that we know about from the sources, and often in the Classical world rather than north of the Alps, given the lack of testimony before Caesar. A prime case is linking the adoption of coinage across Iron Age Europe to the employment of Celtic mercenaries in Hellenistic armies (Nash 1987; Sills 2003; Scheers 2004), a model now coming under more critical appraisal (Pion 2012; Nieto-Pelletier and Olivier 2016). Another example is the persistent dating of the important Tayac gold hoard in Aquitaine by reference to the late 2nd-century BC passage of the Cimbri and their allies through the area (*e.g.* Forrer 1908; Kellner 1970) – although the hoard is probably earlier (Haselgrove 1999; Sills 2003) and looks like a votive deposit.

As a fixed point, the Gallic War remains by far the greatest draw. Thanks to the detail in the *Commentaries* – seemingly borne out by the early discoveries at Alesia – the course of the war provides a rich hunting ground for scholars seeking to date Iron Age gold series and to interpret the record in ways familiar for well-documented later periods. This, however, often runs a risk of circular argument, whereby numismatic observations (*e.g.* a dramatic increase in minting and hoarding; rapid weight loss and debasement) are seen as due to the war, whilst also being used to validate the dating. This is reminiscent of the culture-history era in archaeology prior to the advent of scientific dating, when archaeological reasoning was constantly undermined by the need to make the material yield a chronology as well as explain change, which, as Renfrew (1974, 35) emphasized, it could do only by distorting both. If a supposedly wartime coinage was actually minted over years rather than a few months, then the changes put down to the exigencies of war would not be so rapid after all.

Without a fully independent chronology, the historical value of Iron Age coins must be considered limited. I shall return to the prospects of such a development below but will first examine the role played by the Gallic War in the formation of Iron Age chronologies over the century and a half since the Alesia discoveries and also how later gold coinage in Belgic Gaul and Britain came to be tied to the war. The fault line between insular and continental dating exposed by the Le Câtillon II hoard (de Jersey this volume) is not new. As we shall see, scholarly opinion has gone through similar cycles in Britain and France, but only rarely in step with each other and frequently with discrepant chronological models at any one time.

The dating of Iron Age coinage – from Alesia to Le Câtillon I

Absolute dates do not loom large in either of the books that laid the foundations for modern Iron Age coin studies on both sides on the Channel. Evans (1864) and Blanchet (1905) were both more concerned with localizing different coinages, although Evans does devote a whole chapter to 'Date and Origin', where he describes his method of temporal ordering based on typological descent – later likening the process which gave rise to new varieties to the then newly established Darwinian theory of evolution (Evans 1875). Assuming that the Philippus was first imitated in Gaul around 300 BC and its descendants underwent a fairly uniform reduction in weight over time, Evans arrived at a date of 200–150 BC for Gallo-Belgic broad-flan coins (GBA) – the first gold to circulate in quantity in Britain (Evans 1864, 26, 34; 1875, 486) – which is close to the accepted dating today (Sills 2003). Blanchet has almost nothing to say on the topic, apart from dismissing many of the proposed dates for Gaulish coins as having no scientific basis (1905, 175–178),[5] although he does also lament the efforts put into attributing coinages to individual Gaulish peoples named by Caesar at the expense of dating (Blanchet 1905, 19).

Blanchet followed the *Atlas des Monnaies Gauloises* (La Tour 1892)[6] in seeing the GBA broad flan coins and their Gallo-Belgic successors as Gaulish (1905, 369), whereas Evans thought they were British given the higher number of insular finds (1864, 25). The implication that the circulation of these series on both sides of the Channel was the means of introducing coins to Britain was rapidly taken up in the diffusionist framework that held sway in British archaeology until the 1970s. A continental origin remains the received wisdom and crucial to the dating, although as Burnett (1996) notes, Evans's point about the higher insular frequencies of Gallo-Belgic types – still true today – has never really been answered, leading Burnett to ask why provenance is thought less significant as an argument in this one instance given its primacy in the attribution of most Iron Age coinages (Burnett 1996, 9). The issue is complicated by higher recording rates in Britain via the Celtic Coin Index and Portable Antiquities Scheme (Haselgrove 2005, 138), but otherwise this is a fair point – especially as the insular distributions are almost invariably also more coherent than on the continent.[7]

As well as providing an inventory of hoards on both sides on the Channel, Blanchet included an agenda-setting chapter on circulation, in which he lists Gaulish coin types found in burials and excavated or collected on archaeological sites across France and beyond (Blanchet 1905, 483–538).[8] This showed that some issues have highly localized distributions, dominating sites in a given region, but are rarely found elsewhere, in contrast to the pan-regional distributions of many other types. Notwithstanding his general caution over dating, Blanchet does attribute certain groups of hoards to the Gallic War, linking Arvernian hoards containing coins of Cas or Vercingetorix to the fighting before Alesia and a cluster of gold hoards in Belgic Gaul to Caesar's campaigns in that region, with the Guignicourt-Variscourt hoard singled out as being found only 4 km from the battlefield of 57 BC at Mauchamp (Blanchet 1905, 522–523). The fighting in 56 BC is similarly held responsible for over 40 hoards belonging to the last phase of Armorican coinage (Blanchet 1905, 524–525), buttressed this time by the association of the same coin types with Roman *denarii* to 39 BC in the 1875 Rozel hoard (de Jersey this volume).

The most significant contribution on coin dating at this period was in fact archaeological. In his 1902 paper on the La Tène Iron Age, Joseph Déchelette for the first time invoked the archaeological context of a coin type – in this case, a deformed quadruped potin (LT 5368) derived from butting-bull bronzes of Massalia in Grave 49 at Ornavasso in northern Italy – to challenge its received numismatic dating (Déchelette 1902, 277). As the cemetery ended in the early 1st century BC, Déchelette inferred that the potin – and by implication its prototype (then dated to 49 BC) – must be earlier, also highlighting the occurrence of similar potins in middle La Tène graves in Switzerland. His conclusion was accepted by Blanchet (1905, 252), who also pushed back the date of the Massalia prototype to the 3rd century BC.

At this era, however, most coins lacked an archaeological context or reliable associations and, as Pion (2008, 351) notes, Déchelette's enduring legacy was to treat coins as archaeological objects in their own right. The final volume of his great *Manuel d'Archéologie* included 'des premières monnaies gauloises dans les sépultures' as a characteristic of La Tène II, and 'de nombreuses monnaies gauloises dont beaucoup sont en bronze coulé' as an attribute of La Tène III (Déchelette 1914, 931–932). Two Cisalpine silver coins inscribed Rikos (LT 2169) are figured alongside similar types of pottery vessels found at Ornavasso and Soldo as typical of La Tène II burials in the Alps (Déchelette 1914, 1095, figs 450–451; cf. Déchelette 1902, 279, figs 26–35), and, building on Blanchet, Déchelette discusses the types of coins found at key La Tène III sites such as Bibracte (1914, 954–955). By integrating coinage into a typological framework for the later Iron Age defined by changes in brooch and sword styles, Déchelette bridged the divide that had hitherto existed between archaeology and numismatics (Pion 2008), but at the same time paved the way for significant misuse of Gaulish coins in dating continental late Iron Age sites in the 20th century.

The effects of this marriage of coinage and archaeology were in fact felt first in Britain, where Brooke (1933) proposed that imitation of the Philippus in Gaul only started after 121 BC when the Roman Provincia was established, following the arrival in Rome of vast quantities of the original coins as war booty after the defeat of the Hellenistic successor kingdoms. Attributing the early broad-flan coins (GBA) in Britain to trade, Brooke linked their successors (GBC) to the first of two Belgic invasions inferred by Hawkes and Dunning (1930), responsible for 'Iron Age C' culture and dated around 75 BC. Unlike their predecessors, these new types were copied by indigenous groups. They were soon followed by related uniface staters (GBE) and then about 50 BC by coins with a triple-tailed horse copied from another continental type (GBG); these latter coins were associated with a second Belgic 'invasion', this time of people displaced by the Gallic War, among them Caesar's erstwhile ally, now enemy, Commios, whose name soon appeared on the coins (Hawkes and Dunning 1930, 291–296; Brooke 1933, 130–131). Although Brooke lacked concrete evidence for equating any of the coin types with the archaeological traits used to infer the Belgic invasions (themselves long since discredited), his numismatic dating of the later Gallo-Belgic types and their insular copies to the 25 years ending with the Caesarian conquest of Gaul still essentially holds sway today (*e.g.* Creighton 2000; Sills 2003; 2017; Talbot 2017), even if the precise dates have veered to and fro over the years.

Much closer in its approach to Déchelette was an early paper on British potin coins by Derek Allen. From their association with 'Iron Age A' pottery and sites, Allen attributed these coins to the pre-Belgic inhabitants of south-east England (1936, 356). Broadly contemporary with GBA, they were soon replaced by gold coins in the core area of Belgic settlement (reflected by a wave of potin hoards along the Thames), although perhaps surviving longer in outlying areas. Allen was curiously silent on whether Caesar's famous mention of the use of *aes* for money in Britain (*BG* 5.12) referred to these coins – possibly because on his argument, they were no longer in circulation in the maritime region in 54 BC.

The second half of the 20th century saw a major change in direction, with the Gallic War now assuming a central role in dating Iron Age coinage on both sides of the Channel. On the continent, this movement was led by J.-B. Colbert de Beaulieu and reinforced by his many students. In a series of influential papers from the 1950s onward (*e.g.* Colbert de Beaulieu 1955a; 1955b; 1966; 1970), culminating in his magisterial *Traité de Numismatique Celtique* (1973a), he proposed a four-fold scheme for Gaulish coinage. This was conceived around two major events, both of which Colbert saw as having immediate profound effects on coin production and circulation. The first – dividing his Stages 1 and 2 – was the collapse of a supposed Arvernian hegemony after their defeat in 121 BC by the Romans. The second, forming Stage 3 in its own right, was the Gallic War, which also shaped the nature of post-war coinages (Stage 4) until indigenous minting ended in the reign of Augustus (Colbert de Beaulieu 1973a, esp. 169–250).

Whilst recognizing that Philippi were in fact copied in Gaul at a date close to that of the prototypes, Colbert otherwise echoed Brooke's short chronology by compressing most of Gaulish coinage into the period from 121 BC onward, arguing that minting was monopolized by the Arverni and confined to gold until after their defeat, apart from in Belgic Gaul, where another putative hegemony existed, minting gold based on Tarentine protypes, and on the Atlantic fringes (1973a, 180–181). Each stage was characterized by specific monetary developments (conveniently summarized in Gruel 1989, 30–31 and Pion 2008, 352–354). For the Gallic War, these included (1) the expansion of coin circulation areas through military and population movements; (2) disappearance of gold and of precious metal more generally, balanced by a major increase in bronze issues; and (3) the introduction of cast potins as an emergency currency. Archaeological support for this model rested, however, on the one 'fixed point' provided by Alesia, for which Colbert made a critical error, inferring that the reason for the small number of potins from the 1860s investigations (12% of the Gaulish coins)[9] was because potins were only just appearing in 52 BC (with their main usage after the war), rather than being earlier and on their way out of circulation. To fit his model, Colbert also argued that the long silver series headed by coins inscribed Kaletedou Sula (DT 3193), copying a *denarius* of P. Cornelius Sulla of *c.* 151 BC (Crawford 1974, no. 205/1), must allude to Sulla's dictatorship in the 80s BC (Colbert de Beaulieu 1966), at one fell swoop shortening the lifespan of the Gaulish silver *quinarius* coinages that form the largest single component of the Alesia finds from more than a century to a mere thirty years.

The dating of Gallo-Belgic gold was also now seemingly anchored to the 50s BC, if in a roundabout way, by the 1957 discovery on Jersey of the Le Câtillon I hoard (see de Jersey this volume). Predominantly consisting of late Armorican billon with a few other Gaulish coins and some brooches, and seemingly dating to the Gallic

War (Colbert de Beaulieu 1957; 1973a, 163), its significance resided in the 20 British coins it contained. In a landmark study, Allen (1960) seized on the presence of two worn British B staters and 11 freshly minted South-Western coins in the Le Câtillon hoard as providing a secure *terminus ante quem* for the insular copying of the GBC staters and GBD quarters from which they were ultimately derived. All told, at least three generations of coinage were implied, leading Allen to push the date of GBC and GBD (of which the hoard contained a worn example) back to *c.* 100 BC and restore Evans's mid-2nd-century BC date for their broad-flan predecessors. Since the GBE uniface coins were now the only major series unaccounted for, Allen also concluded that they must have been current at the time of the Gallic War (1960, 113–116). A decade later, in revisiting Kentish potin coins, he expanded on this, linking the many potin hoards along the Thames and a series of coastal gold hoards closing with GBD/E to refugees fleeing from Kent in different directions in 55–54 BC (Allen 1971, 140–141)[10], thereby aligning himself with Blanchet's (1905, 522–523) suggestion that the cluster of Belgic hoards containing uniface staters and other late types related to the Gallic War.

Thus was the stage set for the emergence of the orthodoxy that would dominate continental and British thinking for the rest of the 20th century and which is still influential today. In her epic study of Belgic coinage, Scheers (1972; 1977) proposed that a closely-related group of gold coinages on a common weight standard and module and sharing a single prototype in GBC were minted by the Belgic peoples from 58 BC onward to finance the war against Rome. These issues included GBE uniface staters, GBF/G triple-tailed horse types, S29 'epsilon' staters, S30 'eye' staters, and various derivatives (Figure 13.1). Invoking Colbert's doctrine – including his idea that some peoples could only have issued gold coins after 57 BC when they gained independence from dominant neighbours – Scheers inferred precise dates for successive classes of the different series defined by rapid falls in weight and fineness by correlating them with the various Roman campaigns in Belgic Gaul down to 50 BC, when gold minting ceased altogether.

Cogently argued, based on a comprehensive review of the data and elegant in its simplicity, Scheers' thesis rapidly found widespread acceptance (*e.g.* Kent 1978; Haselgrove 1984; Nash 1987, 114–117; Roymans 1990; Fitzpatrick 1992). In Britain, her scheme led Kent to propose that as the broad-flan coins in Britain were mostly very worn, all the Gallo-Belgic series had been exported in quick succession at the time of the Gallic War to buy the support of the British troops about whom Caesar complains (*BG* 4.20) and that it was this influx of gold that brought about indigenous minting. Kent's inference still holds sway today among many British numismatists (*e.g.* de Jersey this volume; Sills 2017), but required him to argue that the Le Câtillon I hoard must be post-Caesarian (Kent 1978, 315).[11] Importantly for our long-term understanding, Kent (1978, 316–318) emphasized the abrupt change from a silver-rich to a copper-rich gold alloy evident in British coinage around the mid-1st century BC and instigated the first major programme of metal analysis of Iron Age gold types.

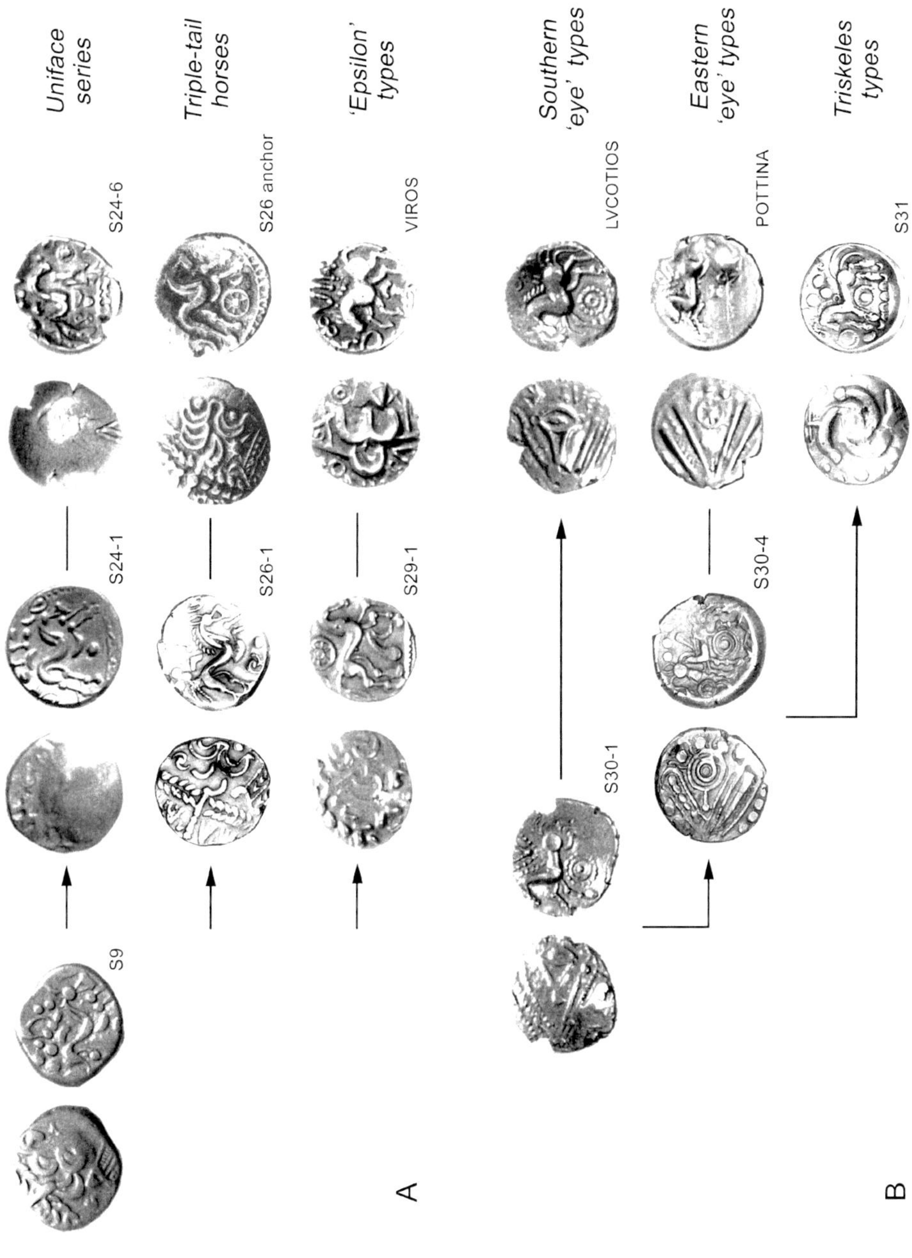

Figure 13.1 The two principal groupings of late Belgic gold coinage. (A) GBC biface staters (S9) and derivatives. (B) S30-1 'eye' staters and derivatives (adapted from Haselgrove 1984, fig. 2). Scale 1:1.

This in turn implied that the earliest insular coinages were made by recycling Gallo-Belgic coins with added silver and copper, if not the timescale by which this process occurred (Cowell *et al.* 1987; Cowell 1992)

For the present author, too, the enormous number of dies used for minting certain classes of GBE and S30 'eye' staters seemingly confirmed Scheers' view that these types were struck during the war. An increase in output on this scale would probably have required the conversion of other precious metal objects into coin and the ultimate effect of the war was to strip Belgic Gaul of nearly all its gold, whether in the form of the many unrecovered hoards closing with uniface coins, through their export to Britain, or due to their removal as booty by the Romans (Haselgrove 1984). The integrity of Scheers' typological scheme and some of her assumptions based on the Colbert doctrine seemed more questionable, however. Instead, I suggested that two discrete groupings could be recognized, one headed by GBC, the other by S30-I 'eye' staters, and as a corollary, that minting of the oldest types might have begun before 57 BC and small-scale production could have continued for some time afterwards (Haselgrove 1984; 1987, 80–84).[12] These adjustments have since been generally accepted (Roymans 1990, 124–125; Delestrée 1996; Pion 2003).

The Colbert doctrine also had a profound impact on the archaeological dating of the Iron Age. This came about in two distinct, but complementary ways. First, Colbert's seemingly firm dating of potins and other coin types commonly found in archaeological contexts to the Gallic War and afterwards forced excavators to date these deposits and thus entire sites to the later 1st century BC (Pion 2008, 354), drastically reducing the length of Déchelette's La Tène III. Second, Colbert's idea that whole sites could be characterized by coin finds alone compounded the situation and led to crucial mistakes. An extreme example is provided by the lengthy debate over the chronological order of the nearby Aisne valley *oppida* at Pommiers and Villeneuve-Saint-Germain. The first site had long been regarded as prime candidate for the Noviodunum of the Suessiones captured by Caesar in 57 BC (*BG* 2, 12). In one of his first major studies, its coin list – dominated by struck bronzes (86%) and with many extra-regional issues (including Roman *denarii*) – was held up by Colbert de Beaulieu (1955b) as typical for a site occupied intensively at the time of the Gallic War – although he admitted that the coins also indicated continuing occupation at the site. Nevertheless, when the valley-bottom fortification at Villeneuve was excavated in the 1970s–80s and its coin list turned out to be almost mutually exclusive and dominated by potins (81%), the logic of the Colbert model dictated that it should be dated *after* Pommiers (Debord 1990; 1995; 2001), despite other diagnostic finds from the sites indicating the reverse (Figure 13.2; Haselgrove 1996; Pion 1996). In a classic case of circularity, a triple-tailed horse stater then classed as British[13] from the closure deposits at Villeneuve was cited as support for a late date for that site, even though the insular gold chronology actually depended on Scheers' scheme, founded on the Colbert doctrine.

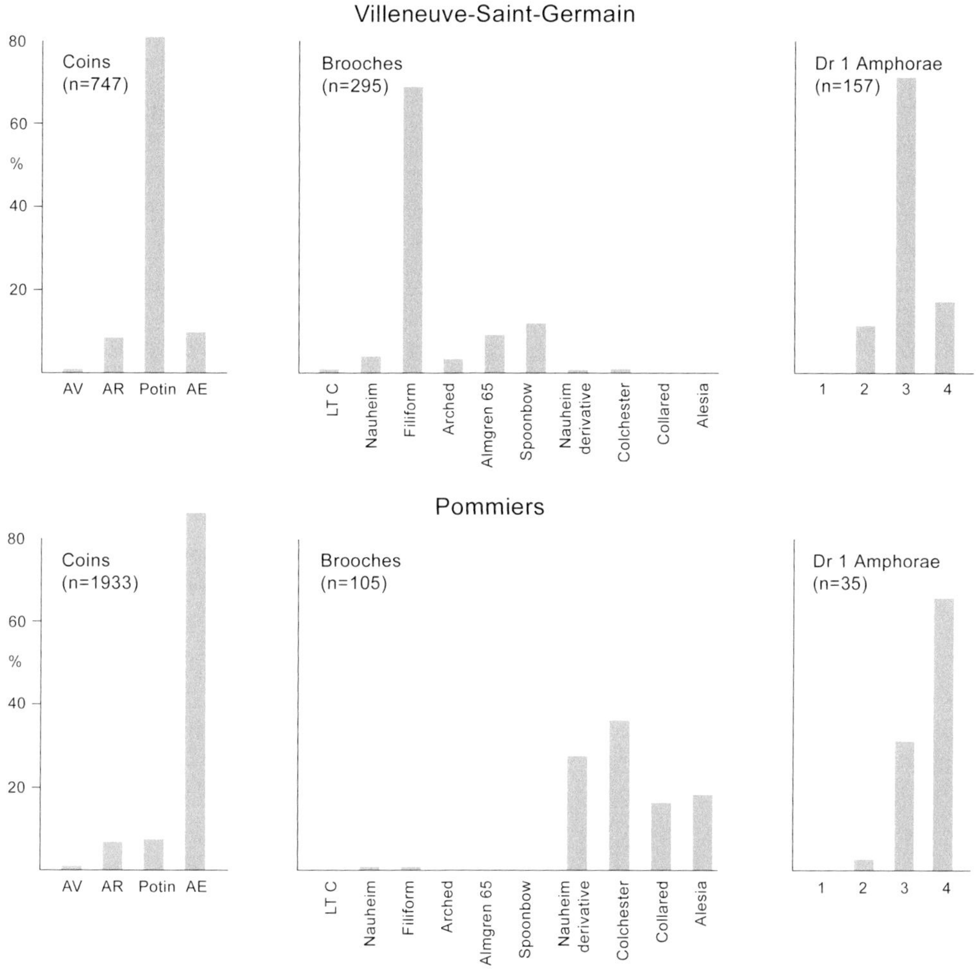

Figure 13.2 Relative frequencies of Gaulish coins, brooch types and Dressel 1 amphora rims at Villeneuve-Saint-Germain and Pommiers, Aisne (after Haselgrove 1996, fig. 8).

Archaeology fights back

Whilst broadly in step with Scheers' scheme for late Belgic gold, anglophone scholars never accepted Colbert's idea of the Arvernian hegemony (*e.g.* Nash 1976) or his dating of Gaulish silver and potin (*e.g.* Allen 1971; 1973). Colbert's counter-arguments were in part driven by this ideology – for instance his dismissal of the Houssen and Lattes-3 silver hoards as pointing to an earlier date for potins[14] – but there was at this stage more justification to his argument that attempts to lengthen the chronology depended on isolated finds from a mere handful of archaeological contexts, many of which could be individually contested (Colbert de Beaulieu 1973b).

This, however, began to change as archaeologists reassessed the material associations of various coin series and new stratified finds began to accrue as rescue excavation gathered pace. For the type site of La Tène, Allen (1973, 496–498) highlighted the contradiction between the received date of the silver and potin coins among the lake deposits, and the mass of weaponry and other objects of late 3rd-century date. Similarly, comparison of the coins and other archaeological finds from the successive late La Tène occupations at the Basel Gasfabrik and Münsterhügel sites pointed firmly to an earlier 1st-century BC date for the local potins (Furger-Gunti and von Kaenel 1976). Most decisively of all, a new study of coins found in La Tène burials (many of them old finds known to Blanchet and Déchelette) reaffirmed a 3rd-century BC date for various Iron Age gold and silver series and an early start for potin (Polenz 1982). On both sides of the Channel, this spurred a renewed interest in stratified coin finds (Brunaux and Gruel 1987; Haselgrove 1987; 1988), although the initial effects were limited owing to the late dating still in force for the late La Tène period (and a lingering reluctance by numismatists to accept the implications of the early La Tène D1 associations for potins identified by Polenz), which was exacerbated in Britain by a lack of independent dating for the later Iron Age and continued reliance on cross-dating with the continent.

Thanks to two key developments this would change entirely in the 1990s. The first was a fundamental reappraisal of late Iron Age chronology, freeing it from the confines of the numismatic model. This came from three directions, first the increasing availability of absolute dates from dendrochronology (Kaenel 1990); second a recalibration of the funerary sequence in the Moselle region (Miron 1986; 1991); and third, work linking the central and northern Gaulish chronologies with the Mediterranean zone (Vaginay and Guichard 1988; Duval *et al.* 1990; Metzler 1995). Cumulatively, these pushed the start of the late La Tène period (now usually subdivided into La Tène D1 and D2 on the German system) back to the mid-2nd century BC, where it has essentially stabilized (Figure 13.3; Kaenel 2006; Barral and Fichtl 2012; see Ralston this volume); the Gallic War is now seen as correlating with the archaeological transition from La Tène D2a to D2b. In parallel, the mounting volume of excavated finds allowed individual series – especially silver and potin – to be fixed in regional chronologies (Delestrée and Lambot 1991; Guichard *et al.* 1993; Pion 1996), leading to a reconsideration of the wider issues around potin chronology (Gruel 1995; Haselgrove 1995). By the turn of the millennium, a starting date for potin during La Tène C2 and for the Kaletedou silver early in La Tène D1, with attendant implications for the dating of other silver and base-metal issues, was generally accepted (Wigg and Riederer 1998; Delestrée 1999; Haselgrove 1999; Gruel 2005; Gruel and Haselgrove 2006) and was adopted for the *Nouvel Atlas des monnaies Gauloises* (Delestrée and Tache 2002; 2004; 2007).

A sufficiently robust chronological framework expressed in terms of the sub-phases of La Tène D1–D2 now exists for us to deduce the main regional silver, potin and bronze series in circulation at the time of the Gallic War, if not always the precise

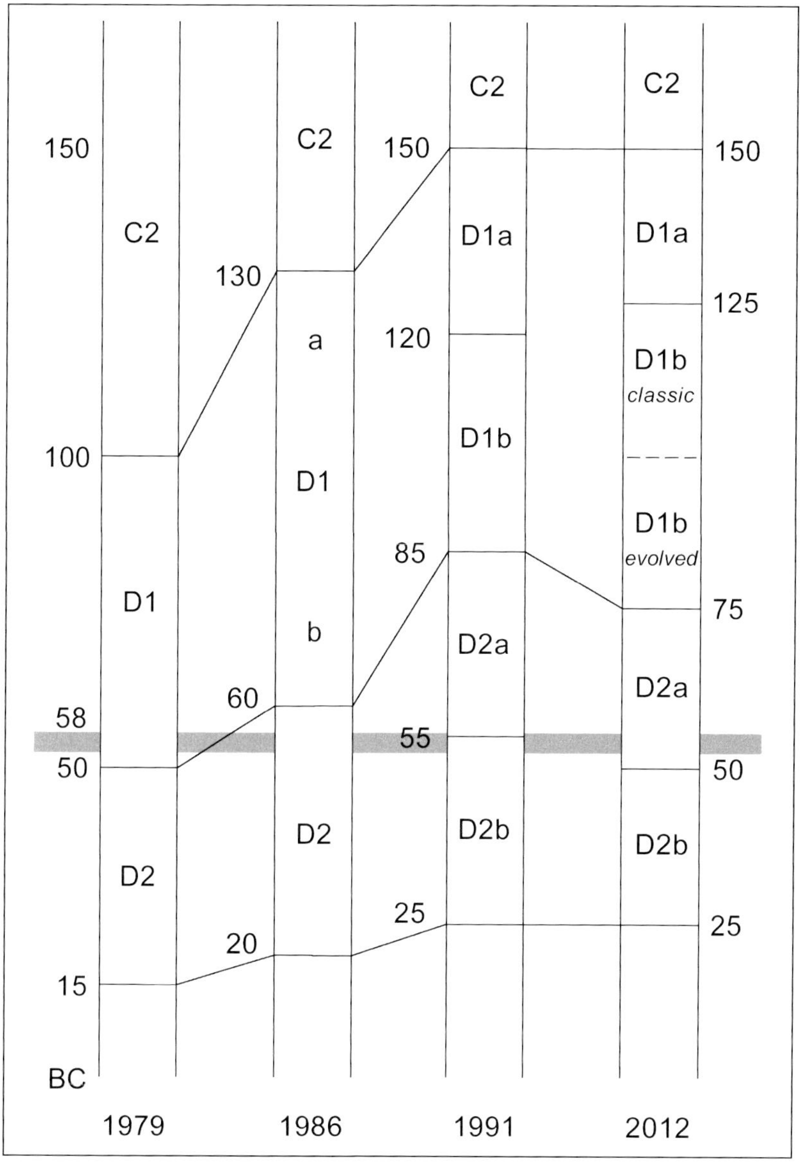

Figure 13.3 Fifty years of relative and absolute chronology for La Tène D (adapted from Kaenel 2006, fig. 7 and Barral and Fichtl 2012, fig. 1).

moment at which particular types were first minted (Figure 13.4). Alesia remains an important site of reference, especially for large sites with long sequences such as Bibracte, where a high degree of residuality can be expected, but also as a means of calibrating the extent to which mainly base metal site losses reflect a circulation pool of which silver coins – often plated – were a major component (Gruel and Popovitch 2007, 65–101). Comparisons of coin lists with Alesia have also been used to postulate military

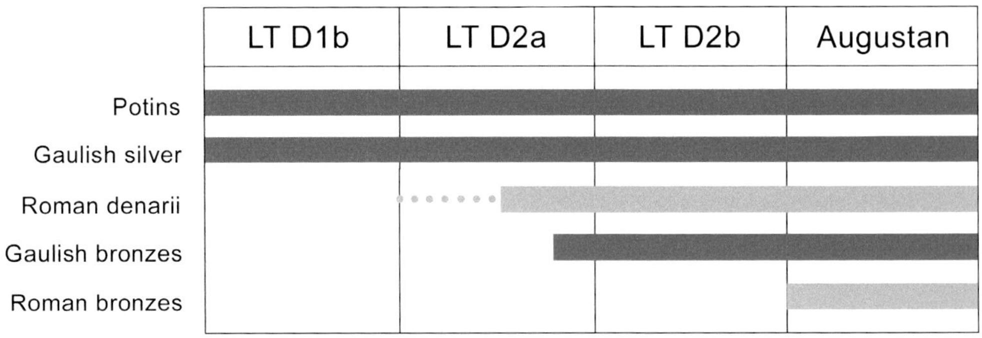

Figure 13.4 The appearance in circulation of Gaulish and Roman coinage at the oppidum *of Bibracte by metal (adapted from Gruel and Popovitch, 2007, fig. 76).*

occupation of Caesarian date at a number of *oppida* in Belgic Gaul, notably La Chaussée-Tirancourt, where there is good structural evidence in the interior (Delestrée *et al.* 2006; Bayard 2018), Liercourt-Erondelle (Delestrée and Boisard 2010) and Pommiers (above). A degree of caution is needed, however, as these coins are mainly surface finds. At Pommiers, the 19th-century finds seem to be a fair proxy for the occupation span (La Tène D2b–Augustan), to judge from the 1980s excavations (Pion 1996), but this is not always true, as shown by another *oppidum* first discussed by Blanchet (1905), Corent in the Auvergne. Here, a short early 1st-century BC occupation inferred from coins and other finds recovered in limited initial investigations, and deployed by Guichard *et al.* (1993) in their major contribution to the chronological debate, has since been shown by large-scale excavations not to be representative of the Iron Age activity, which in fact covers the whole of La Tène D1– D2 (Poux and Demierre 2015, 505–507). At Corent, the demolition of the sanctuary is placed during the Gallic War, based partly on the presence of ten 'legionary' bronzes of Epad (DT III 3607) in the top of the demolition horizon (Poux and Demierre 2015, 523–525). Epad is generally equated to the Epasnactus of the Arverni, 'a loyal friend of Rome' (*BG* 8.44); these coins appear likely to date to the end of the war or shortly thereafter (Delestree and Tache 2007, 152; Pernet this volume).

In Britain, archaeological finds have confirmed a long chronology from the 2nd to the 1st century BC for potins (Holman 2016), parallel to their use in Gaul. Perhaps rashly, Gruel and Haselgrove (2007, 256–257) have suggested that four late Kentish potins found in a mid-1st-century BC context at Corent, less than 8 km from the site of Caesar's defeat at Gergovie, arrived in the Auvergne with his troops in 52 BC following the invasions of Britain. Other Kentish potins have been found in northern France, including some from early military sites (*e.g.* Liercourt-Erondelle); while speculative, it is frankly difficult to think of a better reason why the four outliers should have ended up in central Gaul at this date! If this is correct, the Kentish series was already in its final stages by the time of Caesar's invasions, rather than continuing through the later 1st century BC (Allen 1971).

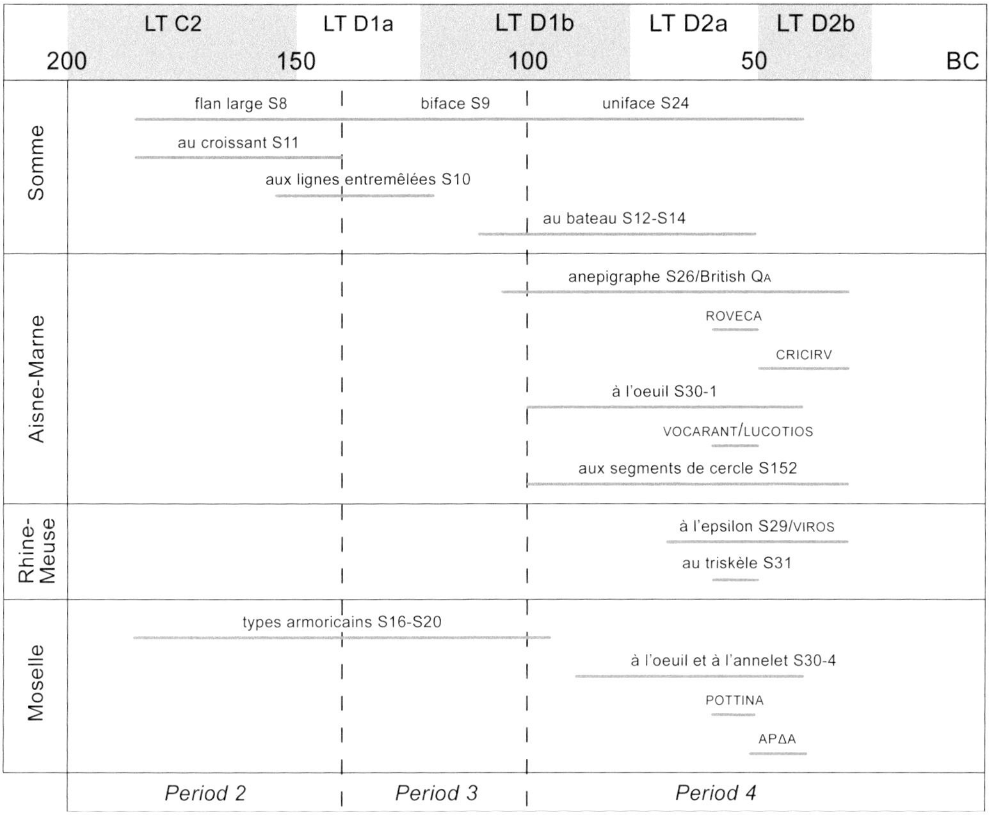

Figure 13.5 The chronology of gold coinages in northern Gaul in the 2nd and 1st centuries BC (adapted from Sillon 2014, fig. 400).

The dating of gold coinage

If most Gaulish base metal and silver coinages can be fairly confidently dated, this is still far from true for gold in Belgic Gaul or both gold and early silver in Britain. Although a broad consensus exists over the mid-1st-century BC end date of Scheers' Gallic War series, by the 1990s there were archaeological grounds to propose that some of these types began significantly earlier and had a longer life span (Pion 1996; Wigg and Riederer 1998; Haselgrove 1999). Twenty years on, there has unfortunately been no major breakthrough. One school of thought (including this author) regards the principal late Belgic gold series as spanning the first two-thirds of the 1st century BC, but with a few exceptions they are not more closely datable (Sillon *et al.* 2011; Doyen 2014; Sillon 2014; 2016; Figure 13.5). Others still prefer to see some, if not all, of these types as wartime coinages, even linked to particular campaigns (*e.g.* Roymans 2004, 31–53; Roymans and Scheers 2012; Sills 2013; 2017).[15] As with the controversy over potin (above), individual gold coin finds from early contexts have been doubted as possibly intrusive or misdated (*e.g.* Sills 2017, 706–707), and there are not yet enough stratified finds to build up consistent trends and thereby expose outliers, as eventually became possible for potins.

This is not the place to rehearse the intricacies of the numismatic arguments used to attribute these gold series to the Gallic War, but I would like to add to my earlier points about methodology. First, without any direct knowledge of why Iron Age coins were minted, the approach is invariably the same (Burnett 1996, 9): to invoke an analogy from another context, usually the Classical world, and support its application with textual evidence or further examples from other places or periods. It is hard, however, to see a definitive way of validating a given model; nor does the source of the analogy being fairly close in space and time to late Iron Age societies in north-west Europe necessarily make them any more fit for purpose. Second, it is just hypothesis that the specific features of these gold coinages (their volume, a decline in weight and fineness, the pattern of hoarding) can *only* be explained in the context of the Gallic War (Burnett 1996, 6–7). There are indeed documented instances linking all these traits with episodes of conflict, as noted earlier, but also many examples without this correlation.[16] Third, and closely related, is the matter of time depth. Here the element of smoke and mirrors is particularly pervasive. Compressed into a short period, the changes appear dramatic, but viewed in an extended timescale of 50–75 years, the same developments become less out of the ordinary – although we still have to explain why they occurred, and indeed also why the rate of change in gold coinage was now much greater compared to the preceding centuries.

One quite simple answer might be a rise in demand for gold coins. New estimates of the number of dies used to strike GBE uniface staters (de Jersey 2009, 265–266; Sills 2017, 702, fig. 159) suggest that these and other late Belgic gold coinages were larger than I calculated 35 years ago (Haselgrove 1984), even at a conservative estimate of output per die.[17] Although de Jersey's (2009) experiments suggest that *c.* 350,000 GBE2 uniface staters could have been produced in a very short period of time, extrapolating the metal resources required for this one issue – 1270 kg of gold, 636 kg of silver and 210 kg of copper – to late Belgic gold coinages in their entirety, arguably strengthens the case for striking over an extended period. At the outset of the war, calling in valuables and earlier coins could have created additional metal stocks (Haselgrove 1984, 91; de Jersey 2009, 267), but it is less easy to see how minting on this scale could have been sustained for a further six years, even with reductions in weight and fineness. There seems to be an implicit assumption, based on the analytical results and the trend line they generate (Cowell *et al.* 1987; Sillon 2014) that each new issue involved the recycling of existing coins adulterated to the new standard – at least I am not aware of anything published to the contrary. Yet large-scale recall and melting down of coins in circulation would surely have been more difficult after 57 BC, and, in any case, we know that large quantities of the earlier uniface staters ended up in Britain (Sills 2017, 701), where they were effectively beyond reach.

On these grounds, a longer timescale for these coinages is perhaps to be preferred and it is high time to start to think about what circumstances could have led to a greatly increased demand for gold coins in La Tène D1 compared to earlier. The obvious answer would seem to lie in the increased monetization from 150 BC onward evident in the rapid proliferation of silver coins throughout Celtic Gaul, and of potin there and in Belgic Gaul. In the latter zone, this could easily have translated into gold, too, being used more frequently and in a wider range of transactions, be they political, economic or socio-religious. Yet the Gallic War model requires us to believe that in the north, gold minting continued essentially at the same level until the 50s, notwithstanding the intensifying use of potin. If we take the opposite view of the chronology, however, minting gold coins in far greater numbers than before, even if spread over longer, would have had a significant impact on metal stocks, which in turn would explain the observed reductions in weight and fineness between issues as well as the care taken in alloying to maintain the colour of the gold. In this scenario, the major change in metal stock in Belgic Gaul around the start of the 1st century BC revealed by metal analysis (Sillon 2014; 2017), probably as a result of the mixing of gold from east of the Rhine with the existing stock, may also be pertinent.

Hoards pose the same problems of perception as minting. In Britain, much ink has been spilled over whether or not a group of broad similar silver hoards from Norfolk, many of which contain Roman *denarii*, constitute a single, short-lived horizon associated with the Boudiccan revolt of AD 60/61– the most recent assessment suggests that they do (Talbot 2017). As noted above, we need to distinguish more systematically between circulation wear and die wear of hoarded coins, as this can have implications both for the dating of different types and the date of deposition. Interpreting these measures, however, again begs questions about how Iron Age coins were produced and used, which we cannot answer except by resorting to analogy, so we need to be cautious in applying them. Interestingly, Icenian gold and silver are rarely found with extreme circulation wear (in contrast to Roman coins in the same hoards), yet hoard content is biased towards the most recent types, as if they come from a revolving pool of coinage (Talbot 2017, 121–123), which rather underlines the difficulties.

Where we reach firmer ground with hoards is that the growing number recovered through controlled investigation on both sides of the Channel are allowing an increasing number of hoards to be placed in an archaeological context or, at least, in a secure landscape setting, from which various patterns are emerging (Roymans *et al.* 2012; Bland *et al.* forthcoming). In the short term this is unlikely to resolve the problem of chronology. Many Belgic gold hoards come from locations with a possible religious significance, such as bogs or springs, but this does not preclude the coins having been hidden in periods of unrest (Haselgrove 1999, 151); emergency hoards could still have been safeguarded in traditional ways by placing them in the safekeeping of the gods with an intention of later recovery (Roymans and Scheers

2012, 20; Bradley 2017, 47). At present, there are certainly no indications that the Gallic War led to a pattern of gold hoarding in a form or forms that differed radically from pre-existing cultural traditions. There are, however, features of the hoarding record that deserve more thorough consideration. Why for example are S30 'eye' staters only rarely found in hoards, whereas the broadly contemporary GBE uniface and S29 'epsilon' staters were both deposited in numerous hoards? Why, too, if Class 5–6 uniface staters were struck in even greater quantity than the preceding types – as the new die estimates suggest (Sills 2017, 702, fig. 159) – do they feature in only two of the 30 recorded hoards containing over five coins (Sills 2017, 703, table 37)? Lastly, if the Gallic War did indeed lead to hoarding on both sides of the Channel, why on the short chronology preferred by most British numismatists do a mere 25 insular hoards close with 'wartime' issues, as against 121 hoards ending with coins attributed to 50–20 BC (de Jersey 2014, 14–23)?

Conclusion – where next?

If we confine ourselves to a broad La Tène D1–D2 dating for the latest Belgic gold, it seems to me that we are on reasonably secure ground, but for most types to assign more precise dates is to pretend to a knowledge which is as yet unattainable (cf. Burnett 1996, 7); unless and until we can develop a robust independent chronology for the major series, we are doomed to largely fruitless discussion.

What prospect is there of this happening? There are grounds for optimism. Archaeological chronology for the late Iron Age is increasingly subject to check and refinement by independent dating methods such as dendrochronology, as at Mont Beuvray and elsewhere (Durost *et al.* 2008; Guichard *et al.* 2018, 205, fig. 59). Thanks to large-scale development-led archaeology on both sides of the Channel, new coins are continually coming to light in secure archaeological contexts – on settlements and in burials – and while gold coins are not common (Martin *et al.* 2016, 51–55), it may be hoped that they too will gradually stack up to provide clear trends and reveal genuine anomalies.

In northern France, excavated finds include a GBC stater, three *globules-à-la-croix* and an Armorican boar stater at Urville-Nacqueville in the Cherbourg peninsula, three from an enclosure ditch and two from a surface spread at this later 2nd-century BC settlement (Lefort 2015). There are also a number of gold hoards from enclosure ditches and buildings, as at Chaize-le-Vicomte, Ifs ZAC-Object'Ifs, Laniscat, and Saint Denis-lès-Sens.[18] Most are of non-Belgic types, but in 2011 two deposits of GBE staters and GBD quarters were discovered in the ditch of a La Tène D2 enclosure at Sin-le-Noble, one of them associated with a torc and ring (Sillon 2014, 405–413). Coins from burials remain rare in any metal, an exception being Vaugrinon, in central France, where six graves contained potins (Riquier 2004).

In Britain, GBE uniface staters have been found excavating Iron Age sites at Northfleet in Kent, and near Cambridge (Sherlock 2018, 20). The lack of an independent archaeological chronology in Britain is starting to be redressed by radiocarbon dating and Bayesian modelling. At Westhampnett, a posterior density estimate for a grave containing a British AF2 quarter stater (Sills 2017, 296) falls between burials with Nauheim brooches and those containing Almgren 65 types (Fitzpatrick *et al.* 2017); this implies an early 1st-century BC date for these insular derivatives of GBD. A radiocarbon date on the wooden core of a torc associated with GBA and GBC-3 staters in Snettisham Hoard F indicates that the torc is of the early 2nd century BC at very latest (Garrow *et al.* 2008). Radiocarbon has also been used to confirm the 3rd-century BC date of a storage pit containing an early half stater of Hesperange type and La Tène C1 pottery at Thézy-Glimont in Picardy (Le Béchennec 2016, 307–308; Sillon 2014). With more radiocarbon determinations it should eventually become possible to model the date ranges of successive gold coinages on both sides of the Channel.

Finally, we may hope that further study of the Le Câtillon II hoard and its relationship to Le Câtillon I could yet help bridge the continental and insular chronologies. Like Le Câtillon I, the 2011 find contained early South-Western issues, much thin silver and various other non-Armorican types, including *globules-à-la-croix* (de Jersey this volume). The Le Câtillon I brooches are La Tène D2a types and no longer require a post-Caesarian date for the hoard (Fitzpatrick and Megaw 1987), which in any case is quite different in character to definite post-war hoards. That being so, we should not overlook its two British B staters, derived at some removes from GBC, and its GBD-3 quarter, a series now seen as coeval with the uniface staters rather than their parent series (Sills 2017). If Allen was correct that these three coins obtained their wear in circulation, they could yet prove as significant for coin chronologies on both sides of the Channel as he surmised. Only time will tell.

Notes

1 The following abbreviations are used in this chapter for coin types: DT = Delestrée and Tache 2002–2007; GB = Gallo-Belgic; LT = de la Tour 1892; RRC = Crawford 1974; S = Scheers 1977.

2 This total excludes two Belgic series in the name of Caesar's legate, Aulus Hirtius, author of *BG* Book 8. Both are more likely to have been struck in 45–44 BC, when Hirtius returned to Gaul as *Imperator* (S153; S162-I; Haselgrove 1999, 152).

3 Some other leaders named on coins must have been known to Caesar. A prime candidate is the Togirix of the common east Gaulish silver series. His late issues – thought to be post-war – bear the legend Q. Julius Togirix (DT 3251), presumably a reward for services rendered to Caesar (always assuming they are one and the same person).

4 Even when imitation is certain, there can be difficulties over dating, as on Hirtius' bronze coins (S162-I), which copy Caesar's elephant *denarii* (RRC 443/1). Burnett *et al.* (1992, 148) argue that S162-I may date to 51–50 BC rather than the 40s because they omit the title Imperator, which occurs on S153 – and that Sydenham's (1952) dating of the elephant *denarii* (54–51 BC) is therefore to be preferred to Crawford's (49–48 BC). I doubt the validity of the argument – Belgic coins do not follow the same conventions as Roman issues and the Hirtius series were issued by different Belgic peoples (Haselgrove 1999, 152, n. 186). A later date is supported by

their circulation pattern and affinities with Treveran types in the name of C. Carinas, Roman governor in 31–30 BC (S162-II). This provides a useful reminder, however, that even Roman coins are not always as securely dated as we might want to believe.

5 *Inter alia*, Blanchet rejects a late 3rd-century BC starting date proposed by Lelewel (1840, 141) for GBE uniface staters, now dated by many scholars to the 50s BC.

6 Another fruit of the research initiated by Napoléon's *Commission de la Topographie des Gaules*, along with the Bibliothèque Nationale catalogue (Muret and Chabouillet 1889).

7 The term Gallo-Belgic is applied to six main series, A–F/G. Given their circulation on both sides of the Channel, Gallo-British would actually seem a more appropriate term, but Gallo-Belgic is too well established to be easily dropped.

8 Including several with Caesarian links (*e.g.* Alesia, Bibracte, Gergovie, Orleans, Pommiers) as well as many other prominent sites (*e.g.* Corent, La Tène, Martburg). In Britain, only a handful of archaeological finds were known even in 1890 when Evans published his Supplement to *The Coins of the Ancient Britons*.

9 The 1990s finds, which are mostly from Camps B and C, raise the proportion of potins to 15.6%.

10 Two key planks in Allen's argument were the association of GBD and GBE in the Weybourne hoard and of GBD, Kentish potins and torcs at Snettisham further around the Norfolk coast. Allen also now accepted that Caesar's mention of *aes* in Britain (*BG* 5, 12) probably referred to Kentish potins.

11 As too had Scheers (1977, 116, 886–887), in her case on the grounds that the light-weight thin silver coins in the hoard, some of them of British origin, were more likely to be a post-war development.

12 What view Allen took of Scheers' scheme is unclear. Although her 1972 paper appeared three years before his death in 1975, the only reference I can find – in his posthumously published Rhind lectures – merely cites Scheers' dating of the Treveran ruler Arda to the 40s BC as supporting the view that Belgic gold coinage did not cease suddenly on Caesar's victory (Allen 1980, 80).

13 Formerly British QA, renamed GBG following the recognition that these coins, which stand at the head of an extensive British series, are probably of Continental origin (Sills 2017, 18–21, 707–9).

14 The publication of the Lattes-3 hoard of monnaies à la croix (Py 2006, 657, 1031–1145) excludes the solitary potin (DT 3509) as not reliably associated – although it was the only 'odd' coin found sieving earth from the findspot. The hoard is dated to the mid-2nd century BC, and as DT 3509 potins are now known from both site and burial finds of this date in their home territory in central Gaul (Riquier 2004), there is no reason to doubt the association at Lattes.

15 Roymans and Scheers (2012, 9, 29), for example, believe that it is now possible to distinguish a late group of coinages struck in the 50s BC, including S29 'epsilon' staters and S31 'triskeles' staters, and an older group, which included the first three classes of GBE uniface staters.

16 Even for Rome, the correlation between minting and conflict is not perfect. Heavy military expenditure in 91–89 BC is reflected in the scale of minting, but not for 110 and 108 BC (Hopkins 1980, 111), and minting under Domitian shows no link to the German wars in his reign (Burnett 1996, 6).

17 De Jersey (2009, 266) uses the same estimate of 1000 coins per die as Haselgrove (1984). Adopting the oft-quoted average of 10,000 coins per die would give an output of 1,353,000 for GBE-2, requiring 12,710 kg of gold. The figure of 10,000 was obtained from striking silver, however, rather than the harder ternary alloys of GBE, but a figure higher than 1000 is not improbable. On different methods of quantifying coinages and the attendant pitfalls, see Bland (2018) and references therein.

18 For further information on gold coin hoards from settlements, see Haselgrove and Webley (2016) and Martin *et al.* (2016).

Bibliography

Allen, D.F. (1936) British tin coinage of the Iron Age. *Transactions of the International Numismatic Congress London 1936*, 351–357.

Allen, D.F. (1960) The origins of coinage in Britain: a re-appraisal. In S.S. Frere (ed.), *Problems of the Iron Age in Southern Britain*, 97–308. London, Institute of Archaeology Occasional Paper 11.

Allen, D.F. (1971) British potin coins: a review. In D. Hill and M. Jesson (eds), *The Iron Age and its Hillforts*, 127–154. Southampton, University of Southampton.

Allen, D.F. (1973) The coins found at La Tène. *Études Celtiques* 13, 477–521.

Allen, D.F. (1980) *The Coins of the Ancient Celts* (ed. D. Nash). Edinburgh, Edinburgh University Press.

Barral, P. and Fichtl, S. (eds) (2012) *Regards sur la chronologie de la fin de l'âge du Fer (IIIe–Ier siècle avant notre ère) en Gaule non méditerranéenne*. Glux-en-Glenne, Collection Bibracte 22.

Bayard, D. (2018). L'occupation des oppida gaulois par l'armée romaine à la fin de la République. L'exemple du 'Camp César' de la Chaussée-Tirancourt (80). In M. Reddé (ed.), *L'armées romaines en Gaule à l'époque républicaine. Nouveaux témoignages archéologiques*, 155–178. Glux-en-Glenne, Collection Bibracte 28.

Besly, E. (2015) Mapping conflict: coin hoards of the English Civil War. In J. Naylor and R. Bland (eds), *Hoarding and Deposition of Metalwork from the Bronze Age to the 20th Century: A British Perspective*, 181–200. Oxford, British Archaeological Reports British Series 615.

Blanchet, A. (1905) *Traité des monnaies Gauloises*. Paris, Leroux.

Bland, R. (2018) Quantifying the size of a coinage: die studies or coin finds. In N.T. Elkins and J. DeRose Evans (eds), *Concordia Disciplinarum. Essays on Ancient Coinage, History, and Archaeology in Honor of William E. Metcalf*, 223–233. New York, American Numismatic Society, Numismatic Studies 38.

Bland, R., Chadwick, A., Ghey, E., Haselgrove, C., Mattingly, D., Rogers, A. and Taylor, J. (forthcoming) *Iron Age and Roman Coin Hoards in Britain*. Oxford, Oxbow Books.

Bradley, R. (2017) *A Geography of Offerings. Deposits of Valuables in the Landscapes of Ancient Europe*. Oxford, Oxbow Books.

Brooke, G.C. (1933) The Philippus in the West and the Belgic invasions of Britain. *Numismatic Chronicle* 13, 88–138.

Brunaux, J-L. and Gruel, K. (eds) (1987) *Monnaies Gauloises découvertes en fouilles*. Paris, Errance, Dossiers de Protohistoire 1.

Burnett, A. (1996) 'Gallo-Belgic' coins and Britain. In B. Raftery (ed.), *Sites and Sights of the Iron Age*, 5–11. Oxford, Oxbow Monograph 56.

Burnett, A., Amandry, M. and Ripollès, P.P. (1992) *Roman Provincial Coinage I: From the Death of Caesar to the Death of Vitellius (44 BC–AD 69)*. London, British Museum Press & Paris, Bibliothèque Nationale.

Colbert de Beaulieu, J.-B (1955a) Numismatique celtique d'Alésia. *Revue Belge de Numismatique* 101, 55–83.

Colbert de Beaulieu, J.-B (1955b) Peut-on dater par la numismatique l'occupation d'un oppidum? L'exemple de Pommiers. *Revue Archéologique de l'Est et du Centre-Est* 6(3), 260–270.

Colbert de Beaulieu, J.-B. (1957) Le trésor de Jersey-11 et la numismatique celtique des deux Bretagnes. *Revue Belge de Numismatique* 103, 47–88.

Colbert de Beaulieu, J.-B. (1962) Les monnaies gauloises au nom des chefs mentionnés dans les *Commentaires* de César. In M. Renard (ed.), *Hommages à A. Grenier*, 419–462. Brussels, Latomus 58.

Colbert de Beaulieu, J.-B. (1966) La monnaie de Caletedu et les zones du statère et du denier en Gaule. *Revue Archéologique du Centre* 18, 101–129.

Colbert de Beaulieu, J.-B. (1970) Les potins dits 'à la tête diabolique', un monnayage indigène de la Gaule en voie de romanisation. *Revue Belge de Numismatique* 96, 97–123.

Colbert de Beaulieu, J.-B. (1973a) *Traité de Numismatique Celtique I. Méthodologie des ensembles*. Paris, Les Belles Lettres.

Colbert de Beaulieu, J.-B. (1973b) Chronologie des bronzes Gaulois et British potin coins. *Revue Belge de Numismatique* 119, 5–41.
Colbert de Beaulieu, J.-B. and Fischer, B. (1998) *Les légendes monétaires. Recueil des Inscriptions Gauloises 4*. Paris, Gallia supplément 45.
Cowell, M. (1992) An analytical survey of the British gold coinage. In M. Mays (ed.), *Celtic Coinage: Britain and Beyond*, 207–233. Oxford, British Archaeological Reports British Series 222.
Cowell, M., Oddy, W. and Burnett, A. (1987) Celtic coinage in Britain: new hoards and recent analyses. *British Numismatic Journal* 57, 1–23.
Crawford, M.H. (1974) *Roman Republican Coinage*. Cambridge, Cambridge University Press.
Crawford, M.H. (1985) *Coinage and Money under the Roman Republic*. London, Methuen.
Creighton, J. (2000) *Coins and Power in Late Iron Age Britain*. Cambridge, Cambridge University Press.
Debord, J. (1990) Les fouilles du site gaulois tardif de Villeneuve-Saint-Germain (Aisne). *Fédération des Sociétés d'Histoire et d'Archéologie de l'Aisne Mémoires* 35, 137–170.
Debord, J. (1995) A propos de la chronologie des sites de Pommiers et de Villeneuve-Saint-Germain (Aisne). *Revue Archéologique de Picardie 1995* 1/2, 205–208.
Debord, J. (2001) Noviodunum Suessionum: Pommiers ou Villeneuve-Saint-Germain? *Mémoires du Soissonais* 2 (1999–2001), 7–30.
Déchelette, J. (1902) Montefortino et Ornavasso, étude sur la civilisation des Gaulois Cisalpins. *Revue Archéologique* I, XL, janvier–juin, 245–283.
Déchelette, J. (1914) *Manuel d'Archéologie préhistorique, celtique et gallo-romaine, II. Archéologie celtique ou protohistorique. Troisième partie: Second âge du fer ou époque de La Tène*. Paris, Picard.
de Jersey, P. (2009) Some experiments in Iron Age coin production and some implications for the production of Gallo-Belgic E. In J. van Heesch and I. Heeren (eds), *Coinage in the Iron Age. Essays in Honour of Simone Scheers*, 257–269. London, Spink.
de Jersey, P. (2014) *Coin Hoards in Iron Age Britain*. London, British Numismatic Society Special Publication 12.
Delestrée, L.-P. (1996) *Monnayages et peuples Gaulois du Nord-Ouest*. Paris, Errance.
Delestrée, L-P. (1999) Les bronzes coulés imités de Marseille dans la région parisienne. *Cahiers Numismatiques* 141, 17–25.
Delestrée, L.-P. and Boisard, C. (2010) Les monnaies gauloises du camp militaire de Liércourt-Érondelle (Somme). In D. Hollard (ed.), *L'armée et la monnaie II*, 21–42, pl. I–III. Paris, Recherches et Travaux de la SÉNA 3.
Delestrée, L.-P. and Tache, M. (2002) *Nouvel Atlas des monnaies Gauloises I. De la Seine au Rhin*. Saint-Germain-en-Laye, Éditions Commios.
Delestrée, L.-P. and Tache, M. (2004) *Nouvel Atlas des monnaies Gauloises II. De la Seine à la Loire moyenne*. Saint-Germain-en-Laye, Éditions Commios.
Delestrée, L.-P. and Tache, M. (2007) *Nouvel Atlas des monnaies Gauloises III. La Celtique, du Jura et des Alpes à la façade Atlantique*. Saint-Germain-en-Laye, Éditions Commios.
Delestrée, L.-P., Boisard, C. and Boulenger, D. (2006) Les monnaies gauloises du site fortifié de la Chaussée-Tirancourt (Somme): coexistence d'un faciès militaire et d'un faciès indigène. In D. Hollard (ed.), *L'armée et la monnaie*, 7–25, pls I–II. Paris, Recherches et Travaux de la SÉNA 1.
Doyen, J.-M. (2014) *Structure et dynamique des flux monétaires chez les Rèmes: modélisation d'un traceur socio-économique entre 275/250 av. et 68 apr. J.-C.* Mémoire HDR, University of Nice-Sophia Antipolis.
Durost, S., Rossignol, B., Lambert, G.-N. and Bernard, V. (2008) Climat, Guerre des Gaules et dendrochronology du chêne (*Quercus* sp.) du Ier siècle av. J.-C. *ArcheoSciences revue d'archéométrie* 32, 31–50.
Duval, A., Morel, J.-P. and Roman, Y. (1990) *Gaule interne et Gaule méditerranéenne au IIe et Ier siècles avant J.-C. Confrontations chronologiques*. Paris, Revue Archéologique de Narbonnaise supplément 21.
Evans, J. (1864) *The Coins of the Ancient Britons*. London, Russell Smith.

Evans, J. (1875) The coinage of the ancient Britons and natural selection. *Notices of the Proceedings of the Royal Institution of Great Britain* 7, 476–487.

Evans, J. (1890) *The Coins of the Ancient Britons. Supplement.* London, Quaritch.

Fischer, B. (2001) Les monnaies gauloises: enseignements et questions. In M. Reddé and S. von Schnurbein (eds), *Alésia. Fouilles et recherches franco-allemandes sur les travaux militaires romains autour du Mont-Auxois (1991–1997)*, 11–19. Paris, Mémoires de l'Académie des Inscriptions et Belles-Lettres 22.

Fitzpatrick, A.P. (1992) The roles of Celtic coinage in south-east England. In M. Mays (ed.), *Celtic Coinage: Britain and Beyond*, 1–32. Oxford, British Archaeological Reports British Series 222.

Fitzpatrick, A.P. and Megaw, J.V.S. (1987) Further finds from the Le Câtillon hoard. *Proceedings of the Prehistoric Society* 53, 433–444.

Fitzpatrick, A.P., Hamilton, D. and Haselgrove, C. (2017) Radiocarbon dating and modelling of a late Iron Age cremation cemetery at Westhampnett, West Sussex, UK. *Archäologisches Korrespondenzblatt* 47 (3), 359–381.

Forrer, R. (1908) Der Goldstaterfund von Tayac-Libourne, ein Dokument des Cimbern-und Tigurinerzuges von 113–105 vor Chr. In R. Forrer, *Keltische Numismatik der Rhein-und Donauland*, 316–43. Strasbourg, Trübner.

Furger-Gunti, A. and von Kaenel, H.M. (1976) Die Keltische Fundmünzen aus Basel. *Schweizerische Numismatische Rundschau* 55, 35–76.

Garrow, D., Gosden, C., Hill, J.D. and Bronk-Ramsey, C. (2009) Dating Celtic art: a major radiocarbon dating programme of Iron Age and early Roman metalwork in Britain. *Archaeological Journal* 166, 79–123.

Gruel, K. (1989) *La monnaie chez les Gaulois.* Paris, Errance.

Gruel, K. (ed.) (1995) *Les potins gaulois: typologie, diffusion, chronologie, état de la question.* Paris, Gallia 52.

Gruel, K. (2005) L'alignement du denier gaulois sur l'étalon romain, datation et impact économique. In J. Metzler and D. Wigg (eds), *Die Kelten und Rom: neue numismatische Forschungen*, 29–38. Mainz, Studien zu Fundmünzen der Antike 19.

Gruel, K. and Haselgrove, C. (2006), Le développement de l'usage monétaire à l'âge du fer en gaule et dans les régions voisines. In C. Haselgrove (ed.), *Les mutations de la fin de l'âge du Fer*, 117–138. Glux-en-Glenne, Collection Bibracte 12/4.

Gruel, K. and Haselgrove, C. (2007) British potins abroad. A new find from central France and the Iron Age in southeast England. In C. Gosden, H. Hamerow, P. de Jersey and G. Lock (eds), *Communities and Connections. Essays in Honour of Barry Cunliffe*, 240–262. Oxford, Oxford University Press.

Gruel, K and Popovitch, L. (2007) *Les Monnaies gauloise et romaines de l'oppidum de Bibracte.* Glux-en-Glenne, Collection Bibracte 13.

Guichard, V., Pion. P., Malacher, F. and Collis, J. (1993) A propos de la circulation monétaire en Gaule chevelue au IIe et Ier siècles av. J.-C. *Revue Archéologique du Centre* 32, 25–55.

Guichard, V., Meunier, A. and Paris, P. (2018) Chronique des recherches sur le Mont Beuvray. *Revue Archéologique de l'Est* 67, 151–211.

Haselgrove, C. (1984) Warfare and its aftermath as reflected by the precious metal coinage of Belgic Gaul. *Oxford Journal of Archaeology* 3, 81–105.

Haselgrove, C. (1987) *Iron Age Coinage in South-East England: The Archaeological Context.* Oxford, British Archaeological Reports British Series 174.

Haselgrove, C. (1988) The archaeology of British potin coinage. *Archaeological Journal* 145, 99–122.

Haselgrove, C. (1995) Les potins 'au personnage courant'. In K. Gruel (ed.), *Les potins gaulois: typologie, diffusion, chronologie, état de la question*, 51–59. Paris, Gallia 52.

Haselgrove, C. (1996) Roman impact on rural settlement and society in southern Picardy. In N. Roymans (ed.), *From the Sword to the Plough: Three Studies on the Earliest Romanization of Northern Gaul*, 127–188. Amsterdam, Amsterdam Archaeological Studies 1.

Haselgrove, C. (1999) The development of Iron Age coinage in Belgic Gaul. *Numismatic Chronicle* 159, 111–168.

Haselgrove, C. (2005) A new approach to analysing the circulation of Iron Age coinage. *Numismatic Chronicle* 165, 129–174.

Haselgrove, C. and Webley, L. (2015) Lost purses and loose change? Coin deposition on settlements in Iron Age Europe. In C. Haselgrove and S. Krmnicek (eds), *The Archaeology of Money*, 85–113. Leicester, Leicester Archaeology Monograph 24.

Hawkes, C. and Dunning, G.C. (1930) The Belgae of Gaul and Britain. *Archaeological Journal* 87, 150–335.

Holman, D. (2016) A new classification system for the Flat Linear potin coinage. *British Numismatic Journal* 86, 1–67.

Hopkins, K. (1980) Taxes and trade in the Roman empire (200 BC–AD 400). *Journal of Roman Studies* 70, 101–125.

Kaenel, G. (1990) La dendrochronologie appliquée au IIe et Ier siècle avant J.C. In A. Duval, J.-P. Morel and Y. Roman, *Gaule interne et Gaule méditerranéenne au IIe et Ier siècles avant J.-C. Confrontations chronologiques*, 321–326. Paris, Revue Archéologique de Narbonnaise supplément 21.

Kaenel, G. (2006) Agglomérations et oppida de la fin de l'âge du Fer. Une vision synthétique. In C. Haselgrove (ed.), *Les mutations de la fin de l'âge du Fer*, 17–39. Glux-en-Glenne, Collection Bibracte 12/4.

Kellner, H.-J. (1970) Der Fund von Tayac, ein Zeugnis des Cimbernzuges? *Jahrbuch der Numismatik und Geldgeschichte* 20, 13–47.

Kent, J.P.C. (1978) The origins and development of Celtic gold coinage in Britain. *Actes du Colloque International d'Archéologie, Rouen*, 313–324. Rouen, Musée départemental des antiquités de Seine-Maritime et Circonscription des antiquités historiques de Haute-Normandie.

Lambot, B. and Delestrée, L.-P. (1991) Des séries de potins du Belgium antérieures au début du Ier siècle avant J.C. *Bulletin de la Société Archéologique Champenoise* 84, 67–79.

La Tour, H. de (1892) *Atlas des Monnaies Gauloises*. Paris, Plon.

Le Béchennec, Y. (2016) Thézy-Glimont (Somme), du site au territoire. In G. Blancquaert and F. Malrain (eds), *Evolution des sociétés gauloises du Second âge du Fer, entre mutations internes et influences externes (Actes du 38e colloque international de l'AFEAF, Amiens 2014)*, 303–316. Amiens, RAP Numero spécial 30.

Lefort, A. (2015). *Contribution bas-normande à une archéologie des relations transmanches à la fin de l'âge du Fer. Échanges matériels et culturels*. Ph.D. thesis, University of Bourgogne-Franche-Comté.

Lelewel, J. (1840) *Études numismatiques et archéologiques, Vol. I: type Gaulois ou Celtique. Atlas*. Brussels, Voglet.

Martin, S., Malrain, F. and Lorho, T. (2016) La circulation monétaire dans les campagnes gauloises de l'âge du Fer. Éléments de synthèse à partir des découvertes répertoriées dans la base de données des établissements ruraux du second âge du Fer. In S. Martin (ed.), *Monnaies et monétisation dans les campagnes de la Gaule du Nord et de l'Est, de l'âge du Fer à l'Antiquité tardive*, 33–59. Bordeaux, Ausonius, Scripta Antiqua 91.

Metzler, J. (1995) *Das Treverische Oppidum auf dem Titelberg*. Luxembourg, Dossiers d'Archéologie du Musée National d'Histoire et d'Art 3.

Miron, A. (1986) Das Gräberfeld von Horath. Untersuchungen zur Mittel- und Spätlatènezeit im Saar-Mosel-Raum. *Trierer Zeitschrift* 49, 7–198.

Miron, A. (1991) Die späte Eisenzeit in Hunsrück-Nahe-Raum: mittel- und spätlatènezeitliche Gräberfelder. In A. Haffner and A. Miron (eds), *Studien zur Eisenzeit im Hunsrück-Nahe-Raum*, 151–169. Trier, Trierer Zeitschrift Beiheft 13.

Muret, E. and Chabouillet, A. (1889) *Catalogue des monnaies gauloises de la Bibliothèque Nationale*. Paris, Plon.

Nash, D. (1975) The chronology of Celtic coinage in Gaul: the Arvernian 'hegemony' reconsidered. *Numismatic Chronicle* (Ser. 7) 15, 204–218.

Nash, D. (1987) *Coinage in the Celtic World*. London, Seaby.

Nieto, S. (2004) Monnaies Arvernes (Vercingétorix, Cas) en orichalque. *Revue Numismatique* 160, 5–25.

Nieto-Pelletier, S. and Olivier, J. (2016) Les statères aux types de Philippe II de Macédoine: de l'Égée à la Gaule, des origines aux imitations. *Revue Numismatique* 173, 171–229.

Pion, P. (1996) *Les habitats Laténiens tardifs de la Vallée de l'Aisne: contribution à la périodisation de la fin du second Âge du Fer en Gaule nord-orientale*. Ph.D. thesis, University of Paris I.

Pion, P. (2003) L'or des Rèmes. In S. Plouin and P. Jud (eds), *Habitats, mobiliers et groupes régionaux à l'âge du Fer*, 387–401. Dijon, Revue Archéologique de l'Est supplément 20.

Pion, P. (2008) 'La monnaie de l'absolu': un siècle de numismatique gauloise dans les chronologies du second âge du Fer. In A. Lehoërff (ed.), *Construire le temps. Histoire et méthodes des chronologies et calendriers des derniers millénaires avant notre ère en Europe occidentale (Actes du 30e colloque international de Halma-Ipel, Lille, 2006)*, 349–358. Glux-en-Glenne, Bibracte 16.

Pion, P. (2012) La monnaie mercenaire: une approche anthropologique des premiers monnayages celtiques au nord-ouest du complexe nord-alpin (IIIe siècle av. J.-C.). In P. Pion and B. Formoso (eds), *Monnaie antique, Monnaie modern, Monnaie d'ailleurs... Métissages et hybridations*, 151–164. Paris, De Boccard.

Polenz, H. (1982) Münzen in latènezeitlichen Gräbern Mitteleuropas aus der Zeit zwischen 300 und 50 vor Christi Geburt. *Bayerische Vorgeschichtsblätter* 47, 28–222.

Popovitch, L. (2001) Les monnaies Romaines. In M. Reddé and S. von Schnurbein (eds), *Alésia. Fouilles et recherches franco-allemandes sur les travaux militaires romains autour du Mont-Auxois (1991-1997)*, 69–84. Paris, Mémoires de l'Académie des Inscriptions et Belles-Lettres 22.

Poux, M. and Demierre, M. (2015) *Le sanctuaire de Corent (Puy-de-Dôme, Auvergne)*. Paris, Gallia supplément 62.

Py, M. (ed.) (2006) *Les monnaies préaugustéennes de Lattes et la circulation monétaire protohistorique en Gaule méridionale*. Lattes, Lattara 19.

Renfrew, C. (1974) British prehistory: changing configurations. In C. Renfrew (ed.), *British Prehistory: A New Outline*, 1–40. London, Duckworth.

Riquier, S. (2004) La nécropole gauloise de 'Vaugrignon' à Esvres-sur-Indre (Indre et Loire). *Revue Archéologique du Centre de la France* 43, 21–113.

Roymans, N. (1990) *Tribal Societies in Northern Gaul: An Anthropological Perspective*. Amsterdam, Cingula 12.

Roymans, N. (2004) *Ethnic Identity and Imperial Power: The Batavians in the Early Roman Empire*. Amsterdam, Amsterdam Archaeological Studies 10.

Roymans, N. and Scheers, S. (2012) Eight gold hoards from the Low Countries. A synthesis. In N. Roymans, G. Creemers and S. Scheers, *Late Iron Age Gold Hoards from the Low Countries and the Caesarian Conquest of Northern Gaul*, 1–46. Amsterdam, Amsterdam Archaeological Studies 18.

Roymans, N., Creemers, G. and Scheers, S. (2012) *Late Iron Age Gold Hoards from the Low Countries and the Caesarian Conquest of Northern Gaul*. Amsterdam, Amsterdam Archaeological Studies 18.

Saulcy, F. de (1867) Numismatiques des chefs gaulois mentionnés dans les *Commentaires* de César. *Annuaire de la Société numismatique et d'archéologie* 2, 1–32.

Scheers, S. (1969) *Les monnaies de la Gaule inspirées de celles de la république Romaine*. Leuven, University of Leuven.

Scheers, S. (1972) Coinage and currency of the Belgic tribes during the Gallic war. *British Numismatic Journal* 41, 1–6.

Scheers, S. (1977) *Traité de numismatique celtique II: La Gaule belgique*. Paris, Les Belles Lettres.

Scheers, S. (1987) La numismatique d'Alésia: quelques précisions. In C. Bémont, C. Deplace, B. Fischer, K. Gruel, C. Peyre and J.-Cl. Richard (eds), *Mélanges offerts au docteur Colbert de Beaulieu*, 747–52. Paris, Le Léopard d'Or.

Scheers, S. (2004) La naissance du monnayage d'or en Gaule d'après les influences étrangères. In K. Strobel (ed.), *Forschungen zur Monetarisierung und ökonomischen Funktionalisierung von Geld in den nordwestlichen Provinzen des Imperium Romanum. Die Entstehung eines europäische Wirtschaftraumes (Akten des 2. Trierer Symposiums zur antiken Wirtschafgeschichte)*, 7–26. Trier, Trierer Historische Forschungen 49.

Sherlock, S. (2018) Big archaeology: The A14 Cambridge to Huntingdon road scheme. *British Archaeology* 162, 16–25.

Sillon, C. (2014) *L'or monnayé dans le Nord de la Gaule. Recherches sur les monnaies d'or frappées dans le Nord de la Gaule entre le IIIe et le Ier siècle avant notre ère*. Ph.D. thesis, University of Orléans.

Sillon, C. (2016) La 'richesse relative des émissions' comme facteur chronologique: un modèle à dépasser. Le cas du nord de la Gaule. *Revue Belge de Numismatique* 162, 113–142.

Sillon, C., Nieto-Pelletier, S. and Doyen, J.-M. (2011) Archéologie et numismatique gauloise: une contribution du Cabinet des Médailles de Bruxelles à l'histoire des Rèmes et des Trévires. *In Monte Artium* 4, 129–151.

Sills, J. (2003) *Gaulish and Early British Coinage*. London, Spink.

Sills, J. (2013) Reversal of fortune: eye staters of the Treveri and Remi. In P.-M. Guihard and D. Hollard (eds), *De Nummis Gallicis. Mélanges de numismatique celtique offerts à Louis-Pol Delestrée*, 173–209. Paris, SÉNA.

Sills, J. (2017) *Divided Kingdoms: The Iron Age Gold Coinage of Southern England*. Aylsham, Chris Rudd.

Sydenham, E.A. (1952) *The Coinage of the Roman Republic*. London, Spink.

Talbot, J. (2017). *Made for Trade: A New View of Icenian Coinage*. Oxford, Oxbow Books.

Vaginay. M. and Guichard, V. (1988). *L'habitat gaulois de Feurs (Loire). Fouilles récentes (1978–1981)*. Paris, Documents d'Archéologie Française 14.

Wigg, D. and Riederer, J. 1998. Die Chronologie der Keltischen Münzprägung am Mittelrhein. In U. Peter (ed.), *Stephanos nomismatikos. Edith Schönert-Geiss zum 65. Geburtstag*, 661–74. Berlin.

Chapter 14

The island of Jersey: Focus of resistance or field of last resort?

Philip de Jersey

The discovery of the Le Câtillon II hoard in Jersey in June 2012, and its subsequent excavation under laboratory conditions, has provided an extraordinary opportunity to re-examine the Gallic War period in the Channel Islands and in the wider Armorican region. The sheer size of the hoard – almost 70,000 coins, plus a dozen gold torcs, silver and bronze ingots, and many other items of precious metal – is unparalleled in Armorica, and indeed further afield: it is by some distance the largest single hoard of Celtic or Iron Age coinage ever uncovered. It is by no means an isolated find, however. There are other hoards from Jersey and indeed at least one, and possibly two or three, more from the same field. These hoards have been interpreted in a fairly consistent fashion since the late 19th century, but such is the volume of material now known from the island that reconsideration of the traditional interpretation is arguably well overdue.

The Jersey hoards

Prior to the discovery of Le Câtillon II in 2012, at least eight or nine hoards of Iron Age coinage had been recovered from Jersey soil (Figure 14.1). The earliest known discoveries, made towards the end of the 18th century, are poorly recorded, but seem to have included 'a number of pieces' found at the Mont de la Ville megalithic monument in 1786 or 1787; perhaps two hundred coins 'in an iron pot ... near the great harbour', *c.* 1795; and 'a considerable quantity' in an earthenware pot near Rozel, *c.*1802 (Hawkes 1937, 124–125; Colbert de Beaulieu 1957a, 49–51). The identity of the 'great harbour' is uncertain and it is just possible, despite the reported difference in vessel, that the last two refer to the same discovery. The few coins which survive from these hoards, or were illustrated at the time, are almost all typical Coriosolite issues (see below).

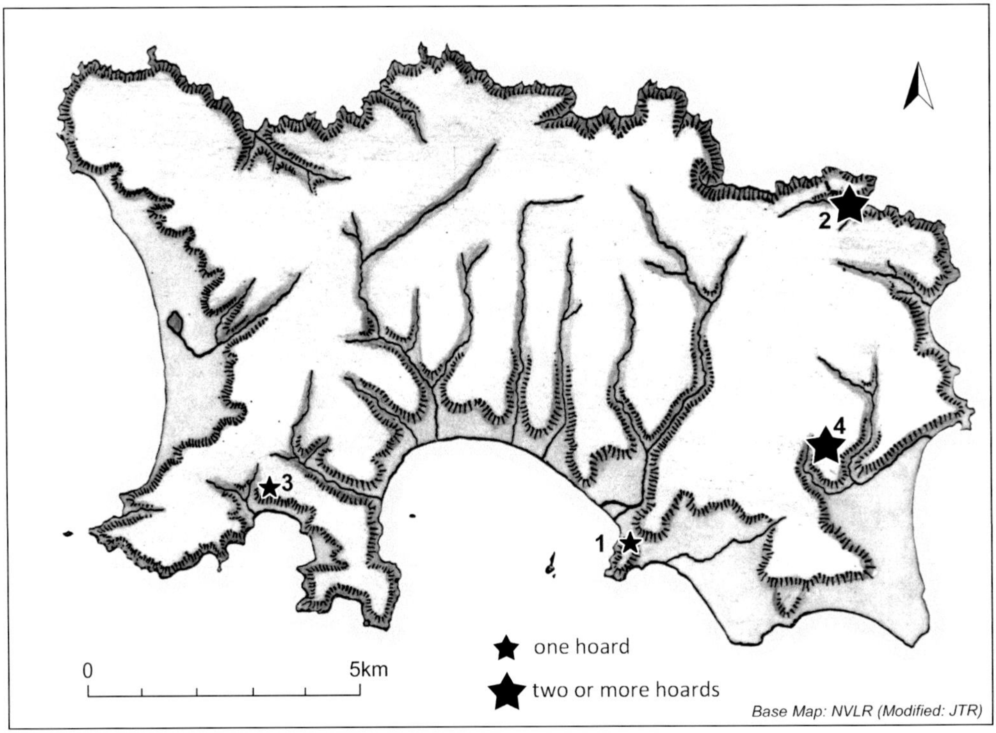

Figure 14.1 Map of Jersey showing the locations of (1) Mont de la Ville; (2) Rozel; (3) La Marquanderie; (4) Le Câtillon. Not marked: 'the great harbour'.

Subsequent discoveries are generally rather better recorded. There are at least four substantial hoards and one smaller find. All have relevance to the following discussion and so their contents will be briefly summarized here.

Rozel, 1820

A cliff fall at Rozel, within the promontory fort of Le Câtel de Rozel (Cunliffe 1992), revealed a large hoard almost entirely composed of Coriosolite billon staters. The Baron de Donop acquired 982 coins – possibly the entire hoard – and illustrated 760 of them in *Les médailles gallo-gaëliques* (1838). Colbert de Beaulieu (1957a, 52) considered the 760 line drawings to show 754 Coriosolite staters, two Coriosolite quarter staters and four 'Unelli' staters – probably equivalent to the 'Rybot types' from La Marquanderie (see below).

Rozel, 1875

One or perhaps more likely two hoards, discovered after heavy rain caused the collapse of a cliff at Rozel (Cable 1876, 29). Colbert de Beaulieu (1957a, 54–56) suggested that there were at least two separate deposits, one consisting mostly of Coriosolite staters

– perhaps several hundred, many of them heavily defaced – and the other a far more heterogeneous mix of central, northern and eastern Gaulish silver, with at least fourteen Roman *denarii* down to 39 BC (de Jersey 1994, 168–170). The contemporary accounts (the most useful of which is de Barthélemy 1884) indicate that this part of the deposit must have included at least 700 coins.

Rozel, 1883

A small hoard of eighteen coins in an earthenware jar, including Coriosolite staters and Roman coins, found close to the 1875 discovery (Cable 1886, 122–123). Cable (1886) suggested that there may have been more coins than the finder admitted. Those examined included a *denarius* of Mark Antony, *c.* 32 BC (Colbert de Beaulieu 1957a, 56).

La Marquanderie, 1935

The largest known hoard of Armorican coinage, until the 2012 discovery, was found in digging the foundations of a house at La Marquanderie, in the south-west of the island, on 22 April 1935. It contained approximately 12,000 staters, all but eight of them issues attributed to the Coriosolitae. The hoard was published by Major N.V.L. Rybot (1952), who identified these eight coins as 'intruders'. Although they have clear stylistic links to other lower Normandy coinages, at least six of them form a distinctive group that remained extremely rare until the discovery of Le Câtillon II, which contains more than one hundred examples. The significance of Rybot's 'intruders' will be considered below.

Le Câtillon I, 1957

On 22 January 1957, Peter Langlois moved a large stone in a field at Le Câtillon, in the parish of Grouville in south-eastern Jersey, to find beneath it something in the order of 2,500–3,000 coins, and various items of jewellery. The precise nature of the discovery was obscured at the time, and the contemporary accounts of the numismatic contents, by Colbert de Beaulieu (1957a; 1957b; 1958a; 1958b; 1959) and Derek Allen (1958; 1960, 297–301), suffered accordingly. It is unlikely now that the exact contents will ever be certain, but it seems to have been a single deposit, consisting of at least 2,280 Coriosolite staters and 43 Coriosolite quarter staters, together with a minimum of 160 other Armorican issues, a few coins from elsewhere in continental Gaul, and – crucially for questions of chronology – some 20 or 21 Gallo-Belgic and British coins. The items which accompanied the coins included fibulae and rings in silver and bronze, pieces of silver chain, a fragment possibly from a gold torc on an iron core, and other iron objects (Fitzpatrick and Megaw 1987).

At least two of these hoards – the non-Armorican element of Rozel (1875) and the small group from the same location (1883) – cannot have been buried before about 35 and 30 BC respectively, given the presence of Roman coins in both. In contrast, La

Marquanderie and Rozel (1820) consist solely of Armorican issues which, according to the conventional chronological framework, could have been deposited in the Gallic War period, or shortly thereafter – for the sake of argument between about 56 BC and 45 BC.

The dating of Le Câtillon I is more difficult, primarily because of uncertainty about the chronology of the British coins and some of the jewellery contained within the hoard. The British coins include six staters and six quarter staters attributed to the Durotriges, all in good silver (Allen 1960, 297–298). On the currently most widely accepted chronology for the British series – which essentially sees the development of a native gold coinage in most regions as consequent on the import of large quantities of Gallo-Belgic gold, during or very soon after the Gallic War – it is difficult to place the silver coinage of the Durotriges before the early 40s BC, if not a little later in the decade. Admittedly the examples of this coinage in Le Câtillon I are heavy and in good silver, which suggests that they date from near the beginning of this series, but we still have to allow time for the stylistic development visible from their predecessors struck in gold; and if the Durotrigan gold cannot have been struck before, say, 54 BC, then the silver coins which followed obviously cannot have been buried in 57 or 56 BC, the years when Caesar's troops were present on Armorican soil. A more realistic date for the burial of Le Câtillon I would thus be in the early or mid-40s BC; if we allow for a very rapid typological progression through gold and silver, then it is just about feasible that the heavy silver coins could have been produced towards the end of the 50s BC, and (on that basis) the hoard buried *c.* 50 BC. But unless our interpretation of the British coinage is seriously at fault, we simply cannot push the Durotrigan material in Le Câtillon I back to the mid-50s BC. This chronological difficulty is still more of an issue for Le Câtillon II, as we will see below.

Colbert de Beaulieu and Allen both considered that Le Câtillon I – and most of the other Coriosolite-dominated Jersey hoards – must have been buried during the Gallic War (de Jersey 2016, 165–166). Allen (1960, 297) commented that 'The date of burial [of Le Câtillon I] must be between Caesar's campaign against the Veneti in 56 BC and the completion of his campaigns in 51 BC'. Colbert was even more strongly in favour of burial in 56 BC, although he qualified this view slightly by suggesting that even if the hoards were not buried in that year, then they must have been assembled in 56 BC (Colbert de Beaulieu 1973, 163 n. 205).

This chronology was increasingly challenged from the late 1970s onwards, partly because of revisions in the dating of the British coinage, including that in Le Câtillon I (Haselgrove 1987, 317–321), and partly because of improvements in the dating of some of the items of jewellery, notably the fibulae (Fitzpatrick and Megaw 1987, 437). As a consequence it was suggested (Fitzpatrick and Megaw 1987) that the Almgren 65 fibulae in Le Câtillon I dated to between about 40 and 20 BC, and consequently the hoard cannot have been buried before that period. Somewhat ironically, it now appears (Andrew Fitzpatrick, pers. comm.) that the dating of the Almgren 65 fibulae may be rather earlier than was considered to be the case thirty years ago, and so their presence in the hoard would not necessarily preclude assembly and/or deposition during the Gallic War. Regardless of the dating of the fibulae, however, the chronology of the British coinage still pushes the date of deposition significantly after the war.

Le Câtillon II, 2012

Early in 2012 Reg Mead and Richard Miles detected a signal in the field at Le Câtillon where the hoard had been found in 1957. They dug a neat hole down to the find and recovered four staters and a quarter stater, before refilling their excavation and disguising its location. They reported their discovery to the Jersey Heritage Trust and in June 2012 an archaeological excavation of 2 m × 2 m was carried out, centred on the location of the metal-detected signal (de Jersey 2012; Miles and Mead 2016). The hoard was removed as a single large block, weighing approximately 750 kg, and taken to the Jersey Heritage laboratory where excavation under laboratory conditions began in September 2014. The final coins (save for a small portion of the hoard which has been left intact for future research) were removed in January 2017; the estimated total, including the preserved portion, is approximately 69,550 coins. In addition to the coins, the hoard contained many other items, including ingots in copper and silver, a dozen gold torcs, smaller items of jewellery in gold, silver and bronze, several glass beads, one

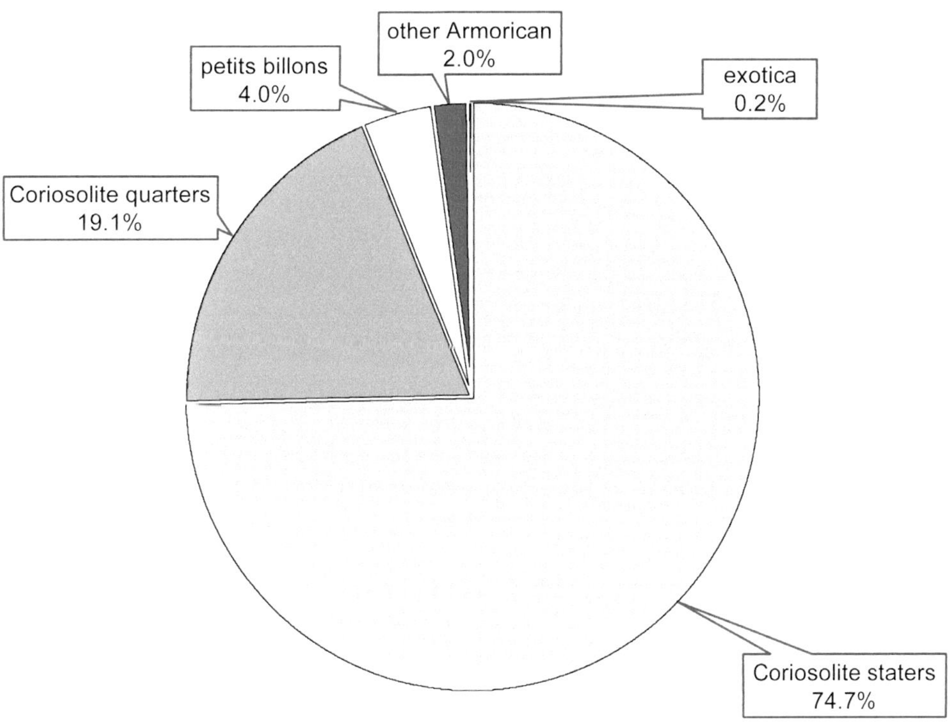

Figure 14.2 Approximate proportions of the main coin types in Le Câtillon II.

Figure 14.3 Coin no. 22585, apparently combining a petit billon *obverse die with a Coriosolite class IV quarter stater reverse. Diameter 11.5 mm, weight 0.72 g.*

late Bronze Age spearhead, and a worked stone. At least two of the ingots have coins visibly projecting from the metal. Most of the non-numismatic material is yet to be studied in detail, and so the following discussion will focus primarily on the evidence of the coinage.

At the time of writing (March 2017) some 56,360 coins have been cleaned and identified. Approximately three-quarters of these (*c.* 42,100) are staters of the Coriosolitae (Figure 14.2). This proportion is unlikely to change significantly as the remaining coins are cleaned, and thus the total number of Coriosolite staters should be in the order of about 52,000. A further 19%, or about 10,800, of the coins cleaned so far are quarter staters of the Coriosolitae. This is an extraordinary figure when it is considered that as recently as 2004, Delestrée and Tache (2004, 92) could write that Coriosolite quarter staters are 'de la plus grand rareté … l'effectif des divisions connues de nous, essentiellement par d'anciennes publications, se monte à quelques dizaines d'individus dont les trois lots du trésor de Jersey 11 [Le Câtillon I] ont fourni l'essentiel'. Preliminary examination of the Coriosolite quarters in Le Câtillon II suggests that this element of the coinage is far more complex than the relatively straightforward six classes of Coriosolite stater, and thus it is not a simple matter of identifying six types of quarter stater which correspond directly to the stater types.

About 2,300 of the coins cleaned so far are examples of the types generally known as *petits billons armoricains* (Gruel and Taccoen 1992). This is a catch-all term for a complex and poorly understood series of coinages, undoubtedly originating from several different regions of Armorica, and possibly spanning both the pre- and post-conquest periods. The *petits billons* have typically been dated to the period between about 40 and 10 BC (Gruel and Taccoen 1992, 180), but there is at least one coin in Le Câtillon II which apparently combines a reverse die of a Coriosolite quarter stater, stylistically identical to class IV staters, with an obverse die otherwise found only on *petits billons* (Figure 14.3). This has various important implications: it suggests, for example, that this *petit billon* type was produced at the same mint as the Coriosolite quarter, and at the same time, presumably before the Gallic War. Other *petit billon* types in Le Câtillon II include coins with features strongly associated with other Armorican coinages, such as the *barrière d'hippodrome* found on staters and quarter staters of the Osismii (as Gruel and Morin 1999, no. 152). There are also a significant number of *petits billons* types in Le Câtillon II which were previously unknown, and as with the Coriosolite quarter staters will require considerable research before they can be placed more securely in their Armorican context.

Other Armorican types (*i.e.* neither Coriosolite, nor *petits billons*) in stater and quarter stater denominations are currently represented by about 1,100 of the cleaned coins. In addition to relatively well-known types traditionally attributed to the Baiocasses, the Osismii and other Armorican tribes, there are two less familiar groups which are of particular interest. One is best described as 'Coriosolitae/Veneti' in style. A few examples have been published in recent catalogues (*e.g.* DT 2294, 2331; DTS 2330A, 2331A, 2333A–B, all of which are attributed solely to the Coriosolitae),[1] but there do not appear to be any provenanced examples from mainland Armorica; it is curious that none seem to have been recorded in any of the previous hoards, either from Brittany or Jersey. They are usually struck in good silver and in terms of style they are clearly related to the early Coriosolite classes (in particular VI and V) and the so-called 'Veneti' billon (de Jersey 2016, 171; see Delestrée 2015, 11 for an appropriately doubtful view of this traditional attribution).

The second Armorican group of particular interest consists of just over one hundred staters and a few quarter staters, which are related to the group of 'intruders' recognized by Rybot (1952, 42–44) in the La Marquanderie hoard. They have stylistic links to coinages from Lower Normandy, for example in the form of the hair (generally between two and four large locks) and in the presence of a lyre (in this case always placed vertically) beneath the horse. Colbert de Beaulieu (1958a, 203) listed them as 'a few coins of the Unelli and the Abrincatui', but paid them less attention than they deserve. Le Câtillon II has provided at least eight major varieties. With a few exceptions, probably dating from the beginning of the series, they are noticeably more poorly engraved than almost all of the other Armorican types in the hoard. They give the impression of hurried production, possibly by an authority with limited skills or resources available. It is tempting – though as yet wholly unsupported by any other evidence – to suggest an association with Viridovix, the Celtic king defeated by Quintus Titurius Sabinus in the south part of the Cotentin in 56 BC (Caesar, *BG* 3.17–19).

The remaining *c.* 110 coins so far identified from Le Câtillon II consist of various 'exotica': coins originating from beyond Armorica. The two largest groups are about twenty-five *globules à la croix*, traditionally attributed to the Senones or the Carnutes (DT 2537), and more than sixty 'thin silver units' purportedly from Hampshire or West Sussex (ABC 911). Almost all of the *globules* have test-cuts, a feature otherwise virtually unknown on this type (John Sills, pers. comm.), and thus may have been regarded essentially as bullion in this context. The thin silver units are intriguing because there are now more known from Le Câtillon II than from the whole of southern Britain; there were four examples in Le Câtillon I (Allen 1960, 298, nos 15–18), but the type is seemingly unknown from the continent. The possibility that it might be a continental production (or even from Jersey?) cannot be ruled out, however.

As with Le Câtillon I, one of the smaller groups of exotica – in this case, two staters and seven quarter staters of the Durotriges – bear a significance far out of proportion to their quantity, in terms of the chronology of the hoard. For the reasons explained in the discussion of Le Câtillon I, above, it is very difficult to place these coins before the early 40s BC, and indeed the examples of these types in Le Câtillon II mostly appear to be rather later in the Durotrigan sequence than those in Le Câtillon I. Once again, therefore, we have to conclude that unless the dating of the British series is at fault, Le Câtillon II cannot have been buried before about 50 BC, at the very earliest, and in fact is unlikely to have been buried until *c.* 40 BC or later.

Le Câtillon: the hoard in context

One of the magnificent benefits of Le Câtillon II, and the means by which it was discovered and then excavated, is that for the first time in Jersey we have the opportunity to truly explore the context of the discovery. We can also make more sense of Le Câtillon I in relation to the 2012 hoard, thanks in particular to the archival research of Robert Waterhouse, Field Archaeologist for La Société Jersiaise, who has established that the two hoards were located about 13 m apart (Waterhouse 2016, 37). Waterhouse's detailed recording of the excavation site, and the records and observations kept by

Figure 14.4 Excavation of Le Câtillon II, showing the surface of the large hoard block (being measured) and the 'Roman' pit (with vertical scale) in the north-east corner of the trench.

the two metal detectorists, Richard Miles and Reg Mead, all serve to demonstrate the unique importance and potential of this site: not just for the island of Jersey, but for the whole Armorican region at the end of the Iron Age.

The 2 m × 2 m excavation which revealed the 2012 hoard also exposed other features of potentially great significance. In addition to the pit which had been dug for the hoard, there was another, smaller pit in the north-east corner of the trench (Figure 14.4). This contained early Roman material, including a *denarius* of Augustus struck in Lyon in 8 or 7 BC (RIC I, 199). Elsewhere in the trench, Waterhouse (2016, 37–38) recorded the presence of metal slag, burnt clay and daub. Given the amount of activity in this area of just four square metres – and the presence of Le Câtillon I, a few metres away – it seems very likely indeed that there will be further traces of occupation elsewhere in the field. The pattern of ploughsoil finds recorded by Miles and Mead (2016, 20, 34) also points to at least one more possible hoard, perhaps scattered from a point towards the north: more than one hundred coins have been recovered in a narrow strip of land on the western edge of the field. Nor should we completely dismiss the 'legend' or rumour told to Reg Mead in about 1980, concerning the discovery of an unreported hoard found when one of the hedgerows was grubbed up some years earlier (Miles and Mead 2016, 18–19). This might just be a garbled version of the 1957 discovery, but if not confused with that find then it implies the presence of at least one more hoard on the site. The potential value of a detailed geophysical survey of the whole field, and the field to the west, across Le Câtillon road, cannot be underestimated.

Although as indicated above there are hints of settlement and occupation in the finds retrieved from the 2012 excavation, as yet we have no clear insight into the nature of the wider site, and thus for the time being we need to turn again to the evidence provided specifically by the hoard – and in particular the dominant numismatic element, the staters of the Coriosolitae.

The coinage of the Coriosolitae

Staters of the Coriosolitae account for some 75% of the hoard's numismatic contents by number, and more than 90% by weight. An association between some at least of the six Coriosolite stater classes – probably the final three, in chronological order I, III and II – with the Gallic War, and specifically with the period of 57–56 BC, has been recognized for many years, and this still seems the most likely explanation of the sudden surge in production. Katherine Gruel (1998, 61) has taken this interpretation further with her suggestion that those three late classes were issued by a coalition of Armorican forces. Their production did not necessarily take place at the same location as the earlier classes, nor was it necessarily the same authority – whether an individual or a coalition of rulers – who sanctioned the production of the 'confederal' coinage. It is clear from die studies that there is a definite break between the three earlier classes – VI, V and IV, in that order – and the three later (Colbert de Beaulieu

1973, 114), but the duration and wider significance of this division is not known. The absolute dating of the earlier classes is still elusive, since there are no examples known from securely-dated archaeological contexts. Even the earliest coins of the series are in relatively poor silver (about 32% for class VI staters), and it is not at all implausible that the series did not begin until the second quarter of the 1st century BC – but it must be admitted that this is little more than a guess, such is the paucity of the evidence.

The association between this coinage and the tribe known as the Coriosolitae seems to have become generally accepted in the later 19th century. There are no inscriptions on the coins to support the attribution, and so the evidence is based solely on findspots. Lambert (1864), in common with other antiquarians and numismatists of his era, focused on the presence of either the boar or the lyre beneath the horse to refine the attribution. Thus the coins with the lyre 'appartiennent aux *Curiosolites*, chez lequels on les retrouve le plus habituellement, ainsi que chez leurs voisins, les *Redones*, d'une part; les *Abrincatuens* et les *Unelliens*, de l'autre' (Lambert 1864, 26), while those with the boar 'appartiennent aux *Abrincatuens* et aux *Unelliens*...' (Lambert 1864, 28). Twenty-five years later, the catalogue of the Bibliothèque Nationale (Muret and Chabouillet 1889, 147–150) presented more or less the modern interpretation in listing both boar and lyre types as coins of the Curiosolitae (*sic*).

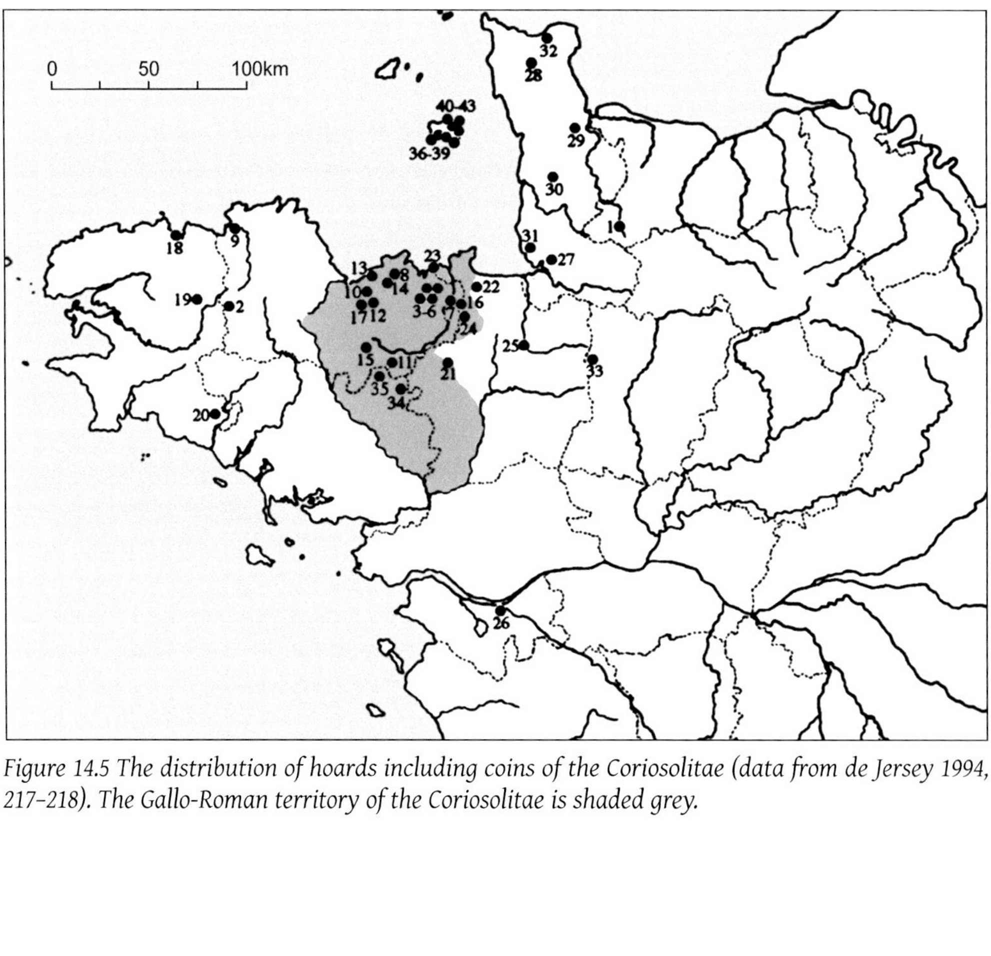

Figure 14.5 The distribution of hoards including coins of the Coriosolitae (data from de Jersey 1994, 217–218). The Gallo-Roman territory of the Coriosolitae is shaded grey.

Single finds to support this attribution are not especially common (de Jersey 1994, 214–216), but those recorded are concentrated principally in three areas: the hinterland of Saint-Malo, in the extreme north-east of the Côtes-d'Armor; the southern part of the Cotentin; and the island of Jersey. The hoards (de Jersey 1994, 217–218), in addition to the obvious concentration on Jersey, are scattered more widely across eastern Côtes-d'Armor and just across the Rance into Ille-et-Vilaine, and intermittently through the Cotentin. The distribution of the hoards in Brittany corresponds reasonably well to the territory ascribed to the Coriosolitae in the early Gallo-Roman period (Figure 14.5), with the exception of a void in the southern third of this region, approximately between the rivers Oust (in the west) and Vilaine (in the east). Hoards are not necessarily reliable indicators of territory (Casey 1986, 61–67), but with the relatively small number of single finds, they represent the strongest evidence we have to make a direct link between this coinage and the Coriosolitae.

We might well ask, however: does this really matter? 'Coriosolite' is a useful label to apply to the coinage – we have to call it something – but to do so invokes numerous assumptions that simply cannot be tested. The division between the first three and the last three coinages of the series has already been mentioned. Neither the early classes nor the late were necessarily produced by or for this tribe, and as we have seen Gruel has suggested that the latter group was a confederal issue. Some elements of the coinage might perhaps have been the output of a ruler in a particular area of the Coriosolite territory. And one of the single greatest problems in resolving these questions is that we have *absolutely no evidence* of where the coinage was manufactured: no minting debris of any sort has been recovered from the supposed Coriosolite territory, or indeed from almost anywhere in Armorica (the single exception appears to be a quarter stater die from the Morbihan; Delestrée 2017, 205).

In the absence of physical evidence of manufacture it seems to be generally assumed that the Coriosolite coinage was produced somewhere in northern Brittany. Colbert de Beaulieu (1973, 128) briefly considered the possibility that it was manufactured in Jersey, noting the 'densité prodigieuse' of finds on the island, but rejected this view on various counts, some more convincing than others (de Jersey 2016, 166–167). As discussed in relation to Le Câtillon I, above, Colbert de Beaulieu and his 20th-century contemporaries considered almost without exception that the coins were carried to Jersey by refugees fleeing the Gallic Wars, and buried on the island between about 56 and 51 BC (Allen 1960, 297; Colbert de Beaulieu 1973, 128). Whether deposition took place during that period or in the decade or two afterwards, we should arguably consider anew the possibility that some of the Coriosolite coinage was produced on Jersey. The fact that the raw materials would have to be transported to the island does not necessarily count against this possibility; it is self-evident that the Jersey hoards were imported at some point, whether as finished coinage or as ingots, coins or other objects destined to be recycled. The shipment of this material would have carried some element of risk, but perhaps that risk was perceived as less significant than that incurred in manufacturing the coins on the Armorican mainland, closer to the threat posed by Rome. If production did take place on the island, that in turn raises intriguing questions about its political and social affiliations: was it effectively part of the territory of the Coriosolitae? This is far from a novel idea – Lemière (1851, 222) asked precisely this question in one of the earliest useful studies of Armorican coinage – and it is no easier to answer now than it was in the mid-19th century. If not actually part of the Coriosolite territory, then presumably the population of the island were at least 'on the same side' as their mainland neighbours. But at present we simply cannot say whether the production process, if it did occur on Jersey, was carried out by inhabitants of the island, or by allies from the mainland – whether of the Coriosolitae or other groups – who were only briefly present on Jersey.

The sheer number of Coriosolite coins now recorded from Jersey is certainly impressive. Le Câtillon II is likely to furnish about 52,000 staters when cleaning is completed, and to this we can add the various hoards mentioned above, giving a total of at least 67,000 Coriosolite staters. Although comparatively insignificant in terms of weight, we should not forget that there are now also in excess of 11,000 quarter staters from the island. Precise figures from mainland Armorica are more difficult to calculate, primarily because of the number of poorly-recorded antiquarian finds, but something in the order of 8,000 Coriosolite staters is a reasonable lower estimate; quarter staters are very scarce indeed, as mentioned above. The largest credibly reported hoard on the mainland is Trébry (Côtes-d'Armor), containing 1,756 staters (Gruel 1981). One early 19th-century discovery (Saint-Dénoual, Côtes-d'Armor; de Jersey 1994, 161) reportedly contained between 1,200 and 1,500 staters, probably of the Coriosolitae, and there are several other antiquarian finds in the high hundreds, though in each case containing fewer than a thousand coins (de Jersey 1994, 217–218). Single finds are still comparatively rare, possibly in part because of the greater restrictions on metal-detecting operating in France, compared to Britain or Jersey. In summary, therefore, it is not unreasonable to estimate that more than eight times as many Coriosolite staters have been found on Jersey than on the Armorican mainland, and that quarter staters are almost exclusively an insular phenomenon.

It is possible to examine the Coriosolite stater figures in a little more detail, with reference to the standard division into six classes. Of the 67,000 coins found in Jersey, approximately 47,000 are class I, II and III issues, the so-called confederal coinage. The great majority (94%) of the 20,000 'early' staters (*i.e.* classes IV, V and VI) found in Jersey are from Le Câtillon II (35.3% of the Coriosolite stater contents): a little less than one thousand were recorded from La Marquanderie (8.6%), and just over one hundred from Le Câtillon I (5.2%).

The breakdown of the six stater classes in Le Câtillon II, compared to other hoards both from Jersey and the mainland, is intriguing (Table 14.1). It differs significantly from both insular and continental hoards in two respects: a relatively high proportion of class V staters, compared to other Jersey hoards, equivalent to the bottom end of the range seen on the Armorican mainland; and a proportion of class II staters, the final issue, which is both much lower than the previous Jersey finds, and markedly

Table 14.1 Proportion of Coriosolite staters by class, arranged chronologically, in nine hoards.

	cl. VI	cl. V	cl. IV	cl. I	cl. III	cl. II
La Marquanderie, Jersey	0.2	3.1	5.3	14.4	22.5	54.4
Rozel, Jersey, 1820	0.2	9.2	5.5	15.1	14.5	55.3
Rozel, Jersey, 1875	0.8	9.6	8.0	15.2	13.6	52.8
Le Câtillon I, Jersey	0.3	2.1	2.8	12.3	16.8	65.6
Le Câtillon II, Jersey	**3.0**	**22.4**	**9.9**	**14.4**	**17.3**	**33.0**
Roz-Landrieux, Ille-et-Vilaine	16.3	63.8	5.1	14.1	4.5	1.9
Merdrignac, Côtes-d'Armor	0.1	40.6	40.6	9.1	0	8.3
Penguilly, Côtes-d'Armor	1.1	27.8	19.7	23.2	16.2	11.6
Trébry, Côtes-d'Armor	0.3	23.1	34.3	24.9	17.0	0.4

Note that there are historical errors in the data for Roz-Landrieux (totalling 105.7%) and Merdrignac (98.7%), which cannot now be resolved.

higher than Armorican comparisons. Quite what this means, however, is difficult to say. It could be interpreted to suggest that Le Câtillon II is chronologically slightly earlier in date than the other Jersey hoards, with a greater proportion of the earlier types of coin and fewer late types, but that seems to be contradicted by the presence of the relatively late Durotrigan issues, as discussed above. Given that all of the Jersey hoards contain the final class II issue – forming between one-third (Le Câtillon II) and two-thirds (Le Câtillon I) of the Coriosolite stater contents – then plainly none of them can have been buried before class II was manufactured and 'circulated', insofar as that term is appropriate. It seems more likely that there has been some additional variation in the factors leading to the assembly of particular hoards, but attempting to identify the factors involved in any one case may be difficult. The variation between Le Câtillon I and Le Câtillon II is a useful example of this point. The two finds are geographically identical, to all intents and purposes, just a few metres apart in the same field, and it is difficult (although not impossible) to conceive that the depositors of one did not know about the presence of the other. And yet there is a tenfold difference in the proportion of class V staters, and one

Figure 14.6 Left-facing Coriosolite quarter stater from Le Câtillon II (coin no. 66001). Maximum diameter 15 mm, weight 1.47 g.

hoard has proportionately half as many class II staters as the other. There are other differences: to give just one example, there were more than 50 'XN' staters in Le Câtillon I, the type generally attributed to the Abrincatui (de Jersey 1994, 103–105), but these coins are entirely absent from Le Câtillon II.

Why? It must surely be a reflection of the source of the coins in each hoard, and the history of each parcel or batch which went to make up each hoard before it was buried for a final time. It is just possible that some light may be shed on these processes by the 3-D spatial recording of the hoard contents (Miles and Mead 2016, 78), which provides an unprecedented opportunity to identify patterns at the level of individual dies. This point is perhaps best explained by a potential case study. There are almost 30 examples in Le Câtillon II of a previously unknown Coriosolite quarter stater, with the unusual feature of the head facing left (Figure 14.6). All but one of these coins is struck from the same pair of dies (the exception is struck from the same obverse and a different reverse). It is reasonable to assume that these left-facing quarters represent a single episode of production at a mint, wherever it was. If they are found to be scattered widely throughout the hoard, then it seems likely that some period of time elapsed between production and final deposition, allowing these coins to disperse from the mint and, to some extent, to circulate. If they are found to be confined to a restricted area of the hoard, it might instead suggest that this batch has stayed more or less intact since production. This type of enquiry – possible only because of the painstaking removal and recording of the coins from the hoard, one by one – presents a new and potentially very valuable source of information on the processes by which the hoard was assembled.

Focus of resistance or field of last resort?

Analysis of Le Câtillon II is still at an early stage. Although most of the coins have now been identified, this is just the first step in what will inevitably be a long process of examination and investigation, given the sheer size of the hoard and the many different objects it contains. Further investigation of the find site is also fundamental to a full understanding of the context of this hoard, and of its 1957 predecessor. In the meantime, we can make some preliminary suggestions as to how this extraordinary discovery fits in with the other hoards from Jersey and with the Gallic War period in the wider Armorican region.

The question of chronology – and specifically the date of deposition of the hoard – has a tendency to dominate all other lines of enquiry, but it is undeniably fundamental to our attempts to make sense of Le Câtillon II. In this respect the presence of a small number of Durotrigan imports is crucially important. As discussed, it is impossible on the current, widely-accepted chronology of the British series to date these Durotrigan coins any earlier than *c.* 50 BC, and there is good reason to suggest that the examples in Le Câtillon II are several years later. As a consequence, the final deposition of Le Câtillon II simply cannot have taken place before about 40 BC, and it is by no means impossible that it was a little later still, perhaps in the 30s BC. There is unfortunately nothing in the vastly greater quantities of Armorican material which provides anything like the same degree of precision in dating, nor in the handful of other 'exotic' coins scattered through the hoard. Unless some key chronological indicator is identified among, for example, the bracelets or fibulae, then the numismatic dating supplied by the Durotrigan coins will remain paramount.

If we accept a date for the burial of Le Câtillon II as, say, 40 or 35 BC, then clearly in a strictly chronological sense it is removed from direct association with the Gallic Wars, although its assembly may still owe almost everything to the events of the mid-50s BC. However one views the Coriosolite coinage, and in particular the three later classes – whether confederal or not, whether produced by the Coriosolitae or another authority, whether struck in Jersey or on the mainland – an association with the incursion of Roman troops in 57 and 56 BC seems by far the most likely explanation of the sudden increase in production. The fact that eight times as many Coriosolite staters have been found on Jersey as on mainland Armorica might suggest that this production took place on the island, but at present there is simply no physical evidence to confirm this, one way or the other. The presence in Le Câtillon II of at least two ingots containing partially-melted coins is undoubtedly significant, but it does not in itself prove that production took place on this site, or indeed anywhere necessarily on Jersey.

How, then, should we explain the gap of perhaps fifteen or twenty years, or more, between the date when most of the coinage assembled in Le Câtillon II was produced, and the date when it was finally buried? The composition of the hoard gives the impression of consisting of every last scrap of precious metal available to the people who gathered it together: every little parcel of coins kept securely since the Roman conquest; all their jewellery, whether pristine or damaged beyond repair; a late Bronze Age spearhead, perhaps a treasured keepsake; the ingots melted down from earlier Armorican coinages; a few Durotrigan coins received from their allies across the Channel. There is a sense of finality about all of this. Does Le Câtillon II represent the treasury of a people for whom the technicality of a Roman conquest in 56 BC was about to become the reality of Roman occupation?

In this scenario we might consider that the island of Jersey did in some sense act as a focus of resistance during the immediate post-conquest period. Coinage and other valuables were brought to the island, whether by refugees desperate to find safety, or as the result of more strategic decisions made by the inhabitants of mainland Armorica; quite possibly in both circumstances. For some time after the Gallic War had ended, the inhabitants of the island continued to live relatively unaffected by the Roman conquest. We have no detail, literary or historical, on events in Armorica during the two or three decades after 56 BC, and the archaeological evidence is very rarely of a precision that can shed any further light on such a short period. But it seems unlikely that a relatively isolated (and difficult to access) location such as Jersey would have been the first target for the new occupying power, especially if it was not perceived as a threat. The Romans may have been aware of the wealth concealed on the island, but they might equally have realized that the inhabitants presented no significant military challenge. In those circumstances they could afford to leave them in peace for a few more years.

When, at last, the time came to occupy the island, the treasure which had been stored on Jersey was buried for a final time: much of it at Le Câtillon, some of it perhaps at other locations on the island, particularly at Rozel. At least two of the Rozel hoards cannot have been buried before the mid or late 30s BC, and it is by no means impossible that the Le Câtillon deposits were made at the same time; it is also worth mentioning the Sark hoard in this context, another treasure perhaps buried *c.* 30 BC (Allen 1971; de Jersey forthcoming). The Roman occupation of Jersey began shortly afterwards, and there are tantalizing glimpses from the Le Câtillon II excavation trench that whether or not the occupiers realized that the field contained treasure, they must have somehow appreciated its significance to the local population, because they chose to continue to occupy the site through the end of the 1st century BC and into the early 1st century AD, and perhaps beyond – only further excavation will tell. For the island population, however, it is fair to say that while for a short time Le Câtillon might have seemed to be a focus of resistance, ultimately it became their field of last resort.

Note

1 The following abbreviations are used in this chapter for coin types: ABC = Cottam *et al.* 2010; DT = Delestrée and Tache 2004; DTS = Delestrée and Tache 2008.

Bibliography

Allen, D.F. (1958) New light on the date of early British coins. *Spink Numismatic Circular* 66/4, 85–87.

Allen, D.F. (1960) The origins of coinage in Britain: a reappraisal. In S.S. Frere (ed.), *Problems of the Iron Age in Southern Britain*, 97–308. London, Institute of Archaeology.

Allen, D.F. (1971) The Sark hoard. *Archaeologia* 103, 1–31.

Barthélemy, A. de (1884) Étude sur les monnaies gauloises découvertes à Jersey en 1875. *Revue Numismatique* ser. 3, 2, 177–202.

Cable, E.K. (1876) Report on coins found at Rozel. *Bulletin of La Société Jersiaise* 1, 29–31.

Cable, E.K. (1886) Roman and Gaulish coins found at Rozel, Jersey. *Bulletin of La Société Jersiaise* 2, 119–123.

Casey, P.J. (1986) *Understanding Ancient Coins.* London, Batsford.

Colbert de Beaulieu, J.-B. (1957a) Le trésor de Jersey-11 et la numismatique celtique des deux Bretagnes. *Revue Belge de Numismatique* 103, 47–88.

Colbert de Beaulieu, J.-B. (1957b) Les trésors de monnaies celtiques de l'île de Jersey et la circulation des monnaies gauloises. *Bulletin de la Société Nationale des Antiquaires de France* 1957, 86–96.

Colbert de Beaulieu, J.-B. (1958a) Armorican coin hoards in the Channel Islands. *Proceedings of the Prehistoric Society* 24, 201–210.

Colbert de Beaulieu, J.-B. (1958b) La récolte de monnaies armoricaines de Jersey-XI. *Annales de Bretagne* 65/1, 44–53.

Colbert de Beaulieu, J.-B. (1959) Un troisième lot de la récolte de Jersey-11. *Revue Belge de Numismatique* 105, 49–57.

Colbert de Beaulieu, J.-B. (1973) *Traité de numismatique celtique I. Méthodologie des ensembles.* Paris, Les Belles Lettres.

Cottam, E., de Jersey, P., Rudd, C. and Sills, J. (2010) *Ancient British Coins.* Aylsham, Chris Rudd.

Cunliffe, B.W. (1992) Le Câtel de Rozel, Jersey: the excavations of 1988–90. *Antiquaries Journal* 72, 18–53.

de Jersey, P. (1994) *Coinage in Iron Age Armorica.* Oxford, Oxford University Committee for Archaeology.

de Jersey, P. (2012) Excavating the largest coin hoard ever seen in the ancient Celtic world. *British Archaeology* 126, 34–36.

de Jersey, P. (2016) Colbert de Beaulieu, the Coriosolitae and the Jersey hoards. *Revue Belge de Numismatique* 162, 159–178.

de Jersey, P. (forthcoming) The coins. In B. Cunliffe and E. Durham (eds), *Sark: A sacred island?* Oxford, Oxford University School of Archaeology.

Delestrée, L.-P. (2015) Le monnayage des Vénètes: du mythe à la réalité. In D. Hollard and K. Meziane (eds), *Numismatique bretonne. Les faux monétaires*, 5–39. Paris, Société d'Etudes Numismatiques et Archéologiques.

Delestrée, L.-P. (2017) Les chaînes de la production monétaire en Gaule: outillage et premiers constats. In J.-M. Doyen and V. Geneviève (eds), *Hekátê triformis: Mélanges de numismatique et d'archéologie en mémoire de Marc Bar*, 199–216. Brussels, Cercle d'Études Numismatiques.

Delestrée, L.-P., and Tache, M. (2004) *Nouvel Atlas des monnaies gauloises, II: De la Seine à la Loire moyenne.* Saint-Germain-en-Laye, Editions Commios.

Delestrée, L.-P. and Tache, M. (2008) *Nouvel Atlas des monnaies Gauloises IV. Supplément aux tomes I–III.* Saint-Germain-en-Laye, Éditions Commios.

Donop, Baron de (1838) *Les médailles gallo-gaëliques.* Hanover, Hahn.

Fitzpatrick, A.P., and Megaw, J.V.S. (1987) Further finds from the Le Câtillon hoard. *Proceedings of the Prehistoric Society* 53, 433–444.

Gruel, K. (1981) *Le trésor de Trébry (Côtes-du-Nord).* Paris, Les Belles Lettres, Etudes de numismatique celtique 1.

Gruel, K. (1998) Estimation du volume des émissions armoricaines. In H. Sebire (ed.), *Guernsey Connections: Papers in honour of Bob Burns*, 61–66. Guernsey, La Société Guernesiaise.

Gruel, K., and Morin, E. (1999) *Les monnaies celtes du Musée de Bretagne.* Rennes, Musée de Bretagne.

Gruel, K., and Taccoen, A. (1992) Petit numéraire de billon émis durant et après la conquête romaine dans l'Ouest de la Gaule. In M. Mays (ed.), *Celtic Coinage: Britain and Beyond*, 165–188. Oxford, British Archaeological Reports British Series 222.

Haselgrove, C.C. (1987) *Iron Age Coinage in South-East England: The archaeological context.* Oxford, British Archaeological Reports British Series 174.

Hawkes, J. (1937) *The Archaeology of the Channel Islands, Vol. II: The Bailiwick of Jersey.* Jersey, La Société Jersiaise.

Lemière, P.-L. (1851) Essai sur les monnaies gauloises de la Bretagne-Armoricaine. *Bulletin Archéologique de l'Association Bretonne* 4, 203–225.

Miles, R., and Mead, R. (2016) *The Jersey hoard: Le Câtillon II* (2nd edn). Jersey, Barnes Publishing.

Rybot, N.V.L. (1952) *Armorican Art. A new and enlarged edition of the article published in the Bulletin of the Société Jersiaise for 1937.* Jersey, La Société Jersiaise.

Waterhouse, R. (2016) *Two Iron Age and Roman Coin Hoards from Le Câtillon, Grouville, Jersey.* Unpublished interim report. Jersey, La Société Jersiaise.

Chapter 15

The second battle of Alesia: The 19th-century investigations at Alise-Sainte-Reine and international recognition of the Gallic period of the late Iron Age

Laurent Olivier

There would seem to be a dark cloud hanging over Alesia, the site where the Gaulish army fighting for liberation was defeated by the Romans. The excavations carried out between 1861 and 1865 at Alise-Sainte-Reine, where Caesar laid his siege, were immediately enveloped in controversy, for the findings, which were based on false premises, were as unsettling as they were unexpected. It was not the location of the site that generated such debate, for that had been well established by the antiquarians of the 18th century, but rather the fact that the artefacts unearthed in the entrenchments – especially the weapons – defied expectations. Scholars at that time proved incapable of recognizing these arms as Gallic, and generally attributed them to Roman craftsmanship. As for the equipment used by Caesar's troops, and which included pieces not of Roman manufacture, it seemed at best atypically Roman, and quite possibly not Roman at all (Quicherat 1865). The climate of uncertainty threw everything into question, even the dating and the very location of the site that had been established by the excavations that Napoléon III had commissioned. One hundred and fifty years later, French research on the Gallic Wars is still suffering the consequences.[1]

The French scholars of the 1860s found themselves at this impasse not because they did not have the wherewithal to identify their finds correctly, but rather because the available data for continental Europe prevented them from seeing that the Gallic arms unearthed at Alise-Sainte-Reine had been made by the Celts. The problem, moreover, did not trouble French archaeologists alone. The finds made in the late 1850s at La Tène, on the banks of Lake Neuchâtel in Switzerland, were not recognized as dating from pre-Roman times either. The majority of scholars believed that these perfectly preserved iron weapons dated from far more recent times, most likely not long before the Middle Ages. The path that eventually led to archaeological recognition of a late Iron Age in Europe, contemporary in part to the Gallic Wars, was filled with twists and pitfalls. And as opposed to the myths that 20th-century historiographers helped propagate, it was not the discovery of the site at La Tène that forced recognition of the late Iron Age in Europe, which was not officially credited until Hildebrand did so in 1876. Rather, it was the realization that some of the arms unearthed at Alise-Sainte-Reine were in fact Gallic – which, at the time, no one was willing to believe.

The invisible Gauls

It has largely been forgotten that until the mid-1860s virtually nothing was known of the material culture of the Gauls living at the time of the Gallic Wars. Of course, numismatists such as Félicien de Saulcy (1807–1880) and Anatole de Barthélemy (1821–1904), to name just the best known, had performed significant work as early as the beginning of the 19th century. They had identified the coinages minted by various Gallic peoples and the links between some of them. But until 1858, when Napoléon III charged scholars on the *Commission de la Topographie des Gaules* with the task of searching for material remains of the conquest of Gaul, nothing was known of either the funerary rites or the dwellings of the Gallic peoples. It was not even known what their pottery, weaponry, and jewellery looked like. The archaeology of the Gauls was at that stage solely the province of numismatists.

The pre-Roman past of the Gauls had essentially been reconstructed from Classical sources. Caesar's *Commentaries on the Gallic War* were among the most important of these, along with passing references made by various Greek and Roman historians and geographers such as Poseidonios, Strabo and Cassius Dio. In the 1820s, the French historian Amédée Thierry (1797–1873) compiled these fragmentary and incomplete sources into his monumental *Histoire des Gaules:* the great history of the Gauls 'from their most distant past to their total submission to Roman dominance' (Thierry 1828). In effect, the history of the Gauls existed only on paper as a narrative, and the protagonists of this centuries-long tale had all the trappings of characters in a story.

And yet, striking pieces crafted by pre-Roman Gauls had already been discovered. In 1841, a splendid bronze helmet richly decorated with gold leaf and red enamel inlay was dredged from the bed of the Seine at Amfreville-sous-les-Monts (north-west France), but the experts who examined it – among them Viollet-le-Duc (1814–1879) – judged it to be too lovely, 'too delicate' to have been crafted by barbaric Gauls. They dated it to the early Middle Ages (Viollet-le-Duc 1862, 226). The Celts, or Gauls, were conspicuous by their absence. Their invisibility was attributed to what Greek and Roman historical sources had presented as the extremely unrefined nature of their civilization.

La Tène: a missed opportunity

In the early 1850s, Swiss lakes began yielding an abundant crop of prehistoric objects made of ceramic, bronze and worked or polished stone. Collectors and researchers

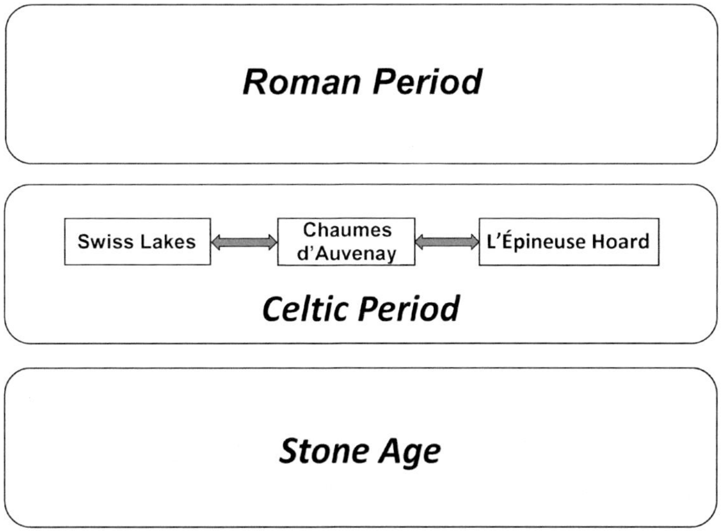

Figure 15.1 The chronology of the 'Celtic' period, as it was seen at the beginning of the 1860s.

noted that the different locations at which these items were found yielded distinct assemblages that could be divided between 'stone age' pieces, none of which was made of metal, and 'bronze age' pieces from areas where metalworking had been common practice. The director of the museum in Lausanne, Frédéric Troyon (1815–1866), dated these 'Celtic' antiquities to a 'Helvetian' period that he associated with the discoveries at Hallstatt, where a rich collection of goods had been unearthed by the Austrian directing the excavations, Johann Georg Ramsauer (1795–1874) (Figure 15.1).

In November 1857, a fellow who 'fished for lacustrine collectibles' and did work for the great collector of prehistoric antiquities, Friedrich Schwab (1803–1869), brought back an unusual assortment of finds. In barely an hour he had fished out some 40 iron objects that had been lying on the bottom of Lake Neuchâtel at a place called La Tène, where the water ran only 60 cm deep. There were swords, some in perfect condition, and spearheads, as well as tools such as axes and sickles (Figure 15.2). For Dr Ferdinand Keller, the great expert in lacustrine archaeology, who reviewed these finds, they were clearly rather recent, dating from the Roman era or perhaps even medieval times (Keller 1858, 151).

As luck would have it, the sister of Hans Kopp, the treasure-fisher working for Schwab, was a cook in the household of Édouard Desor (1811–1882),[2] a geologist and naturalist from Neuchâtel. Desor had gone to do research in Scandinavia in 1846, and while there had met the famous antiquarian Christian Thomsen (1788–1865), the inventor of the three-age system. In 1852, on his return from America, Desor naturally took an interest in the discoveries made in the Swiss lakes, in particular the spectacular finds from La Tène. Desor had his own theory about these finds, quite different from the one elaborated by Schwab, who believed all the iron pieces

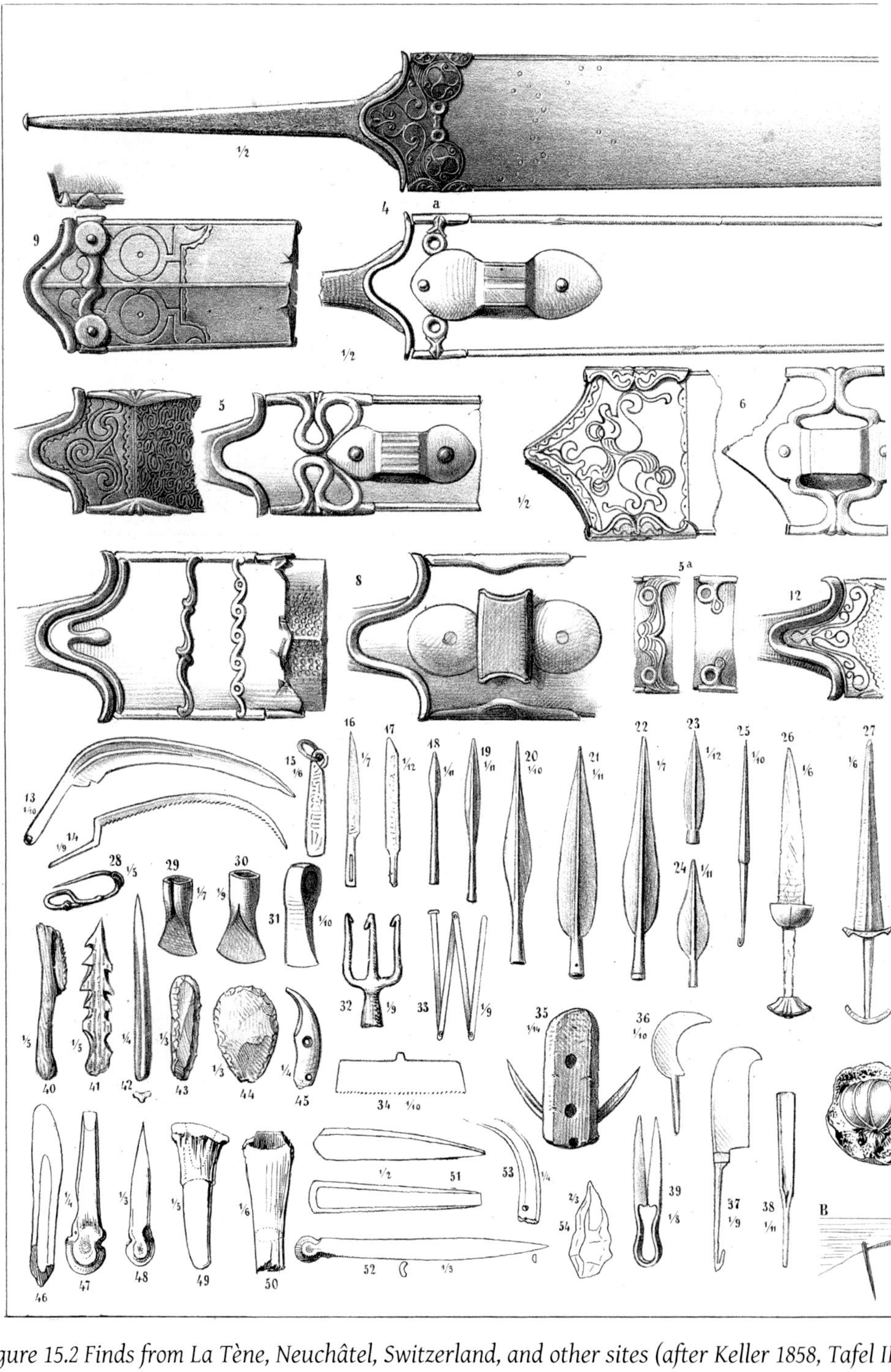

Figure 15.2 Finds from La Tène, Neuchâtel, Switzerland, and other sites (after Keller 1858, Tafel III).

to be Roman. As early as 1860, Desor theorized that the Swiss lake sites represented distinct groupings that corresponded to either the Stone, the Bronze or the Iron Ages, 'much like paleontological deposits'. It followed from this reasoning that the Swiss lake sites offered a microcosm of prehistoric chronology and that the finds at La Tène could logically be attributed to the Iron Age, which until then had yielded none (Desor 1860). But Desor was preaching in the wilderness, for at the time there was no archaeological evidence to support his interpretation. In fact, it seemed completely unjustified. There was no way to date the finds from La Tène, for at that time, they were unlike anything else.

The European Iron Age in the 1850s

What is more, there was no room for this kind of Iron Age whose existence, at the time, was limited to La Tène, or more precisely, to the items held by Schwab and Desor. European scholars allowed that there had been a 'Celtic period' that pre-dated the Roman conquest, but there was no agreement as to what it contained. By the end of the 1850s, when they had almost all learned of the spectacular finds from the Hallstatt cemetery in Lower Austria, it was generally agreed that these finds reflected the part of the Iron Age that came directly after the Bronze Age.

In western Europe, scholars recognized that certain objects found in graves located beneath tumuli in the Alsace, Lorraine and Burgundy regions of north-eastern France were similar in type and shape to those found at Hallstatt. The 'Hallstatt Period' thus seemed to have a corresponding 'Tumulus Period' that was contemporary with it, but its dating remained a largely approximate affair. Most scholars imagined it to have extended as far as the centuries that immediately preceded the Roman conquest. For one thing, the finds from La Tène were not at all like those from Hallstatt; for another, there was no place for a new Iron Age, for nothing equivalent to the discoveries made by Schwab and Desor had yet been found elsewhere. For want of anything better, scholars clung to the status quo.

Astonishing discoveries in Burgundy

In 1859, Felicien de Saulcy (1807–1880), president of the *Commission on Gaulish Topography,* dug on the Chaumes d'Auvenay plateau in Ivry-en-Montagne (Burgundy). Scholarly tradition, deriving from the work of the 18th-century antiquarians, held that it was in this part of France that the battle of 58 BC had taken place and from which a migrant Helvetian population had been driven out. The finds made here, which included a bronze knife with a perforated handle and a set of bronze pins with vasiform heads, clearly recalled those from the Swiss lakes that Troyon had designated 'Helvetian' (Figure 15.3; Bertrand 1861).

That stood as proof, it was thought, that the burial mounds on the Chaumes d'Auvenay plateau had been erected by the Helvetians whom Caesar had ruthlessly

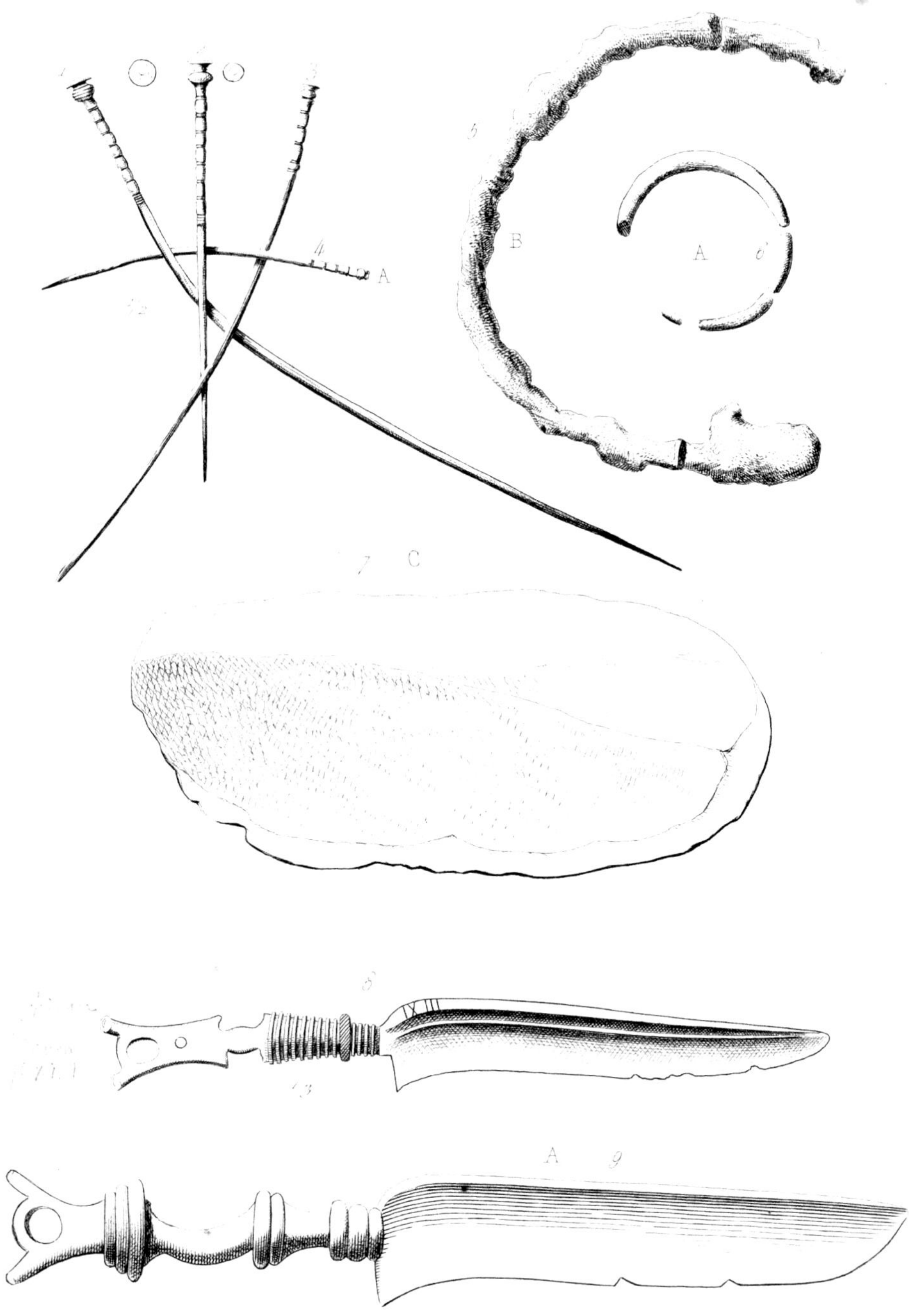

Figure 15.3 Grave goods from the tumuli in Chaumes d'Auvenay, Côte-d'Or (after Bertrand 1861).

driven off the land. The seemingly haphazard arrangement of the mounds, which were spread out over several miles, and the presence of graves situated on top of others within certain tumuli, were put down to the fact that 'the people administering the funeral rites were pressed for time and carried out their work in haste' (Saulcy 1860, 337).

The finds from this plateau were thus seen to date to 'a transitional period between the pure Celtic and the Gallo-Roman eras'. An iron bracelet found in one grave, which was of the same type as those made of bronze, allowed scholars to place these supposedly 'Helvetian' burials at the junction between the Bronze and Iron Ages, which they dated 'not that much further back than the beginning of our own era' (Bertrand 1861, 4). This was how the finds from Ivry-en-Montagne allowed scholars to conclude with confidence that the weapons of the Gauls living at the time of the Gallic Wars were made exclusively of bronze (Bertrand 1861, 8).

A sensational discovery at Alise-Sainte-Reine

In November 1860, bronze weapons and tools were found in a ditch near the Ferme de l'Épineuse, at the foot of Mont Auxois, which, according to the wisdom of the day, was the site of the siege of Alesia (Figure 15.4). A study of these pieces found them to be akin to those found on the Chaumes d'Auvenay plateau. In addition to a sword, there was a knife and a pin with a vasiform head which, here again, were analogous to the pieces from the Swiss lakes that Troyon had attributed to a 'Helvetian' period.

This unexpected discovery offered further proof, so it seemed at the time, that these pieces were of Gaulish manufacture and dated from the period of the Roman conquest, just as the 'Helvetian' finds from the Chaumes d'Auvenay plateau had allowed scholars to make a similar determination. The presence of bronze Gaulish weapons thus represented, so it was believed, an indisputable piece of evidence placing the site of the siege of Alesia at Mont Auxois (Rossignol 1861).

This is why Emperor Napoléon III, who was working on a book on Julius Caesar,3 immediately charged the archaeologists on the *Commission* with the task of excavating near the site at l'Épineuse to study and map Caesar's fortifications. The enthusiasm that marked the outset of the project soon gave way to disappointment: Caesar's siegeworks were nowhere to be found... and for good reason. As we now know, neither the pieces unearthed at l'Épineuse nor those found in the graves on the Chaumes d'Auvenay plateau were contemporary with the Gallic War. They actually belonged to the end of the Bronze Age, around eight centuries before the siege of Alesia (Olivier and Triboulot 2000).

Where are the Gauls? Disappointment at Alise-Sainte-Reine

At the beginning of the 1860s, French archaeologists believed that they were capable of reconstructing the equipment used by Gallic warriors at the time of the Gallic

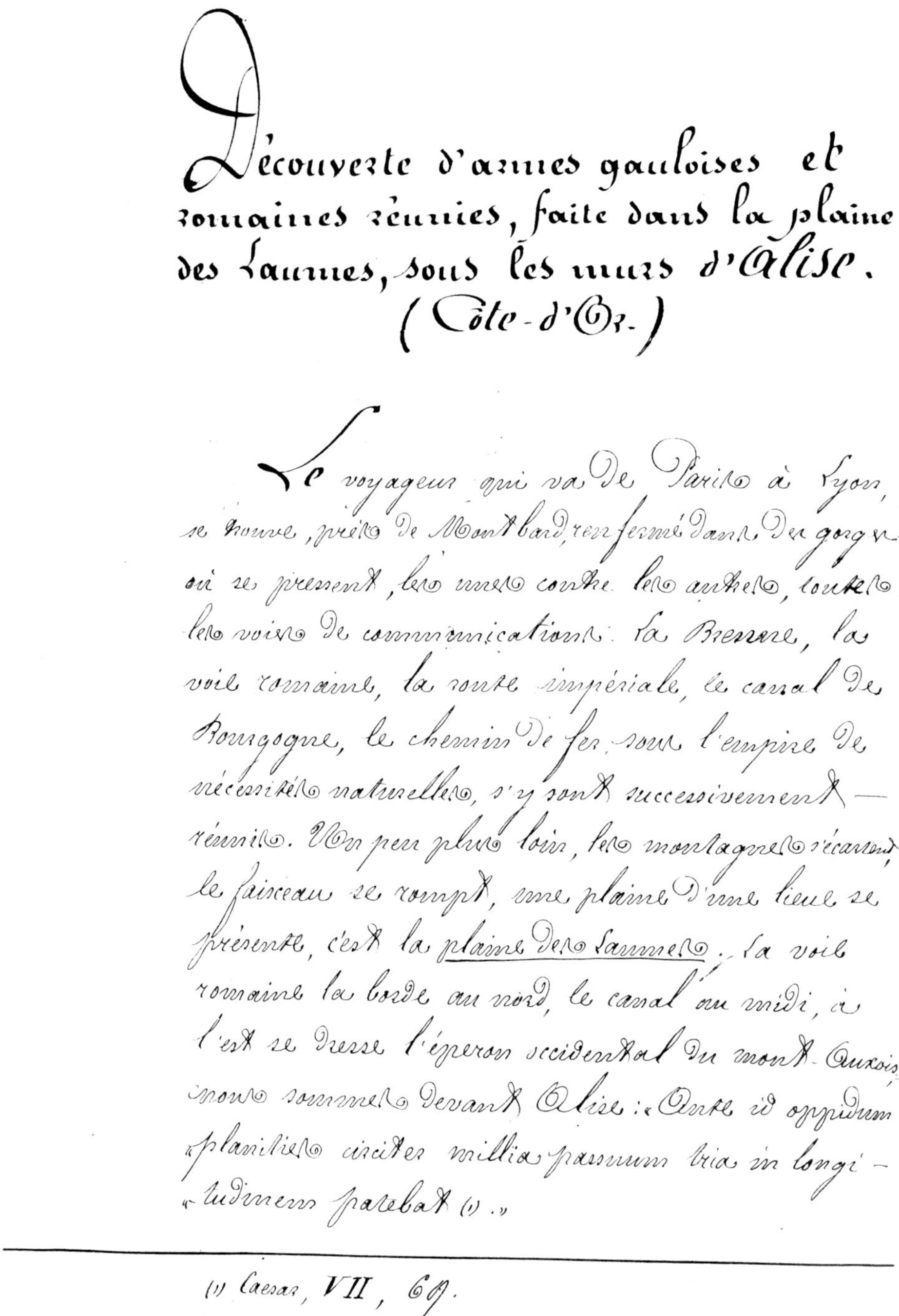
Découverte d'armes gauloises et romaines réunies, faite dans la plaine des Laumes, sous les murs d'Alise. (Côte-d'Or.)

Le voyageur qui va de Paris à Lyon, se trouve, près de Montbard, renfermé dans des gorges où se pressent, les unes contre les autres, toutes les voies de communication. La Brenne, la voie romaine, la route impériale, le canal de Bourgogne, le chemin de fer, sous l'empire de nécessités naturelles, s'y sont successivement réunis. Un peu plus loin, les montagnes s'écartent, le faisceau se rompt, une plaine d'une lieue se présente, c'est la plaine des Laumes. La voie romaine la borde au nord, le canal au midi, à l'est se dresse l'éperon occidental du mont Auxois, nous sommes devant Alise : « Ante id oppidum « planities circiter millia passuum tria in longi- « tudinem patebat (1). »

(1) Caesar, VII, 69.

Figure 15.4 Claude Rossignol's account of the discoveries at l'Épineuse, Côte-d'Or, 1860 (Archives of the Musée d'Archéologie nationale, Saint-Germain-en-Laye).

Figure 15.5 Emmanuel Frémiet's Gallic Warrior, *commissioned by Napoléon III in 1862 (Musée d'Archéologie nationale, Saint-Germain-en Laye).*

Wars. They were convinced that they used bronze for their weaponry and that it was identical to the finds from l'Épineuse, which the 'Helvetian' discoveries from the Swiss lakes allowed them to date roughly to the 1st century BC. This explains why, in 1862, when Napoléon III had Emmanuel Frémiet (1824–1910) sculpt a Gaulish chief from the time of the Gallic Wars, the figure was bedecked with bronze equipment that we now know with certainty to date from the very end of the Bronze Age, somewhere in the 8th century BC: a Villanovan helmet with a crest, body armour like that found at Véria (eastern France), and an antenna sword from northern Italy (Olivier *et al.* 2017; Figure 15.5).

At the site in Alise-Sainte-Reine, in the spring of 1861, a highly laborious start led to a change in strategy. Instead of continuing to work 'blind', it was decided to dig a long exploratory trench from the Plaine des Laumes towards the plateau of Mont Auxois, the idea being that if Caesar's trench system was in fact there, they would run into it somewhere (Olivier 2010; Olivier and Reddé 2015). The change in tactics paid off. About 300 m from the farm of l'Épineuse, 'right at the base of the slope', the trench ran into a large ditch whose dark soil fill contrasted sharply with the surrounding substrate. These were the siege lines encircling the base of the plateau that were to contain the Gauls. The investment included a circumvallation on the inside and a contravallation towards the outside designed to protect the besieging forces from an attack initiated from without (Figure 15.6).

Gradually, the digging uncovered the line of the Roman trenches that stretched some 30 km in all. The work soon began to yield numerous Gallic and Roman coins, as well as the remains of iron weapons: hundreds of spearheads, *pilum* heads, arrowheads, ballista projectile heads, swords... but not a single piece of bronze. As the number of pieces unearthed kept mounting – especially Gallic coins, nearly 500 in all – a disconcerting question began to arise with increasing persistence: where were the Gauls' weapons? Given the number of Gaulish troops involved, their weapons should have been at least as numerous as those of the Romans.[4] Why, as they came closer and closer to completing the circuit of the Roman siege lines, had they failed to come upon any?

Reffye identifies the Gallic arms from Alesia (1864)

Jean-Baptiste Verchère de Reffye (1821–1880) was a weapons engineer appointed ordnance officer by Napoléon III; he would later revolutionize canon design with the invention of the rifled breech-loading canon. He was one of 'the emperor's men' sent to oversee and assist the archaeologists in the research Napoléon III had charged them to carry out. At Alise-Sainte-Reine, he oversaw the work on Roman weapons. He studied their ballistic capabilities, especially those of artillery pieces, and replicated them at his research centre in Meudon. As part of his work for the committee organizing what was to become the Musée des Antiquités National[5] at Saint-Germain-en-Laye, which was created in 1862, he was asked to look for items that could be included in the new archaeological museum's collections.

In December 1863, Reffye went to see Colonel Schwab at his home in Bienne, which had been transformed into a veritable museum of lacustrine antiquities. Reffye was especially interested in the pieces from La Tène, of which he hoped to negotiate, on behalf of the Emperor, cast replicas that could be displayed at the future museum in Saint-Germain, for the Colonel had refused to part with his beloved finds that were coveted by all the great museums of Europe, including the British Museum and the Römisch-Germanische Zentralmuseum at Mainz. What Reffye discovered in Schwab's elegant quarters left him flabbergasted. The iron weapons that had been retrieved

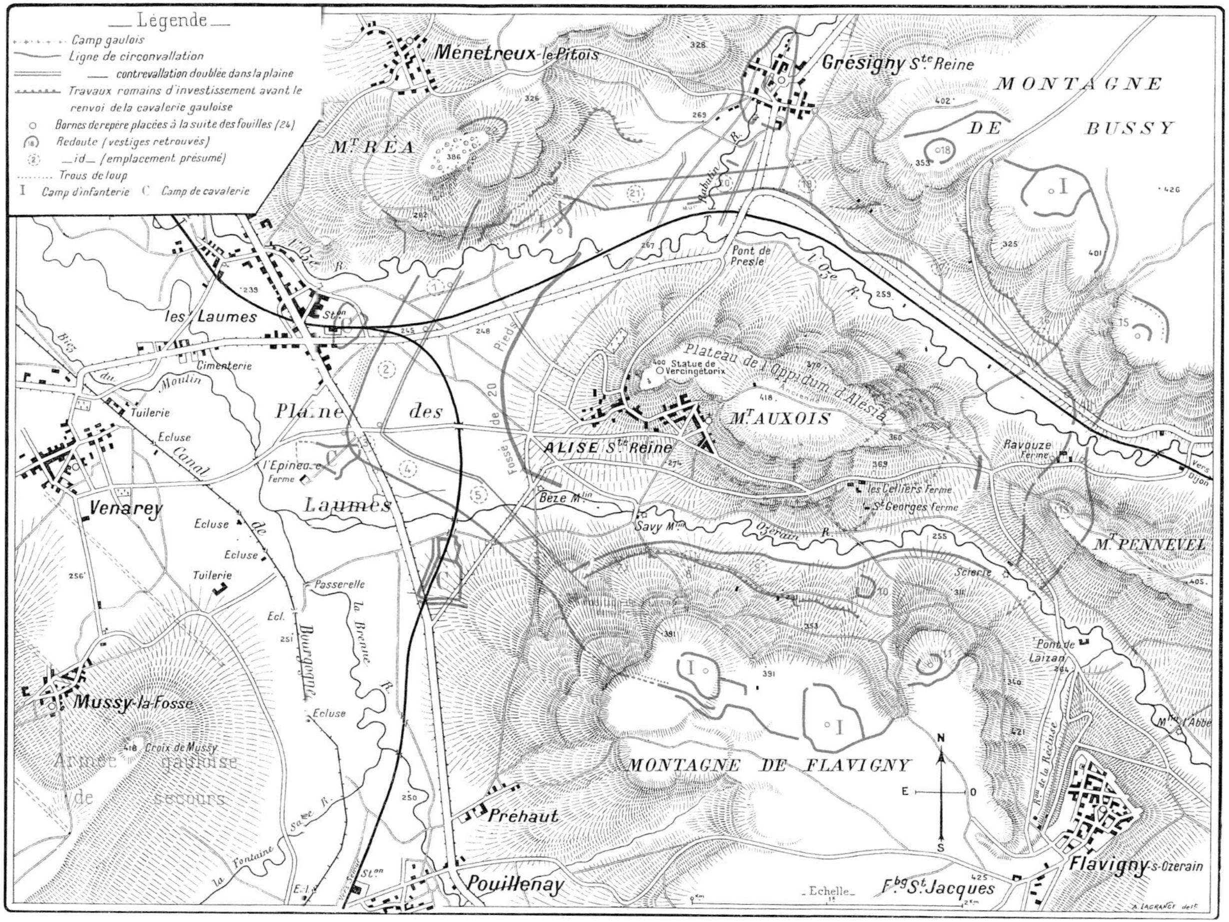

Figure 15.6 Map of the siegeworks ct Alise-Sainte-Reine, Côte-d'Or, 1861–1865 (Archives of the Musée d'Archéologie nationale, Saint-Germain-en-Laye).

from Lake Neuchâtel, especially the swords, were of the same kind as those unearthed at Alise-Sainte-Reine: the same double-edged blades, the same tanged hilts with a rectangular cross-section, the same iron-plate scabbards (Figure 15.7; Reffye 1864).

As Reffye immediately sensed, the 'lacustrine' weapons were neither Roman nor medieval; they were authentically Gaulish. Whereas until that time, no one had been able to situate them chronologically, they had at last been identified through comparison with the finds at Alise-Sainte-Reine. Desor, who had earlier dated them to the Iron Age, effectively had his interpretation confirmed. Conversely, the finds from La Tène authenticated the Gallic origins of some of the weaponry found at Alise-Sainte-Reine. All this was further confirmed by the dating of the battle site of 52 BC, whose location was attested by the variety of coins minted by the different Gallic peoples of the coalition forces that Caesar had spoken of. As Reffye pointed out, the hypothesis that the Gauls' weapons were made of bronze had to be abandoned (Reffye 1864, 349).

Gaulish graves in the Marne (1865)

Over the remainder of 1864, events began to unfold at an accelerated pace. Negotiations with Colonel Schwab having stalled, his rival, Édouard Desor, seized the moment. He sent the conclusions he himself had drawn from the La Tène site to Napoléon III's cabinet, to have them accredited. The Emperor wasted no time in responding. Desor was offered 4,000 francs, a sizeable sum at the time, for his collection. The objects discovered at La Tène were considered the equal of the finds from Alesia and seen as potentially some of the most prestigious holdings of the Musée des Antiquités National, which was to open to the public three years later, to coincide with the *Exposition Universelle* that would be held in Paris in 1867.[6]

During this same period, in May 1864, the curators from the museum at Saint-Germain learned of a discovery that at first went relatively unnoticed. A farmer named Denis Machet, from the village of Saint-Étienne-au-Temple in the Marne department in north-east France had for some time been digging up ancient graves that held 'weapons, necklaces, brooches, urns, and so on' (Beaune 1864, 40, no. 85). In the course of nearly twenty years, Machet had come across some 350 of them. The site on which this one-man digging machine worked included different groups of graves, the largest of which, about 300, manifestly dated to Roman times. Other groups, though, were markedly different. They held bodies adorned with bronze 'necklaces', fibulae and bracelets, with black earthenware urns sitting nearby. Above all, some of the tombs held the skeletons of warriors who had been buried with their arms. The iron swords and spearheads that accompanied them were completely absent from the graves from the Roman period.

When other graves containing iron weapons were discovered in Saint-Étienne-au-Temple at the beginning of 1865, the newly appointed curator, Alexandre Bertrand (1820–1902), decided to organize excavations there on behalf of the Musée des Antiquités National. With Machet's help, four tombs were opened in May 1865. One

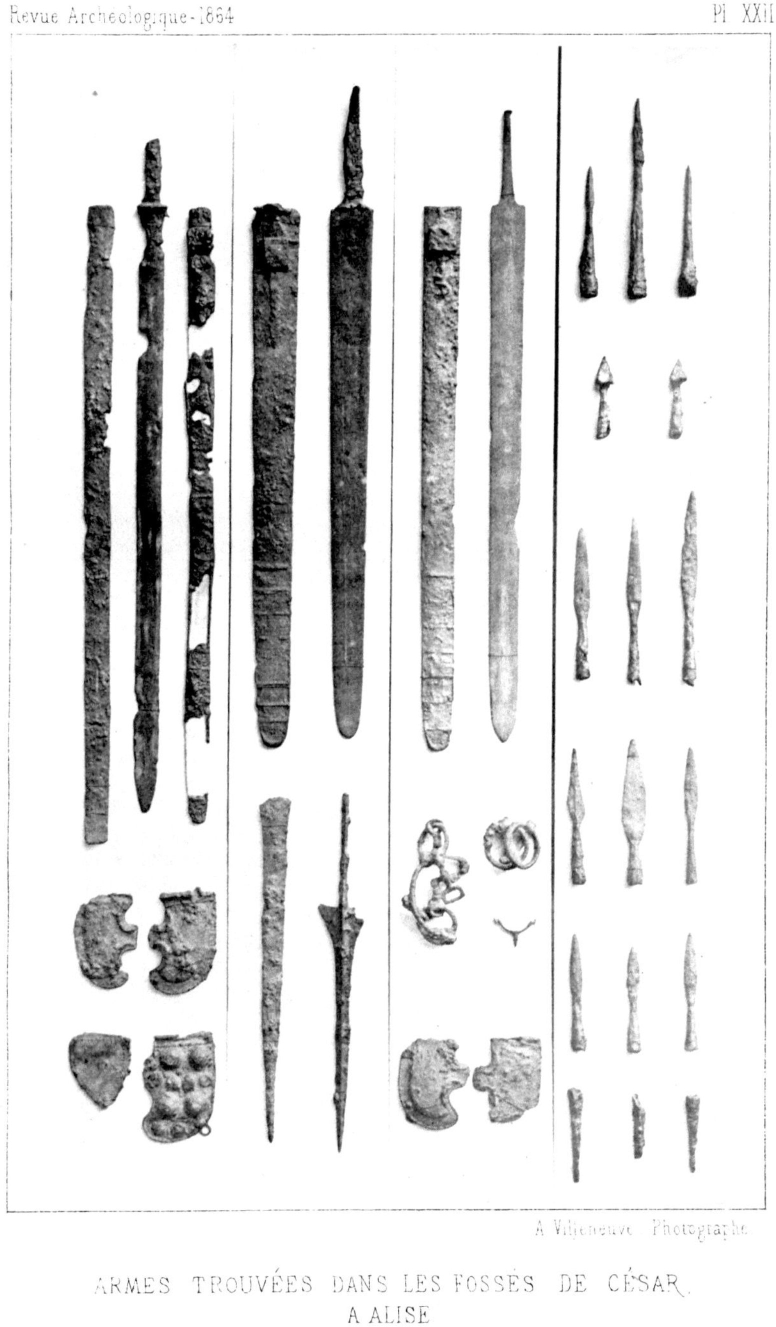

Figure 15.7 Weapons found in the trenches of Caesar's army at Alise-Sainte-Reine (after Reffye 1864, pl. XXII).

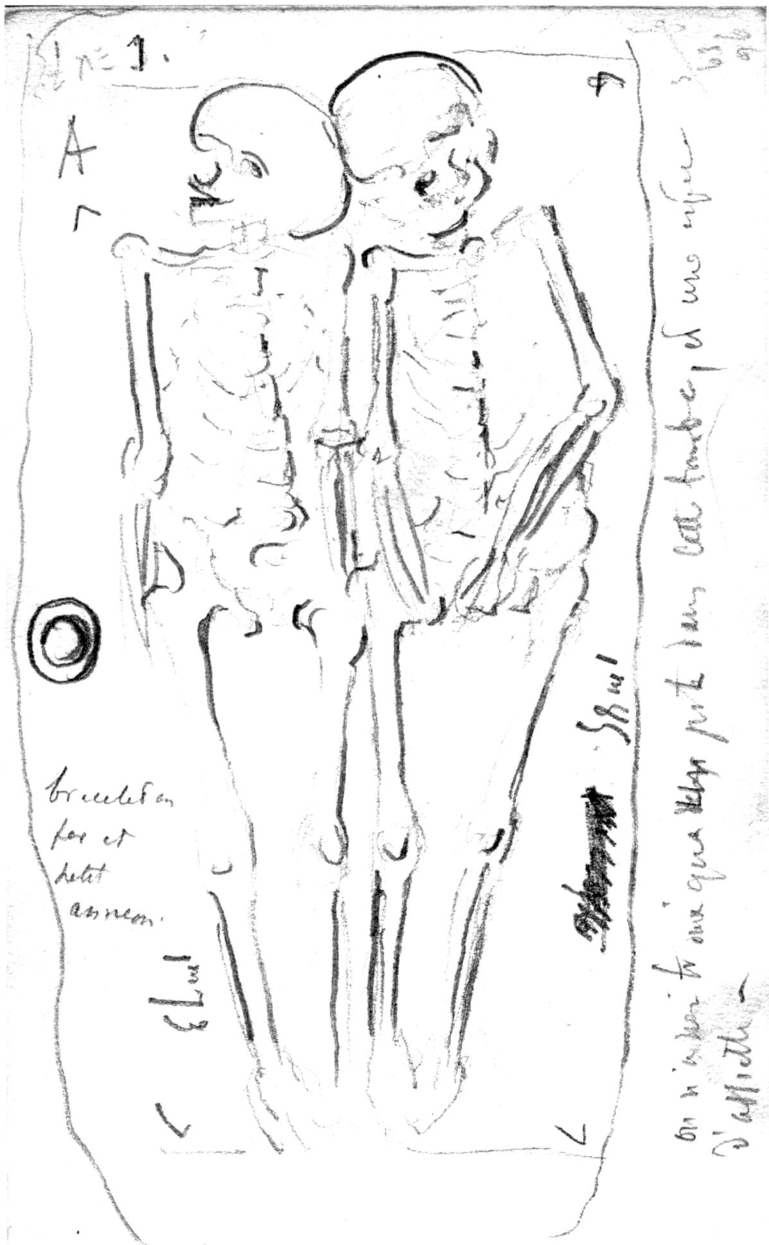

Figure 15.8 Gaulish grave discovered in 1865 at Saint-Étienne-au-Temple, Marne (Archives of the Musée d'Archéologie nationale, Saint-Germain-en-Laye).

of them contained a warrior with an iron sword in an iron plate scabbard lying at his side and the remains of his shield positioned where his body would have been (Figure 15.8). These were the very first graves to be determined to be Gaulish. As Reffye put it (1865), 'the grave goods established that the Saint-Étienne-au-Temple tombs belonged to the Gaulish era and seemed to pre-date the Roman conquest'.

The Gallic period of the Iron Age (1864–1866)

The Gaulish origin of the graves from Saint-Étienne-au-Temple would not be definitively authenticated until June 1866, when a strange sculpture made its way from the Musée Calvet in Avignon to Saint-Germain, after Napoléon III ordered that a copy of it be made for the Musée des Antiquités National. The stela found in Mondragon (south-eastern France) in 1834 depicts an upright male figure wrapped in a full fringed cloak, holding an oval shield in front of him, his sword hanging down on his right side (Figure 15.9). Alexandre Bertrand recognized the equipment to be that of the Gallic warriors described by the Greek historian Diodorus Siculus.[7] He also realized that the arms on the relief were displayed in the same way they had been found in the Gallic warrior's grave he had worked on in April 1865. His on-site notes describe a man buried with a sword at his side and a shield resting on top of his body (Bertrand 1867, 70, pl. XIII). Diodorus had also mentioned the fibulae Gallic warriors used to keep their cloaks fastened, and an iron clasp of this kind was in fact found in the warrior grave at Saint-Étienne-au-Temple. As Bertrand noted, the representational iconography of the Greeks offered corroboration for the archaeological finds; Greek and Roman historical sources confirmed them both. This was the irrefutable proof that allowed scholars to determine the graves unearthed in the Marne department to be of Gallic origin (Olivier forthcoming). The existence of a new archaeological period, which had until then existed in historical sources alone, had been demonstrated.

A number of common points linked the weapons found at Alise-Sainte-Reine to those from La Tène as well as to the grave goods from Saint-Étienne-au-Temple (Figure 15.10), whose technological and stylistic features clearly separated them from the Tumulus and Hallstatt periods. Thus, there arose the need to insert a new period between the Hallstatt era and the Roman conquest: the Gallic Period. Scholars from the museum at Saint-Germain-en-Laye suggested that it be called the 'Marnian Period', since that department was the area where its existence had been clearly demonstrated. Still, as it was thought to extend over little more than the two or three centuries following the Hallstatt period, it was difficult to present it as an archaeological period *per se*.

Revelations at Bologna (1871)

The situation remained unchanged until the Prehistoric Anthropology and Archaeology Congress that took place at Bologna in 1871. The dating of pieces from

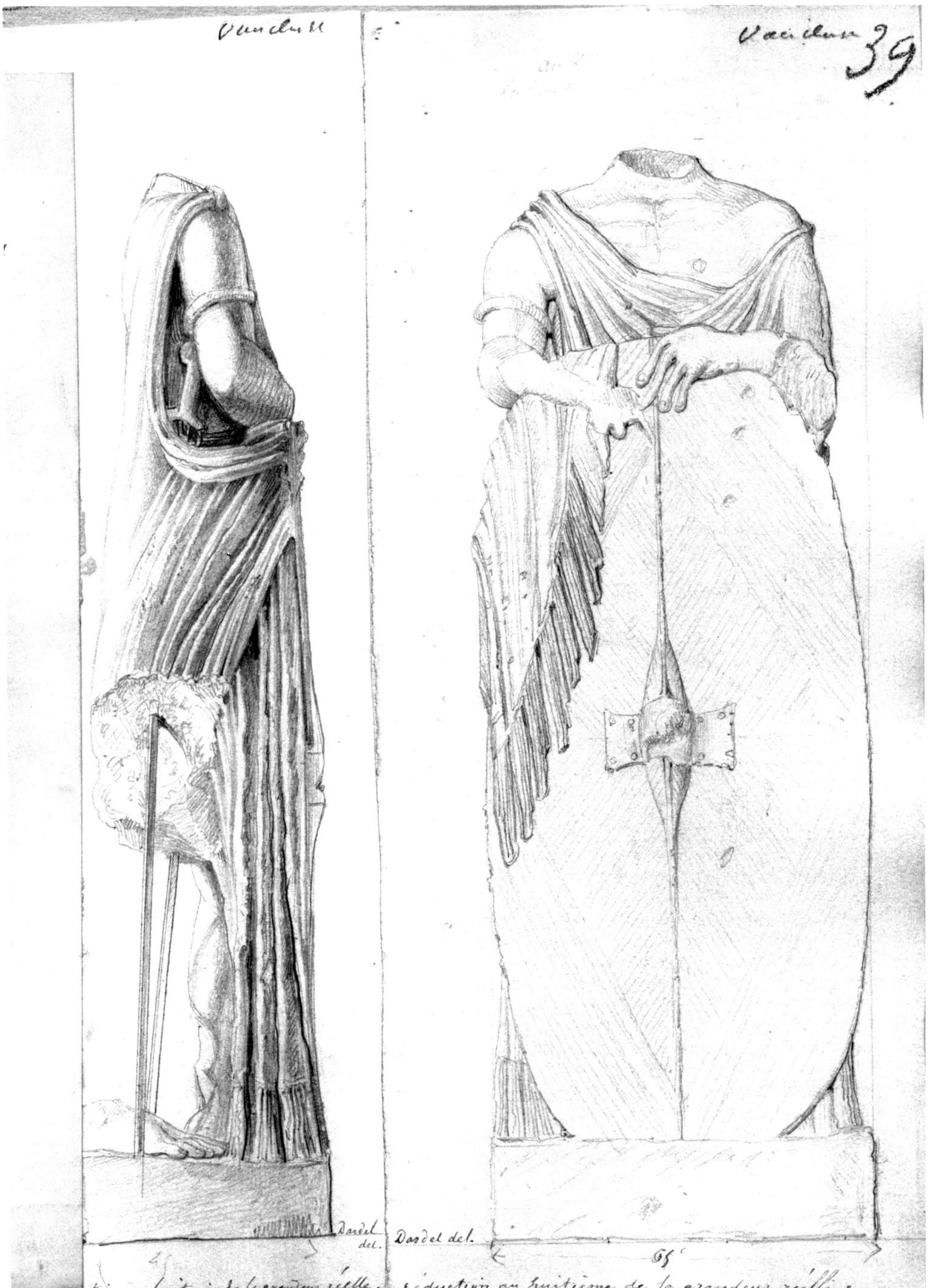

Figure 15.9 Gallic warrior sculpture found at Mondragon, Vaucluse (Archives of the Musée d'Archéologie nationale, Saint-Germain-en-Laye).

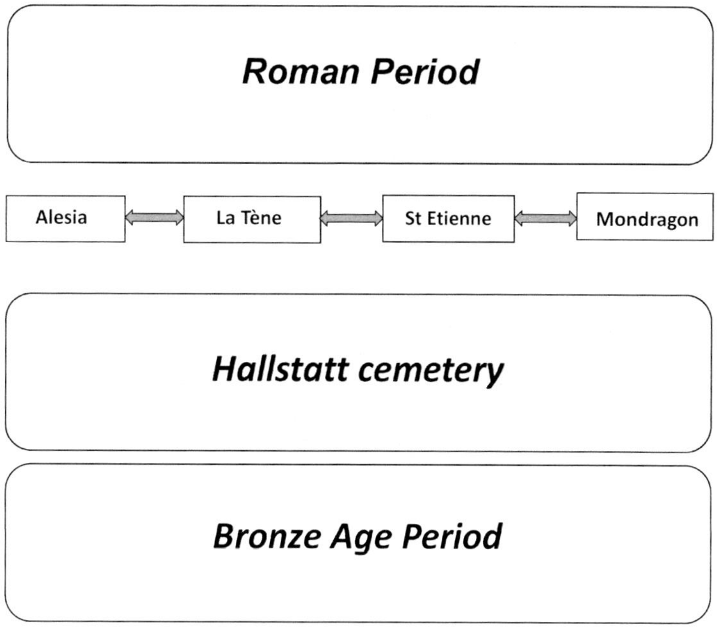

Figure 15.10 The chronology of the later Iron Age as elaborated following the discoveries at Saint-Étienne-au-Temple, 1865.

a cemetery in Villanova, northern Italy, whose connections to the Hallstatt cemetery were manifest, allowed scholars to situate the beginning of the Hallstatt period 'nine or ten centuries, if not more' before the Common Era. Similarly, some of the objects found in north Italian graves at Certosa and Marzabotto seemed to be contemporary with the Etruscan period. The Marzabotto cemetery was of especial interest in that it contained the very same types of objects – swords in iron scabbards, bronze fibulae with the foot bent back towards the bow – found in the Gaulish cemeteries in Marne (Figure 15.11). The French graves thus dated to the same period, between the 5th and 4th centuries BC.

In the wake of the Bologna Congress, it became clear, as Gabriel de Mortillet pointed out in 1873, that a new Gallic 'Marnian' period had followed the Hallstatt period and that it represented a second Iron Age (Mortillet 1875). It was at this time too that scholars recognized the need to distinguish between a 'late' phase corresponding to the finds from Alesia and La Tène, and an 'early' one characterized by the finds from Marne (Figure 15.12). This was the revelation that marked the Bologna Congress, and of which the Swedish archaeologist Hans Hildebrand (1842–1913) was unaware when, at the Stockholm Congress in 1874, he suggested adopting the eponymous terms Hallstatt and La Tène to designate the first and second Iron Ages, whose existence had clearly been established on the European continent (Hildebrand 1876).

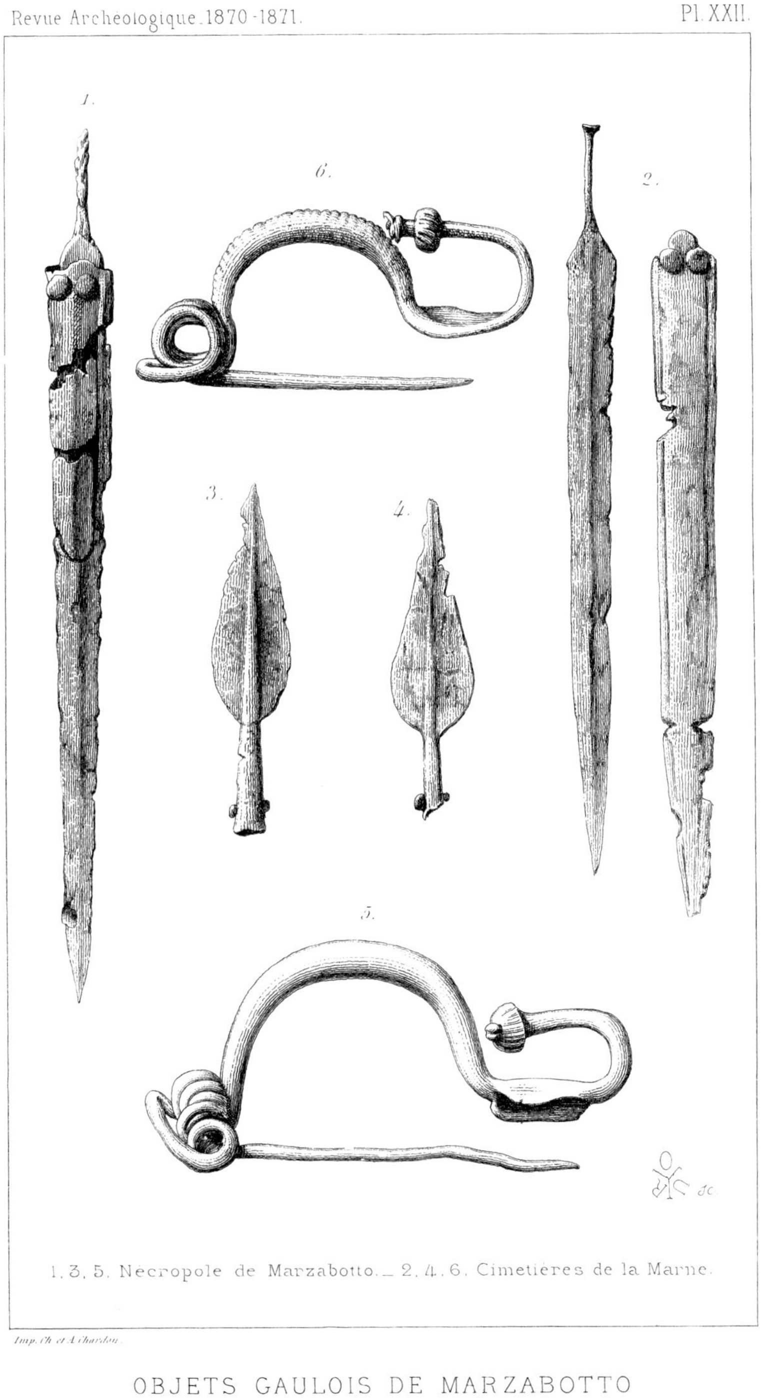

Figure 15.11 'Gaulish finds from Marzabotto', Emilia-Romagna, Italy (after de Mortillet 1871, pl. XXII).

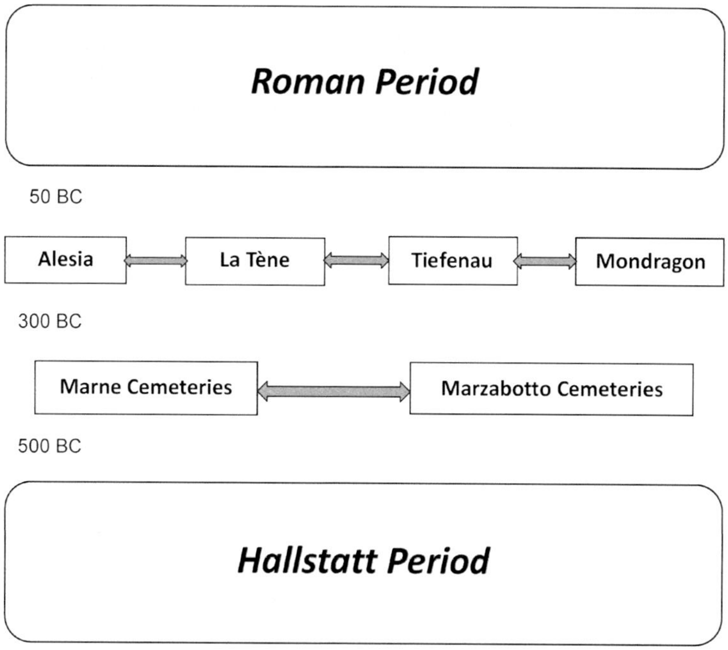

Figure 15.12 The chronology of the later Iron Age as elaborated after the Congress of Bologna, 1871.

Adopting Tischler's chronology (1885)

The periodization of the late Iron Age was not definitively fixed until the mid-1880s. The new chronology proposed by the German archaeologist Otto Tischler (1843–1891) was essentially based on that of Hildebrand (Tischler 1885). Moreover, in designating the European late Iron Age 'La Tène', Tischler effectively accredited Desor's precociously intuitive understanding that continental Europe's chronology was necessarily aligned with Scandinavia's, which had been established by Danish scholars, in particular Christian Thomsen and Jens Worsaae (1821–1885).

In assembling the archaeological data for continental Europe, Tischler distinguished three successive phases, each characterized by particular types of objects, known as type fossils, that had been attested in given regions or on particular sites. For example, the finds from the Marne cemeteries were indicative of objects belonging to the *early* phase, those from La Tène to the *middle* phase, and those from Mont Beuvray to the *late* phase of the newly named La Tène period (Figures 15.13 and 15.14).

In 1914, Joseph Déchelette (1862–1914) would base his European chronology of the late Iron Age on this system and substitute La Tène I, II and III for Tischler's early, middle and late (Déchelette 1914). In so doing, Déchelette introduced a radically new approach to the chronology of protohistoric times. By emphasizing the presence of identical kinds of objects across Europe, Déchelette's chronology effectively accredited the then new concept of a homogeneous and unilinear archaeological

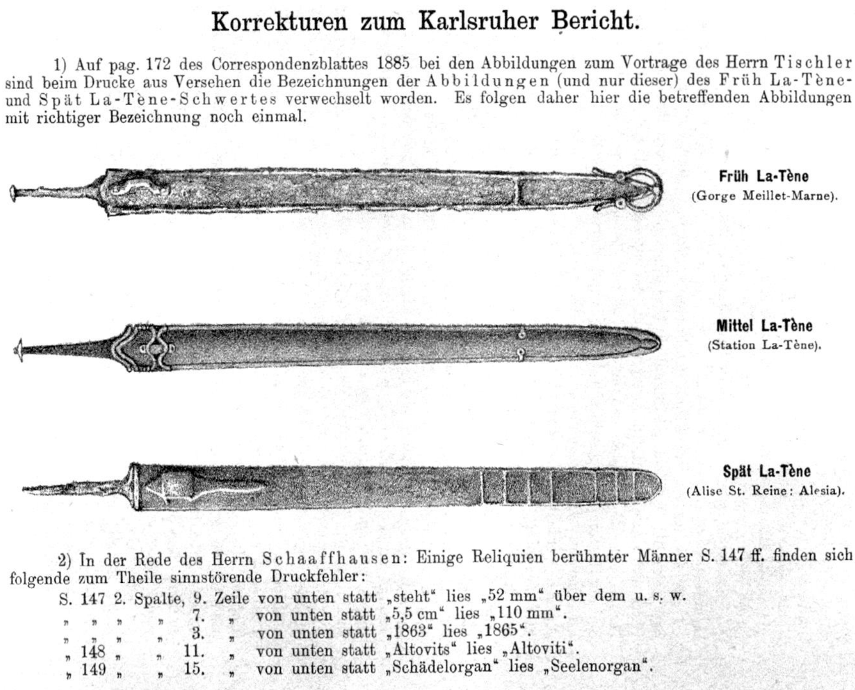

Korrekturen zum Karlsruher Bericht.

1) Auf pag. 172 des Correspondenzblattes 1885 bei den Abbildungen zum Vortrage des Herrn Tischler sind beim Drucke aus Versehen die Bezeichnungen der Abbildungen (und nur dieser) des Früh La-Tène- und Spät La-Tène-Schwertes verwechselt worden. Es folgen daher hier die betreffenden Abbildungen mit richtiger Bezeichnung noch einmal.

Früh La-Tène
(Gorge Meillet-Marne).

Mittel La-Tène
(Station La-Tène).

Spät La-Tène
(Alise St. Reine: Alesia).

2) In der Rede des Herrn Schaaffhausen: Einige Reliquien berühmter Männer S. 147 ff. finden sich folgende zum Theile sinnstörende Druckfehler:

S. 147 2. Spalte, 9. Zeile von unten statt „steht" lies „52 mm" über dem u. s. w.
„ „ „ „ 7. „ von unten statt „5,5 cm" lies „110 mm".
„ „ „ „ 3. „ von unten statt „1863" lies „1865".
„ 148 „ „ 11. „ von unten statt „Altovits" lies „Altoviti".
„ 149 „ „ 15. „ von unten statt „Schädelorgan" lies „Seelenorgan".

Figure 15.13 Chronological distinctions between swords of the La Tène Iron Age (after Tischler 1885).

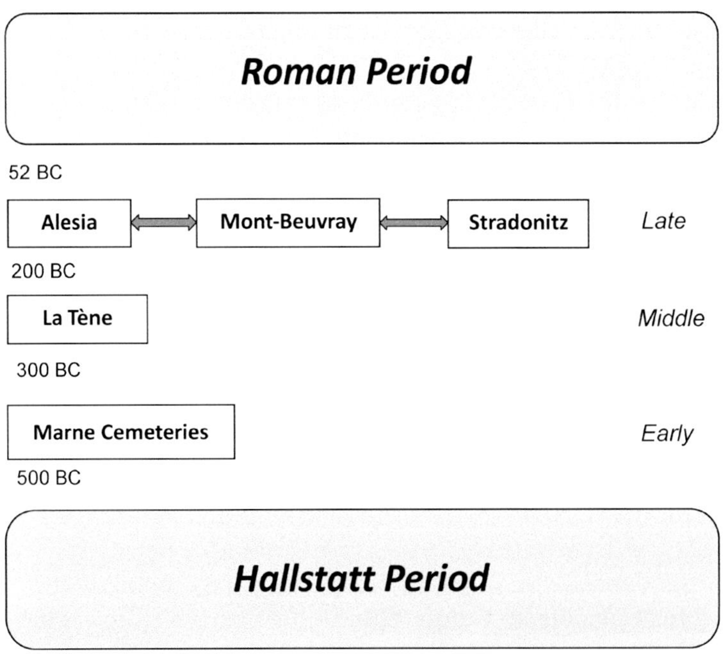

Figure 15.14 The chronology of the later Iron Age as elaborated in the work of Otto Tischler, 1885.

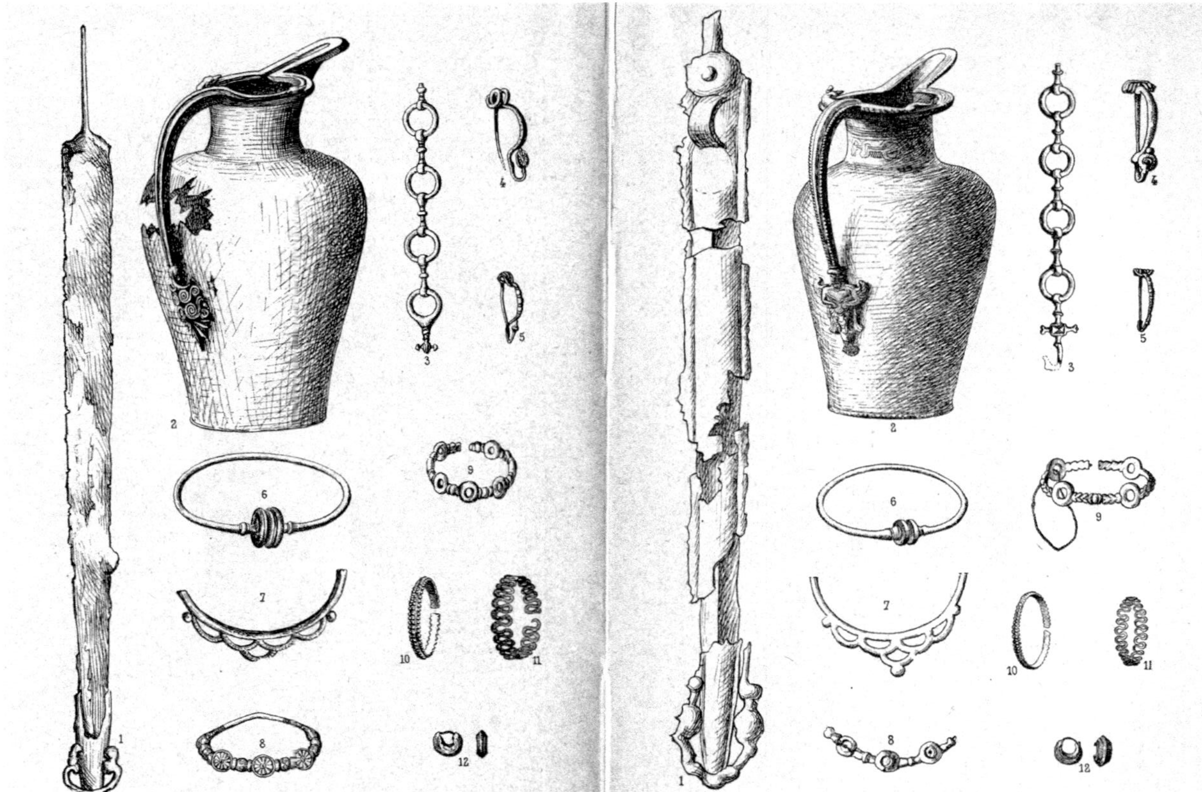

Fig. 385. — Objets divers provenant des sépultures gauloises de la Marne. Périodes de La Tène I et II [1].

1. N°s 1, 2, 5-7, 9, 12, d'après Morel, *Champagne souterraine*, pl. 2, fig. 10 ; pl. 8, fig. 2 ; pl. 26, fig. 3 ; pl. 34, fig. 17 ; pl. 26, fig. 2 ; pl. 13, fig. 16 ; pl. 3, fig. 13 ; — N° 3, d'après Bosteaux-Paris, AFAS, Nantes, 1898, II, p. 556 ; — N°s 4, 10, 11, d'après DAG, pl. (sans n°) ; — N° 8, d'après Bosteaux-Paris, AFAS, Limoges, 1890, p. 592, fig. 2

Fig. 386. — Objets divers provenant des sépultures gauloises de la Bohême. Périodes de La Tène I et II [1].

1. N°s 1, 3-11, d'après Pič, *Starožitnosti*, II, 1, pl. I, fig. 5 ; pl. XXVI, fig. 1 ; pl. VIII, fig. 4 ; pl. hors texte (après la p. 15), fig. 31 ; pl. XI, fig. 6 ; pl. VI, fig. 11 ; pl. XI, fig. 11 ; p. 11, fig. 10 ; pl. VIII, fig. 8 ; pl. II, fig. 4 ; — N°s 2, 12, d'après Pič, *Starožitnosti*, I, 2, pl. XXXI, fig. 1, 3.

Figure 15.15 Comparison of finds dating from the early and middle periods of La Tène from Bohemia and the Marne department (Déchelette 1914, figs 285–286).

timeframe within which each typological phase was strictly synchronous over the area of Celtic civilization (Figure 15.15).

Conclusion and perspectives: the role of Alesia in building European Iron Age chronology

Contrary to what has filtered down into the history of protohistoric archaeology, the finds from Alise-Sainte-Reine played a major role in establishing the European late Iron Age. They were, in their way, the foundation on which it was built. Archaeological knowledge progressed through a remarkable succession of reassessments, with each new discovery forcing a re-evaluation of those that preceded it. Throughout the decade that stretches roughly from 1865 to 1875, which is when the chronology of the European late Iron Age was established, the finds from Alesia were key both to establishing the links by which given discoveries were related to one another and to situating them chronologically through cross-dating (Figure 15.16).

It was the weaponry found at Alesia that effectively allowed scholars, in 1864, to authenticate the discoveries made at La Tène, which had until then defied identification. Then, beginning in 1865, came the digs at Saint-Étienne-au-Temple which corroborated the Gallic origins of the artefacts found at Alesia and La Tène

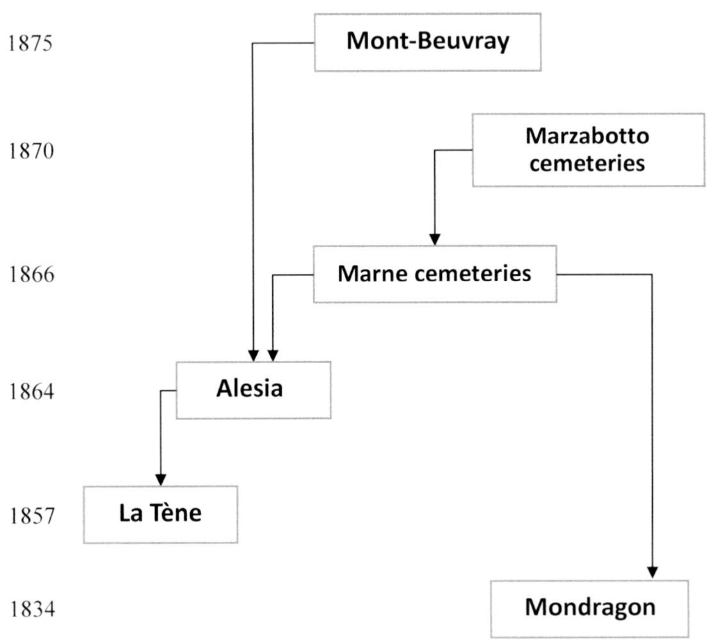

Figure 15.16 The key discoveries and their contribution to the development of European late Iron Age chronology.

and, above all, allowed scholars to reassess the figure on the stela discovered decades before at Mondragon. When matched against Diodorus' description of Gallic weapons, the relief sculpture provided the first chronological anchor point that manifestly pre-dated the Roman conquest. Then, at the Congress of Bologna in 1872, when scholars became aware of the Celtic grave goods from Marzabotto, this prompted chronological reassessment of the finds from both Alise-Sainte-Reine and the Celtic cemeteries of north-eastern France, which, from that point on, clearly seemed to pre-date Alesia. And finally, it was the excavations at Mont Beuvray that, beginning in the mid-1870s, led scholars to reassess the typo-chronological position of the finds from Alesia.

Above all, one notes that the relatively belated chronological syntheses effected first by Tischler, then by Déchelette, depended on a critical mass of data, both large in number and homogeneous, on which to base a system at once well founded and relatively general. This point was not reached until the 1880s, some twenty years after the first discoveries at Alise-Sainte-Reine and the cemeteries of north-eastern France. These chronological syntheses radically altered the way we perceive the archaeological time of these periods. Thinking was no longer based on isolated objects, but rather on series of them. Most of all, the chronology of the various Iron Ages ceased to be considered as the product of individual examples taken together (as Tischler continued to see them) – Alise-Sainte-Reine, La Tène, the Marne – and instead was understood as the manifestation of the 'universal archaeological time' prevalent across the whole of 'Celtic' Europe, as Déchelette had proposed.

Notes

1 Witness, for example, the interminable debate over the location of the siege of Alesia, which some once placed at Alaise (central-eastern France; Delacroix 1860) and others, more recently, at Syam (also central-eastern France; Berthier and Wartelle 1990; Porte 2014).

2 On 28 October 1858, Hans Kopp returned from a fishing trip at La Tène and presented his sister with 'a magnificent 10-pound trout for the evening meal' and Desor with 'a sabre, a spearhead, and a strange-looking fishhook, all of them of iron'. 'Hansli' would thereafter do work for the scholar from Neuchâtel as well.

3 Napoléon III, *Histoire de Jules César,* Paris, Imprimerie nationale, 2 vols, 1865–1866.

4 The first iron sword, unearthed in 1861, was immediately assumed to be of Roman manufacture [Unattributed introductory note on the digs at Alise-Saint-Reine] (*Revue archéologique,* 1861–1862, 141–142).

5 Musée d'Archéologie nationale since 2005.

6 At the Prehistoric Anthropology and Archaeology Congress held in Paris in 1867, Desor categorized the pieces from La Tène as belonging to a second 'Gallic Iron Age' that followed the Hallstatt era (Mortillet 1867, 381).

7 *Library of History* 5.30.

Bibliography

Beaune, P. (1864) Antiquités gallo-romains et mérovingiennes. Camp d'Attila, canton de Suippes, renseignemens [*sic*] du Dr. Remy. Marne. Manuscript note, in *Collections du musée de Saint-Germain*, 40, no. 85. Saint-Germain-en-Laye, Archives of the Musée d'Archéologie nationale.

Berthier, A. and Wartelle A. (1990) *Alésia*. Paris, Nouvelles éditions latines.

Bertrand, A. (1861) Les tombelles d'Auvenay (Côte-d'Or). *Revue Archéologique* 4, 1–11.

Bertrand, A. (1867) Le guerrier gaulois du musée Calvet, à Avignon. *Revue Archéologique* 16, 69–72.

Déchelette, J. (1914) *Manuel d'archéologie préhistorique, celtique et gallo-romaine, II. Archéologie celtique ou protohistorique. Troisième partie: Second âge du Fer ou époque de La Tène*. Paris, Picard.

Delacroix, A. (1860) *Alaise et Séquanie. Extrait de la revue des races latines*. Besançon, Bulle.

Desor, E. (1860) Quelques considérations sur les habitations lacustres des lacs de Suisse et d'Italie. *Almanach de Neuchâtel*, 1–16.

Hildebrand, H. (1876) Sur les commencements de l'âge du Fer en Europe. *Congrès internationaux d'anthropologie et d'archéologie préhistoriques, compte rendu de la VIIe session, Stockholm 1874*, 592–601.

Keller, F. (1858) Pfahlbauten. Zweiter Bericht. *Mittheilungen der Antiquarischen Gesellschaft in Zürich* 14, 6, 113–156.

Mortillet, G. de (1867) Congrès d'anthropologie et d'archéologie préhistorique, 2e session Paris, 17–30 août 1867. *Matériaux pour l'Histoire positive et philosophique de l'Homme* 3, 369–387.

Mortillet, G. de (1871) Les Gaulois de Marzabotto dans l'Apennin. *Revue Archéologique* 22 (1870–1871), 288–290.

Mortillet, G. de (1875) Tableau archéologique de la Gaule. *Matériaux pour l'Histoire positive et philosophique de l'Homme*, 273.

Olivier, L. (2010) À propos d'un vase-conteneur du Bronze final provenant des fouilles du siège d'Alésia. Victor Pernet et les fouilles impériales d'Alise-Sainte-Reine (Côte-d'Or). *Antiquités nationales* 40 (2009), 51–68.

Olivier, L. (forthcoming) La statue de Mondragon et l'authentification de l'armement gaulois aux origines de l'archéologie celtique des années 1860. In O. Cavalier (ed.), *Le « guerrier » de Mondragon. Recherches sur une œuvre celtique de la fin de l'époque hellénistique*. Milan, Éditions Silvana.

Olivier, L., Pernet, L. and Bastien, C. (2017) Les emprunts iconographiques du *Chef gaulois* d'Emmanuel Frémiet: une image de l'archéologie gauloise au début des années 1860. In O. Hébert and L. Péchoux (eds), *Gaulois, images, usages et stéréotypes (Actes du colloque de Clermont-Ferrand «Quand l'usage fait l'image: Les Gaulois, de la manipulation historique au stéréotype. Nouvelle enquête historiographique», 18–19 Septembre 2014)*, 75–95. Autun, Éditions Mergoil.

Olivier L. and Reddé M. (2015) *L'Album des fouilles d'Alise* redécouvert dans les archives de la Commission de la Topographie des Gaules. *Antiquités nationales* 45 (2014), 69–79.

Olivier L. and Triboulot B. (2000) Les fouilles de Félix de Saulcy dans la nécropole des 'Chaumes d'Auvenay' à Ivry-en-Montagne (Côte-d'Or) et les inhumations précoces de la fin du Bronze final dans le nord-est de la France. *Antiquités nationales* 31, 117–139.

Porte, D. (2014) *Alésia, la supercherie dévoilée*. Paris, Pygmalion, Gérard Watelet.

Quicherat, J. (1865) Examen des armes trouvées à Alise-sainte-Reine. Dissertation relative à la question d'Alésia. *Revue Archéologique* 11, 81–99.

Reffye (Verchère de), J.-B. (1864) Les armes d'Alise. Lettre à M. le Docteur F. Keller, Président de la Société des Antiquaires de Zurich. *Revue Archéologique* 10, 337–349.

Reffye, (Verchère de) J.-B. (1865) *Comptes-rendus des séances de la commission consultative pour l'organisation du musée de Saint-Germain*. Saint-Germain-en-Laye, Archives of the Musée d'Archéologie nationale.

Rossignol, C. (1861) *Découverte d'armes gauloises et romaines réunies, faite dans la plaine des Laumes, sous les murs d'Alise (Côte-d'Or)*. Manuscript. Saint-Germain-en-Laye, Archives of the Musée d'Archéologie nationale.

Saulcy, F. de (1860) Guerre des Helvètes. Première campagne de César. *Revue archéologique* 2, 165–186; 242–259; 313–344.

Thierry, A. (1828) *Histoire des Gaulois depuis les temps les plus reculés jusqu'à l'entière soumission de la Gaule à la domination romaine* (3 vols). Paris, Jules Labitte.

Tischler, O. (1885) Über die Gliederung der La-Tène-Periode und die Dekorierung der Eisenwaffen in dieser Zeit. *Correspondenz-Blatt der deutschen Gesellschaft für Anthropologie, Ethnologie und Urgeschichte* 14, 157–161.

Viollet-le-Duc, E. (1862) Casque antique trouvé dans un ancien bras de la Seine. *Revue archéologique* V, 1862, 224–227.